XIX Ibero-American Conference on Software Engineering (CIBSE 2016)

AA004965

Quito, Ecuador
27-29 April 2016

Editors:

Efrain R. Fonseca C.
Cecilia Hinojosa
Juan Pablo Carvallo
Gleison Santos
Martin Solari
Marcos Kalinowski
Tayana Conte
Ignacio Panach
Lidia Lopez
Eduardo Kinder Almentero
Omar Gomez
Carlos Cares
Sabrina Marczak

ISBN: 978-1-5108-2718-9

Printed from e-media with permission by:

Curran Associates, Inc.
57 Morehouse Lane
Red Hook, NY 12571

Some format issues inherent in the e-media version may also appear in this print version.

Copyright© (2016) by the authors
All rights reserved.

Printed by Curran Associates, Inc. (2016)

For permission requests, please contact CIbSE - IberoAmerican Conference on Software Engineering at the address below.

CIbSE - IberoAmerican Conference on Software Engineering
c/o Luca Cernuzzi
Universidad Católica "Nuestra Seóra de la Asunción",
Campus Universitario, Asunción
Barrio Santa Ana, C.C.1683, C.P. 1364
Asunción - Paraguay

Phone: +595 21 334650
Fax: +595 21 310587

lcernuzz@uca.edu.py

Additional copies of this publication are available from:

Curran Associates, Inc.
57 Morehouse Lane
Red Hook, NY 12571 USA
Phone: 845-758-0400
Fax: 845-758-2633
Email: curran@proceedings.com
Web: www.proceedings.com

CIBSE 2016

XIX Ibero-American Conference on Software Engineering

http://cibse.espe.edu.ec

April 27-29, 2016, Quito, Ecuador

Hosted by:

Universidad de las Fuerzas Armadas ESPE, Sangolquí, Ecuador

Editors:

Efraín R. Fonseca C.
Cecilia Hinojosa
Juan Pablo Carvallo
Gleison Santos
Martin Solari
Marcos Kalinowski
Tayana Conte
Ignacio Panach
Lidia Lopez
Eduardo Kinder Almentero
Omar Gomez
Carlos Cares
Sabrina Marczak

ESPE
UNIVERSIDAD DE LAS FUERZAS ARMADAS
INNOVACIÓN PARA LA EXCELENCIA

Proceedings

XIX Ibero-American Conference on
Software Engineering

http://cibse.espe.edu.ec

CIBSE 2016 - Quito, April 27-29th, 2016

Local Organizers:

Proceedings of XIX Ibero-American Conference on Software Engineering

Editors:

Efraín R. Fonseca C.
Cecilia Hinojosa
Juan Pablo Carvallo
Gleison Santos
Martin Solari
Marcos Kalinowski
Tayana Conte
Ignacio Panach
Lidia Lopez
Eduardo Kinder Almentero
Omar Gomez
Carlos Cares
Sabrina Marczak

Published by:

Universidad de las Fuerzas Armadas ESPE
Campus Sangolquí, Av. Gral. Rumiñahui s/n Sangolquí – Ecuador
Phone: +59323989400
Email: rpublicas@espe.edu.ec

Copyright 2016 by the authors.

Message From Conference and General Program Chairs

Welcome to the 19th Ibero-American Conference on Software Engineering!

Ecuador is glad to receive this event by the second time, first CIBSE 2010 and now CIBSE 2016.

This event is particularly important in our country because it allows us to show cutting-edge articles in this area. From that point of view, CIBSE is quite useful to show and understand what Software Engineering is in our country and abroad.

CIBSE is a flagship event in the field of Software Engineering, with the participation of a vibrant Ibero-American community. It was conceived as a space dedicated to the dissemination of research results and activities, as it encourages dialogue between scientists, educators, professionals, and students of Software Engineering. CIBSE has distinct characteristics as it welcomes contributions in three languages: Portuguese, Spanish or English. It is backed by 18 previous conferences held in various countries:

Brazil-Torres (IDEAS'98),
San Jose, Costa Rica (IDEAS'99),
Cancun, Mexico (IDEAS'00),
Heredia, Costa Rica (IDEAS'01),
Havana, Cuba (IDEAS'02),
Asunción, Paraguay (IDEAS'03),
Arequipa, Peru (IDEAS'04),
Valparaiso, Chile (IDEAS'05),
La Plata, Argentina (IDEAS'06),
Isla Margarita, Venezuela (IDEAS'07),
Recife, Brazil (IDEAS'08),
Medellín, Colombia (IDEAS09),
Cuenca, Ecuador (CIbSE'10),
Rio de Janeiro, Brazil (CIbSE'11),
Buenos Aires, Argentina (CIbSE'12),
Montevideo, Uruguay (CIbSE'13).
Pucon, Chile (CIbSE'14).
Lima, Peru (CIbSE'15)

CIbSE is an evolution of the successful IDEAS (Iberoamerican Workshop on Environments and Software Requirements Engineering) which began in 1998. It was strengthened with the integration of two specialized events: the Workshop on Requirements Engineering (WER) in 2010 and the Experimental Software Engineering Latin American Workshop (ESELAW) in 2011. Last year CIbSE also added an Industrial Track. As a result, CIbSE consists of four tracks. The issues related to Requirements Engineering are discussed under the WER track, the ESELAW track handles Experimental Software Engineering topics. The Industrial track covers software engineering issues in industry.

All remaining Software Engineering themes are discussed under the SET Track. CIBSE also hosts a Doctoral Symposium for Ph.D. students whose research area includes topics of Software Engineering, Requirements Engineering or Experimental Software Engineering.

This event is of particular importance to our country, since it allows the local, academic and industrial communities, to review and attend the presentation of cutting-edge articles in the field of software engineering, and thus, understand the state of the practice in this highly relevant field at a regional and international level.

We hope that you will enjoy your stay at Quito and make the most of CIbSE'16!

Gleison Santos and
Juan Pablo Carvallo

General Program chairs

Efraín R. Fonseca C.
and Cecilia Hinojosa

General Conference chairs

GENERAL INDEX
Wednesday, April 27

Session: SET - Systems Modelling

Session: WER - Requirements Specification

Session: Tutorials

Thursday, April 28

Session: Industrial track

Session: Tutorials

Session: Doctoral Symposium

Friday, April 29

Session: SET - Software Quality

Session: Tutorials

This page intentionally left blank.

LIST OF AUTHORS

Acosta Ramìrez, René
Alencar, Fernanda
Alex Federico
Angelica Toffano
Aquino, Nathalie
Araújo, João
Armijos Roblero,
Assis, Denise
Astudillo, Hernan
Avila Paldes, Roberto
Azevedo, Roberto,
Barbosa Dósea, Marcos
Barcelos, Leonardo
Barrantes, Mario
Becker, Pablo
Bezerra, Allan
Blum Haddad, Flavia Belintani
Bravo, Leonardo
Brenes, Enrique
Brito, Isabel Sofia
Brito, Maria
Bulcão-Neto, Renato
Caballero, Ismael
Calazans, Seidel
Canhadas Genvigir, Elias
Carretero, Ana G.
Carvalho Oliveira, Camila
Castro-Herrera, Carlos
Castro, Jaelson
Cernuzzi, Luca
Colaço Júnior, Methanias
Condori-Fernández, Nelly
de La Vara, Jose Luis
De Souza Silva, Bruno
de Souza, Simone R. S.
Delamaro, Marcio E.
Dias-Neto, Arilo
Dieste, Oscar
Dora, Graciela
Esparcia-Alcazar, Anna I.
Ferreira Aguiar, Luiz Gustavo
Fonseca C., Efraín R.
Fontão, Awdren
França, Heyde
Franch, Xavier
Gallego, Mauricio
García Molina, Jesús J.
Genero, Marcela
Gomes, Roberta
Gonçalves, Enyo
González, Magalí
Hadad, Susana
Holanda, Ana
Jaqueira, Aline
Jenkins, Marcelo
Lencastre, Maria
Lima, Paulo
López, Iván
Lucena, Marcia
Maciel, Teresa
Madrigal, Denisse
Magdala, Miriam
Marín, Beatriz
Martínez, Alexandra
Matalonga, Santiago
Maya, Ricardo D.
Melo Mariano, Ari
Mendes, Emilia
Mendes, Ingrid
Mighetti, Juan Pablo
Miriam M. Pinto
Monsalve Arteaga, Carlos Teodoro

Moreira Da Silva, Thiago
Murillo-Morera, Juan
Nascimento, André Vinícius R. P.
Noel, Rene
Olsina, Luis
Papa, María Fernanda
Pastor López, Óscar
Pedruce, Letícia
Penteado, Rosângela
Pereira de Azevedo Sousa, Silvia
Pereira, Marcos
Pereira, Tarcísio
Piattini, Mario
Pimentel, João
Porto, Faimison
Quesada-López, Christian
Ramos, Ricardo
Raura, Geovanny
Reis, Rodrigo
Renata Guizzardi,
Reyes Ch., Rolando P.
Reyes Román, José Fabián
Ribeiro Castro, Eduardo José
Rivera, Belén
Rocca, José Ignacio
Roldán Martínez, David
Romero, José A.
Rosso, Nicolas
Rueda Molina, Urko
Sá Filho, Celso
Santana Santos, Tauany Lorene
Silva Schuenemann, Lourenço
Silva, Paulina
Simao, Adenilso
Soares, Michel
Solari, Martin
Sousa, Aêda
Souza, Paulo S. L.
Souza, Simone
Souza, Thiago
Teodoro Da Silva, Rebeca
Travassos, Guilherme Horta
Ullón, Ruben H.
Valverde Giromé, Francisco
Verdecia Díaz, Yadirka
Vilela, Jéssyka
Vilela, Ricardo F.
Vos, Tanja E. J.
Wieringa, Roel,

KEYNOTES

WER 2016 Keynote
Dealing with Non-Functional Requirements in Model-Driven Development

Xavier Franch

Universidad Politécnica de Cataluña, Barcelona, España

Franch@essi.upc.edu

Abstract. Software systems cannot be successful without taking non-functional requirements (NFRs) into account. But still there seems to be a lopsided emphasis on the functionality of the system, even though the functionality is not useful or usable when NFRs do not hold. MDD is not an exception to this rule. In this keynote, we will first analyse the state of the art in MDD with respect to NFR treatment. Besides a general landscape, we will provide details on one particular domain (service-based systems) and one particular modeling approach (goal-oriented). Next, we will reflect on the possible ways to fit NFRs in the MDD process and the consequences of each alternative. At the end, we will discuss a research agenda. During the talk, we will report some preliminary observations coming from the NFR4MDD project.

ESELAW 2016 Keynote
Improving and Estimating the Value of Decisions

Emilia Mendes

Blekinge Institute of Technology and University of Oulu

emilia.mendes@bth.se

Abstract. In his call to arms paper, which gave origin to Value-based Software Engineering (VBSE), Boehm (back in 2003) very clearly put forward that much of the current software engineering practice and research is carried out in a value neutral setting, where: Every requirement, use case, object, test case, and defect is treated as equally important; "Earned value" systems track project cost and schedule, not stakeholder or business value; A "separation of concerns" is practiced, in which the responsibility of software engineers is confined to turning software requirements into verified code. As part of three-year research project (2015-2017) funded by the Finnish Funding Agency for Technology and Innovation, we are collaborating with four ICT companies to help them improve their decision-making relating to software or software-intensive products, and to be able to predict the overall value of their decisions. All companies already employ a value-based approach to decision making; however decisions are based on tacit knowledge, in the sense that decision makers' mental models have not been explicitated, and alternatively combined and used with the help of data visualization tools/'what-if' scenarios in support of their decision-making processes. The goal and main contribution of this keynote is to detail our proposed framework towards value estimation, in addition to some preliminary empirical results, in order to support those companies who wish to improve their value-based decision making, and to predict the value of their decisions. As will be detailed later, the proposed framework also includes the theory of organizational knowledge creation and the Expert-based Knowledge Engineering of Bayesian Networks process.

SET 2016 Keynote
Is It Possible to Build General, Empirically-Backed Knowledge in Software Engineering?

Oscar Dieste

Universidad Politécnica de Madrid, Madrid, Spain

odieste@fi.upm.es

Abstract. The application of empiricism to Software Engineering (IS) brings the possibility to obtain knowledge comparable to the knowledge produced in other engineering disciplines. A large share of the research community has embraced this methodology. We have obtained a great amount of results, primarily research papers, so far. Nevertheless, we have been unable to generalize particular findings into pieces of knowledge, or theories having predictive values in more or less generic contexts.

What could be the reasons that restrict our ability to build general, empirically-backed knowledge in IS? Some *accidental* difficulties are well known: the (relative) youth of empirical IS, the scarcity of replications, and the limited external validity of studies conducted using students as experimental subjects. Should we have time enough, create an adequate reward structure so that researchers are persuaded to replicate, and get practitioners and companies involved in the research, then we will be able to build general knowledge.

However, right now, I am not that sure that this is *completely true*. Far from my intention the commencement of an epistemological debate in IS. Simply put, I have been observing that many other accidental difficulties exist, which jointly interact to give origin to impressive obstacles that deserve the name of *essential* difficulties. The core problem is our inability to assess in a reasonable precise manner the *context effects*. Having unlimited time/resources at our disposal, it is theoretically possible to ascertain the influence of context; in practice, resources are limited and the context effects remain uncertain.

I wonder whether the right approach is the other way around, i.e.: start the research with some promising technology (/phenomenon) of apparently general character. For instance, we could start the research using students, and later try to establish its usefulness (/truth) in particular contexts, keeping away from pretensions of generality. This reflection is not totally my original. A.M. Davis & A. Hickey y R. Wieringa have expressed similar opinions, although starting from different premises (theirs theoretical, mine from the trenches).

Keywords. Empiricism, theory, replication, students, practitioners, industry, experiment, case study, synthesis, meta-analysis, context

This page intentionally left blank.

Track 1: Software Engineering Technology (SET 2016) Preface

On behalf of the Program Committee we would like to welcome you to the edition of the Software Engineering Track (SET 2016), part of the XIX Ibero-American Con-ference on Software Engineering (CIbSE 2016), held from April 27 to 29 in Quito – Ecuador.

Software Engineering is a discipline that tackles a wide range of topics related to software development processes. Even though Software Engineering is not new in the short history of computer science, there are still important challenges. In a world where new technologies are growing exponentially, the software development process affects different areas such as the economy, communications, social re lationships, comfort and security among many others. In such context, SET 2016 agglutinates a set of research papers with the aim to advance in the development of quality software from an engineering point of view. SET 2016 is a Latin American forum bringing together academic, industrial and commercial communities to make a step forward to improve software development processes. This year, SET received 32 paper submis-sions from 13 countries. These papers were written in one of the three official idioms: Portuguese, Spanish, and English. All the submitted papers were revised by at least 3 reviewers from the SET´16 Program Committee. At the end of the reviewing process, seven high-quality papers were accepted to be published and presented at the SET Track, representing an acceptance rate of 21.87%.

The program of SET 2016 is organized in 2 technical sessions:

1. Systems Modelling
2. Software Quality

We would like to acknowledge and thank all authors who submitted papers. You made SET 2016 possible by sharing your expertise with us. We also would like to thank all the members of the Program Committee for following an excellent and me-ticulous reviewing process. Your dedication has resulted in the selection of high-quality papers for the Software Engineering Track.

Ignacio Panach and Tayana Conte
PC co-chairs SET 2016

Program Committee

Adelaide Bianchini, USB, Venezuela
Adler Diniz de Souza, UNIFEI, Brasil
Agustina Buccella, Universidad Nacional del Comahue, Argentina
Alejandra Garrido, Universidad Nacional de la Plata, Argentina
Alejandro Catalá, Universidad de Castilla La Mancha
Andreia Malucelli, PUCPR, Brasil
Antonio Brogi, University of Pisa, Italy
Arilo Claudio Dias-Neto, UFAM, Brasil
Beatriz Marín, Universiad Diego Portales, Chile
Breno França, COPPE/UFRJ, Brasil
Bruno Gadelha, UFAM, Brasil
Carlos Cetina, Universidad San Jorge, Spain
Claudia Pons, Universidad Nacional de La Plata, Argentina
Claudio Sant'Anna, Federal University of Bahia, Brazil
Daniel Riesco , National University of San Luis, Argentina
Daniel Romero, Universidad de Asunción, Paraguay
Daniela Godoy, ISISTAN Research Institute, Argentina
Davi Viana (UFAM/ FUCAPI), Brasil
David Ameller, Universitat Politècnica de Catalunya, Spain
Diego Vallespir, Universidad de la República, Uruguay
Dolors Costal, Universitat Politècnica de Catalunya, Spain
Eduardo Figueiredo, UFMG, Brasil
Elena Navarro, University of Castilla-La Mancha, Spain
Ernest Teniente, Unversitat Politècnica de Catalunya, Spain
Estefanía Serral, Research Centre for Management Informatics, Belgium
Eugenio Scalise, UCV, Venezuela
Fabio M Costa, UFG, Brasil
Francisco Ruiz, Universidad de Castilla La Mancha, Spain
Francisco A. C. Pinheiro, Universidade de Brasilia, Brasil
Francisco Valverde, Universitat Politècnica de València, Spain
Gabriel Tamura, Icesi, Colombia
Gastón Mousques, Universidad ORT, Uruguay
Giovanni Giachetti, Universidad Andrés Bello, Chile
Gonzalo Rojas, Universidad de Concepción, Chile
Gustavo Rossi, LIFIA, Argentina
Hernán Astudillo, Universidad Técnica Federico Santa María, Chile
Igor Steinmacher (UTFPR), Brasil
Javier González Huerta, Valencia, Spain
Jesus Garcia-Molina, Universidad de Murcia, Spain
João Falcão E Cunha, Universidade do Porto, Portugal
Jose Antonio Macías, Universidad Autónoma de Madrid, Spain
Jose Luis De La Vara, Universidad Carlos III de Madrid, Spain
Jose Norberto Mazon, Universidad de Alicante, Spain
Juan Hernández, Quercus Software Engineering Group, Spain
Juan Pablo Carvallo , Universidad del Azuay, Ecuador
Kawtar Benghazi, Universidad de Granada, Spain
Kleinner Farias, PUC-Rio, Brasil
Lourdes Moreno, Universidad Carlos III de Madrid, Spain
Luca Cernuzzi, Universidad Católica, Paraguay
Luis Olsina, Universidad Nacional La Plata, Argentina
Luz Marcela Ruiz, Universitat Politécnica de València, Spain
Marcello Thiry, UNIVALI, Brasil
María Cecilia Bastarrica , Universidad de Chile, Chile
Miguel Katrib, Universidad de la Habana, Cuba

Nelio Cacho, UFRN, Brasil
Nelly Bencomo, Aston University, UK
Nelly Condori-Fernández, VU University, Amsterdam
Nestor Garay-Vitoria, Universidad Del País Vasco, Spain
Norah M. Villegas, Icesi, Colombia
Omar Gómez, Universidad Autónoma de Yucatán, Mexico
Rafael Prikladnicki, PUCRS, Brasil
Raul Mazo, Paris 1, Francia
Regina Braga, UFJF, Brasil
Renata Guizzardi, Univ. Federal do Espirito Santo, Brasil
Ricardo Soto, Pontificia Univ. Católica de Valparaíso,Chile
Ricardo Ramos, Univasf, Brasil
Rodrigo Quites Reis, UFPA, Brasil
Rosana Braga, Univ. Sao Paulo, Brasil
Roxana Giandini , Universidad Nacional de la Plata, Argentina
Sabrina Marczak, PUCRS, Brasil
Sheila Reinehr, PUCPR, Brasil
Silvia Rueda, Universitat de València, Spain
Silvia Teresita Acuña, Universidad Autónoma de Madrid, Spain
Toacy Oliveira, UFRJ, Brasil
Vicente Pelechano , Universitat Politècnica de València, Spain
Víctor López, Universidad de Castilla La Mancha, Spain
Victor Santander, Universidad Estadual do Oeste do Paraná, Brasil
Vitor Souza, FUES, Brasil

Aditional Reviewers

Johnatan Oliveira
Matias Pol'La
Mario Beron
Maria Jose Villanueva
Miguel A. Teruel
Sebastián Pizard
Andre Menolli
Martin Garriga
Rodrigo Olivares
Victoria Torres
Pablo Becker
John Wilmar Castro Llanos

SET INDEX

Session 1: Systems Modelling

Session 2: Software Quality

Including haplotypes treatment in a Genomic Information Systems Management

José F. Reyes Román[12], Óscar Pastor[1], Francisco Valverde[1] and David Roldán M.[1]

[1] Research Center on Software Production Methods (PROS). DSIC. Universitat Politècnica de València. Camino Vera s/n. 46022, Valencia, Spain
[2] Department of Engineering Sciences. Universidad Central del Este (UCE). Ave. Francisco Alberto Caamaño Deñó. 21000, San Pedro de Macorís, Dominican Republic.
e-mail: {jreyes | opastor | fvalverde}@pros.upv.es, darolmar@upvnet.upv.es

Abstract. The study and comprehension of the human genome is a major challenge due to its high level of complexity. The application of Next Generation Sequencing (NGS) technologies contributes to the generation of large amounts of new data that is increasing every day. This huge data growth, if not managed properly, could lead to information heterogeneity and inconsistency. As a consequence, data quality is compromised. To face this problem, we have proposed a *Conceptual Schema of the Human Genome* (CSHG), intended to understand and improving our conceptual definition of the domain. Due to the constant increase in genomic data there is a need of mechanisms to update and supporting this conceptual model. In this paper, we enrich the CSHG with the integration of haplotypes. Our goal is to improve the understanding of the relationship between genotype and phenotype, because we have detected that they are more complex than expected. With our solution we expand our genomic knowledge, with the aim of providing conceptual models for improving diagnosis in medical contexts where *Genomic Information Systems* (GeIS) play a key role.

Keywords: haplotypes, GeIS, conceptual modeling, genetic diagnosis, statistical models

1. Introduction

The large amounts of data generated in genomic environments arise the need to build structures to organize, process and use that data to take advantage of all the new knowledge to improve our understanding of the human genome.

Several previous works [1-3] show how the use of *conceptual models* allow us to provide a definition of a domain, so that we can understand it better, identifying the entities involved and their relationship. These studies focused on describing the genome of eukaryotic cells, the interaction between proteins, transcriptome, and others. There were also studies focused specially in the proteins topic by Ram [8], [23]. Also, Pastor *et. al.* describes the Conceptual Schema of Human Genome (CSHG) [4]. However, this conceptual schema requires to be constantly aligned with the new genomic knowledge. Specifically, in this paper we extend the model to include the specification of *haplotypes* (which will be defined in Section 2). As for haplotypes, this model should be extended in two ways:

- *Integrating treatment of haplotypes.*

- *Application of statistical models.*

In this context, the goal of our work (*that is part of a wider research*) is to extend the *Conceptual Schema of the Human Genome* with the integration of haplotypes and statistical models to improve its expressiveness. This way, we foresee the creation of a powerful and reliable genomic data repository based on this holistic conceptual schema.

To achieve this goal, the article is divided into the following sections: Section 2 presents the background of this work and the concept of haplotypes. Section 3 explains the research methodology used in the development of this work. Section 4 shows the related work focused on how haplotype information is currently structured and stored in popular genomic data repositories. Section 5 shows our proposal about the conceptual modeling of haplotypes. Section 6 describes the conceptual alignment that we suggest to formalize haplotype information. Finally, section 7 presents the conclusions and future work.

2. Background: Understanding the Haplotype Concept

We detected the relevance of including haplotypes treatment in our CSHG studying the genetic implications for the pathology of *Alcohol Sensitivity*, where we perform an intensive research regarding genes and variations that were associated for predisposition to suffer the disease [5-6].

From a Bioinformatics point of view, Haplotypes are a set of SNP's[1] that are inherited and found together on a chromosome. *Haplotypes* are defined as a group of SNP of a gene that are very close and they tend to be inherited together. This means that a haplotype of the alleles is not separated in recombination phase and can be transmitted in blocks, allowing combinations of variations to a gene that affects certain phenotypes [7-8].

Currently, there is a significant set of genetic diseases where the influence of haplotypes has been well-stablished such as *breast cancer* [9-10], *alcohol sensitivity* [11-12], and others [13-14]. If haplotypes are considered in the diagnosis process, the outcome can be improved as assessed probabilities indicate the level of risk in genomic diagnosis more accurately. In our preliminary studies we detect a "*haplotype case*" with the gene GABRA2. We find the existence of a haplotype composed of three variations: rs279871, rs279836 and rs279845 [48]; initially we were working with individual variations[2], without considering relationships between them and without considering the variation rs279845 [11-12].

1 A single nucleotide polymorphism (SNP), is a variation at a single position in a DNA sequence among individuals. Recall that the DNA sequence is formed from a chain of four nucleotide bases: A, C, G, and T [*Scitable by Nature Education*].

2 Variation: Naturally occurring genetic differences among organisms in the same species [*Scitable by Nature Education*].

The rs279871 form a haplotype with rs279836 and rs279845		
rs279871	RefSNP Alleles: A/G	Ancestral Allele: A
rs279836	RefSNP Alleles: A/T	Ancestral Allele: T
rs279845	RefSNP Alleles: A/T	Ancestral Allele: A

After obtaining this new knowledge we realized that our conceptual schema should be improved to achieve an integration of information in a more appropriate manner. If we treat this concept effectively, we can improve the results generated in the genetic diagnoses.

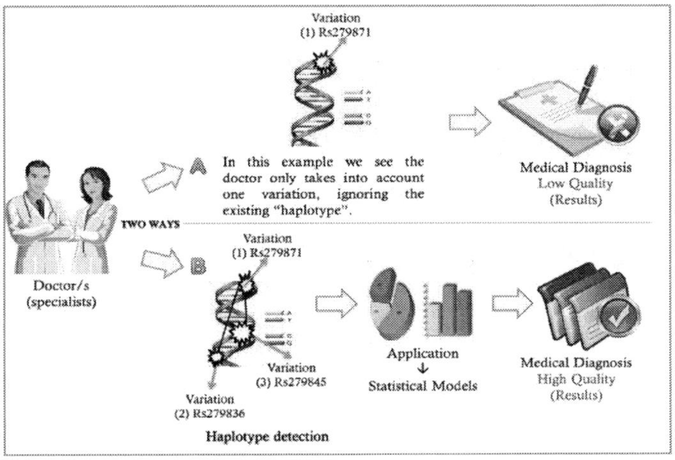

Figure 1. *Differences between Genetic Analysis on "variations" and "variations + haplotypes"*

Figure 1 shows the differences in genetic analysis focused only on individual variations against existing studies on variations plus haplotypes in a reference sample. This figure explains (in the way: A) in this situation the doctor looks for a change in the sample associated with a specific disease; merely check the variation (SNP) in the analyzed sample. With this information we have generated a report that is used to inform about the existence of the variation. The figure (following the path B) explains the ideal process, we try to project in our solution. The doctor looks for the variations and evaluates if exist combinations between all the variations, trying to find haplotypes on different alleles through the analysis of frequencies of each one. In order to obtain this data, we should apply different statistical models that help us to present a more detailed and comprehensive genetic report.

The Haplotypes studies enhance the variation detection rate (with combinations or not) for a specific disease [17]. The reason is that each allele or variation represents a frequency of occurrence in each population, and with this information we can improve the generation of genetic diagnosis [17].

3. Research Methodology

This work discussed and analyzes only a part of a wider PhD research. This study is based on the presentation of the "*Solution Design*" [15]; and that is why we introduce our research methodology using the *–Engineering Cycle–* proposed by Roel Wieringa, which includes the following steps [16]:

a. Implementation Evaluation / Problem Investigation
In this phase we focus on describing the problem and submit initial proposals for the resolution of the case [15]. Our work with haplotypes and variations explain the necessity of extend our CSHG, because all the possible combinations between variations, help us to improve the impact of diagnosis of genetic diseases.

b. Solution Design
One of the steps taken to design our solution was to investigate in depth the state of the art on the subject and then proceed to apply analysis and evaluation techniques to obtain the relevance and the impact factor of haplotypes for genetic diagnosis. Our solution is based on an integrative approach of heterogeneous genomic data sources using conceptual models as the main formalism. Our goal is to gather and represent the available knowledge using an unambiguous representation and establish concise relationships among data. From these models, we will develop a high-quality data repository using a Model-driven development (MDD) approach [41].

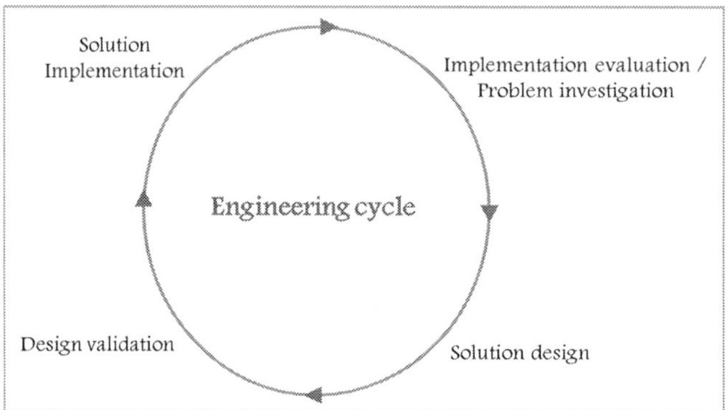

Figure 2. *Engineering Cycle by Roel Wieringa*

c. Design Validation
Design validation is a knowledge task [15]. We are going to develop a data integration framework based in our CSHG that integrates the haplotypes treatment in the genomic diagnosis.

d. Solution Implementation
Finally, the implementation of our solution will be tested with a selected group of physicians that work in the genetic analysis domain, and also with a group of users to obtain a feedback about functionality, usability and the value of the provided information.

4. Related Work

Currently there are -*scarce*- work focused on modeling "*haplotypes*". There have been various studies in order to achieve a conceptual definition for the entire human genome, but this knowledge quickly becomes obsolete due to the continuous evolution of the domain. Our research focuses on the integration and use of information about haplotypes in the genomic information repositories, such as information systems and databases. For those reasons, firstly we analyze some of the most important genomic repositories, in order to evaluate the existing schemas and structures to display and storage haplotypes. Next we detail each analyzed repository:

- **dbSNP**
  This repository facilitates an ER schema which identifies the representation of data about: population, SNP allele frequencies and the summary of populations. dbSNP collects these data in the view "*Frequency calculation submitted by SNP and population*" with construction number 118 dated 11/17/2003. Within this view we find a table called "*b125_SNPMapInfo_35_1*" related "*SNP*" table, where there is only one attribute related with haplotypes - "*hap_cnt*"- [45].

Attribute	*dbSNP_Description*
-hap_cnt	The number of contigs that have the group_term (in ContigInfo) with ""*haplotype*"" suffix that the SNP aligns to.

- **Ensembl**
  Ensembl schema does not provide any explicit relationship with haplotypes. But it is noteworthy that in the "*features_analyses_core*" view we detect some entities that could be linked to treatment, such as: the table "*Marker_map_location*" and the attribute "*lod_score*"; which is a statistical data used in population genetics and in the LD calculations [38] [46].

- **UCSC Genome Bioinformatics**
  In this case, there is not available a schema that defines the data. But with the help of the "*Gene Sorter*" tool [40] we could check the different data provided from a gene. Within this information there is some data associated haplotypes in the block "*Common Gene haplotype Alleles*", which are generated from the platform of 1000 Genomes (http://www.1000genomes.org/). From the data presented we make an outline (draft) of the structure to compare with our solution [39] [47].

Additionaly, we can find a set of databases focused on collecting data associated with haplotypes and populations frequencies as: *HapMap* [18], *ALFRED* [19], *YHRD* [20], *D-HaploDB* [21], and others [4], [8]. The problem with this kind of repositories is that is complex to manage and access to the haplotypes information, showing us the large amounts of dispersed information. An example of this is that the data is stored in multiple text files (* .txt, * .csv, etc.), avoiding the treatment of data in a more efficient manner. After analyzing different data sources (*and schemas*) that store haplotypes information, we have identified three main issues:

P1. Complexity in data management

Presentation of data ambiguously, and in many cases difficult to understand and manipulate. e.g., in the case of dbSNP and Ensembl, the haplotype data is not shown explicitly users. For dbSNP and UCSC, the first sample taken from HapMap data and the second data generated from the 1000 Genomes Project. In our studies, we detected some cases of inconsistency of data between these repositories.

P2. High dispersion and data redundancy

Different data sources with large amounts of information (structured and unstructured) and different formats. e.g., formats like: *.zip; *.csv; *.txt; *.xml; *.fasta; and others.

P3. There is no clear conceptual definition of the concept of "haplotypes"

This is found to see that many of these repositories did not provide a suitable structure (schema) to manage haplotypes. And in other cases they did not represented this concept. e.g., in the cases we studied, we saw that for dbSNP and Ensembl their databases schemas are available, but we found a lot differences at conceptual level on how they represent haplotypes. For UCSC we did not find a conceptual definition. dbSNP in its definition only shows an attribute associated with the concept of haplotypes; Ensembl not provide a clear definition in his schema; UCSC presents data about haplotypes, but this repository does not have a conceptual definition of their work.

As the genomic environment is continuously evolving, additional knowledge is incorporated. There are several sources of data showing information on haplotypes, as in the cases mentioned above, but the problem lies primarily in the complexity of management and interpretation of the data (*the importance, relevance, etc.*) (P1) [43].

A further disadvantage identified in the haplotype data is the *large dispersion* and *data redundancy* (P2) [43]. Using a conceptual modelling approach, we will tackle these problems with a comprehensive data processing to complement existing genetic diagnostics.

5. Conceptual Modeling of Haplotypes

The application of data management techniques in genomic environment could be thwarted or affected by the different characteristics that define it, such as: *high conceptual complexity*, *large amounts of data* and the *constant evolution* in the community. Our research group has been able to generate a *Conceptual Schema of the Human Genome (CSHG)* [24], which has evolved and grown over the years, giving the scientific community a thrust in understanding the human genome.

The latest version of the CSHG (v3) is classified into five views [44], which are:

(1) *Structural view*: this describes the genome structure (species, chromosomes, etc.).

(2) *Transcription View*: shows the components and concepts related to protein synthesis.
(3) *Variation View*: This view models the knowledge related to the differences in the DNA sequence of different individuals.
(4) *Pathway View*: in the area of biochemical pathways or metabolic pathways are a series of chemical reactions occurring within a cell.
(5) *Bibliography and data bank View*: contains information on sources where you have extracted the data, and a series of bibliographic reference documents for anyone wishing to obtain more information regarding any topic described here [22], [24].

In our CSHG (v3) currently we work with *precise variations*. For the treatment of haplotypes is necessary to manage others concepts like: *frequencies (allelic and genotypic)* and *populations* [25], this data that have been difficult to manage in the genomic field. This new scenario implies that the data loading process should also consider the concepts represented in the left side (Frequency generalization) of Figure 3. Currently only entities highlighted in green are considered as haplotypes are not loaded. Figure 4 presents our proposal to integrate the haplotypes into the CSHG, where we found a number of added or extended classes. As we can see the variations area, defined by their "*description*" is preserved as in the current version. In this figure we can notice that the part of variations defined by its "*frequency*" has to implement changes that are necessary for working with the haplotype data and statistical models.

The insertions and changes made to the schema are explained as follows: the "*Haplotype*" class, which is associated with the "*SNP*" class, is added, reflecting the relationships present in a Haplotype-SNP by the combination of two or more SNPs. The attributes that define "*Haplotype*" class in the schema are: "*id_reference*" which defines an identifier a link between the different SNPs and haplotype; the "*id_haplotype*" corresponds to the identifier of the haplotype, as the "*variation_id*" that identifies the associated variation. The haplotype should be based in scientific resource to confirm its medical value, for this reason we created the class called "*Hap_Bib_Ref*", that help us the join with the classes "*Haplotype*" and "*Bibliography reference*", allowing thus maintain our repository linked to various research works about haplotypes.

Our idea of integrating haplotypes strengths the conceptual schema and also assess levels of incidence or risk of "*variations*" in predisposing genetic diseases. The figure 3 presents the current state of the "*variation view*", indicating classes (green boxes) that are currently loaded into our repository. The variations are presented in two groups that are by: *frequency* and *description*. The first is classified according the variation frequency into the population (occurrence). In this case, there are two types: mutations and polymorphisms. The alteration that occurs in any part of the genetic code is known as a mutation. And when a single nucleotide change between genomes of individuals of the same species occurs is known as polymorphism (occurring in at least 1% of the population). The second group it conforms to the description given by the variations, classified in two types: *precise* and *imprecise*. The precise variations are those that indicate their position in the chromosome, and imprecise variations only described their phenotypic effect but do not have their location within the chromosome.

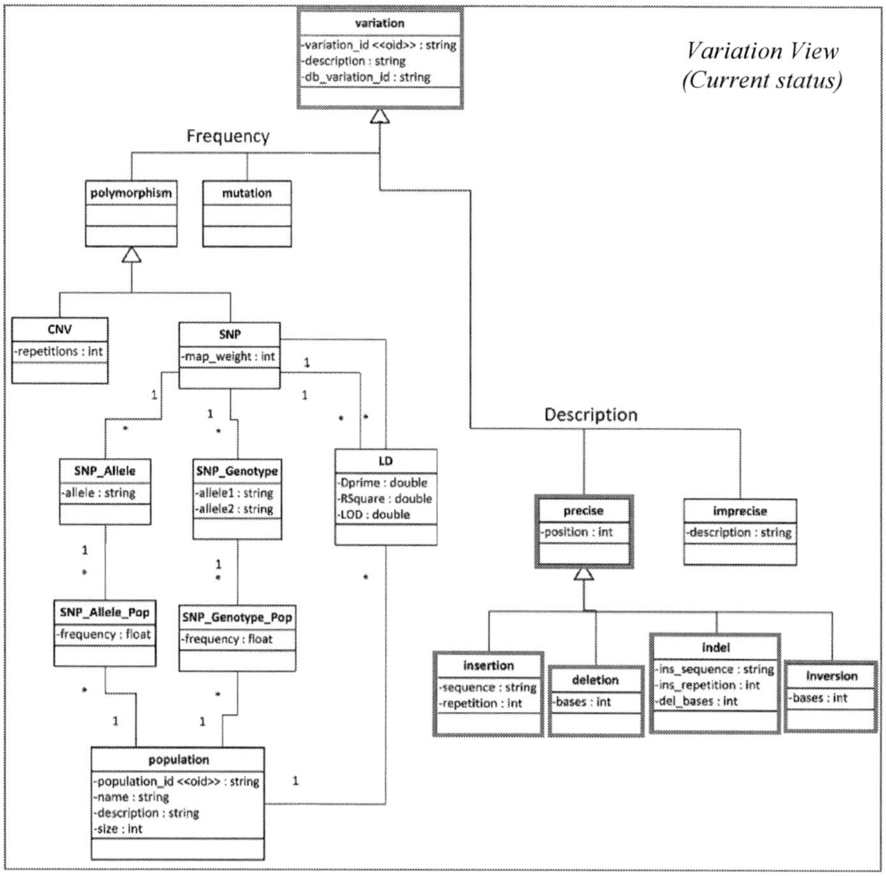

Figure 3. *Current status of the "Variation View"*

The "*SNP*" class of our CSHG becomes the root-class where new concepts appear. Although the conceptualization of the following classes is represented in our original proposal, "*SNP_Allele*"; "*SNP_Allele-Pop*"; "*SNP_Genotype*"; "*SNP_Genotype-Pop*"; "P*opulation*"; "*LD*", the data related to them were not treated and neither have been loaded in our repository, may be by any of the following causes: (a) the unavailability of data (sources, resources, etc.) or (b) before, we did not know an appreciable or tangible value for this data.

A SNP is associated with many alleles ("*SNP Allele*"), and these sets have a frequency of alleles in a population in specific ("*SNP_Allele-Pop*"). Similarly, a SNP has several genotypic data ("*SNP Genotype*") defined by "*allele1*" and "*allele2*" (the reference allele and the allele changed within genotype); each allele represent a frequency within a population. The "*Population*" class is used to group all the populations that have been studied for the analysis of variations in the human genome.

This class consists of the following attributes: "*population_id*" that serves as an identifier of the population; the identifier of the source "*pop_db_id*"; the name of the population "*pop_name*" and geographical region "*geo_region*". Also in this class we associated the new class "*Pop_OriginDB*" which we use to define the sources that provide the above populations. In this class we define the following attributes: "*pop_orig_id*" which is the identifier of the repository; the "*name*" and "*description*" of the source, and the "*URL_pop*" which has the URL of population data file.

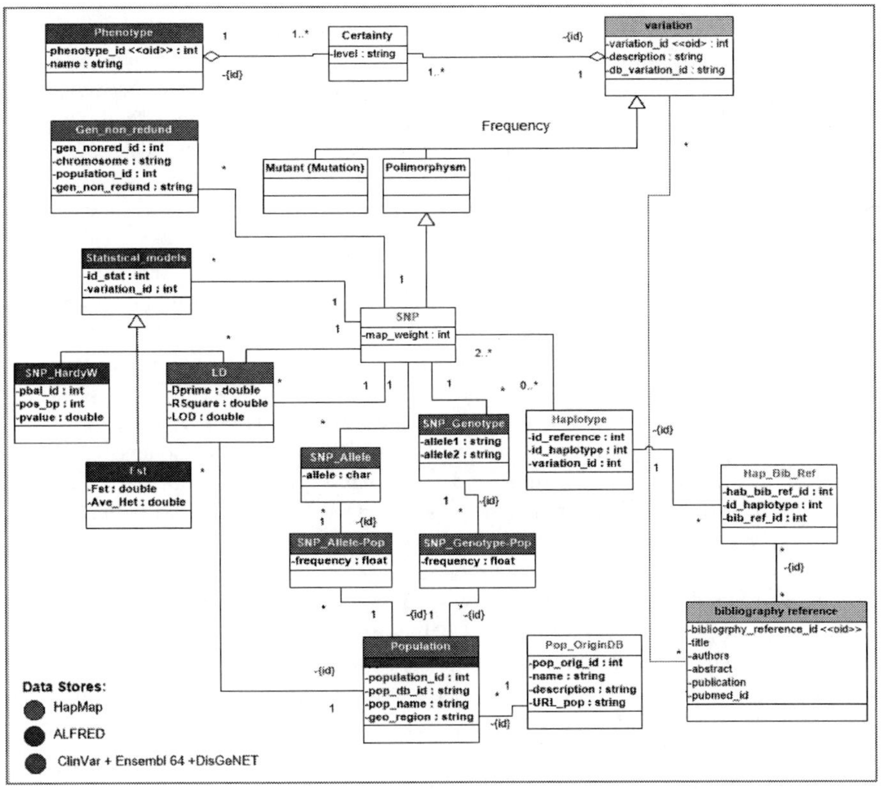

Figure 4. *Haplotype integration to the CSHG – Phase II*

Another novelty on the schema is the addition of the "*Statistical_models*" class, which has been defined with the objective of unify the statistical models that are applied to the data related with variations [26-28], specifically on changes in the value of "*variation_id*", considering that for a SNP or variation can be applied from zero to many statistical models. Three subclasses of this superclass are derived: "*SNP_HardyW*", "*Fst*" and "*LD*".

The conceptual definition of these classes allows us to tackle very important concepts in the world of genomics, called "*Population Genetics*". The population genetics is the study of the forces that alter the genetic makeup of a species. This focus associated with micro-evolutionary mechanisms like: mutation, natural selection, gene flow and genetic drift [29-30].

The "*SNP_HardyW*" class represents the Hardy-Weinberg model (also known as panmictic balance), which is used to calculate the genotype frequencies from allele frequencies [31-32]; we take data from the data sources and apply it into the model. This class has the following characteristics: unique identifier of the "*pbal_id*" class; chromosomal position in base pairs "*pos_bp*"; and the P-value "*pvalue*" which indicates the level of significance smallest possible that we can choose.

Another statistical value used in population genetics, is the calculation of "*fixation indices*", which allow us to measure the differentiation of the population due to genetic structure, facilitating the comparison of genetic variability within and between populations. To do this we define the "*Fst*" class, containing the values: "*Fst*" for fixation index and the "*Ave_Het*" that indicates the average heterozygosity. The "*LD*" class defines the "*Linkage disequilibrium*", which occurs when the genotypes in the two loci are not independent of another. To calculate the LD, we found three statistical parameters (*biological*) which are: (1) the sensitivity index "*DPrime*", which measures the imbalance between the alleles interact. (2) The coefficient of determination "*RSquare*" which serves to determine the quality of the model, to replicate the results, and the proportion of variation in the results presented in the model. (3) LOD score "*LOD*" with this value we refer to the logarithm of the odds of two genes or loci are linked and thus are inherited together more often than usual. The "*LD*" class is related to the "*SNP*" class indicating that a SNP can have zero to many LD.

In this extension of the CSHG we integrate all the existing data about phenotypes that are in different repositories, we suggested the "*Phenotype*" class, which join to the "*Variation*" class through the intermediate class "*Certainty*", used as the indicator of the incidence level between phenotype-variation.

Finally, the "*Gen_non_redund*" class, help us to presents the results of the cleaned dataset (without redundancy), for sets for SNP-genotyping and population. For this class we assign a unique identifier to the data without redundancy "*gen_nonred_id*"; information about chromosome and the studied population, the attributes are "*chromosome*" and "*population_id*" respectively; and total non-redundant data after performing filtering "*gen_non_redund*".

6. Conceptual Alignment

To evaluate this work, we have check if the concepts are suitable to support the information provided by popular haplotypes repositories: trying to represent a good conceptual alignment with validated databases from the community. The figure 4 shows the extended schema and at the bottom points out data repositories that we have studied. The main data source is the *HapMap* Project in its third phase. The dataset from HapMap according to our *variation view* is contained in the following directories: (a) *frequencies* and (b) *ld_data*. First, "*frequencies*" is a directory that contains the above SNPs with their frequency in each population. Due to the large amount of information, they cluster all of them into two groups: the frequencies of SNP variations type taking into account only one allele of the chromosome ("*Allele_freqs*"), and frequencies of SNP rate variations taking into account the two alleles ("*Genotype_freqs*").

The Linkage disequilibrium data [33] is provided through the "*LD_data*" directory, for the large amount of information is divided by: chromosomes and populations. Information about population "*Population*" and not redundant genes "*Gen_non_redund*" is found in specific sections of the main web. The "*Statistical_models*" class consists of the extracted data in HapMap for "*LD*", and provided by the ALFRED repository for frequencies and statistical processes applied to biological field. The frequencies dataset from *ALFRED* corresponds to a file called "*FreqByChrom*" available from their website; these frequencies have been obtained for each chromosome according to the studied population. This repository also facilitates the extraction of information about populations that they used. For the "*phenotypic*" entity, we find several data sources from which we can extract all the information classified in multiple repositories, such as: *ClinVar*, *Ensembl* and *DisGeNET* (sorted by their scientific relevance) [34-37]. The following is a summary table that brings together the schema elements (updated) with their origin data sources:

Schema element (name)	**Data source (origin)**
SNP_Allele	HapMap
SNP_Allele-pop	HapMap
SNP_Genotype	HapMap
SNP_Genotype-pop	HapMap
Gen_non_redund	HapMap
Population	HapMap; ALFRED
Statistical_models	ALFRED
Fst	ALFRED
SNP_HardyW	ALFRED
LD	HapMap
Phenotype	ClinVar; Ensembl; DisGeNET

7. Conclusions and Future Work

The application of Conceptual models in the bioinformatics field is essential to develop a *Genomic Information Systems* (GeIS). The extension of the previous proposed CSHG is a must, because of recent advances in genomic data repositories. We believe that our conceptual alignment is correctly, because it extends the genetic knowledge in the CSHG through the integration of new concepts, thus achieving a valid conceptual representation for the different data sources analyzed.

Future research work is oriented in the implementation of an ETL process [42] using our conceptual model. Also, the study and treatment of *haplogroups*, which include people with a similar genetic profile who share a common ancestor. Other interesting work is the inclusion of data mining techniques to achieve a better exploitation of acquired knowledge.

Acknowledgements

The authors thanks to the members of the PROS Center Genome group for fruitful discussions. In addition, it is also important to highlight that this work has been supported by the Ministry of Higher Education, Science and Technology (*MESCyT*). Santo Domingo, Dominican Republic.

References

1. Paton *et al.*, 2000. Conceptual Modelling of Genomic Information. BIOINFORMATICS, Vol. 16 no. 6, pages 548-557
2. Pastor *et al.*, 2010. Enforcing Conceptual Modeling to Improve the Understanding of Human Genome. Valencia, Spain. APCCM2010
3. Paton *et al.*, 2002. Conceptual data modelling for bioinformatics. Henry Stewart Publications 1467-5463. Briefings in Bioinformatics. Vol 3. No 2. 166–180
4. Martin *et. al.*, 2011. Integrating Human Genome Variation Data: An Information System Approach, DEXA, pp.65-69.
5. Sánchez *et. al.*, June, 2000. Sensibilidad al Alcohol y la Predisposición a beber. Ciencia al Día Internacional, Número 2, Volumen 3, ISSN 0717-3849.
6. M. Dick *et. al.*, May, 2003. Candidate Genes for Alcohol Dependence: A Review of Genetic Evidence From Human Studies. Vol. 27, No. 5. Alcoholism: Clinical & Experimental Research.
7. Drogodependencias: Farmacología. Patología Psicología. Legislación, Pedro Lorenzo Fernández, Edición 3, Editor Médica Panamericana, 30/06/2009 - 725 páginas, ISBN: 8498354684, 9788498354683
8. Reyes, J. F., 2013. Integración de Haplotipos al Modelo Conceptual del Genoma Humano utilizando la Metodología SILE. Tesis de Máster en Ing. Software, Métodos Formales & SI, Universitat Politècnica de València (UPV), Valencia, España.
9. Campos *et. al.*, 2004. Análisis del haplotipo en portadores de la mutación 6857delAA en el gen BRCA2 en 4 familias con cáncer de mama u ovario hereditario. Servei de Genètica. Hospital de la Santa Creu i Sant Pau. Barcelona. Laboratorio de Genética Molecular Humana. Departamento de Biología Celular y Molecular. (13-5-2004).
10. Sifuentes Álvarez *et. al.*, 2012. Asociación del cáncer de mama con los polimorfismos T-66G y G-156GG del gen SPP1 y las concentraciones séricas de osteopontina. Ginecol Obstet Mex 2012; 80(1):22-29. ISSN-0300-9041 Volumen 80, núm. 1, enero 2012
11. The Effects of Alcohol on the Brain (2013). http://www.scripps.edu/newsandviews/e_20020225/koob2.html
12. Edenberg *et. al.*, March 2012. Variations in GABRA2, encoding the alpha 2 subunit of the GABA(A) receptor, are associated with alcohol dependence and with brain oscillations. Indiana University School of Medicine, Indianapolis 46202, USA. edenberg@iupui.edu. http://www.ncbi.nlm.nih.gov/pubmed/15024690
13. Gabriel *et al.*, 2002. The Structure of Haplotype Blocks in the Human Genome. Pages: 1-10. 10.1126/science.1069424
14. Fonseca *et. al.*, 2008. Deletions Identification in Female Carriers of Duchenne's Muscular Distrophy. Laboratorio de Biología Molecular y Celular. Instituto de Ciencias Básicas. Facultad de Medicina. Universidad del Rosario. Acta Med Colomb vol.33 no.2 Bogotá Apr./June 2008.

15. Wieringa, R., 2013. Introduction to design science methodology. Slides based on a book on Design Science methodology. 8-4-2013 REFSQ 2013 Doctoral Symposium
16. Wieringa, R., 2009. Design Science as Nested Problem Solving. Department of Electrical Engineering, Mathematics, and Computer Science. University of Twente, the Netherlands. DESRIST ´09, May 7-8, 2009. Malvern, PA, USA.
17. Roitt, 2008. Inmunología. Fundamentos. Ed. Médica Panamericana. ISBN9500608995, 9789500608992. 528 pages.
18. Gibbs *et al.*, 2003. "The international HapMap project." Nature 426.6968: 789-796.
19. Cheung *et al.*, 2000. "ALFRED: an allele frequency database for diverse populations and DNA polymorphisms." Nucleic Acids Res. 28.1: 361-363.
20. Willuweit *et. al.*, 2007. "Y chromosome haplotype reference database (YHRD): update." Forensic Science International: Genetics 1.2: 83-87.
21. Higasa *et al.*, 2007. "D-HaploDB: a database of definitive haplotypes determined by genotyping complete hydatidiform mole samples." Nucleic Acids Research 35. suppl 1: D685-D689.
22. Martin, A., 2012. Human genome conceptual modeling: An ontological framework for the design and implementation of genomic Information Systems. RCIS 2012: 1-6
23. Ram *et. al.*, 2004. "Modeling the semantics of 3D protein structures," Conceptual Modeling–ER 2004, pp. 696-708.
24. Pastor *et. al.*, 2010. "Enforcing conceptual modeling to improve the understanding of human genome." Research Challenges in Information Science (RCIS), 2010. IEEE.
25. The International HapMap Consortium*, 2005. A haplotype map of the human genome. Vol 437|27 October 2005|doi:10.1038/nature04226
26. Stephens *et. al.*, 2001. A New Statistical Method for Haplotype Reconstruction from Population Data. The American Journal of Human Genetics. Volume 68, Issue 4, April 2001, Pages 978–989
27. Fallin *et. al.*, 2000. Accuracy of Haplotype Frequency Estimation for Biallelic Loci, via the Expectation-Maximization Algorithm for Unphased Diploid Genotype Data. The American Journal of Human Genetics. Volume 67, Issue 4, Oct. 2000, P947–959
28. Schaid *et. al.*, 2002. Score Tests for Association between Traits and Haplotypes when Linkage Phase Is Ambiguous. The American Journal of Human Genetics. Volume 70, Issue 2, February 2002, Pages 425–434
29. Genética de Poblaciones, 2003. UVIGEN. Universidad de la República Uruguay. http://uvigen.fcien.edu.uy/utem/Popgen/popintro.html
30. Barbadilla *et. al.*, 2009. "Genética de Poblaciones." Departamento de Genética y Microbiología. Universidad Autónoma de Barcelona.
31. Modelo de Hardy-Weinberg, 2015. Atlas of Genetics and Cytogenetics in Oncology and Haematology (10/03/2015).
32. Barrett *et. al.*, 2005. "Haploview: analysis and visualization of LD and haplotype maps." Bioinformatics 21.2: 263-265.
33. Reich *et. al.*, 2001. "Linkage disequilibrium in the human genome." Nature 411.6834: 199-204.
34. Landrum *et. al.*, 2014. "ClinVar: public archive of relationships among sequence variation and human phenotype." Nucleic Acids Res. 42. D1: D980-D985.
35. Johnston *et. al.*, 2013. "Databases of genomic variation and phenotypes: existing resources and future needs." Human molecular genetics: ddt384.
36. Hubbard *et. al.*, 2002. "The Ensembl genome database project." Nucleic acids research 30.1: 38-41.
37. Piñero *et. al.*, 2015. "DisGeNET: a discovery platform for the dynamical exploration of human diseases and their genes." Database 2015: bav028.
38. Hubbard *et. al.*, 2002. The Ensembl genome database project. Nucleic Acids Res., 30(1), 38-41.

39. Karolchik *et. al.*, 2014. The UCSC genome browser database: 2014 update. Nucleic Acids Research, 42(D1), D764-D770.
40. Kent *et. al.*, 2005. Exploring relationships and mining data with the UCSC Gene Sorter. Genome research, 15(5), 737-741.
41. Pastor *et. al.*, 2008. Model-driven development. Informatik-Spektrum, 31(5), 394-407.
42. Munoz *et. al.*, 2011. ETL process modeling conceptual for data warehouses: a systematic mapping study. Latin America Transactions, IEEE, 9(3), 358-363.
43. Martinez F., A., 2012. Wiki-Genome: A model-driven genome data management environment. IEEE RCIS 2012, pp. 1-6.
44. Pastor *et. al.*, 2012. Conceptual modeling of human genome: Integration challenges. In Conceptual Modelling and Its Theoretical Foundations. Springer Berlin Heidelberg, (pp. 231-250).
45. dbSNP ER Schema, 2015. NCBI. ftp://ftp.ncbi.nih.gov/snp/database/b124/mssql/schema/erd_dbSNP.pdf
46. Ensembl: Core Schema, 2015. Ensembl. http://www.ensembl.org/info/docs/api/core/core_schema.html#top
47. UCSC Genome Bioinformatics: Haplotypes representation, 2015. UCSC. https://genome.ucsc.edu/goldenPath/help/haplotypes.html
48. Reyes *et. al.*, 2016. Use of GeIS for Early Diagnosis of Alcohol Sensitivity. Proceedings of the 9th International Joint Conference on Biomedical Engineering Systems and Technologies (BIOSTEC 2016) - Volume 3: BIOINFORMATICS, pages 284-289.

Una Propuesta Basada en Model Driven Architecture para el Soporte de Rich Internet Applications

Iván López, Magalí González, Nathalie Aquino y Luca Cernuzzi

Universidad Católica "Nuestra Señora de la Asunción", Asunción, Paraguay
ivalop81@gmail.com
{mgonzalez, nathalie.aquino, lcernuzz}@uca.edu.py

Abstract. Las Rich Internet Applications (RIA) han surgido para permitir aplicaciones en la Web con características similares a las de escritorio. Este trabajo se enfoca en las características RIA relacionadas a la validación local de datos y a la inclusión de widgets interactivos de amplia utilización para extender Model Oriented Web Approach (MoWebA). MoWebA es una aproximación de desarrollo de aplicaciones Web fundamentada en los principios de Model Driven Architecture (MDA). En ese contexto, este trabajo extiende MoWebA para dar cobertura a las Rich Internet Applications (RIA), dando lugar a MoWebA4RIA. Se han extendido los metamodelos y perfiles de MoWebA para dar soporte a las características mencionadas. De manera correspondiente, se adaptaron las reglas de transformación y el compilador de modelo a texto para generar interfaces enriquecidas usando jQuery UI y jQuery Validation Plugin. Finalmente, se ha realizado una ilustración de la propuesta, a fin de demostrar las nuevas capacidades de MoWebA4RIA.

Keywords: Model Driven Architecture (MDA), Model Oriented Web Approach (MoWebA), Rich Internet Applications (RIA)

1 Introducción

El término Rich Internet Application (RIA) fue introducido en el 2002 por la empresa Macromedia, que en ese entonces abordaba limitaciones en cuanto a la riqueza de las interfaces, medios y contenidos de las aplicaciones Web. Las RIA son aplicaciones Web que exhiben widgets, comportamientos y características que están presentes en las aplicaciones de escritorio. Poseen una mayor capacidad de respuesta, son más seguras y presentan una interfaz más avanzada con respecto a las aplicaciones del modelo Web tradicional [2][4].

Las RIA tienen cuatro características principales [3]: i) es posible almacenar datos en el lado cliente, o bien distribuir el almacenamiento entre el cliente y el servidor; ii) es factible distribuir la ejecución de la lógica de negocios entre el cliente y el servidor, o bien llevar a cabo operaciones complejas, específicas de dominio, o de validación de datos directamente en el lado cliente; iii) las interfaces de usuario ofrecen una mayor riqueza ya que permiten manejar eventos en el lado cliente, ofertan una amplia variedad de widgets interactivos, siguen un paradigma de página única, y dan soporte a contenido multimedia; y iv) se crean mecanismos para reducir al mínimo la transferencia de datos entre el cliente y el servidor, dando soporte a comunicaciones asíncronas entre ellos.

Debido a los avances propuestos por las RIA, muchas metodologías de desarrollo basadas en modelos y enfocadas en las aplicaciones Web tradicionales (como OOHDM [12], OOH [15], WebML [14], UWE [8][13] , OOWS [1], entre otras) han tenido que evolucionar, agregando nuevos modelos o extendiendo los existentes, para dar cobertura a las características de las RIA.

Los trabajos de Wright y Dietrich [5], y el de Preciado et al. [6] exponen la necesidad de metodologías sistemáticas para el desarrollo de las RIA y llevan a cabo estudios presentando las diversas metodologías Web existentes para ese fin. Toffetti [3] presenta un estudio más exhaustivo y reciente enfocado en hacer comparativas entre las diversas metodologías. Busch y Koch [9] presentan además un estado del arte de las aplicaciones RIA.

En el contexto de este trabajo, se ha realizado un nuevo análisis comparativo entre las metodologías de desarrollo Web basadas en modelos para las RIA. Las metodologías consideradas en el análisis derivan de la evolución de enfoques dirigidos por modelos que fueron concebidos originalmente para el diseño y desarrollo de aplicaciones Web tradicionales y son: OOHDM-RIA [12], OOH4RIA [15], WebML-RIA [14], Patrones RIA con UWE [13], UWE-R [8] y UWE+RUX [7]. Cada una de estas metodologías es comparada con respecto a las cuatro características principales de las RIA.

Tabla 1. Comparación de metodologías de desarrollo Web basadas en modelos en relación a las características de las RIA

Características RIA / Metodologías de desarrollo Web basadas en modelos		**OOHDM-RIA**	**OOH4RIA**	**WebML-RIA**	**Patrones RIA con UWE**	**UWE-R**	**UWE+RUX**
Almacenamiento en lado cliente		-	-	sí	-	-	-
Lógica de negocios en lado cliente	Operaciones complejas	-	-	sí	-	-	-
	Operaciones específicas de dominio	-	-	-	-	sí	-
	Validación de datos local	sí	sí	sí	-	-	sí
Interfaces enriquecidas	Manejo de eventos en lado cliente	-	-	sí	sí	sí	sí
	Widgets interactivos	sí	sí	-	sí	sí	sí
	Paradigma de página única	sí	sí	sí	sí	-	sí
	Contenido multimedia	-	sí	-	-	sí	sí
Comunicación cliente-servidor	Sincronización de datos	-	-	sí	-	sí	sí
	Actualizaciones parciales de página	sí	sí	sí	sí	sí	sí
	Push y pull	-	-	sí	-	sí	-

Muchas de las metodologías citadas han logrado una notable evolución incorporando los avances propuestos por las RIA. Sin embargo, como se puede observar en la Tabla 1, ninguna de las metodologías ofrece cobertura completa a todas las características de las RIA, de allí la necesidad de proponer extensiones a tales metodologías, o bien, de promover nuevas.

Recientemente se ha propuesto un nuevo enfoque, denominado Model Oriented Web Approach (MoWebA) [10] [11], para el desarrollo de aplicaciones Web, fundamentado en los principios propuestos por el Object Management Group (OMG - http://www.omg.org/). Este enfoque está basado en los estándares de Model Driven Architecture (MDA - http://www.omg.org/mda/) y ofrece un esquema de modelado en capas para la separación de conceptos.

En el marco de este trabajo, en lugar de extender alguna de las metodologías Web analizadas, se ha optado por extender MoWebA para que de soporte a las características RIA orientadas a datos en el lado cliente y widgets interactivos, en aplicaciones Web para PCs. Los motivos de elegir MoWebA son: i) está basado en estándares ampliamente aceptados, UML, mientras que entre las metodologías analizadas, solo OOH4RIA, Patrones RIA con UWE y UWE-R poseen un lenguaje de modelado cien por ciento basado en UML; ii) propone un enfoque de modelado orientado a la navegación dinámica centrada en la interacción del usuario y del contexto (y no del dominio), lo cual lo vuelve bastante atractivo para estos entornos y lo diferencia de las demás propuestas analizadas; iii) incorpora un modelo específico de arquitectura (ASM - Architectural Specific Model), no considerado por ninguna propuesta estudiada, que establece una clara separación entre los modelos independientes de la plataforma y los que incorporan detalles de la arquitectura; iv) finalmente, se tiene el interés de que MoWebA siga evolucionando e incorpore características RIA.

Para lograr el objetivo mencionado, los metamodelos y perfiles relacionados a la capa de presentación de MoWebA han sido mejorados y extendidos para dar soporte a la validación de datos en el lado cliente y a los widgtes interactivos. Además, se adaptaron las reglas de transformación del compilador de modelo a texto a fin de generar interfaces enriquecidas en código HTML y Javascript.

El resto del artículo se estructura como se explica a continuación. En la sección 2 se introduce el enfoque MoWebA. En la sección 3 se presentan las extensiones que se han realizado en los metamodelos de MoWebA para dar soporte a las RIA, así como, el proceso de transformación para generar las nuevas interfaces enriquecidas. En la sección 4 se presenta una ilustración de la propuesta. Finalmente, la sección 5 presenta un análisis de los resultados obtenidos y los posibles trabajos futuros.

2 La Aproximación MoWebA (Model Oriented Web Approach)

MoWebA [10] [11] adopta los principios de MDA y propone un enfoque que incluye un proceso de modelado y un proceso de transformación. En el proceso de modelado se especifican los diagramas necesarios para contemplar las fases CIM (Computational Independent Model), PIM (Platform Independent Model), ASM (Architectural Specific Model) y PSM (Platform Specific Model). Esta propuesta provee un modelado basado en la navegación como punto de referencia principal, en donde la navegación se encuentra orientada a funciones. Las fases del proceso de modelado se resumen a continuación.

- **Modelado del problema:** en esta fase se incluyen el CIM y el PIM. El CIM está orientado al modelado de los requisitos funcionales. El PIM está orientado al modelado del problema sin considerar aspectos de la arquitectura o plataforma. A partir de aquí es posible llevar a cabo transformaciones para obtener los modelos específicos de la arquitectura y de la plataforma de manera semi-automática.
- **Modelado de la solución:** en esta fase se incluyen el ASM y el PSM. Es en esta fase en la que todos los detalles de la arquitectura y plataforma destino se definen, permitiendo generar a partir de aquí, el código de la aplicación de manera automática. En MoWebA se plantea tener siempre el mismo PIM para una aplicación dada y a partir de este, se podrán generar diferentes ASM para diferentes arquitecturas destino. Finalmente, a partir de un ASM, se podrán generar diferentes PSM para diferentes plataformas destino. Como se puede ver, MoWebA separa aspectos arquitectónicos y de plataforma específica, y esto hace que la aproximación sea bastante prometedora para la implementación de las RIA, debido a que las RIA constituyen una arquitectura y existen numerosas plataformas destino para desplegarlas.
- **Código fuente:** incluye al ISM (Implementation Specific Model), que corresponde al código generado automáticamente y al código manual agregado, en caso de ser necesario, para obtener la aplicación final.

Cabe mencionar que todos los modelos de la aplicación pueden refinarse, dado que todas las fases son iterativas e incrementales.

La capa de presentación de MoWebA, para la cual ha sido definida la propuesta de extensión, tiene como fin principal facilitar la interacción de los usuarios con la aplicación y proveerles los elementos necesarios para que puedan realizar sus tareas (introducir datos, activar procesos, navegar, etc.) de la mejor manera posible. MoWebA propone dos diagramas para ella: el diagrama de contenido y el diagrama de estructura. El diagrama de contenido permite especificar los diferentes elementos que serán presentados en la interfaz. Se compone de un conjunto de páginas de presentación, las que, a su vez, se componen de uno o más elementos de interfaz. Los elementos de interfaz definen un conjunto de atributos clasificados de la siguiente manera: atributos estáticos, que son los atributos propios de la clase de presentación y sirven para representar información no asociada a la capa de datos, como por ejemplo, el titulo de la página web; y atributos de enlace, que representan la transición de un estado a otro, como un submit de un formulario.

El diagrama de estructura permite representar las diferentes regiones de una pantalla. Cada región puede estar compuesta de subregiones. Con el diagrama de estructura se pueden definir diferentes estructuras por aplicación.

Cabe destacar que actualmente MoWebA no soporta la arquitectura RIA. Más detalles de la capa de presentación pueden ser consultados en [10] [11].

3 Una propuesta de extensión a MoWebA: MoWebA4RIA

Las RIA cubren una gran variedad de características que abarcan varias capas de una aplicación (presentación, lógica de negocio, persistencia y comunicación cliente-servidor). En este trabajo, se ha decidido enfocar la extensión hacia las presentaciones enriquecidas considerando a los widgets y en la lógica de la aplicación del lado cliente, dejando como trabajo futuro las demás características. Para identificar los widgets a ser considerados, se ha realizado primeramente una revisión de aquellos más utilizados a partir de un conjunto de sitios web muy demandados (como Facebook, gmail, amazon, entre otros). El proceso de extensión de MoWebA para que de soporte a las RIA (presentación y lógica del lado cliente) ha consistido de los siguientes pasos. Primero, se han mejorado y extendido los metamodelos de la capa de presentación de MoWebA. Las principales extensiones se han realizado en el metamodelo de contenido, donde se han agregado nuevos elementos enriquecidos (widgets) y propiedades de validación local de campos de entrada. Segundo, las mejoras y extensiones de los metamodelos de contenido y estructura han sido reflejadas en los perfiles (UML profiles) correspondientes de MoWebA. Estos perfiles son los que definen la sintaxis concreta de MoWebA. Tercero, se definieron las reglas de transformación para las plataformas jQuery UI (https://jqueryui.com/) y jQuery Validation (http://jqueryvalidation.org/). Si bien existen diferentes tecnologías para el desarrollo e implementación de las RIA, las basadas en Javascript o librerías Ajax son las más utilizadas debido a que utilizan tecnologías de uso abierto y estandarizado como Javascript, HTML y CSS. Además, según el sitio de encuestas sobre tecnologías para la Web, W3Tech, jQuery es utilizado por más del 67,9% de todos los sitios Web a nivel mundial, siendo el de mayor popularidad [16]. Las transformaciones definidas en este trabajo son de modelo a texto (M2T) y fueron definidas en las plantillas de transformación de contenido y estructura, respectivamente, que han sido implementadas utilizando la herramienta Acceleo (https://eclipse.org/acceleo/), ampliamente conocida y relacionada con el proyecto Eclipse. Como resultado del proceso, MoWebA ha evolucionado a MoWebA4RIA. A continuación, se presentan más detalles del proceso descripto.

3.1 Metamodelos y Perfiles de Contenido y Estructura de MoWebA4RIA

La Fig. 1 presenta los metamodelos de contenido (Content) y de estructura (Layout) de MoWebA4RIA. Estos metamodelos fueron obtenidos luego de aplicar mejoras y extensiones a sus versiones originales correspondientes de MoWebA. Los elementos de ambos metamodelos fueron catalogados en diferentes colores. Aquellos que ya existían en los metamodelos originales de MoWebA aparecen en color salmón. Los que ya existían y han sufrido modificaciones, aparecen en color celeste. Y los nuevos, que no existían en los metamodelos orginales de MoWebA, aparecen en color verde.

En relación al metamodelo de contenido, un diagrama de presentación (PresentationDiagram) se compone de páginas (PresentationPage), las que a su vez se componen de elementos de interfaz (PDElements). Los elementos de interfaz pueden ser compuestos (CompositeUIElement) o simples (UIElement). Un elemento compuesto de interfaz puede contener a otros elementos que pueden ser compuestos o simples. Un elemento de interfaz puede acceder al modelo de datos y tener condiciones (UICondition) del tipo "order by" o "group by". Además, un elemento de interfaz contiene las propiedades horizontalOrder y verticalOrder para indicar una prioridad en el orden de despliegue en pantalla horizontal o vertical de un elemento simple o compuesto que se encuentra definido en una misma región que otro elemento en una misma página. Por su parte, los Panels permiten aglomerar varios elementos compuestos de interfaz. Además, cada panel forma parte de un elemento enriquecido de interfaz, ya sea un Accordion o un Tabs.

Los elementos simples de interfaz, ya sean tradicionales o enriquecidos, se clasifican en elementos de entrada, de salida, y de control. Los elementos de entrada (InputElement) se encargan de obtener una entrada desde la interfaz de usuario (TextInput, List, Password, Email, DatePicker, AutoSuggest); los de salida (OutputElement), de desplegar información en la interfaz (Text, HtmlText, Multimedia, ToolTip); y los de control (ControlElement), de obtener órdenes de navegación o de cambio de página (ExternalLink, Button, Anchor).

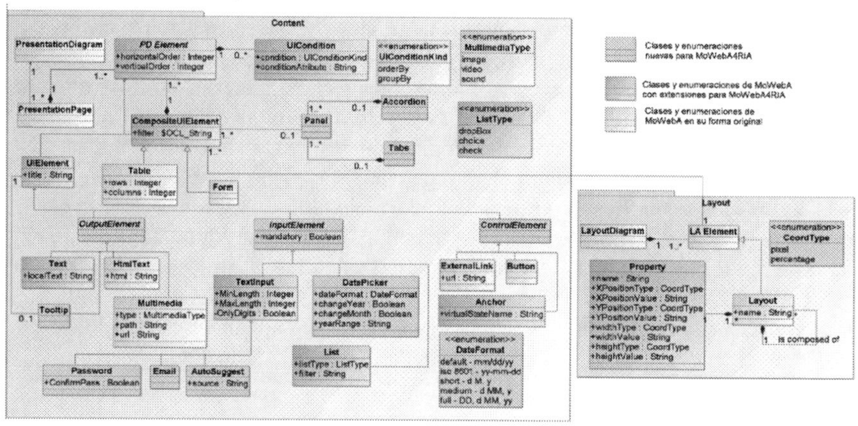

Fig. 1. Metamodelos de contenido (Content) y de estructura (Layout) de MoWebA4RIA

Luego de una explicación general del metamodelo de contenido, se presentan a continuación más de detalles de cada uno de sus nuevos elementos enriquecidos incorporados a la propuesta MoWebA: nuevos widgtes y opciones de validación local de datos.

- **AutoSuggest:** permite desplegar un listado de palabras sugeridas a partir de una fuente de datos definida por el atributo source (que puede ser introducida como listado, o bien a través de un archivo xml). También es posible obtener el listado de palabras desde el modelo de datos de MoWebA.
- **DatePicker**: contiene a los atributos dateFormat, changeYear, changeMonth y yearRange. El dateFormat corresponde a un tipo de dato enumerable que permite seleccionar formatos de fecha. El atributo changeYear es un valor booleano que

indica la ausencia o presencia de un rango de años desplegable en el DatePicker. El rango de años se especifica en el atributo yearRange. Por último, el atributo booleano changeMonth permite desplegar una lista con todos los meses del año.

- **ToolTip**: permite enriquecer con mensajes personalizados a cualquiera de los elementos de entrada, salida o control.
- **Live Validation**: corresponde a un conjunto de extensiones que permite llevar a cabo validaciones locales a elementos de interfaz del tipo TextInput, Email, Password y List. Para dar soporte a las validaciones se han agregado nuevos atributos en las clases correspondientes (por ejemplo, los atributos MinLength, MaxLength y OnlyDigits de la clase TextInput).
- **Accordion y Tabs**: permiten encapsular elementos de interfaz dentro de paneles colapsables para presentar información en una cantidad limitada de espacio.

En cuanto al metamodelo de estructura, un diagrama de estructura (LayoutDiagram) se compone de elementos de estructura (LAElement, Layout). A su vez, un elemento de estructura se puede componer de otros elementos de estructura. Además, cada elemento de estructura se asocia a varios elementos de propiedades (Property) que permiten definir valores para diversos atributos relacionados a las coordenadas de la posición de un elemento en la interfaz y a sus dimensiones.

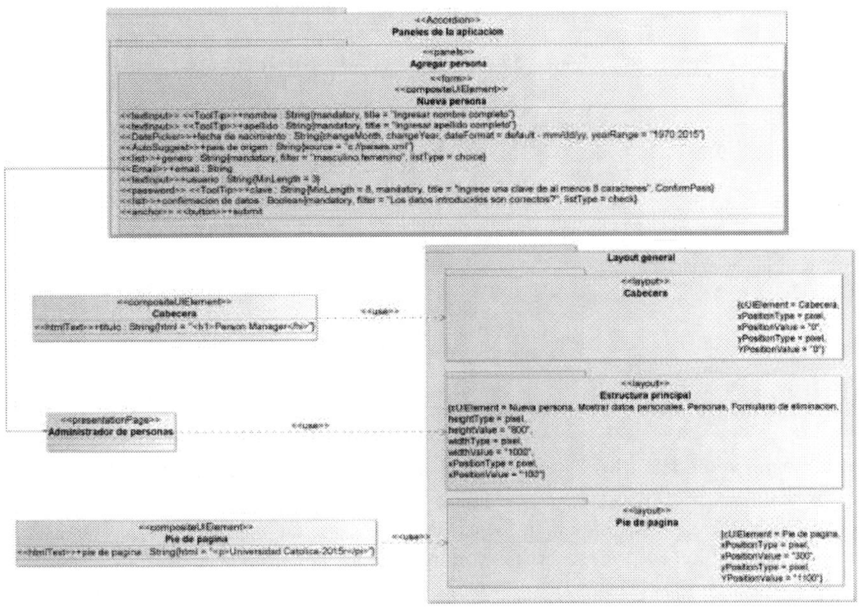

Fig. 2. Parte del PIM de capa de presentación modelado con MoWebA4RIA para una aplicación de administración de personas

A partir de los metamodelos de contenido y estructura se han derivado los perfiles UML correspondientes para MoWebA4RIA. Estos perfiles definen la sintaxis concreta de MoWebA4RIA. Con los metamodelos y perfiles definidos, es posible utilizar MoWebA4RIA para modelar los PIM de capa de presentación de una aplicación dada. La Fig. 2 presenta un ejemplo de PIM de capa de presentación modelado con MoWebA4RIA para una aplicación sencilla que permite administrar personas (listarlas, agregarlas o eliminarlas de un sistema). El ejemplo incluye varios elementos que forman parte de la extensión que se ha realizado en este trabajo, como el Accordion, paneles, etc.

3.2 Transformación para la Generación de Interfaces Enriquecidas

El proceso que se debe realizar para generar aplicaciones con interfaces enriquecidas con MoWebA4RIA se representa en la Fig. 3.

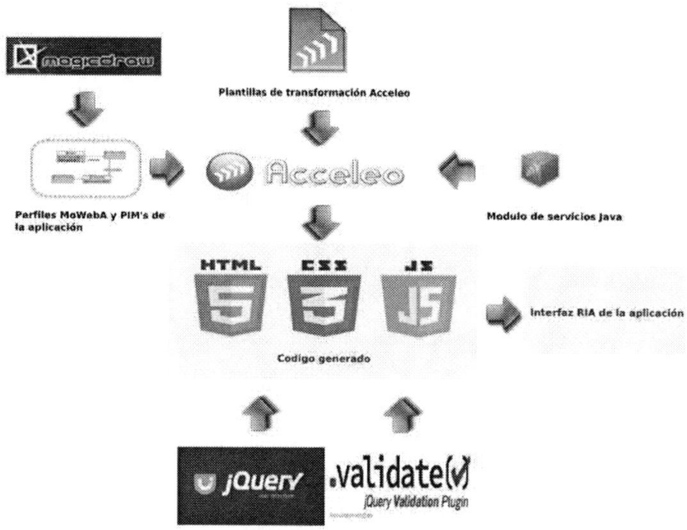

Fig. 3. Proceso de desarrollo para generar interfaces enriquecidas con MoWebA4RIA

Primeramente se modelan los PIM que representan a una aplicación particular utilizando los distintos perfiles UML de MoWebA4RIA (no sólo los de presentación, sino también los correspondientes a la lógica de negocios, navegación, etc.). Posteriormente, tanto los PIM como los perfiles son exportados al formato XMI del Eclipse Modeling Framework (EMF - https://www.eclipse.org/modeling/emf). Esto se lleva a cabo a fin de tener compatibilidad con la herramienta de transformación Acceleo, que toma como entrada modelos UML basados en el metamodelo Ecore[1]. Por medio de plantillas de transformación y módulos de servicio Java (Java Service Wrappers), que

[1] Ecore es un metamodelo nativo del Eclipse Modeling Framework para describir los modelos.

forman parte de Acceleo, es posible llevar a cabo las transformaciones necesarias sobre los modelos de entrada para obtener los archivos fuentes (.html, .css y .js) que representan a la aplicación en sí. Como parte de este trabajo, se han definido las plantillas de transformación necesarias para ejecutar las transformaciones. Cabe destacar que estas plantillas pueden ser utilizadas para generar otras aplicaciones, siempre que las mismas hayan utilizado la extensión MoWebA4RIA para modelarlas.

Para los widgets Accordion, Tabs, DatePicker, ToolTip y AutoSuggest se genera código HTML y Javascript correspondiente a la librería JQuery UI. Para los diversos tipos de validación local se genera código Javascript correspondiente al jQuery Validation plugin. Se genera también código CSS para estructurar cada uno de los elementos de interfaz (enriquecidos o no).

Finalmente, las librerías Javascript jQuery UI y jQuery Validation Plugin se invocan desde el código fuente generado para desplegar y utilizar las funcionalidades enriquecidas de la aplicación en uso.

4 Ilustración de la Propuesta

Con la intensión de ilustrar de una manera práctica las nuevas capacidades ofrecidas por MoWebA4RIA, y a la vez, de realizar ciertas comparaciones entre MoWebA y MoWebA4RIA, que sirvan como validación preliminar, los autores han implementado, con ambos enfoques, un sistema de administración de personas (Person Manager). Los requisitos del Person Manager, se refieren básicamente a poder agregar, editar, eliminar y listar a las personas de un sistema.

Se han definido cinco preguntas de investigación (PI) para guiar el análisis de las comparaciones entre la implementación del Person Manager con MoWebA y la implementación con MoWebA4RIA. A continuación se presentan las cinco preguntas de investigación junto con los datos que se han recabado para contestarlas y los análisis realizados a partir de dichos datos.

- **PI1:** ¿Consume una mayor cantidad de tiempo modelar la aplicación aplicando MoWebA4RIA que MoWebA?

  La Tabla 2 presenta el tiempo, en minutos, que se ha tardado para modelar la aplicación del PersonManager con MoWebA y con MoWebA4RIA.

Tabla 2. Tiempo de modelado y cantidad de generaciones de código hasta obtener la interfaz final al implementar el Person Manager con MoWebA y con MoWebA4RIA

	Tiempo de modelado (minutos)		Cantidad de generaciones de código hasta obtener la interfaz final	
	MoWebA	MoWebA4RIA	MoWebA	MoWebA4RIA
Agregar persona	50	56	3	4
Listar persona	27	28	1	1
Eliminar persona	29	30	2	3
Totales	106	114	6	8

Con MoWebA4RIA se tardó 8 minutos más en el proceso de modelado que con MoWebA. Esto se debe principalmente a que con MoWebA4RIA es necesario definir un mayor número de propiedades en cada uno de los elementos que forman parte de la extensión, a diferencia de MoWebA. Esto concuerda con la intuición en el sentido de que cuanto mayor es el nivel de detalle en el modelo, mayor tiempo de modelado se requiere. Sin embargo, se puede considerar que este hecho no constituye una limitante demasiado grave, teniendo en cuenta que ese tiempo extra de modelado permite a la interfaz de la aplicación Person Manager enriquecerse notablemente.

- **PI2:** ¿Para cuál de los enfoques es necesaria una mayor cantidad de generaciones de código para obtener la interfaz de usuario final?
  La Tabla 2 presenta la cantidad de generaciones de código que se han realizado hasta obtener la interfaz final del PersonManager con MoWebA y con MoWebA4RIA. Una vez que los modelos de la aplicación se encontraban listos, el siguiente paso era generar código fuente a partir de ellos. Cuando a alguno de los modelos le faltaba definir alguna propiedad para alguno de sus elementos, entonces el código fuente generado en primera instancia, no reflejaba el resultado esperado. En estos casos, iterativamente se volvían a hacer cambios al modelo y luego se generaba de vuelta la aplicación. Un leve incremento en el número de generaciones para el enfoque MoWebA4RIA se pudo apreciar a partir de los datos recabados, con respecto a MoWebA. Debido a que los requerimientos RIA requieren un mayor nivel de detalle en los modelos de MoWebA4RIA, existe una mayor posibilidad de cometer errores u omisiones y, por ende, será necesaria una mayor cantidad de generaciones de código para ir depurando la aplicación.
- **PI3:** Desde el punto de vista de las presentaciones enriquecidas, ¿qué ventajas aportan las características RIA presentes en la aplicación implementada con MoWebA4RIA con respecto a MoWebA?
  El enfoque MoWebA4RIA ofrece numerosas ventajas con respecto a las presentaciones enriquecidas, evitando recargas innecesarias de las páginas por medio del widget Accordion y presentando widgets interactivos como los hDatePicker, AutoSuggest y ToolTip. El enfoque MoWebA no contempla tales elementos enriquecidos y navegar por cada una de sus páginas implica recargar completamente cada una de ellas. En la Fig. 4 se pueden apreciar los elementos enriquecidos presentes en la versión de MoWebA4RIA, en contrapartida a MoWebA, para el Person Manager.
- **PI4:** Desde el punto de vista de la lógica de negocios en el lado del cliente, ¿qué ventajas aportan las características RIA presentes en la aplicación implementada con MoWebA4RIA con respecto a MoWebA?
  El enfoque MoWebA4RIA permite llevar a cabo diversas validaciones en los campos de entrada de la aplicación, como campos que deben ser obligatorios, longitudes mínima y máxima de caracteres en un campo, validaciones de claves y formato de email. En contraparte el enfoque MoWebA, no soporta ningún tipo de validación. En la Fig. 5 se pueden apreciar los diversos tipos de validaciones locales presentes en la versión de MoWebA4RIA, en contrapartida a MoWebA, para el Person Manager.

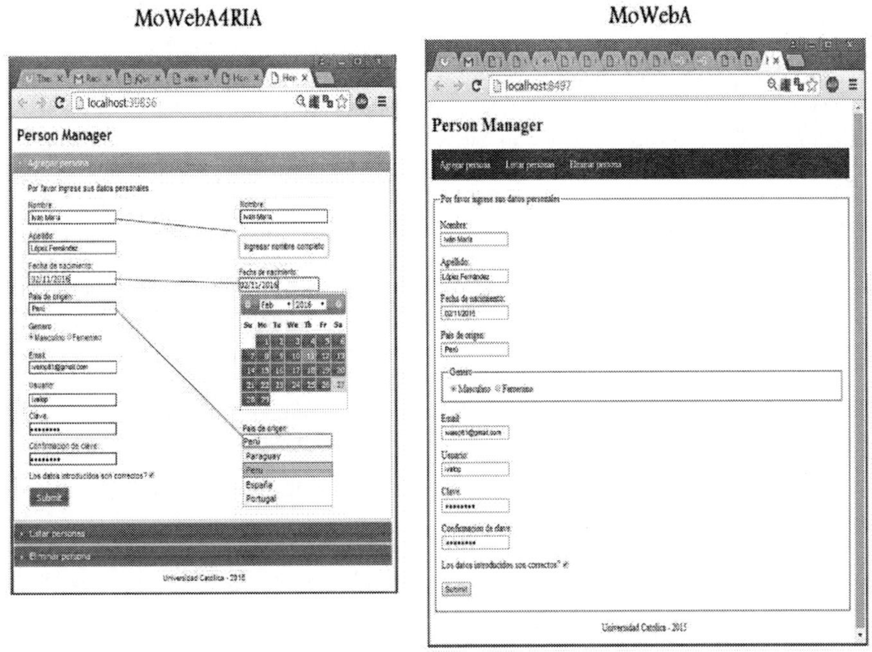

Fig. 4. Person Manager implementado con MoWebA4RIA y con MoWebA, desde el punto de vista de las presentaciónes enriquecidas

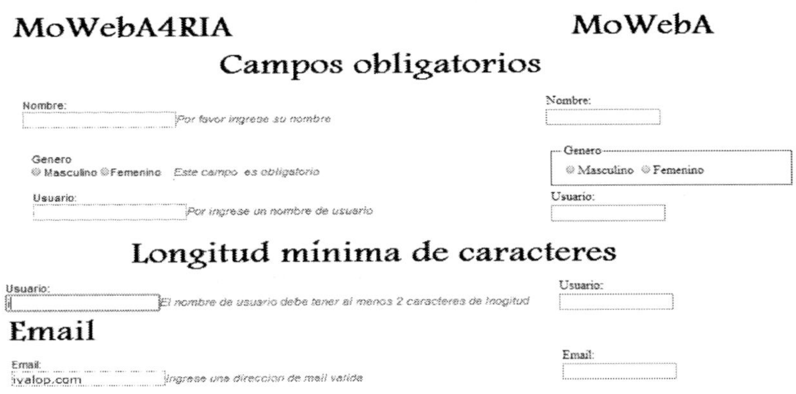

Fig. 5. Person Manager implementado con MoWebA4RIA y MoWebA, desde el punto de vista de la lógica de negocios en el lado del cliente

- **PI5**: Para cada una de las vistas del Person Manager, ¿qué cantidad de líneas de código para la interfaz de usuario se pudieron generar de manera automática a partir de los modelos, en cada uno de los enfoques implementados?
  La Tabla 3 presenta la cantidad de líneas de código resultantes de implementar el Person Manager con MoWebA y con MoWeba4RIA. Analizando primeramente el tamaño total del Person Manager para ambos enfoques, se puede apreciar que la versión de MoWebA posee 123 líneas de código menos que la versión de MoWebA4RIA (equivalente a un 32% menos). Esto se debe a que con MoWebA no se genera código Javascript en la interfaz de usuario, ya que su interfaz no posee elementos enriquecidos interactivos. El código que fue implementado manualmente en la aplicación, 53% (para el enfoque MoWebA) y 43% (para MoWebA4RIA) respectivamente, corresponde a código para refinar la aplicación final y código para el acceso a la capa lógica y de dominio de la aplicación. De ahí se puede concluir que el 47% del código del Person Manager fue generado de manera automática para el enfoque MoWebA y el 57% para el enfoque MoWebA4RIA.

Tabla 3. Cantidad de líneas de código al implementar el PersonManager con MoWebA y con MoWebA4RIA

	MoWebA			**MoWebA4RIA**		
	Líneas de código automáticas	**Líneas de código manuales**	**Totales**	**Líneas de código automáticas**	**Líneas de código manuales**	**Totales**
Agregar persona	51	56	107	135	56	191
Mostrar persona	1	45	46	3	45	48
Eliminar persona	7	27	34	31	27	58
Estructura y código común para todas las vistas (cabecera, estructura y pie de página)	67	10	77	52	38	90
Totales	126	138	264	221	166	387

Como se puede notar, si bien MoWebA4RIA implica un mínimo mayor esfuerzo de tiempo e iteraciones, al mismo tiempo ofrece la posibilidad de generar aplicaciones más enriquecidas conforme las RIA. Esto también se refleja en la automatización de la generación de código.

5 Conclusiones y Trabajos Futuros

En este trabajo se presenta MoWebA4RIA, una extención de MoWebA para incorporar las principales características y tecnologías de las RIA. La extensión abarca el metamodelo de contenido, agregando una nueva reestructuración y clasificación de los elementos de interfaz, separando a los distintos componentes de interfaz en elementos de entrada, salida y control. Además, para enriquecer la implementación, algunos widgets interactivos comunes en las aplicaciones RIA se han agregado, precisamente Accordion, Tabs, AutoSuggest, DatePicker, ToolTip y LiveValidation. La extensión ha incorporado también mejoras en el metamodelo de estructura. Para la definición de la sintaxis concreta de la presentación, se han incoporado las extensiones con sus respectivos widgets en los perfiles de contenido y estructura.

Con la herramienta de transformación Acceleo, se implementaron las plantillas de transformación para la presentación. La transformación genera código para cada uno de los elementos definidos en el perfil de contenido, a partir de los PIM de entrada, en donde, para los widgets se genera código para la plataforma destino jQueryUI y jQuery validation plug-in. A partir del perfil de estructura, se genera código CSS con las posiciones de los elementos de interfaz según fueron establecidas en el PIM de entrada. Finalmente, una ilustración de la propuesta se llevó a cabo para comparar los aportes de MoWebA4RIA con respecto a MoWebA.

Entre los trabajos futuros, como primer paso nos interesa migrar a un entorno totalmente abierto, con el uso de Papyrus como herramienta de modelado. Por otro lado, consideramos que podrían incluirse otras características RIA a MoWebA, no sólo a nivel de la presentación, sino también en la comunicación cliente-servidor, en la lógica de negocios (no limitadas a las validaciones locales) y ofrecer cobertura de persistencia de datos en el lado del cliente, incluyendo también a los ambientes de dispositivos móviles. Otro trabajo futuro interesante sería realizar transformaciones para otros frameworks o plataformas destino RIA. Se prevé además la realización de validaciones más rigurosas, como casos de estudios o experimento, de la extensión propuesta, que incluya también comparaciones con otras propuestas que extienden a RIA (como OOH4RIA, WebML-RIA, etc.). Finalmente, resultaría de mucho interés explorar la posibilidad de no enriquecer directamente el PIM sino definir un ASM específico para RIA, siguiendo así una de las originalidades de MoWebA, no contemplada por otras propuestas. Con este aporte, se logrará incorporar conceptos y propiedades de arquitecturas en un nuevo modelo (ASM), manteniendo siempre la independencia de la plataforma (en el PIM) y disponer de un mecanismo de adaptación a la evolución dinámica de aplicaciones.

Agradecimientos. Este trabajo ha sido desarrollado con el apoyo financiero del Consejo Nacional de Ciencia y Tecnología (CONACYT, Paraguay) en el marco del proyecto MejorMDD (14-INV-056).

Referencias

1. Valverde F and Pastor O. Applying interaction patterns. In Towards a Model-Driven Approach for Rich Internet Applications Development.Proc. 7th Int. Workshop on Web-Oriented Software technologies, IWWOST 2008, 2008.

2. Martínez-Ruiz F J. *A Development Method for User Interfaces of Rich Internet Applications*. PhD thesis, Université catholique de Louvain, Belgium, August 2010.
3. Toffetti G, Comai S, Preciado J C, and Linaje M. State-of-the art and trends in the systematic development of rich internet applications. *J. Web Eng.*, 10(1):70–86, March 2011.
4. Allaire J. Requirements for rich internet applications. http://download.macromedia.com/pub/flash/whitepapers/richclient.pdf, March 2002.
5. Wright J and Dietrich J. Survey of existing languages to model interactive web applications. In *Proceedings of the fifth Asia-Pacific conference on Conceptual Modelling - Volume 79*, APCCM '08, pages 113–123, Darlinghurst, Australia, 2008. Australian Computer Society, Inc.
6. Preciado J C, Linaje M, Sanchez F, and Comai S. Necessity of methodologies to model rich internet applications. In *Proceedings of the Seventh IEEE International Symposium on Web Site Evolution*, WSE '05, pages 7–13, Washington, DC, USA, 2005. IEEE Computer Society.
7. Preciado J C, Linaje M, Morales-Chaparro R, Sanchez-Figueroa F, Zhang G, Kroiβ C, and Koch N. Designing rich internet applications combining *UWE* and rux-method. In *Proceedings of the 2008 Eighth International Conference on Web Engineering*, ICWE '08, pages 148–154, Washington, DC, USA, 2008. IEEE Computer Society.
8. Machado L, Filho O, and Ribeiro J. *UWE*-r: an extension to a web engineering methodology for rich internet applications. *WSEAS Trans. Info. Sci. and App.*, 6(4):601–610, April 2009.
9. Busch M and Koch N. Rich internet applications state-of-the-art. Technical report 0902, Programming and Software Engineering Unit (PST), Institute for Informatics, Ludwig-Maximilians-Universität München, Germany, December 2009.
10. González M, Casariego J, Bareiro J, Cernuzzi L, and Pastor O. Una propuesta *MDA* para las perspectivas navegacional y de usuarios. In *XXXVI Conferencia Latinoamericana de Informática (CLEI) - ISBN 978-99967-612-0-1*, page 58, Asunción, Paraguay, 2010.
11. González M, Cernuzzi L, and Pastor O. Una aproximación para aplicaciones web: *MoWebA*. In *XIV Congreso Iberoamericano en Software Engineering – CibSE*, Río de Janeiro, Brasil, 2011.
12. Urbieta M, Rossi G, Ginzburg J, and D. Schwabe. Designing the interface of rich internet applications. In *Proceedings of the 2007 Latin American Web Conference*, LA-WEB '07, pages 144–153, Washington, DC, USA, 2007. IEEE Computer Society.
13. Koch N, Pigerl M, Zhang G, and Morozova T. Patterns for the model-based development of Rias. In *Proceedings of the 9th International Conference on Web Engineering*, ICWE '9, pages 283–291, Berlin, Heidelberg, 2009. Springer-Verlag.
14. Fraternali P, Comai S, Bozzon A, and Carughi G T. Engineering rich internet applications with a model-driven approach. *ACM Trans. Web*, 4(2):7:1–7:47, April 2010.
15. Meliá S, Gómez J, Pérez S, and Dáz O. A model-driven development for gwt-based rich internet applications with ooh4ria. In *Proceedings of the 2008 Eighth International Conference on Web Engineering*, ICWE '08, pages 13–23, Washington, DC, USA, 2008. IEEE Computer Society.
16. Usage of Javascript Libraries for Websites, http://w3techs.com/technologies/overview/javascript_library/all, December 2015.

BVCCON-TOOL: A Modeling Tool to Support Dynamic Business Process Configuration Approach

Tarcísio Pereira[12], Fernanda Alencar[1], and Jaelson Castro[1]

Federal University of Pernambuco - UFPE[1]
{tcp,jbc}@cin.ufpe.br,fernanda.ralencar@ufpe.br
Federal Institute of Sertão Pernambucano - IF-Sertão[2]

Abstract. BVCCoN (Business Process Configuration with NFRs and Context-Awareness) is the only approach that takes into account non-functional requirements, variability, and contextual information in business process configuration. Modeling steps of BVCCoN approach are too complex and consume much time and effort. To address this shortcoming, we present BVCCoN-Tool, a modeling tool based on a metamodel that is capable of supporting all modeling steps of BVCCoN approach. Our usability evaluation suggests that our tool was considered useful by the users, and it performs tasks that it claims to do. **Tool demonstration video:** https://youtu.be/oXon8WwPSMQ

Keywords: business process configuration · tool · metamodel.

1 Introduction

BVCCoN (Business Process Configuration with NFRs and Context-Awareness) [13] approach deal with business process variability, its configuration uses NFRs (Non-Functional Requirements) and contextual information. The configuration process relies on contextual information to identify change opportunities. Besides that, NFRs can define essential constraints that the business process must comply. Hence, NFR is used as qualitative criteria to drive configuration of business process models and the application of context-awareness to deal with changes in the environment.

The process in BVCCoN approach is composed of five main tasks: 1) *Elicit Variability* - Variability elicitation starts by analyzing a reference model in BPMN. With the help of a set of questions and applying these questions to the model elements, is possible to identify some variations in the way the process is performed. This raw data will be analyzed and then be represented as variants, variation point or as contextual information; 2) *Describe Variability* - is expressed regarding variants and variation points. Variation Points indicate where the process can vary, using begins and ends points. The idea is to indicate how and where the main flow (reference process) can change; 3) *Analyze Context* - Next step is to associate contexts to process variants. Contexts describe states of the world that can affect the process. Contextual information is represented by logical expressions that can be assessed through data monitoring; 4) *Link NFRs and Variants* - NFRs are used to describe quality attributes that may be relevant for the stakeholders. BVCCoN uses qualitative analysis, where the analyst expresses the way he believes a variant may affect the process configuration in a controlled range: from the most positive (++) to the most negative (– –); and 5) *Perform Configuration* - The last step of BVCCoN approach generates a new business process model as output. In this step is considered the Variation Point and the Variants of the process model, and how they impact non-functional requirements. This information can be used to support the configuration itself. It can be performed based on Variants selection for the most critical NFRs. To see the details and how the approach works, the reader can consult [13] or [12].

BVCCoN approach is too complex, because it is related to business process model, non-functional requirements model, and context information model. All of these models are built in the steps 2, 3, and 4 of the approach, so we can say that more than half of approach execution is performed through the construction of models. These models are connected, in other words, there is a dependency between these models. The user needs to have at the end of these phases, models that represent them. The lack of a tool that helps the user to perform the modeling steps makes the process slower, hard to understand and error prone [13].

To address this shortcoming, we present BVCCoN-Tool, a modeling tool based on a metamodel that is capable of supporting all modeling steps of BVCCoN approach. We also presented a usability evaluation with post-graduated students in Computer Science to evaluate the *usefulness of the system* of the proposed tool. Our usability evaluation suggests that our tool was considered useful by the users, and it performs tasks that it claims to do.

The remainder of this article is structured as follows: Section 2 describes the process to develop the tool. It presents the metamodels and the technologies that were used; In section 3 we present the BVCCoN-Tool, it's interface and the way to use it; Usability evaluation of the tool with focus on usefulness of the system is presented in Section 4; A discussion of the related works is given in Section 5. The article ends with a conclusion and an outlook for future works in Section 6.

2 BVCCoN-Tool Development

BVCCoN approach covers three perspectives in the business process configuration: variability description, non-functional requirements, and contextual information. These three perspectives and concepts are described by their respective metamodels.

2.1 Variability Metamodel

The main concepts related to variability are: *VariationPoint* and *Variants*. The first one indicates the local inside the process model that can change, and the second one are pieces of the process that can be added to be part of the process model. *VariationPoints* and *Variants* are represented as business process elements (see Figure 1). The *begins* and *ends* links access the BPMN metamodel for a relationship with the *FlowElements* artifacts. The *Variants* can be associated with one or more *VariationPoints*. To represent the variability dependency relationship is used the Operator attribute that can be OR, AND and XOR. Associated with these operators, we can found the patterns, which are information that tell us how the variants will be positioned in the business process model. The *WorkFlowPatterns* can represent sequence, parallelism, optional behavior, among others. The *Variants* are related with the *VariationPoints* through *Patterns*. The *Variants* has some restrictions: requires and excludes. The first one requires the presence of another variant, and the second one excludes a variant. All of this information can be seen in Figure 1.

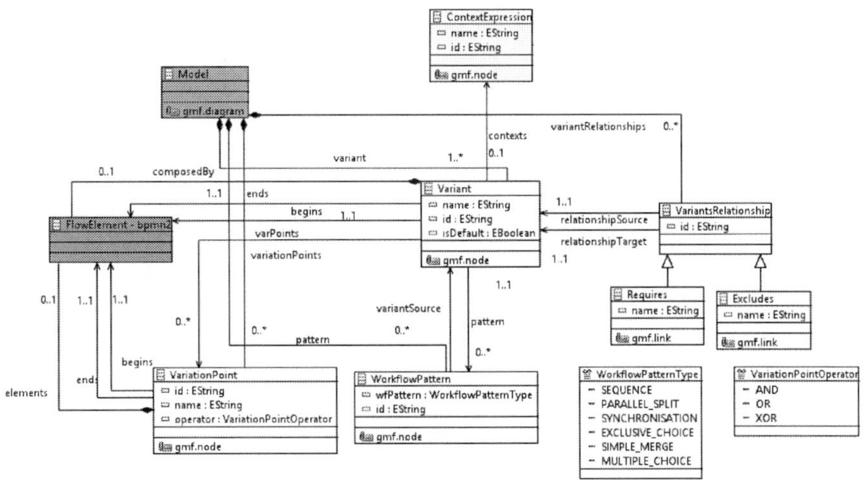

Fig. 1. Variability Metamodel - BVCCoN.

2.2 Context Metamodel

A context tree is composed by expressions/variables that need to be evaluated to check if the context holds. According to Figure 2, the main concept is a *Predicate*. A *Predicate* can be a *Statement* a *Facts* or a *PredicateDecomposition*. A *Statement* is a world predicate that can not be verified by an actor and it can be decomposed in others statements or facts. Unlike statements, *Facts* can be verified and associated to *Variables* that express values evaluated by predicate formula. *Predicates* can be decomposed by others predicates using the

AndDecomposition, *OrDecomposition* and *NotDecomposition* operators. *ContextExpressionLink*, *PredicateLink*, and *CELink* are used to perform links between the elements described before. Context trees are drawn into the compartment represented by the *ContextModel* class. Lastly, *ContextModel* and it's elements are inside the main model called "Model".

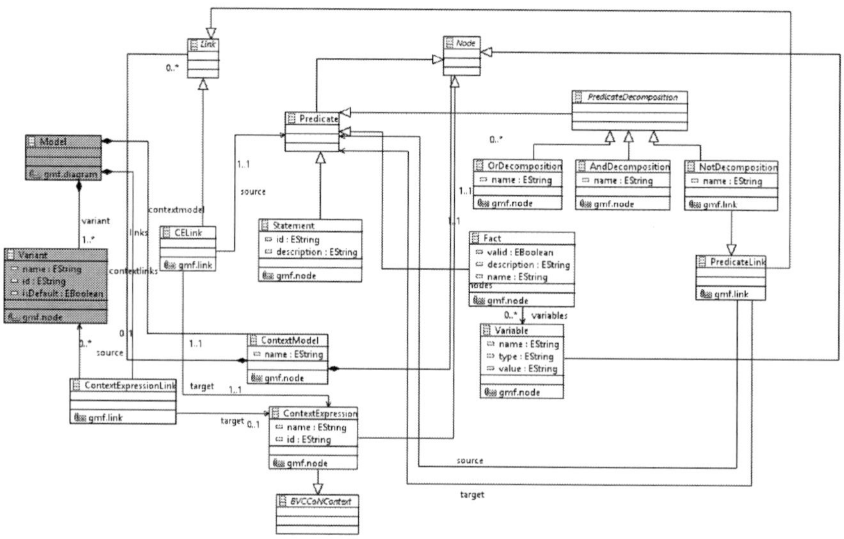

Fig. 2. Context Metamodel - BVCCoN.

2.3 NFR Metamodel

According to Figure 3, the main concepts are *NFRSoftgoal*, *NFRSoftgoalContribution* and *NFRSoftgoalContributionOperational*. These concepts are used to describe the NFR catalogs, NFR decompositions and to represent contributions between NFRs and contributions from Variants to RNFs. The contribution relationships represented by *NFRSoftgoalContribution* has subtypes like: AndContribution and OrContribution, they are used to decompose NFRs during the definition of NFRs catalog. Contribution relationships represented by *NFRSoftgoalContributionOperational* has subtypes like: *BreakContribution*, *HurtContribution*, *EqualContribution*, *HelpContribution*, and *MakeContribution*, ranging respectively from negative to positive impact. The kind of relationships with contributions is used to represent preferences between *Variants*. The contribution links and *NFRSoftgoal* node are drawn into the compartment represented by the class *NFRModel*. Finally, *NFRModel* and its elements are inside the main model called *"Model"*.

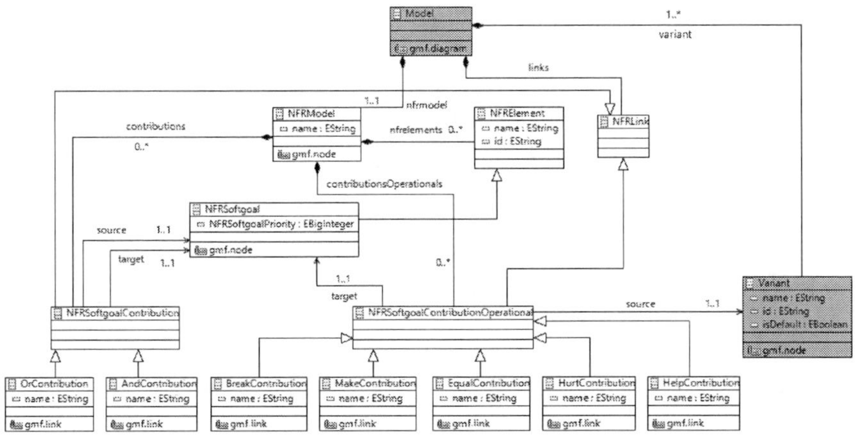

Fig. 3. NFR Metamodel - BVCCoN.

2.4 Technologies

To develop the BVCCoN-Tool, we used a set of unified modeling frameworks, tools and patterns implementation found in Eclipse community [1]. Among the modeling frameworks, we highlight EMF (Eclipse Modeling Framework) [14], that supports the metamodel specifications and provides functionality to automatic code generation in Java, the GMF (Graphical Modeling Framework) [4], that is a model-driven approach to developing graphical editors based on Eclipse and Epsilon [5]. The last is a family of language and tools for code generation, model-to-model transformation, model validation, comparison, migration, and refactoring of metamodels. Besides that, it uses XMI (Metadata Interchange) to store, manipulate, recover and interchange of metadata.

To develop the tool, we choose one of the three views of BVCCoN approach, and we code the metamodel in Emfatic language of Epsilon Framework [2]. Then, we performed some changes to the metamodel be according to abstract syntax. Besides that, with EuGENia [3] annotations in the metamodel we also defined a concrete syntax to get an enriched metamodel. Listing 1.1 demonstrates a piece of the NFR metamodel. In particular, the annotations represent the following issues.

- Line 2: the *NFRModel* is a compartment where the NFR Elements are drawn. An Eclass that must be annotated like *gmf.node.*
- Line 16: each *NFRSoftgoal* is an *NFRElement.* It's graphical representation is a rectangle with dash lines.
- Line 24: each *NFRSoftgoalContribution* is represented like a link between his source and target *NFRSoftgoal.*
- Line 30: in the diagram, each *OrContribution* is a kind of *NFRSoftgoalContribution.* It is a link which representation is a continuous line labeled with the word "OR".

Listing 1.1. A piece of the NFR Metamodel written in Emfatic Language

```
@gmf.node(label="name", label.placement="internal", label.icon
    ="false", figure="rounded", border.color="0,0,0", size
    ="500,200")
class NFRModel{
        attr String[1] name="NFR Model";
        @gmf.compartment
        val NFRElement[*] nfrelements;
        val NFRSoftgoalContribution[*] contributions;
        val NFRSoftgoalContributionOperational[*]
            contributionsOperationals;
}

class NFRElement{
  !ordered attr String[1] name;
  id attr String[1] ~id;
}

@gmf.node(label.placement="internal", label.icon="false",
    label="name", size="100,30", border.color="0,0,0", border.
    style="dash")
class NFRSoftgoal extends NFRElement{
  !ordered attr EBigInteger[1] NFRSoftgoalPriority = "0";
}

class NFRLink {

}

class NFRSoftgoalContribution extends NFRLink {
  !ordered ref NFRSoftgoal[1] source;
  !ordered ref NFRSoftgoal[1] target;
}

@gmf.link(source.decoration="none", target.decoration="none",
    source="source", target="target", color="0,0,0")
class OrContribution extends NFRSoftgoalContribution {
        attr String name="OR";
}
```

Then, it's time to generate an Ecore metamodel from the metamodel built in Emfatic. Ecore metamodel is composed by the following elements: *Eclass* (used to represent a metaclass); *EAttribute* (used to represent an Eclass attribute); *EReference* (used to describe associations between classes); and *EEnum* (used to describe enumerations); In sequence, the EuGENia tool was used to abstract the configuration and execution details of GMF. EuGENia generates graphical tools from an Ecore metamodel with annotations written in Emfatic language. The output of the last step is a graphical editor. Then, EVL (Epsilon Validation Language) was used to add validations and make minor adjustments in the graphical editor GMF. Figure 4 depicts the bvccon-tool development process discussed above.

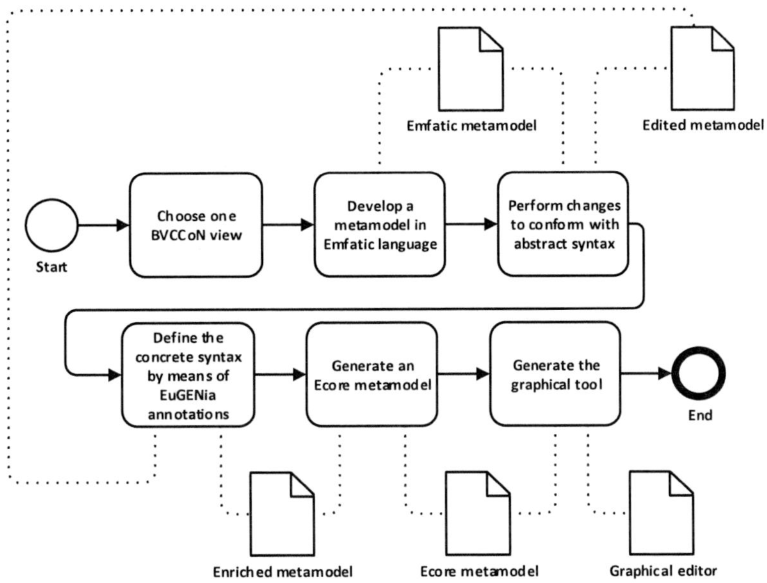

Fig. 4. BVCCoN-Tool development process

The main challenges we faced while developing the tool were: (1) Join three different metamodel in one. At this point, we analyze the main elements of each metamodel to find a way to connect them and at the same time, be according to BVCCoN approach. (2) Import BPMN models to BVCCoN-Tool. It was the great challenge of the process since we had to study BPMN metamodel and define a way to import any BPMN process created in other tools to be used in our tool by the *Variant* and *Variation Point* elements. The solution we find was import the BPMN metamodel defined by OMG (Object Management Group) inside our BVCCoN-Tool project and use it as a second metamodel. Thus, some BVCCoN-Tool elements can refer to BPMN elements.

3 Presentation of BVCCoN-Tool

In Figure 5, we present the graphical interface of BVCCoN-Tool. It is important to note that: 1) in area "A" there are the bvccon model constructors; 2) in area "B" we can see the workspace where the models are designed and 3) in are "C" the properties of each bvccon constructor can be configured. The modeling task starts with a click in the desired constructor (area "A") and after in the local that it should appear in the workspace (area "B"). Then, the designer can edit the properties of the constructor (area "C") and add new constructors. Beyond these basic features, BVCCoN-Tool has others features, for example: create text notes, definition of colors to the constructors, visualization of many schemes in different tabs, zoom control and undo or redo an action. More information about BVCCoN-Tool (including its download link, documentation, and explanatory videos) can be found at https://sites.google.com/site/bvccontool/.

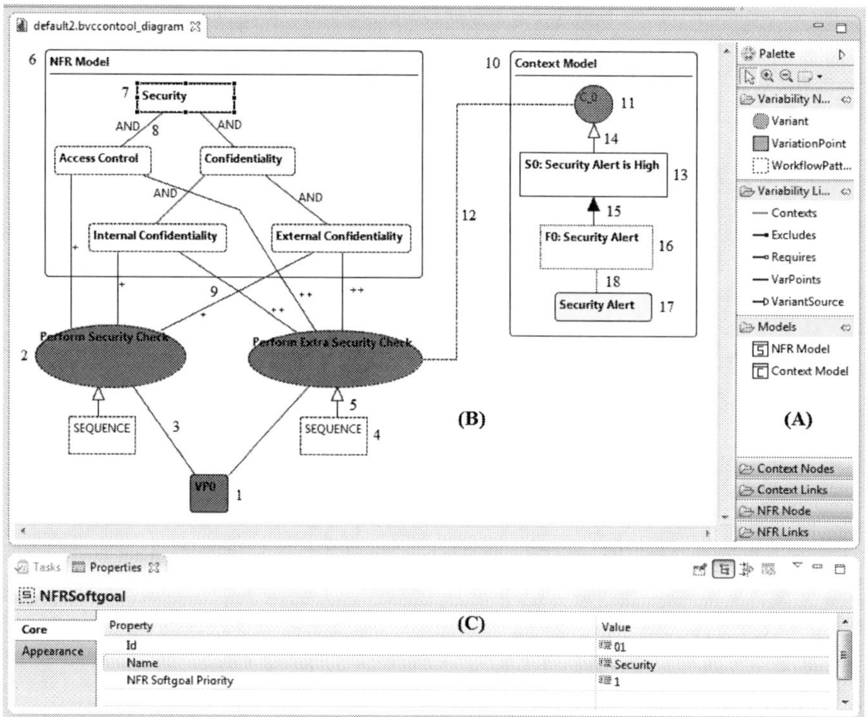

Fig. 5. BVCCoN-Tool Graphical Interface.

With the purpose to model a simple scheme that covers almost all bvccon constructors, Figure 5 depicts a symbolic schema of an airport domain where the user has to perform check-in. The task in evidence is called Perform Security Check, and it occurs at the moment that the user has to go to the boarding gate. This task can be performed in two different ways. The first one is default (Variant Perform Security Check), no context is validated, and it contributes positively to the following NFRs: Access Control, Internal Confidentiality, and External

Confidentiality. The second one occurs when the context called S0: Security Alert is High is validated as true. So, the Variant Perform Extra Security Check is activated, and it contributes more positively than the first Variant to the NFRs cited before. Because of space limitations, it was not possible to model a scheme that covers all bvccon constructors.

We can see in Figure 5: 1) Variation Point indicates the local in the process model that can change; 2) Variants are process parts that can be added to be part of the process model. It can be associated with one or more variation point; 3) VarPoints are used to links between Variant and Variation Point; 4) WorkflowPatterns are information that tell how the variants will be positioned in the business process model. It can represent parallelism, optional behavior, among others); 5) Variants Source are used to links between WorkflowPattern and Variant; 6) NFR Model is a compartment where NFRs model is built; 7) NFR Node represents non-functional requirements; 8) NFR Links are represented by AndContribution and OrContribution (links between NFR Node); 9) NFR Links can also be represented by Break Contribution, Make Contribution, Equal Contribution, Hurt Contribution and Help Contribution (links between Variants and NFR Node); 10) Context Model is a compartment where trees contexts are projected; 11) Context Expression is composed by predicate formula; 12) Contexts are links between Variants and Context Expression; 13) Statement is a world predicate that can be decomposed in other statement or facts; 14) CELink are links between Statement and Context Expression; 15) Predicate Link are links between And/Or Decomposition to Statement, Facts to Statement, and Facts to And/Or Decomposition; 16) Facts are verified and associated to variables; 17) Variable express the values assessed by predicate formula and 18) Variables are links between Variable and Facts.

The metamodel of BVCCoN-Tool was built in a way that it can prevent syntactic errors. For example, the metamodel of non-functional requirements view was adapted from *NFRFramework* so it can be consistent with BVCCoN approach and prevent some syntactic errors. The only type of relationship between NFR Nodes are And/Or Contribution. Before adjustment, others types of relationships were allowed. Figure 6 illustrates this error (marked with an x), as well the way to fix it.

4 Usability Evaluation

In order to evaluate our tool, we conducted a usability evaluation. The scenario used to perform the usability evaluation was the same as described in section 3, Check-in at airports. We used the questionnaire of the method PSSUQ (The Post Study System Usability Questionnaire) [8], that predicts four different factors from the responses obtained from the evaluation questionnaire: *Overall Satisfaction*, *Usefulness of the System*, *Information Quality* and *Interface Quality*. Survey responses were based on a visual scale of 5 levels: "strongly agree" (5), "agree" (4), "neutral" (3), "disagree" (2) and "strongly disagree" (1). This method is suitable for usability testing in laboratory environments, it is accord-

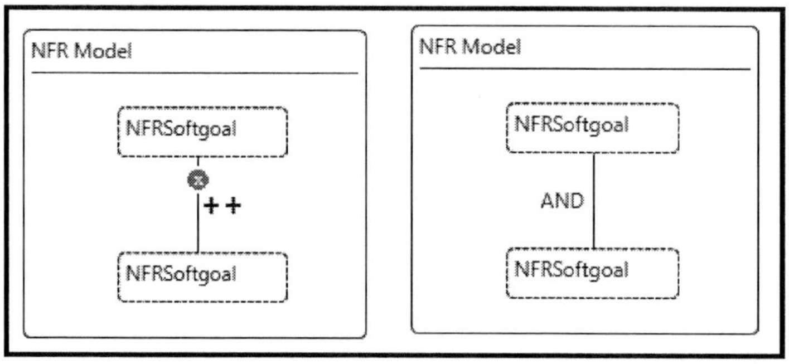

Fig. 6. Syntactic error avoided by BVCCoN-Tool.

ing to our context, and it is based on a set of tasks with the user answering the questionnaire after their execution. For reasons of space, we present the principal evaluation factor, the *Usefulness of the System*, so that we can analyze if the tool was considered useful by the users performing tasks that the tool proposes to do.

Users who participated in the usability test are graduate students in Computer Science from Federal University of Pernambuco institution. They were attending the Requirements Engineering discipline and thus possessed some contact with modeling tools. In all, 15 users participated in the test. For this evaluation, users had to perform a sequence of tasks whose goal was to build part of the check-in scenario an airport, since the entire scenario requires more time for the test run. This scenario was chosen to explore the use of the maximum resources that the tool offers.

4.1 Results

To analyze the results collected in the questionnaire in the form of Likert scale [9], we used the method proposed by [10]. Table 1 presents data collected from the questionnaire. The answers were given by 15 participants (A-O) to a questionnaire of 19 items. We will present the results related to System Usefulness, so, the items analyzed are related to number 1 until 8, that correspond to the following statements: 1) Overall, I am satisfied with how easy it is to use this system, 2) It was simple to use the system, 3) I could effectively complete the tasks and scenarios using this system, 4) I was able to complete the tasks and scenarios quickly using this system, 5) I was able to efficiently complete the tasks and scenarios using this system, 6) I felt comfortable using this system, 7) It was easy to learn to use this system and 8) I believe I could become productive quickly using this system. In the right part of the table it is shown the sum of the number of responses for each participant grouped by Likert scale of points, it shows how many times each participant selected 5, 4, 3, 2 and 1 as response.

Table 1. Usefulness of the System

	1	2	3	4	5	6	7	8	Total	5	4	3	2	1
A	5	4	5	4	4	4	5	4	**35**	3	5	0	0	0
B	4	4	5	5	5	4	4	4	**35**	3	5	0	0	0
C	4	3	4	5	5	3	4	3	**31**	2	3	3	0	0
D	4	4	4	3	3	4	4	2	**28**	0	5	2	1	0
E	5	5	5	5	5	4	4	5	**38**	6	2	0	0	0
F	4	4	4	3	4	4	4	2	**29**	0	6	1	1	0
G	4	4	4	4	4	3	4	4	**31**	0	7	1	0	0
H	4	4	4	4	3	4	4	4	**31**	0	7	1	0	0
I	4	4	5	5	3	4	4	4	**33**	2	5	1	0	0
J	5	5	5	4	5	4	4	3	**35**	4	3	1	0	0
K	2	3	4	2	3	1	3	2	**20**	0	1	3	3	1
M	4	4	2	4	4	3	3	2	**26**	0	4	2	2	0
N	3	3	4	3	4	3	4	4	**28**	0	4	4	0	0
O	4	4	3	4	3	4	4	4	**30**	0	6	2	0	0

According to the method [10] used to analyze data, it needs to perform a manual analysis to identify whether the participants answers were consistent. Participant L is not in Table 1 because he marked "strongly agree" for the 19 items of the questionnaire, making a bias for research. Therefore, it was excluded from analysis. The rest of the participants who answered the questionnaire shows consistency in their responses.

Using Table 1, we calculate the average of all responses. We sum the data from "Total" column and divide by the total number of participants. Thus, the average is 30.71 (430/14). Therefore, the average of all participants is greater than the average 24 ("no opinion"), implying that in general our tool has been considered useful by the users. That is, the tool performs tasks that it claims to do. In this specific case (*Usefulness of the System*), only one participant (K) belongs to the unfavorable group. His average (20) was lower than average related to no opinion (24). Thus, 13 last participants are part of the favorable group. The tool also has presented a good usability in the others aspects such as overall satisfaction, information quality, and interface quality. All material, questionnaires, results and user tasks are available at [11] by the following electronic address: http://bit.ly/21B0CLl.

5 Related Works

In order to compare the tools related to business process configuration, we took into account the modeling aspects of the tools, since they are the core of any business process configuration approach.

BVCCoN-Tool is a tool more complete. It allows modeling different perspectives related to business process (non-functional requirements, variability, and context information), without the need to extend an existing modeling language or use a language only to cover some perspective cited before. In contrast, the tool proposed by Lapouchnian et al. (2007) [7] mixes the process information with variability description and softgoals.

Different from Lapouchnian et al. (2007) [7], La Rosa (2009) [6] tool deals with business process variability and contextual information. Even sharing some characteristics in common with other tools, BVCCoN-Tool shows more advantages than disadvantages when considering the scenario of dynamic process configuration. Table 2 reports a summary of the tools related to criteria discussed above.

Modeling Aspects	Quaestio [6]	OpenOME [7]	BVCCoN-Tool [12]
1. Variability Description	YES	YES	YES
2. Non-Functional Requirements (Softgoal)	NO	YES	YES
3. Contextual Information	YES	NO	YES
YES	66.66%	66.66%	100%
NO	33.33%	33.33%	0%

Table 2. Comparative Analysis of Case Tools for Business Process Configuration

6 Conclusion and Future Work

Due to importance and complexity of the BVCCoN approach described in [13], it was necessary develop a tool to support the approach. Thus, this paper presented the BVCCoN-Tool, which has the following strengths: 1) import BPMN model - to set the attributes of elements called Variant and Variation Point, is necessary to import BPMN models; 2) using BVCCoN-Tool is possible to model three views independently - non-functional requirements, business process variability, and contextual information.

The tool was built to supports the modeling steps of BVCCoN approach, however, it can also be used to model NFRs during requirements engineering process of software development approaches, by business analysts, to describe business process variability and by any professional who wishes to model contextual information. (it is important to note that BVCCoN-Tool is the unique modeling tool to support these three views); 3) interactive feedbacks - the tool is based on metamodel, so it prevents the modeling of diagrams with syntax errors, showing a prohibited sign, which acts as a marker to indicate for the user to realize that some concept is not well understood; and 4) Usefulness of the system - by means of a usability evaluation, our tool was considered useful by the users, having an overall acceptance.

Even though we have not yet evaluated the tool in any industrial setting, the feedback from the usability evaluation and the use example we have performed has been very encouraging. We found evidence that our tool can serve as vehicle for improving the quality of the models and time consuming of BVCCoN approach. Some issues are still open, and others came up from the results achieved. This way, the following items must be considered in future works: 1) the next stage to bringing the tool into practice is to execute a pilot project in the industry; 2) perform other usability evaluation; and 3) extend the tool to automate the configuration of dynamic business process.

References

[1] Eclipse: Eclipse Modeling Project (2013), `http://www.eclipse.org/modeling/`, http://www.eclipse.org/modeling/. ltimo acesso em Novembro/2013

[2] Eclipse: Epsilon (2013), `http://www.eclipse.org/epsilon/`, http://www.eclipse.org/epsilon/. ltimo acesso em Outubro/2013

[3] Eclipse: EuGENia (2013), `http://www.eclipse.org/epsilon/doc/eugenia/`, http://www.eclipse.org/epsilon/doc/eugenia/. ltimo acesso em Outubro/2013

[4] Eclipse: Graphical Modeling Project (GMP) (2013), `http://www.eclipse.org/modeling/gmp/`, http://www.eclipse.org/modeling/gmp/. ltimo acesso em Outubro/2013

[5] Kolovos, D.: An extensible platform for specification of integrated languages for model management. Doutorado, The University of York (2008)

[6] La Rosa, M., van der Aalst, W.M., Dumas, M., ter Hofstede, A.H.: Questionnaire-based variability modeling for system configuration. Software & Systems Modeling 8(2), 251–274 (2009)

[7] Lapouchnian, A., Yu, Y., Mylopoulos, J.: Requirements-driven design and configuration management of business processes. In: Business Process Management, pp. 246–261. Springer (2007)

[8] Lewis, J.R.: Ibm computer usability satisfaction questionnaires: psychometric evaluation and instructions for use. International Journal of Human-Computer Interaction 7(1), 57–78 (1995)

[9] Likert, R.: A technique for the measurement of attitudes. Archives of psychology (1932)

[10] McClelland, J.A.: Tcnica de questionrio para pesquisa. Revista Brasileira de Fsica 1(1), 93–101 (1976)

[11] Pereira, T.C.: Bvccon-tool: uma ferramenta para apoiar uma abordagem de configuração de processos de negócio dinâmicos (2014)

[12] Pereira, T.C.: BVCCoN-Tool: Uma Ferramenta para Apoiar uma Abordagem de Configurao de Processos de Negcio Dinmicos. Master's thesis, Universidade Federal de Pernambuco, Recife, Pernambuco, Brasil (2014)

[13] Santos, E.B.: Business Process Configuration with NFRs and Context-Awareness. Doutorado, Universidade Federal de Pernambuco (2013)

[14] Steinberg, D., Budinsky, F., Merks, E., Paternostro, M.: EMF: eclipse modeling framework. Pearson Education (2008)

Visualization of automated test results obtained by the TESTAR tool

Urko Rueda, Anna I. Esparcia-Alcazar, and Tanja E.J. Vos

Research Center on Software Production Methods (PROS)
Universitat Politècnica de València
Camino de vera s/n 46022, Valencia, Spain
{urueda,aesparcia,tvos}@pros.upv.es
http://www.testar.org

Abstract. Bigger and more complex software systems demand quality practices that are seldom carried out in real industry. A common practice is to provide a post-release maintenance service of products to correct defects reported by the end user. In previous work we presented TESTAR, a technology-agnostic tool for automated testing of applications from their GUI. Here we introduce state-transition graph models derived from TESTAR test results as a tool for visualisation of what has been tested, to which extent and which software defects were found. We discuss how such models enable to perform quality assessment of software products by inspecting and debugging the system behaviour from the GUI perspective. This constitutes a step forward in aid of software developers and testers, since the User Interface is commonly the means end-users encounter potential software defects.

Keywords: Automated Testing, User Interface Models, Quality Assessment, Visualization

1 Introduction

Visualisation is a historical mechanism that contributes to human understanding of large sets of information. From city, bus and metro maps to UML models for software design, presentation slides to communicate to attendees, hardware resources graphs to display their usage by different applications processes, the list is numerous. In computer science it does not matter how smart a system could be, human control is still critical in most scenarios, including software design and software testing.

In previous work we presented TESTAR [8] and its successful application to various industrial systems [9]. TESTAR is capable of automated test generation and executes test cases based on a tree model that is automatically derived from the application's GUI through accessibility API technologies. Since this structure is built automatically during testing, the GUI is not assumed to be fixed and tests still run even when the GUI has been modified. This reduces the maintenance problem that threatens most current state-of.the-art approaches in GUI testing, like Capture-Replay [26, 24, 14, 15, 11] and Visual Testing [29, 3].

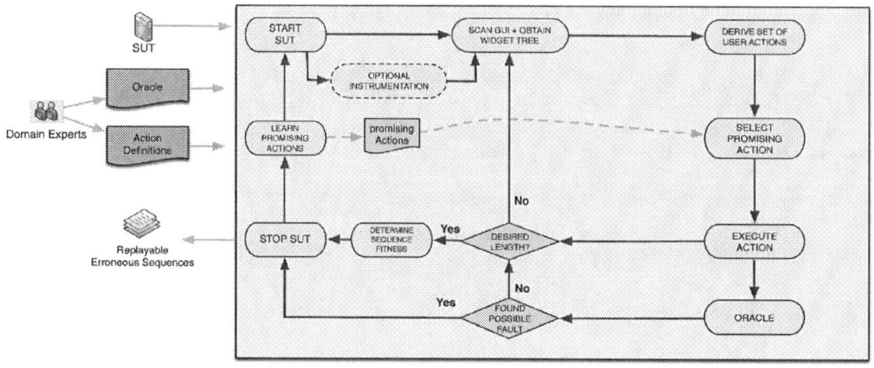

Fig. 1. TESTAR testing cycle

The TESTAR tool [25] carries out automated testing, Figure 1, on the SUT's GUI by deriving sets of possible actions for each state that the GUI is in, and automatically selecting and executing appropriate ones until a stopping criteria is reached. A tester can take full control of tests, by modifying a TESTAR default provided testing protocol which enable to establish the stopping criteria, which actions are available from the GUI, oracles, etc. Oracles are used to detect faulty behaviour when a system crashes or freezes. Besides these simple,"free" oracles, the tester can easily specify regular expressions that detect patterns of suspicious titles in widgets that might pop up during the execution. For more sophisticated and powerful oracles, the tester can enrich the default TESTAR (Java-based) protocol that is used to drive the tests.

SUT GUI states are computed as the set of hierarchical widgets (user interface elements) that conform its GUI, called widget trees in TESTAR. These widget trees are gathered through the Operating System's Accessibility API, an assistive technology that has the capability to detect and expose the GUI widgets and their corresponding properties[1].To illustrate the concept, the left part of Figure 2 shows the GUI of a very simple application, with its corresponding widget tree on the right. It has a titlebar (with text *Example*), a menu bar, a button, a text-field and a slider. It also includes an example of actions that could be performed by the user: dots for clicks, ABC text for text-input, arrows for drag&drop operations in the slider.

TESTAR has been deployed in various industrial environments [25], which has allowed us to receive feedback from the end users. Companies have been keen to take up TESTAR, yet they would appreciate a visualisation aid in order to see what has happened and what has been tested. We are also aware such an aid would enable us to debug testing performance, check which parts of the application GUI were exercised, and how TESTAR achieved to crash or reveal software defects.

[1] Such as display position, widget size, ancestor widgets, etc.

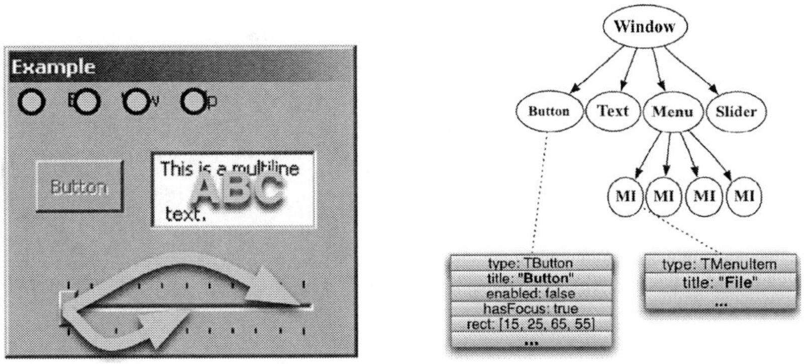

Fig. 2. An example GUI state (left) and its corresponding widget tree (right)

Here we present the results of our work on visualisation of the TESTAR outputs. The functionality described in the paper is already supported by the tool (https://github.com/STaQ-PROS-UPV/TESTAR). Section 2 gives an overview of related work in the area. Section 3 introduces the main contribution of this paper, namely the TESTAR graphical models, including a description of how they can be used for quality assessment. Finally, in section 4 we present some conclusions and outline areas for future work.

2 Related work

Model extraction using dynamic GUI crawling is a popular research topic when adopting model-based testing (MBT). It addresses the challenge of the effort and expertise required on crafting the application models. In [5] an overview is given of the existing body of knowledge on GUI testing, showing that 52% of the studied papers were about Model-Based GUI Testing approaches. It was found that the models that were mostly used to generate tests were Event Flow Graphs (EFG) and Finite State Models (FSM). Moreover, most approaches are limited to specific programming language environments.

Work related to EFG models has mostly been carried out by the GUITAR team [23] and is based on reverse engineering (called ripping [18]) of a EFG GUI model that represents all possible interaction sequences with the GUI widgets. Such a model is then used for test case derivation. GUITAR (available at http://guitar.sourceforge.net/wiki/index.php) was initially developed for Java applications, but extensions have been made for iPhone, Android and Web applications. Murphy Tools [1, 2] is a GUI Driver tool based on GUITAR, that presents a dynamic reverse engineering tool for Java GUI applications, and an iterative process of manually providing valid input values and automatically improving the created state-models. Murphy Tools automatically extracts models of the GUI of applications as the user interacts with them. Then, the models are used to drive testing. This approach differs from TESTAR in two ways. First, the manual work required to exercise the applications for models population. Secondly, tests are guided by the extracted models. The effectiveness of the tests would rely directly on the goodness of extracted models. In contrast, TESTAR approach performs automated testing without the need of models. It is true that models are still extracted and, what is more, the models can be applied for more intelligent testing (i.e compared to randomly selecting GUI actions) when GUI space exploration is a main concern.

FSM models are used in [16] where tests are generated for AJAX applications using Hill-Climbing and Simulated Annealing on an approximate model that is obtained from the applications Document Object Model tree. [20, 21] present a tool called Crawljax that uses dynamic analysis to construct a FSM of an AJAX application using web crawling, from which a set of test cases is generated. WebMate [10] is another model extractor for web applications. It extracts a so-called a usage model, a graph where nodes correspond to states of the application and a transition represents a single interaction with the application. In [19] we can find automated crawling of web applications' models. They focus on Javascript and DOM to dynamically analyse candidate events to perform on the GUI and that would change the application state. Yet, in contrast to TESTAR, the tester does not have control over the events that would be interesting to perform. This is mainly because such approaches are focused to craft a model of the application, while TESTAR seamlessly drives testing on tester controlled testing protocol.

In [22] an FSM based approach is presented called GUI Test Automation Model (GUITam) for constructing the state models by dynamic analysis. The GUITam Runner works for C++ applications.

With the increased availability of mobile platform applications in our daily life there is a trend to switch testing from traditional desktop platform to the mobile context. In [28] static analysis is combined with dynamic GUI crawling to test Android applications. They use static analysis of the application source code to extract the actions supported by the GUI of the application. Next, they use dynamic crawling to build a FSM of the application by systematically exercising the extracted events on the live application. They compare their approach to the Android version of GUITAR.

The iCrawler tool [13] is a reverse engineering tool for iOS mobile applications that also uses an FSM.

Other types of models are used too. In [4] a so-called GUI tree is used as a model to perform crash testing on Android mobile apps (the nodes represents user interfaces of the app, while edges describe event-based transitions). Similar to [20], the model is obtained by a so-called GUI-Crawler that walks through the application by invoking the available event-handlers with random argument values. From the GUI-tree test cases are obtained by selecting paths starting from the root to one of the leaves. The application under test is instrumented to detect uncaught exceptions that would crash the app. Morgado et al. present

ReGUI tool [12] that uses dynamic analysis to generate Spec# and GraphML GUI models to test windows applications.

In [17] a tool called AutoBlackTest is presented that does dynamic analysis for model extraction and test suite generation for GUI applications. The tool uses IBM Rational Functional Tester (RFT) to extract the list of widgets present in a given GUI, to access their state and to interact with them. RFT supports a range of technologies to develop GUIs and offers a programmatic interface that is independent from the technology used to implement the GUI of the application under test.

Maintenance is one of the major drawbacks when using capture & replay tools, as changes to the user interface can result in laborious manual adaption work. Therefore, approaches to automating test suite maintenance [11] become crucial. In this line, work by Leotta et al. e.g. focuses on making existing approaches more robust to changes to the application [15]. Sun and Jones perform analysis of the underlying application programmable interface (API) in order to generate GUI tests [27].

3 TESTAR State-Transition Graphs

TESTAR testing cycle iterates a pair of action selection and execution for each UI state the SUT is in. Each UI state is represented by an unique identificator, and each action from that concrete state is also represented by an unique identifier. TESTAR populates the graphs by pairs of state-ID and action-ID as actions are being executed in a test sequence. A TESTAR graphing utility retrieves such pairs of states and actions and populates the test graphs.

To be able to visualise TESTAR test runs, we have defined the TESTAR State-Transition Graph, in which each node represents a unique GUI state and has an associated unique state identifier. The graph edges, which have an associated unique action identifier, represent a state transition caused by a user-action, such as left/right clicks, text input and drag&drop operations. An example is given in Figure 3, which shows a fragment of the corresponding TESTAR State-Transition Graph Model for a test run.

Each node contains a label xxx (y), where *xxx* represents the state identifier and *y* the number of times the state was traversed on a test execution. Similarly, labels for actions include identifier, number of repetitions and an extra parameter between square brackets which indicates the action sequence number in the test execution. In this way we have the ability to explore the executed test action by action. We discuss the quality assessment of applications in Section 3.5.

Nodes[2] and links in dashed lines, which include the label *unexplored*, refer to actions that are available from a given GUI state, but that were not executed during a test. The number of actions that were not executed appears between brackets.

[2] The number following the label *unexplored* within nodes merely refers to the count of states not fully explored

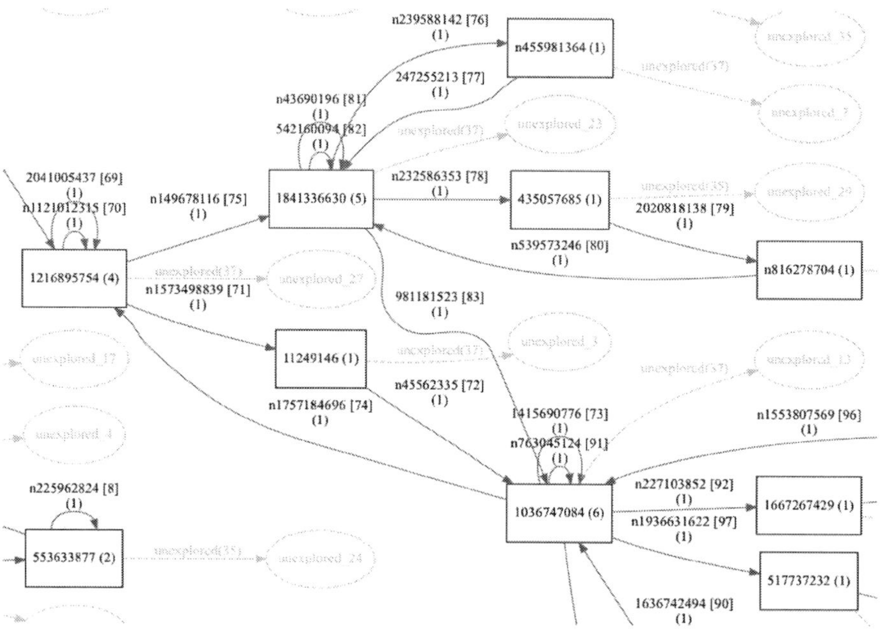

Fig. 3. Fragment of the TESTAR graph (tiny) for a 99-action test sequence for Windows calculator

3.1 Unique identifiers for states and actions

TESTAR reports test runs as a sequence of actions, each of which is a transition from two GUI states that might be the same (the GUI does not change) or different (the action produced an GUI change). Providing unique identifiers to those states and actions could potentially help in the inspection and analysis of test results. Several applications can be think of: quick search and jump to concrete states and actions by their unique id, cross test run matching were a state from test run X can be localised into a test run Y, etc. In the end, we believe these identifiers are essential to support debugging when there is a need to jump into concrete states and actions.

To make states and actions uniquely identified even across different runs of the SUT, we need to assign a unique and stable identifier to each state and action. TESTAR allows us to derive the complete GUI state of the SUT (i.e. the widget tree as explained in Section ??), so that we can inspect the property values of each visible widget. For instance, it gives access to the title of a button, its position and size and tells us whether it is enabled. This gives us the means to create a unique identifier for a click on that button: It can be represented as combination of the button's property values, like its title, help text or its position in the widget hierarchy (which parents / children the button has). The properties selected for the identifier should be relatively "stable". The title of a window, for example, is quite often not a stable value (opening new documents in Word will change the title of the main window) whereas its tool tip or help text is less likely to change.

Each action type (i.e. a click or a keystroke) may have parameters. For example, a click action has two parameters: the button (i.e. left or right) and the clicking position (x and y coordinates). The action identifier used for the graph link takes parameters into account. Hence, the action that types the text *foo* will have a different identifier than the action that types *boo*. What is more, the identifier also depends on the state the action is performed. This approach will enable to precisely locate an action in the graph by its unique identifier. The same approach can be applied to represent GUI states: one simply combines the values of all stable properties of all widgets on the screen.

3.2 Reusing the TESTAR graphs

TESTAR GUI models are state-transition diagrams/graphs described with plain text graph description language (DOT), which makes them reusable by third party tools. The DOT format is illustrated in the following sample code.

```
digraph DOT { rankdir=LR;
START [shape=point, height=0.3, style=solid, color=black];
START -> state_1;
state_1 -> state_2 [label="transition"];
state_2 -> state_2 [label="loop"]; state_2 -> END; }
```

It mainly consists of links between nodes, e.g. transition from state 1 to state 2; graphical properties can be set for different graphical representations.

The rationale behind using this simple dot format is that it offers enough capabilities for the representation of the UI test sequences from the perspective of acquiring an overview of the execution. Node labels can be applied to UI states identifiers and link labels to state' actions identifiers. The graphical properties of the dot format would also enable to remark special characteristics of the test sequences, as for example a varying color to indicate a higher repetition of certain actions. At a glance, the colors would be indicators of how much were the different parts of the UI exercised.

3.3 Test results graphs

TESTAR graphs comes in three varying details: *minimal*, without states and actions identifiers, *tiny*, which incorporates identifiers to the minimal version and *screenshoted*, which embeds GUI screenshot to states and GUI action target screenshot to transitions.

A *minimal* detailed version will help improve visualisation and get an overview of the SUT GUI space explored by a test sequence; an example of this can be found in Figure 4. This is done by removing the identifiers from states and actions, and the order of actions in the test which happen to crowd the graphs

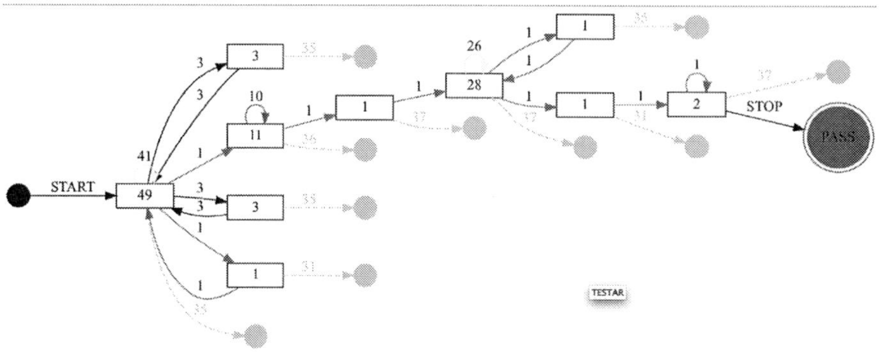

Fig. 4. Windows calculator TESTAR Graph (minimal) for 99 actions test sequence

with too much information for a simple overview of the complete test sequence. This is indeed more crucial the bigger the graphs are.

For a regular *tiny* version, the graphs provide enough information to search and identify the states and actions from test runs. The order, between brackets, in the actions enable to trace a test run action by action. This version is less readable than the minimal one due to the extra information displayed, but will enable to debug and match a test run to its corresponding GUI state-transition graph.

TESTAR also keeps a *screenshot-version* of the graphs, see Figure 5, that can be directly used for test documentation. Embedding the GUI screenshots for graph states and actions GUI target screenshots (e.g. the widget screenshot for a button click) provides more meaningful information about test runs. It allow to read which GUI states were exercised by a test run and the SUT behaviour after each executed action.

3.4 Abstracting the graphs

Some actions tend to populate the graphs almost to infinite, which would be problematic for graph visualisation due to their large extension. For example, a text-field widget might accept any kind of text input, which translates into nearly infinite ways of populating the text-field. The corresponding graph would consist of a different state for each different text input: *stateX, input-a, state-a, input-b, state-b, ..., input-n, state-n.* In this concrete sequence, if we start at state *X*, giving the input "a" for a text field will end in the state *b*, and so on with the input "b" to input "n". To avoid such expansion of the graph and maintain it more scalable, we present next an **abstraction mechanism**.

We have shown above how the graph states and actions identifiers are computed to uniquely identify them. States consider the widget properties *Role*, *Title* and *Shape*, while actions do take into account the GUI state from which it is performed and its event parameters (i.e. *some text* in a typing action).

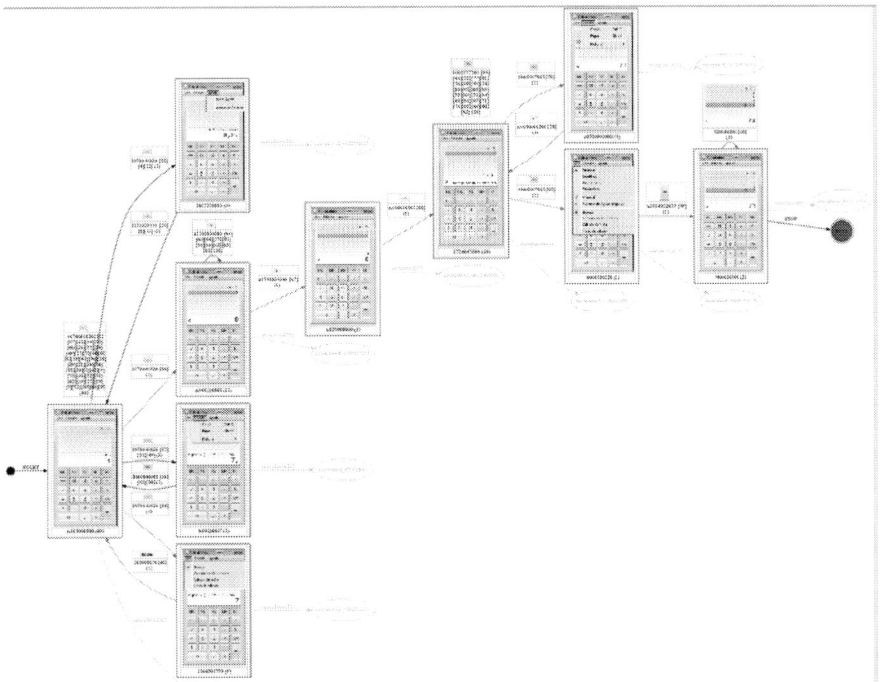

Fig. 5. Windows calculator TESTAR Graph (screenshot) for 99 actions test sequence

We can achieve abstraction by recoding the identifiers. Abstract state identifiers are computed by only considering the *Role* property of a widget. Thus, we can abstract the GUI by looking into its widgets hierarchy and widget types. For actions, the abstract identifier is calculated by discarding event parameters, concretely *mouse position* and typed texts. For the former, in the example, a left/click mouse action is performed at a fixed coordinate (the mouse position), but we are only interested on the action type (thus, ignoring the coordinates). For the latter, typing some text is abstracted ignoring what is typed.

Then, each unique state and action has an associated abstract identifier (a cluster of states or actions respectively) that enables TESTAR to cluster the graphs, collapsing states and actions into a simpler representation of the GUI model. Clusters are reported together with graphs, for example (cluster uses the abstract identifier):

```
  Cluster (5) 1151628151 contains:
(1) n1626056442 (2) 1669305354 (3) n86735519
```

We would like to remark that the current version of TESTAR screenshot version of the abstracted graphs are merely illustrative because each abstracted state and action is the combination of many states and actions, respectively. The combination of several screenshots into a single abstracted screenshot is out of the scope of this paper. However, we can jump into the non-abstracted graphs to get a precise scenario of states and actions for our test sequence.

3.5 An example of application: quality assessment

The TESTAR approach aims to automate testing in industry, independently of the size and complexity of applications and the technology underneath. Such a technology-agnostic automation approach needs to be largely independent of the source code, especially as companies are reluctant to share their source code and are not keen on instrumentation or injection. Consequently, we need to complement our approach with quality metrics that are also independent of the source code. This way we can provide industry with quality indicators about the testing activities done with TESTAR. Being aware of the extent at which our software applications are being tested, it can provide and indicator of how reliable we could expect our software to be. While traditional testing provides metrics on code coverage and mutation metrics, indicators of how much of the code was exercised, a technology-agnostic black-box (testing outside the code or binary) testing approach like TESTAR requires alternative approaches to report the extent at which software are exercised/stressed.

The TESTAR graphing utility presented in this paper provides SUT GUI space exploration metrics. It reports, every X actions, on the number of unique and abstracted states and actions that were traversed/executed during a test. For example, a test run of 50 actions with a sampling every 10 actions may report the next exploration curve data:

```
________________UNIQUE ________ABSTRACT ___________TOTAL
   #, states, actions, states, actions, unique, abstract
   1,      4,      10,      2,       2,     14,        4
   2,      7,      20,      3,       3,     27,        6
   3,     13,      30,      5,       6,     43,       11
   4,     16,      40,      6,       7,     56,       13
   5,     22,      50,      6,       7,     72,       13
```

Additionally, TESTAR also reports the number of states for which there were discovered actions that were not explored/executed. The corresponding test report of the previous exploration curve data would include metrics for unexplored states and actions and a test verdict (PASS or FAIL):

```
______________________________STATES
total, unique, abstract, unexplored (with unexplored actions)
   51,     22,        6,         21 (total = # actions + 1)

_____________________________ACTIONS
total, unique, abstract, unexplored (discovered but unexecuted)
   50,     50,        7,        638
```

```
____________TOTAL
 unique, abstract, ... VERDICT
     72,       13, ...    PASS
```

Looking to this sample metrics we can make several observations. First, the exploration curve indicates how fast a test sequence is exploring the UI of the application. The last 10 executed actions does not increase the number of abstract states and actions explored (6 and 7 respectively). It could suggest a possible stopping criteria of the test sequence when we want to broad exercise the UI of the application. In contrary, the last 10 actions also suggest that a specific part of the UI is being stressed. This might be also interesting to discover faults that may arise by hard stressing a concrete part of the UI.

Secondly, the unexplored states and actions metrics provide indicators of un-exercised parts of the UI. Again, this may contribute to decide on the tests stopping criteria. The ideal testing would continue until no unexplored states or actions are reported. Yet, the screenshot version provides information on which unexplored UI parts should be further tested.

A TESTAR graph, from an executed test, depicts which SUT GUI states are reached by concrete actions. It provides (specially the screenshot versions) a straightforward documentation of how our system behaves. Most importantly, this documentation can be obtained automatically as soon as a new product version is available for testing. The graph will sketch how exactly the system reacts to user actions. The feedback received from our industrial partners indicates that this is a good way to proceed with test quality reporting in TESTAR.

4 Conclusions

TESTAR is a technology-agnostic automated testing solution that enables analyses of the quality of software from their GUI through a customised tester testing protocol, which enable to control which actions can be performed on the GUI, which actions should be executed and how to detect defects or suspicious behaviour through implementing SUT specific oracles.

In this paper we have presented an approach to visualisation that enables TESTAR to provide visual information of test runs. Test visualisation helps testers to directly inspect and analyse how the SUT was exercised in the search of potential failures. Without this feature we will only know whether a test pass or fails and, if reported, the raw sequence of actions that were performed. However, raw actions force to reproduce them in the GUI to check what was executed. Mechanisms to visually check how the tests performed are helpful if we want to get a deep insight of how the SUT was tested and what made a SUT to reveal a failure. In this line, TESTAR screenshoted graphs enable to inspect and analyse the tests. Even more, these graphs can be used as test documentation, from which human testers might perform manual tests (e.g. for failure reproducibility) Other than testers, developers can also benefit from this information which makes them aware of concrete test sequences that break the SUT. TESTAR is also able to measure the size and complexity on GUI basis based on the number of GUI states and transitions explored by test runs. We have also introduced how to assess the quality of software products looking into the reported data and graphs models.

We are confident that TESTAR will help software industry to adopt testing automation and that it will enable to reduce the maintenance costs on new software releases. TESTAR is not oriented to update test artifacts, but to keep a working testing protocol (i.e. widgets/actions recognition, oracles) that will yet run on new releases. However, we are aware that there is still manual work to perform, the most critical part being the oracles definition. We foresee that oracles should be a new trending topic in testing development that will be mixed into the traditional software development methodologies. For example, a SUT working with a database should provide the mechanisms to check the data consistency: a) in the database itself, b) in the data sent from the SUT to the database and c) in the data retrieved from the database to the SUT GUI.

We are aware that one potential problem with our visualisation approach stems from the fact that bigger systems would produce bigger graphs with a higher amount of nodes/states. This is a critical scalability problem, specially on screenshoted versions of graphs, that could potentially introduce technical difficulties for inspecting and assessing the models. Addressing this potential problem is left for future work. Yet, our plan is to break the graphs into small interconnected portions. Each portion could be associated with concrete portions of the whole application GUI. We have already worked with graphs comprising of more than 250 abstract states and more than 500 abstract actions, due to test sequences of 5000 actions over the windows calculator. Although the graphs are big, we can easily jump to interesting parts by searching the identifiers of states and actions. More advanced inspecting features will be also incorporated (e.g. state centered re-graphing, displaying the closest interconnected states and actions).

Finally, we acknowledge that the TESTAR approach relies on the applications accessibility compliance, as TESTAR makes use of the platform native Accessibility API to retrieve the widget-trees presented in this paper. However, we expect to address the issue by supplying specific drivers that provides application widget-trees and events handling. We have already succeed on this line by supporting the Android platform for mobile phones.

An empirical evaluation of the visualization approach is also left for a consequent publication.

5 Acknowledgement

This work was partly funded by FITTEST project, ICT-2009.1.2 no 257574, SHIP project (EACEA/A2/UHB/CL 554187) and the PERTEST project (TIN2013-46928-C3-1-R).

References

1. Aho, P., Menz, N., Rty, T., Schieferdecker, I.: Automated java gui modeling for model-based testing purposes. In: Information Technology: New Generations (ITNG), 2011 Eighth International Conference on. pp. 268–273 (April 2011)
2. Aho, P., Suarez, M., Kanstren, T., Memon, A.: Murphy tools: Utilizing extracted gui models for industrial software testing. In: The Proceedings of the Testing: Academic & Industrial Conference (TAIC-PART). IEEE Computer Society (2014)
3. Alegroth, E., Nass, M., Olsson, H.: Jautomate: A tool for system- and acceptance-test automation. In: Software Testing, Verification and Validation (ICST), 2013 IEEE Sixth International Conference on. pp. 439–446 (March 2013)
4. Amalfitano, D., Fasolino, A., Tramontana, P.: A gui crawling-based technique for android mobile application testing. In: Software Testing, Verification and Validation Workshops (ICSTW), 2011 IEEE Fourth International Conference on. pp. 252–261 (March 2011)
5. Banerjee, I., Nguyen, B., Garousi, V., Memon, A.: Graphical user interface (gui) testing: Systematic mapping and repository. Information and Software Technology (2013)
6. Bauersfeld, S., Vos, T.E.J.: User interface level testing with TESTAR; what about more sophisticated action specification and selection? In: Proceedings of the Seventh Seminar on Advanced Techniques and Tools for Software Evolution, SATToSE 2014. pp. 60–78 (July 2014)
7. Bauersfeld, S., Wappler, S., Wegener, J.: A metaheuristic approach to test sequence generation for applications with a GUI. In: Proceedings of the Third International Symposium on Search Based Software Engineering (SSBSE 2011). pp. 10–12 (September 2011)
8. Bauersfeld, S., Vos, T.E.J.: Guitest: a java library for fully automated gui robustness testing. In: Proceedings of the 27th IEEE/ACM International Conference on Automated Software Engineering. pp. 330–333. ASE 2012, ACM, New York, NY, USA (2012), http://doi.acm.org/10.1145/2351676.2351739
9. Bauersfeld, S., Vos, T.E.J., Condori-Fernández, N., Bagnato, A., Brosse, E.: Evaluating the TESTAR tool in an industrial case study. In: 2014 ACM-IEEE International Symposium on Empirical Software Engineering and Measurement, ESEM 2014, Torino, Italy, September 18-19, 2014. p. 4 (2014)
10. Dallmeier, V., Pohl, B., Burger, M., Mirold, M., Zeller, A.: Webmate: Web application test generation in the real world. 2014 IEEE Seventh International Conference on Software Testing, Verification and Validation Workshops 0, 413–418 (2014)
11. Grechanik, M., Xie, Q., Fu, C.: Maintaining and evolving gui-directed test scripts. In: Proceedings of the 31st International Conference on Software Engineering. pp. 408–418. ICSE '09, IEEE Computer Society, Washington, DC, USA (2009), http://dx.doi.org/10.1109/ICSE.2009.5070540
12. I.Morgado, Paiva, A., Faria, J.: Dynamic reverse engineering of graphical user interfaces. Int. Journal on Advances in Software 5(3 and 4), 224–246 (2012)
13. Joorabchi, M., Mesbah, A.: Reverse engineering ios mobile applications. In: Reverse Engineering (WCRE), 2012 19th Working Conference on. pp. 177–186 (Oct 2012)
14. Kaner, C.: Avoiding shelfware: A managers view of automated gui testing. http://www.kaner.com/pdfs/shelfwar.pdf (2002)
15. Leotta, M., Clerissi, D., Ricca, F., Spadaro, C.: Comparing the maintainability of selenium webdriver test suites employing different locators: a case study. In:

Proceedings of the 2013 International Workshop on Joining AcadeMiA and Industry Contributions to testing Automation. pp. 53–58. JAMAICA 2013, ACM, New York, NY, USA (2013), http://doi.acm.org/10.1145/2489280.2489284
16. Marchetto, A., Tonella, P.: Using search-based algorithms for ajax event sequence generation during testing. Empirical Software Engineering 16(1), 103–140 (2011), http://dx.doi.org/10.1007/s10664-010-9149-1
17. Mariani, L., Pezzè, M., Riganelli, O., Santoro, M.: Autoblacktest: A tool for automatic black-box testing. In: Proceedings of the 33rd International Conference on Software Engineering. pp. 1013–1015. ICSE '11, ACM, New York, NY, USA (2011), http://doi.acm.org/10.1145/1985793.1985979
18. Memon, A., Banerjee, I., Nguyen, B., Robbins, B.: The first decade of gui ripping: Extensions, applications, and broader impacts. In: Proceedings of the 20th Working Conference on Reverse Engineering (WCRE). IEEE Press (2013)
19. Mesbah, A., van Deursen, A., Lenselink, S.: Crawling AJAX-based web applications through dynamic analysis of user interface state changes. ACM Transactions on the Web 6(1), 1–30 (2012)
20. Mesbah, A., van Deursen, A.: Invariant-based automatic testing of ajax user interfaces. In: Proceedings of the 31st International Conference on Software Engineering. pp. 210–220. ICSE '09, IEEE Computer Society, Washington, DC, USA (2009), http://dx.doi.org/10.1109/ICSE.2009.5070522
21. Mesbah, A., van Deursen, A., Lenselink, S.: Crawling ajax-based web applications through dynamic analysis of user interface state changes. ACM Trans. Web 6(1), 3:1–3:30 (Mar 2012), http://doi.acm.org/10.1145/2109205.2109208
22. Miao, Y., Yang, X.: An fsm based gui test automation model. In: Control Automation Robotics Vision (ICARCV), 2010 11th International Conference on. pp. 120–126 (Dec 2010)
23. Nguyen, B.N., Robbins, B., Banerjee, I., Memon, A.: Guitar: an innovative tool for automated testing of gui-driven software. Automated Software Engineering pp. 1–41 (2013)
24. Nguyen, B.N., Robbins, B., Banerjee, I., Memon, A.M.: Guitar: an innovative tool for automated testing of gui-driven software. Autom. Softw. Eng. 21(1), 65–105 (2014)
25. Rueda, U., Vos, T.E.J., Almenar, F., Martínez, M.O., Esparcia-Alcázar, A.I.: TESTAR: from academic prototype towards an industry-ready tool for automated testing at the user interface level. In: Canos, J.H., Gonzalez Harbour, M. (eds.) Actas de las XX Jornadas de Ingeniería del Software y Bases de Datos (JISBD 2015). pp. 236–245 (2015)
26. Singhera, Z.U., Horowitz, E., Shah, A.A.: A graphical user interface (gui) testing methodology. IJITWE 3(2), 1–18 (2008)
27. Sun, Y., Jones, E.L.: Specification-driven automated testing of GUI-based Java programs. In: Proceedings of the 42nd annual Southeast regional conference. pp. 140–145. ACM (2004)
28. Yang, W., Prasad, M.R., Xie, T.: A grey-box approach for automated gui-model generation of mobile applications. In: Proceedings of the 16th International Conference on Fundamental Approaches to Software Engineering. pp. 250–265. FASE'13, Springer-Verlag, Berlin, Heidelberg (2013)
29. Yeh, T., Chang, T.H., Miller, R.C.: Sikuli: Using gui screenshots for search and automation. In: Proceedings of the 22Nd Annual ACM Symposium on User Interface Software and Technology. pp. 183–192. UIST '09, ACM, New York, NY, USA (2009), http://doi.acm.org/10.1145/1622176.1622213

Um Estudo de Caso para Avaliação de um Modelo para Teste de Usabilidade em Aplicação Móvel

Ingrid do Nascimento Mendes[1], Arilo Claudio Dias-Neto[1], Rodrigo dos A. Cruz Reis[1], Allan J. S. Bezerra[1,2]

[1] Instituto de Computação, Universidade Federal do Amazonas. Manaus, AM, Brasil
{inm, arilo}@icomp.ufam.edu.br, rdgdosanjos@gmail.com

[2]Samsung Ocean Center, UEA, Manaus, AM
allan.jsb@oceanbrasil.com

Abstract. Usability is considered one of the quality characteristics that have direct relation with the success/failure of a mobile application. Several attributes need to be evaluated in this applications aiming to assure an interaction of quality between user and application, such as effectiveness, efficiency, level of satisfaction, learning facility, errors, memorization, and cognitive load of the users while they use the application. In this work, we describe a case study that applied and evaluated the model PACMAD (*People At the Centre of Mobile Application Development*) for usability testing in a mobile application, considering the seven attributes cited above. Metrics and guides are proposed to support the model instantiation for each evaluation attribute and they can be adopted by software organizations. The results pointed out possible usability problems in the application under testing, suggesting the applicability of the proposed model instantiation for usability testing in mobile applications.

Resumo. A usabilidade é considerada uma das características de qualidade que possui relação direta com o sucesso/fracasso de uma aplicação desenvolvida para dispositivos móveis. Diversos atributos precisam ser avaliados nestas aplicações a fim de assegurar uma interação de qualidade entre o usuário e aplicação, tais como eficácia, eficiência, nível de satisfação, facilidade de aprendizado, erros, memorização e carga cognitiva do usuário enquanto utiliza a aplicação. Neste trabalho, é descrito um estudo de caso para aplicação e avaliação do modelo PACMAD (*People At the Centre of Mobile Application Development*) para testes de usabilidade em uma aplicação móvel considerando os sete atributos citados acima. Métricas e guias são propostos para instanciação do modelo para cada atributo de avaliação e podem ser adotados por organizações de software. Os resultados apontaram possíveis problemas relacionados à usabilidade da aplicação sob teste, indicando a aplicabilidade da instanciação proposta do modelo para testes de usabilidade em aplicações móveis.

Palavras-chave: Teste de Usabilidade, Aplicações Móveis, PACMAD.

1 Introdução

Desde seu surgimento, aplicações móveis estão em constante evolução em tecnologia e disseminação na sociedade. Dentre as características de qualidade de software presentes na série de normas ISO/IEC 25000 [1], Duh et al. [2] apontam a usabilidade como fator crítico para a popularidade e sucesso de uma aplicação móvel. Usabilidade pode ser definida como a medida pela qual um produto pode ser usado por usuários específicos para alcançar objetivos específicos em um contexto de uso específico [3].

Nos últimos anos, abordagens de análise e medição de usabilidade têm sido propostas e/ou evoluídas na literatura técnica [4]. Neste artigo, é descrito um estudo de caso para avaliação de uma proposta de instanciação do modelo PACMAD (*People At the Centre of Mobile Application Development*) [5], que propõe sete atributos para testes de usabilidade em uma aplicação móvel (eficácia, eficiência, satisfação, facilidade de aprendizagem, memorização, erros e carga cognitiva). Para instanciação deste modelo, foram utilizadas métricas oriundas de diversos trabalhos de pesquisa publicados na literatura técnica a fim de avaliar os resultados providos pela aplicação do modelo PACMAD em uma aplicação móvel selecionada no contexto desta pesquisa. Como resultado, foram obtidos dados que proveem indícios da aplicabilidade da instanciação do modelo PACMAD para avaliação da usabilidade de uma aplicação móvel a partir dos sete atributos analisados. Além disso, o modelo possibilita a descoberta de problemas de usabilidade na aplicação móvel, que depois de corrigidos podem melhorar sua usabilidade. Como contribuição, são apresentados guias de apoio à aplicação dos atributos que compõem o modelo PACMAD para avaliação de usabilidade de aplicações móveis.

O artigo está estruturado da seguinte forma: Na Seção 2 serão apresentados conceitos sobre teste de usabilidade em aplicações móveis e trabalhos relacionados. Na Seção 3 será mostrado como foi projetado e conduzido o estudo de caso proposto neste trabalho que visou a instanciação do modelo PACMAD. Na seção 4 serão discutidas as análises sobre os resultados obtidos ao longo do estudo, além de guias de apoio à aplicação dos atributos que compõem o modelo PACMAD para realização de testes de usabilidade em aplicações móveis. Na seção 5 são apresentadas as ameaças à validade observadas com a condução deste estudo de caso. E por fim, na Seção 6 serão apresentadas as conclusões sobre os resultados obtidos, e trabalhos futuros são descritos visando a sua continuidade.

2 Teste de Usabilidade em Aplicações Móveis

O teste de usabilidade em aplicações desenvolvidas para dispositivos móveis deve levar em conta a variedade de dispositivos, com diferentes tamanhos e resolução de tela. Dependendo da plataforma do dispositivo, seus elementos visuais deverão seguir um guia com a padronização correta de disposição de elementos de interface, como botões, janelas e cores, para não comprometer aspectos funcionais do sistema [6].

2.1 Técnicas de Teste de Usabilidade

Existem diversas técnicas para avaliação de usabilidade publicadas na literatura técnica, podendo estas serem aplicadas em aplicações móveis. Elas podem ser classificadas em Empíricas e Não Empíricas [7].

As técnicas empíricas envolvem a utilização de participantes representando usuários da aplicação sob teste. Como exemplos de técnicas empíricas, podem ser citadas: Observação de campo (observação do usuário no ambiente real), Experimento Controlado (técnica formal com objetivo de remover distrações, isolando os efeitos estudados), Registro verbal (usuário realiza tarefas e fala para uma câmera sobre um tópico pré-determinado pelo avaliador), Registro de uso (uso de dispositivos de registro automático que captam as interações do usuário com a interface). Essas técnicas podem ser aplicadas de forma isolada ou até mesmo de forma combinada em um ambiente construído exclusivamente para isso, chamado de Laboratórios de avaliação de usabilidade.

Existem técnicas de avaliação de usabilidade que não utilizam participantes. Isso pode ser necessário em situações onde possa haver dificuldade para encontrar o público alvo (usuários com as características requeridas) ou até mesmo quando há confidencialidade da aplicação. Sendo assim, as avaliações são feitas por especialistas e são denominadas como Não-Empíricas. São exemplos de tais técnicas: Avaliação de Perito (análise aprofundada feita por peritos que indicam uma lista com problemas importantes), Lista de Verificação (*checklist* - verifica se uma interface está de acordo com propriedades que asseguram que uma interface é fácil de usar), Percurso Cognitivo (especialista percorre a interface em busca de erros que resultam em dificuldades que usuário terá para completar a tarefa), Avaliação Heurística (grupo de especialistas examina a interface e procura problemas que violem boas práticas).

2.2 Trabalhos Relacionados

Neste trabalho, serão aplicadas duas técnicas empíricas, pois se deseja observar a interação de participantes com a aplicação. São elas: experimento controlado (com o objetivo de remover distrações) e registro de uso (para detectar as reações dos participantes). As técnicas de teste de usabilidade devem ser aplicadas com o apoio de abordagens que visam a avaliação e medição da usabilidade em aplicações móveis. Inicialmente, a usabilidade de aplicativos móveis vinha sendo avaliada por meio das heurísticas de Nielsen [8]. No entanto, um estudo apresentado em [9] avaliou que as heurísticas de Nielsen são deficientes em identificar problemas de usabilidade nesta categoria de aplicações.

Em [10] e [11] são apresentados estudos que avaliam e caracterizam abordagens de apoio à avaliação de usabilidade em aplicações móveis. De 2004 até 2013, houve um aumento considerável em abordagens para avaliação de usabilidade em aplicações móveis, e essas avaliações cobrem os três tipos de aplicações: web, nativas e hibridas [12]. Dentre os atributos utilizados para avaliação da usabilidade [5], foi visto também que maior parte das abordagens analisadas no estudo optam por utilizar satisfação, eficácia, eficiência e facilidade de aprendizagem como métricas em seus estudos.

Em [13], são documentadas deficiências de técnicas de modelagem, como GOMS (*Goals-Operators-Methods-Selection rules*) e princípios de facilidade de aprendizado são definidos: previsibilidade, sintetização, consistência, generalização e familiaridade.

Grossman et al. [14] apresentam um levantamento de métricas (mapeadas em 7 grupos, nos quais as métricas que foram utilizadas neste trabalho pertencem ao grupo 'Métricas com base no desempenho de tarefas') e metodologias para o atributo facilidade de aprendizado. Com base nos resultados de um estudo de usuário conduzido com software desktop, os autores afirmaram que, em comparação com um protocolo *Think-Aloud* tradicional, o protocolo de *Question-suggestion* (mesmo protocolo utilizado neste trabalho, onde o avaliador fornece aconselhamento para o participante no decorrer da execução da tarefa) é uma metodologia mais eficiente para identificação de problemas de capacidade de aprendizado em software, e sugeriram uma série de diretrizes de design, distribuídas entre cinco categorias para melhorar a capacidade de aprendizado de aplicações. A cerca da carga cognitiva, Haji et al. [15] constatam por meio de simulação em um complexo cirúrgico que a utilização combinada das medidas desempenho, esforço mental e complexidade da tarefa é extremamente vantajosa em pesquisas de design.

Os dois últimos trabalhos mencionados não tratavam do ambiente mobile. No entanto, Heo et al. [16] propõem um framework para avaliar a usabilidade de aparelhos celulares com um modelo hierárquico, considerando as características particulares dos aparelhos, que suporta abordagens de avaliação baseadas em tarefas e em interface por meio de quatro conjuntos de listas de verificação, um método de quantificação e um processo de avaliação. Um estudo de caso também é conduzido pelos autores para verificar a aplicabilidade do framework e melhorar sua estrutura. Entretanto, é importante considerar que a estrutura pode ser difícil de ser usada em testes de usabilidade reais, podendo ser melhor aproveitado em inspeções de usabilidade.

Em [17] foi construído um framework para avaliar a usabilidade de ferramentas MDD (*Model-Driven Development*), e uma avaliação foi conduzida para ilustrar sua aplicabilidade. Os autores afirmam que a precisão dos resultados em uma avaliação de usabilidade depende da forma como a avaliação foi concebida (por exemplo, uma má seleção de tarefas de modelagem poderia concentrar toda a avaliação em uma pequena parte da ferramenta). A ferramenta INTEGRANOVA foi avaliada em termos dos atributos eficácia, eficiência e satisfação, e algumas melhorias foram propostas.

Aquino et al. [18] apresentam uma avaliação de usabilidade de interface gráfica de usuário de sistemas multi-plataforma (desktop e web) gerados por MDE (Model-driven engineering). Um experimento foi realizado medindo a usabilidade em termos dos atributos satisfação, eficácia e eficiência e concluiu que a eficiência foi afetada por dispositivos diferentes e também por diferentes plataformas, e que a satisfação tende a ser afetada por diferentes dispositivos.

A maioria dos trabalhos citados não trata de aplicações móveis e suas especificidades, e os que tratam focam em um pequeno conjunto de atributos. A seguir será discutido o modelo PACMAD, focado em avaliação de usabilidade em aplicações móveis e que foi instanciado nesta pesquisa.

2.3 Modelo de Avaliação de Usabilidade em Aplicações Móveis

Harrison et al. [5] propuseram um modelo de avaliação de usabilidade chamado PACMAD (*People At the Centre of Mobile Application Development*). Este modelo de usabilidade foi projetado para lidar com as limitações dos modelos existentes, quando aplicado a dispositivos móveis, e identifica sete atributos utilizados para definir a métrica para avaliação da usabilidade de uma aplicação móvel:

- **Eficácia**: é a capacidade de um usuário específico concluir uma tarefa específica em um contexto específico.
- **Eficiência**: é a capacidade do usuário para completar a sua tarefa com rapidez e precisão. Este atributo reflete a produtividade de um usuário ao utilizar a aplicação.
- **Erros**: é usado para refletir o quão bem o usuário possa concluir as tarefas desejadas sem erros. A taxa de erro de usuários pode ser usada para inferir a simplicidade de um sistema. Ao compreender a natureza desses erros, é possível evitá-los em futuras versões da aplicação.
- **Facilidade de Aprendizagem**: é a facilidade com a qual um usuário pode obter proficiência com uma aplicação. Ele geralmente reflete o tempo que uma pessoa leva a se tornar capaz de usar a aplicação de forma eficaz.
- **Memorização**: é a capacidade de um usuário reter a forma de usar uma aplicação de forma eficaz. Pode ser medida pedindo aos participantes para executarem uma série de tarefas depois de se tornar proficientes com o uso do software e, em seguida, pedindo-lhes para realizar tarefas semelhantes depois de um período de inatividade.
- **Carga cognitiva**: é o impacto que a utilização do dispositivo móvel tem sobre o desempenho do usuário. Por exemplo, um usuário pode querer enviar uma mensagem de texto durante a caminhada. Neste caso, a velocidade de caminhada

do usuário será reduzida, pois ele está se concentrando em enviar a mensagem, o que irá distrai-lo ao andar.

- **Satisfação**: é a percepção do nível de conforto e prazer proporcionados ao usuário através do uso da aplicação. Isso geralmente é medido subjetivamente e varia entre usuários individuais.

Neste trabalho, o modelo PACMAD será instanciado em um estudo de caso contendo métricas para todos os sete atributos de avaliação de usabilidade em aplicações móveis propostos no modelo, a ser descrito na próxima seção.

3 Projeto e Execução do Estudo de Caso

O estudo de caso foi conduzido no Laboratório de Engenharia de Software da Universidade Federal do Amazonas em duas sessões de cerca de 15 minutos cada.

3.1 Seleção dos Participantes e Ambiente do Estudo

Participaram de forma voluntária 12 estudantes – 5 homens/7 mulheres – de graduação e pós-graduação em computação da Universidade Federal do Amazonas, com média de idade de 25,5 anos. Os participantes foram identificados de A1 a A12. É importante ressaltar que todos os 12 participantes concordaram em participar do estudo de caso através de TCLE[1].

Para conduzir o estudo, foi utilizado um dispositivo móvel com a plataforma Windows Phone 8.1 projetado em um computador desktop usando a ferramenta *Project My Screen*[2]. Tal projeção foi gravada utilizando o editor *Camtasia Studio*, o que possibilitou a análise posterior dos dados. Esta plataforma foi escolhida por fazer parte de um projeto de Pesquisa e Desenvolvimento entre a UFAM e um instituto de pesquisa sediado em Manaus que trabalha com a plataforma Windows.

3.2 Seleção da Aplicação a ser Avaliada

Com o objetivo de escolher uma aplicação alvo do estudo de caso, os participantes responderam a uma enquete em que deveriam marcar somente aquelas que conheciam em uma lista de 11 aplicações disponíveis na *Windows Phone Store* (loja de aplicativos Windows), para que fosse possível identificar as aplicações menos conhecidas, tornando viável capturar o real primeiro contato do participante com a aplicação. Ao final, foi escolhida a aplicação Vacinas[3], que é um guia de saúde que auxilia pessoas no controle da vacinação de crianças com até 10 anos de idade, pois foi o aplicativo menos conhecido dentre os participantes (apenas 1 participante conhecia).

3.3 Classificação da Experiência dos Participantes

A fim de verificar o conhecimento prévio dos participantes, eles foram submetidos a 5 questões relacionadas a domínio da: tecnologia (plataforma e aplicativos) e tarefa (vacinação). A primeira questão perguntava se o participante conhecia a aplicação Vacinas, a fim de identificar quais participantes realizariam o primeiro contato com esta aplicação durante o estudo de caso. A segunda questão perguntava se o participante possuía/utilizava um smartphone, para que então este fosse direcionado à

---

[1] Termo de Consentimento Livre e Esclarecido.

[2] Disponível em: http://www.microsoft.com/enus/download/details.aspx?id=42536

[3] Disponível em: http://goo.gl/IFvWPC

próxima questão. A terceira questão relacionava-se com os tipos de aplicações móveis que o participante costuma usar, os quais deveriam escolher entre até 10 opções. Foi considerado: marcar até 3 opções implicava em baixa experiência; 4 a 7 opções, média experiência; e 8 a 10 opções, alta experiência. A quarta questão coletava quais funcionalidades da plataforma *Windows Phone* o participante sabia utilizar, entre 5 opções. Escolher 0 ou 1 opção implicava em baixa experiência; 2 ou 3 opções, média experiência; e 4 ou 5 opções, alta experiência. Finalmente, a quinta questão era uma assertiva de 4 relações sobre vacinação, em que acertar 0 ou 1 era considerado baixa experiência, 2 ou 3 acertos, média experiência e 4 acertos, alta experiência.

Todos os participantes possuíam smartphone, mas apenas um (A10) conhecia a aplicação Vacinas. Assim, tornou-se possível observar o comportamento deste em relação aos demais. A caracterização dos participantes deu-se então somente a partir das questões 3 a 5. Se o participante obtivesse o mesmo tipo de experiência (entre baixa, média e alta) em duas ou três das questões mencionadas, este era categorizado neste tipo de experiência; caso as três questões possuíssem tipos de experiências diferentes, este era considerado com média experiência. A Tabela 1 apresenta o resumo da caracterização dos 12 participantes do estudo.

Tabela 1. Caracterização dos Participantes do Estudo.

ID	Sexo	Q1	Q2	Q3	Q4	Q5	Resultado
A01	M.	Não	Sim	Média	Baixa	Baixa	**Baixa**
A02	F	Não	Sim	Média	Baixa	Média	**Média**
A03	M	Não	Sim	Média	Baixa	Média	**Média**
A04	F	Não	Sim	Média	Média	Alta	**Média**
A05	F	Não	Sim	Média	Baixa	Alta	**Média**
A06	M	Não	Sim	Média	Baixa	Alta	**Média**
A07	M	Não	Sim	Alta	Média	Baixa	**Média**
A08	F	Não	Sim	Alta	Média	Média	**Média**
A09	F	Não	Sim	Alta	Alta	Alta	**Alta**
A10	F	Sim	Sim	Alta	Alta	Alta	**Alta**
A11	M	Não	Sim	Alta	Alta	Média	**Alta**
A12	F	Não	Sim	Baixa	Alta	Alta	**Alta**

3.4 Instanciação das Métricas para o Modelo PACMAD

O modelo PACMAD apresenta sete atributos para avaliação da usabilidade em aplicações móveis. No entanto, este não fornece as métricas a serem usadas para sua aplicação. Assim, neste trabalho foram definidas métricas para os sete atributos de avaliação que compõem o modelo PACMAD, citados na segunda seção deste artigo.

Para avaliar a **Eficácia**, foi observada a medida: completar ou não um conjunto de tarefas preestabelecidas, citada por [5] e [19].

A **Eficiência** foi avaliada por meio das métricas: número de tentativas, teclas (excluindo as teclas digitadas em campos de texto para entradas de dados) e o tempo que cada participante levou para completar cada tarefa, como feito em [5] e [19].

O atributo **Erros** foi verificado por número de erros cometidos em respostas a um questionário aplicado durante a utilização do aplicativo, conforme descrito em [19].

Facilidade de Aprendizagem foi medida por meio da repetição de pares de tarefas semelhantes em cada sessão, como o que foi realizado em [20].

Memorização foi medida por meio da realização de tarefas semelhantes em duas sessões, a segunda após um período de tempo de 3 dias – padrão para todos os participantes – a fim de verificar o desempenho após um período de tempo inativo, similar ao que foi feito em [20].

Carga cognitiva foi observada por meio de métricas utilizadas em [21]: experiência do usuário, explicada acima, nível de distrações no ambiente – no qual foi simulado um ambiente com baixa e média distração – e complexidade da interface – observada por meio das telas em que os participantes mais tiveram problemas.

Satisfação foi medida por meio da atitude dos participantes em relação a aplicação Vacinas após utilizá-la, coletada por meio de questionário, feito também em [19], como será aprofundado a seguir.

3.5 Execução do Estudo

Os participantes foram orientados a se imaginarem no seguinte cenário:

Você possui dois filhos: Pedro, de 2 anos, e Sabrina, de 7 anos, e deseja gerenciar as vacinas tomadas por eles utilizando o aplicativo Vacinas.

Durante as duas sessões, os participantes foram submetidos à lista de tarefas apresentada na Tabela 2, onde está ainda indicada a quantidade ideal de teclas necessárias para conclusão de cada tarefa. É importante ressaltar que os pares de tarefas 1-2, 3-4 e 5-6 são semelhantes e foram executados nessa mesma ordem.

Tabela 2. Lista de Tarefas a Serem Cumpridas.

ID	Tarefa	#Teclas
1	Adicione 1 filho com nome Pedro, data de nascimento 25/01/2013 e sexo "M"	7
2	Adicione 1 filha com nome Sabrina, data de nascimento 12/07/2007 e sexo "F"	7
3	Crie um atalho para o filho Pedro na tela inicial do Windows Phone.	2
4	Crie um atalho para a filha Sabrina na tela inicial do Windows Phone.	2
5	Confirme que o filho Pedro tomou a 1ª dose da vacina contra a Febre Amarela na data de hoje.	4
6	Cadastre e confirme a vacina BCG-ID em vacinas tomadas da filha Sabrina na data de hoje	9

Ainda na primeira sessão, os participantes foram orientados a, após realizarem as tarefas, responder ao questionário apresentado na Tabela 3.

Tabela 3. Questionário Pós Sessão 1.

ID	Pergunta	Resposta Esperada
A	Qual a data da última vacina que o filho Pedro irá tomar?	Maio de 2016
B	Quais são as próximas vacinas da filha Sabrina?	Febre Amarela e Tríplice Viral
C	Quantas doses tem a vacina Meningocócica C?	2 doses
D	O filho Pedro ainda precisa tomar quantas doses da vacina Pentavalente?	3 doses

4 Análise dos Resultados

A seguir são descritas análises sobre os atributos avaliados e alguns problemas encontrados na aplicação sob teste.

4.1 Análise do Atributo Eficácia

A Fig. 1 reporta os participantes que não concluíram cada uma das 6 tarefas que compuseram o estudo. É possível observar que a maior quantidade de tarefas incompletas/incorretas ocorreu nas tarefas 3, 4 e 6.

Além disso, observa-se que apenas 19 das 72 tarefas (6 tarefas x 12 participantes) não foram concluídas, representando 26% do total de tarefas. Isso seria um indício da eficácia da aplicação em relação à sua usabilidade, porém ainda com possibilidade de melhorias. Nas tarefas 3 e 4, observam-se dificuldades dos participantes em encontrar o botão para criar atalho para uma criança na tela inicial do *Windows Phone*, que se encontrava na *app bar* da tela inicial de uma criança e era representado pela imagem de um alfinete. Na tarefa 6, ocorreram problemas devido a alguns participantes cadastrarem corretamente a vacina, mas esquecerem de confirmá-la, o que gerava um alerta informando sobre a confirmação da vacina para a data escolhida.

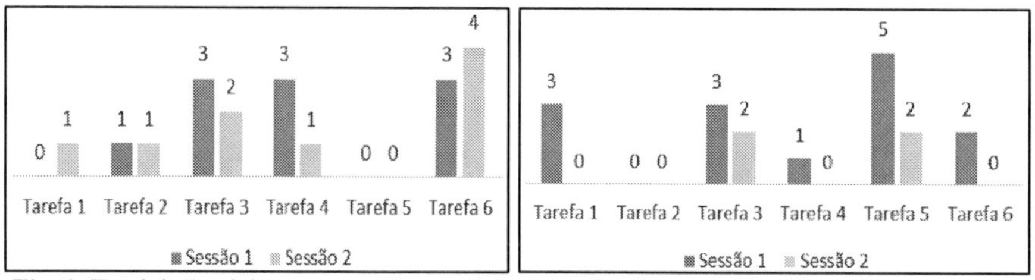

Fig. 1. Total de Participantes que não concluíram tarefas (à esquerda) e Total de tentativas de repetição por tarefa (à direita).

A Fig. 1 (à direita) reporta o total de tentativas extras feitas por participante para cada tarefa que compôs o estudo. É possível observar que a maior quantidade de tentativas extras ocorreu nas tarefas 5 (7 tentativas extras nas 2 sessões), 3 (5 tentativas extras) e 1 (3 tentativas extras). Este resultado era de certa forma esperado, e uma justificativa para este alto número nessas tarefas é que elas foram as primeiras tarefas dos pares (1-2; 3-4; 5-6) definidos no estudo, conforme descrito na Tabela 2.

> **Guia de apoio (Eficácia):** uma organização pode definir um limite mínimo a ser atingindo para as medidas de eficácia (tarefas não concluídas e tentativas extras) de forma a considerá-las satisfatórias em um projeto de desenvolvimento de aplicações móveis.

4.2 Análise do Atributo Eficiência

Analisando o número de teclas extras usadas pelos participantes do estudo para conclusão das tarefas (Fig. 2 à esquerda), observa-se que as duas primeiras tarefas foram as que mais requisitaram teclas extras, seguidas pelas tarefas 5 e 6. Uma justificativa é que estas tarefas representam o primeiro contato dos participantes com a aplicação móvel (e em alguns casos com a plataforma *Windows Phone*). À medida que as tarefas vão sendo realizadas, a necessidade por teclas extras tende a diminuir.

Comportamento similar pode ser observado na avaliação do tempo requerido para a conclusão das tarefas (Fig. 2 à direita), onde novamente as tarefas 1 e 2 obtiveram um tempo maior para conclusão, quando comparada às demais. As tarefas 5 e 6 também obtiveram um alto tempo, em média, para serem concluídas.

Interpretando os resultados na aplicação avaliada, novos problemas de usabilidade foram observados e estariam relacionados à inserção da data de nascimento no cadastro de uma criança (tarefas 1 e 2), pois o teclado virtual sobrepunha a caixa de entrada da data. Além disso, no cadastro de uma nova vacina (tarefas 5 e 6), o botão de adicionar vacina no início da lista de vacinas já cadastradas não estaria intuitivo e resultou em tempo extra, segundo os participantes do estudo.

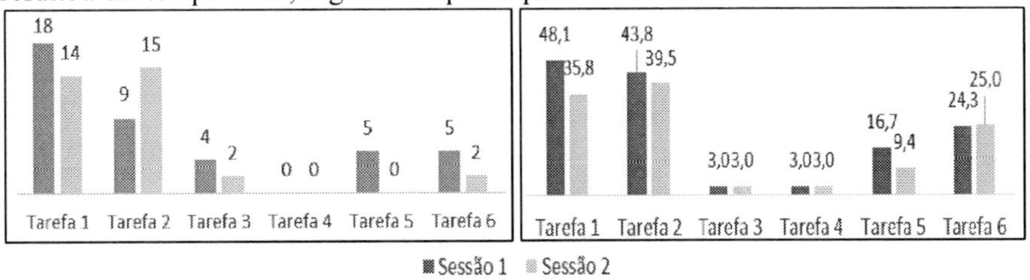

Fig. 2. Total de teclas extras para conclusão das tarefas (à esquerda) e Média de tempo para conclusão das tarefas (à direita).

Guia de apoio (Eficiência): uma organização pode observar tarefas (ou funcionalidades) de uma aplicação móvel que resultam em mais esforço para conclusão como um medidor de eficiência da usabilidade. As tarefas que apresentarem um comportamento diferenciado das demais podem ser candidatas a terem suas características de usabilidade adaptadas.

4.3 Análise do Atributo Erros

A análise de **Erros** foi feita a partir do questionário aplicado junto aos participantes após a Sessão 1 do estudo. Nesses resultados, foi percebido que 5 participantes erraram a quantidade de doses restante de uma determinada vacina para uma criança já cadastrada (Questão D). Para todas as demais questões, todos os participantes acertaram suas respostas.

Dentre as 4 questões (A a D) respondidas pelos participantes, essa foi a única que obteve problemas, e até os participantes que acertaram a resposta percorreram um caminho errado dentro da aplicação para encontrar essa resposta (com exceção do participante A09). Isso se deve ao fato de que os participantes não perceberam que o degradê na imagem da vacina representava a quantidade de doses dela.

Guia de apoio (Erros): uma organização pode preparar um questionário a ser respondido pelos avaliadores a fim de assegurar que, além de concluir as tarefas, eles estejam seguros das informações trabalhadas ao longo da utilização da aplicação. Respostas incorretas podem representar indícios de problemas de usabilidade, visto que apesar de concluir as tarefas, os avaliadores não possuem domínio total sobre os dados manipulados pela aplicação.

4.4 Análise do Atributo Aprendizagem

A **Aprendizagem** é observada analisando os resultados apresentados na Fig. 1 e Fig. 2, onde é possível observar que os participantes obtiveram um melhor desempenho nas tarefas 2, 4 e 6, pois já haviam realizado uma tarefa semelhante anteriormente (as tarefas 1, 3 e 5, respectivamente).

Observando os números, o total de teclas extras usadas nas tarefas 1, 3 e 5 ao longo das 2 sessões foi 43, enquanto que nas tarefas 2, 4 e 6 foi 31 (redução de 28%). Analisando o total de tentativas extras nas 2 sessões para as tarefas 1, 3 e 5, o valor obtido foi 15, enquanto que para as tarefas 2, 4 e 6 este número foi 3 (redução de 80%).

Guia de apoio (Facilidade de aprendizagem): a equipe de testes pode preparar um conjunto de tarefas similares distribuídas em uma mesma sessão de teste. Observando o comportamento dos participantes e a curva das métricas de eficácia e eficiência entre as duplas de tarefas similares, é possível obter indícios do quanto o fator aprendizado contribui para a execução das tarefas, e assim comparar os resultados obtidos com um oráculo definido.

4.5 Análise do Atributo Memorização

A **Memorização** pode ser vista analisando os resultados apresentados na Fig. 1 e Fig. 2, em que é possível observar que na segunda sessão os participantes obtiveram um melhor desempenho em todas tarefas (com exceção da tarefa 2, onde ocorreu um maior número de teclas extras).

Isso seria um indício de que a aplicação Vacinas é de fácil memorização, pois o número de teclas extras caiu de 41, na primeira sessão, para 33 na segunda sessão (redução de 20%); e o número de tentativas extras caiu de 14, na primeira sessão, para 4, na segunda (redução de 71%).

Guia de apoio (Memorização): observar o comportamento dos participantes e a curva das métricas de eficácia e eficiência em uma mesma tarefa ou em tarefas similares considerando diferentes momentos (sessões) de uso da aplicação. Novamente, pode ser construído um oráculo para considerar os resultados obtidos como sendo satisfatórios.

4.6 Análise do Atributo Carga Cognitiva

A **Carga Cognitiva** foi avaliada sob três perspectivas: (1) experiência do usuário, (2) nível de distrações no ambiente e (3) complexidade da interface.

Em relação ao item 3, durante a análise de eficácia e eficiência já foram destacadas as telas da aplicação que requerem um maior esforço (medido por número de teclas ou tentativas para a conclusão das tarefas) por parte de seus usuários. Em relação ao item 1, foi possível observar que, em geral, quanto maior a experiência prévia do participante, melhor o seu desempenho nas tarefas em relação ao número de teclas extras requeridas para a conclusão das tarefas e tarefas concluídas com sucesso.

Tabela 4. Teclas Extras por Nível de Experiência.

Sessão	Expertise	Tarefa 1	Tarefa 2	Tarefa 3	Tarefa 4	Tarefa 5	Tarefa 6
	Baixo ou Médio	8,8	7,9	2,6	2,0	4,5	9,7
#1	Alto	8,0	7,8	2,3	2,0	4,3	9,3
	%	9%	1%	16%	0%	6%	4%
	Baixo ou Médio	8,9	8,8	2,2	2,0	4,0	9,2
#2	Alto	7,3	7,0	2,3	2,0	4,0	9,5
	%	22%	26%	-4%	0%	0%	-4%

Analisando o número de teclas extras (Tabela 4), apenas na Tarefa 6 o desempenho de participantes com alta experiência foi inferior aos participantes com experiência baixa ou média, o que ocorreu em virtude de apenas 2 participantes de alta experiência terem concluído esta tarefa, resultando em poucos pontos para cálculo da média. Analisando os dados no geral, participantes com alta experiência utilizaram, em média, 5,2 teclas extras, enquanto que participantes com experiência baixa ou média utilizaram, em média, 6 teclas extras, resultando em uma diferença de 15%.

Além disso, analisando a proporção de tarefas não concluídas, os participantes com experiência alta obtiveram um desempenho de 0,75 tarefas não concluídas por participante (3 tarefas não concluídas em um grupo com 4 pessoas), enquanto que os participantes com experiência baixa ou média obtiveram um desempenho de 2 tarefas não concluídas por participante (16 tarefas não concluídas em um grupo com 8 pessoas). Isso resulta em uma diferença de 166% entre os dois grupos.

Em relação ao item 2, foi possível observar que o aumento das distrações no ambiente teve impacto na realização das tarefas 2, 4 e 6 na segunda sessão do estudo. Analisando o tempo requerido para conclusão das tarefas por pares (Tarefas 1-2, Tarefas 3-4, Tarefas 5-6) na sessão 2, observa-se que o tempo requerido para realizar a Tarefa 2 (39,5s), em média, foi superior ao tempo para realizar a Tarefa 1 (35,8s), apesar de ter sido realizada posteriormente. Um aumento de 10% no tempo. O mesmo ocorreu com o par de Tarefas 5-6, onde a segunda tarefa (Tarefa 6) requereu mais tempo, em média, para ser concluída pelos participantes (25s na tarefa 6 versus 9,4s na tarefa 5), um aumento de 166% no tempo. Apenas no par Tarefas 3-4 não foi observada variação no tempo em virtude da distração, pois estas são tarefas simples que demandam um curto tempo para conclusão.

Estes resultados sugerem a importância da avaliação do atributo Carga Cognitiva na avaliação da usabilidade de uma aplicação móvel, uma vez, que este atributo pode influenciar diretamente no uso da aplicação e, consequentemente, em seu sucesso e popularidade em seu nicho de mercado.

Guia de apoio (Carga cognitiva): selecionar métricas que mais se aplicam no escopo da aplicação móvel, entre expertise do usuário (descoberto por meio de aplicação de questionário com os participantes), nível de distrações no ambiente (simulando situações sem interrupções, com ruídos ao fundo e/ou com várias atividades sendo realizadas paralelas ao uso da aplicação) e outras. Após isso, pode-se verificar a influência dessas informações nos resultados obtidos para as métricas de eficácia e eficiência e comparar com um oráculo estabelecido para considerar os resultados satisfatórios.

4.7 Análise do Atributo Satisfação

Referente ao atributo **Satisfação**, na segunda sessão, após a realização das tarefas, os participantes foram orientados a responder a um questionário referente à aplicação Vacinas. As respostas dos participantes estão apresentados na Tabela 5. Para a análise, as duas primeiras opções (Não e Não Muito) são assumidas como respostas negativas, enquanto que as duas últimas (Um Pouco e Sim) são assumidas como respostas positivas. A terceira opção é considerada neutra.

Nos resultados, é possível observar que para a primeira questão, 11 (92%) participantes apresentaram respostas positivas em relação à facilidade em aprender a usar a aplicação Vacinas, o que se comprova nas análises dos atributos eficácia e eficiência em usos subsequentes dentro de uma mesma sessão do estudo.

Tabela 5. Resultado do Questionário Pós-Aplicação.

	Não	Não Muito	Talvez	Um Pouco	Sim
1. É fácil aprender a usar?	0	1	0	6	5
2. É fácil fazer o que preciso?	0	0	0	6	6
3. É fácil se tornar habilidoso?	0	0	3	0	9
4. É fácil de usar?	0	2	1	4	5
5. Pretendo usar?	5	0	3	1	3

Na segunda questão, todos os 12 participantes tiveram respostas positivas sobre ser fácil fazer o que foi solicitado na aplicação, o que pode ser visto na completude das 6 tarefas propostas.

Na terceira questão, 9 (75%) dos participantes apresentaram respostas positivas sobre ser fácil se tornar habilidoso, o que se comprova nas análises dos atributos eficácia e eficiência em usos subsequentes dentro das duas sessões conduzidas. Os outros 3 participantes apresentaram respostas neutras.

Com relação à facilidade de usar (questão 4), as respostas foram variadas dentro das escalas apresentadas. No entanto, 9 (75%) dos participantes acreditaram ser fácil o uso da aplicação Vacinas. Apenas 2 (16%) participantes apresentam respostas negativas em relação à facilidade em usar a aplicação.

Por último, foi questionado se os participantes pretendiam usar a aplicação em teste. Nesta análise, 5 (41%) participantes apresentaram respostas negativas, 4 (33%) apresentaram respostas positivas e os demais foram neutros. Acredita-se que este resultado foi diversificado pelo fato de os participantes não corresponderem ao público alvo para aplicação, por não possuírem filhos de até 10 anos de idade.

Guia de apoio (Satisfação): criar questões acerca do sentimento dos participantes em relação ao uso da aplicação. Pode ser feita a atribuição de uma escala de Likert às questões e então o estabelecimento de níveis para considerar os resultados obtidos como sendo satisfatórios.

5 Ameaças à Validade

As ameaças à validade foram organizadas em 4 categorias [22]: validade de construção, interna, externa, e de conclusão.

Em relação à **Validade de Construção**, as ameaças mais comuns estão relacionadas com: (i) participante manipular seus dados com expectativas pessoais sobre a avaliação de seus resultados, algo não presente neste estudo pois o desempenho individual do participante não foi avaliado, pois mesmo sendo estudantes, o estudo não fez parte de uma disciplina; e (ii) o formulário de avaliação induzir o participante a ter resultados favoráveis ao pesquisador, no entanto os formulários de coletada de dados foram oriundos de pesquisas científicas que apontavam medidas a serem consideradas para avaliação de usabilidade em aplicações móveis.

Em relação à **Validade Interna**, a medida tempo para conclusão de uma determinada tarefa, referente ao atributo eficiência, mostrou-se extremamente útil em categorizar o desempenho da amostra em cada sessão. Entretanto, está sujeita a falhas, devido a instantes em que o participante olhou para a lista de tarefas ou foi interrompido por pequenas distrações externas. No entanto, acredita-se que esta ameaça seria minimizada com a uniformidade no processo de coleta do tempo por meio de uma ferramenta de monitoramento adotada no estudo.

Em relação à **Validade Externa**, os participantes não correspondem ao público alvo da aplicação Vacinas, que seriam pais de crianças de até 10 anos de idade. No entanto, acredita-se que com o fim de avaliar a aplicabilidade do modelo de avaliação de usabilidade, e não a aplicação em si, esta ameaça seria minimizada.

Em relação à **Validade de Conclusão**, isso envolve a correta análise e interpretação estatística do resultado, confiabilidade das medidas e confiabilidade da implementação dos tratamentos. Em relação à quantidade ideal de participantes, Bastien [23] afirma que há estudos sobre o assunto desde a década de 90, porém não há resposta final sobre o número ideal. Segundo o estudo descrito em [23], com quatro ou cinco participantes, 80-85% dos problemas de usabilidade de uma interface poderiam ser descobertos. Neste estudo, a população foi composta por 12 participantes.

6 Conclusão

Neste trabalho, foi apresentado um estudo de caso que avaliou a aplicabilidade de uma instanciação do modelo PACMAD para testes de usabilidade em uma aplicação móvel chamada Vacinas. Neste estudo, duas técnicas empíricas (que requerem a participação de pessoas) para avaliação da usabilidade em aplicações móveis foram utilizadas: experimento controlado e registro de uso.

Para instanciação do modelo PACMAD, métricas oriundas de diversos trabalhos científicos foram utilizadas a fim de avaliar os resultados providos pela aplicação do modelo PACMAD para sete atributos relacionados à usabilidade de software: eficácia, eficiência, satisfação, facilidade de aprendizagem, memorização, erros e carga cognitiva. Como resultado, o modelo pode ser aplicado em sua totalidade e possibilitou a identificação de problemas relacionados aos sete atributos avaliados e que podem servir como diretriz para melhorias na usabilidade da aplicação sob teste. Além disso, guias de apoio foram providos de forma a facilitar a replicação da instanciação por outros testadores. Assim, a instanciação proposta pode ser adotada por organizações de software para avaliação de usabilidade de suas aplicações móveis.

Como trabalho futuro, está prevista formalização de uma abordagem de apoio a testes de usabilidade em aplicações móveis a partir do modelo PACMAD, composta por processos, atividades, métricas, diretrizes e roteiros de artefato, visando contribuir na condução de testes de usabilidade em aplicações móveis. Além disso, novos estudos estão previstos com outras aplicações móveis utilizando o seu público alvo a fim de investigar o impacto disto na aplicação do modelo e na avaliação da aplicação.

Agradecimentos

Os autores agradecem à FAPEAM e INDT pelo apoio financeiro.

Referencias Bibliográficas

1. International Organization for Standardization, "ISO/IEC 25000 - Software engineering - Software product Quality Requirements and Evaluation (SQuaRE) - Guide to SQuaRE", ISO/IEC, Mar. 2011.
2. H. Duh, G. Tan, V. Chen. (2006). "Usability evaluation for mobile device: a comparison of laboratory and field tests". Proceedings of the 8th conference on Human-computer interaction with mobile devices and services (MobileHCI). pp. 181-186.
3. J. Spool, W. Schroeder. (2001). "Testing Web sites: five users is nowhere near enough", Proceedings of the Conference Extended Abstracts on Human Factors in Computing Systems, CHI'2001, ACM Press, New York.
4. J. Kjeldskov, J. Stage (2004). "New techniques for usability evaluation of mobile systems".

In: International Journal of Human-Computer Studies, pp. 599-620.
5. R. Harrison, D. Flood, D. Duce. (2013). "Usability of mobile applications: literature review and rationale for a new usability model". Journal of Interaction Science, p 1-16.
6. D. Zhang, B. Adipat. (2005). "Challenges, methodologies, and issues in the usability testing of mobile applications", International Journal of Human Computer Interaction, vol. 18, no. 3, pp. 293-308.
7. E. R. Brandão, A. M. Moraes (2006). "Publicidade on-line, ergonomia e usabilidade: o efeito de seis tipos de banner no processo humano de visualização do formato do anúncio na tela do computador e de lembrança da sua mensagem". Rio de Janeiro, 400 p. Dissertações de Mestrado – Departamento de Artes & Design, PUC-RJ.
8. J. Nielsen (1994). "Usability inspection methods". In: Conference companion on Human factors in computing systems. ACM, p. 413-414.
9. J. O. Machado-Neto, (2013) "Usabilidade da interface de dispositivos móveis: heurísticas e diretrizes para o design". Tese de Doutorado. Universidade de São Paulo.
10. F. Nayebi, J.M. Desharnais, A. Abran (2012). "The State of the Art of Mobile Application Usability Evaluation". In: 25th IEEE Canadian Conference on Electrical Computer Engineering (CCECE'2012), pp.1-4.
11. J. Kjeldskov, J. Paay. (2012). "A longitudinal review of Mobile HCI research methods". In: International Conference on Human-computer interaction with mobile devices and services (MobileHCI'12), pp. 6978.
12. N. P. Huy, D. VanThanh. (2012). "Evaluation of mobile app paradigms". Proceedings of International Conference on Advances in Mobile Computing & Multimedia, pp. 25-30.
13. S. Kristoffersen (2008). Learnability and Robustness of User Interfaces - Towards a Formal Analysis of Usability Design Principles. In International Conference on Software and Data Technologies - ICSOFT, pp. 261-268.
14. T. Grossman, G. Fitzmaurice, R. Attar (2009). "A Survey of Software Learnability: Metrics, Methodologies and Guidelines". Proceedings of the SIGCHI Conference on Human Factors in Computing Systems, pp. 649-658.
15. F. A. Haji et al. (2015). "Measuring cognitive load: performance, mental effort and simulation task complexity". MEDICAL EDUCATION 2015; 49: pp. 815–827.
16. J. Heo, D. Hamb, S. Park, C. Song, W. Yoon (2009). A framework for evaluating the usability of mobile phones based on multi-level, hierarchical model of usability factors. Interacting with Computers, Vol 21, pp.263–275.
17. N. Fernández, J. Panach, A. Baars, T. Vos, Ó. Pastor (2013). An empirical approach for evaluating the usability of model-driven tools. Science of Computer Programming, Vol. 78, pp. 2245–2258.
18. N. Aquino et al. (2010). Usability Evaluation of Multi-Device/Platform User Interfaces Generated by Model-Driven Engineering. In: ACM-IEEE International Symposium on Empirical Software Engineering and Measurement (ESEM'10). ACM, New York, 10 pages.
19. M. Masoodian, N. Lane. (2003). "An empirical study of textual and graphical travel itinerary visualization using mobile phones". Proceedings of the Fourth Australian User Interface Conference on User Interfaces, 18, pp. 11–18.
20. M. Ziefle. (2002). "The influence of user expertise and phone complexity on performance, ease of user and learnability of different mobile phones". Behavior & Information Technology, 21, 303–311.
21. D. Flood, P. Germanakos, R. Harrison, F. Mc Caffery. (2012). "Estimating cognitive overload in mobile applications for decision support within the medical domain". 14th International conference on Enterprise Information Systems (ICEIS 2012), Wroclaw.
22. G. H. Travassos, D. Gurov, E. A. Amaral. (2002), "Introdução à Engenharia de Software Experimental". COPPE/UFRJ, Rio de Janeiro, Relatório técnico: RTES-590/02.
23. J. M. C. Bastien (2010). "Usability testing: a review of some methodological and technical aspects of the method". International Journal of Medical Informatics. Vol 79(4), pp. e18-e2.

Evaluación del nivel de madurez de datos usando MAMD: un estudio de caso

Ana G. Carretero, Ismael Caballero, Mario Piattini

{AnaIsabel.Gomez, Ismael.Caballero, Mario.Piattini}@uclm.es
Grupo de Investigación Alarcos. Escuela Superior de Informática
Paseo de la Universidad 4, 13071, Ciudad Real (España)

Abstract. Las organizaciones son cada vez más conscientes de que cuanto mejor sean los datos, mayor será el rendimiento que se podrá obtener de ellos. Para maximizar este rendimiento, es preciso que institucionalicen un conjunto de buenas prácticas relacionadas con la gestión de datos, el gobierno de datos, y la gestión de calidad de datos.

Como fruto de nuestras investigaciones, hemos desarrollado el ***Modelo de Mejora de Datos MAMD,*** que es un marco de evaluación y mejora del nivel de madurez organizacional de la gestión de datos, el gobierno de datos, y la gestión de calidad de datos.

En este artículo se explica cómo se ha usado MAMD para evaluar el nivel de madurez organizacional de gestión de datos, gobierno de datos y gestión de calidad de datos de *una biblioteca universitaria*.

Keywords: Calidad de Datos, Gestión de Calidad de Datos, Gestión de Datos, Gobierno de Datos, Modelo de Madurez, MAMD

1 Introducción

En los datos reside el potencial de las organizaciones para desarrollar su misión y encontrar nuevas vías para innovar en un mercado cada día más competitivo. Ello implica mejorar las formas existentes - y si es posible encontrar otras nuevas- para explotar los datos que poseen. En línea con esto, las organizaciones, están empezando a ser cada vez más conscientes de que cuanto mejor sean los datos, más rendimiento (por ejemplo a nivel económico) podrán obtener de ellos. Por tanto, parece razonable pensar que las organizaciones deberían invertir suficientes recursos en desplegar soluciones para que los datos tengan un nivel de calidad proporcional a su uso previsto y otros futuros usos.

Por consiguiente, asegurar la calidad de los datos es una tarea que debe planificarse con suficiente tiempo, realizarse con objetivos claros alineados a la estrategia de la organización, y dedicando los recursos humanos, materiales y económicos adecuados. Sólo así se podrán garantizar resultados proporcionales al potencial de la organización. Este aseguramiento de la calidad de los datos debe realizarse mediante la implantación de programas integrados de gestión de datos, gobierno de datos, y gestión de calidad de datos.

Para facilitar la mejora de los procesos software de las organizaciones existen alternativas basadas en estándares como COBIT [1], CMMI [2] o ISO/IEC 15504 [3], entre otros. Pero que lamentablemente ni abordan específicamente el problema de los datos, ni resulta sencillo particularizarlos para tratar conjuntamente las disciplinas de gestión de datos, el gobierno de datos, y la gestión de calidad de datos. No obstante, en los últimos tiempos están surgiendo iniciativas orientadas a procesos como DMM [4] o ISO 8000-60 [5] que están tratando de abordar la forma en la que las organizaciones pueden afrontar la implantación de estos planes. Tras un estudio detallado, concluimos que DMM tenía dos problemas importantes: no era de fácil aplicación y estaba enfocado principalmente al sector financiero. Por otro lado, ISO 8000-60, aunque era de más fácil aplicación y de propósito general, no incluía explícitamente aspectos de procesos de gobierno de datos, y tampoco abordaba completamente los procesos de gestión de datos.

Para paliar estas carencias, y como principal resultado de nuestra investigación hemos desarrollado el **Modelo de Madurez de Datos MAMD**. Nuestro objetivo era desarrollar un marco de trabajo que permitiera a las organizaciones desarrollar proyectos de mejora continua basados en PDCA para la implantación progresiva de mejoras para que pudieran tener un mayor rendimiento de los datos. MAMD consta de dos componentes principales:

- Un modelo de referencia de procesos que extiende ISO 8000-61 [6] con los procesos de gobierno de datos, y algunos procesos de gestión de datos, y
- Un modelo de evaluación y mejora basado en ISO/IEC 33000 [7].

La contribución de este artículo es doble: por un lado presentar brevemente los componentes del modelo, y por otro describir un estudio de caso que hemos realizado para validar empíricamente MAMD.

El resto del artículo está estructurado como sigue: la sección 2 presenta brevemente los componentes de MAMD. La sección 3 describe cómo se ha utilizado MAMD para evaluar el nivel de madurez organizacional de gobierno de datos, gestión de datos y gestión de calidad de datos de una biblioteca universitaria a la que se denominará *BUX* por motivos de confidencialidad. Finalmente la Sección 4 recoge algunas conclusiones que se han obtenido como resultado de la evaluación e introduce algunas líneas de trabajo futuro que consideramos necesarias para mejorar MAMD.

2 Modelo de Mejora de Datos

Como se comentó en la introducción, **MAMD** consta de un modelo de referencia de procesos que reagrupa los procesos propuestos de gestión de calidad de datos en ISO 8000-61 y los extiende con los procesos específicos de gobierno de datos y de gestión de datos, y un modelo de evaluación de procesos basado en las distintas partes de la familia ISO/IEC 33000. Los siguientes apartados describen ambos componentes.

2.1 Modelo de Referencia de Procesos

De acuerdo a lo establecido en la cláusula 5.3.1 de ISO/IEC 33004 [8], se define un modelo de referencia de procesos como un conjunto de procesos que de forma colectiva puede dar soporte al modelo de procesos organizacional. El modelo de referencia de procesos de MAMD está compuesto por 18 procesos agrupados en las áreas gestión de datos, gobierno de datos, y gestión de calidad de datos. A continuación se recogen los procesos que hemos identificado mediante el mapeo de ISO 8000-61, DMM, COBIT, y DAMA, y se describe el objetivo de cada uno de ellos.

Procesos Relacionados con la Gestión de datos.

- **DM.1. Gestión de requisitos de datos.** Recopilar y validar los requisitos referentes a los datos necesarios para gestionar con éxito la organización.
- **DM.2. Gestión de la infraestructura tecnológica.** Especificar y mantener la infraestructura tecnológica necesaria para dar soporte al significado de los datos compartidos entre las aplicaciones.
- **DM.3. Gestión de datos históricos.** Mantener y ejecutar las políticas necesarias para la gestión de datos históricos de la organización.
- **DM.4. Gestión de seguridad de datos.** Definir y habilitar mecanismos para hacer posible la confidencialidad, integridad, accesibilidad o disponibilidad, autenticidad, imposibilidad de rechazo, consistencia, aislamiento y auditoría de los datos.
- **DM.5. Gestión de la configuración.** Definir los procesos por los que una organización demanda, determina, aprueba e implementa los planes alcanzables y evalúa los cambios del ciclo de vida de los datos.
- **DM.6. Gestión de datos maestros.** Identificar los conceptos relevantes para el dominio del negocio de la organización y el alineamiento de la estrategia organizacional de datos en torno a dichos datos maestros.
- **DM.7. Diseño de datos.** Crear un modelo de datos consistente, completo y extensible que cubra la visión de los datos de los datos maestros de todas las unidades organizacionales y que esté alineado con la estrategia organizacional de datos.
- **DM.8. Establecimiento de Fuentes y destinos de datos.** Identificar y caracterizar cada una de las fuentes y destinos de los datos usados en los procesos de negocio organizacionales, así como los acuerdos y las interacciones con los proveedores y clientes.
- **DM.9. Integración de datos.** Asegurar la integridad de los datos mediante el control de flujo y las relaciones con los datos transferidos a los sistemas de aplicaciones o bases de datos.

Procesos Relacionados con la Gestión de la Calidad de los Datos.

- **DQM.1. Medición de la calidad de datos.** Establecer los recursos necesarios para satisfacer los requisitos, y medir los niveles de calidad de datos de acuerdo a los criterios de medición.

- **DQM.2. Mejora de la calidad de datos.** Implementar un ciclo de mejora continua basado en el modelo PDCA para la mejora de los datos en los repositorios organizacionales.

Procesos Relacionados con el Gobierno de Datos.

- **DG.1. Establecimiento de estrategias de datos.** Identificar y priorizar los objetivos de gestión de datos, y trabajar de acuerdo a esa priorización para dar soporte a los objetivos estratégicos empresariales.
- **DG.2. Gestión del ciclo de vida y valor de datos.** Identificar el grado de importancia que tienen los datos para los diferentes procesos de negocio en las correspondientes etapas.
- **DG.3. Establecimiento de estándares, políticas, buenas prácticas y procedimientos.** Establecer aquellos estándares, políticas, buenas prácticas y procedimientos para la gestión de los datos, gestión de la calidad de datos y el gobierno de datos a fin de poder dar soporte el mejor soporte posible a la estrategia de calidad de datos.
- **DG.4. Gestión de recursos humanos.** Gestionar adecuadamente las necesidades para la formación específica requerida para los recursos humanos específicamente destinados a la gestión de los datos, gobierno de los datos y a gestión de la calidad de los datos.
- **DG.5. Gestión de recursos financieros.** Desarrollar planes para el aprovisionamiento y mantenimiento de recursos financieros que puedan dar soporte a la estrategia de datos de la organización.
- **DG.6. Monitorización de las estrategias organizacionales de datos.** Desarrollar y medir los indicadores claves para la monitorización de la consecución de la estrategia de gestión de datos y comprobar que realmente está siendo alineada a la estrategia organizacional de datos.
- **DG.7. Gestión de cambios en las estrategias de datos.** Mantener coherente la estrategia organizacional de datos de acuerdo a la evolución de los objetivos estratégicos empresariales.

Para llegar a este modelo de referencia de procesos se han estudiado los modelos de madurez de datos existentes más importantes como DAMA [9], ISO 8000-61, DMM, aunque por motivos de restricción del artículo no se incluyen. También, se han estudiado las relaciones entre los diferentes procesos de MAMD con los procesos de DMM e ISO 8000-61, que son los más importantes y actuales. Dicha relación se describe en la tabla 1.

2.2 Modelo de evaluación

El modelo de evaluación está basado en ISO/IEC 33020 [10], y por tanto incluye una metodología de evaluación que consta de cinco pasos –por problemas de espacio, estos pasos se introducen como parte del estudio de caso en la Sección 3-, y un modelo de madurez organizacional.

Tabla 1. Relaciones entre los procesos de MAMD, DMM e ISO 8000-61.

MAMD	DMM	ISO 8000-61
DM.1	DO 4.1	I 1.1
DM.2	PA 5.1, PA 5.2, PA 5.3	DRS 2.1
DM.3	PA 5.5	
DM.4	SP 6.4	DRS 2.4
DM.5	SP 6.5	
DM.6	DMS 1.1, DG 2.1	
DM.7	DG 2.2, DG 2.3	
DM.8	DO 4.3	DMS 2.2
DM.9	PA 5.4	I 1.8, DMS 2.2
DQM.1	SP 6.1, DQ 3.1, DQ 3.3	I 1.5, I 1.7, I1.10
DQM.2	SP 6.1, DQ 3.1, DQ 3.3	I1.11,I1.12,I1.14
DG.1	DMS 1.1, DQ 3.1, DG 2.1, DMS 1.2	I 1.2, I 1.4, I 1.5
DG.2	DO 4.2	
DG.3	DG 2.1, DMS 1.2, DQ 3.1, DQ 3.2, PA 5.2	I 1.3, I 1.9
DG.4	DMS 1.3	RP 3.2
DG.5	DMS 1.5	
DG.6	DG 2.1, DMS 1.1	I 1.7
DG.7	DMS 1.1	

La evaluación del nivel de madurez organizacional se corresponde con una evaluación de tipo 1 (véase cláusula 4.6.1.1 de ISO/IEC 33002 [11], y por tanto se tienen que inspeccionar al menos cuatro instancias de cuatro procesos organizacionales que están en el alcance de la evaluación. Como resultado de la evaluación, se obtendrá un determinado nivel de madurez.

Los niveles de madurez que se proponen en MAMD, junto con su significado y los procesos que se incluyen, se detallan a continuación:

- **Nivel de Madurez 0 o Inmaduro:** La organización no puede demostrar la implementación efectiva de las buenas prácticas del modelo de referencia de procesos. Por lo tanto, no hay garantías de que estén utilizando adecuadamente sus datos.
- **Nivel de Madurez 1 o Básico:** La organización puede demostrar que utiliza un conjunto de buenas prácticas orientadas a proporcionar el soporte mínimo necesario para la gestión de los datos necesarios en sus procesos de negocio. Pero no se presta especial atención ni al gobierno de los datos ni a la calidad de datos. Esto implica la ejecución de las actividades de los siguientes procesos del modelo de referencia de procesos de MAMD:

— DM.1.Gestión de requisitos de datos
— DM.2.Gestión de infraestructura tecnológica
— DM.5.Gestión de la configuración
— DM.8.Establecimiento de fuentes y destinos de datos.

- **Nivel de Madurez 2 o Gestionado**: La organización puede demostrar que utiliza un conjunto de buenas prácticas orientadas a garantizar que los datos usados en sus procesos de negocio están alineados con la estrategia organizacional. Por lo tanto, hay garantías de que la organización tiene implementado los procesos necesarios de gobierno de datos mínimo como para asegurar el éxito en sus procesos de negocio. Esto implica institucionalizar y ejecutar, no sólo las buenas prácticas de los procesos del nivel 1, sino además los siguientes procesos del modelo de referencia de procesos de MAMD:

- DM.3.Gestión de datos históricos
- DM.4.Gestión de seguridad de datos
- DG.1.Establecimiento de estrategias de datos
- DG.2.Gestión del ciclo de vida y valor de los datos
- DG.3. Establecimiento de estándares, políticas, buenas prácticas y procedimientos.

- **Nivel de Madurez 3 o Establecido:** La organización puede demostrar que utiliza un conjunto de buenas prácticas orientadas a gestionar la calidad de los datos para garantizar que los datos usados en sus procesos de negocio tienen los niveles adecuados de calidad. Esto implica que los procesos de negocio se benefician en la ejecución de los siguientes procesos dentro del modelo de referencia de procesos de MAMD, así como los procesos incluidos en el nivel 2:

- DM.9. Integración de datos
- DQM.1. Medición de calidad de datos
- DM.6. Gestión de datos maestros
- DM.7. Diseño de datos
- DQM.2. Mejora de calidad de datos
- DG.4. Gestión de recursos humanos

- **Nivel de Madurez 4 o Predecible:** La organización puede demostrar que utiliza un conjunto de buenas prácticas orientadas a monitorizar que las estrategias organizacionales de datos son realmente efectivas. Para alcanzar este nivel una organización debe ejecutar todos los procesos del modelo de referencia de procesos del nivel 3 y además el siguiente proceso del modelo de referencia de procesos:

- DG.6. Monitorización de las estrategias organizaciones de datos

- **Nivel de Madurez 5 o Innovando:** La organización puede demostrar que utiliza un conjunto de buenas prácticas orientadas a garantizar que las estrategias de datos van evolucionando a medida que evolucionan las estrategias organizacionales. Una organización estará en nivel de madurez 5, cuando además de monitorizar sus estrategias de datos (nivel 4), ejecuta los siguientes procesos del modelo de referencia de procesos orientadas a actualizar las estrategias de datos, no sólo para mejorar defectos conocidos sino que podría ser utilizada para mejorar el rendimiento global:

- DG.5. Gestión de recursos financieros
- DG.7. Gestión de cambios en las estrategias de datos.

El nivel de madurez se computa en función del nivel de capacidad que tienen los procesos del modelo de referencia de procesos incluidos en la evaluación. El nivel de capacidad se computa teniendo en cuenta el grado de institucionalización de las buenas prácticas y de los atributos de procesos descritos en ISO/IEC 33020.

Para realizar el cómputo del nivel de capacidad de dichos procesos hay que realizar una inspección de los distintos tipos de evidencias (directas, indirectas, entrevistas y documentación) que se recolectarán para cada una de las instancias de los procesos de negocio que se han escogido para realizar la evaluación. Como resultado del nivel de capacidad se obtendrá una calificación de {*Not Achieved (N)*, *Partially Achieved (P)*, *Full Achieved (F)*, *Largely Achieved (L)*} para cada uno de los atributos de proceso de acuerdo a lo especificado en ISO/IEC 33020.

Con respecto a la mejora, el objetivo de la organización será alcanzar un mayor nivel de madurez organizacional. Ello implica institucionalizar progresivamente cada vez más procesos y llevar los procesos institucionalizados a niveles de capacidad mayores, con el objetivo de garantizar mejores niveles de calidad para los procesos organizacionales. Por razones de espacio, en este artículo no se cubrirá la mejora.

3 Ejemplo de aplicación

En esta sección se van a describir los resultados obtenidos en el estudio del caso de aplicación de MAMD a la Biblioteca de la Universidad X (BUX - por motivos de confidencialidad), que ha permitido refinar y validar el modelo. La evaluación se ha realizado siguiendo los principios de evaluación expuestos en ISO 33010 [12].

3.1 Descripción de la organización

La BUX da soporte a una comunidad universitaria formada – a fecha de 2014 - por 31.203 alumnos, 1.044 miembros del personal de administración y servicio y 2.227 miembros del personal docente e investigador repartidos en varios campus con un total de 13 puntos de servicio y 3 salas de lecturas que permiten un ratio de 6,6 alumnos por puestos de lectura .

En 2014, la BUX gestionó un fondo bibliográfico de 1.140.509 volúmenes informatizados, así como el acceso a 46.411 revistas electrónicas y 487.077 libros electrónicos, aparte de otros muchos servicios. De estos recursos, se contabilizaron un total de 289.388 préstamos de material de fondo bibliográfico, se contabilizaron un total de 339.279 descargas de libros electrónicos y se realizaron un total de 588.520 búsquedas en las bases de datos de referencias. Todo ello soportado por un total de 78 profesionales de distintas categorías y rangos repartidos por todas las instalaciones y con un presupuesto de 1.321.172 € para su ejecución durante 2015.

A parte de la gestión de material bibliográfico, la BUX también gestiona otros servicios como préstamo de equipamiento para la docencia y el aprendizaje, cursos de formación, gestión de redes sociales,... Toda esta actividad está soportada por una infraestructura tecnológica gestionada por el *Centro de Cálculo de la Universidad*, que permite el uso no solo de los equipos que utiliza el personal, sino también de los 964 puestos de consultas fijos y portátiles repartidos por todas las salas de lectura. Además se emplean recursos humanos y tecnológicos en la integración de datos provenientes de otras instituciones.

3.2 Alcance de la evaluación

Como se trataba de una experiencia piloto, y como parte del estudio de caso era determinar el esfuerzo de la evaluación, se decidió evaluar sólo hasta el nivel 2 de madurez de la BUX. Como es una evaluación del nivel de madurez organizacional, se requiere una evaluación de clase 1. Esto implica la inspección de evidencias de institucionalización de mejores prácticas recogidas en el modelo de referencia de procesos en al menos cuatro instancias de procesos de la organización: uno principal y tres auxiliares. Pero en aras de simplificar el esfuerzo por parte del personal de la BUX, se decidió elegir sólo tres procesos, que se identificaron durante la fase de planificación (véase Sección 3.3).

3.3 Planificación de la evaluación

Se podrían distinguir dos momentos importantes durante la planificación: (1) un primer contacto inicial con los directivos de la BUX, en donde se decidieron los procesos que iban a ser analizados durante la evaluación, y (2) un segundo en el que tras haber decidido los procesos, se planificó quiénes y cuándo, en función de su nivel de responsabilidad sobre los procesos elegidos, iban a participar para aportar evidencias durante la evaluación.

Con respecto a la identificación de los procesos, y teniendo en cuenta el interés de los directivos de la BUX en optimizar los procesos de la biblioteca que, siendo los más críticos en su día a día, eran los más sensibles a la hora de estar afectados por problemas basados en niveles inadecuados de calidad, se eligieron instancias de los siguientes procesos, y se nos explicó con detalle su funcionamiento:

- Proceso Principal (PP): Procedimiento de catalogación.
- Proceso Auxiliar 1 (PA1): Procedimiento de circulación de fondos
- Proceso Auxiliar 2 (PA2): Procedimiento de carga de usuarios / usuarios externos

Se planificó la evaluación para que se realizara durante tres días y se entrevistó a personal del punto de servicio de una de las localizaciones que eran o bien responsable, o bien estaban relacionados con los tres procesos identificados.

3.4 Recolección de evidencias

Para recoger datos necesarios para la evaluación se preparó un guion de trabajo que incluía una lista de comprobación con los resultados esperados, y un cuestionario con preguntas específicas para las personas que participan en la ejecución de los procesos seleccionados.

El cuestionario, que cubría los procesos incluidos en el nivel 1 y en el nivel 2 de MAMD (véase sección 2.2) y los atributos de procesos AP.1.1, AP.2.1, AP.2.2, incluía preguntas para las personas identificadas durante la planificación (véase sección 3.3). Los atributos de procesos se describen en ISO/IEC 33020 en la cláusula 5.2 y la escala ordinal para calcular el nivel de capacidad en la cláusula 5.3. Aparte de las respuestas, los trabajadores de la BUX aportaron otras evidencias, como la documentación pertinente (véase Tabla 2). Es importante resaltar el hecho de que todos los procesos típicos en los de la BUX están convenientemente documentados mediante Instrucciones Técnicas y Manuales de Procesos accesibles públicamente. Por razones de espacio no se puede incluir el catálogo completo de las evidencias obtenidas. Sólo se incluyen las conclusiones resultado de las inspecciones y entrevistas llevadas a cabo para cada uno de los procesos evaluados en el modelo de referencia de procesos.

Tabla 2. Documentación aportada por el equipo de trabajo de la BUX.

Proceso	Documentación aportada
PP	Proceso Técnico de Documentos (BIB-34). Instrucciones técnicas (IT 08, 09, 10). Manual de Proceso Técnico de la Biblioteca. Manual de AbsysNet. Manual MARC21. Modelo Z39-50 y captura desde Catálogo Colectivo REBIUN [13].
PA.1	Préstamo de Fondos (BIB-35). Normativa de acceso y préstamo BUX. Manual de AbsysNet. Manual GTBIB [14].
PA.2	Gestión de Usuarios (BIB-15). Normativa de acceso y préstamo BUX. Manual de AbsysNet. Procedimiento técnico de carga de usuarios desde aplicaciones CCUX

- **DM.1. Gestión de requisitos de datos.** En el PP, completamente descrito en los documentos BIB-37 y en las instrucciones técnicas IT 08, IT 09, IT10 (véase Tabla 2) se han identificado adecuadamente los requisitos de datos, y se obtienen evidencias documentadas y a través de las entrevistas de que el proceso DM.1 se ejecuta en el PP. Esto satisfaría el AP.1.1. En esta situación, ya no haría falta buscar evidencias para DM.1. en PA1 y en PA2, pero dada la oportunidad de poder realizar el caso de estudio, se decidió buscarlas y se encontraron documentadas tanto en el documento BIB-35 (véase Tabla 2) para PA1, como en el documento BIB-15 (véase Tabla 2) para PA.2. Al indagar por los aspectos específicos de AP.2.1 y AP.2.2 (véase Cláusula 5.2 de ISO 33020 para una descripción más detallada), es posible llegar a la conclusión de que en cualquiera de las tres instancias de los procesos elegidos, la gestión de requisitos de datos como tal es ampliamente gestionada así como la gestión de los productos de trabajo. Con respecto a la gestión del proceso, descubrimos que se identifican los objetivos a la hora de gestionar los requisitos, y se planifica el proceso, aunque no se monitoriza, y aunque se dedican los recursos suficientes a hacer las tareas, las personas responsables de ejecutar el proceso se eligen ad hoc, sin una asignación prestablecida. Con respecto a la gestión de los productos de trabajo, pudimos observar que aunque existen plantillas predefinidas para la recolección de requisitos de datos y se realizan varios controles y revisiones de los documentos generados, todas estas tareas se realizan de forma ad hoc.

- **DM.2.Gestión de infraestructura tecnológica**. El PP está soportado adecuadamente por una infraestructura tecnológica integrada completamente en los servicios TIC de la UX, y mantenida y actualizada convenientemente por el centro de cálculo de la Universidad de acuerdo a las mejoras que se introducen en los diferentes procesos de negocio. La gestión de la infraestructura propiamente dicha se realiza por tanto de forma externalizada, pero en la BUX existen responsables técnicos que se encargan de recopilar, validar e informar de los cambios que hay que hacer en la infraestructura tecnológica requisitos al centro de cálculo Por ejemplo, en el caso del PP, una de las principales herramientas para el procedimiento de catalogación es Absys, y todas las especificaciones necesarias se gestionaron adecuadamente.
- **DM.5. Gestión de la configuración**. La BUX está plenamente adaptada a la normativa existente en la red de bibliotecas de su país. Ello implica tener en cuenta y propagar a los procesos de la biblioteca las correspondientes modificaciones y evoluciones en la definición de los datos, que son gestionadas. Por ejemplo, en el caso del PP, cuando se asimiló el formato MARC 21 [15], se llevó a cabo un proceso de gestión de configuración y versionado del modelo de los datos para que las nuevas definiciones fueran coherentes en todas las aplicaciones implicadas. Los entrevistados nos informaron que dado que los cambios en los modelos de los datos no es algo que no ocurra frecuentemente, y que la BUX responde reactivamente ante ellos, no consideran necesario desarrollar unos procedimientos específicos para la gestión de la configuración de los datos; por tanto no existe formalmente una definición detallada del proceso, y cuando se ha tenido que realizar se ha hecho ad hoc.
- **DM.8.Establecimiento de fuentes y destinos de datos**. Los entrevistados nos explicaron que tanto las fuentes de destinos de los datos estaban perfectamente identificadas para cada uno de las instancias de los procesos que se habían elegido para la evaluación. En ese sentido, el proceso estaba convenientemente gestionado – aunque no se habían especificado claramente quién tendría que hacerse responsable de ejecutar el proceso y, en el caso del PP, normalmente recaía sobre el responsable del fondo documental-. Tanto en el caso del PP, como de los procesos auxiliares, todas las fuentes y destinos de los datos estaban agrupada en sus correspondientes catálogos que son gestionados y puestos a disposición del resto de los trabajadores.
- **DM.3.Gestión de datos históricos**. La BUX mantiene una serie de políticas muy detalladas, entre las que se encuentran las correspondientes a la gestión de datos históricos. En el caso del PP, descatalogar un libro significa mover sus datos del fondo documental en producción al fondo documental descatalogado y gestionar las consecuencias de que un documento pase a estar descatalogado (por ejemplo, cancelar los préstamos asignados a los usuarios). Este proceso es realizado por el responsable del fondo documental, que es el único que tiene autoridad para descatalogar una obra. En el caso, del PA.1, se tiene como política borrar los datos correspondientes a la circulación de fondos que tenga más de tres años de antigüedad. Con respecto al PA.2, se tiene como política borrar los datos de los usuarios al comienzo

del curso siguiente al que terminaron sus estudios. Sí que pudimos constatar que la ejecución de la gestión de datos históricos en cualquiera de las instancias de los procesos está completamente automatizada, con lo que los productos de trabajo están adecuadamente gestionados.

- **DM.4.Gestión de seguridad de datos**. La BUX es muy cuidadosa en lo que se refiere a los datos personales. De hecho hereda de la UX la totalidad de los procedimientos de protección de los datos. Esto se traduce en que para cualquiera de las tres instancias de los procesos observados, se gestiona adecuadamente el acceso a los datos, impidiendo que usuarios no autorizados consulten o modifiquen datos. No obstante, los datos más sensibles se mueven en el proceso PA.1, ya que son datos de usuarios y las obras que le son prestadas, y que pueden revelar información confidencial acerca de aspectos sensibles de los usuarios de la BUX. En el otro extremo estaban los datos de las obras, cuya gestión no requería especial protección. Precisamente por eso, se decidió inspeccionar la instancia de PA.1. Se concluyó que la ejecución de las políticas correspondiente a la gestión de datos históricos efectivamente se realiza por las personas a quienes se les ha asignado la responsabilidad de hacerlo, que es un proceso planificado que usa los recursos que le han sido asignados, aunque no se monitoriza y está perfectamente adecuado. Por otro lado, el catálogo de política de seguridad responde a un esquema madurado a lo largo de la vida de la BUX, y que por tanto se documenta, controla y transfiere de forma precisa.
- **DG.1.Establecimiento de estrategias de datos**. Es interesante resaltar el hecho de que aunque los directivos de la BUX no son conscientes de estar realizando lo que se entiende por gobierno de datos, en realidad llevan haciéndolo mucho tiempo. En este sentido son conscientes de la importancia de tener los datos adecuados y de la necesidad de tener una estrategia para los datos alineada con la propia estrategia de la BUX, por ejemplo, para poder comunicarse con otras bibliotecas de otras universidades o para poder integrar datos de usuarios externos. Así, cada una de las instancias de los procesos observados durante la evaluación da muestras de la aplicación de las estrategias de los datos. No obstante, aunque hay una aplicación evidente, el proceso de establecimiento de estrategia de datos no está en absoluto definido ni especificado explícitamente, y todas las iniciativas se han hecho ad hoc por directivos de la BUX de una forma independiente y, en muchas ocasiones sin poder dedicar recursos al proceso de establecimiento de las estrategias de datos, aunque sí dedicando recursos a las iniciativas que han surgido para implementar esas "inspiradas" estrategias de datos.
- **DG.2.Gestión del ciclo de vida y valor de los datos**. Al igual que en el caso de la evaluación del DG.1, no existen evidencias de una definición explícita del proceso de gestión del ciclo de vida y valor de los datos. Siempre se ha hecho de forma ad hoc, pero sin ser consciente de que se estaba realizando. De las entrevistas se desprende la inquietud de los directivos de la BUX de disponer de los mejores datos posibles en la mejor forma posible, y de ser conscientes de la necesidad de implementar mecanismos para los datos, pero sin asociarlo al hecho de que diferentes datos pueden tener diferente valor, y que este puede cambiar a lo largo de su ciclo de vida.

- **DG.3. Establecimiento de estándares, políticas, buenas prácticas y procedimientos**. Como parte de la gestión de la BUX, se han definido e implementado adecuadamente una serie de políticas, buenas prácticas y procedimientos que están basadas en las políticas generales de la UX. Muchas de estas políticas están orientadas fuertemente a gestionar adecuadamente los datos y de alguna forma su calidad; además cuando es posible se asimilan como parte de las políticas estándares internacionales. Por ejemplo, se identifican para PP algunos estándares acordados en la CRUE que instan a usar ISO 2709 [16]. Se tiene por tanto un catálogo de políticas de datos, y se asume que tiene que ser elaborado por los directivos de la BUX como parte de las responsabilidades de su trabajo, pero aunque se gestiona el catálogo de políticas, en ningún momento se gestiona el proceso propiamente dicho: no se asigna responsabilidades, ni se asignan explícitamente recursos, ni se planifica, ni por supuesto se monitoriza.

3.5 Validación de los datos

El equipo de evaluación confirmó la objetividad de las evidencias recogidas y las validó con respecto a otras evidencias proporcionadas para los mismos procesos. Se consideró que el conjunto de evidencias aportadas era suficiente y bastante representativa para el propósito y alcance de la evaluación.

3.6 Derivación de los resultados

Basándose en las conclusiones sobre las evidencias recogidas (véase sección 3.4) y, siguiendo las líneas guías proporcionadas en la cláusula 4.2 de ISO 33010 para la evaluación de los atributos de procesos, se procedió a derivar los resultados para cada uno de ellos - mostrados como {N, P, L, F} en la Tabla 3.

Tabla 3. Calificación de los atributos de procesos y computación del nivel de madurez organizacional de gestión de datos, gobierno de datos, y gestión de calidad de datos en la BUX.

AP.2.2	L	F	P	L	L	F	N	N	L
AP.2.1	L	F	P	L	F	F	P	N	N
AP.1.1	F	F	F	F	F	F	F	F	F
	DM.1	**DM.2**	**DM.5**	**DM.8**	**DM.3**	**DM.4**	**DG.1**	**DG.2**	**DG.3**
	Nivel de Madurez 1				**Nivel de Madurez 2**				

Para considerar un nivel de madurez consolidado es preciso que todos los procesos incluidos en el nivel anterior estén en el estado "F", y los procesos de ese nivel estén en un estado al menos "L": por ejemplo se considera que el nivel de madurez 2 está consolidado, cuando habiendo obtenido todos los procesos del nivel 1 una "F" para el atributo de proceso AP.1.1, todos los procesos nuevos han obtenido una "F" para el atributo AP.1.1, y todos los procesos –tantos los que pertenecen al nivel 1 como los que pertenecen al nivel 2, han obtenido al menos una "L" para los atributos de procesos AP.2.1 y AP.2.2. En base a esto se derivó el nivel de madurez organizacional de gobierno de datos, gestión de datos y gestión de calidad de datos de acuerdo al modelo MAMD. Estos resultados se muestran en la Tabla 3.

Como puede observarse, todos los procesos del nivel de madurez 1 tienen evaluados el AP.1.1 como F (*Fully achieved*) lo que consolida el nivel de madurez 1. No obstante, algunos de los procesos incluidos en el nivel de madurez 1 (DM.5) como otros incluidos en el nivel de madurez 2 (DG.1, DG.2, DG.3) no han obtenido la calificación mínima requerida de L (*Largely Achieved*) para los atributos de procesos AP.2.1 y/o AP.2.2, con lo que, incluso teniendo consolidado el nivel de madurez 1, no es posible consolidar el nivel de madurez 2.

3.7 Informar de los resultados.

Finalmente tras la evaluación, se celebró una reunión con los directivos de la BUX para informarles de los resultados de la evaluación. En esta reunión no sólo se informó del nivel de madurez obtenido (nivel de madurez 1 o básico), sino que se especificaron los puntos fuertes (muchos de los procesos están documentados y se heredan numerosas políticas de la BUX) y las no conformidades con respecto a MAMD (no están asignadas ni convenientemente documentadas las responsabilidades de la mayoría de los procesos, es necesarios definir los procesos correspondientes a DG.1, DG.2, y DG.3).

Finalmente, el equipo de evaluación recomendó la planificación y ejecución de un proyecto de mejora para resolver las no conformidades obtenidas y poder alcanzar el nivel de madurez 2.

4 Conclusiones y Trabajos futuros

Hemos constatado que la aplicación de MAMD puede proporcionar realmente beneficios para las organizaciones, beneficios que resultan de trabajar con datos que tienen niveles adecuados de calidad. En cualquier caso, es necesario aplicar MAMD en más estudios de caso, y aprovechar las lecciones aprendidas para refinar mejor el modelo.

También queremos establecer cuantitativamente hasta qué punto mejorar el nivel de madurez de gestión de datos, gobierno de datos y gestión de calidad de datos supone una ventaja clara para las organizaciones.

5 Agradecimientos

Queremos agradecer al personal de la BUX su gentil colaboración durante la realización de este estudio de caso. A continuación se listan los proyectos que financian esta investigación: (1) proyecto GEODAS: Gestión para el Desarrollo Global de Software mediante Ingeniería de Negocio y Entornos Avanzados de Colaboración (Ministerio de Economía y Competitividad y Fondo Europeo de Desarrollo Regional FEDER, TIN2012-37493-C03-01); (2) proyecto VILMA: Visualización y Medición de la cAlidad del proceso, proyecto y producto software, financiado por la Consejería de Educación, Ciencia y Cultura de la Junta de Comunidades de Castilla La Mancha, y Fondo Europeo de Desarrollo Regional FEDER, (PEII-2014-048-P); y (3) proyecto

GOVINDA, ITC-20151200, cofinanciado por el Centro para el Desarrollo Tecnológico Industrial (CDTI) dentro de FEDER-INNTERCONECTA 2015.

6 Referencias

1. ISACA: COBIT 5: Enabling Information (2013)
2. Team, C.P.: Capability Maturity Model® Integration (CMMI SM), Version 1.1. CMMI for Systems Engineering, Software Engineering, Integrated Product and Process Development, and Supplier Sourcing (CMMI-SE/SW/IPPD/SS, V1. 1) (2002)
3. ISO/IEC-JTC1/SC7: ISO/IEC 15504-1:2004, Information Technology - Process Assessment - Part 1: Concepts and Vocabulary. International Organization for Standarization, Geneva, Switzerland (2004)
4. SEI: DMM: Data Management Maturity Model. SEI, Pittsburgh (2014)
5. ISO: ISO 8000-60: Data Quality Management : The Overview of Process Assessment ISO (2015)
6. ISO: ISO 8000-61: Data quality: Information & data quality management process reference model. ISO (2015)
7. ISO: ISO/IEC 33000: Information technology: Process assessment. ISO (2015)
8. ISO: ISO/IEC 33004: Information technology: Process assessment: Requirements for process reference, process assessment and maturity models. ISO (2015)
9. Mosley, M., Brackett, M., Earley, S., Henderson, D. (eds.): The DAMA Guide to Data Management Body of Knowledge (DAMA-DMBOK Guide)-First Edition. Data Management International (2009)
10. ISO: ISO/IEC 33020: Information technology: Process assessment: Process measurement framework for assessment of process capability. ISO (2015)
11. ISO: ISO/IEC 33002: Information technology: Process assessment: Requirements for performing process assessment. ISO (2015)
12. ISO: ISO/IEC 33010: Information technology: Process assessment: Guide to performing assessment ISO (2015)
13. BUX, Modelo Z39-50 y captura desde Catálogo Colectivo REBIUN, http://www.rebiun.org/documentos/Documents/GTCATALOGO/Manualdeprocedimiento_CatalogoColectivo_enero2014.pdf, 12/12/2015
14. BUX, Manual GTBIB, http://www.gtbib.net/manual/sod/indice.htm, 12/12/2015
15. BUX, Manual MARC21, http://www.bne.es/es/Micrositios/Guias/Marc21/, 12/12/2015
16. ISO: ISO 2709: Information and documentation: Format for information exchange. ISO (2008)

Hacia la Evaluación y Mejora de Software dirigidas por Metas Multinivel y Estrategias

Belén Rivera, Pablo Becker, Fernanda Papa, Luis Olsina

GIDIS_Web, Facultad de Ingeniería, UNLPam, General Pico, LP, Argentina
{riveramb, beckerp, pmfer, olsinal}@ing.unlpam.edu.ar

Abstract. En cualquier organización, los proyectos de medición y evaluación (ME) operacionalizan metas de necesidad de información que dan soporte a metas principales o de negocio, las cuales pueden estar formuladas a distintos niveles organizacionales, como operativo, táctico y estratégico. Para saber si se alcanzan las metas de negocio, se necesita establecer metas de necesidad de información las cuales pueden requerir satisfacer objetivos de ME. A su vez, una estrategia ayuda a alcanzar las metas de un proyecto mediante sus actividades y métodos bien establecidos. Se debe seleccionar la estrategia apropiada según el objetivo de ME y/o cambio propuesto. Por lo tanto, como contribución en este artículo se especifica una base y marco conceptual que enlaza conceptos de meta de negocio y necesidad de información con conceptos de proyecto, estrategia y requerimientos no funcionales. Para ilustrar al enfoque propuesto, se realiza una prueba de concepto sobre una aplicación de red social con el fin de enlazar metas de negocio con objetivos de mejora, de necesidad de información y de ME. Se discute además el uso de patrones de estrategia específicos para dar soporte a metas de ME y cambio.

Keywords: Metas Multinivel. Evaluación. Proyecto. Estrategia. Ontología.

1 Introducción

Toda organización debiera establecer objetivos o metas de negocio a niveles estratégico, táctico y operativo, y las organizaciones de software no deberían ser la excepción. Basili *et al.* [3] sostienen que una cuestión crítica en una organización es la falta de vinculación entre las metas de nivel estratégico con las de nivel operativo. El correcto establecimiento de metas de negocio a diferentes niveles organizacionales determina gran parte del éxito en realizar proyectos [17]. Por lo tanto, si las metas que se formulan a nivel operativo no están alineadas con alguna meta de nivel táctico o estratégico, la organización puede mal direccionar sus esfuerzos y malgastar recursos.

Para alcanzar una meta de negocio a menudo es necesario contar con cierta información. Por lo tanto, una organización también debe establecer metas de necesidad de información. Se puede decir que una meta de necesidad de información es una meta de soporte a las metas de negocio, y por ende una meta de necesidad de información siempre está relacionada con una meta de negocio. Un tipo particular de meta de necesidad de información es la meta de medición y evaluación (ME). Este tipo de meta permite conocer en qué medida se está alcanzando una meta de negocio, y también brinda información necesaria para alcanzarla, como se verá más adelante.

Por otra parte, las diferentes metas establecidas se operacionalizan mediante proyectos. La gestión de proyectos permite organizar el trabajo, es decir, planificar, ejecutar y controlar las actividades y recursos del ciclo de vida adoptado para el proyecto [18]. A su vez, en un proyecto se debería considerar estrategias que ayuden a alcanzar las metas. Una estrategia define un curso de acción a seguir, es decir, especifica qué debe hacerse y cómo para alcanzar el objetivo propuesto. Por lo tanto, según [16] es deseable que una estrategia cuente con tres capacidades integradas, a saber: *una especificación del proceso*, *una especificación de métodos* y *un marco conceptual de dominio* (ver definiciones en Tabla 1). Estrategias que ayudan a alcanzar metas de necesidad de información de ME son por ejemplo GQM (*Goal Question Metric*) [2] y GOCAME (*Goal-Oriented Context-Aware Measurement and Evaluation*) [14], mientras que SIQinU (*Strategy for Improving Quality in Use*) [12] es un ejemplo de estrategia para mejora. SIQinU permite realizar cambios dirigidos por ME, por lo que se la considera una estrategia de medición, evaluación y cambio (MEC), a diferencia de las primeras que son clasificadas como estrategias de ME. Además existen estrategias de desarrollo como por ejemplo UP (*Unified Process*).

Por ello, es de suma importancia que las organizaciones cuenten con un enfoque sistemático que les permita establecer y alinear metas a diferentes niveles organizacionales, además de definir proyectos y estrategias en pos de alcanzar tales metas. Si bien en la literatura revisada existen enfoques que consideran algunos de estos aspectos, no se encuentran integrados, o carecen de una base conceptual robusta (como una ontología), tal cual se discute en la Sección 2. Por lo tanto, en este artículo presentamos un enfoque que permite a las organizaciones de software establecer metas de necesidad de información de ME para dar soporte a metas de negocio formuladas a diferentes niveles organizacionales. Es más, el enfoque propuesto contribuye a la selección de estrategias para proyectos de ME y MEC.

En resumen, las contribuciones de este trabajo son: i) *extender la base conceptual* del marco de ME previamente desarrollado [4, 20], para enlazar conceptos de meta de negocio y necesidad de información con conceptos de proyecto, estrategia, requerimientos no funcionales y vistas de calidad; ii) *ilustrar el enfoque propuesto* mediante una prueba de concepto en donde se vinculan metas de negocio a diferentes niveles organizacionales con metas de necesidad de información y de ME; y iii) *discutir el uso de patrones de estrategia* para dar soporte a metas de ME y MEC.

El resto del artículo está organizado como sigue. La Sección 2 analiza trabajos relacionados a enfoques y estrategias de ME/MEC que consideren metas multinivel, y que estén soportadas por bases conceptuales, ya sean estructuradas en glosarios u ontologías. La Sección 3 especifica la base conceptual de metas de negocio, proyecto y estrategia definiendo los principales términos, atributos y relaciones. La Sección 4 presenta una prueba de concepto que ejemplifica la relación entre metas de negocio y de necesidad de información, utilizando como escenario la mejora de la aplicación móvil Facebook. La Sección 5 discute la importancia de contar con patrones de estrategia para dar soporte a metas de ME y MEC. Finalmente, la Sección 6 resume las principales contribuciones y líneas de avance de esta investigación.

2 Trabajos Relacionados

En Ingeniería de Software existen algunos trabajos que indican la importancia del alineamiento de metas de medición (a nivel operativo) con metas de negocio de niveles superiores (táctico y estratégico) [1, 3, 7, 17]. Esta vinculación es vital en la toma de decisiones ya que las metas de necesidad de información de ME brindan información útil para conocer en qué medida se ha alcanzado una meta de negocio, además de ofrecer, en algunos casos, información necesaria para alcanzarla, por ejemplo, favoreciendo el diseño e implementación de cambios. No obstante, observando la literatura específica del área, no hemos detectado enfoques que consten de bases conceptuales robustas (como ontologías) que integren términos como *meta de negocio*, *nivel organizacional*, *necesidad de información*, *necesidad de información de ME*, *estrategia*, *proyecto*, etc., excepto en [1]. Además, teniendo presente que una estrategia es un recurso valioso que ayuda a alcanzar metas de un proyecto, cabe remarcar que, como discutido en [16], existen pocas estrategias que cuenten con las tres capacidades integradas, a saber: una especificación del proceso, una especificación de métodos y un marco conceptual de dominio.

Un trabajo relacionado a estrategias integradas es GQM$^+$Strategies [3], que comprende un enfoque orientado a metas para diseñar e implementar proyectos de medición de software, a distintos niveles organizacionales. A diferencia de su antecesor, GQM [2], las metas de negocio que define permite alinearlas a distintos niveles de una organización a través del establecimiento de estrategias. Las estrategias definen objetivos para alcanzar las metas, y, para esto, pueden necesitar que se definan y satisfagan metas de niveles inferiores. En definitiva estas metas de negocio son asociadas a metas de medición usando GQM. GQM$^+$Strategies tiene una base terminológica estructurada en forma de glosario en la que se definen los principales términos involucrados, sin embargo, carece de cierta riqueza semántica al no estar estructurada en una ontología. En [16] se presenta un estudio comparativo de estrategias integradas de ME el cual concluye que GQM$^+$Strategies satisface en buena medida las tres capacidades deseables de una estrategia integrada, aunque su aspecto más débil es la calidad de las capacidades del marco conceptual de dominio.

Otro de los trabajos revisados es [17] el cual describe un proceso que permite definir metas de medición que ayudan a comprender aspectos de metas de negocio de la organización. El proceso inicia indicando que la organización debe plantear las metas de negocio en algún nivel organizacional, de las cuales surgirán interrogantes relacionados a qué se quiere saber y cómo lograrlo. Estos interrogantes o preguntas permiten identificar información cuantitativa a través de la descomposición de la meta principal de negocio en submetas relacionadas. Con la lista de submetas y las preguntas se identifican los atributos y entidades asociadas, siguiendo el modelo y plantillas de GQM. Esta guía constituye una referencia valiosa, dado que detalla el proceso de medición a través de la descomposición de metas, y provee plantillas que permiten formalizar las metas e instanciar el proceso. Como base conceptual usa los términos que define GQM, careciendo de un glosario que incluya términos como meta de negocio, nivel organizacional, necesidad de información y estrategia.

Adicionalmente, en [7] se describe un enfoque que combina los aspectos más destacados de la estrategia descripta previamente [17] y el enfoque *Balanced Scorecard* [11] para descomponer metas estratégicas en submetas que ayuden a identificar y definir medidas e indicadores. En esta derivación se utiliza el enfoque GQIM (*Goal-Question-Indicator-Measurement*) [7] que permite a la organización sistemáticamente establecer metas para cada uno de los cuadrantes que define *Balanced Scorecard* y desarrollar un conjunto de medidas e indicadores. GQIM incluye un glosario con la definición de algunos términos, que no se encontraban en GQM. Sin embargo, GQIM no pone énfasis en el empleo de estrategias integradas para alcanzar metas de negocio a partir de metas de necesidad de información, tal como se discute en nuestra propuesta.

Por último, aunque no menos importante, en [1] se define una subontología de metas de medición, argumentando que la medición debe estar alineada con metas organizacionales de manera de producir datos útiles para la toma de decisión. La ontología propuesta por los autores contiene términos, relaciones y restricciones relacionadas con el alineamiento entre medición, metas y organización. En este trabajo los autores sostienen que los indicadores constituyen las medidas que pueden ser usadas para juzgar el nivel de logro o satisfacción de metas, aunque no describen el uso de estrategias para alcanzarlas. A diferencia de [1], nuestra propuesta establece formalmente el uso de estrategias integradas para alcanzar las metas y también especifica que las metas de necesidad de información de ME están vinculadas a metas de negocio para conocer en qué medida éstas se están alcanzando.

3 Enlazando Conceptos de Meta de Negocio y Necesidad de Información con los Conceptos de Proyecto y Estrategia

En [20] se presenta el marco conceptual C-INCAMI (*Contextual-Information Need, Concept Model, Attribute, Metric and Indicator*) para el dominio de ME, el cual está formado por seis paquetes (componentes conceptuales), a saber: *non-functional requirements, measurement, evaluation, context, quality view* y *project.* Los términos, atributos y relaciones de estos componentes surgen a partir de la ontología de ME documentada en [13, 14] y de la ontología de vistas de calidad formalizada en [20]. Además, cabe mencionar que los términos para *measurement* y *evaluation,* fueron semánticamente enriquecidos con la ontología de proceso presentada en [4].

Si bien C-INCAMI cuenta con los términos necesarios para especificar requerimientos no funcionales (como entidad, atributo, necesidad de información de ME, etc.) no considera que una necesidad de información de ME da soporte a una meta de negocio, lo cual es importante para mostrar el alineamiento entre metas a diferentes niveles organizacionales. Por otra parte, el componente *project* existente en [14] no considera términos como estrategia y tampoco se relaciona con el término meta. Por lo tanto, en esta sección se presenta al nuevo componente denominado *business goal* y una extensión del componente *project* (ver Fig. 1). Básicamente, estos componentes permiten especificar metas a distintos niveles organizacionales, que se operacionalizan mediante proyectos y son alcanzadas por medio de estrategias. En las tablas 1, 2 y 3 se encuentran definiciones de términos, relaciones y atributos de la base conceptual resaltadas a seguir en *itálica.* Además, cabe remarcar que al definir los diferentes términos y atributos se han revisado documentos como [1, 3, 5, 9, 18], con el fin de tener cierta adherencia o contraste a fuentes reconocidas.

Una organización (*Organization*) es una entidad que comprende personas y que está estructurada y gestionada para establecer y perseguir metas, y que afecta o es afectada por el contexto en el que se encuentra. La organización establece (*establishes*) metas (*Goal*) u objetivos. Una meta contiene una declaración explícita (*statement*) sobre el fin o propósito que se quiere alcanzar en un período de tiempo. El propósito (*purpose*) de una meta es el fundamento por el cual se quiere lograr la misma. Por ejemplo, para metas de necesidad de información de ME (*ME Information Need*), propósitos específicos pueden ser: comprender, mejorar, predecir. El período de tiempo (*timeframe*) establecido para concretar la meta puede ser de corto, mediano, o largo plazo. A su vez, las metas que establece una organización pueden clasificarse en metas de negocio (*Business Goal*) y metas de necesidad de información (*Information Need Goal*). Las metas de negocio son las metas principales que la organización se fija considerando la misión (*mision*) y la visión (*vision*).

Es importante mencionar que una meta de negocio puede ser formulada a (*isFormulatedAt*) diferentes niveles organizacionales (*Organizational Level*), como operativo, táctico o estratégico. A su vez, una meta de negocio puede descomponerse en submetas (*subGoal*). Por último, las metas de necesidad de información son metas de soporte a las metas principales o de negocio (*isSupportedBy*). Usualmente brindan información útil para conocer en qué medida se ha alcanzado una meta de negocio.

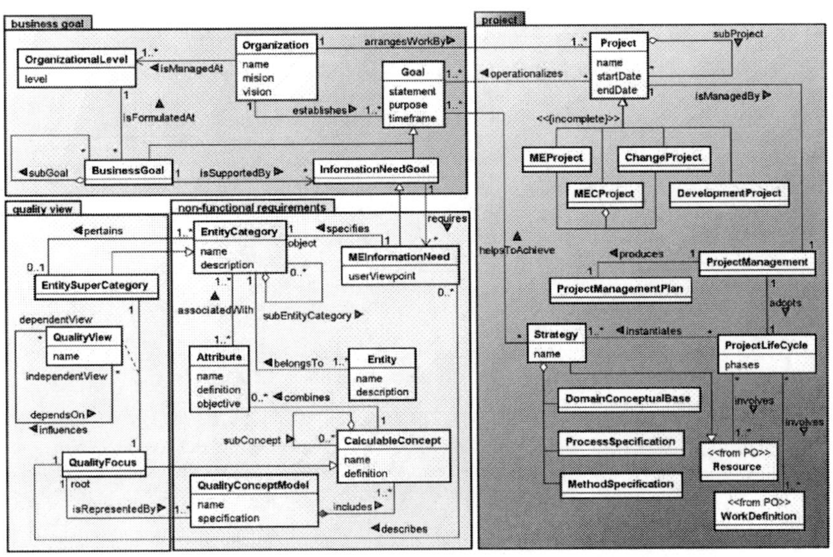

Fig. 1. Conceptos principales del dominio de Metas de Negocio (paquete *business goal*) y relaciones con algunos conceptos del dominio de Proyecto (paquete *project*) y de Requerimientos no funcionales (*non-functional requirements*). Nota: PO significa *Process Ontology*; ME, *Measurement and Evaluation*; y MEC, *Measurement, Evaluation and Change*.

Tabla 1. Definición de términos de las subontologías de *metas de negocio* y *proyecto*.

Term	Definition
Business Goal	It is a main or primary Goal that the Organization intends to achieve.
Change Project	It is a Project for operationalizing a Business Goal with the purpose of changing the current state of an entity. Note: Different kinds of changes (e.g., adaptive, perfective, corrective changes) can be made in maintenance projects
Development Project	It is a Project for operationalizing a main Business Goal with the purpose of building a new product or system.
Domain Conceptual Base	It is a terminological base in which, for a given domain, the main terms or concepts are explicitly defined. Note: A Conceptual Base can be structured for instance in a glossary, taxonomy, or ontology, amongst other ways.
Goal (synonym **Objective**)	The statement of the aim to be achieved by the Organization which considers the propositional content of a purpose in a given time frame.
Information Need Goal	It is a Goal intended to get insight for a given Business Goal. Note: Information Need, as per [9], is defined as "Insight necessary to manage objectives, goals, risks, and problems".
MEC Project	It is a Project for operationalizing a Business Goal with the purpose of improving an entity. Note: A MEC Project comprises both Change and ME Project where changes in the entity are driven by measurement and evaluation.
ME Information Need	It is an Information Need Goal driven by measurement and evaluation activities.
ME Project	It is a Project for operationalizing a ME Information Need
Method Specification	It is the representation of a method. Note 1: Method is the specific and particular way to perform the specified steps in the description of a Work Definition. Note 2: The specific and particular way of a Method –i.e. how the described steps in a work definition should be made- is represented by a procedure and rules [4].
Organization	It is an entity comprising people that is structured and managed to establish and pursue organizational Goals and is affected by and affects to its environment or context. Note: Most organizations have a level-oriented management structure that determines relationships between the different members and the activities, and subdivides and assigns roles and authority to perform different tasks.
Organizational Level	It represents an abstract level in which Organization's Business Goals are formulated and can be managed by Projects. Note: Usually, long-term Business Goals are formulated at strategic Organizational Level, while short-term Business Goals are formulated at operational Organizational Level
Process Specification	It is a model which relates a set of process elements such as activities, tasks, inputs and outputs, pre- and post-conditions, artifacts, roles, amongst others. Note 1: A process specification can consider different process perspectives such as functional, behavioral, informational and organizational [6]. Note 2: Usually, process specifications primarily state what to do rather than to represent how to do activity descriptions
Project	It is an entity representing a temporary and goal-oriented endeavor with definite start and finish dates, which considers a managed set of interrelated activities, tasks and resources aimed at producing and modifying unique work products (i.e., artifacts, services or results) for satisfying a given requester need.
Project Life Cycle	The series of phases that a Project passes through from its initiation to its closure [18]. Note: Examples of phases to be managed in any Project are planning, scheduling, monitoring, among others.
Project Management	It is the set of managerial processes and activities intended to achieve the Project Goal. Note: The application of knowledge, skills, tools, and techniques to project activities to meet the project requirements, as per [18].

Project Management Plan	The document that describes how the Project will be executed, monitored, and controlled [18].
Resource	Asset assigned to a Work Definition. Note: An asset is an entity (e.g., agent, people, Strategy, method, tool, etc.) with added value for an Organization [4].
Strategy	Principles, patterns, and particular domain concepts and framework that can be specified by a set of core processes, in addition to a set of appropriated methods and tools, as core Resources, for helping to achieve the Project's Goal. Note: An integrated strategy comprises three capabilities simultaneously, namely: (i) a domain conceptual base; (ii) process perspective specifications; and, (iii) method specifications [16].
Work Definition	Abstract entity which describes the work by means of consumed and produced work products, conditions and involved roles. Note: Work represents a process, an activity or a task [4].

Tabla 2. Definición de algunas relaciones en los componentes *metas de negocio* y *proyecto*.

Relationship	Definition
arrangesWorkBy	An Organization organizes its work or effort by means of Projects for the achievement of its established Goals.
establishes	An Organization *establishes* and pursues Goals as part of its Mission, and in alignment with its Vision.
helpsToAchieve	A Strategy gives support for achieving one or more organizational Goals.
involves	The realization of a Project Life Cycle *involves* Resources and Work Definitions, among other aspects.
isManagedAt	An Organization *is managed at* Organizational Levels, such as strategic, tactical and operational levels.
produces	A Project Management process *produces* a Project Management Plan as artifact.
subGoal	A Business Goal can be divided into *sub-goals*, which are in turn Business Goals at lower granularity levels.

Tabla 3. Definición de algunos atributos de los términos en *metas de negocio* y *proyecto*.

Term	Attribute	Definition
Goal	**statement**	An explicit declaration of the aim to be achieved. Note: A statement is usually a written assertion in a high-level or natural language.
	purpose	The rationale for achieving a specified Goal. Note: Examples of ME Information Need's specific purposes are: understand, improve, etc.
	timeframe	A set period of time in which the Goal is pursued or is expected to be achieved. Note: A timeframe of a Goal can range from short-, mid-term to long-term period of time.
Organization	**mission**	It states the organization's core purpose and focus. Note: A mission statement normally remains unchanged over time.
	vision	It describes what an organization wants to aspire to, and what specific motivation binds together the organization's stakeholders. Note: A vision reflects the realization of the organization's values.
Organizational Level	**level**	It is the name that labels the abstract level in which an Organization's Business Goal is formulated. Note: Usually, a long-term Business Goal is formulated at a Strategic Level, while a short- or mid-term Business Goal is formulated at an Operational or Tactical Level.
Project Life Cycle	**phases**	A phase of a Project Life Cycle is a group of strongly-related processes and activities defined in a given order. Note 1: A phase ends with a milestone, such as the completion of a deliverable like a project plan. Note 2: A Project Life Cycle has many phases such as Planning, Scheduling, Monitoring, among others.

Una meta de necesidad de información puede a su vez requerir (*requires*) de metas de necesidad de información de ME (*ME Information Need*). Estas son un tipo más específico de metas que están dirigidas por actividades de ME. Una necesidad de información de ME especifica un objeto (*Entity Category*) a ser evaluado considerando un foco de calidad (*Quality Focus*), tal como se puede observar en los componentes *non-functional requirements* y *quality view* respectivamente.

Una organización organiza el trabajo (*arrangesWorkBy*) mediante proyectos (*Project*) que permiten operacionalizar (*operationalizes*) las metas establecidas. Hemos definido proyecto en [4] como "*una entidad que representa un esfuerzo temporal y orientado a metas, con una fecha de inicio y fin determinados, que considera un conjunto de actividades, tareas y recursos interrelacionados dirigidos a producir y modificar productos de trabajo únicos (artefactos, servicios o resultados) para satisfacer una necesidad del solicitante*".

Existen diferentes tipos de proyectos. Por ejemplo, un proyecto de desarrollo (*Development Project*) es aquel que operacionaliza una meta de negocio que tiene como propósito construir un nuevo producto software o sistema. Particularmente, en este trabajo nos interesan los proyectos de ME (*ME Project*), que operacionalizan metas de necesidad de información de ME, y los proyectos de MEC (*MEC Project*) que operacionalizan metas de negocio junto a metas de necesidad de información de ME, con el propósito de mejora. En este último tipo de proyecto los cambios son dirigidos por ME, por lo tanto se compone de subproyectos de ME y de cambio (*Change Project*). Un proyecto de cambio operacionaliza una meta de negocio con el propósito de cambiar o modificar el estado actual de una entidad. Los cambios pueden ser adaptativos, perfectivos, correctivos o evolutivos. En la Sección 4 se realiza una prueba de concepto para una meta de mejora mediante un proyecto de MEC.

La gestión de proyecto (*Project Management*) es el conjunto de procesos destinados a alcanzar la meta del proyecto. En [18] se define esta actividad como "*la aplicación del conocimiento, habilidades, herramientas y técnicas a las actividades del proyecto para alcanzar los requerimientos del proyecto*". La gestión de proyecto produce (*produces*) un plan (*Project Management Plan*), esto es, el documento que describe cómo el proyecto será ejecutado, monitoreado y controlado. Además, un proyecto adopta (*adopts*) un ciclo de vida (*Project Life Cycle*) que indica las fases por las que atraviesa, desde su inicio hasta su fin.

El ciclo de vida involucra al menos recursos (*Resource*) y definiciones de trabajo (*WorkDefinition*), e instancia (*instantiates*) estrategias (*Strategy*). Una estrategia se define como "*principios, patrones y conceptos de un dominio y marco particular que pueden ser especificados por un conjunto de procesos principales además de un conjunto de métodos y herramientas apropiadas como recursos fundamentales para ayudar a alcanzar la meta del proyecto*" [4]. Como indicado en la Sección 1, el principio de una estrategia integrada [16] es contar con tres capacidades tales como: 1) un marco conceptual de dominio (*Domain Conceptual Base*), 2) una especificación del proceso (*Process Specification*) y 3) una especificación de métodos (*Method Specification*). El marco conceptual de dominio incluye una base terminológica para un dominio en particular (en nuestro caso para el dominio de ME), en la que se define explícitamente los principales términos que se agrupan en componentes. La segunda capacidad describe principalmente qué hacer. Es un modelo que relaciona un conjunto de elementos de proceso tales como actividades, tareas, entradas y salidas, pre y poscondiciones, artefactos, roles, entre otros. Puede ser especificado desde diferentes perspectivas, como funcional, de comportamiento, entre otras [6]. La tercera capacidad representa cómo se deben llevar a cabo las descripciones de las actividades. En pocas palabras, es la representación del método. Claramente, una estrategia es un recurso que ayuda a alcanzar (*helpsToAchieve*) una meta. En nuestra investigación nos hemos enfocado en estrategias de ME o MEC, es decir aquellas destinadas a alcanzar metas que son operacionalizadas por proyectos de ME o MEC.

Para concluir esta sección, cabe aclarar que los términos incluidos en el nuevo componente *business goal* son los mínimos y necesarios para describir metas y lo mismo para el componente *project* que relaciona términos como proyecto y estrategia. Como el lector podrá conjeturar, por ejemplo, para el término *Project Management* muchos otros términos específicos podrían relacionarse, no representados en nuestra base conceptual dado el alcance y foco de nuestro objetivo de investigación.

4 Ilustrando Metas de Mejora: Caso de Facebook

A seguir, presentamos una prueba de concepto instanciando los términos de las subontologías propuestas, ilustrando un caso de evaluación y mejora de un sistema, dirigido por metas multinivel y estrategias. Se utilizará el estudio de evaluación de la aplicación Facebook para smartphones [15] con el fin de detectar problemas de usabilidad y recomendar acciones de cambio para mejorar las debilidades encontradas. Cabe aclarar que en [15] no se tuvo en cuenta metas a diferentes niveles organizacionales, sino que solo se consideró una meta del proyecto, a nivel operativo.

Supongamos que la organización "*XYZ*" establece a nivel estratégico la siguiente meta de negocio "*Incrementar el 20% de usuarios de la aplicación móvil Facebook para el próximo año*", la cual es operacionalizada por un proyecto concreto. Para esta meta, según la Fig. 2, se establecen las siguientes submetas: (1) "*Incrementar 5% la publicidad de la aplicación móvil Facebook*" (a nivel táctico), y (2) "*Mejorar un 10% la usabilidad de la aplicación móvil Facebook en 6 meses*" (a nivel operativo).

Respecto de la submeta de negocio (2), se puede alcanzar realizando cambios dirigidos por ME, a la aplicación móvil Facebook, y así mejorarla. Por lo tanto, esta submeta de negocio es operacionalizada por un proyecto de MEC. Para esta submeta se puede establecer una meta de necesidad de información que le de soporte, por ej. "*Analizar si la usabilidad ha mejorado en un 10% luego de realizarse cambios en la aplicación*", y así comprender en qué medida se ha alcanzado la submeta de negocio. Notar que la submeta (1) no será analizada dado que seguramente requerirá de subobjetivos, proyectos y estrategias relacionadas con el área de marketing, lo cual está fuera del alcance de este artículo.

Como parte de la gestión del proyecto de MEC antes citado y de su ciclo de vida, se instancia la estrategia GOCAME para cambios ("*GOCAMEC*") con el propósito de mejorar una vista de calidad. En [19] analizamos cómo instanciar estrategias a partir de un patrón de estrategia, discusión que reanudaremos en la Sección 5.

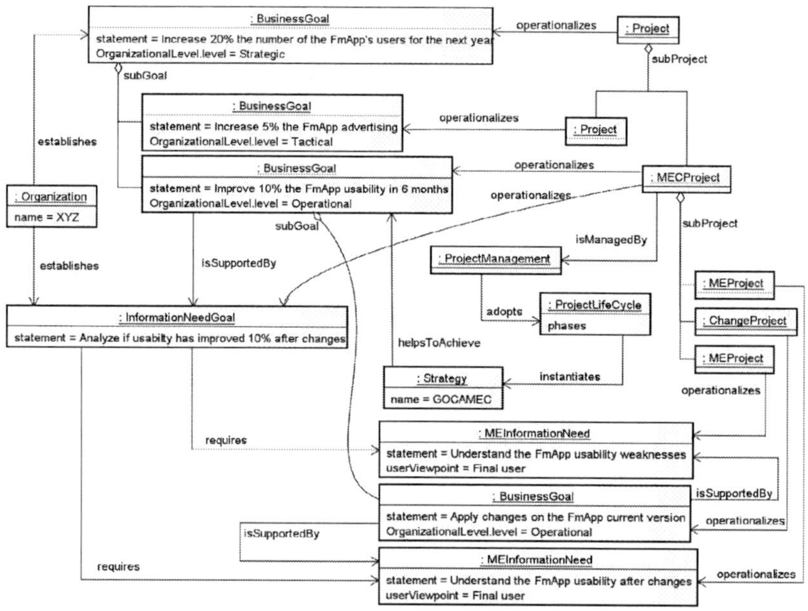

Fig. 2. Instanciación de un escenario, donde una Meta de Negocio de nivel estratégico se descompone en submetas que son soportadas por Metas de Necesidad de Información que requieren a su vez de metas de Necesidad de Información de Medición y Evaluación. Nota: FmApp significa *Facebook mobile Application* y ME, *Measurement and Evaluation*.

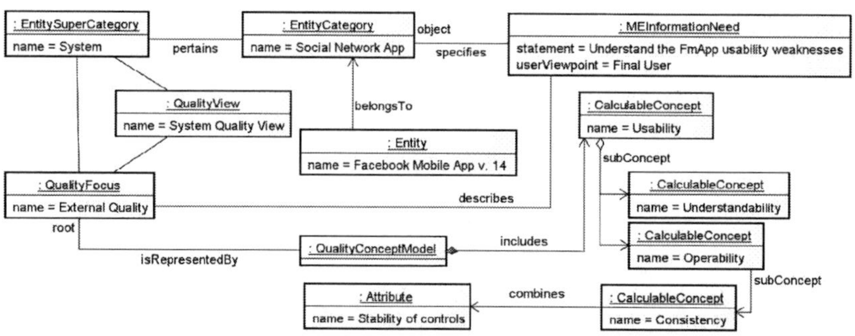

Fig. 3. Instanciación de una Meta de Necesidad de Información de ME.

Por ejemplo, GoMEC_1QV (*Goal-oriented Measurement, Evaluation and Change for one Quality View*) es un patrón de estrategia aplicable a proyectos de MEC para una vista de calidad. Este patrón tiene como propósito comprender la situación actual de una entidad y mejorarla, con respecto a un foco de calidad, en un contexto dado, mediante el empleo sistemático y disciplinado de procesos y métodos de medición, evaluación, análisis y cambio [19]. En síntesis, este patrón de estrategia embebe tres submetas tales como: comprender el estado actual del ente, realizar los cambios, y comprender el estado ulterior (la mejora) del ente. Para nuestro caso, las tres submetas que instancia la estrategia GOCAMEC son: "*Comprender debilidades de usabilidad de la aplicación móvil Facebook*"; "*Aplicar cambios en la versión actual de la aplicación móvil Facebook*"; y "*Comprender la usabilidad de la aplicación móvil Facebook luego de los cambios*". Analizando la Fig. 2, de las tres submetas, la segunda es una de negocio que se operacionaliza por medio de un proyecto de cambio. Las submetas restantes son de necesidad de información de ME, que se operacionalizan mediante proyectos de ME. Estos tres subproyectos componen a su vez al proyecto de MEC que se lleva a cabo usando la estrategia GOCAMEC.

Por otra parte, una meta de necesidad de información de ME, especifica (*specifies*) una categoría de entidad y describe (*describes*) un foco de calidad (ver Fig. 1, paquete *non-functional requirements*). La Fig. 3 instancia a dichos términos para la meta de necesidad de información de ME "*Comprender debilidades de usababilidad de la aplicación móvil Facebook*". Concretamente, el foco es "*Calidad Externa*" y se representa por (*isRepresentedBy*) un modelo de calidad que incluye a "*Usabilidad*" como concepto calculable (característica), y a "*Understandability*" y "*Operability*" como subcaracterísticas. A su vez, las subcaracterísticas combinan atributos (notar que la Fig. 3 solo incluye un atributo a fin de no sobrecargar el diagrama; el árbol completo se puede ver en [15]). La categoría de entidad es "*Aplicación de red social*" y pertenece a la supercategoría de entidad "*Sistema*". Tal como se observa en el paquete *quality view* de la Fig. 1, el foco y la supercategoria de entidad determinan la vista de calidad. Para nuestro ejemplo, la vista considerada es "*Calidad de Sistema*".

En definitiva, empleando la estrategia GOCAMEC se puede apreciar la mejora lograda luego de realizar las mediciones y evaluaciones (usando indicadores) para cada ciclo (notar que se podría requerir más de un ciclo de cambio, dentro del tiempo establecido). Por ende, la estrategia permite "*analizar si la usabilidad ha mejorado en un 10% luego de realizarse cambios en la aplicación*", y así comprender en qué medida se ha alcanzado la submeta de negocio relacionada que indicaba "*mejorar un 10% la usabilidad de la aplicación móvil Facebook en 6 meses*".

Resumiendo, esta prueba de concepto ha ilustrado que una meta de negocio a nivel estratégico puede descomponerse en submetas de niveles inferiores, y que las metas de necesidad de información (particularmente las de ME) brindan soporte a las metas de negocio. Este alineamiento entre metas multinivel permite organizar de un modo eficaz el trabajo en proyectos, y favorece a tomar decisiones más justificadas.

5 Discusión sobre Patrones de Estrategia y su Utilidad para dar Soporte a Metas

En todo proyecto es necesario instanciar estrategias que provean un curso de acción específico que ayuden a alcanzar la meta establecida. Por ej., en proyectos donde el propósito de la meta es *comprender* la situación actual de una entidad, se deben instanciar estrategias de ME; y donde el propósito es *mejorar* una entidad, realizando cambios dirigidos por ME, se deben instanciar estrategias de MEC. Además, al momento de seleccionar una estrategia de MEC se debe tener presente la cantidad de vistas de calidad involucradas. En [20] especificamos la subontología de vistas de calidad y definimos vista de calidad (*Quality View*) como la asociación entre una supercategoría de entidad (*Entity SuperCategory*) y un foco de calidad (*QualityFocus*) (ver Fig. 1). Para el escenario de la Fig. 3, la "*Vista de Calidad de Sistema*" asocia el foco "*Calidad Externa*" y la supercategoría "*Sistema*". Considerando el propósito de una meta y la cantidad de vistas de calidad involucradas, en esta sección describimos el concepto de patrón de estrategia y su utilidad al momento de instanciar estrategias.

La experiencia adquirida al desarrollar y utilizar estrategias de ME y MEC como GOCAME y SIQinU nos ha permitido observar que a menudo los proyectos, aunque con diferentes metas, comparten el mismo propósito y cantidad de vistas. Así, una misma estrategia puede aplicarse a diferentes proyectos de ME o MEC, y por ende, es posible desarrollar un conjunto de patrones de estrategia que brinden una solución flexible e instanciable [19]. Los patrones de estrategia establecen un curso de acción genérico indicando qué actividades deben ser instanciadas para alcanzar la meta. A su vez proveen especificaciones de métodos que indican cómo llevar a cabo las actividades genéricas que el patrón propone. Además cuentan con la especificación de un marco conceptual del domino en el cual se aplican. En definitiva, un patrón de estrategia provee una solución (estructura) que se corresponde con el principio de las tres capacidades integradas comentadas en la Sección 3, a saber: una especificación del proceso, una especificación de métodos, y un marco conceptual de dominio.

Retomando el escenario de la Sección 4, la declaración (*statement*) de la meta de negocio "*mejorar un 10% la usabilidad de la aplicación móvil Facebook en 6 meses*" embebe el propósito (*purpose*) de *mejorar* en un período (*timeframe*) de 6 meses. A su vez, para esta meta la única vista a considerar es la de *Calidad de Sistema*, ya que la entidad a evaluar y mejorar es la aplicación móvil Facebook (cuya supercategoría es *Sistema*) considerando subcaracterísticas de *Usabilidad* (que forman parte del foco *Calidad Externa*). Dado que se busca *mejorar una vista de calidad*, el patrón adecuado a seleccionar e instanciar es GoMEC_1QV. En [19] se indica que este patrón "*se aplica a proyectos de MEC donde el propósito es comprender y mejorar la entidad evaluada y que involucra una sola vista de calidad, como por ejemplo la Vista de Calidad de Sistema, la Vista de Calidad de Producto software, entre otras*". En la Fig. 3 observamos que para alcanzar esta meta se utiliza la estrategia GOCAMEC, la cual personaliza el proceso definido en este patrón. A su vez, esta meta involucra a tres submetas que GOCAMEC debe instanciar y que surgen de las actividades que la especificación del proceso del patrón prescribe.

Supongamos que otra meta de negocio de nivel operativo sea "*mejorar un 10% la satisfacción del usuario contemplando potenciales mejoras en la aplicación móvil Facebook, en 6 meses*". Por un lado, Satisfacción es una característica incluida en el modelo de Calidad en Uso [10], la cual se relaciona con la vista de Calidad de Sistema en Uso [20]. Por otro lado, dado que se propone realizar cambios sobre la aplicación móvil Facebook, también intervendrá la vista de Calidad de Sistema, sabiendo de antemano que la Calidad Externa influye a la Calidad en Uso. Esta declaración (*statement*) de la meta permite seleccionar e instanciar al patrón GoMEC_2QV. Este patrón de estrategia se aplica cuando el propósito de la meta es *mejorar* una entidad a partir de cambios realizados en otra entidad relacionada, considerando *dos vistas de calidad*. En este escenario, la mejora esperada de la satisfacción de usuario (vista de Calidad de Sistema en Uso) se alcanza realizando cambios/mejoras sobre la aplicación Facebook (vista de Calidad de Sistema) a partir del conocimiento que se tiene de las relaciones de *dependencia* (*dependsOn*) e *influencia* (*influences*) entre estas dos vistas de calidad [10, 20]. Por lo tanto, a diferencia del patrón de estrategia GoMEC_1QV, ahora se involucran a dos vistas de calidad bajo la premisa de que comprender problemas de calidad en uso ayuda a derivar atributos de calidad externa relevantes que, si se mejoran, pueden impactar positivamente en la calidad en uso del sistema. En definitiva, esta meta involucra a un conjunto de cinco submetas que la estrategia SIQinU [12] instancia y que surgen de las actividades que la especificación del proceso del patrón GoMEC_2QV prescribe.

En síntesis, un patrón de estrategia, es una solución reusable en proyectos con metas diferentes pero con propósitos comunes. Los patrones de estrategia que se instancian por medio de estrategias ME/MEC embeben el conocimiento que permite determinar cuáles son las submetas que requiere la meta de necesidad de información que da soporte a la meta de negocio a alcanzar.

6 Conclusiones y Trabajo Futuro

En este artículo hemos presentado una propuesta que considera la vinculación entre metas de ME a nivel operativo con metas de negocio a distintos niveles organizacionales. Además, se ha tenido en cuenta la selección de patrones de estrategia que permiten a su vez instanciar estrategias específicas que ayudan a alcanzar la meta establecida del proyecto.

Respecto a las contribuciones listadas en la Introducción, cabe concluir que se ha extendido la base conceptual del marco C-INCAMI mediante la incorporación de dos componentes: el de metas de negocio (paquete *business goal*), y el de proyecto (paquete *project*). Estos componentes contienen conceptos y relaciones de metas de negocio, metas de necesidad de información, proyecto, estrategia, entre otros, que a su vez están vinculados a términos de los componentes de requerimientos no funcionales y vistas de calidad, tal cual presentamos en la Sección 3. Es importante recalcar que los términos, relaciones y atributos incluidos en los nuevos componentes son los mínimos y necesarios para describir metas multinivel, proyectos y estrategias.

Luego en la Sección 4, hemos ilustrado el enfoque propuesto mediante una prueba de concepto en donde se vinculan metas de negocio a diferentes niveles organizacionales con metas de necesidad de información y de ME considerando como escenario la mejora de la aplicación móvil Facebook. Para operacionalizar la meta del proyecto mediante actividades y métodos de medición, evaluación, análisis y cambio, se ha discutido en la Sección 5 la utilidad de los patrones de estrategia, particularmente a los patrones GoMEC_1QV y GoMEC_2QV, los cuales permiten instanciar estrategias concretas de MEC para una y dos vistas de calidad.

Como trabajo futuro, se prevé modelar a la subontología de requerimientos funcionales y vincular sus términos con el concepto de meta de negocio del paquete *business goal* tal como hemos vinculado a la subontología de requerimientos no funcionales con el concepto de meta de necesidad de información. Para este fin, será valiosa también la consulta de ontologías fundacionales, como la documentada en [8].

Referencias

1. Barcellos M. P., Falbo R., Rocha A. R..: A Strategy for Preparing Software Organizations for Statistical Process Control. Brazilian Computer Society Journal, 19(4), pp. 445-473, (2013)
2. Basili V., Caldiera G., Rombach D.: Goal, Question, Metric Paradigm, Encyclopedia of Software Engineering, J.J. Marciniak, Ed., John Wiley & Sons, Vol., pp. 528-532, (1994)
3. Basili V., Lindvall M., Regardie M., Seaman C., Heidrich J., Jurgen M., Rombach D.,Trendowicz A.: Linking Software Development and Business Strategy through Measurement. IEEE Computer, 43:(4), pp. 57–65, (2010)
4. Becker P., Papa F., Olsina L.: Process Ontology Specification for Enhancing the Process Compliance of a Measurement and Evaluation Strategy. CLEI Elec J. 18:(1), pp. 1-26, (2015)
5. CMMI: Capability Maturity Model Integration Dev. v.1.3, CMU/SEI-2010-TR-033, (2010)
6. Curtis B., Kellner M., Over J.: Process Modelling. Com. of ACM, 35:(9), pp.75-90, (1992)
7. Goethert W., Fisher M.: Deriving Enterprise-Based Measures Using the Balanced Scorecard and Goal-Driven Measurement Techniques. Software Engineering Measurement and Analysis Initiative, CMU/SEI-2003-TN-024, (2003)
8. Guizzardi G., Falbo R., Guizzardi R: Grounding Software Domain Ontologies in the Unified Foundational Ontology (UFO): The case of the ODE Software Process Ontology. In IDEAS'08, Recife, Brazil, pp. 127-140, (2008)
9. ISO/IEC 15939: Software Engineering - Software Measurement Process, (2002)
10. ISO/IEC 25010: Systems and Software Engineering - Systems and Software Quality Requirements and Evaluation (SQuaRE) - System and Software Quality Models, (2011)
11. Kaplan R. S., Norton D. P.: The Balanced Scorecard: Translating Strategy into Action. Harvard Business Press, (1996)
12. Lew P., Olsina L., Becker P., Zhang L.: An Integrated Strategy to Understand and Manage Quality in Use for Web Applications, Req. Eng. Journal, 17:(4), pp. 299-330, (2012)
13. Olsina L., Martín M.: Ontology for Software Metrics and Indicators. Journal of Web Engineering, Rinton Press, USA, 2:(4), pp. 262-281, (2004)
14. Olsina L., Papa F., Molina H.: How to Measure and Evaluate Web Applications in a Consistent Way. Web Engineering: Modelling and Implementing Web Applications, Springer HCIS, Rossi G., Pastor O., Schwabe D., Olsina L. (Eds.), Ch.13, pp. 385-420, (2008)
15. Olsina L., Santos L., Lew P.: Evaluating Mobileapp Usability: A Holistic Quality Approach, In: 14th Int'l Conference on Web Engineering, ICWE 2014, Casteleyn S., Rossi G., and Winckler M. (Eds.): Springer, LNCS 8541, pp. 111-129, (2014)
16. Papa M.F.: Toward the Improvement of a Measurement and Evaluation Strategy from a Comparative Study, In LNCS 7703, Springer: Current Trends in Web Engineering, ICWE Int'l Workshops, Grossniklauss M. and Wimmer M. (Eds.), pp. 189-203, (2012)
17. Park R. E., Goethert W. B., Florac W. A.: Goal-Driven Software Measurement. A Guidebook. Carnegie-Mellon, Software Engineering Inst., TR. CMU/SEI-96-HB-002, (1996)
18. PMBOK: A Guide to the Project Management Body of Knowledge. 5th Edition, (2013)
19. Rivera M.B., Becker P., Olsina L.: Strategy Patterns for Measurement, Evaluation And Improvement Projects (In Spanish). In CIbSE'15, Lima, Perú, pp. 166-180, (2015)
20. Rivera B., Becker, P., Olsina L.: Extending the Conceptual Base for a Holistic Quality Evaluation Approach. 1st Argentine Symposium on Ontologies and their Applications (SAOA'15) Rosario, Argentina, ceur-ws.org/Vol-1449/, pp. 121-130, (2015)

This page intentionally left blank.

Track 2: 13th Experimental Software Engineering Latin America Workshop (ESELAW 2016) Preface

Welcome to the thirteenth edition of the Experimental Software Engineering Latin American Workshop (ESELAW 2016) held in Quito, Ecuador, at Universidad de las Fuerzas Armadas (ESPE), from the 27th to the 29th of April, 2016.

Over more than a decade, ESELAW has become an important forum for researchers and practitioners to report on and discuss new research results in Experimental Software Engineering, bringing together Latin America's academic, industrial and commercial communities. The workshop encourages the exchange of ideas to understand the strengths and weaknesses of software engineering technologies, focusing on the process, design and structure of experimental studies, as well as on results from specific studies. To strengthen its goal of becoming a landmark event on Experi-mental Software Engineering in Ibero-America, since 2011 ESELAW has been held in the context of CIbSE – the leading research forum on Software Engineering in Ibero-America.

ESELAW 2016 received a total of 40 full paper submissions, written in the three official languages of the conference (Spanish, Portuguese and English). The papers were peer-reviewed by three members of the Program Committee, composed of prom-inent researchers from an international community. After a careful revision process, 12 full high-quality scientific works were accepted (acceptance rate of 30 %), which shows the rigor of the process and the quality of the resulting program.

Emilia Mendes will give this year's keynote with the title: Improving and Estimat-ing the Value of Decisions. The program has been structured in 3 technical sessions: Session 1 - Development process and research methodology, Session 2 - Predictive models and estimation and Session 3 - Software testing and security.

We would like to acknowledge all people that have made possible the organization of ESELAW 2016: the authors who submitted their papers; the Program Committee members and the additional reviewers who made detailed revisions helping authors to build a high-quality program; and the organizing committee members who handled all the complexity of arranging an event such as CIbSE 2016. Finally, we want to offer a warm welcome to all speakers, authors, students and general audience who attend ESELAW 2016. We hope you enjoy the event.

Marcos Kalinowski and Martin Solari
ESELAW 2016 Program Committee co-chairs

ESLAW 2016 Program Committee

Raúl Antonio Aguilar Vera	Universidad Autónoma de Yucatán- Facultad de Matemáticas
Eduardo Almeida	CESAR - Recife Center for Advanced Studies and Systems
Marco Araujo	IF Sudeste MG
Claudia P. Ayala	Technical University of Catalunya
Ellen Barbosa	ICMC/USP
Monalessa Barcellos	UFES
Jose Antonio Cruz-Lemus	University of Castilla-La Mancha
Marcio Delamaro	Universidade de São Paulo
Arilo Claudio Dias-Neto	Federal University of Amazonas
Oscar Dieste	Universidad Politecnica de Madrid
Sandra Fabbri	UFSCar
Eduardo Figueiredo	Federal University of Minas Gerais
Felix Garcia	Alarcos Research Group, Information and Systems Department, Escuela Superior de informática, University of Castilla-La Mancha
Marcela Genero	University of Castilla-La Mancha
Marco Gerosa	IME - USP
Miguel Goulão	CITI, Departamento de Informática, Faculdade de Ciências e Tecnologia, Universidade Nova de Lisboa
Omar S. Gómez	Technical School of Chimborazo
Clemente Izurieta	Montana State University
Marcelo Jenkins	UCR
Marcos Kalinowski	Universidade Federal Fluminense
José Carlos Maldonado	ICMC-USP
Paulo Masiero	University of São Paulo
Santiago Matalonga	Universidad ORT Uruguay
Gerardo Matturro	Universidad ORT Uruguay
Emilia Mendes	The University of Auckland por Blekinge Institute of Technology, Sweden and University of Oulu, Finland
Daniel Méndez-Fernández	Technische Universität München
Oscar Pastor Lopez	Universitat Politécnica de Valencia
Rafael Prikladnicki	PUCRS
Fabio Q. B. Da Silva	Federal University of Pernambuco
Gabriela Robiolo	Universidad Austral
Gleison Santos	UNIRIO

Sergio Soares	Informatics Center - CIn/UFPE
Martin Solari	Universidad ORT Uruguay
Simone R. S. Souza	ICMC/USP
Rodrigo Spinola	Universidade Salvador
Guilherme Travassos	COPPE/UFRJ
Juan Pablo Ucán Pech	UADY
Auri Marcelo Rizzo Vincenzi	Instituto de Informática/Universidade Federal de Goiás
Raul Wazlawick	UFSC
Dietmar Winkler	Vienna University of Technology

Additional reviewers

Belgamo, Anderson
Borges, Vanessa
Brito, Maria
Carvallo, Juan Pablo
Cordeiro de Magalhães, Cleyton Vanut
Dias Valle, Pedro Henrique
Farias, Mário
Fernandes, Eduardo
Fontão, Awdren
Hackenberg, Georg
Hautmann, Benedikt
Kalinowski, Marcos
Machado, Ivan
Meireles, Silvia
Mendes, Thiago
Neves Esteca, Antonio Marcos
Ognawala, Saahil
Oliveira, Rafael A. P.
Ribeiro, Danilo
Rocca, Ignacio
Rodrigues, Anderson
Santos Nepomuceno, Vilmar
Santos, Ronnie E. S.
Saraiva, Juliana
Silva, Luciano
Silva, Rodolfo A.
Souza, Mauricio

ESELAW INDEX

Session 3: Software testing and security

Trabajo colaborativo en ambientes MDD: Un mapeo sistemático

Nicolás Rosso, Beatriz Marín

Escuela de informática y telecomunicaciones,
Universidad Diego Portales, Chile
{nicolas.rosso,beatriz.marin}@mail.udp.cl

Resumen El desarrollo de software dirigido por modelos (Model Driven Development - MDD por sus siglas en inglés) presenta importantes beneficios como por ejemplo la reducción del tiempo de desarrollo, la mejora en escalabilidad, y la mejora en la mantenibilidad del software. Bajo este paradigma es interesante conocer cómo interactúa un equipo de desarrollo en un ambiente MDD. El objetivo principal de este estudio es encontrar evidencia de estudios que contemplen el trabajo colaborativo en ambientes MDD. Para lograr este objetivo se ha realizado un mapeo sistemático de la literatura sobre trabajo colaborativo en ambientes MDD. Este trabajo presenta los resultados del mapeo sistemático y los desafíos que deben ser resueltos para proponer una metodología de trabajo colaborativo en un ambiente MDD.

1 Introducción

MDD utiliza modelos conceptuales en diferentes niveles de abstracción para generar el código del software mediante sucesivas transformaciones de modelos. Es decir, MDD [25], pone especial foco en la fase de diseño estableciendo que si el diseño se realiza bajo ciertos estándares y estructuras rigurosas pre-definidas (modelos conceptuales), la generación de código se puede realizar de forma automática, a través de un compilador de modelos que sólo necesite configuraciones mínimas de entorno.

La arquitectura dirigida por modelos - MDA [38] por sus siglas en inglés es el estándar promovido por el Object Managment Group que soporta MDD. MDA define 4 niveles para la transformación de modelos [23]: *(1) Modelo independiente de cómputo*, que se enfoca en el ambiente y los requisitos del sistema (p.ej., el diagrama de casos de uso); *(2) Modelo independiente de la plataforma*, que toma en cuenta las partes del sistema que se construirán, y define su funcionamiento interno, sin definir la plataforma en la que será implementada (p.ej., los diagramas conceptuales y de interacción); *(3) Modelo específico de la plataforma*, que define las características de la plataforma en la que se construirá el software; *(4) Modelo del código*, que es finalmente el código generado de forma automática.

Este paradigma trae importantes beneficios al desarrollo de software, como la producción de software de mayor calidad, ya que se evitan los errores manuales de programación debido a que el código se genera automáticamente a partir de transformaciones de modelo. Además, presenta mejoras en la mantenibilidad, ya que se cuenta con la especificación del software completa y actualizada para el código. Otro beneficio es la reducción del tiempo de desarrollo, ya que parte de las fases de análisis y diseño integran de forma automática la fase de construcción, esto gracias a la automatización del código, donde cada elemento del modelo representa una cantidad considerable de lineas de código [31].

Al utilizar MDD como paradigma de desarrollo, es importante tener en cuenta cómo participan los diferentes roles de los equipos de trabajo utilizando este paradigma, por lo que se vuelve interesante conocer: *¿Cómo interactúan los equipos de trabajo en proyectos desarrollados con MDD?*.

El manejo al interior de grupos de trabajos y como interactúan sus roles, es un área que se reconoce como trabajo colaborativo [7], que en síntesis cambia el manejo de grupos tradicionales enfocados sólo en resultados, por una gestión más horizontal que busca crear bases de conocimiento sólidas para llegar a resultados en base a la colaboración entre pares, y no a la realización de tareas de forma separada y segregada sin interacción entre los roles de un equipo de desarrollo.

El trabajo colaborativo es esencial en el desarrollo de software, por esto es que en este artículo se presentan los resultados de un mapeo sistemático de la literatura que busca evidencia de cómo se realiza trabajo colaborativo para un equipo de desarrollo en un ambiente MDD. La principal motivación de este mapeo sistemático es poder encontrar evidencia de cómo se lleva a cabo el trabajo en un proyecto real en ambientes MDD, y cómo se deberían tener en cuenta los conceptos del trabajo colaborativo para facilitar la adopción de MDD.

El artículo esta estructurado de la siguiente forma: La sección II presenta el trabajo relacionado. La sección III presenta el método utilizado para realizar el mapeo. La sección IV muestra cómo se realizó la revisión de forma detallada, y la sección V se presenta el análisis de los resultados y las amenazas a la validez del estudio. Finalmente, la sección VI presenta las conclusiones de la investigación.

2 Trabajos relacionados

El modelado colaborativo es una forma novedosa de enfrentar las fases de diseño en la empresa, ya que deja el concepto en donde sólo una persona trabaja sobre un modelo, y en su lugar, especifica ciertas estructuras de trabajo para poder generar modelos considerando un equipo de desarrollo [29]. Un símil es la programación en pareja *(PairProgramming)* [41], en donde se detalla cómo dos personas trabajan sobre una misma solución, definiendo roles y formas de trabajo colaborativo. Así, se buscaría llevar las ventajas que la programación en parejas genera a la etapa de diseño mediante el modelado colaborativo.

Esta idea se puede encontrar en [29], que presenta cómo se trabaja en la integración de modelos, identificando 3 métodos principales: (1) La integración de modelos es realizada de forma automática, (2) la integración se decide por el grupo de modelado, y (3) un híbrido de éstas. Asimismo, define como desafío el tamaño de los grupos de modelado, ya que muestra que no deberían haber grupos de trabajo más grande que 7 personas para que un líder pueda mantener el orden sobre el modelo.

Además, el trabajo presentado en [29] menciona la importancia de incluir a los stakeholders en la etapa de resolución de conflictos para la unión de modelos, asegurando que mejora la eficiencia y rectitud de los modelos en una etapa final, y lo deja como trabajo futuro. Otro de los desafíos es la elección de un punto de inicio del modelo, es decir, para trabajar con colaboración de modelos se debe seleccionar un modelo que genere consenso, y en base a éste realizar las modificaciones, la elección de este punto y quien realiza este modelo inicial son vitales para las siguientes iteraciones sobre el modelo. Como desafío final, en [29] se propone para la integración de submodelos realizados en paralelo la creación de reglas estrictas que permitan realizar este proceso de forma ordenada. Así, este trabajo presenta información de gran utilidad para poder entender el trabajo colaborativo en un ambiente MDD.

El trabajo presentado en [26] es un estudio terciario de modelado colaborativo. La búsqueda arrojó sólo un estudio [28] en las bibliotecas Springer y Google Scholar. Este trabajo está basado en modelado gráfico, dejando fuera el modelado de artefactos o arquitecturas. Si bien da lineamientos de cómo se debe trabajar en un ambiente de colaboración, al no estar enfocado a fases de diseño de productos de software se debe considerar esta inspección como el origen para poder armar la revisión de trabajo colaborativo en MDD.

3 Método de investigación

Un mapeo sistemático es un estudio secundario que busca identificar y clasificar toda la investigación relacionada a un tema en particular [26]. Un mapeo es similar a una revisión sistemática de la literatura (SLR), pero se diferencia principalmente en que no se enfoca en buscar evidencias empíricas como una SLR.. En resumen, un mapeo sistemático presenta una idea general de la información encontrada asociada a un tema.

El proceso definido por Kitchenham [16] consiste en: definir las preguntas de investigación, realizar la búsqueda de estudios primarios, definir criterios de inclusión y exclusión, y aplicarlos para seleccionar los estudios, extraer la información relevante, y finalmente, la construcción del mapeo.

3.1 Pregunta de investigación

La pregunta de investigación refleja el objetivo de la revisión, que en este caso es identificar y clasificar todos los estudios que muestren evidencia de trabajo colaborativo en un ambiente de desarrollo de software dirigido por modelos. Para poder lograr este objetivo se ha definido la siguiente pregunta:

RQ1: ¿Qué evidencia existe de trabajo colaborativo utilizando desarrollo de software dirigido por modelos?

En particular, se han considerado las siguientes características relevantes para este estudio: Desarrollo dirigido por modelos, diagrama de clases o UML, herramienta colaborativa, herramienta MDD, caso de estudio, roles modelado y etapas de desarrollo.

La revisión está estructurada por los siguientes criterios PICOC [39], por su sigla en inglés:

- **Población:** Estudios sobre desarrollo de software basados en modelos.
- **Intervención:** Estudios sobre trabajo en equipo.
- **Comparación:** Los trabajos son comparados en base a las características presentadas anteriormente.
- **Resultado:** Identificar una metodología de desarrollo para MDD basada en la colaboración.
- **Contexto:** No existen restricciones de contexto es decir, se buscan evidencias tanto en la industria como en la academia.

3.2 Estrategia de búsqueda y selección de de bibliotecas digitales

La selección de bibliotecas digitales como fuente de información se debe a que la búsqueda en formatos físicos tiene una dificultad importante en la facilidad de acceso, ya que aunque se cuente con una buena biblioteca del tema, es prácticamente imposible poder contar con la cantidad de fuentes que las bibliotecas digitales entregan. En estas bibliotecas digitales se ingresa un string de búsqueda, que corresponde a una frase con operadores lógicos, construida con los conceptos a buscar. Este string de búsqueda debe representar completamente la pregunta de investigación, sin dejar información fuera de la búsqueda.

Para realizar el string de búsqueda se desglosó la pregunta en los siguientes conceptos claves: Modelado colaborativo y MDD. Se trabajó con los conceptos en inglés, y se buscaron las distintas formas en que estos conceptos pueden presentarse en la literatura. Así, el string de búsqueda es:

- *("collaborative modeling" OR "cooperative modeling" OR "collaborative process modeling") AND(("MDD")OR("MDA")OR("MDE")OR("model driven development")OR("model-driven development")OR("model driven engineering")OR("model-driven engineering") OR("model driven architecture")OR("model-driven architecture"))*

El proceso de búsqueda se realizó en 3 bibliotecas distintas, ACM Digital Library, IEEE Xplore y Springer Link. Además, se complementó con Google Scholar, revisando que los trabajos que son seleccionados en las bibliotecas digitales aparezcan en la búsqueda realizada en Google Schoolar.

La selección de las bibliotecas se realizó debido a la fidelidad respecto a la calidad de las publicaciones que contienen. Son bibliotecas con gran reconocimiento, que poseen evaluadores destacados y, además, cuenta con la condicionante que para publicar en ellas se tienen que tener estudios avanzados en el área.

3.3 Selección de estudios

Para seleccionar los estudios lo primero es entrar a la biblioteca digital seleccionada, luego ingresar el string de búsqueda en el campo requerido, para poder agregar los criterios de inclusión las bibliotecas cuentan con filtros tipo checkbox, si es que no lo tienen como en el caso de Google Scholar, se filtran en el momento de la lectura de título y abstract. Los criterios de inclusión y exclusión se presentan en la Tabla 1. Con todo esto se empieza la lectura de título y abstract. Con la información obtenida se define si un estudio podría ser útil, si no lo es, se pasa a otro estudio, si puede serlo, se lee la introducción, con esta información ya se puede decidir si un estudio se agrega a la lista de aceptados, si es que no se agrega se puede optar por leer el estudio completo, o rechazarlo y seguir con el siguiente estudio. Este proceso se puede ver claramente en la Figura 1, que muestra un BPMN con el proceso de selección de estudios.

Tabla 1. Criterios de inclusión y exclusión

Criterios de inclusión	Criterios de exclusión
- Sólo se incluirán estudios realizados en inglés. - Se considerarán estudios posteriores al 2004, ya que en este año se identifican las primeras publicaciones de MDD cómo una tecnología real de desarrollo. - En bibliotecas que no sean específicas en ciencias de la computación, se seleccionarán sólo estudios referentes a esta categoría.	- Se excluyeron documentos como tesis, prólogos, introducciones, etc. Es decir cualquier estudio que no este presentado en un formato de artículo científico.
- Estudios que sólo abarquen desarrollo de software y no otras áreas de las ciencias de la computación.	- Estudios ya seleccionados en revisiones anteriores.

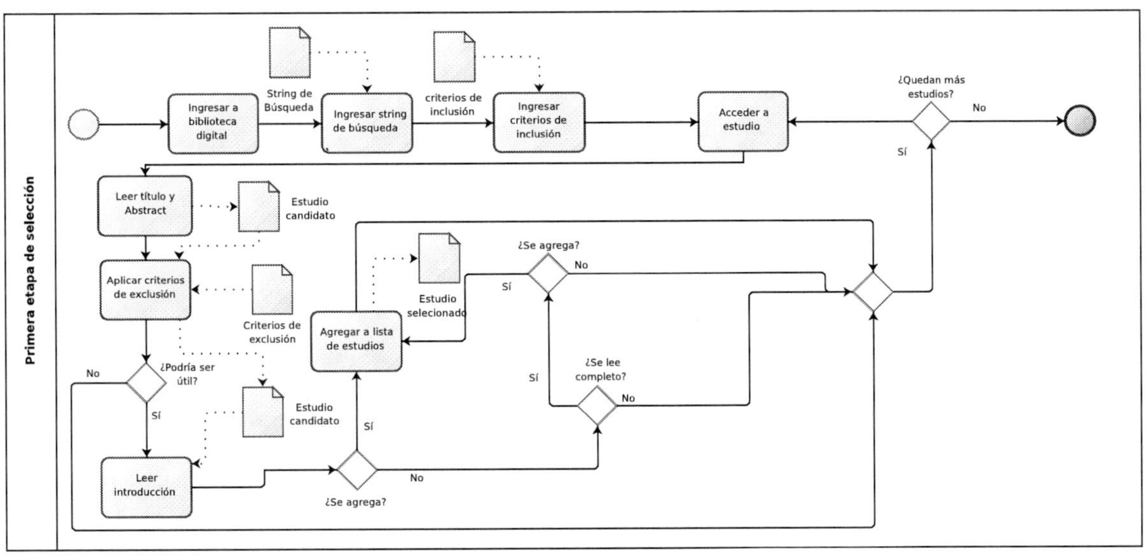

Fig. 1. Proceso de selección de estudios.

3.4 Extracción de Datos

Una vez ejecutada la búsqueda de información, es necesario seleccionar aquella que sea relevante para la investigación. Para ello se ideó una tabla que permite evaluar los estudios encontrados y con ello poder resumir la información extraída. La tabla se crea en base a las guías propuestas en [15].

Estos conceptos se desprenden de lo que se considera debe tener trabajo colaborativo en ambientes MDD, es decir los conceptos Desarrollo dirigido por modelos, Diagrama de clases, UML, Herramienta colaborativa, Herramienta MDD, Caso de estudio, Roles de modelado y Etapas de Desarrollo. Para cada concepto se define un valor booleano, con valor Sí si el concepto es mencionado en el estudio y No en caso contrario. Luego, se realiza una evaluación dependiendo del grado de profundidad en una escala Likert de 1 a 5. Es importante aclarar que la evaluación no es sobre la calidad del estudio, sino que es sobre cuánto se adecua el concepto a la pregunta de investigación y su nivel de profundidad y utilidad.

4 Ejecución de la revisión

La ejecución de la revisión comenzó en 03-05-2014 y terminó el 15-07-2014. La última actualización, presentada en este estudio, finalizó el 11-12-2015.

Se definieron dos iteraciones, la primera consiste en filtrar los estudios encontrados por una revisión del contenido del título y de contenido del resumen, y además en caso de ser necesario la introducción. La segunda etapa fue la lectura completa de los estudios, buscando la presencia de los contenidos de la Tabla 3, y con ésto llegar a los estudios que finalmente constituirán el mapeo. Los resultados de la primera iteración se presentan en la Tabla 2:

Tabla 2. Resultados de estudios encontrados

Bibliotecas	**Encontrados**	**Útiles**
Springer Link	119	8
ACM Digital Library	117	6
IEEE Xplore Digital Library	0	0
Google Scholar	284	13
Total	*520*	*27*

Uno de los mayores problemas de la ejecución fue los extraños resultados en IEEE Xplore Digital Library, que no arrojó resultados, por esto mismo se realizaron esfuerzos generalizando aún más el string de búsqueda para poder encontrar resultados asociados a la pregunta de investigación. Sin embargo, los esfuerzos al ampliar el espectro de búsqueda no proporcionaron resultados por muy general que fueran los cambios que se le realizaran al string de búsqueda.

Se buscó certificar que los estudios que se encontraron útiles en Springer Link aparecieran en la búsqueda realizada en Google Scholar, utilizando este método para corroborar el string de búsqueda y su validez, los resultados fueron satisfactorios por lo que se continúo utilizando el string planteado.

Otro de los hechos que causaron extrañeza fue que estudios encontrados en Google Scholar estaban presentes en IEEE Xplore. Una de las explicaciones a esto es que Google Scholar funciona diferente, ya que busca en todo el documento a diferencia de IEEE Xplore que busca en la metadata.

En la segunda iteración se toman los 27 estudios encontrados, ver la Tabla 2, y se someten a evaluación según los conceptos presentados anteriormente. Sólo se dejan como estudios útiles los que tienen al menos un concepto presente y poseen una evaluación mayor a 1, o más de un concepto presente. Se pueden ver todos los estudios analizados, y los conceptos que fueron encontrados para cada uno en la Tabla 3.

Tabla 3. Trabajos con presencia de conceptos

	MDD	Diagrama de clases	UML	Herramienta colaborativa	Herramienta MDD	Caso de estudio	Roles de modelado	Etapas de desarrollo
[34]	Sí	No	Sí	No	No	Sí	No	Sí
[36]	No	No	Sí	Sí	No	No	No	No
[33]	No	No	Sí	Sí	No	No	No	No
[27]	No	Sí	Sí	Sí	No	No	No	No
[6]	Sí	Sí	No	Sí	No	Sí	Sí	No
[40]	Sí	Sí	Sí	Sí	No	Sí	No	No
[24]	No	No	No	No	No	No	No	No
[30]	No	No	No	No	No	No	No	No
[14]	Si	No	No	No	No	No	No	Si
[10]	No	No	No	Si	No	No	No	No
[21]	No	No	No	No	No	No	No	No
[19]	Si	No	No	No	No	No	No	Si
[4]	Si	No	No	No	No	No	No	Si
[20]	No	No	No	No	No	No	No	No
[18]	Sí	No	No	Sí	No	No	No	No
[12]	Sí	Sí	Sí	Sí	No	Sí	No	No
[2]	No	Sí	No	Sí	Sí	No	No	No
[8]	No	No	No	Sí	No	No	No	No
[11]	No	No	No	No	No	No	No	No
[22]	Sí	Sí	Sí	Sí	Sí	No	No	No
[9]	No	No	No	No	No	No	No	No
[37]	No	No	No	No	No	No	No	No
[13]	No	Sí	No	Sí	No	No	No	No
[3]	No	No	No	Sí	No	No	No	No
[5]	Sí	No	Sí	Sí	No	No	No	No
[17]	No	No	No	Sí	No	Sí	No	No
[32]	No	No	No	Sí	No	No	No	No

Existen sólo 19 estudios que cumplen con las características definidas, ver Tabla 4. Estos estudios son los que fueron analizados y valorados.

Tabla 4. Resultados de papers encontrados

Bibliotecas	**Útiles**
Springer Link	6
ACM	3
Google Scholar	10
Total	*19*

Como se dijo previamente la valoración se confecciona en base a los términos presentados en la Tabla 3, por lo que primero se debe mostrar el resultado de la evaluación a cada estudio (Ver Tabla 5).

Tabla 5. Evaluación de conceptos

	MDD	Diagrama de clases	UML	Herramienta colaborativa	Herramienta MDD	Caso de estudio	Roles de modelado	Etapas de desarrollo
[34]	3	0	2	0	0	1	0	4
[36]	0	0	1	3	0	0	0	0
[33]	0	0	3	4	0	0	0	0
[27]	0	4	2	4	0	0	0	0
[6]	2	5	0	5	0	1	2	0
[40]	2	5	2	2	0	1	0	0
[14]	3	0	0	0	0	0	0	3
[19]	1	0	0	0	0	0	0	2
[4]	1	0	0	0	0	0	0	3
[18]	2	0	0	4	0	0	0	0
[12]	1	2	2	2	0	1	0	0
[2]	0	1	0	2	1	0	0	0
[8]	0	0	0	2	0	0	0	0
[22]	2	1	1	3	1	0	0	0
[13]	0	1	0	2	0	0	0	0
[3]	0	0	0	2	0	0	0	0
[5]	1	0	2	2	0	0	0	0
[17]	0	0	0	1	0	1	0	0
[32]	0	0	0	2	0	0	0	0

5 Análisis de resultados y amenazas

Realizada la evaluación de cada estudio, se hace un análisis de los valores obtenidos para cada concepto en los 19 estudios, el resultado de este análisis se muestra en la Figura 2. Se utiliza la mediana ya que es menos susceptible a valores atípicos.

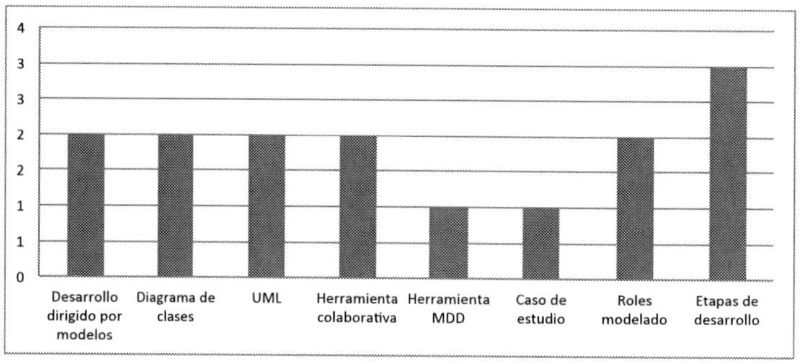

Fig. 2. Mediana de conceptos sin valores nulos.

Además, estos valores promedios sólo se pueden entender si se sabe cuántos estudios fueron encontrados para cada valor (Ver la Figura 3).

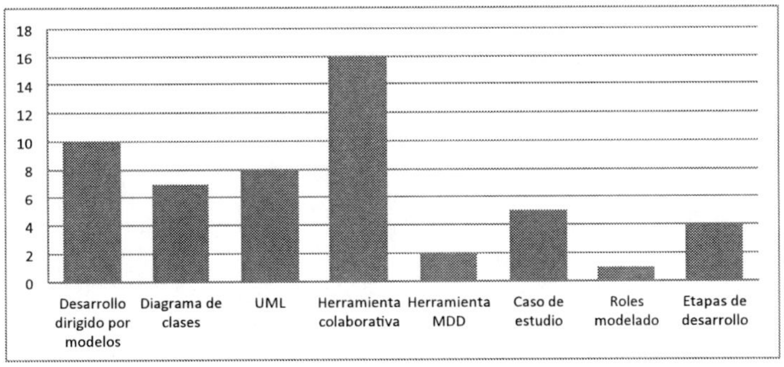

Fig. 3. Cantidad de estudios para cada concepto.

Se puede tender a pensar que si estos estudios se han seleccionado deben tener al menos los conceptos definidos en el string de búsqueda. Sin embargo, muchos de los estudios mencionan la utilidad que una herramienta de modelado colaborativo puede tener en desarrollo de software dirigido por modelos, pero no se profundiza en ésto, simplemente lo nombran como un posible impacto dentro de los estudios. Tampoco es presentado en ningún estudio como trabajo futuro, es decir, el foco que se presenta en todos los estudios que se revisaron no se acerca a integrar los dos focos de la pregunta, que son la colaboración en el modelado y el desarrollo de software dirigido por modelos.

Otra forma de ver los datos es sopesar cuántos conceptos hay presentes al mismo tiempo en cada estudio. Se debe tener en cuenta que los conceptos *UML* y *diagrama de clases* son contados con la operación lógica OR, debido a que son complementarios y existiendo al menos uno de los dos es suficiente, no presentaría un valor agregado al estudio que aparezcan ambos conceptos. En base a lo anteriormente descrito, se presenta la Figura 4 que muestra cuantos estudios tienen una cantidad de conceptos presentes:

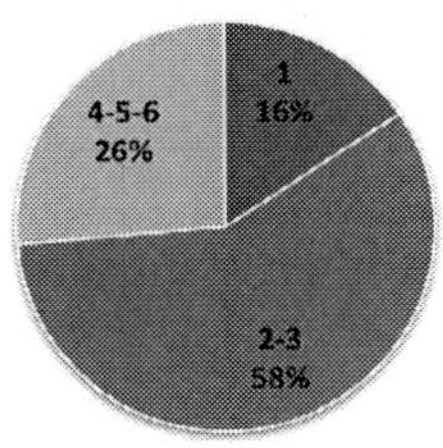

Fig. 4. Cantidad de conceptos presentes por estudio.

Con esto ya se tiene una idea de que prácticamente no se encuentran estudios en la actualidad que estén en la orientación que busca este mapeo. Esto se aprecia ya que un 58% de los estudios encontrados tienen solo 1 concepto que pueda ser evaluado (Figura 4). Estos conceptos son los que se encuentran en la Tabla 3.

El 42% que queda se podría decir que puede estar más cerca a lo que se está buscando. La forma de saberlo es poder observar qué grupos son los que se están formando. Para esto, se definieron cinco grupos de conceptos que reflejan cuáles serían relevantes si se presentasen juntos en el mismo estudio.

1. El primer grupo contiene lo mínimo de lo que se espera de un estudio al realizar esta investigación, es decir, que contenga los siguientes conceptos: Desarrollo de software dirigido por modelos; Herramienta de modelado colaborativo; Roles de modelado; y diagrama de clases o UML.
2. El segundo corresponde a un sub-grupo del anterior, sacando el concepto de roles de modelado.
3. El tercer grupo busca los siguientes conceptos, siendo el que se considera más completo: Herramienta colaborativa; Herramienta de desarrollo de software dirigido por modelos; Roles de modelado; y etapas de desarrollo.
4. El cuarto grupo es una generalización de lo presentado anteriormente, sólo buscando los siguientes conceptos: Desarrollo de software dirigido por modelos; Roles de modelado; Etapas de modelado.
5. Para finalizar, el quinto grupo está descrito por los siguientes conceptos: Herramienta de modelado colaborativo; y herramienta de desarrollo de software dirigido por modelos.

Los grupos están definidos para poder encontrar estudios que presenten información relacionada a nuestra pregunta de investigación, pero no de forma separada, más bien integrando el trabajo colaborativo con el desarrollo MDD. Al definir estos grupos se espera observar claramente cuántos de todos estos estudios pueden ser realmente útiles. El resultado es presentado en la Figura 5.

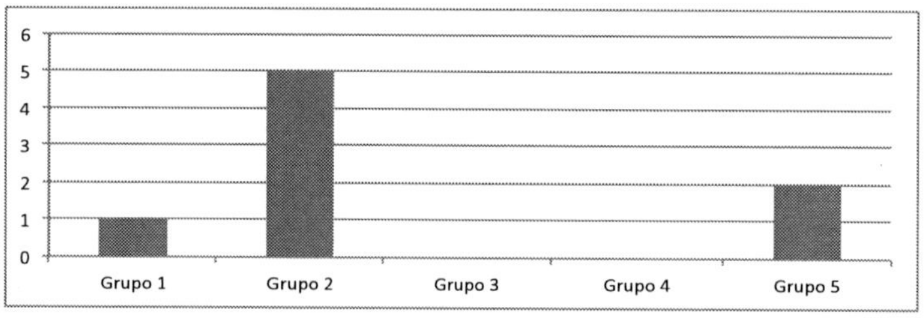

Fig. 5. Grupos de estudios.

Se aprecia en la Figura 5, que solo un estudio [6] cuenta con lo definido en el primer grupo, siendo éste el que más se acerca a lo buscado. Dentro de los datos que se encuentran en la tabla consolidada (Ver Tabla 5) sobre este estudio, se puede ver que tiene 5 de los 8 conceptos presentes, y además tiene una evaluación promedio de estos conceptos de 3, por lo que se puede considerar como el estudio más relevante dentro de la revisión.

Adicionalmente, se observa que para los grupos 3 y 4 no se encontraron estudios asociados. Esto representaría uno de los principales resultados de la investigación, debido a que muestra que al menos dentro de las bases de datos buscadas no se encontraron estudios que traten estos conceptos. Este mapeo propone como tema central el trabajo colaborativo en un ambiente MDD, y es importante señalar que si bien dentro de los estudios se habla de estos temas en común, en ninguno se trata con la profundidad que se podría esperar, ya que todos los estudios encontrados se centran principalmente en cómo hacer unión de modelos y cómo hacer que estos sean escalables y sujetos a control de versiones a través de los algoritmos que ellos mismos proponen.

5.1 Respuesta a la pregunta de investigación

RQ1: ¿Qué evidencia existe de trabajo colaborativo utilizando desarrollo de software dirigido por modelos?

En los resultados del mapeo no se encontró un estudio que conjuntamente hable de modelado colaborativo y MDD. Sin embargo, dos estudios presentan por separado estos conceptos: Modelado colaborativo con trabajo en MDD a nivel de diagramas en [6] y MDA llevado a la colaboración pero sin la definición de metodologías y roles en [34].

Además de estos dos estudios principales, existen otro grupo de estudios que hablan de la resolución de conflictos en la unión de modelos y manejo de versiones, que se puede realizar de forma síncrona o asíncrona [33]; esto quiere decir que si es asíncrona una persona es encargada de resolver los conflictos a mano, y manejar el mismo el documento final de modelado. Y la otra, que se propone en mayor medida, es la síncrona, que requiere de una arquitectura cliente-servidor, donde el servidor será el encargado de administrar las versiones de modelo, resaltar conflictos, y esperar resolución por parte de los distintos usuarios del modelo.

Para este tipo de resolución de conflictos son presentadas varias herramientas, siendo la más recurrente AMOR [1], que presenta el análisis de conflictos a través de una interfaz simple. Es importante señalar que AMOR es un plug-in de Eclipse [35], ya que esto permite una variedad e integración con otras herramientas de desarrollo que otros software de modelado no presentan.

5.2 Amenazas a la validez

La evaluación que se realiza de los estudios puede considerarse parcial, ya que no se entrega un método que permita replicar la misma evaluación, debido a que se define con nota 1 si el concepto es solamente mencionado, y nota 5 si el foco central del estudio es el trabajo colaborativo en ambientes MDD. Para mitigar esta amenaza, las notas intermedias se evaluaron mediante una escala Likert entre estos dos valores.

Si bien los conceptos en la Tabla 3 debieran estar presentes, ya que se infieren de los conceptos de trabajo colaborativo, o de MDD, éstos no se buscaron de forma explícita, por lo que una de las razones por las que no se encontraron fue porque no se estaban buscando aisladamente y con presencia clara en el string de búsqueda para cada concepto. Para mitigar esta amenaza, se considera que todos los contenidos que se buscaron derivan directamente de la pregunta de investigación, y para poder responder a ésta se debe explicar estos conceptos.

6 Conclusiones

Hoy en día es necesario contar con técnicas que permitan realizar el desarrollo de software de manera colaborativa y eficiente, y en este trabajo se ha realizado un mapeo sistemático de la literatura asociada a este tema. Los resultados muestran que si bien algunos estudios pueden tratar temas similares, no se encontró ninguno que cuente con el nivel de profundidad deseado, ya que se enfocaban principalmente en la unión de modelos, que si bien es algo necesario para llevar a cabo un modelado colaborativo, no es lo único a considerar para poder planificar un desarrollo de software dirigido por modelos en un ambiente colaborativo.

A pesar de que no se encontró una respuesta clara y completa, ya que dentro de la pregunta de investigación se desprenden dos conceptos importantes que no son respondidos en ningún estudio al mismo tiempo, sí se puede decir que se encontraron partes de esta respuesta. Entre ellas existen conceptos importantes como el plug-in para eclipse [1] que es una solución al modelado colaborativo que de forma simple busca emular el proceso de colaboración realizado en el desarrollo del código en un ambiente de modelado. El otro estudio importante es [34], que presenta varios de los conceptos buscados, presenta un ejemplo concreto de colaboración en MDA, definiendo un proceso de 12 pasos, y se centra en la colaboración del modelado y sus interacciones, pero sin definir la colaboración como un elemento a considerar en interacción de roles.

El principal beneficio que otorga esta investigación es demostrar con certeza que aún cuando se encontraron documentos que se pueden acercar a señalar herramientas para trabajo colaborativo, no realizan un análisis detallado de equipos de desarrollo, y de las etapas que lo conforman como el que se planteó inicialmente al analizar el trabajo colaborativo en ambientes MDD.

Hay desafíos que enfrentar como la correcta definición de los roles que participan en un proceso de desarrollo colaborativo, la especificación de la interacción que tienen estos roles, las actividades necesarias que se deben llevar a cabo para generar software utilizando MDD, y la construcción de herramientas que permitan llevar la gestión del proyecto de acuerdo al avance en las especificaciones bajo el paradigma MDD. Teniendo en cuenta que no se ha encontrado un trabajo que enfrente estos desafíos de manera conjunta, se hace necesario enfocarse en ellos para poder brindar una respuesta adecuada, en esa línea se define como trabajo futuro inmediato la creación de una metodología de trabajo colaborativo para un ambiente MDD. Además, en base a la metodología creada, se realizará un estudio empírico que permita hacer una evaluación clara de cómo afecta a MDD trabajar en un entorno colaborativo de desarrollo.

7 Agradecimientos

Este trabajo ha sido financiado por Universidad Diego Portales y FONDECYT (Chile) bajo el proyecto TESTMODE Ref. 11121395.

Referencias

1. Altmanninger, K., Kappel, G., Kusel, A., Retschitzegger, W., Schwinger, W., Seidl, M., Wimmer, M.: Amor – towards adaptable model versioning. 1st Int. Workshop on Model Co-Evolution and Consistency Management pp. 4–50 (2008)
2. Barteit, C., Molter, G., Schumann, T.: A model repository for collaborative modeling with the jazz development platform. IEEE pp. 1–10 (2009)
3. Bartelt, C.: Conflict analysis at collaborative development of domain specific models using description logics. IEEE pp. 1–9 (2011)
4. Bittar, T.J., Fortes, R.P., Lobato, L.L., Watanabe, W.M.: Web communication and interaction modeling using model-driven development. In: 27th ACM Int. Conference on Design of Communication. pp. 193–198. ACM (2009)
5. Brosch, P., Kargl, H., Langer, P., Seidl, M., Wieland, K., Wimmer, M., Kappel, G.: Conflicts as first-class entities: A uml profile for model versioning. Springer Berlin Heidelberg 6627, 184–193 (2011)
6. Brosch, P., Seidl, M., Konrad Wieland, M.W., Langer, P.: We can work it out: Collaborative conflict resolution in model versioning. Springer London pp. 207–214 (2009)
7. Carmel, E.: Global software teams: Collaborating across borders and time zones (1999)
8. Cicchetti, A., Muccini, H., Pelliccione, P., Pierantonio, A.: Towards a framework for distributed and collaborative modeling. IEEE pp. 149–154 (2009)
9. Dengler, F., Happel, H.J.: Collaborative modeling with semantic mediawiki. ACM pp. 1–2 (2010)
10. Espinazo-Pagán, J., García-Molina, J.: A homogeneous repository for collaborative mde. In: 1st Int. Work. on Model Comparison in Practice. pp. 56–65. ACM (2010)
11. Filipe Del Nero Grillo, Renata Pontin de Mattos Fortes, Lucredio, D.: Towards collaboration between sighted and visually impaired developers in the context of model-driven engineering. Anais do Simp. Brasileiro de Informática na Educação pp. 1–11 (2014)
12. Gallardo, J., Bravo, C., Redondo, M.A.: A model-driven development method for collaborative modeling tools. J. of Network and Computer Applications 35, 1086–1105 (2012)
13. Gallardo, J., Bravo, C., Redondo, M.A., de Lara, J.: Modeling collaboration protocols for collaborative modeling tools: Experiences and applications. Journal of Visual Languages & Computing 24, 10–23 (2013)
14. de Jesus Almeida, C.C., de Oliveira, A.A.: Qualitas: A proposal of process model development software driven models. In: 7th Euro American Conference on Telematics and Information Systems. pp. 28:1–28:4. ACM (2014)
15. Keele, Staffs: Guidelines for performing systematic literature reviews in software engineering. In: Technical report, Ver. 2.3 EBSE Technical Report. EBSE (2007)
16. Kitchenham, B.A., Budgen, D., Brereton, P.: Using mapping studies as the basis for further research – a participant-observer case study. Inf. Softw. Technol 53(6), 638–651 (2011)
17. Koegel, M., Naughton, H., Helming, J., Herrmannsdoerfer, M.: Collaborative model merging. ACM pp. 27–34 (2010)
18. Kolovos, D.S., Rose, L.M., Matragkas, N., Paige, R.F., Guerra, E., Cuadrado, J.S., De Lara, J., Ráth, I., Varró, D., Tisi, M., Cabot, J.: "a research roadmap towards achieving scalability in model driven engineering ". ACM pp. 1–10 (2013)

19. Loniewski, G., Insfran, E., Abrahão, S.: A systematic review of the use of requirements engineering techniques in model-driven development. In: 13th Int. Conf. on MDE Languages and Systems: Part II. pp. 213–227 (2010)
20. Marth, K., Ren, S.: Model-driven development with euml-arc. In: 27th Annual ACM Symposium on Applied Computing. pp. 1877–1882. ACM (2012)
21. Medeiros, A.L., Batista, T., Chavez, C.: Marisa-dp – from architecture to design: An mdd approach. In: 15th Workshop on Early Aspects. pp. 37–42. ACM (2009)
22. Michaux, J., Blanc, X., Shapiro, M.: A semantically rich approach for collaborative model edition. ACM Symposium on Applied Computing pp. 1–7 (2011)
23. Pastor, O., España, S., Panach, J.I., Aquino, N.: Model-driven development: Piecing together the mda jigsaw puzzle. Informatik-Spektrum 31(5), 394–407 (2008)
24. Pastor, O., Molina, J.C.: OO-method implementations. In: Model-Driven Architecture in Practice, pp. 289–291. Springer-Verlag Berlin Heidelberg (2007)
25. Pastor, O., Ruiz, M., España, S.: From requirements to code: A full model-driven development perspective. Springer Berlin Heidelberg 303, 56–70 (2013)
26. Petersen, K., Feldt, R., Mujtaba, S., Mattsson, M.: Systematic mapping studies in software engineering. British Computer Society pp. 68–77 (2008)
27. Phalp, K., Grimm, F., Xu, L.: Supporting collaborative work by preserving model meaning when merging graphical models. S. Berlin Heidelberg pp. 262–269 (2012)
28. Renger, M., Kolfschoten, G.L., de Vreede, G.J.: Challenges in collaborative modeling: a literature review. Springer Berlin Heidelberg 10, 61–77 (2008)
29. Renger, M., Kolfschoten, G.L., Vreede, G.J.D.: Challenges in collaborative modelling: a literature review and research agenda. Int. J. of Simulation and Process Modelling (2008)
30. Roa, J., Chiotti, O., Villarreal, P.: A verification method for collaborative business processes. Springer Berlin Heidelberg 99, 293–305 (2012)
31. Selic, B.: The pragmatics of model-driven development. Software, IEEE 20(5), 19–25 (2003)
32. Stephen Barrett, Patrice Chalin, G.B.: Model merging falls short of software engineering needs. INFERENCE pp. 1–10 (2008)
33. Taentzer, G., Ermel, C., Langer, P., Wimmer, M.: A fundamental approach to model versioning based on graph modifications: from theory to implementation. Springer Berlin Heidelberg 13, 239–272 (2014)
34. Tan, W., Ma, L., Xu, Z., Mao, J.: Application mda in a collaborative modeling environment. Springer Berlin Heidelberg 4740, 225–230 (2007)
35. The Eclipse Foundation: Eclipse (April 2015), `http://eclipse.org/`
36. Thum, C., Schwind, M., Schader, M.: Slima lightweight environment for synchronous collaborative modeling. Springer Berlin Heidelberg 5795, 135–151 (2009)
37. Tomaz, L., Nt, J., Xexeo, G., Souza, J.: Collaborative process modeling and reuse evaluation. In: Collaborative Computing: Networking, Applications and Worksharing, 2009. CollaborateCom 2009. pp. 1–9 (2009)
38. Valverde, F., Valderas, P., Fons, J., Pastor, O.: A mda-based environment for web applications development: From conceptual models to code. 6th Int. Workshop on Web-Oriented Software Technologies pp. 164–178 (2007)
39. Walker, J.J.: Systematic reviews in the social sciences: a practical guide. Sociology of Health and Illness 2, 318–319 (2007)
40. Wieland, K., Langer, P., Seidl, M., Wimmer, M., Kappel, G.: Turning conflicts into collaboration. Springer Netherlands 22, 181–240 (2013)
41. Williams, L., Kessler, R.R., Cunningham, W., Jeffries, R.: Strengthening the case for pair programming. IEEE software pp. 19–25 (2000)

Simulação de Ecossistemas de Software Móvel: Estado da Arte, Desafios e Oportunidades

Allan Bezerra[1,2], Awdren Fontão[1], Arilo Dias-Neto[1]

[1]Grupo de Experimentação e Teste de Software – ExperTS, ICOMP-UFAM, Manaus, AM
{allan.bezerra, awdren, arilo}@icomp.ufam.edu.br

[2]Samsung Ocean Center, UEA, Manaus, AM
allan.jsb@oceanbrasil.com

Resumo. Em um Ecossistema de Software Móvel (MSECO), fabricantes disponibilizam uma plataforma para desenvolvedores criarem aplicações móveis (*Apps*) e disponibilizá-las para consumo de seus usuários, possibilitando assim, a oferta de um número maior de soluções e serviços. Uma diversidade de fatores pode influenciar no sucesso e desempenho de um *App* ou de um MSECO ao longo do tempo, dificultando a construção de boas soluções nesse cenário de incerteza. Nesse contexto, o uso de simulação mostra-se como uma importante ferramenta para apoio à tomada de decisão, experimentando de forma controlada diferentes cenários em um MSECO e minimizando risco na busca pela criação de um *App* popular. Este artigo descreve a caracterização de métodos e ferramentas para simulação de MSECO a partir da condução de um estudo de Mapeamento Sistemático da Literatura. Como resultado, dos 289 artigos inicialmente retornados na busca, foram identificados 18 trabalhos relacionados ao tema. Eles foram analisados sobre a perspectiva do *App*, Usuário e Desenvolvedor. Observou-se que a maioria dos modelos foi avaliada em um contexto acadêmico, sem avaliação na indústria. Os dados encontrados nesse estudo mostram não apenas o estado-da-arte sobre simulação em MSECO, mas ainda os desafios e oportunidades de pesquisa relacionadas ao tema sobre uma perspectiva de aplicação prática na indústria de desenvolvimento de *Apps*.

Abstract. In a Mobile Software Ecosystem (MSECO), manufacturers provide a platform for developers to create mobile applications (*Apps*) and make them available for consumption of their users, enabling to offer a high number of solutions and services. A variety of factors may influence the success and performance of *App* or a MSECO over time, making the constructions of good solutions to this uncertainty scenario. In this context, the use of simulation would be an important tool to support decision making, providing in a controlled manner different scenarios in a MSECO and minimizing risk in the pursuit of creating a popular *App*. This paper describes the characterization of methods and tools for simulation of MSECOs from the conduction of a Systematic Literature Mapping study. As results, from the 289 papers initially returned in the search, we identified 18 works dealing with this research topic. They were analyzed from the perspective of the App, User and Developer. We observed that most of the models were evaluated in an academic context, not rated in the industry. The findings in this study show not only the state of the art of simulation in MSECO, but also the challenges and research opportunities related to the topic about the perspective of practical application in the apps development industry.

Palavras-chave: Ecossistema de Software, Simulação, Aplicações Móveis, Mapeamento Sistemático.

1 Introdução

A popularização dos smartphones trouxe um aumento significativo na demanda e utilização de aplicações móveis (*Apps*) pelos consumidores. Isso formou uma complexa rede de criação e fornecimento de Software. Diversos desenvolvedores externos atuando no contínuo desenvolvimento de novos produtos. O conjunto desses elementos e suas interações forma um ambiente denominado Ecossistema de Software. No trabalho de Jansen *et al.* [1], Ecossistema de Software é definido como um conjunto de atores que funcionam como uma unidade e interagem com um mercado de software ou serviço. No contexto de plataformas móveis, é adotado o termo Ecossistema de Software Móvel (MSECO).

Nesse ambiente, existem três atores de grande relevância: o mantenedor da plataforma, o desenvolvedor de *Apps* e os Usuários finais. Em um MSECO, os fabricantes disponibilizam uma plataforma para desenvolvedores criarem *Apps* e disponibilizá-las para consumo nas Lojas de *Apps*, possibilitando assim a oferta de um número maior de soluções e serviços para os usuários finais [2]. O aparelho deixa de ser uma plataforma isolada e se torna uma plataforma aberta para a criação e publicação de soluções desenvolvidas por terceiros.

O conceito de plataformas permite a distribuição massiva de inovação em uma escala que ultrapassa as cadeias de geração de produtos convencionais [3]. Esse modelo de colaboração externa tem se tornado vantajoso para muitas dessas empresas [4][5]. Diversas empresas responsáveis por plataformas móveis (ex: Google, Samsung, Microsoft) têm voltado seus investimentos para um cenário de desenvolvimento externo, permitindo assim entregar mais valor às plataformas dessas empresas.

Nesse cenário, onde há uma similaridade muito grande entre o *hardware*, a grande diferenciação para essas plataformas é a qualidade dos *Apps* disponíveis para o usuário final. A oferta ou não de um determinado *App* passou a ser fator de decisão no processo de escolha entre uma Plataforma ou outra. Essa dinâmica criou um mercado lucrativo chamado de *App Economy* (Economia de *Apps*). Para exemplificar o tamanho desse mercado, em apenas um MSECO, o *iOS App Store* da Apple distribuiu U$10 bilhões para os desenvolvedores em 2014, superando números de mídias tradicionais, como o mercado americano de filmes [6].

Com milhares de *Apps* disponíveis, uma diversidade de fatores pode influenciar no sucesso e desempenho de um *App* ou de um MSECO, ao longo do tempo, dificultando a construções de boas soluções nesse cenário de incerteza. Conhecer as características que impactam diretamente a popularidade de um aplicativo é primordial para se projetar *Apps* melhores, sobre a perspectiva do usuário.

Entender a dinâmica envolvendo MSECO pode ser um diferencial entre o sucesso ou o fracasso de um *App*. Diante dessa necessidade, o uso de simulação mostra-se como uma importante ferramenta para apoio a tomada de decisão, experimentando de forma controlada diferentes cenários em um MSECO e minimizando risco na busca pela criação de um *App* popular. Em MSECO, isso permite, por exemplo, avaliar previamente o nível de aceitação de um aplicativo baseado em suas características e do ecossistema no qual a aplicação será inserida. Entretanto, para isso ser possível, é importante entender quais ferramentas estão disponíveis na literatura técnica que viabilizem uma simulação confiável de um MSECO.

Este trabalho tem como motivação caracterizar métodos e ferramentas para simulação de MSECO, em especial aqueles que observam a dinâmica envolvendo Lojas de *Apps*. A partir da definição de questões de pesquisa, foi realizado um Mapeamento Sistemático da Literatura utilizando duas bases para a busca de estudos primários: *Scopus* e *IEEE Explorer*. Após a aplicação de filtros, os dados dos trabalhos relevantes foram extraídos através de formulários. Dos 289 inicialmente retornados na busca, foram identificados 18 artigos relacionados ao tema, que foram analisados sobre a perspectiva do *App*, do Usuário e do Desenvolvedor.

Como resultado prévio, observou-se que a maioria dos modelos encontrados foram avaliados em um contexto acadêmico, sem avaliação na indústria. Além disso, os modelos encontrados apresentam dificuldades para a utilização por um desenvolvedor de *Apps* interessado em avaliar previamente o potencial do seu aplicativo. Entender os modelos existentes e adaptá-los pode tornar mais viável o seu uso por desenvolvedores e organizações que criam *Apps*. Os dados encontrados nesse estudo mostram não apenas o estado-da-arte sobre simulação em MSECO, mas ainda os desafios e oportunidades de pesquisa relacionadas ao tema sobre uma perspectiva de aplicação prática na indústria de desenvolvimento de *Apps*.

O artigo está organizado da seguinte forma. Na seção 2 é apresentada a fundamentação teórica deste trabalho, descrevendo conceitos sobre Ecossistemas de Software Móvel e Simulação em Engenharia de Software. A seção 3 descreve o estado da arte em simulação de ecossistemas de software móvel, formalizado através da realização de um mapeamento sistemático da literatura. A Seção 4 apresenta a análise dos resultados encontrados a partir do mapeamento sistemático realizado. Na seção 5 são apresentados os desafios e oportunidades de pesquisa em MSECO. Por fim, a Seção 6 apresenta as conclusões e trabalhos futuros.

2 Fundamentação Teórica

2.1 Ecossistema de Software Móvel (MSECO)

Moore *et al.* [7] definem um ecossistema como uma comunidade com fins econômicos, apoiada por um conjunto de organizações e indivíduos que estão em constante interação. Na área de Computação, um Ecossistema de Software (ECOS) é definido como um conjunto de atores que funcionam como uma unidade e interagem com um mercado de software ou serviço [1]. No contexto de plataformas móveis, é adotado o termo Ecossistema de Software Móvel (MSECO, do inglês ***M**obile **S**oftware **Eco**system*).

Em [8], os autores apresentam um mapeamento sistemático sobre MSECO, que identificou as principais características e benefícios, além dos principais elementos que compõem um MSECO, que são:

- **Aplicação Móvel (*App*):** consiste em um software para plataforma móvel, produzido por um desenvolvedor ou uma equipe de desenvolvedores, e que pode ser adquirido por usuários. Deve obedecer ao mínimo de qualidade requerido pela loja de aplicações móveis.
- **Loja de Aplicações Móveis (*App Store*):** é um canal de distribuição dos *Apps* de uma plataforma aos seus usuários potenciais. Torna-se um ambiente de mercado altamente competitivo, onde desenvolvedores necessitam prover software para uma extensa base de usuários.
- **Organização Central (*Keystone*):** organização responsável por gerir um MSECO, além de prover estratégias para atrair e incentivar desenvolvedores externos e usuários a participarem do MSECO. Mantém uma comunidade

virtual que agrega valor a aplicações móveis, desenvolvedores e usuários finais.

- **Desenvolvedor:** papel responsável pelo desenvolvimento de aplicações móveis a serem disponibilizados no MSECO, respondendo aos requisitos dos usuários. No contexto de MSECO, os desenvolvedores são normalmente externos à organização central.
- **Comunidade:** uma estrutura de colaboração e coordenação de atividades dentro de um ecossistema, composta por elementos externos e internos.

Cada um dos elementos do MSECO possui uma responsabilidade e um desempenho esperados que dependem da gestão da organização central, que é quem precisa garantir o funcionamento do ecossistema e atingir metas, tais como aumentar a quantidade de desenvolvedores e o número de aplicações móveis disponíveis na loja de aplicações móveis. A organização central precisa empreender esforços na disponibilização de uma estrutura para que o MSECO possa se expandir (orquestração). O desenvolvedor precisa criar e disponibilizar aplicações móveis que atendam da melhor forma os nichos existentes de usuários e obter visibilidade dentro da loja devido à qualidade das aplicações desenvolvidas [9].

Santos *et al.* [10] classificam Ecossistemas de Software Móvel sob três dimensões centrais presentes em todo ecossistema, como forma de identificar e classificar oportunidades de pesquisa e desafios: Técnico, Negócios e Social.

- **Técnico:** esta dimensão tem como objetivo analisar o ecossistema através de analogias com outros tipos de ecossistema, como o natural, o de negócios e o social. O objetivo é obter e derivar métodos e modelos para organização, classificação e avaliação de ecossistemas e o ciclo de vida de suas plataformas.
- **Negócios:** foca no fluxo de conhecimento, por exemplo, artefatos, recursos e informação. Isto é executado a partir do estabelecimento dos objetivos e planos de ação do ecossistema por meio de programas e projetos. A inovação ligada com um ecossistema para o Mercado de software e o entendimento de como planejar estratégias são onde poderão ser atingidos os objetivos.
- **Social:** foca nos *stakeholders* de um ecossistema por meio do balanceamento de proposições e percepção de utilidade (como os elementos interagem, expandem e modificam o conhecimento dentro de um ecossistema, e como interagem entre si), promoção (como o engajamento dos participantes é reconhecido), e conhecimento (como as redes sociais formadas pelos indivíduos os ajudam em suas contribuições para o ecossistema).

2.2 Simulação de Sistemas

Banks [11] define simulação como uma metodologia indispensável para a resolução de muitos problemas do mundo real. A simulação é utilizada para descrever e analisar o comportamento de um sistema, permitindo assim responder previamente a diversas perguntas sobre o sistema real. Isso passa e ser um diferencial competitivo, permitindo o teste prévio de cenários importantes para o sistema e minimizando custos e riscos no processo decisório.

Barros *et al.* [12] aplicam simulação no contexto de gerenciamento de projetos de desenvolvimento de Software. Nesse trabalho, diferentes situações de projetos são representadas em modelos de cenários, permitindo que um gerente verifique o impacto de teorias, procedimentos, ações, mudanças e estratégias gerenciais que podem ser aplicadas ou impostas durante a execução de um projeto de software. Os modelos de cenário utilizados são descritos por meio de formulações matemáticas e avaliados por meio de simulações. Esse trabalho é um exemplo prático da aplicação de simulação em problemas reais, reforçando a importância do seu uso como apoio ao processo de decisão, reduzindo riscos e minimizando custos em projetos de software.

A respeito de simulação, há diversos conceitos relacionados que devem ser levados em consideração, que incluem: sistema, eventos, variáveis de estado do sistema, entidades e atributos, processamento de lista, atividades e atrasos, e finalmente, um modelo computacional que permita a simulação [11]. Para produzir um modelo, é necessário construir uma abstração da realidade. Esso modelo não deve representar todos os aspectos de um Sistema a ser estudado. Em vez disso, o modelo deve ser desenvolvido de forma simples, representando apenas os aspectos importantes para avaliar as variáveis do Sistema que se quer medir. Assim, o modelo pode descrever um Sistema em algum momento de captação ou em múltiplos níveis de captação com o objetivo de representar o Sistema de uma forma confiável, que permita a simulação computacional [13]. Muitas vezes, é difícil decidir quais os aspectos relevantes que devem ser incluídos no modelo de simulação.

O trabalho de França *et al.* [14] apresenta as dificuldades em se utilizar simulação em experimentos envolvendo engenharia de Software. O autor destaca, ainda, que a falta de informações sobre a maioria dos estudos baseados em simulação, e seus modelos, restringem à replicação desses estudos. França *et el.* Relatam ainda que a falta de um modelo e de informações claras sobre o processo de execução da simulação podem ser uma ameaça a validade dos resultados, comprometendo a confiança dos resultados. Em um trabalho seguinte [15], os mesmos autores apresentam um conjunto de práticas e recomendações para suportar o projeto de estudos baseados em simulação.

Nesse trabalho, o foco é em simulação aplicada no contexto de Ecossistemas de Software Móvel, representando aspectos principais desse Ecossistema, como Usuários, Desenvolvedores e Aplicativos, e suas interações. É importante entender quais são os métodos, técnicas e ferramentas de simulação existentes na literatura técnica. Para isso, foi conduzido um Mapeamento Sistemático, que é apresentado na próxima seção.

3 Mapeamento do Estado da Arte sobre Simulação em MSECO

3.1 Definição do Objetivo

O objetivo desse estudo é inspirado no trabalho de França *et al.* [14], focando em simulação de Ecossistemas de Software Móvel (MSECO), seus benefícios, desafios, oportunidades de pesquisa, aplicações, métodos e ferramentas.

O levantamento do estado da arte sobre Simulação em MSECO foi realizado por meio de um Mapeamento Sistemático da Literatura, com o objetivo de caracterizar modelos e ferramentas de simulação de dinâmica em MSECO com relação aos seus objetivos, plataformas, área foco, estratégias de simulação e métodos de avaliação. O processo utilizado foi baseado no apresentado por Kitchenham *et al.* [16].

3.2 Questões de Pesquisa e String de Busca

A principal questão de pesquisa foi "Quais os métodos e/ou ferramentas existentes na literatura que dão suporte a Simulação de Ecossistemas de Software Móvel? ". A partir dessa questão principal, algumas questões secundárias foram elaboradas, tais como:

- **RQ1**: Quais as principais características abordadas nos trabalhos envolvendo simulação de MSECO?
- **RQ2**: Quais são os modelos, algoritmos ou estratégias para simulação da dinâmica de MSECO no contexto de lojas de aplicativos?
- **RQ3**: Como os resultados simulados são verificados com dados reais de ecossistemas? Em qual MSECO o modelo ou simulador é aplicado?

A *string* de busca foi modelada a partir da estrutura analítica PICO (do inglês *Population*, *Intervention*, *Comparison* e *Outcomes*) [16], conforme a Tabela 1.

Tabela 1. Estrutura PICO para o Mapeamento Realizado

População	Trabalhos em Ecossistemas de Software
Intervenção	Aplicações e Plataformas Móveis
Comparação	*<não se aplica>*
Resultado	Algoritmos, Modelos ou Simuladores

Os termos comerciais que representam os principais Ecossistemas de Software Móvel foram utilizados na composição da *string* de busca, uma vez que alguns trabalhos não utilizam o termo formalmente utilizado na literatura *Software Ecosystem*, e dão ênfase as plataformas onde foram realizados os estudos. Assim, a *string* aplicada no estudo foi a seguinte:

> *(("software ecosystem*") **AND** ("app*" OR "game*" OR "embedded" OR "mobile" OR "microsoft" OR "nokia" OR "blackberry" OR "apple" OR "google" OR "android" OR "ios" OR "windows") **AND** ("algorithm*" OR "model*" OR "simulat*"))*

3.3 Planejamento do Estudo

Para seleção dos dados, foram selecionadas como fonte, base de trabalhos científicos disponíveis no portal CAPES Periódicos[1]. As fontes deveriam estar acessíveis via *web*, por meio de máquinas de buscas. Portanto, no contexto deste mapeamento, não foi considerada a busca manual. Para essa seleção dos trabalhos, foram adotados os critérios a seguir: 1) Permitir a consulta de artigos em bibliotecas digitais, congressos, simpósios e revistas; 2) Preferencialmente, presença de mecanismos de busca por meio de palavras-chaves; 3) Ter os estudos disponíveis em inglês.

Nesse trabalho, foram selecionadas as bases *Scopus*[1] e *IEEExplorer*[2]. Essas bases foram selecionadas por atender aos critérios definidos anteriormente, por indexarem

[1] http://www.scopus.com
[2] http://ieeexplore.ieee.org

trabalhos relevantes no domínio de Engenharia de Software e, principalmente, como é o caso da *Scopus*, indexar outras bases de dados. Santos *et al.* [17] apontam a alta cobertura e sensitividade da combinação das duas bibliotecas na realização de buscas por estudos primários em mapeamentos sistemáticos.

Para a seleção dos trabalhos, foram definidos previamente alguns critérios de inclusão que auxiliem na seleção de trabalhos. Os trabalhos que não atendessem a pelo menos um dos critérios de inclusão foram excluídos. São eles:

- I1: deve ser relacionado a *Mobile Software Ecosystem* (MSECO).
- I2: deve apresentar modelos de simulação de MSECO.
- I3: deve apresentar características da dinâmica de simulação de MSECO.

Definidos esses pontos, a fase de seleção dos trabalhos ocorreu em duas etapas. Na primeira, os trabalhos foram selecionados de acordo com os critérios de inclusão definidos a partir da leitura do título, resumo e palavras-chave. Na segunda etapa, os trabalhos selecionados na etapa anterior foram integralmente lidos, permitindo assim um entendimento mais profundo do conteúdo, esclarecendo pontos duvidosos e selecionando os trabalhos relevantes de acordo com os critérios de inclusão definidos anteriormente. Os trabalhos selecionados nessa segunda etapa foram elegíveis para a extração. A extração de dados foi realizada em formulário baseado no trabalho de França *et al.* [14], permitindo responder às questões de pesquisa definidas (Tabela 2).

Tabela 2. Formulário de Extração.

Dados Extraídos
Identificação do Trabalho: *[Título, Autor, Ano, Fonte]*
Nome do Método Proposto: *[nome definido pelos autores]*
Característica de Simulação: *[selecionada entre as opções a seguir, separada por categoria]* • ***App***: *[Características do App, modelos de monetização, Predição de popularidade].* • ***Usuário***: *[Modelo de Preferências do Usuário, Forma de descoberta de novos Apps, Influência do meio na seleção de Apps]* • ***Desenvolvedor***: *[Ciclo de Desenvolvimento, Modelos de Monetização de Apps, Rede de colaboração e reuso]*
Ferramenta para simulação apresentada: *[selecionada entre as opções a seguir]* • *Heurísticas, Modelo e Simulador de MSECO*
MSECO utilizado: *[selecionada entre as opções a seguir]* • *Android, Apple, Microsoft Windows Phone, Blackberry e Outro.*
App Store **utilizada:** *[selecionada entre as opções a seguir]* • *Google Play, App Store, Market Place, Loja Alternativa Android e Outra.*
Forma de Validação: *[selecionada entre as opções a seguir]* • *Validação com amostra específica de caráter acadêmico.* • *Validação com dados reais de MSECO.* • *Sem validação.*
Vantagens do modelo proposto: *[texto descrevendo as vantagens reportadas]*
Desvantagens do modelo proposto: *[texto descrevendo as desvantagens reportadas]*
Desafios apresentados: *[texto descrevendo os desafios sugeridos]*
Principais Resultados do Trabalho: *[texto resumindo os resultados]*

3.4 Execução do Estudo

O presente mapeamento sistemático foi realizado entre os meses de Junho e Agosto de 2015. A Tabela 3 resume a quantidade de trabalhos retornados por cada base e o número de trabalhos selecionados em cada fase de filtro do mapeamento. Foram retornados 289 trabalhos durante a pesquisa. Após a aplicação do 1° Filtro (seleção baseada no título, resumo e palavras-chave), 51 trabalhos foram selecionados. Dando continuidade, foram selecionados 18 trabalhos no 2° Filtro (baseado na análise do texto completo do trabalho) para extração dos dados. O tema envolvendo Simulação e MSECO é recente, o que justifica a quantidade restrita de trabalhos disponíveis na literatura.

Tabela 3. Número de Trabalhos retornados por fase

Biblioteca Digital	Trabalhos Retornados	Trabalhos 1° Filtro	Trabalhos 2° Filtro
Scopus	223	41	16
IEEExplorer	66	10	2
Total	**289**	**51**	**18**

A lista completa com as referências dos artigos selecionados após o 2° Filtro está apresentada na Tabela 4.

A próxima seção descreve a análise dos resultados deste mapeamento sistemático, visando responder às questões de pesquisa apresentadas nesta seção.

4 Análise dos Resultados

O termo Ecossistemas de Software Móvel começou a aparecer na literatura após o lançamento das primeiras lojas de aplicativos em 2007 e 2008. No estudo realizado neste trabalho, os primeiros trabalhos abordando simulação no contexto de MSECOS são do ano de 2011, indicando uma pequena diferença de tempo entre o surgimento da área e do tema MSECO e o surgimento dos primeiros trabalhos que descrevem simulação em MSECO. A Tabela 5 apresenta a distribuição dos artigos por ano de publicação.

Nas próximas subseções, serão analisadas as questões de pesquisa apresentadas para este mapeamento sistemático.

4.1 RQ1: Quais as principais características abordadas nos trabalhos envolvendo simulação de MSECO?

Os 18 trabalhos foram analisados para entender com qual propósito simuladores de MSECO são utilizados. Para, isso tomou-se como base os 3 principais elementos envolvidos na dinâmica de um MSECO [8]: *Apps*, Usuários e Desenvolvedores.

Os trabalhos que têm como foco central *Apps* estão preocupados em entender os fatores que influenciam a popularidade de um *App* e como a tendência de subida ou decida de um gráfico de popularidade é impactado. Observando sob o ponto de vista do Usuário, os trabalhos estão interessados no comportamento do usuário e como o processo de descoberta e download de *Apps* acontece. Analisando a dinâmica do Desenvolvedor, é importante observar os diferentes perfis e estratégias utilizadas por eles no desenvolvimento e lançamento de novos *Apps*.

Tabela 4. Referências dos Trabalhos Selecionados.

ID	Artigos Selecionados
ID1	H. Zhu, C. Liu, Y. Ge, H. Xiong, E. Chen, "Popularity Modeling for Mobile Apps: A Sequential Approach.," *IEEE Trans. Cybern.*, 2015.
ID2	R. Baeza-yates, D. Jiang, B. Harrison, "Predicting The Next App That You Are Going To Use," *Proc. Eighth ACM International Conference Web Search Data Min.*, 2015.
ID3	G. R. Larocque, J. Bhatti, A. Arsenault, "Integrated modelling software platform development for effective use of ecosystem models," *Ecol. Modell.*, 2014.
ID4	M. Li, K.-Y. Goh, H. Cavusoglu, "Investigating Developers Entry To Mobile App Platforms: a Network Externality View", *22nd European Conf. on Info. Systems*, 2014.
ID5	A. Ghose, S. P. Han, "Estimating Demand for Mobile Applications in the New Economy," *Management Science*, 2014.
ID6	D. G. Taylor, M. Levin, "Predicting Mobile App Usage for Purchasing and Information-Sharing," *Int. J. Retail Distrib. Manag.*, 2014.
ID7	Q. Wang, "Zoom in iOS Clones: Examining the Antecedents and Consequences of Mobile App Copycats", In 35th Int. Conference on Information Systems, 2014, pp. 1–17.
ID8	E. Knauss, D. Damian, A. Knauss, A. Borici, "Openness and requirements: Opportunities and tradeoffs in software ecosystems", *IEEE 22nd Int Requir. Eng. Conf. (RE)*, 2014.
ID9	T. Petsas, A. Papadogiannakis, M. Polychronakis, E. Markatos, T. Karagiannis, "Rise of the Planet of the Apps: A Systematic Study of the Mobile App Ecosystem," *Proceedings of the 2013 conference on Internet measurement conference*, 2013.
ID10	S. L. Lim, P. J. Bentley, "Investigating app store ranking algorithms using a simulation of mobile app ecosystems," *2013 IEEE Congr. Evol. Comput. CEC 2013*.
ID11	S. Jansen, E. Bloemendal, "Defining app stores: The role of curated marketplaces in software ecosystems," *Lect. Notes Bus. Inf. Process.*, vol. 150 LNBIP, 2013.
ID12	A. Karatzoglou, L. Baltrunas, K. Church, B. Matthias, Hmer, "Climbing the app wall: enabling mobile app discovery through context-aware recommendations," *Proc. 21st ACM Int. Conf. Inf. Knowl. Manag.*, 2012.
ID13	S. L. Lim, P. J. Bentley, "App Epidemics: Modelling the Effects of Publicity in a Mobile App Ecosystem," *13th Int. Conf. on the Synthesis and Simulation of Living Systems (ALIFE'13)*, 2012.
ID14	C. Shin, J.-H. Hong, A. K. Dey, "Understanding and prediction of mobile application usage for smart phones," *Proc. 2012 ACM Conf. Ubiquitous Comput. - UbiComp*, 2012.
ID15	P. Bentley, S. Lim, "How to be a Successful App Developer: Lessons from the Simulation of an App Ecosystem," 2012.
ID16	E. Yu and S. Deng, "Understanding software ecosystems: A strategic modeling approach," in *CEUR Workshop Proceedings*, 2011.
ID17	H. Zhu, H. Xiong, S. Member, Y. Ge, "Discovery of Ranking Fraud for Mobile Apps," 2015.
ID18	D. Yang, W. Liu, Q. Cui, J. Li, Y. Yang, Q. Wang, "Modeling the Number of Active Software Users," *Empir. Softw. Eng. Meas. (ESEM), 2011 Int. Symp.*, 2011.

A Tabela 6 apresenta a classificação dos trabalhos encontrados de acordo com as características instanciadas a partir do cruzamento entre os elementos de um MSECO (*App*, Usuário, Desenvolvedor) definidos em [8], e dimensões de ecossistemas

(Técnica, Negócios e Social), apresentadas em [10]. Os trabalhos ID3, ID8 e ID11 não respondem diretamente à questão de pesquisa RQ1, por isso não aparecem mapeados na Tabela 6.

Tabela 5. Distribuição dos trabalhos por ano de publicação.

Ano de Publicação	Total de Trabalhos	Trabalhos (ID)
2011	2	16, 18
2012	4	12, 13, 14, 15
2013	3	9, 10, 11
2014	6	3, 4, 5, 6, 7, 8
2015	3	1, 2, 17

Tabela 6. Distribuição dos trabalhos por característica resultante de elemento x dimensão.

Elemento	Dimensão	Descrição da Característica. Foco em...	Trabalhos (ID)
App	Técnica	Funcionalidades e serviços providos pelos *Apps*	7, 10, 13, 15
	Negócios	Diferentes modelos de precificação (gratuito e pago)	15
	Social	Entendimento do comportamento do *App* na sociedade (ex: analisando/predizendo sua popularidade)	1, 9, 10, 16, 17
Usuário	Técnica	Modelagem de preferências (positivas e negativas) do usuário quanto a características presentes em *Apps*	2, 10, 12, 14, 15, 18
	Negócios	Modelagem de diferentes meios de descoberta de Apps	15
	Social	Influência do meio na seleção de *Apps* (inclusão de comportamento "viral")	13, 15
Desenvolvedor	Técnica	Definição ou representação, mesmo que mínima, de um ciclo de desenvolvimento de *App*	15
	Negócios	Estratégias que resultam em modelos para monetização dos *Apps*	5, 6
	Social	Definição de perfil de desenvolvedores e na interação entre esses perfis	4, 15

4.1 RQ2: Quais são os modelos, algoritmos ou estratégias para simulação da dinâmica de MSECO no contexto de lojas de aplicativos?

Identificados os trabalhos, é importante observar a contribuição de cada um deles para a simulação de um MSECO, classificando em 3 níveis. No nível 1, foram considerados trabalhos que apresentam técnicas isoladas de algum dos elementos da dinâmica de um MSECO. No nível 2, foram classificados trabalhos que apresentam modelos mais formais para simulação de MSECO. No nível 3, foram identificados trabalhos mais maduros, que apresentam um simulador com um conjunto de parâmetros e referências que permitam a simulação de MSECO. Essa classificação foi consolidada na Tabela 7.

A grande maioria dos trabalhos apresentam técnicas que tratam de forma isolada algum aspecto do *App*, do Usuário ou do Desenvolvedor, elementos primordiais de um MSECO. As técnicas encontradas foram apresentadas de forma isolada, o que dificulta uma análise prévia do efeito da combinação dessas técnicas em um ambiente de simulação, que busca reproduzir cenários compatíveis com o real. Por exemplo, para o aspecto do crescimento do número dos usuários, os trabalhos ID10, ID13 e ID15 sugerem um modelo de crescimento baseado em modelos de ecologia, sem abordar o impacto e influência de outros elementos.

Tabela 7. Distribuição dos trabalhos por contribuições apresentadas.

Contribuições apresentadas	Trabalhos (ID)
1) Apresenta técnicas para simulação	2, 3, 4, 5, 6, 7, 11, 12, 14, 17
2) Apresenta modelo para simulação	1, 18
3) Apresenta uma ferramenta de simulação	9, 10, 13, 15

Os trabalhos ID9, ID10, ID13 e ID15, apresentam resultados mais completos e maduros, disponibilizando um simulador e permitindo assim a sua replicação. O trabalho ID9, por exemplo, sugere um modelo onde um pequeno conjunto de *Apps* é responsável por um número grande de downloads de um MSECO, seguindo assim a regra de Pareto. Os trabalhos ID10, ID13 e ID15 abordam o simulador chamado *AppEco*, instrumentado com parâmetros de entrada e permitindo a simulação de vários aspectos de um MSECO. O código do *AppEco* está disponível para *download*[3].

4.2 RQ3: Como os resultados simulados são verificados com dados reais de ecossistemas? Em qual MSECO o modelo ou simulador é aplicado?

O melhor cenário para validação de uma simulação envolvendo MSECO é com dados reais da dinâmica envolvendo os elementos desse ecossistema. Entretanto, a maioria dos estudos encontrados não apresenta validação formal ou simplesmente não valida seus resultados, conforme apresentado na Tabela 8. Isso pode ser explicado pelo fato de que boa parte dos MSECOs, incluindo as principais iOS e Android, não disponibilizam publicamente informações de suas lojas de aplicativos que detalhem a dinâmica dos 3 principais atores envolvidos em um MSECO: *Apps*, Usuários e Desenvolvedores. Essa é uma das grandes dificuldades da aplicação dos resultados dos estudos por desenvolvedores e empresas da indústria.

Nesse cenário, destacam-se três estratégias alternativas bem definidas para validação dos trabalhos: 1) relatórios de terceiros que evidenciam dados reais das lojas. Esses relatórios apresentam dados de um MSECO, entretanto, os dados costumam representar um pequeno espaço de tempo, por conta disso, apresentam pouca representatividade; 2) validação através de lojas alternativas, coleta de forma exaustiva os dados por meio de um *web crawler*[4] (ID9); e 3) Caracterização das curvas de crescimento dos elementos de um MSECO: *App*, Usuários e Desenvolvedores (ID10, ID13 e ID15). Essa

[3] www.appeco.co.uk

[4] *Web Crawler* é um programa de computador que visita sistematicamente um conjunto de sites na *Internet* coletando informações.

abordagem garante limites superiores para as quantidades desses elementos na simulação, tentando equiparar resultados simulados com os dados reais.

Poucos trabalhos foram encontrados envolvendo o MSECO Android, em especial a *GooglePlay*, a principal loja de aplicativos em termos de número de downloads, aplicativos e usuários atualmente.

Tabela 8. Distribuição dos trabalhos – Tipo de Validação

Validação	**MSECO**	**Loja de Apps**	**Trabalhos (ID)**
Sem validação	-	-	3, 6, 8, 11, 14, 16
Em amostra de carácter acadêmico	Android	*Google Play*	2, 5, 12
	iOS	*App Store*	1, 4,7
Dados Reais de MSECO	Android	*Google Play*	-
	Baseado em Android	*SlideMe*	9
	iOS	*App Store*	10, 13, 15

Os desafios e oportunidades de pesquisa em Simulação de Ecossistemas de Software Móvel são apresentadas na seção 5.

5 Desafios/Oportunidades de Pesquisa em Simulação de MSECO

O mapeamento da literatura realizado neste trabalho permitiu uma análise sobre o uso de Simulação para Ecossistemas de Software Móvel. Diante disso, e tomando como base os dados extraídos dos trabalhos selecionados, foram listados alguns desafios e oportunidades. Esses desafios apresentam oportunidades de pesquisa que contribuirão para um cenário que permitiria a aplicação de simulação no contexto de MSECO, com uma margem maior de confiabilidade. A seguir esses desafios e oportunidades são apresentados de acordo com as dimensões de um MSECO:

- **Técnica**: Na área técnica, desafios estão relacionados à construção de soluções que permitam a aplicação de simulação por desenvolvedores e empresas usando dados e modelos que representem cenários próximos aos reais. Como principais oportunidades/desafios, podem ser citados:
  1. Como adequar os modelos existentes para avaliar o impacto de cada fase do desenvolvimento de um *App* no seu sucesso?
  2. Como ampliar a matriz de características de *Apps* apresentado em ID10, identificando célula e sua influência na popularidade de *App*?
  3. Como adequar os modelos para verificar a popularidade de um *App* de acordo com o nível de maturidade de um MSECO?
  4. Como avaliar o impacto do processo de Verificação e Validação no sucesso de um *App*?
- **Negócios**: Na dimensão de negócios, os desafios de pesquisa estão diretamente ligados à necessidade do desenvolvedor de maximizar o retorno provido por cada *App* do seu portfólio. Diante disso, destacam-se os desafios:
  1. Como criar um modelo que permita avaliar o impacto de diferentes estratégias de monetização (download pago, publicidade, etc) na popularidade de um *App*?
  2. Como estimar o preço de um *App* baseado no histórico de *Apps* com as

mesmas características?
3. Como ampliar os modelos existentes para permitir diferentes valores de precificação de Apps?

- **Social**: Na dimensão social, os desafios que se destacam são:
  1. Como ampliar os modelos identificados para permitir a representação de diferentes fatores culturais no comportamento do Usuário?
  2. Qual o comportamento geral dos modelos identificados em MSECOs mais amplos, como *Android/GooglePlay*?
  3. Como o processo de feedback do Usuário impacta no comportamento dos desenvolvedores e nos indicadores de um MSECO?
  4. Como o reuso de componentes de terceiros impacta na produtividade e qualidade dos *Apps* de um desenvolvedor?

Como continuidade dessa pesquisa, buscamos utilizar simulação de MSECO com o objetivo de aplicar os resultados na Indústria de *Apps*, dando suporte ao processo de decisão envolvendo o desenvolvimento de *Apps*. A seguir, são apresentadas as conclusões e trabalhos futuros relacionados a esta pesquisa.

6 Considerações Finais e Trabalhos Futuros

Com milhares de *Apps* disponíveis, uma diversidade de fatores pode influenciar no sucesso e desempenho de um *App* ou de um MSECO ao longo do tempo, dificultando assim a construções de boas soluções nesse cenário de incerteza. Entender a dinâmica envolvendo MSECO pode ser um diferencial entre o sucesso ou o fracasso de um *App*. O uso de simulação mostra-se como uma importante ferramenta para apoio à tomada de decisão. Este trabalho teve como motivação caracterizar métodos e ferramentas para simulação de MSECO, em especial aqueles que observam a dinâmica envolvendo Lojas de *Apps*.

Os resultados encontrados foram analisados sob a perspectiva do *App*, Usuário e Desenvolvedor. A grande maioria dos trabalhos encontrados apresenta heurísticas isoladas envolvendo os principais elementos de um MSECO. Observou-se que a maioria dos modelos foi avaliada em um contexto acadêmico, sem avaliação uma validação mais ampla.

Os desafios apresentados na seção anterior se apresentam como trabalhos futuros, e eles têm como foco a pesquisa e desenvolvimento na área de simulação em MSECO. Em um cenário mais voltado ao uso de simuladores, há um grande desafio na aplicação prática por desenvolvedores e organizações. As técnicas, modelos encontrados abordam dinâmicas isoladas e de difícil replicação. É um desafio a adequação e integração para um uso prático e realista dos simuladores na indústria, permitindo uma maior interação na simulação para que se tenha, enfim, ferramentas que apoiem a tomada de decisão em no processo de governança em MSECO.

AGRADECIMENTOS

Os autores agradecem a UFAM, FAPEAM, UEA e SAMSUNG pelo apoio para a realização desse trabalho. Parte dos resultados apresentados neste artigo foi obtida por meio de atividades de P&D do projeto SAMSUNG OCEAN, patrocinado pela Samsung Eletrônica da Amazônia Ltda., sob os termos da lei federal No. 8.248/91.

REFERÊNCIAS

[1] S. Jansen, A. Finkelstein, S. Brinkkemper, "A sense of community: A research agenda for software ecosystems", 31st International Conference on Software Engineering (ICSE 2009), pp. 2–5, 2009.

[2] S. Jansen, E. Bloemendal, "Defining app stores: The role of curated marketplaces in software ecosystems", Lect. Notes Bus. Inf. Process., vol. 150 LNBIP, pp. 195–206, 2013.

[3] A. Tiwana, "Platform Ecosystems: Aligning Architecture, Governance, and Strategy". MORGAN KAUFMANN, 2014.

[4] P. Bosch-Sijtsema, J. Bosch, "Aligning innovation ecosystem strategies with internal R&D", In IEEE ICMIT, 7th international conference on management of innovation and technology, pp. 424–430, 2014.

[5] J. Bosch, "From Software Product Lines to Software Ecosystems", Proc. 13th International Software Product Line Conference, pp. 111–119, 2009.

[6] R. Meyer, "The App Economy Is Now 'Bigger Than Hollywood'", In: The Atlantic, Disponível em: http://goo.gl/S0nFNz, acessado em: 01/03/2016.

[7] J. F. Moore, "Predators and prey: a new ecology of competition", Harvard Bus. Rev., vol. 71, no. 3, pp. 75–86, 1993.

[8] A. Fontao, A. C. Dias-neto, R. Santos, "Mobile Software Ecosystem (MSECO): A Systematic Mapping Study", In Proceedings of the 39th Int. Conf. Computers, Software & Applications (COMPSAC), pp. 653-658, 2015.

[9] A. Fontao, A. Dias-Neto, R. Santos, "MSECO-SUP: Support Process in Mobile Software Ecosystems", In Simposio Brasileiro de Engenharia de Software, Belo Horizonte, pp. 31-40, 2015.

[10] R. Santos, C. L. Werner, "A Proposal for Software Ecosystems Engineering", in Proceedings of the Workshop on Software Ecosystems, pp. 40–51, 2011.

[11] J. Banks, "Introduction to Simulation", in Proceedings of the 1999 Winter Simulation Conference, pp. 7–13, 1999.

[12] M. Barros, "Gerenciamento de Projetos Baseado em Cenários: Uma abordagem de Modelagem Dinâmica e Simulação", Tese de Doutorado da COPPE-UFRJ, 2001.

[13] J. A. Sokolowski, C. M. Banks, "Modeling and Simulation Fundamentals: Theoretical Underpinnings and Practical Domains". WILEY, 2010.

[14] B. França, G. Travassos, "Are we prepared for simulation based studies in software engineering yet?", CLEI Electronic Journal, vol. 16, no. 1, paper 8, 2013.

[15] B. França, "Guidelines for Experimentation with Dynamic Simulation Models in the context of Software Engineering", Tese de Doutorado da COPPE/UFRJ, 2015.

[16] B. Kitchenham, S. Charters, "Guidelines for performing Systematic Literature Reviews in Software Engineering", Technical Report, Keele University, vol. 2, p. 1051, 2007.

[17] J. Santos, A. Santos, M. Mendonça, "Investigating bias in the search phase of Software Engineering secondary studies", in Proceedings of 12th Workshop on Experimental Software Engineering, pp. 1-14, 2015.

[18] A. Fontao, R. Santos, A. Dias-Neto, "Research Opportunities for Mobile Software Ecosystems", in Workshop on Distributed Software Development, Software Ecosystems and Systems-of-Systems (WDES), pp. 97-98, 2015.

Procesos de Software Orientados a la Usabilidad Un Mapeo Sistemático de la Literatura

José Ignacio Rocca, Martin Solari

jrocca@uni.ort.edu.uy, martin.solari@ort.edu.uy

Universidad ORT Uruguay

Abstract. Las principales tendencias tecnológicas de software (Internet of Things, computación ubicua, sistemas contextuales, etc.) promueven la adopción masiva de aplicaciones por parte de usuarios en contextos heterogéneos. El software está cada vez más presente en la vida diaria de las personas y la usabilidad es de crítica importancia para su adopción y utilidad. Por otro lado, los procesos de software y metodologías permiten generar productos de calidad a partir de la sistematización del desarrollo. El objetivo de este trabajo es presentar un mapeo sistemático de la literatura que permita identificar y categorizar propuestas de procesos de software orientados al desarrollo de productos usables. Como parte del mapeo se definió un protocolo para realizar la búsqueda. Se detectaron 31 propuestas de procesos de software orientados a la usabilidad y los resultados indican que el 66% de los procesos propuestos cuentan con evidencia de aplicación mediante casos de estudio industriales o académicos, no obstante, se detectó que solo el 40% de las propuestas pueden ser replicadas utilizando la información disponible. De igual manera se observó que el 75% de las propuestas de proceso analizadas no tuvieron evolución en su investigación, replicación o adaptación.

1 Introducción

1.1 Procesos de software y usabilidad

Los procesos de software proveen un enfoque sistemático para el desarrollo y evolución del software. El SWEBOK [1] los define como un conjunto interrelacionado de actividades y tareas que transforman entradas en salidas. Feiler y Humphrey [2] también coinciden en esta definición pero agregan que, los procesos de software no representan una prescripción rígida sino un conjunto de criterios adaptables para desarrollar y evolucionar productos de software en distintos contextos. Existen múltiples razones para especificar y definir los procesos de software, como ser, facilitar el entendimiento, la comunicación y coordinación entre equipos. Brindar soporte a la gestión de proyectos, viabilizar la mejora continua y sobre todo para mejorar la calidad de los productos resultantes. Existe evidencia experimental [3] que avala esta visión respecto de la importancia de los procesos en el desarrollo y mantenimiento de software.

La naturaleza intangible y parametrizable del software permite la existencia de diversos tipos de proceso. Por un lado existen procesos de software que son guiados por un enfoque de gestión predictiva, basados en procesos y planes bien definidos y documentados, donde las fases del desarrollo se van cumpliendo linealmente con feedback de los usuarios a demanda. Por otro lado, existen los procesos basados en enfoques adaptativos o ágiles, donde se trabaja en iteraciones cortas de desarrollo, con apertura a cambios, con visibilidad y colaboración frecuente hacia los usuarios. Si bien, ambos tipos de procesos son de utilidad en determinados contextos, existen de modo transversal a estas visiones, procesos (predictivos o adaptativos) que se enfocan en asegurar un determinado atributo de calidad del producto, como ser la mantenibilidad, seguridad o usabilidad.

La usabilidad se define como la eficacia, eficiencia y satisfacción con la que un producto permite alcanzar objetivos específicos a los usuarios en un contexto de uso determinado [4]. Los conceptos claves de esta definición son el objetivo o tarea, el usuario y el contexto. La usabilidad incluye un conjunto de sub-atributos y componentes como ser: prevención de errores, facilidad de aprendizaje, eficiencia en la tarea, facilidad para recordar, estética y accesibilidad [5] que son claves para el éxito de los productos. Esta definición fue modificada y normalizada años después por la familia de normas ISO/IEC 25000 [6] que definen en detalle las características que debe poseer un producto de software de calidad.

1.2 Motivación

Hoy en día la usabilidad es un atributo de calidad clave de los sistemas de software. Las principales tendencias de tecnologías de la información (TI) de la actualidad [7] [8] incluyen la computación en todos lados (Computing Everywhere), el internet de las cosas (Internet of Things) y la importancia de sistemas contextuales (Context Rich Systems). Esto significa que el software no solo debe satisfacer las necesidades de los usuarios de teléfonos móviles sino que también de una amplia gama de dispositivos wearables (por ejemplo, relojes y lentes) además de pantallas táctiles en lugares públicos y de trabajo. La ubicuidad de conectividad y proliferación de dispositivos hacen converger el mundo físico y el mundo virtual, generando que el software sea adoptado en forma masiva por un público de usuarios más heterogéneo posibilitando un conjunto más diverso de tareas.

Los gerentes de tecnología consideran la usabilidad como un factor clave para decidir compras de productos de software [9] mientras que múltiples estudios indican que desarrollar software buscando asegurar la usabilidad es más rentable desde el punto de vista de costos [10]. De igual forma, se ha estudiado el impacto e importancia que la usabilidad tiene en la adopción de aplicaciones por parte de usuarios no técnicos [11]. Condiciones similares, dieron origen a la disciplina de ingeniería de la usabilidad (Usability Engineering en inglés, UE) [5] por Jakob Nielsen y remarcan la importancia de desarrollar software cada vez más usable.

La disciplina de la ingeniería de software enfrenta nuevos desafíos para desarrollar software cada vez más usable. Sin embargo buena parte de los métodos de ingeniería de software no especifican explícitamente prácticas para asegurar la usabilidad a lo largo del ciclo de vida del desarrollo. Las disciplinas de diseño centrado en el usuario (User Centered Design en inglés, UCD), interacción hombre-computadora (Human Computer Interaction en inglés HCI), y la ingeniería de usabilidad (UE) definen modelos de procesos y métodos que tienen poca adopción en la industria de software que todavía utiliza métodos tradicionales de desarrollo [12], [13]. En el contexto actual, la comunidad de la ingeniería de software necesita un enfoque sistemático para integrar la usabilidad a los procesos de desarrollo de software.

El objetivo de este trabajo es presentar los resultados de un mapeo sistemático de la literatura como medio para identificar y caracterizar el estado actual de las propuestas de procesos de software orientados a la usabilidad y que puede facilitar y promover la integración de la usabilidad en los procesos de software. A continuación se detalla el trabajo previo relevante. En la sección 3 se presenta la metodología y el protocolo de búsqueda utilizado. En la sección 4 se presentan los resultados obtenidos. Finalmente en las secciones 5 y 6 se presentan las conclusiones y trabajo futuro a realizar como parte de la investigación en el área.

2 Trabajo previo

2.1 Integración de la usabilidad en el desarrollo de software

Varios estudios exploran los problemas y obstáculos existentes a la hora de integrar los enfoques mencionados con la ingeniería de software. Para Seffah [9] en primer lugar, existen diferentes definiciones de usabilidad dado que el término ha evolucionado desde la definición original de IEEE [14] que refleja el conocimiento inicial al respecto. De igual manera en ciertos ambientes industriales y académicos se entiende por usabilidad simplemente diseño gráfico o de interfaz de usuario o estética de las pantallas. Seffah también señala que existe una brecha cultural entre las disciplinas antes mencionadas y la ingeniería de software. Tanto UE, UCD y HCI toman en consideración, aspectos de psicología y cognición para establecer teorías que usualmente no forman parte ni se integran al cuerpo de conocimiento de la ingeniería de software. Tanto los expertos en usabilidad como los ingenieros de software poseen distintas capacidades y enfoques culturales lo cual amplía la brecha antes mencionada entre estas disciplinas.

Otro problema es la falta de entrenamiento en técnicas y métodos específicos orientados a la usabilidad. Esto también fue señalado por varios estudios [12], [15] mediante encuestas realizadas en universidades. Particularmente Collazos et al. [15] marca que a pesar del crecimiento en número, existen pocos cursos de HCI, UCD o UE obligatorios en la currícula de las carreras de grado de ciencias de la computación de las universidades iberoamericanas.

2.2 Propuestas de procesos

Es posible decir la ingeniería de la usabilidad (UE) [5] puede ser considerada la primer propuesta de proceso de software orientado a la usabilidad. El ciclo de vida propuesto por Nielsen marca como aspectos claves:

- conocer a los usuarios,
- desarrollar el software de forma iterativa, permitiendo la participación de los usuarios durante el diseño de la aplicación.
- uso de prototipos
- evaluaciones de usabilidad mediante heurísticas o experimentos con usuarios.

Así mismo, se detectaron trabajos previos que presentan propuestas de procesos de software orientados a la usabilidad. Los trabajos detectados poseen distinto foco y nivel de evidencia. Por ejemplo, se aborda la importancia de la usabilidad en dominios web [16], la integración de UCD a la ingeniería de software [17] o la integración de prácticas específicas en esquemas de desarrollo guiado por modelos (MDD). En ese sentido, Panach et al. [18] definieron primitivas para incorporar aspectos de funcionalidad que se relacionan con la usabilidad dentro de un método MDD. Respecto a la definición y mejora de procesos de software como medio para alcanzar productos de calidad de software, se detectó un mapeo sistemático [19] que concluye que la usabilidad es uno de los principales atributos de calidad, que son mejorados y asegurados mediante iniciativas de mejora de procesos de software.

Se detectaron además estudios secundarios que fueron consideradas por sintetizar los resultados de estudios primarios en las áreas de interés del mapeo.

Da Silva et al. [20] analizan como los aspectos de usabilidad son alcanzados en el marco de proyectos ágiles. Su conclusión principal es que existen diferentes tácticas para integrar la usabilidad, por ejemplo trabajar con expertos en diseño centrado en el usuario dentro del equipo de proyecto, apoyarse en prototipos o realizar iteraciones de diseño al comienzo del proyecto (en inglés little design up front). En este estudio se identifican prácticas y artefactos comunes utilizado por los equipos ágiles para alcanzar los requisitos de usabilidad. A partir de los estudios identificados, los autores proponen un modelo de procesos para integrar UCD en proyectos ágiles.

Sohaib et al. [21] investigan las tensiones existentes entre los métodos ágiles y las prácticas de ingeniería de la usabilidad (UE). El trabajo detecta que las principales tensiones son entre la filosofía de diseño en instancias tempranas propuesta por UE y la entrega continua de valor propuesta por las metodologías ágiles. De cualquier forma se concluye que ambos enfoques son integrables mediante por ejemplo el apoyo de especialistas en usabilidad en el equipo.

Salah et al. [22] analizaron cuales son los principales desafíos que los profesionales podrían encontrar cuando se adopta un enfoque integrado entre el diseño orientado al usuario y la agilidad. El estudio además presenta una taxonomía donde se ordenan los principales desafíos y las prácticas clave que posibilitan la integración entre estos enfoques. De igual manera que el estudio de Sohaib, el principal desafío detectado fue la falta de tiempo al comienzo de los proyectos para definir aspectos de usabilidad, además de la brecha entre los equipos de desarrollo y los expertos en usabilidad que fue destacada. El estudio presenta las prácticas clave para simplificar la integración entre UCD y los métodos ágiles.

El estudio de Jurca et al. [23] mapea la evidencia empírica existente sobre Agile-UX, una propuesta que integra usabilidad y agilidad. Sus conclusiones marcan que aún hay escasa evidencia rigurosa publicada de la aplicación de esta propuesta de proceso.

Por otro lado, Brhel et al. [24] presenta cuáles son los principios y valores comunes que permiten constituir un enfoque híbrido entre UCD y Agile. A partir de la clasificación en 4 niveles de integración (procesos, prácticas, social y tecnológico) de los trabajos analizados, se infieren y definen 5 principios genéricos para posibilitar la integración de ambos enfoques.

Por último Silva et al. [25] detecta mediante un mapeo cuáles son los métodos, técnicas y prácticas utilizados en los procesos de desarrollo de software que mejoran la usabilidad. El mapeo concluye que la mayoría de los enfoques de integración de prácticas se dan en la fase de verificación y validación de los productos. Por otro lado se detecta que existe falta de métodos y prácticas que puedan integrarse en etapas tempranas del proceso de desarrollo de software.

Los distintos estudios secundarios poseen foco en analizar la integración en contextos ágiles o analizar la integración de prácticas y técnicas de usabilidad en el ciclo de desarrollo. El presente estudio, tiene un enfoque más amplio al considerar propuestas de procesos de software tanto ágiles como predictivas, y considerar enfoques de integración para etapas tempranas y tardías del ciclo de desarrollo.

3 Método de investigación

3.1 Mapeo sistemático de la literatura

Los mapeos sistemáticos de la literatura son un método de investigación que brinda una visión general de un área. Los mapeos son de utilidad para categorizar y relevar el nivel de evidencia empírica disponible sobre un área de conocimiento permitiendo ahorrar tiempo y esfuerzo a los investigadores. Esta metodología es utilizada frecuentemente como base para ejecutar trabajos de investigación futuros [26]. No obstante esto, deben ser realizados con rigor y amplitud para poder ser utilizados como plataforma de investigación a futuro por otros investigadores de la comunidad. Para la definición y ejecución del mapeo sistemático se utilizaron las guías propuestas por Kitchenham y Charters [27].

3.2 Preguntas de investigación

En el contexto mencionado anteriormente, resulta relevante preguntarse:

- RQ1: ¿Qué procesos de software o metodologías se orientan al desarrollo de aplicaciones usables?
- RQ2: ¿Qué nivel de evidencia empírica existe del uso de este tipo de procesos?
- RQ3: ¿Cuál es el origen conceptual de las propuestas de procesos de software orientadas a la usabilidad?
- RQ4: ¿Qué tan replicables son las propuestas de procesos de software publicadas?

Para facilitar la detección de sinónimos y armado de la cadena de búsqueda se analizó la RQ1 utilizando el método PICOC (Population, Intervention, Comparison, Outcome, Context) [27] .

Population: Procesos de desarrollo de software.

Intervention: Técnicas, métodos o prácticas orientadas a la usabilidad que se integran en los procesos.

Comparison: No aplica, dado que el presente mapeo solo pretende detectar y definir procesos de software orientados a usabilidad.

Outcomes: Definición de activos específicos para el proceso de software orientado a usabilidad.

Context: No aplica dado que se pretende detectar propuestas de procesos para cualquier contexto y luego categorizar las mismas.

3.3 Proceso de búsqueda

En función de la pregunta de investigación y el PICOC aplicado, se realizaron búsquedas exploratorias para evaluar palabras clave (keywords) e identificar su relevancia en dentro de los resultados obtenidos. El objetivo de estas búsquedas fue definir 3 términos sinónimos de Software, Process y Usability. La Tabla 1 presenta las palabras clave derivadas a partir de la pregunta de investigación y las búsquedas exploratorias realizadas.

Término 1	Término 2	Término 3
Software	Process	Usability
Program	Life cycle	HCI
Application	Model	UCD
	Methodology	UX

Tabla 1 Sinónimos de búsqueda.

A partir de los sinónimos de los distintos términos especificados se genera la cadena de búsqueda. Para ejecutar las búsquedas se utilizaron los motores de búsqueda accesibles mediante el portal Timbó [1]de la Agencia Nacional de Investigación e Innovación (ANII) de Uruguay. Se seleccionó Scopus como motor de búsqueda para detectar la literatura y evidencia relevante ya que es la base de datos de abstracts y citas más importante disponible mediante el portal Timbó. Dentro de Scopus se agregaron filtros por área de conocimiento Computer Science. La cadena de búsqueda utilizada fue: *(Software OR Program OR Application) AND (Process OR Life cycle OR Model OR Methodology) AND (Usability OR HCI OR UCD OR UX).*

3.4 Criterios de inclusión y exclusión

Se consideran relevantes y se incluyen aquellos resultados de búsqueda que:

[1] El portal provee acceso a más de 19.000 revistas, 34.000 libros electrónicos, actas de conferencias, bases de datos de abstract y citas, etc. Las colecciones habilitadas incluyen: Scopus, Springer, Jstor, IEEE, The Cochrane Library y Science Direct entre otras. Más información en: http://timbo.org.uy/

- Presenten evidencia de una propuesta de proceso de software que integra prácticas y métodos de usabilidad.
  - La propuesta de proceso integra prácticas o técnicas de usabilidad a lo largo del ciclo de vida del desarrollo (no se enfoca únicamente a una técnica aplicada en una única fase del proceso).
  - La propuesta de proceso integra más de un rol dentro del equipo de software.
  - La propuesta de proceso no fue previamente identificada.
- Estén escritos en inglés.
- No se trate de un workshop, panel, tutorial o seminarios para asegurar cierto nivel de detalle y calidad.
- Sea posible acceder al texto completo mediante Timbó Portal.

Aquellos estudios que sean mencionados como trabajo previo relevante de los artículos ya detectados usando la cadena de búsqueda, serán agregados en forma manual por parte del investigador aplicando snowballing en la bibliografía.

No se consideran relevantes y se excluyen aquellos resultados de búsquedas que:
- No concuerden con los criterios de inclusión.

3.5 Extracción de datos

Como estrategia de extracción de datos se definió un formulario a partir de las preguntas de investigación identificadas anteriormente.

Con referencia a la RQ1 (*¿Qué propuestas de proceso se orientan a la usabilidad?*), se pretendió identificar aquellas propuestas de procesos que cumplan con los criterios de inclusión definidos. Se identificó, el nombre de la propuesta de proceso y su año.

Como parte del formulario y asociado a la RQ2 (*nivel de evidencia empírica*) se busca evaluar si el proceso orientado a la usabilidad propuesto presenta algún tipo de evaluación empírica reportada, ya sea industrial o académica. Las opciones para este campo fueron codificadas con los siguientes valores:

- Propuesta genérica: para el caso que el estudio únicamente presente la propuesta del proceso.
- Propuesta y evidencia de aplicación: para el caso en el que el estudio presente tanto la propuesta de proceso como evidencia de la aplicación industrial o académica del mismo.
- Evidencia de aplicación: para el caso en el que el estudio se trate únicamente de un proceso instanciado en un caso.

Relacionada a la RQ3 (*origen conceptual de las propuestas de procesos*) se decidió evaluar si las propuestas de procesos identificadas provienen desde la ingeniería de software o desde otras disciplinas asociadas a la usabilidad. Los valores codificados para este aspecto del formulario fueron:

- Ágil: para el aquellos procesos con origen en metodologías ágiles.
- Predictivo: para aquellos procesos que no se presentan como ágiles y son adaptaciones de procesos predictivos como ser (UP, Waterfall, RAD, etc)

- UCD: para aquellas propuestas de procesos cuyo origen conceptual es la disciplina de diseño centrado en el usuario (UCD)
- UE: procesos que explícitamente se basan en la propuesta Usability Engineering de Nielsen.
- Cognitiva/psicología: procesos basados en aspectos de psicología provenientes del área de HCI.
- No aplica (N/A): para aquellas propuestas de procesos que no tiene un origen conceptual claramente identificable.

Por último, con referencia a la RQ4 (replicabilidad del proceso), se definió si la propuesta de proceso presentada en el estudio es replicable utilizando la información disponible. Para esto se utilizó un campo codificado como Si o No. Para evaluar si la propuesta puede ser replicada, se analizó en detalle los estudios involucrados y se determinó si es posible instanciar el proceso orientado a la usabilidad con la información disponible. Por ejemplo: si el proceso está representado en una notación estándar (BPMN, SPEM, Diagrama de flujo) o está especificado mediante prosa o que haya sido replicado por algún investigador en forma independiente de los que lo propusieron originalmente.

3.6 Estudios considerados

Se ejecutó la búsqueda en Scopus en Abril de 2015 obteniendo como resultado preliminar 1584 entradas posibles. Luego de realizar un primer filtro aplicando los criterios de inclusión y exclusión sobre título y abstract, se obtuvieron 80 estudios a ser analizados con mayor detalle. Como resultado de un segundo filtro sobre el texto completo de los artículos, se detectaron 25 artículos que representaban propuestas de procesos de software orientados a la usabilidad Por otro lado, de los 80 estudios filtrados inicialmente, 14 fueron marcados para una revisión conjunta por parte de un segundo investigador. De esos 14 estudios, 2 fueron considerados propuestas relevantes para el mapeo. De igual manera, se incluyeron 4 estudios que no fueron detectados por la búsqueda de Scopus y resultaron propuestas de proceso relevantes al ser referenciadas e identificadas como trabajo previo por otras propuestas consideradas en el mapeo. En la Tabla 2 se presentan estos resultados.

Fuente	#Papers	Filtro 1	Filtro 2	Revisión	Total
Scopus	1584	80	25	2	27
Otros	-	-	-	4	4

Tabla 2. Estudios considerados.

4 Resultados del mapeo

En esta sección se describen las características de los estudios seleccionados como relevantes para el mapeo. En primer lugar, el Gráfico 1 presenta la evolución en el tiempo de las propuestas. Se observa un interés creciente en las propuestas de procesos orientados a la usabilidad en los últimos años. Desde 2009 a 2014 se ha detectado el 64,51% del total de las propuestas de proceso identificadas en el mapeo. Dado que este mapeo se ejecutó a comienzos de 2015, no todas las publicaciones que se realizaron durante 2015 pudieron ser consideradas al no estar indexadas por los buscadores.

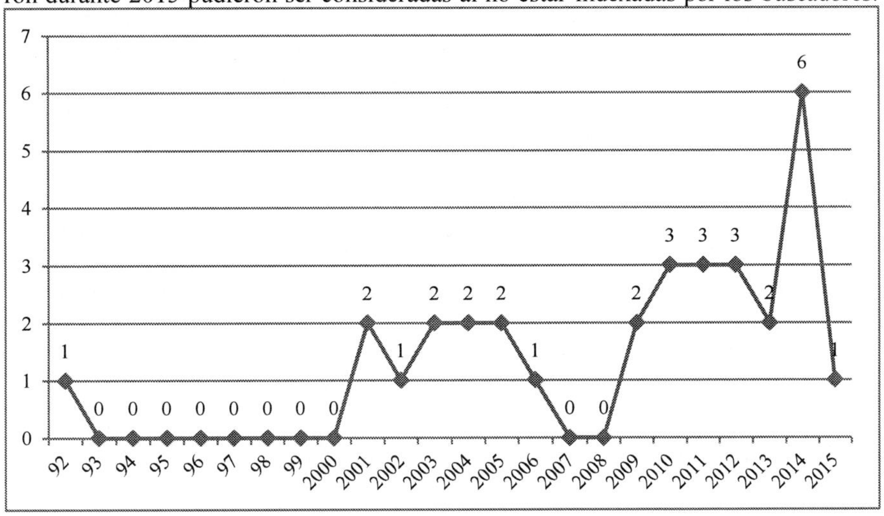

Gráfico 1. Propuestas de proceso por año.

Por otro lado, en la Tabla 3 se presenta el resumen de los resultados de acuerdo a las preguntas de investigación definidas para el mapeo y el formulario de extracción de datos diseñado.

	Resultados	**Cantidad**	**Porcentaje (%)**
RQ1. Procesos	Propuestas de proceso identificadas	31	100
RQ2. Evidencia	Propuesta y evidencia de aplicación	20	64,52
	Propuesta genérica	10	32,26
	Evidencia de aplicación	1	3,23
RQ3. Origen conceptual de las propuestas	Ágil	8	25,81
	Predictivo	10	32,26
	UCD	3	9,68
	UE	2	6,45
	Cognitiva/psicología	2	6,45
	N/A	6	19,35
RQ4. Propuesta replicable	No	17	54,84
	Si	14	45,16

Table 3. Resumen de resultados.

Con referencia a la RQ1, en total, el estudio de mapeo identificó 31 propuestas de procesos de software orientados a la usabilidad. En la mayoría de los casos, los autores identifican la propuesta de proceso orientado a la usabilidad utilizando un nombre propio para el proceso (70,97%), como ser: Usage centered engineering, RUPi, AgileUX, UP/U, Extreme Usability (XU), etc.

Si se analizan los resultados para la RQ2, es posible decir que sólo el 32,26 % de las propuestas de proceso identificadas se detectan como propuestas genéricas o sin evidencia de aplicación en proyectos industriales o académicos. El 67,74% de las propuestas de proceso posee algún nivel de validación empírica.

Por otro lado, en relación al origen conceptual de las propuestas (RQ3), es posible decir que la mayoría de las propuestas de proceso provienen de la ingeniería de software y representan adaptaciones tanto de procesos predictivos (UP, RUP, Waterfall, Spiral y otros) como de procesos ágiles (Scrum o XP). Se detectó que un 22,58% de las propuestas provienen desde áreas de conocimiento vinculadas con la Usabilidad como ser UE, UCD o HCI.

Por último se detectó que sólo el 45,16% de las propuestas de proceso pueden ser replicadas e instanciadas utilizando la información disponible.

5 Discusión

En primer lugar creemos que el reciente interés por definir y proponer procesos de software orientados a la usabilidad acompaña el aumento de la demanda de este atributo de calidad por parte de las comunidades profesionales y los usuarios finales.

A partir del análisis de los datos de la RQ3, observamos que esto se ve sustentado por la integración de propuestas interdisciplinarias (HCI, UCD y UE) dentro del área de conocimiento de la ingeniería de software. Claramente la definición de procesos y aspectos metodológicos es utilizada como medio para compartir e integrar el conocimiento entre las disciplinas, buscando acortar la brecha existente entre ambas. Si bien a nivel de proceso se presentan avances, creemos que el problema de la integración entre las áreas de conocimiento no está completamente resuelto y continúa siendo de interés para las comunidades de investigación.

Continuando con el análisis de los datos obtenidos por la RQ3, como era de esperar por el trabajo previo realizado, la mayor parte de las propuestas de procesos que se detectaron tienen su origen conceptual en la ingeniería de software. En ese sentido, creemos que es importante remarcar que el número de propuestas de proceso con origen ágil o predictivo es similar. Esto implica que la criticidad e importancia que cobra la usabilidad es tal, que es independiente del marco metodológico de base que se utilice para integrarla en los procesos. La usabilidad es abordada y desarrollada en ambos contextos (ágiles y predictivos) y debe ser contemplada de manera integral a nivel de proceso.

Con referencia a la RQ2 que analiza el tipo de evidencia utilizada, el 85,70% de los procesos son validados mediante estudios de caso. Por otro lado se identificaron 3 estudios que condujeron experimentos para evaluar los procesos. Esto resulta esperable debido a que la complejidad y dimensión del fenómeno a estudiar (el proceso de desarrollo de software usable) dificulta la aplicación de un enfoque reduccionista. Los procesos que presentan evidencia de aplicación han sido evaluados tanto en ambientes académicos como industriales. Para aquellos estudios evaluados en ambientes industriales se analizó el dominio de aplicación. La medicina fue el dominio más utilizado, seguido por la educación, en ambos casos aplicando tecnologías tanto web como mobile. En ese sentido, creemos que es importante contar con mayor número de validaciones en diversos contextos de aplicación.

Con referencia a la RQ4, se analizó cómo se realizó la especificación de los procesos en los estudios. Se detectó que sólo el 12,90% de los estudios analizados utilizó una notación específica (SPEM, UML o BPMN) para documentar el proceso propuesto. El 87,00% restante utiliza la prosa o imágenes (sin una notación normalizada) para definir y documentar el proceso propuesto en el estudio. Creemos que este aspecto afecta la capacidad de instanciar y replicar los procesos a partir de la información disponible dado que la definición de un proceso utilizando únicamente prosa puede resultar ambigua. Otro aspecto importante que creemos que afecta la replicación de los procesos, se refiere a la evolución en el tiempo de las propuestas. En ese sentido se detectó que sólo el 16,00% de los estudios identificados tuvieron evolución y fueron utilizados como base para otros estudios en el área de conocimiento. La realización de estudios de seguimiento es un factor que puede facilitar la instanciación de procesos, pero en general el seguimiento de los mismos no es realizado por parte de investigadores externos o independientes.

Los bajos niveles de replicabilidad y evolución de las propuestas de proceso, además de su escaso nivel de documentación dificultan y limitan la investigación futura en el área. De igual manera afectan la difusión y el entrenamiento a las comunidades profesionales de ingeniería de software que desean aplicarlos en contextos industriales. Es necesario trabajar en procesos que posean mayores niveles de validación empírica y replicación por parte de investigadores independientes, en mejorar la documentación y material de capacitación disponible y por último apoyar la difusión de los procesos a las comunidades profesionales.

5.1 Amenazas a la validez

Hemos identificado las siguientes limitantes y amenazas a la validez para el mapeo presentado.

El uso de Scopus como único motor de búsqueda representa una amenaza a la validez sobre los resultados obtenidos y los procesos identificados. Mediante snowballing y búsquedas exploratorias en otras librerías digitales como ser IEEE se detectaron propuestas de procesos que fueron incluidas en forma manual.

Otra limitante detectada está relacionada con la falta de sinónimos estandarizados para las palabras relacionadas con Usabilidad. Por ejemplo existen artículos que utilizan el término UCD, otros User centered design y otros User-centered-design. Esto también se detectó con el término Human Computer Interaction y representa una limitante que posee la cadena de búsqueda utilizada.

Por otro lado otra limitante relevante a destacar, es que la búsqueda fue ejecutada en Abril de 2015, en lugar de considerar un año natural. Esto dificulta la replicabilidad de los resultados obtenidos, al ser incierto el nivel de indexación de Scopus en dicho mes.

Por último otra amenaza a la validez identificada es que sólo un investigador analizó la totalidad de las propuestas de procesos definidas como relevantes. Esto puede generar sesgo en la clasificación y análisis de los procesos considerados.

A pesar de las amenazas y limitantes asociadas al mapeo, creemos que los resultados obtenidos son satisfactorios, estableciendo el estado de arte de los procesos de software orientados a la usabilidad y brindando una buena base teórica para futuros estudios en el área.

6 Conclusiones

En el contexto tecnológico actual la usabilidad toma un papel clave en la aceptación, adecuación y éxito del software moderno. Las aplicaciones de software son adoptadas por diversos tipos de usuarios para ejecutar distinto tipo de tareas en contextos heterogéneos. La definición de procesos de software es un medio para la sistematización del trabajo, la difusión del conocimiento y buenas prácticas y el establecimiento de una base para la mejora continua. Los procesos de software orientados a la usabilidad permiten definir un conjunto de actividades y tareas, prácticas, métodos y herramientas, artefactos y roles que posibilitan el desarrollo de software usable.

El estudio presenta el estado de arte actual en el área de procesos de software orientados a la usabilidad. Se elaboró un protocolo de búsqueda y ejecutó un mapeo sistemático de la literatura que identifica y discute las principales características de las propuestas de procesos de software orientados a la usabilidad.

Como resultado del mapeo se identificaron 31 propuestas de procesos orientados a la usabilidad. Durante los últimos años, la definición de procesos de software orientados a la usabilidad ha ido en aumento, siendo utilizado como uno de los medios para acortar la brecha existente entre la ingeniería de software y las disciplinas de usabilidad. La mayor parte de los procesos, cuenta con evidencia de instanciación tanto en ámbitos industriales como académicos.

Existen propuestas de procesos que provienen de áreas diversas como la cognición, la psicología, el diseño centrado en el usuario y otros campos relacionados. Esto nos muestra que la integración entre las disciplinas es posible a nivel de procesos. Por último las propuestas de proceso detectadas poseen bajos niveles de replicabilidad, documentación o difusión hacia la comunidad profesional de la ingeniería de software.

Como parte del trabajo futuro, se seleccionará un proceso orientado a la usabilidad y se realizará una replicación en el contexto de proyecto real. Se buscará instanciar y adaptar el proceso seleccionado en el marco de un proyecto académico-industrial. Se medirán los resultados obtenidos respecto de la usabilidad del producto final, la flexibilidad y el peso del proceso. De esta forma será posible ampliar el conocimiento disponible en el área.

7 Referencias

[1] Ieee, *Guide to the Software Engineering Body of Knowledge Version 3.0 (SWEBOK Guide V3.0)*. 2014.

[2] P. H. Feiler and W. S. Humphrey, "Software process development and enactment: concepts and definitions," *Softw. Process 1993 Contin. Softw. Process Improv. Second Int. Conf.*, vol. Berlin, Ge, pp. 28–40, 1993.

[3] N. Ashrafi, "The impact of software process improvement on quality: in theory and practice," *Inf. Manag.*, vol. 40, no. 7, pp. 677–690, Aug. 2003.

[4] "'Software Engineering - Product quality. Part 1: Quality model,'" *Software Engineering - Product Quality - Part 1: Quality Model*. .

[5] J. Nielsen, "The usability engineering life cycle," *Computer (Long. Beach. Calif).*, vol. 25, no. 3, 1992.

[6] ISO/IEC, "ISO/IEC 25000 - Software engineering - Software product Quality Requirements and Evaluation (SQuaRE) - Guide to SQuaRE," ISO/IEC, 2005.

[7] Gartner, "Gartner: Top 10 Strategic IT Trends For 2015," 2015. [Online]. Available: http://www.forbes.com/sites/peterhigh/2014/10/07/gartner-top-10-strategic-it-trends-for-2015/. [Accessed: 01-May-2015].

[8] Forrester, "Forrester Top Technology Trends." [Online]. Available: http://www.forbes.com/sites/peterhigh/2013/11/25/forrester-top-technology-trends-for-2014-and-beyond/. [Accessed: 01-Jul-2015].

[9] A. Seffah and E. Metzker, "The obstacles and myths of usability and software engineering," *Commun. ACM*, vol. 47, no. 12, pp. 71–76, Dec. 2004.

[10] A. Marcus, *Cost-Justifying Usability*. Elsevier, 2005.

[11] T. Ijaz and F. Andlib, "Impact of usability on non-technical users: Usability testing through websites," in *2014 National Software Engineering Conference*, 2014, pp. 37–42.

[12] P. S. Pyla, M. a. Perez-Quinones, J. D. Arthur, and H. R. Hartson, "What we should teach, but don't: proposal for cross pollinated HCI-SE curriculum," *34th Annu. Front. Educ. 2004. FIE 2004.*, pp. 16–21, 2004.

[13] T. Granollers, "User Centred Design Process Model . Usability Engineering and Software Engineering Integration .," pp. 2000–2002, 2003.

[14] A. September, "IEEE Standard Glossary of Software Engineering Terminology/IEEE Std 610.12-1990," *Office*, vol. 1990. p. 96, 1990.

[15] C. Collazos, T. Granollers, and C. Rusu, "A survey of human-computer interaction into the computer science curricula in iberoamerica," *Proc. - 2011 8th Int. Conf. Inf. Technol. New Gener. ITNG 2011*, pp. 151–156, 2010.

[16] A. Sivaji, A. Abdullah, and A. G. Downe, "Usability testing methodology: Effectiveness of heuristic evaluation in E-government website development," *Proc. - AMS 2011 Asia Model. Symp. 2011 - 5th Asia Int. Conf. Math. Model. Comput. Simul.*, pp. 68–72, 2011.

[17] L. L. Constantine and L. A. D. Lockwood, "Usage-centered engineering for Web applications," *IEEE Softw.*, vol. 19, no. 2, pp. 42–50, 2002.

[18] J. I. Panach Navarrete, N. Juristo Juzgado, and Ó. Pastor, "Introducing usability in a conceptual modeling-based software development process," *Lect. Notes Comput. Sci. (including Subser. Lect. Notes Artif. Intell. Lect. Notes Bioinformatics)*, vol. 7532 LNCS, no. 20080026, pp. 525–530, 2012.

[19] G. A. García-Mireles, M. Á. Moraga, F. García, and M. Piattini, "Approaches to promote product quality within software process improvement initiatives: A mapping study," *J. Syst. Softw.*, vol. 103, pp. 150–166, May 2015.

[20] T. da Silva, A. Martin, F. Maurer, M. Silveira, and T. Silva da Silva, "User-Centered Design and Agile Methods: A Systematic Review," in *Agile Conference (AGILE), 2011*, 2011, pp. 77–86.

[21] O. Sohaib and K. Khan, "Integrating Usability Engineering and Agile Software Development :," in *2010 International Conference on Computer Design and Applications, ICCDA 2010*, 2010, vol. 2, no. Iccda, pp. 32–38.

[22] D. Salah, R. F. Paige, and P. Cairns, "A systematic literature review for agile development processes and user centred design integration," in *Proceedings of the 18th International Conference on Evaluation and Assessment in Software Engineering - EASE '14*, 2014, pp. 1–10.

[23] G. Jurca, T. D. Hellmann, and F. Maurer, "Integrating Agile and User-Centered Design: A Systematic Mapping and Review of Evaluation and Validation Studies of Agile-UX," in *Agile Conference (AGILE), 2014*, 2014, pp. 24–32.

[24] M. Brhel, H. Meth, A. Maedche, and K. Werder, "Exploring principles of user-centered agile software development: A literature review," *Inf. Softw. Technol.*, vol. 61, pp. 163–181, 2015.

[25] N. M. C. V. and T. C. Williamson Silva, "Integrating the Usability into the Software Development Process A Systematic Mapping Study," pp. 105–113, 2015.

[26] B. a. Kitchenham, D. Budgen, and O. Pearl Brereton, "Using mapping studies as the basis for further research - A participant-observer case study," *Inf. Softw. Technol.*, vol. 53, no. 6, pp. 638–651, 2011.

[27] B. Kitchenham and S. Charters, "Guidelines for performing Systematic Literature Reviews in Software Engineering," *Engineering*, vol. 2, p. 1051, 2007.

Pruebas de Hipótesis en experimentos de Ingeniería de Software: Desviaciones respecto a la teoría

Rolando P. Reyes Ch.[1], Oscar Dieste[2] y Efraín R. Fonseca C.[1]

[1] Universidad de las Fuerzas Armadas ESPE, Sangolquí, Ecuador,
rpreyes@armada.mil.ec, erfonseca@espe.edu.ec,
[2] Universidad Politécnica de Madrid, Campus Montegancedo, España
odieste@fi.upm.es

Resumen: *Antecedentes:* Existen evidencias en las ciencias (e.g: Medicina, Psicología) respecto al uso incorrecto de las técnicas estadísticas. *Objetivo:* Estudiar si es posible el uso inadecuado de técnicas estadísticas en Ingeniería de Software Experimental (ISE). *Método:* Hemos seleccionado un error estadístico usual (uso inadecuado de las pruebas de 1-cola y 2-colas) y mediante un survey realizado a los autores del Congreso Empirical Software Engineering and Measurement y de la Revista Empirical Software Engineering, hemos recabado información acerca de las creencias de los investigadores y ejemplos de uso de las pruebas de 1-cola y 2-colas. *Resultados:* Existen evidencias de la existencia de un uso discutible de las pruebas de 1-cola y 2-colas, tales como la no definición de la cola asociada con la hipótesis alternativa, ó el cambio de tipo de cola. *Conclusión:* Al igual que otras disciplinas, la ISE puede estar usando incorrectamente las técnicas y conceptos estadísticos.

Palabras Claves: Pruebas de Hipótesis, Desviaciones, Errores, 1-cola, 2-colas, Survey.

1. Introducción

La Ingeniería de Software Experimental (ISE) es una de las ciencias más jóvenes dentro del campo científico [1] y al igual que otras disciplinas experimentales, utiliza técnicas estadísticas como el medio para interpretar los resultados en sus estudios [2].

Las técnicas estadísticas requieren de un adecuado conocimiento de las matemáticas que no siempre poseen los investigadores (en general, no específicamente en IS). En la literatura, es sencillo encontrar referencias a errores estadísticos comunes para todas la ciencias [3,4,5,6], entre los que se encuentran: sample size, p-value, niveles de significación, pruebas de hipótesis, entre otros. Sin embargo, no hemos logrado encontrar estudios que evidencien la presencia de estos fenómenos en la ISE, a pesar de la existencia de temas relacionados [7,8]. En el caso de la ISE, buena parte de sus investigadores se han formado a sí mismos en las distintas técnicas estadísticas mediante guías prácticas, libros, experimentos publicados, entre otros [7]. Este hecho, unido a nuestra costumbre de asignar un carácter algorítmico a cualquier procedimiento, aunque no revista de carácter sistemático puede provocar que se tomen decisiones no óptimas o incluso equivocadas en el uso de técnicas estadísticas dentro de la ISE [7,9].

El objetivo de este trabajo es explorar en qué medida existen problemas asociados con el uso de las técnicas estadísticas en ISE. Debido a su carácter exploratorio, no es factible estudiar muchas técnicas. Por ello, nos hemos decantado por explorar solo un concepto estadístico: El tipo de colas (1-cola o 2-colas) de los test. Este concepto es particularmente importante, ya que tiene relación con varios aspectos de la investigación experimental (hipótesis, tests, p-valores, etc.). Por otra parte, el concepto de 1-cola, 2-colas y las pruebas de hipótesis están relacionados con la aparición de falacias, confusiones, conceptos erróneos, malos usos y posiblemente abusos en la literatura científica [10,11,12,13].

Para indagar sobre esta interrogante, proponemos la aplicación de un survey como estratégica empírica. Preguntaremos a investigadores de ISE en qué circunstancias es correcto usar 1-cola ó 2-colas (así como otros aspectos asociados), de lo que inferiremos la existencia de errores o confusiones. Para dar mayor validez y representatividad a los resultados obtenidos del survey, hemos utilizado como población de estudio a los autores de artículos que reportan experimentos en el Congreso Empirical Engineering and Measurement (ESEM) y en la Revista Empirical Software Engineering (EMSE).

Los resultados obtenidos evidencian la existencia de algunas prácticas dudosas en su uso, así como en aspectos relacionados: hipótesis de investigación, hipótesis estadísticas, test estadísticos, entre otros.

La estructura del artículo es la siguiente: en la sección II, se analiza la literatura referente a la problemática y estudios similares en otras disciplinas. En la sección III, se detalla el diseño del survey como método de investigación. En la sección IV, se presentan los resultados e interpretación. Finalmente, en la sección V, enunciamos las conclusiones obtenidas.

2. Antecedentes

2.1. Errores Estadísticos en las Distintas Disciplinas

El uso inadecuado de las técnicas estadísticas ha sido un tema estudiado durante varios años en el campo de las ciencias médicas [14,15,16]. Sin embargo, actualmente despierta un creciente interés en otras áreas, como por ejemplo, la Psicología [17,18] o la Educación [19]. El uso inadecuado de las técnicas estadísticas ha sido lo suficientemente importante como para ser tratado en monografías específicas [3,4,5,6].

El estudio acerca del uso inadecuado de las técnicas estadísticas toma habitualmente la forma de revisión de literatura, normalmente en revistas especializadas. Los estudios ponen en manifiesto publicaciones con técnicas estadísticas inadecuadas [14], incompletas [16] o con serios errores estadísticos, tales como: uso inadecuado del sample size [15,16,17], p-value [15,17], niveles de significación [17,12], pruebas de hipótesis [12,14], entre otros. Como puede observarse en las referencias los errores en el uso de las técnicas estadísticas son comunes entre disciplinas.

2.2. Errores Estadísticos en Ingeniería de Software Experimental

Los antecedentes descritos anteriormente nos hacen pensar que podría también estar ocurriendo un uso incorrecto de las técnicas estadísticas en la ISE. Sin embargo, después de buscar trabajos similares en nuestra comunidad acerca de esta problemática, encontramos poca información que podría estar relacionada. A modo de excepción, Dyba et al. [7] evaluó cuantitativamente el uso del poder estadístico dentro de la ISE en 103 experimentos controlados de las principales revistas y congresos en la ISE. Los resultados arrojaron que el uso del poder estadístico cae sustancialmente por debajo de los estándares normalmente aceptados. También Miller [8] evaluó la técnica estadística del meta-análisis. Sus resultados demuestran que esta técnica estaría siendo utilizada incorrectamente en los experimentos de ISE. Ambos trabajos sugieren que se podría estar dando un uso incorrecto de las técnicas estadísticas en ISE.

2.3. Pruebas de *1-cola* y *2-colas*

Uno de los problemas más frecuentemente mencionados en la literatura hace referencia a las pruebas de 1-cola y 2-colas. Ello es sorprendente, ya que se trata de un procedimiento estadístico ampliamente utilizado en el ámbito empírico [20], sencillo y definido de modo riguroso en la literatura [21,22]. Sin embargo, a pesar de ello, este concepto estadístico se ha convertido un tema controvertido que se ha generado debates entre los bayesianos y frequentistas desde hace más de medio siglo [10,11,12], mostrado ser un concepto expuesto a falacias, confusiones, errores, malos usos y posiblemente abusos [13].

Más específicamente, la Psicología [11,23], Medicina [23] y Ecología [10] han desarrollado gran cantidad de estudios referente a esta temática. Los resultados indican que los autores de algunos artículos informan incorrectamente las pruebas de hipótesis [11,23] utilizadas, reportan cálculos estadísticos aparentemente inadecuados [10], utilizan la prueba de *1-cola* cuando debe utilizarse una prueba de *2-colas* [11,23], o simplemente los autores no se habrían molestado en indicar la prueba de cola utilizada [24].

Nos preguntamos si la prueba de 1-cola y 2-colas, es utilizado también de forma dudosa en la ISE. De ser así, ello podría sugerir la existencia de otros problemas, quizá mayores. Utilizaremos un survey como estrategia empírica de investigación.

3. Método de Investigación

3.1. Preguntas de Investigación

En un trabajo previo [25], determinamos que los experimentadores de la ISE construyen de manera apropiada su hipótesis de investigación. Sin embargo, al momento de definir analíticamente la hipótesis estadística, en diversas ocasiones no lo hacen. En estudios de otras ciencias, se considera a este fenómeno como un problema de traducción (o formulación) de una hipótesis de investigación a su correspondiente hipótesis estadística [12], debido a la falta de una *vinculación lógica exacta* entre ambos tipos de hipótesis. Por tal motivo, nuestra primera RQ es:

RQ1: *¿Existe una vinculación lógica exacta entre la hipótesis de investigación y la hipótesis estadística en los experimentos de la ISE?*

Los experimentadores de la ISE no describen en algunos casos el tipo de prueba de hipótesis utilizada en sus estudios (e.g:*1-cola,2-colas*). Esto dificulta establecer la existencia de un posible uso inadecuado de las prueba de hipótesis (e.g: falta de correspondencia entre el tipo de cola y el test estadístico utilizado). Existen presunciones en otras disciplinas (e.g: Psicología [11], Ecología [24]) que sugieren un uso preferente de la prueba de *1-cola* sobre la prueba de *2-colas* o viceversa. En razón a ello, nuestra segunda y tercera RQs son:

RQ2: *¿Existe un uso preferente de la prueba de 1-cola en la ISE?*

RQ3: *¿Existe un uso preferente de la prueba de 2-colas en la ISE?*

3.2. Diseño de la Encuesta

El diseño del survey está basado en las guías para creación y conducción de surveys para ISE propuestas por Kitchenham et al. [26] y Punter et al. [27]. El survey abordará aspectos cuantitativos y cualitativos acerca del uso de pruebas de hipótesis. Ello nos permitirá, por un lado, lograr producir estadístico descriptivos, y por otro lado, obtener información importante para responder a las preguntas de investigación propuestas en este estudio.

Construcción de la encuesta El survey consta de un total 19 preguntas obligatorias y 6 preguntas opcionales que están relacionadas con las respuestas a las preguntas obligatorias. El survey se encuentra alojado en un servidor del Grupo de Investigación en Ingeniería del Software Empírica (GRISE) de la Universidad Politécnica de Madrid(UPM), específicamente en el enlace: http://grise.upm.es/htdocs/sites/extras/15.

Esperamos que los participantes puedan proporcionar sus respuestas en menos de 10 minutos (dependiendo del feedback aportado). Suponemos que un survey en este tiempo no fatigará a los encuestados [26]. La mayoría de preguntas son cerradas con el fin de no dar lugar a interpretaciones erróneas y/o la provisión de una respuesta irrelevante o confusa. En los casos restantes, proporcionaremos definiciones y aclaraciones en las preguntas del survey, con fin de evitar una posible mala interpretación.

Instrumento de evaluación Se adoptó un proceso de dos etapas de evaluación del survey. En primer lugar, un experimentador con experiencia en experimentación (O. Dieste) revisó el cuestionario y proporcionó información sobre su legibilidad, comprensibilidad y ambigüedades potenciales. Su retroalimentación nos condujo a la eliminación de 5 preguntas obligatorias y creación de 8 nuevas preguntas obligatorias y opcionales. En segundo lugar, dos experimentadores (M. Solari y O. Gómez, no incluidos como autores), pilotaron la encuesta. Durante esta revisión se mejoraron 4 preguntas opcionales.

3.3. Población

La población para este survey, fueron autores de artículos del Congreso ESEM y la revista EMSE. Consideramos que los artículos en estas publicaciones son representativas de la investigación de la mejor calidad y relevancia en ISE. Ello nos permitirá una mejor capacidad de observación del fenómeno de estudio [26].

Para seleccionar artículos experimentales, se aplicaron los siguientes criterios de inclusión: (1) deben perseguir el objetivo de comparar diferentes poblaciones, procesos, métodos o herramientas [7], (2) emplear estadística inferencial, (3) asignar en forma aleatoria o no, de sus unidades experimentales a tratamientos. El único criterio de exclusión utilizado fue que los artículos aplicasen métodos no frecuentistas (ej. método bayesiano).

Se obtuvieron un total de 221 correos electrónicos de autores únicos; 106 correos electrónicos pertenecientes al ESEM y 115 correos electrónicos pertenecientes al EMSE.

3.4. Recopilación de datos

La recolección de datos para los autores del congreso ESEM inició el 30.10.2015 y finalizó el 14.11.2015. La recolección de datos para los autores de la revista EMSE inició el 15.11.2015 y finalizó el 01.12.2015. Separamos la recolección de datos en ambas comunidades para poder trazar resultados del survey a comunida-des en caso de que fuera preciso.

La encuesta fue anunciada a todos los autores mediante correo electrónico. Se envió un recordatorio en la mitad del tiempo de cada survey. Un total de 28 personas respondieron al survey. De las encuestas respondidas, 20 fueron completadas satisfactoriamente y 8 fueron dejadas sin completar, por lo que no fueron considerados como parte de este estudio. El ratio de respuesta es de $\frac{28}{221} = 12,7\,\%$, en línea con los ratios de respuesta de otros surveys en la ISE [28].

3.5. Amenazas a la validez

Se discuten las amenazas generales a la validez de acuerdo a las cuatro perspectivas presentadas por Wohlin et al. [29].

Validez de la Conclusión: Este tipo de validez se refiere al grado en que las conclusiones obtenidas se derivan de los datos obtenidos [26]. Dado que no usamos técnicas estadísticas, la única amenaza posible es la falta de representatividad de la sub-población escogida. Creemos que esta amenaza no opera, ya que hemos escogido encuestados que poseen alto nivel de experiencia en experimentación dentro de la ISE.

Validez Interna: Este tipo de validez hace referencia a que no existan otras variables influyentes en el estudio, excepto las que estamos estudiando [26]. En el contexto de este survey, la aparición de otras variables influyentes sólo deberían aparecer por errores en la formulación o comprensión de las preguntas del survey.

Para evitar este problema, proporcionamos una introducción en nuestro survey con el fin de familiarizar al encuestado acerca del contexto del estudio y su propósito. También proporcionamos información acerca de la intención de las preguntas, añadiendo definiciones de la terminología utilizada para evitar posibles ambigüedades.

Para mitigar las confusiones, se ordenaron a las preguntas del survey en bloques, de acuerdo a la temática de las RQs. De esta manera, esperamos se espera que los encuestados no pierdan el contexto del tema abordado, y por lo tanto se ayude a mitigar las amenazas de la omisión de preguntas por fatiga, confusión o desconocimiento.

Por otra parte, para garantizar la veracidad de los datos, hemos brindado confidencialidad y anonimato a las respuestas a los autores. Esto permite que los encuestados tengan mayor libertad y confianza para completar la encuesta, evitando la amenaza potencial de que el encuestado no desee contestar a preguntas donde exista el riesgo de cometer errores en algunos conceptos estadísticos, o se revele información comprometida.

Finalmente, tratamos de mitigar el posible sesgo en las respuestas mediante respuestas pre-definidas con un campo de texto adicional, a fin de dar la posibilidad al encuestado de introducir texto libre que sustente la respuesta seleccionada.

Validez del Constructo: Este tipo de validez se refiere a la relación entre una teoría detrás de un investigación y su observación [26]. Para ello, se realizó un estudio previo acerca de los errores estadísticos, así como de la teoría de pruebas de hipótesis, con la finalidad de diseñar el survey. El survey fue evaluado por un experimentador con experiencia y piloteado por dos experimentadores con experiencia no relacionados con la presente investigación.

Validez Externa: La validez externa se refiere a la generalización [26]. Creemos que los resultados son válidos externamente debido a que la sub-población seleccionada es muy representativa de los investigadores en la Ingeniería de Software Empírica.

4. Resultados e Interpretación

4.1. *Características generales de los encuestados:*

El 55 % de encuestados poseen una experiencia en investigación empírica entre 5 a 10 años y el 25 % de encuestados poseen más de 10 años. En lo que respecta a la participación en experimentos controlados, el 30 % de encuestados han realizado entre 2 a 5 experimentos y el 45 % más 5 experimentos. El 35 % de encuestados se formó en pruebas de hipótesis a partir de explicaciones y experiencias de otros investigadores. El 25 % de encuestados se han autoeducado en diversos materiales como tutoriales o guías prácticas. El 25 % de encuestados han tomado cursos formales universitarios.

4.2. RQ1: *¿Existe una vinculación lógica exacta entre la hipótesis de investigación y la hipótesis estadística en los experimentos de la ISE?*

Tabla 1. Respuestas relacionadas con la pregunta de investigación - RQ1

Pregunta Survey	Opciones Respuesta	Total	% Total
Do you define the research hypotheses (or similar, e.g.: Aim / Research Questions) in experimental reports ?	Never.	0	0 %
	In some experiments.	1	5 %
	Always	19	95 %
	No answer.	0	0 %
Do you define statistical hypotheses in analytical form (H_0 and H_1) in experimental reports?	Never.	1	5 %
	In some experiments.	5	25 %
	Always.	14	70 %
	No answer	0	0 %
Do you specify in experimental reports the type of tail associated with the null hypothesis / alternative hypothesis BEFORE running your experiment?	Never.	2	10 %
	In some experiments.	5	25 %
	Always.	13	65 %
	No Answer.	0	0 %
Do you consider that there is a clear connection or relationship between research hypothesis and statistical hypothesis?	Yes.	13	65 %
	Sometimes.	6	30 %
	No.	1	5 %

Los resultados relacionados a esta pregunta de investigación se muestran en la Tabla 1. Desglosaremos la respuesta a esta pregunta en 4 tópicos:

1. ***Definición de la Hipótesis de investigación:*** La importancia de la hipótesis de investigación radica en ser la declaración anticipada de las bases para el diseño de cualquier estudio [30]. Un 95 % de los encuestados indican que siempre definen la hipótesis de investigación. Solo un investigador indica que no la define. Sin embargo, en su respuesta aclaratoria, el investigador resalta que *"Some experiments are not appropriate for null hypotheses, for example case studies."*. Consideramos que esta respuesta es correcta, aunque nuestra intención no era abarcar casos de estudio. Por lo tanto, todos los encuestados concuerdan en que la definición de la hipótesis de investigación es importante.
2. ***Formulación Analítica de la Hipótesis Estadística:*** La formulación analítica (H_0, H_1) ayuda a definir rigurosamente la orientación de una investigación [12]. Un 70 % de los encuestados formulan analíticamente la hipótesis estadística). Sin embargo, un 25 % de encuestados manifiesta que definen la hipótesis solo *en algunos experimentos*, debido a lo siguiente:

- *1) "When we don't know in advance whether we will have enough subjects for experiment A so we revert to experiment B".*
- *2) "Sometimes English definitions are clear enough. A formal analytical definition may introduce unnecessary cognitive overhead for the reader."*
- *3) "Some studies are exploratory in nature. They dont require a specific hypothesis, It depends on the context."*

Respecto a 1), no parece que la cantidad de sujetos experimentales tengan relación con la formulación (H_0, H_1). Respecto a 2) es cierto que en estudios de carácter exploratorio no es necesaria una formulación analítica (H_0, H_1) y, en principio, una definición clara de la Hipótesis de Investigación sería suficiente. No obstante, la formulación analítica (H_0, H_1) en estudios confirmatorios parece ser importante a pesar de suponer una supuesta sobrecarga cognitiva al lector [12]. Respecto a 3) estamos de acuerdo con la respuesta dada.
Un investigador señala que *nunca* se debería definir la formulación analítica de la hipótesis estadística. En su respuesta aclaratoria indica que *"I define the hypothesis as Research Question. Do not use formal H_0 y H_1"*. Al igual que 2), si bien ello puede ser totalmente correcto, de esta forma puede existir ambigüedad respecto a los test de inferencia que realizar.

3. ***Especificar el tipo de cola asociada a la Hipótesis Nula:*** Definir la cola antes de iniciar un experimento ayuda al investigador definir claramente el fenómeno a investigar, evitando escoger a propósito la direccionalidad para obtener resultados significativos [21]. Un 65 % de encuestados indican que la cola debería ser especificada. Un 25 % de encuestados manifiesta que *en algunos experimentos* definen la cola atendiendo a ciertas matizaciones:
   - *1) "The experimental design has not always been so rigorous to specify all the analysis details before running the experiment."*
   - *2) "Often this is implicit because the direction of the effect is assumed obvious or the direction of effect rarely comes up in hypothesis generation"*
   - *3) "I hardly ever think about this (despite my formal education in experimentation). I use the default two-tailed version most of the time. Always use two-tailed. but sometimes i might forget to specify it."*
   - *4) "Because I learned myself and sometimes my students and I forgot about it."*

   Respecto a 1) y 2), la matización parece acertada si los estudios son de carácter exploratorio. En caso contrario, la cola podía ser oportunisticamente seleccionada. Respecto a 3), nada podemos objetar. El uso de la prueba de 2-colas es recomendable cuando la dirección de los efectos es desconocido, como ocurre generalmente en Ingeniería de Software. No obstante, usar una prueba de 2-colas por defecto puede implicar el gasto innecesario de recursos (e.g: tamaño muestral) en las investigaciones. Respecto a 4), la auto-educación podía motivar que aspectos relevantes de la teoría estadística pero no percibidos como tales por los investigadores, fueran pasados por alto, transmitiendo además dicho sesgo a generaciones futuras de investigaciones.
   Dos investigadores señalaron que *nunca* se debería definir la cola antes de iniciar un experimento. En el primer caso, el encuestado asegura que *"I*

make sure that that's clear from the hypothesis definition", se trata de un caso extremo de respuesta 2) anterior.

4. ***Relación entre Hipótesis de Investigación e Hipótesis Estadística:*** La Hipótesis de Investigación es la declaración sintáctica y semántica de una relación esperada o prevista entre dos o más variables, y la Hipótesis Estadística es una formulación analítica sobre la base de la Hipótesis de Investigación, con el fin de describir los patrones en los datos empíricos para probar su verdad o falsedad en relación a una o varias distribuciones o parámetros de una distribución [30]. Un 65 % de encuestados tienen claro que existe esta relación. Sin embargo, un 30 % de encuestados manifiesta que en algunos experimentos no existe esta relación debido a:
   - *1) "It is not clear the magnitude of the effects until you measure them. If you have large datasets it is always possible to have "statistically"significant results that have no practical meaning whatsoever.".*
   - *2) "Sometimes the way you describe the hypothesis and the way the statistical method is used makes interpretation not easy.".*
   - *3) "I don't think there is a clear mapping from statistical constructs to research constructs."*
   - *4) "Some research questions are broader than the statistical hypotheses".*

   El encuestado 1), está haciendo probablemente referencia a la posibilidad de que resultados estadísticamente significativos no posean relevancia en la práctica (e.g: los efectos asociados sean muy pequeños). Esto no invalida la relación entre hipótesis de investigación y estadística. Respecto a 2) entendemos que hace referencia a que, en ocasiones, el análisis estadístico que requiere un conjunto de datos no pude trazarse fácilmente a las hipótesis de investigación. Esto ocurre con frecuencia en estudios exploratorios, aunque nos parece más raro que pueda suceder en estudios confirmatorios. Es muy posible que los encuestados 3) y 4) hagan referencia a esta especial relación entre hipótesis de investigación y estadística en estudios exploratorios.
   Un investigador señala que *nunca* existe tal relación. No aclaró las razones de su respuesta.

4.3. RQ2: *¿Es posible la existencia de desviaciones en la aplicación de la prueba de 1-cola en la ISE?*

Los resultados relacionados a esta pregunta de investigación se muestran en la Tabla 2. Desglosaremos la respuesta a esta pregunta en 2 tópicos:

1. ***Situaciones en las que se utiliza la prueba de 1-cola:*** Los encuestados plantean dos escenarios de uso de las pruebas de 1-cola. Respecto al primer escenario, el 85 % de los encuestados indican que el uso de 1-cola *depende del conocimiento sobre el fenómeno y que debe existir una evidencia empírica suficiente y consistente del efecto en una dirección* ó, lo que es lo mismo, *se usa cuando la hipótesis es direccional, del tipo* $A > B$. Este primer escenario es coherente con lo expuesto en la literatura, donde se indica que para usar una prueba de 1-cola debe poseerse evidencia empírica suficiente

Tabla 2. Respuestas relacionadas a responder a la pregunta de investigación - RQ2

Pregunta Survey	Opciones Respuesta	Total	% Total
Do you believe that 1-tailed tests should be used?	Free Text	20	100 %
Which types of studies do you believe 1-tailed tests apply to?	Exploratory studies.	7	35 %
	Confirmatory studies.	15	75 %
	Observational studies.	4	20 %
	Others.	6	30 %
What are the reasons that drive you to choose the direction of a 1-tailed test?	I choose the direction indicated in previous research by other authors.	11	55 %
	I choose the direction on the basis of the commonly accepted knowledge in the SE community.	11	55 %
	I choose the direction on the basis of formal and informal literature, regardless of being empirically validated.	5	25 %
	I choose the direction arbitrarily, without any given reason.	0	0 %
	I choose the direction according to the results of my own research.	3	15 %
	Other.	10	50 %
Did you ever have a 1-tailed test with $u_1 \leq u_2$ in the first instance, but you changed it later $u_1 \geq u_2$ in your research.?	Yes.	19	95 %
	No.	1	5 %
	No Answer.	0	0 %

y consistente sobre el fenómeno bajo estudio [7,4]. Respecto al segundo escenario, el 15 % de los encuestados han sido radicales en su formulación, sustentando que *la prueba de 1-cola nunca debería ser usada o al menos debería ser evitada en la ISE.* Esta visión del uso de los test de 1-cola está ciertamente presente en ISE (e.g: ver [31]), y tiene sentido desde el punto de vista de la inmadurez de la ISE. Sin embargo, cabria preguntarse si la negativa a aplicar pruebas de 1-cola podría representar un gasto innecesario de tiempo y recursos en ciertos contextos de investigación.

2. ***La prueba de 1-cola y su direccionalidad:*** Con respecto a la direccionalidad, el 95 % de encuestados no cambia la direccionalidad durante el curso de su investigación. Solo un encuestado indica que lo hace con el fin de *"To check that I didn't miss anything in the other direction."*. El mismo encuestado, en respuestas a tópicos anteriores respondió que utiliza la prueba de 1-cola en estudios confirmatorios *"based on common knowledge accepted in the ISE, and formal and informal literature validated."*. Suponemos que el investigador podría tener incertidumbre acerca de la direccionalidad del efecto y que explorar en otra direccionalidad podría darle una seguridad extra durante su investigación. No obstante, cambiar la direcciòn de la cola no es una práctica recomendada en la literatura especializada [5,10]

Tabla 3. Respuestas relacionadas a responder a la pregunta de investigación - RQ3

Pregunta Survey	Opciones Respuesta	Total	% Total
In which situations do you believe that 2-tailed tests should be used?	Free Text	20	100 %
Which types of studies do you believe 1-tailed tests apply to?	Exploratory studies.	14	70 %
	Confirmatory studies.	11	55 %
	Observational studies.	12	60 %
	Others.	5	25 %
Did you ever change a 2-tailed hypothesis into a 1-tailed one?	Yes.	4	20 %
	No.	16	80 %
When you switched the 2-tailed hypothesis into a 1-tailed one, did it turn out that a statistically significant result came to light?	Yes.	2	10 %
	No.	2	10 %
	No Answer.	0	0 %

3. ***Estudios que utilizan la prueba de 1-cola*** Normalmente, la prueba de 1-cola se usa en estudios confirmatorios, los cuales están basados en estudios anteriores donde se insinúa al menos la direccionalidad del efecto. Un 75 % de encuestados utiliza esta prueba en estudios confirmatorios. Sin embargo, un 35 % de encuestados lo utilizan en estudios exploratorios (e.g: estudios correlacionales), un 20 % de encuestados lo utilizan en estudios observacionales (sin aclarar respuesta) y un 30 % de encuestados en otros estudios (e.g: replicaciones). En estos casos, coincide que los encuestados contestaron en *algunos experimentos* o *nunca* respecto al punto 2 de la sección 4.2. De igual forma aquellos encuestados que utilizan la prueba de 1-cola únicamente en estudios confirmatorios, contestaron que *siempre* respecto al punto 2 de la misma sección. Aparentemente quienes han trabajado en estudios confirmatorios definen analíticamente H_0 y H_1 y utilizan la prueba de 1-cola. Sin embargo, cuando el encuestado trabaja en otros tipos de estudios, y no se define claramente H_0 y H_1 y puede existir incertidumbre respecto al tipo de cola.

4.4. RQ3: *¿Es posible la existencia de desviaciones en la aplicación de la prueba de 2-colas en la ISE?*

Los resultados relacionados a esta pregunta de investigación se muestran en la Tabla 3. Desglosaremos la respuesta a esta pregunta en 3 tópicos:

1. ***Situaciones en las que se utiliza la prueba de 2-colas:*** Las pruebas de 2-colas permiten explorar los posibles efectos de un fenómeno sin eliminar la posibilidad de obtener resultados en ambas direcciones [12]. Los encuestados plantean dos escenarios de uso de las pruebas de 2-colas. Respecto al primer escenario, un 75 % de encuestados utilizan una prueba de 2-colas en cualquier tipo de estudio donde sea necesario falsear la hipótesis nula. Respecto al segundo escenario, un 25 % de los encuestados poseen puntos de vista diferentes y posiblemente enfrentados. Por ejemplo, un encuestado indica que la

prueba de 2-colas debe ser usada *"Always or in most cases. Especially when there is no strong prior knowledge on the direction based on previous comparisons"*. Contrariamente otro encuestado indica que *"Never use it. A 2-tailed test is a bogus test which only has a statistical meaning but never a practical meaning. We should always known from a theoretical model in which direction things should go."*.

2. ***Estudios que utilizan la prueba de 2-colas:*** Un 70 % de encuestados utilizan las prueba de 2-colas en estudios exploratorios. No obstante, la prueba de 2-colas se utiliza mayoritariamente en todo tipo de estudios. Un 55 % de encuestados utilizan la prueba de 2-colas en estudios confirmatorios y un 60 % en observacionales. Un investigador en su respuesta aclaratoria indicó que *"two-tailed tests are more conservative, therefore I think they can be valuable in all types of studies"*. Esta es probablemente la razón del alto porcentaje de uso de la prueba de 2-colas. No obstante, aquí es aplicable también lo indicado anteriormente respecto al uso inadecuado de recursos.
3. ***Prueba de 2-colas vs. Prueba de 1-cola:*** El uso de una prueba de 1-cola luego de ejecutar una prueba de 2-colas, cuando no se logró en primera instancia rechazar la hipótesis nula, no parece del todo apropiado, así se obtenga un resultado significativo [10]. Un 80 % de encuestados conoce esta situación. Sin embargo, un 20 % de encuestados realiza este cambio. En las aclaraciones sobre el cambio de elección del tipo de cola se respondió que *"Because sometimes you realize that for some constructs although a 2-tailed hypothesis seems ok, it does make sense in practice"* o *"Because I discovered an error y my perception"* o *"we came to realize that a clear direction of the effect was to be expected"*. Quienes indicaron estas respuestas afirmaron que luego del cambio obtuvieron resultados significativos.

5. Discusión y Conclusiones

Los resultado obtenidos para RQ1 evidencian que la hipótesis de investigación y su formulación analítica no están siendo definidas en todos los casos, con mayor frecuencia cuando los estudios son de carácter exploratorio. En este caso, las preguntas de investigación desempeñan el papel de las hipótesis de investigación. Por otra parte, RQ2 pone en manifiesto que la prueba de 1-cola, es mayoritariamente bien entendida. Sin embargo, encontramos evidencias aisladas de cambio de direccionalidad de la 1-cola, que a pesar ser justificadas por fines de chequeo, denota inseguridad del uso de 1-cola. RQ3 muestra que los investigadores son conscientes que la prueba de 2-colas es más conservadora en la teoría, lo que ha motivado que el uso de la prueba de 2-colas sea frecuente en todos los tipos de estudio de la ISE. Sin embargo, al mismo tiempo hemos observado casos aislados de cambio del tipo de cola (2-colas hacia 1-cola) dentro de un mismo estudio.

Un aspecto interesante fue que se encontraron posiciones enfrentadas entre aquellos que defienden el uso de la prueba de 2-colas frente al uso de la prueba de 1-cola o vicevera. A pesar que dichas posturas enfrentadas son casos aislados en la ISE, comunidades como la Psicología han sufrido (y sufren) controversias sobre el uso de las pruebas de 1-cola o 2-colas [11,23,32], sin haber llegado a una solución satisfactoria por el momento.

Las pruebas de hipótesis son un concepto estadístico sencillo. Sin embargo, los resultados obtenidos apuntan a la existencia de incertidumbre en su uso. Creemos que lo mismo, incluso más acentuado puede ocurrir con conceptos y técnicas más complejas. Este estudio solo representa un primer paso en la dirección de contestar tal pregunta. Ello será el objeto de futuras investigaciones.

Agradecimientos: Esta investigación ha sido parcialmente financiada por el proyecto TIN 2014-60490-P (Ministerio de Economía y Competitividad, Gobierno de España), SENESCYT, ESPE y Armada del Ecuador.

Referencias

1. L. Snyder *et al.*, *Academic careers for experimental computer scientists and engineers.* National Academies Press, 1994.
2. U. of York. NHS Centre for Reviews and Dissemination, *Undertaking systematic reviews of research on effectiveness: CRD's guidance for those carrying out or commissioning reviews*, ser. CRD report. NHS Centre for Reviews and Dissemination, University of York, 2001.
3. S. W. Huck, *Statistical misconceptions.* Routledge, 2009.
4. P. I. Good and J. W. Hardin, *Common errors in statistics (and how to avoid them).* John Wiley & Sons, 2012.
5. C. M. Anderson-Cook, "Common errors in statistics (and how to avoid them)," *The American Statistician*, vol. 58, no. 4, 2004.
6. A. Vickers, *What is a P-value anyway?: 34 stories to help you actually understand statistics.* Addison-Wesley Longman, 2010.
7. T. Dybå, V. B. Kampenes, and D. I. Sjøberg, "A systematic review of statistical power in software engineering experiments," *Information and Software Technology*, vol. 48, no. 8, pp. 745–755, 2006.
8. J. Miller, "Can results from software engineering experiments be safely combined," in *Software Metrics Symposium, 1999. Proceedings. Sixth International.* IEEE, 1999, pp. 152–158.
9. H. Midi, A. R. Imon, and A. Jaafar, "The misconceptions of some statistical techniques in research," *Jurnal Teknologi*, vol. 47, no. 1, pp. 21–36, 2012.
10. C. M. Lombardi and S. H. Hurlbert, "Misprescription and misuse of one-tailed tests," *Austral Ecology*, vol. 34, no. 4, pp. 447–468, 2009.
11. C. Burke, "A brief note on one-tailed tests." *Psychological Bulletin*, vol. 50, no. 5, p. 384, 1953.
12. H.-C. Cho and S. Abe, "Is two-tailed testing for directional research hypotheses tests legitimate?" *Journal of Business Research*, vol. 66, no. 9, pp. 1261–1266, 2013.
13. X. R. Li and X.-B. Li, "Common fallacies in applying hypothesis testing," in *Information Fusion, 2008 11th International Conference on.* IEEE, 2008, pp. 1–8.
14. G. E. Welch and S. G. Gabbe, "Review of statistics usage in the american journal of obstetrics and gynecology," *American journal of obstetrics and gynecology*, vol. 175, no. 5, pp. 1138–1141, 1996.

15. D. G. Altman, "Statistical reviewing for medical journals," *Statistics in medicine*, vol. 17, no. 23, pp. 2661–2674, 1998.
16. C. H. Olsen, "Review of the use of statistics in infection and immunity," *Infection and immunity*, vol. 71, no. 12, pp. 6689–6692, 2003.
17. I. Ercan, Y. Yang, G. Özkaya, S. Cangur, B. Ediz, I. Kan *et al.*, "Misusage of statistics in medical research," 2008.
18. R. S. Nickerson, "Null hypothesis significance testing: a review of an old and continuing controversy." *Psychological methods*, vol. 5, no. 2, p. 241, 2000.
19. J. W. Creswell, *Educational research: Planning, conducting, and evaluating quantitative.* Prentice Hall, 2002.
20. R. E. Walpole, R. H. Myers, S. L. Myers, and K. Ye, *Probability and statistics for engineers and scientists.* Macmillan New York, 1993, vol. 5.
21. R. Fisher, "The design of experiments (1966)," *Oliver and Boyd Ltd., Edinburgh*, 1935.
22. J. Neyman and E. S. Pearson, "On the problem of the most efficient tests of statistical hypotheses," *Philosophical Transactions of the Royal Society*, vol. 231, no. 694-706, pp. 289–337, 1933.
23. M. Bakker and J. M. Wicherts, "The (mis) reporting of statistical results in psychology journals," *Behavior Research Methods*, vol. 43, no. 3, pp. 666–678, 2011.
24. G. D. Ruxton and M. Neuhäuser, "When should we use one-tailed hypothesis testing?" *Methods in Ecology and Evolution*, vol. 1, no. 2, pp. 114–117, 2010.
25. N. Juristo, O. Dieste, and R. Reyes, "The good, the bad and the ugly of the hypothesis in the experimental software engineering," *Enviado al Empirical Software Engineering Journal (EMSE)*, 2016.
26. B. A. Kitchenham and S. L. Pfleeger, "Personal opinion surveys," in *Guide to Advanced Empirical Software Engineering.* Springer, 2008, pp. 63–92.
27. T. Punter, M. Ciolkowski, B. Freimut, and I. John, "Conducting on-line surveys in software engineering," in *Empirical Software Engineering, 2003. ISESE 2003. Proceedings. 2003 International Symposium on.* IEEE, 2003, pp. 80–88.
28. J. L. de la Vara, M. Borg, K. Wnuk, and L. Moonen, "Survey on safety evidence change impact analysis in practice: Detailed description and analysis," 2014.
29. C. Wohlin, P. Runeson, M. Höst, M. C. Ohlsson, B. Regnell, and A. Wesslén, *Experimentation in software engineering.* Springer Science & Business Media, 2012.
30. G. R. McPherson, "Teaching & learning the scientific method," *The American Biology Teacher*, vol. 63, no. 4, pp. 242–245, 2001.
31. A. Arcuri and L. Briand, "A hitchhiker's guide to statistical tests for assessing randomized algorithms in software engineering," *Software Testing, Verification and Reliability*, vol. 24, no. 3, pp. 219–250, 2014. [Online]. Available: http://dx.doi.org/10.1002/stvr.1486
32. H. D. Kimmel, "Three criteria for the use of one-tailed tests." *Psychological Bulletin*, vol. 54, no. 4, p. 351, 1957.

Feature Subset Selection for Instance Filtering Methods on Cross-project Defect Prediction

Faimison Porto and Adenilso Simao

Instituto de Ciências Matemáticas e de Computação
Universidade de São Paulo
PO Box 668, 13560-970, São Carlos, SP, Brazil
{faimison,adenilso}@icmc.usp.br

Abstract. The defect prediction models can be a good tool on organizing the project's test resources. However, not all companies maintain an appropriate set of historical defect data. In this case, the companies can build an appropriate dataset from known external projects. This approach, called Cross-project Defect Prediction (CPDP), solves the lack of defect data, although introduces heterogeneity on data. This heterogeneity can compromises the performance of CPDP models. Recently, filtering methods were proposed in order to decrease the heterogeneity of data by selecting the most similar instances from the training dataset. This similarity between instances is calculated based on the available features of the dataset. On this study, we propose that using only the most relevant features on this calculation can result in more accurate filtered datasets and better prediction performances. We present an empirical evaluation of different methods used for selecting the most relevant features. We evaluate different configurations of four Feature Selection (FS) methods and two metric subsets. We used 36 versions of 11 open source projects on experiments. The results indicate that the defect prediction performance can be improved by using the evaluated approach. In addition, we investigated which methods present better performances. The results do not indicate a method with general better performances, i.e., the most appropriate method for a project can vary according to the project characteristics.

Keywords: Software quality assurance · Cross-project defect prediction · Instance filtering · Feature selection · Network metrics · Code metrics

1 Introduction

Software testing activities are crucial for quality assurance in the software development process. Applying those activities, however, can be expensive and the available resources can be limited. The defect prediction models aim at predicting the likely defective parts of the software. Thus, the cost and efficiency of test can be improved by prioritizing the most critical software parts [2].

Building a good defect prediction model demands an accurate training dataset [31]. Commonly, software companies do not maintain sufficient or appropriate defect data [11]. In this case, the training dataset can be constructed by agglomerating instances from known external projects. This approach, called Cross-project Defect Prediction (CPDP), solves the lack of defect data [25]. However, the heterogeneity of data can compromises the defect prediction performance, as discussed in [31] and [28].

Alternative methods were proposed in order to improve the performance of CPDP models. Among these methods, we can highlight the filtering methods proposed by Turhan et al. [25] and Peters et al. [19]. These methods aim at building an accurate filtered dataset by selecting the most similar instances from the CPDP training dataset. Both methods make use of the Euclidean distance on measuring the similarity between instances. This similarity measure, though, originally considers the entire set of features of the dataset.

We propose that using only the most relevant features on measuring the similarity between instances can improve the performance of the mentioned filtering methods. In order to select the most relevant features of a dataset we refer to the Feature Selection (FS) methods, widely investigated and adopted on the data mining literature [29]. We evaluate four distinct FS methods: Information Gain [4], Relief [12], CFS [29], and Sparcl [27]. We also compare the use of two specific subset of features: code metrics [10] and network metrics [30]. We call the evaluated methods as *Instance Filtering methods based on Feature subset Selection* (IFFS).

Thus, we present an empirical evaluation of the mentioned IFFS methods aiming to answer the following research questions:

- RQ1: Can IFFS methods lead to better performance on CPDP?
  – The results indicate a positive answer. For all evaluated projects, at least one FS method presented better performance in relation to the original filtering methods.
- RQ2: Which IFFS methods present better performance on CPDP?
  – The results do not reveal a unique method with general good performance. Instead, the most appropriate method depends on the project characteristics.

This paper is organized as follows. Section 2 provides the necessary background of the related subjects as well as the related works proposed in the literature. Section 3 shows the experimental setup and methodology. Section 4 presents the obtained results and the answers for the research questions. Section 5 presents the threats to validity. Finally, Section 6 concludes the paper and sketches future work.

2 Background and Related Works

2.1 Defect Prediction

Constructing a good defect prediction model for binary classification problems encompasses two main issues: 1) building an accurate training dataset and 2) applying an appropriate classification algorithm. A training dataset consists of a table of elements (software parts) associated with their respective independent variables (software characteristics) and the dependent variable (or class attribute: defective or not-defective).

Some studies in the literature were proposed in order to identify the most relevant independent variables. Basili et al. [1] presented seminal studies in this context by using object oriented metrics. Ostrand et al. [18] proposed prediction models for industrial large-scale systems by using code metrics and historical defect information. Zimmermann and Nagappan [30] proposed the use of social network analysis metrics (also called network metrics) extracted from the software dependency graph. Further, other metrics were investigated such as developer related metrics [20], organizational metrics [16], process metrics [6], change related metrics [7], and antipatterns related metrics [23]. On this study, we use both code metrics and network metrics once they can be automatically extracted just from the source code. Thus, no historical or additional data is required. Furthermore, some works in the literature indicate that better prediction performances can be obtained by combining these two metrics sets [7, 30].

2.2 Cross-project Defect Prediction

The dependent variable information can be extracted from historical defect data. When available, those data can be mined and associated with the respective defective software parts [32, 10]. However, in practice, not all software companies maintain clear records about defects or do not have sufficient data from previous projects. In this case, the training dataset can be composed by external projects with known defect information. In the literature, this approach is called Cross-project Defect Prediction (CPDP). On this approach, available projects from different application domains and with different characteristics can be agglomerated in a heterogeneous dataset. However, the heterogeneity of data may compromises the efficiency obtained from the defect prediction models [31].

Some alternative approaches were proposed in the literature in order to improve the performance obtained from CPDP models. Representative approaches on this context are Metric Compensation [26], Nearest Neighbour Filter [25], Transfer Naive Bayes [14], TCA+ [17], and Clustering Filter [19]. Among these approaches we highlight the filtering methods proposed by Turhan et al. [25] and Peters et al. [19] once they consist of simple and effective methods. Both filtering methods aim to select the most similar (and relevant) instances from the CPDP training dataset, as shown below.

2.3 Instance Filtering methods

Given a cross-project training dataset and a test dataset to be predicted, the filtering methods aim at selecting only the most relevant training instances. The resulting filtered dataset may improve the efficiency obtained from CPDP models.

Turhan et al. [25] proposed a filtering method based on the nearest neighbor filter. On this method, here called Burak filter, each test instance is compared with the entire training dataset. The comparison is based on the Euclidean distance and considers the entire set of independent variables. Then, for each test instance, the k most similar training instances are selected to compose the filtered dataset. This method is illustrated in Figure 1(b), where for each test instance the two most similar training instances are selected. As illustrated, the same training instance can be similar with more than one test instance. The instance labeled with 'L' is not included in the filtered dataset.

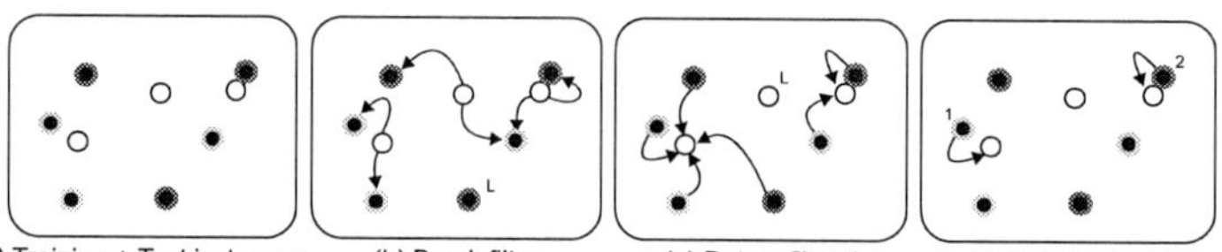

Fig. 1: Illustration of the procedure executed for each filtering method evaluated. On Figure (a), the colored instances represent the cross-project training data and the white instances represent the test data. See text for more details. (Adapted from Peters et al. [19])

The method proposed by Peters et al. [19] select the most similar instances from a different perspective. First, the training instances are clustered considering all the test instances as centroids. The clustering process makes use of the K-means algorithm with Euclidean distance [8]. As a result, each training instance is associated with its most similar centroid (test instance). This first step is illustrated in Figure 1(c). Note that a test instance can be not selected (label 'L'). Second, for each test instance (not labeled with 'L') is selected the most similar training instance to compose the filtered dataset. This second step is illustrated in Figure 1(d). The instances labeled with '1' and '2' represent the most similar instances and the resulting filtered dataset.

2.4 Feature Subset Selection

Both instance filtering methods presented above make use of the Euclidean distance on measuring the similarity between instances. The set of independent variables for an instance m can be represented by a vector $X_m = \{x_1^m, x_2^m, ..., x_n^m\}$, where $|X_m| = n$ is the number of variables (or features). The Euclidean distance between two instances i and j can be defined as

$$d(X_i, X_j) = \sqrt{\sum_{k=1}^{n}(x_k^i - x_k^j)^2}. \tag{1}$$

Let S be a subset of features composed of the most relevant features in X. We propose that using only the most relevant features on the Euclidean distance (i.e., $d(S_i, S_j)$ on Equation 1) can lead to a more accurate filtered dataset and then to a more efficient defect model. In order to select the most relevant features $S \subset X$, we evaluate different Feature Selection (FS) methods.

The FS methods have been widely investigated in the data mining literature [29]. Traditionally, the FS methods are applied in high dimensional data in order to reduce the data dimensionality by removing the irrelevant and the redundant features [29]. We focused on a specific category of FS methods called *filter model* once they are not dependent on the data mining algorithm. We evaluate three supervised methods: Information Gain [4], Relief [12], and CFS [29]; and one unsupervised method: Sparcl [27]. The supervised methods select the most relevant features based on the class attribute. The unsupervised methods, however, select the most relevant features based on their characteristics only, independently of the class attribute.

These different methods represent part of the most important FS methods known in the literature. An specialized feature selection text can be found in [29, 27].

3 Experimental Setup

We conducted an *in silico* experimentation in order to evaluate the performance of IFFS methods. We evaluate two filtering methods - Burak Filter [25] and Peters Filter [19] - combined with feature subset selection. We analysed either Feature Selection (FS) methods and specific Software metric Subsets (SS). All experiments and data analysis were made by using the R Project Platform [21].

3.1 Data Collection

Software Projects The experiments on this study were conducted based on 36 versions of 11 Java open source projects, available in the PROMISE repository[1]. The collection and preparation of defect data was made and provided by Jureczko and Madeyski [10]. Each instance in a dataset represents a Java class. For this study, we converted the dependent variable to a binary classification problem (1, for number of defects > 0; or 0, otherwise). Table 1 list the number of instances, number of defects, and defect rate for each of the analysed datasets.

We evaluate two distinct metrics sets as the independent variables: code metrics (CODE) and network metrics (NET). These metrics are numerical and can be automatically extracted directly from the source code files.

Code Metrics The code metrics set is composed of 19 metrics and include complexity metrics, C&K (*Chidamber and Kemerer*) metrics, and structural code metrics. This metric set has been reported as good quality indicators on literature, as discussed in [10]. These metrics can be extracted by using the Ckjm[2] tool. Further details can be found in [10].

[1] `http://openscience.us/repo/`

[2] `http://gromit.iiar.pwr.wroc.pl/p_inf/ckjm`

Table 1: Summary of the analysed datasets.

Dataset	# Instances	# Defects	% Defects	Dataset	# Instances	# Defects	% Defects
ant-1.3	125	20	0.16	pbeans-2.0	51	10	0.2
ant-1.4	177	39	0.22	poi-1.5	222	131	0.59
ant-1.5	292	32	0.11	poi-2.0	293	36	0.12
ant-1.6	349	92	0.26	poi-2.5	360	223	0.62
ant-1.7	493	139	0.28	poi-3.0	413	260	0.63
forrest-0.6	6	1	0.17	synapse-1.0	155	16	0.1
forrest-0.7	29	5	0.17	synapse-1.1	220	60	0.27
forrest-0.8	32	2	0.06	synapse-1.2	252	86	0.34
ivy-1.1	111	63	0.57	velocity-1.4	186	138	0.74
ivy-1.4	239	16	0.07	velocity-1.5	204	137	0.67
ivy-2.0	351	40	0.11	velocity-1.6	217	76	0.35
log4j-1.0	82	30	0.37	xalan-2.4	409	79	0.19
log4j-1.1	76	31	0.41	xalan-2.5	717	359	0.5
log4j-1.2	123	117	0.95	xalan-2.6	776	328	0.42
lucene-2.0	195	91	0.47	xalan-2.7	762	754	0.99
lucene-2.2	245	142	0.58	xerces-1.2	385	71	0.18
lucene-2.4	337	200	0.59	xerces-1.3	398	69	0.17
pbeans-1.0	26	20	0.77	xerces-1.4	275	168	0.61

Network Metrics The network metrics set were extracted in two steps. First, it was constructed the dependency graph for each analysed software version. Each class file is represented by a vertex and any dependency relationship between two vertices is represented by an edge on the graph. This process was made by using the PF-CDA tool[3]. The inner classes vertices of a same parent class was treated as a unique vertex. For example, vertices with names "A", "A$B" and "A$C" were all contracted to the parent vertex "A".

Once created the dependency graph, we extracted the network metrics data. Table 2 briefly describes the metrics analysed on this study. The metric set can be grouped in two categories: the ego metrics and the global metrics. The ego metrics refers to the metrics extracted from the *ego network*. Given a vertex v, its ego network contains all vertices directly connected to v and their respective connections. The global metrics refers to the metrics extracted from the original entire graph. In addition, some metrics can be extracted from three different kinds of networks according to the direction of edges: incoming edges (In), outgoing edges (Out), or undirected edges (All). We analysed 24 different network metrics. From these 24 metrics, considering all their variations (In, Out, All), we extracted a total of 54 network metrics. We computed these metrics by using the igraph package [5]. The analysed metrics were selected according to availability at igraph package or feasibility to implement.

3.2 Feature Subset Selection

We analysed the FS methods: CFS (FS_CFS) [29], Information Gain (FS_IG) [4], Relief (FS_RLF) [12], and Sparcl (FS_SPC) [27]. The first three are supervised methods. Thus, the feature selection is performed from the training data in which the class attribute is known. The Sparcl method is unsupervised. And thus, can be performed from both training (FS_SPC_Tr) and test data (FS_SPC_Te) once

[3] `http://www.dependency-analyzer.org/`

Table 2: The analysed network metrics. The metrics were computed for incoming (In), outgoing (Out), and/or undirected (All) dependencies. (Descriptions adapted from Zimmermann and Nagappan [30] and Herzig et al. [7])

Ego Network Metrics	
Metric Name	**Description**
$\text{Size}^{In\ Out\ All}$	# nodes connected to the ego network
$\text{Ties}^{In\ Out\ All}$	# directed ties corresponds to the number of edges
$\text{Pairs}^{In\ Out\ All}$	# ordered pairs is the maximal number of directed ties
$\text{Density}^{In\ Out\ All}$	% of possible ties that are actually present
$\text{WeakComp}^{In\ Out\ All}$	# weak components in neighborhood
$\text{nWeakComp}^{In\ Out\ All}$	# weak components normalized by size
$\text{TwoStepReach}^{In\ Out\ All}$	% nodes that are two steps away
$\text{ReachEfficiency}^{In\ Out\ All}$	TwoStepReach normalized by size
$\text{EgoBetween}^{In\ Out\ All}$	% shortest paths between neighbors through ego
$\text{nEgoBetween}^{In\ Out\ All}$	EgoBetween normalized by the size
EffSize^{All}	size of the ego network minus the average number of ties between their nodes

Global Network Metrics	
Metric Name	**Description**
$\text{Degree}^{In\ Out\ All}$	# dependencies for a node
$\text{Closeness}^{In\ Out\ All}$	Total length of the shortest paths from a node (or to a node) to all other nodes
$\text{Reach}^{In\ Out\ All}$	How far a node can receive or send information in the network
$\text{Spread}^{In\ Out\ All}$	How wide a node can receive or send information in the network
$\text{Radiality}^{In\ Out\ All}$	Radial centrality of a node
Eigenvector^{All}	Measure the influence of an node in a network
Betweenness^{All}	Measure for a node in how many shortest paths between other nodes it occurs
Power^{All}	Bonacich Power centrality measure
Clustering^{All}	% of adjacent vertices to a vertex be connected
Page Rank^{All}	Google's PageRank value. Generalization of Eigenvector metric
$\text{Eccentricity}^{All}$	Distance of the shortest path from a vertex to the farthest vertex on the network
Hub^{All}	Kleinberg's Hub measure. Generalization of Eigenvector metric
Authority^{All}	Kleinberg's Authority measure. Generalization of Eigenvector metric

no class attribute information is required. The methods FS_IG, FS_RLF, and FS_SPC provides a rank of weights that measures the relevance of each feature, according to some criterion. Deciding the best k features to compose the feature subset is not a trivial task [29]. Thus, for each method we analysed four different values of $k = \{5, 10, 15, 20\}$ in order to approximate the best k configuration. Considering all methods and their variations of k, we analysed 17 FS methods for each filtering method. We used the R packages 'FSelector' [22] and 'sparcl' [27] with the implemented FS methods.

In addition, we investigated two distinct metric subsets: code metrics (SS_CODE) and network metrics (SS_NET). For each metric subset, we applied a Pearson correlation test in order to disregard the metrics considered redundant, with correlation greater than 0.90 [24]. We also analysed the performance with the original set of features (Orig), as a comparative reference.

3.3 Experiment Design

The experiment design is presented in Figure 2. We considered all projects and versions presented in Table 1. First, we joined all datasets in one unique Cross Project Dataset (CPD). Then, we conducted a cross project analysis. Consider a project P with $V(P)$ versions and a specific version v_i of $V(P)$. For each

$v_i \in V(P)$, we used v_i as test and $CPD - V(P)$ as training. In this way, we can analyse the prediction performance disregarding any bias from the different versions of a same project. Next, the training data were filtered by applying the Burak and Peters filters combined with the studied feature subsets presented above. The filtered training data are then used to construct the defect prediction models.

```
projects = [ant, forrest, ivy, log4j, lucene, pbeans, poi, synapse, velocity, xalan, xerces]
FOR EACH project IN projects
    versions[project] = getAllVersions(project)
END FOR
CPD = joinAllProjects(versions) //all cross-project data

//evaluated FS methods and metric subsets
IFFS = [FS_CFS, FS_IG, FS_RLF, FS_SPC_Tr, FS_SPC_Te, SS_CODE, SS_NET]
filters = [Burak, Peters] //instance filtering methods
learner = [RF] //Random Forest defect predictor

FOR EACH project IN projects
    CPTrain = CPD - versions[project] //all datasets except project versions
    FOR EACH version IN versions[project]
        FOR EACH filter IN filters
            FOR EACH feature_subset IN IFFS
                filtered_train = filter(CPTrain, feature_subset)
                IFFS_predictor = learner(RF, filtered_train)
                [gmeasure, recall, pf] = IFFS_predictor(version) //evaluate predictor on test
            END FOR
            //original filtering method as comparative reference
            filtered_train = filter(CPTrain, all_features)
            orig_predictor = learner(RF, filtered_train)
            [gmeasure, recall, pf] = orig_predictor(version)
        END FOR
    END FOR
END FOR
```

Fig. 2: Pseudocode with the experiment design.

3.4 Prediction Models

The models were constructed by using the Random Forest Algorithm [3]. This algorithm has shown good performances compared with others classification algorithms [13]. Lessmann et al. [13] argue that Random Forest is the current state-of-the-art defect predictor. Random Forest is an ensemble of classifiers based on decision trees. This algorithm presents robustness to redundant and irrelevant attributes. Although, it can produce overfitting models.

In [30] and [7] the authors argue that network metrics can lead to better prediction performance when combined with code metrics. Thus, we considered both metric sets CODE and NET as predictors on experiments. Again, the features with high Pearson correlation (> 0.90) were disregarded. The remaining set with non redundant features is composed of 20 code metrics and 35 network metrics.

3.5 Performance Measures

We analysed three performance measures: recall, probability of false alarm (pf), and g-measure [9]. Those measures has the focus on the defective class [15]. Table 3 present the confusion matrix and the analysed measures.

The *recall* measures how much of the existing defects were found. The *pf* can be described as the probability of an instance predicted as defective do not be a real defective instance. The optimal pf is 0% and the worst result is 100%. The *g-measure* is the harmonic mean between recall and 1-pf (the specificity).

Table 3: Performance measures.

(a) Confusion matrix.

		Actual	
		yes	no
Predicted	yes	TP	FP
	no	FN	TN

(b) Analysed measures.

recall (pd)	$\frac{TP}{FN+TP}$
pf	$\frac{FP}{TN+FP}$
g-measure	$\frac{2*pd*(1-pf)}{pd+(1-pf)}$

4 Results

RQ1: Can IFFS methods lead to better performance on CPDP?

Table 4 shows the prediction performances obtained for each project. The performance on the *noFilter* column are reported by the g-measure (g). All other columns are reported by the relative value $\Delta g = g - g_{noFilter}$, i.e., negative values show lower performance and positive values show higher performance in relation to *noFilter*. To better visualization we multiply the values by 100. The bold values indicates the higher Δg obtained for the respective project row. The projects are presented in decreasing order considering the higher Δg value. The last row presents the mean value for each column. The columns *Best FS* present the best performance among all the evaluated FS methods. The columns *NET* and *CODE* present the performance obtained by considering the feature subsets SS_NET and SS_CODE.

We can analyse this table in different perspectives. First, we can notice that the columns *Best FS* presented better performance than *Orig* in all cases for both filtering methods. It means that at least one of the evaluated FS methods perform better than the original method. The FS methods presented the highest performances in most projects, as highlighted by the bold values. These improvements in performance can be crucial to define if a prediction model is appropriate or not for practical use. Zimmermann et al. [31] present a large experiment on cross-prediction feasibility. Their results show that only 3.4% of the studied models presented a prediction performance considered appropriate to practical use. They considered a successful defect model when accuracy,

Table 4: Performance obtained for the analysed IFFS methods for both Burak and Peters Filters. All performances are presented in relation to *noFilter*. Positive values means better performance and negative values means lower performance. The bold values indicate the highest performance for a project row.

		Burak Filter (Δg)				Peters Filter (Δg)			
Project	**noFilter (g)**	**Orig**	**NET**	**CODE**	**Best FS**	**Orig**	**NET**	**CODE**	**Best FS**
forrest-0.6	0	0	0	0	**94.29**	0	8.33	58.07	58.52
velocity-1.4	7.84	6.49	2.1	-7.58	**49.78**	-1.74	-0.73	11.75	45.5
xerces-1.4	33.27	-2.6	-5.61	3.88	**45.15**	20.97	25.28	15.31	38.34
velocity-1.5	9.21	7.15	6.61	0.43	27.13	-2.22	5.85	10.49	**41.34**
log4j-1.1	45.49	4.37	31.98	25.79	**39.86**	11.81	16.91	22.89	30.8
pbeans-1.0	33.96	-0.42	12.96	-10.41	20.38	0	0	15.85	**33.68**
lucene-2.4	15.55	-4.57	-4.09	10.85	10.56	3.9	-0.53	24.79	**31.49**
log4j-1.0	43.61	21.68	20.39	8.39	**30.64**	24.14	18.31	18.91	27.84
velocity-1.6	18.37	-6.3	-2.43	-8.12	17.26	-0.92	0.18	13.64	**28.99**
log4j-1.2	26.12	-4.36	-4.25	3.45	2.56	-18.23	-17.01	5.56	**28.4**
poi-2.5	15.26	7.58	0.44	19.99	16.93	17.95	-0.05	17.93	**27.58**
poi-3.0	26.12	3.42	5.42	4.77	12.45	12.03	-9.85	16.29	**22.55**
lucene-2.2	31.38	-18.4	-3.31	-0.75	5.16	-4.41	**20.09**	13.47	19.74
xerces-1.3	46.53	-3.15	-5.26	6.48	19.21	4.21	15.9	14.23	**19.97**
synapse-1.1	35.81	-0.41	-20.41	-13.93	11.51	-11.9	2.78	6.25	**17.57**
synapse-1.2	45.3	2.79	3.07	-3	**13.61**	-5.54	-32.53	6.89	11.04
xerces-1.2	36.68	-3.07	-3.76	3.65	**13.5**	1.39	8.3	6.78	11.82
synapse-1.0	56	-3.27	-1.49	-4.51	**13.23**	-8.98	6.78	-0.46	11.83
lucene-2.0	54.66	2.07	4.89	10.28	**12.69**	-7.06	3.3	-0.46	5.65
forrest-0.8	58.6	-45.08	-58.6	-0.69	**12.55**	-53.25	-36.66	11.68	-3.7
poi-2.0	59.14	5.87	-5.9	7.93	**11.7**	5.91	-5.89	7.39	7.03
ant-1.3	64.94	-0.73	-12.64	4.9	**11.21**	-6.74	-27.9	-5.32	3.31
ivy-1.1	63.18	-0.01	0.15	-15.3	**11.03**	4.92	-4.58	-17.42	7.42
ant-1.6	64.24	3.69	3.18	-12.68	**10.48**	1.91	-5.43	-0.55	9.27
ant-1.5	63.68	2.14	5.67	-9.85	**9.19**	2.2	7.97	-16.96	9.04
xalan-2.4	65.74	2.11	4.61	-1.34	**8.8**	1.01	-3.24	-0.55	6.52
xalan-2.7	42.05	-9.23	-3.89	-2.48	**6.18**	-4.64	-3.57	-10.38	4.91
ivy-1.4	72.38	-2.6	2.42	-5.85	**5.71**	1.59	-2.52	0.6	3.37
ant-1.7	73.43	-0.13	1.16	-0.93	**4.69**	-4.36	-8.46	-4.67	-0.31
ant-1.4	58.93	-5.59	-7.83	-2.37	1.76	-5.54	-16.63	-9.81	**4.68**
poi-1.5	59.72	-5.19	-10.94	-8.48	**4.54**	-18.99	-13.8	-14.99	-2.58
forrest-0.7	56.55	-23.86	-23.64	-38.32	**4.2**	-32.16	-39.48	-19.81	3.72
pbeans-2.0	60.74	0.8	-0.31	-1.86	**3.88**	-21.42	-42.9	-13.2	-3.66
xalan-2.6	55.15	-8.71	-2.28	-5.45	**2.79**	-7.48	-6.98	-6.69	0.97
xalan-2.5	46.76	-4.64	-1.22	-3.23	**2.71**	-11.75	-2.23	-8.63	2.27
ivy-2.0	76.73	-1.62	-5.97	**0.66**	0.46	-5.75	-17.21	-2.27	-1.41
Mean	**45.09**	**-2.39**	**-2.25**	**-1.27**	**15.77**	**-3.4**	**-4.52**	**4.63**	**15.65**

precision, and recall presents performance greater than 75%. Peters et al. [19] considered both performance thresholds of 60% and 75% for the g-measure. In Figure 3 we compare the percentage of projects with performance greater than 60% and 75% for the methods *noFilter*, original Burak, original Peters, Burak FS and Peters FS (with reference to the *Best FS* column). The original methods perform slightly better than *noFilter*. The highest performances are presented by the filtering methods associated with FS. Considering $g \geq 60$, Peters FS and Burak FS presented successful performance for more than 50% of projects. For the threshold $g \geq 75$, the method Burak FS presents practical use for almost 20% of projects.

RQ2: Which IFFS methods present better performance on CPDP?

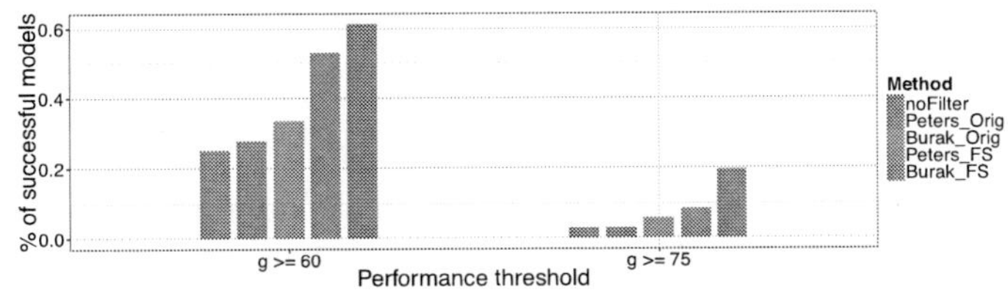

Fig. 3: Rate of successful models for practical use, considering the thresholds $g \geq 60$ and $g \geq 75$.

The best performances obtained for each project are not dominated by one or just a few IFFS methods. Instead, each project has exclusive characteristics that promotes one or other IFFS method. Thus, we analysed the best performances by counting the frequency in which a method is among the top 5 best performances for a project. We consider all the 41 analysed methods, $((17\,FS + 2\,SS + Orig) * 2\,filters) + noFilter$. By this approach we can present the results more clearly. The methods with higher frequency leads to better performances for a larger amount of software projects.

Table 5: Frequency in which a IFFS method performs among the top 5 prediction performances for a project.

Method	Freq.	Method	Freq.	Method	Freq.
BURAK_FS_IG_10	11	PETERS_FS_RLF_5	6	BURAK_FS_IG_20	4
PETERS_SS_CODE	10	PETERS_FS_IG_5	6	BURAK_SS_NET	4
BURAK_FS_IG_5	9	PETERS_FS_RLF_15	6	PETERS_FS_SPC_Te_5	4
PETERS_FS_SPC_Tr_5	9	PETERS_FS_IG_10	5	BURAK_FS_RLF_15	4
BURAK_FS_SPC_Te_5	8	NO_FILTER	5	PETERS_FS_RLF_10	4
BURAK_FS_RLF_10	7	PETERS_FS_IG_15	5	PETERS_FS_IG_20	3
BURAK_FS_SPC_Tr_10	7	BURAK_FS_SPC_Te_20	5	BURAK_FS_RLF_5	3
BURAK_FS_SPC_Te_10	7	BURAK_FS_SPC_Te_15	5	PETERS_SS_NET	3
BURAK_SS_CODE	6	PETERS_FS_SPC_Te_10	5	BURAK_FS_CFS	3
BURAK_FS_SPC_Tr_5	6	BURAK_FS_SPC_Tr_15	4	PETERS_FS_SPC_Te_20	3

Table 5 shows the 30 methods with highest frequencies among the best performances. The method with the highest frequency (BURAK_FS_IG_10, where the postfix 10 represents the k configuration used on FS_IG) covers almost 30% of all projects, followed by PETERS_SS_CODE with frequency 10. The metric subset SS_CODE presents better performance in relation to SS_NET. The originals filter methods (with no feature subset selection) do not appear between the first 30 most frequent methods. The prediction with no filter, however, performed better for 5 projects. This result partially contradicts the results presented by Turhan et al. [25] and Peters et al. [19], in which the instance filtering improves the prediction performance. However, some differences can be highlighted between their works and ours. First, we assumed that both original methods consider all features on filtering instances. However, in their works the experiments are conducted considering only the CODE metric set once only this set is available (i.e., the NET metric set is not available for analyses). Furthermore, the experiments of Turhan et al. [25] are on the cross-company context and the analysed projects were developed by different companies. The projects considered on this study were generally developed by the Apache Foundation (except for the Pbeans project). This aspect can influence on the level of heterogeneity on data and then improve the performance of prediction by using *noFilter*. Lastly, the authors of Peters et al. [19] restrict the testing domain to software projects with less than 100 instances, differently of us (see Table 1).

By observing the filters separately, we can note that the Burak filter is present in 6 of the first 8 most frequent methods. Those frequencies, however, are not mutually exclusive and may count the same project for several methods. For example, it is necessary 10 of the first most frequent methods to cover all the 36 projects.

5 Threats to Validity

The results indicates that the performance of CPDP models can be improved by applying the evaluated methods. However, some sources of bias can be highlighted from the conducted experiments. First, the evaluated dataset is composed only by Java open source projects. Also, the majority of the evaluated projects belongs to a unique company. These bias can reduce the heterogeneity of data and influence on the experiment results. Furthermore, the number of defects found for each software part is an approximate estimation and does not represent the real number of existent bugs [10]. Other datasets with different sources can be used in order to improve the generality of results.

The models on this study were constructed by using only one classification algorithm, sustained by the performance results presented in Lessmann et al. [13]. However, the data mining is an active research field and other algorithms may lead to different results.

6 Conclusion

On this study we investigated the performance of CPDP models by applying filtering methods associated with feature subset selection. We evaluated 19 methods derived from different configurations of four distinct Feature Selection methods and two metric subsets. The results show that for all the analysed projects at least one of the 19 evaluated methods present better performance in relation to the original filtering methods. We also investigated which of the evaluated methods present better performance. We present a rank ordered by the frequency in which a method is between the best top five performances for a project. The most frequent method is present in only 11 of the 36 analysed projects. It indicates that the most appropriate method for a project depends on the characteristics of the project being predicted.

These conclusions instigate further investigation in order to identify the most appropriate method to be applied for a project, given its characteristics. We also plan to extend the set of evaluated methods by considering different Feature Selection methods.

Acknowledgments

The authors acknowledge the support granted by FAPESP (grant 2013/01084-3).

References

[1] Basili, V., Briand, L., Melo, W.: A validation of object-oriented design metrics as quality indicatorss. IEEE Trans. Softw. Eng. 22, 751–761 (1996)

[2] Bener, A., Menzies, T.: Guest editorial: learning to organize testing. Automated Software Engineering 19(2), 137–140 (2012)

[3] Breiman, L.: Random forests. Machine Learning 45(1), 5–32 (2001)

[4] Cover, T.M., Thomas, J.A.: Elements of Information Theory. Wiley-Interscience, New York, NY, USA (1991)

[5] Csardi, G., Nepusz, T.: The igraph software package for complex network research. InterJournal Complex Systems, 1695 (2006)

[6] Hassan, A.E.: Predicting faults using the complexity of code changes. In: IEEE 31st Int. Conf. on Soft. Eng. pp. 78–88. IEEE (2009)

[7] Herzig, K., Just, S., Rau, A., Zeller, A.: Predicting defects using change genealogies. In: IEEE 24nd Int. Symp. on Soft. Reliab. Eng. IEEE (2013)

[8] Jain, A.K.: Data clustering: 50 years beyond k-means. Pattern Recognition Letters 31(8), 651 – 666 (2010)

[9] Japkowicz, N., Shah, M.: Evaluating Learning Algorithms: A Classification Perspective. Cambridge University Press (2011)

[10] Jureczko, M., Madeyski, L.: Towards identifying software project clusters with regard to defect prediction. In: Proc. of the 6th Int. Conf. on Pred. Mod. in Soft. Eng. pp. 9:1–9:10 (2010)

[11] Kitchenham, B.A., Mendes, E., Travassos, G.H.: Cross versus within-company cost estimation studies: A systematic review. IEEE Trans. Softw. Eng. 33(5), 316–329 (2007)

[12] Kononenko, I.: Estimating attributes: Analysis and extensions of relief. In: Machine Learning: ECML-94. pp. 171–182. Springer Berlin Heidelberg (1994)

[13] Lessmann, S., Baesens, B., Mues, C., Pietsch, S.: Benchmarking classification models for software defect prediction: A proposed framework and novel findings. IEEE Trans. Softw. Eng. 34(4), 485–496 (2008)

[14] Ma, Y., Luo, G., Zeng, X., Chen, A.: Transfer learning for cross-company software defect prediction. Inf. Softw. Technol. 54(3), 248–256 (2012)

[15] Menzies, T., Dekhtyar, A., Distefano, J., Greenwald, J.: Problems with precision: A response to "comments on 'data mining static code attributes to learn defect predictors'". IEEE Trans. Softw. Eng. 33(9), 637–640 (2007)

[16] Nagappan, N., Murphy, B., Basili, V.: The influence of organizational structure on software quality: An empirical case study. In: 30th Int. Conf. on Soft. Eng. pp. 521–530 (2008)

[17] Nam, J., Pan, S.J., Kim, S.: Transfer defect learning. In: 35th Int. Conf. on Soft. Eng. pp. 382–391. IEEE Press (2013)

[18] Ostrand, T.J., Weyuker, E.J., Bell, R.M.: Where the bugs are. In: Proc. of the 2004 ACM SIGSOFT Int. Symp. on Soft. Test. and Analy. pp. 86–96. ACM (2004)

[19] Peters, F., Menzies, T., Marcus, A.: Better cross company defect prediction. In: Proc. of the 10th Work. Conf. on Mining Soft. Rep. pp. 409–418. IEEE (2013)

[20] Pinzger, M., Nagappan, N., Murphy, B.: Can developer-module networks predict failures? In: Proc. of the 16th ACM SIGSOFT Int. Symp. on Found. of Soft. Eng. pp. 2–12. ACM (2008)

[21] R Core Team: R: A Language and Environment for Statistical Computing. R Foundation for Statistical Computing, Vienna, Austria (2014)

[22] Romanski, P., Kotthoff, L.: FSelector: Selecting attributes (2014), `http://CRAN.R-project.org/package=FSelector`, r package version 0.20

[23] Taba, S.E.S., Khomh, F., Zou, Y., Hassan, A.E., Nagappan, M.: Predicting bugs using antipatterns. In: Proc. of the 2013 IEEE Int. Conf. on Soft. Maint. pp. 270–279. IEEE (2013)

[24] Torgo, L.: Data Mining with R, learning with case studies. Chapman and Hall/CRC (2010)

[25] Turhan, B., Menzies, T., Bener, A.B., Di Stefano, J.: On the relative value of cross-company and within-company data for defect prediction. Emp. Soft. Eng. 14(5), 540–578 (2009)

[26] Watanabe, S., Kaiya, H., Kaijiri, K.: Adapting a fault prediction model to allow inter language reuse. In: Proc. of the 4th Int. Work. on Pred. Models in Soft. Eng. pp. 19–24. ACM (2008)

[27] Witten, D.M., Tibshirani, R.: A framework for feature selection in clustering. Jour. of the Amer. Statist. Assoc. 105(490), 713–726 (2010)

[28] Zhang, F., Mockus, A., Keivanloo, I., Zou, Y.: Towards building a universal defect prediction model. In: 11th Work. Conf. on Mining Soft. Rep. pp. 182–191. ACM (2014)

[29] Zhao, Z., Morstatter, F., Sharma, S., Alelyani, S., Anand, A., Liu, H.: Advancing feature selection research - asu feature selection repository. Tech. rep., Arizona State University (2011)

[30] Zimmermann, T., Nagappan, N.: Predicting defects using network analysis on dependency graphs. In: 30th Int. Conf. on Soft. Eng. pp. 531–540 (2008)

[31] Zimmermann, T., Nagappan, N., Gall, H., Giger, E., Murphy, B.: Cross-project defect prediction: A large scale experiment on data vs. domain vs. process. In: 7th Joint Meet. of the Euro. Soft. Eng. Conf. and the ACM SIGSOFT Symp. on The Found. of Soft. Eng. pp. 91–100. ACM (2009)

[32] Zimmermann, T., Premraj, R., Zeller, A.: Predicting defects for eclipse. In: 30th Int. Work. on Pred. Models in Soft. Eng. (2007)

An Empirical Validation of an Automated Genetic Software Effort Prediction Framework Using the ISBSG Dataset

Juan Murillo-Morera[1], Christian Quesada-López[1], Carlos Castro-Herrera[2], Marcelo Jenkins[1]

[1] Center for ICT Research, University of Costa Rica
[2] Intel Corporation, Costa Rica
{juan.murillomorera, cristian.quesadalopez}@ucr.ac.cr,
carlos.castro.herrera@intel.com, marcelo.jenkins@ecci.ucr.ac.cr

Abstract. Background: The complexity of providing accurate software effort prediction models is well known in the software industry. Several prediction models have been proposed in the literature using different techniques, with different results, in different contexts. **Objectives:** This paper reports a benchmarking study using a genetic approach that automatically generates and compares different learning schemes (preprocessing+attribute selection+learning algorithms). The effectiveness of the software development effort prediction models (using function points) were validated using the ISBSG R12 dataset. **Methods:** Eight subsets of projects were analyzed running a $M \times N$-fold cross-validation. We used a genetic approach to automatically select the components of the learning schemes, to evaluate, and to report the learning scheme with the best performance. **Results:** In total, 150 learning schemes were studied (2 data preprocessors, 5 attribute selectors, and 15 modeling techniques). The most common learning schemes were: Log+ForwardSelection+M5-Rules, Log+BestFirst+M5-Rules, Log+LinearForwardSelection+SMOreg, ForwardSelection+SMOreg and ForwardSelection+ SMOreg, BackwardElimination+SMOreg, LinearForwardSelection+SMOreg, and Log+Best First+SMOreg. **Conclusions:** The results show that we should select a different learning schemes for each datasets. Our results support previous findings regarding that the setup applied in evaluations can completely reverse findings. A genetic approach that automatically selects best combination based on a specific dataset could improve the performance of software effort prediction models.

Keywords: Effort prediction model, learning schemes, genetic approach, experiment, ISBSG dataset, function points.

1 Introduction

The complexity of providing accurate software effort prediction models is well known. The need for accurate effort predictions for projects is one of the most important issues in the software industry [1]. Software functional size measurement (FSM) and effort prediction models based on software size have been studied for many years, but many software companies are still using expert judgment as their preferred estimation method, producing inaccurate estimations and severe schedule overruns in many of their projects [2]. Software functional size has proved to be one of the main effort-and-cost drivers [3], [4]. Function point analysis (FPA) [3], [5], [6] was the first proposal for a FSM and it is one of the most used FSM methods in the industry [6]. FSM methods analyze software requirements, transactions and data that are meaningful to the final user. They are identified and classified in a set of basic functional size components (BFC) and counted according to defined complexity criteria. Details about FPA method can be found in the FPA manual. In this study, we used function point measures to create the effort prediction models.

Several studies evaluating different effort prediction techniques have been published [7], [8]. The results of these studies are not univocal and are often highly technique-and dataset-dependent. Since there are many models that can be fitted to certain datasets, a crucial issue is the selection of the most efficient prediction model [9]. Additionally, the results of different studies are difficult to compare due to different empirical setups and data preprocessing, possibly leading to contradictory results. The issue of which modeling technique to use for software effort estimation remains an open research question [8]. An automated selection and combination of techniques in alternative ways could improve the overall accuracy of the prediction models for specific datasets [8].

This paper reports on a benchmarking study that automatically generates and compares different learning schemes (preprocessing + attribute selection + learning algorithms) through a genetic approach using subsets of the ISBSG R12. This study evaluates the effectiveness of software effort prediction models based on function point measures. We investigated the performance of effort prediction models based on a) base functional components (BFC) and b) unadjusted function point size (UFP) to compare if these models based on BFC could perform as well as models based on UFP. In total 150 learning schemes which include the combination of two data preprocessors, five attribute selectors, and fifteen modeling techniques represented our search space. A sub-set of learning scheme selected by the genetic search is applied to eight sub-datasets. The better learning schemes are selected by the genetic approach through the elitism technique.

The remainder of the paper is structured as follows. section 2 briefly provides information about previous studies in effort prediction and the different data preprocessing, attribute selector, and learning algorithm techniques employed in this study; section 3 describes the genetic approach to automatically generate effort prediction models; section 4 shows the experimental design. In section 5 the analysis and interpretation of results are presented. Finally, section 6 outlines conclusions and future work.

2 Related Work

Several formal models have been used in software effort prediction models using a number of data mining techniques [7] [8]. These include various regression techniques, neural networks, tree/rule-based models, and lazy learning. [7]. Most of studies evaluate only a limited number of modeling techniques on a dataset which limits the generalizability of the results. The results of different studies are difficult to compare due to different empirical setups, data preprocessing, and dataset characteristics. Thus, determining which modeling technique to use for software effort estimation remains an open research question [8]. Kitchenham and Mendes states: "one of the main problems with evaluating techniques using one or two datasets is that no one can be sure that the specific datasets were not selected because they are the ones that favor the new technique" [10]. The main contribution of our research is that our approach addresses the question of: How to select the data preprocessing, the attributes selection technique and the learning algorithms **automatically** according to the characteristics of a specific data set?. The main objective is to increase the prediction performance. The automatic selection of the learning schemes (preprocessing + attributes selection + learning algorithms) was determined using a genetic approach. We selected this approach because according to the literature "there are very few studies that examine the effectiveness of evolutionary algorithms". The "future studies may focus on the predictive accuracy of evolutionary algorithms for software prediction" [11]. Table 1 presents a summary of techniques and algorithms based on [12]. The data preprocessing step is represented by the tag (PP), the attribute selector step is represented by the tag (AS) and the learning algorithm step is represented by the tag (LA).

Table 1. Machine learning techniques

Tag	Name	Description/Function
PP	None	Data unchanged.
PP	MathExpression	All the numeric values are replaced by their logarithmic values.
AS	Backward Elimination	Starts with the whole set of attributes and eliminates one attribute in each iteration until no single attribute elimination improves the evaluation of the subset.
AS	Forward Selection	Starts from an empty set and evaluates each attribute individually to find the best single attribute.
AS	BestFirst	Greedy hill climbing with backtracking.
AS	LinearForwardSelection	Extension of BestFirst that considers a restricted number of the remaining attributes when expanding the current point int the search.
AS	RankSearch	Sort the attributes and rank promising.
LA	GaussianProcesses(GP)	Gaussian processes for regression.
LA	LeastMedSq(LMS)	Robust regression using the median rather than the mean.
LA	LinearRegression(LR)	Standard multiple linear regression.
LA	MultilayerPerceptron(MP)	Backpropagation neural network.
LA	RBFNetwork(RBFN)	Implements a radial basis function network.
LA	SMOreg(SMO)	Sequential minimal optimization algorithm for support vector regression.
LA	AdditiveRegression(AR)	Enhances the performance of a regression method by iteratively fitting the residuals.
LA	Bagging(BGN)	Combines different models means amalgamating the various outputs into a simple prediction.
LA	ConjunctiveRule(CR)	Simple conjunctive rule learner.
LA	DecisionTable(DT)	Builds a simple decision table majority classifier.
LA	M5Rules(M5R)	Obtains rules from model trees built using M5.
LA	ZeroR(ZR)	Predicts the majority class (if nominal) or the average value (if numeric).
LA	DecisionStump(DS)	Builds one-level decision trees.
LA	M5P(M5P)	M5 Model tree learner.
LA	REPTree(RT)	Fast tree learner that uses reduced-error pruning.

3 Proposed Framework

To build the prediction models, we followed the framework proposed by Song [13] (Figure 1, **Learning Scheme Evaluator, Step-1 to Step-5**), with the major difference of using the genetic algorithm to select the parts of the learning scheme, instead of evaluating only the parts of the learning scheme of a group established by combinations. Our framework consists of two components: 1) Learning Schemes Generator and Evaluator and 2) Effort Prediction. The learning schemes, generator and evaluator component is characterized by the generating and the evaluation of learners. The best learning scheme is selected according to the maximum Correlation Coefficient (CC) calculated in the fitness function. Moreover, the effort prediction component is characterized by the generation of the predictor. Our main contribution in this paper is represented by Figure 1, **Learning Scheme Generator, Step-1, Step-2 and Step-3**.

3.1 Learning Schemes Generator and Evaluator

The learning scheme generator is characterized by the selection of the best learning scheme according to the maximum Correlation Coefficient (CC) value calculated and the configuration selected by the genetic approach (see Figure 1, section Learning Scheme generator). The evaluator component (see Figure 1, section Learning Scheme Evaluator), is represented by the fitness function based on Song methodology [13].

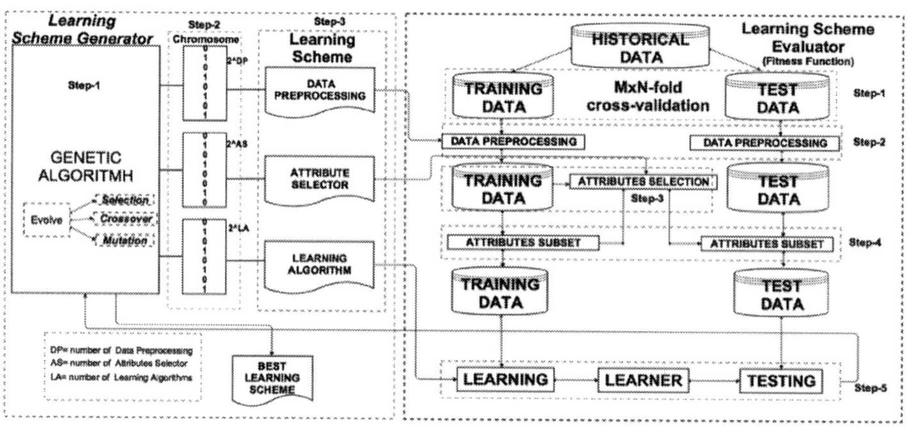

Fig. 1. Learning Schemes Generator and Evaluator. Adapted from [14]

The main steps of this component are detailed below:

1. The historical data was randomized and divided into a training set and a test set. This was done using a $M \times N$-fold cross-validation (Figure 1, **Evaluation, Step-1**).

2. The selected data preprocessing technique was applied to both the training and the test set (Figure 1, **Evaluation, Step-1**), resulting in modified training and test data.
3. The chosen attribute selection technique was applied only to the training set (Figure 1, **Evaluation, Step-1**) and the best subset of attributes was chosen.
4. The attributes selected were then extracted for both training and test set (Figure 1, **Evaluation, Step-1**).
5. The Learning algorithm was built using the training set, and evaluated with the test set.

3.2 Effort Prediction

The main objective of this component is to build a predictor for new data while the main objective of the generator of the learning scheme (first component) is to build a learner and select the best one with respect to its Correlation Coefficient (CC). A predictor is built using the best learning scheme identified in the previous stage. Once it is ready, this predictor can be used to calculate the final performance score using new data (i.e. predicting on new data). This is simulated by running the predictor on the newData dataset that were reserved when doing the 90-10 splits. We applied a N-PASS, where $N = 10$. After N iterations the mean is calculated. This final CC represents our CC of prediction. Our effort prediction component is based on [14].

3.3 Genetic Approach

This section describes the genetic configuration used in this paper: Chromosome, Operators and Fitness Function. The first application of our framework has been applied in the prediction defect context [14]. The genetic configuration and the proposed framework of this research is an adapted version of our this study.

Chromosome. The chromosome of a genetic algorithm represents the set of possible combinations within the search space. It is commonly represented as a binary chain of 0s and 1s. In this paper, the chromosome is composed of three parts: Data preprocessing (DP) (see Table 1), Attribute Selector (AS) (see Table 1), and Learning Algorithms (LA) (see Table 1); effectively constructing a triplet of $< DP, AS, LA >$. For DP, we considered two possibilities, represented by a binary chain of 1 bit ($2^1 = 2$). For AS, we consider five possible techniques, also represented by a binary chain of 3 bits ($2^3 = 8$). For LA, we consider fifteen different possibilities, which require 4 bits to represent ($2^4 = 16$). With this chromosome representation, the goal of the GA is to find the chromosome that maximizes a fitness function. We worked with only combinations inside the range proposed. For example, the range of the attribute selection is between $1-5$. This means that combinations with attribute selection set $6-8$ are not valid.

Fitness Function. The final value of the Correlation Coefficient (CC) is calculated in the prediction phase. The N-PASS is a strategy to avoid the variability of the final result of the Correlation Coefficient (CC) [13], where the fitness score of a chromosome is calculated as the average of 10 runs. The whole dataset is split randomly in two data sets: histData and newData. The histData represents the 90% of the whole dataset, used for training and testing. The newData represents the 10% of the whole dataset, representing a new project; we repeat this for each PASS. In the evaluation phase. This algorithm performs a $M \times N$-fold cross-validation; where multiple rounds are performed with the different partitions to reduce the variability. The validation results are averaged over the rounds. Finally, in the prediction phase we generated the final value of the CC using the unseen new data and the best learning scheme (LS) calculated in the evaluation phase. This solution is used in the prediction phase.

Operators. The operators of selection, reproduction, crossover and mutation used, were configured using the default values provided by the WEKA genetic search [12]. The Learning Scheme Generator, shown in figure 1, is responsible for evaluating and selecting the different learning schemes. The selection is done via the elitism technique of the genetic algorithm.

Finally, the best learning scheme, in our case; the chromosome (with its data preprocessing, attribute selector and learning algorithm) was selected by the genetic algorithm.

4 Experimental Design

4.1 Dataset Selection

The subset of data projects for our study was selected from the ISBSG R12 database according to the criteria shown in Table 2 based on recommendations in [15], [16], [8], [17], [18], [19]. Projects for which all functional components (UFP and BFC) of function points were missing were discarded. For our study, we selected the variables related to FPA functional size components (BFC), effort of software development, and context attributes according to recommendation in [20]. The list of variables selected is: Input count, Output count, Interface count, File count, Enquiry count, Functional size, Work Effort, Development Type, Relative Size, Team Size Group, Development Platform, Architecture, Language Type, Program Language. The description of context variables can be found in [21], [22].

Two groups of datasets were used. The first dataset group is represented by 72 projects ($\geq$ 2008, Rating A). Twenty-nine of them are from 2008, twenty-five from 2009, thirteen from 2010, and five from 2011. The smallest project size is 24 UFPs, the average is 240 UFPs, and the largest project is 1,337 UFPs. The second dataset group is represented by 202 projects ($\geq$ 2005, Rating A or B). Forty-three of them are from 2005, 34 from 2006, 46 from 2007, 35 from 2008, 26 from 2009, 13 from 2006, and 5 from 2011. The smallest project size is 6 UFP, the average is 247 with a median of 184 UFP, and the largest project is 1,337 UFP. The dataset is positively skewed for all variables indicating the quantity of small and medium projects is higher than the number of large projects. Most of the projects were small (between 32-99 UFP) and medium size (between 102-993 UFP). Extra small projects (between 6-28 UFP) and large projects (between 1,018-1,337 UFP) show lower productivity than small and medium size projects. Data indicates that the use small teams in small and medium size projects is better in terms of productivity. A completed description of the ISBSG database could be found in [18], [21], [22].

Before applying the framework, the two used datasets were split manually in four subsets of data. The first subset (72-UFP and 202-UFP) selected unadjusted function points size (UFP) as a predictor and effort of software development as the dependent variable. The second subset selected (72-BFC and 202-BFC) basic functional components size (BFC) as a predictor and effort of software development as the dependent variable. The third subset (72-UFP-CTX and 202-UFP-CTX) selected unadjusted function points size (UFP) and context attributes (nominal) as predictors and effort of software development as the dependent variable. The fourth subset (72-BFC-CTX and 202-BFC-CTX) selected basic functional components size (BFC) and context attributes (nominal) as predictors and effort of software development as dependent variable. Nominal variables were transformed by dummy coding, where each variable was coded as a 0 or 1 by applying a nominal to binary filter.

Table 2. Project Selection Criteria.

Criteria	Values	Motivation
Count Approach	IFPUG 4+	Latest FPA standard and counting rules.
Data Quality	A	Only data with a high level of quality and integrity.
UFP Rating	A or B, A	Counting data with a high level of quality and integrity.
Year of project	$\geq 2005, \geq 2008$	New projects using new technologies.
Application group	BA	Business application is one of the main development areas in sindustry.
Resource Level	1	Only development team effort included.

4.2 Learning Schemes

The learning schemes are composed of three parts: Data Preprocessing, Attribute Selector and Learning Algorithm. This section details the different techniques used for each part. In total, we tested 150 different learning schemes [12] (see Table 3). A complete description of the techniques and algorithms is presented in the section 2 (Related Work).

Table 3. Learning Scheme (DP, AS, LA)

Data Preprocessing (DP)			Attribute selector (AS)			Learning Algorithm (LA)							
1 None	None	1 BE	Backward Elimination	1 GP	GaussianProcesses	6	SMO	SMOreg	11	M5R	M5Rules		
2 Log	Logartihmic	2 FS	Forward Selection	2 LMS	LeastMedSq	7	AR	AdditiveRegression	12	ZR	ZeroR		
		3 BF	BestFirst	3 LR	LinearRegression	8	BGN	Bagging	13	DS	DecisionStump		
		4 LFS	LinearForwardSelection	4 MP	MultilayerPerceptron	9	CR	ConjunctiveRule	14	M5P	M5P		
		5 RS	RankSearch	5 RBFN	RBFNetwork	10	DT	DecisionTable	15	RT	REPTree		

4.3 Evaluation Criteria

The prediction accuracy of the models was tested on the new data and the following statistics (used in [8] [23] [24] [17]) were applied: magnitude of relative error (MRE), magnitude of error relative (MER), balanced relative error

(BRE), and number of predictions within % of the actual ones (Pred25). MRE is the difference between the actual effort and the predicted effort. This difference should be as small as possible. Large deviations will have a significant impact on the costs related to the development of software. The MRE value of individual predictions can be averaged, resulting in the Mean MRE (MMRE). The MMRE can be highly affected by outliers. To address this shortcoming, the MdMRE metric has been proposed which is the median of all MREs. This metric can be considered more robust to outliers, and is therefore preferred over the MMRE. A complementary accuracy measure is Pred. Pred is simply the percentage of estimates that are within $m\%$ of the actual value (the % of the estimates with MRE ≤ 0.25). Typically m is set to 25 so the indicator reveals what proportion of estimates are within a tolerance of 25% [8]. This evaluation is conducted because the presence of an association does not necessarily imply that an accurate predictive model can be built.

4.4 Experimental Description

The experimental process had the following characteristics:

1. In the generation phase we used the following configuration: Mutation (10%) and Crossover (60%). As operator of selection we used Roulette. We set the elitism to (2%).
2. In the evaluation phase we applied a strategy for the selection of attributes named Filter [12]. It was used with the objective of selecting the attributes for each subset. We used this strategy because it is computationally less costly than Wrapper [12] [13]. The main difference between Filter and Wrapper is the internal cross-validation used by the Wrapper.
3. We executed a total of 20 generations with 20 genetic individuals using the standard configuration of WEKA's geneticSearch [12]. Each genetic individual was represented by a learning scheme (see section 5.2 Learning Schemes).
4. We set $N-PASS = 10$, and calculated the average of Correlation Coefficient after $N-PASS$ runs. For each $PASS$ we randomly selected 90% of the data as the historical.
5. A $N = 10$ x $M = 10$-fold cross-validation was used to evaluate each learning scheme. The modules were selected randomly. Further the evaluation metrics: correlation coefficient (CC), mean magnitude of relative error (MMRE), mean magnitude of error relative (MMER), mean balanced relative error (MBRE) and PRED10 to PRED50 were calculated and their average calculated after N x M-fold cross-validation.
6. The fitness function of each genetic individual executed in 1000 holdout experiments, ($N - PASS = 10$) and $N = 10$ x $M = 10$-fold cross-validation. The mean of the 1000 CC measures was reported as the evaluation performance per genetic individual. The historicalData (90%) was preprocessed considering the preprocessing techniques. Then, the predictor was used to predict defects with the newData (10%), which was preprocessed in the same way as that of the historical data.
7. The search space presented a total of 150 combinations (see section 4.2).

8. The prediction performance per metric was calculated as the total average. In this phase we used historical data and new data, both selected randomly.

4.5 Statistical Tests

Part of the procedure described in [8] [25] is conducted to statistically test the results of the benchmarking experiment. To compare the performance of models on a single dataset, the nonparametric Mann-Whitney test and Kruskal-Wallis test were applied on performance metrics: correlation coefficient (CC), MdMRE, Pred25. The Mann-Whitney U test was used to compare differences between two independent groups not normally distributed. The Kruskal-Wallis test is a nonparametric test that can be used to determine if there are statistically significant differences between two or more groups of an independent variable on a continuous variable. This test is considered the nonparametric alternative to the one-way ANOVA, and an extension of the Mann-Whitney U test to allow the comparison of more than two independent groups.

5 Analysis and Interpretation of Results

This section reports on the results of the prediction models based on techniques discussed in subsection 4.2 on the selected datasets detailed in subsection 4.1.

The results of the different modeling techniques (learning schemes) of the evaluation stage, as explained in subsection 4.2, are presented in Table 4 and Table 5 ordered by each dataset. For each model, data preprocessing (DP), attribute selector (AS), and learning algorithm (LA) are detailed. In addition, the mean magnitude of relative error (MMRE), median magnitude of relative error (MdMRE), mean magnitude of error relative (MMER), mean balanced relative error (MBRE), Pred25, and correlation coefficient results are provided. The models were ranked according to their performance on each accuracy metric. The best performing metrics are shown in bold. In Table 6, the results of selected modeling techniques (learning schemes) of the prediction stage are presented. For each model, accuracy metrics are detailed.

The Mann-Whitney and the Kruskal-Wallis statistical tests were applied to test performance differences between prediction models (learning schemes) evaluating the correlation coefficient (CC), MdMRE, and Pred25. The Kruskal-Wallis test resulted in a p-value close to zero (p-values close to 0.000) indicating the existence of significant differences across the applied techniques in all performance metrics (CC, MdMRE, and Pred25). The Mann-Whitney test was conducted for models based on total function points (UFP) and models based on basic functional components (BFC). This test was conducted between 72-UFP and 72-BFC, 72-UFP-CTX and 72-BFC-CTX, 202-UFP and 202-BFC, and 202-UFP-CTX and 202-BFC-CTX and evaluated across performance metrics.

The Mann-Whitney test indicated that some models based on BFCs are equivalent to the model based on UFP in terms of some performance metrics:

1. Comparing models between 72-UFP and 72-BFC, CC (.241), MMER (.075), MBRE (.336), and Pred25 (.246) retains the null hypothesis. The best models

Table 4. Models Performance (72)

DP	AS	LA	CC	MMRE	MMER	MBRE	MdMRE	Pred25
72-UFP								
None	FS	SMO	**0.76**	**0.58**	**0.46**	**0.72**	0.30	**0.38**
None	BF	LMS	**0.76**	**0.58**	0.52	0.76	0.30	0.33
None	LFS	LMS	**0.76**	**0.58**	0.52	0.76	0.30	0.33
Log	FS	LMS	**0.76**	**0.58**	0.52	0.76	0.30	0.34
Log	FS	SMO	**0.76**	**0.58**	**0.46**	**0.72**	**0.29**	**0.38**
72-BFC								
None	BE	M5P	**0.76**	0.73	0.35	0.70	**0.32**	0.33
None	FS	LMS	0.68	**0.66**	0.63	0.93	**0.32**	0.33
None	FS	M5P	**0.76**	0.72	0.41	0.75	**0.32**	**0.34**
None	BF	M5P	**0.76**	0.70	0.31	0.65	**0.32**	**0.34**
None	LFS	M5P	**0.76**	0.72	0.05	0.40	**0.32**	0.33
Log	BE	M5P	**0.76**	0.71	0.19	0.54	**0.32**	**0.34**
Log	FS	SMO	0.70	0.67	0.51	0.83	**0.32**	0.32
Log	FS	M5P	**0.76**	0.71	0.26	0.20	**0.32**	**0.34**
Log	BF	LMS	0.69	**0.65**	0.14	0.46	**0.32**	0.33
Log	BF	SMO	0.70	0.67	0.50	0.82	**0.32**	0.32
Log	BF	M5P	**0.76**	0.71	**0.04**	**0.04**	**0.32**	**0.34**
Log	LFS	LMS	0.69	**0.66**	0.56	0.87	0.31	0.33
Log	LFS	M5P	**0.76**	0.71	0.06	0.33	**0.32**	**0.34**
72-UFP-CTX								
None	FS	LMS	0.80	**0.50**	0.40	0.56	0.27	0.38
None	FS	LR	**0.84**	0.57	**0.01**	**0.12**	**0.26**	**0.42**
None	FS	SMO	**0.84**	0.55	0.31	0.16	0.28	0.38
None	BF	SMO	**0.84**	0.54	0.28	0.45	0.28	0.38
None	LFS	LR	0.80	0.58	0.36	0.54	0.27	**0.42**
None	LFS	SMO	**0.84**	0.54	0.02	0.17	0.28	0.38
Log	FS	LR	**0.84**	0.57	0.35	0.45	**0.26**	**0.42**
Log	FS	SMO	**0.84**	0.55	0.10	0.27	0.28	0.38
Log	LFS	LMS	0.76	**0.50**	0.30	0.45	0.27	0.38
Log	LFS	LR	0.79	0.58	0.02	0.20	0.27	**0.42**
Log	LFS	SMO	**0.84**	0.53	0.05	0.21	0.28	0.39
72-BFC-CTX								
None	FS	LMS	0.72	**0.61**	0.37	0.62	**0.29**	0.36
None	FS	LR	0.76	0.67	0.40	0.11	0.30	**0.37**
None	FS	SMO	**0.77**	0.62	**0.01**	**0.04**	**0.29**	**0.37**
None	BF	SMO	**0.77**	0.62	0.30	0.56	0.30	0.36
None	LFS	SMO	**0.77**	0.62	0.22	0.61	0.30	**0.37**
Log	FS	LMS	0.72	**0.60**	0.19	0.41	0.30	0.36
Log	FS	SMO	**0.77**	0.62	0.11	0.06	0.30	0.36
Log	LFS	LR	0.74	0.68	**0.00**	0.28	0.31	**0.37**
Log	LFS	SMO	**0.77**	0.63	0.24	0.49	0.30	0.36

Table 5. Models Performance (202)

DP	AS	LA	CC	MMRE	MMER	MBRE	MdMRE	Pred25
202-UFP								
None	BE	LMS	**0.70**	0.63	0.67	0.92	**0.40**	0.30
None	BE	SMO	**0.70**	0.63	**0.60**	**0.86**	**0.40**	**0.31**
None	FS	LMS	**0.70**	**0.62**	0.67	0.91	**0.40**	0.30
None	FS	SMO	**0.70**	**0.62**	**0.60**	**0.86**	0.39	**0.31**
None	BF	LMS	**0.70**	**0.62**	0.67	0.92	**0.40**	0.30
None	BF	SMO	**0.70**	0.63	**0.60**	**0.86**	**0.40**	**0.31**
None	LFS	LMS	0.69	**0.62**	0.66	0.92	**0.40**	0.30
None	LFS	SMO	**0.70**	0.63	**0.60**	**0.86**	0.39	**0.31**
Log	BE	LMS	**0.70**	0.63	0.67	0.92	**0.40**	0.30
Log	FS	LMS	**0.70**	**0.62**	0.67	0.92	**0.40**	0.30
Log	FS	SMO	**0.70**	0.63	**0.60**	**0.86**	**0.40**	**0.31**
Log	BF	LMS	**0.70**	**0.62**	0.66	0.92	**0.40**	0.30
Log	BF	SMO	**0.70**	0.63	**0.60**	**0.86**	**0.40**	**0.31**
Log	LFS	LMS	**0.70**	**0.62**	0.66	0.92	**0.40**	0.30
Log	LFS	SMO	**0.70**	0.63	**0.60**	**0.86**	**0.40**	**0.31**
202-BFC								
None	BE	LMS	0.66	**0.65**	0.68	0.95	0.41	0.30
None	BE	SMO	**0.67**	**0.65**	0.63	**0.91**	**0.39**	**0.31**
None	FS	LMS	0.66	**0.65**	0.68	0.95	0.41	0.29
None	FS	SMO	**0.67**	**0.65**	0.63	**0.91**	**0.39**	**0.31**
None	BF	LMS	0.66	**0.65**	0.68	0.95	0.41	0.29
None	BF	SMO	0.66	**0.65**	0.63	**0.91**	**0.39**	**0.31**
None	LFS	GP	**0.67**	0.87	**0.53**	1.01	0.45	0.30
None	LFS	LMS	0.66	**0.65**	0.68	0.95	0.41	0.29
None	LFS	SMO	**0.67**	**0.65**	0.63	**0.91**	**0.39**	**0.31**
Log	BE	LMS	**0.67**	**0.65**	0.63	**0.91**	0.41	0.30
Log	BE	SMO	**0.67**	**0.65**	0.63	**0.91**	**0.39**	**0.31**
Log	FS	SMO	**0.67**	0.66	0.63	0.92	0.40	**0.31**
Log	BF	SMO	0.66	0.66	0.63	**0.91**	**0.39**	**0.31**
Log	LFS	LMS	0.66	**0.65**	0.68	0.95	0.41	0.30
Log	LFS	SMO	**0.67**	**0.65**	0.63	**0.91**	**0.39**	**0.31**
202-UFP-CTX								
None	BE	LMS	0.74	0.71	0.55	0.82	**0.38**	0.31
None	BE	SMO	0.75	0.71	0.07	0.32	0.39	**0.32**
None	FS	LMS	0.73	0.66	0.51	0.75	**0.38**	0.31
None	BF	LMS	0.74	0.66	0.15	0.40	**0.38**	0.31
None	BF	SMO	0.75	0.68	0.25	0.50	0.39	**0.32**
None	LFS	LMS	0.74	0.61	0.53	0.76	0.37	**0.32**
None	LFS	SMO	0.75	0.66	**0.01**	**0.02**	**0.38**	**0.32**
Log	BE	LMS	0.73	0.72	0.41	0.68	**0.38**	**0.32**
Log	BE	SMO	0.73	0.72	1.91	2.15	0.39	**0.32**
Log	FS	LMS	0.74	0.65	0.45	0.69	**0.38**	0.31
Log	BF	SMO	0.75	0.67	0.24	0.49	**0.38**	**0.32**
Log	LFS	LMS	0.74	**0.62**	0.32	0.56	0.37	**0.32**
Log	LFS	SMO	**0.76**	0.66	0.10	0.09	**0.38**	**0.32**
202-BFC-CTX								
None	BE	SMO	0.74	0.74	0.26	0.52	**0.38**	**0.33**
None	BE	M5P	0.71	0.76	0.31	0.65	0.42	0.30
Log	BE	LMS	0.72	**0.71**	0.45	0.69	**0.38**	0.31
Log	BE	SMO	**0.73**	0.74	**0.12**	**0.06**	**0.38**	**0.33**
Log	BE	M5P	0.71	0.75	0.43	0.78	0.42	0.29
Log	FS	SMO	0.69	0.75	0.40	0.74	0.43	0.28
Log	BF	LMS	0.60	**0.70**	0.66	0.96	0.41	0.28

based on total UFP perform as well as models based on BFC for these metrics.

2. Comparing models between 72-UFP-CTX and 72-BFC-CTX, the test resulted in a p-value close to zero (p-values close to 0.000) indicating the existence of significant differences across the applied techniques in all performance metrics (CC, MdMRE, and Pred25).

Table 6. Best Models Performance in Effort Prediction Stage

Dataset	DP	AS	LA	CC	MMRE	MdMRE	Pred25
72-UFP	Log	FS	LR	0.76	0.80	0.48	0.23
72-BFC	Log	BF	M5P	0.84	0.55	0.28	0.33
72-UFP-CTX	None	LFS	SMO	0.83	0.56	0.20	0.46
72-BFC-CTX	None	FS	SMO	0.88	0.56	0.35	0.30
202-UFP	None	FS	SMO	0.63	0.67	0.43	0.29
202-BFC	None	BE	SMO	0.71	0.66	0.41	0.32
202-UFP-CTX	None	LFS	SMO	0.74	0.65	0.39	0.34
202-BFC-CTX	Log	BE	SMO	0.73	0.66	0.48	0.27

3. Comparing models between 202-UFP and 202-BFC, MMER (.305), MdMRE (.744), and Pred25 (.870) retains the null hypothesis. The best models based on total UFP perform as well as models based on BFC for these metrics.
4. Comparing models between 202-UFP-CTX and 202-BFC-CTX, MMER (.535), MBRE (.360), and Pred25 (.172) retains the null hypothesis. The best models based on total UFP perform as well as models based on BFC for these metrics.

Further research on evaluating accuracy of prediction models based on a subset of basic functional components (BFC) is needed to confirm some of the presented results. We provide box-plots capturing group means and variance for each dataset and performance metrics in figure 2. Results shows variability between models performance.

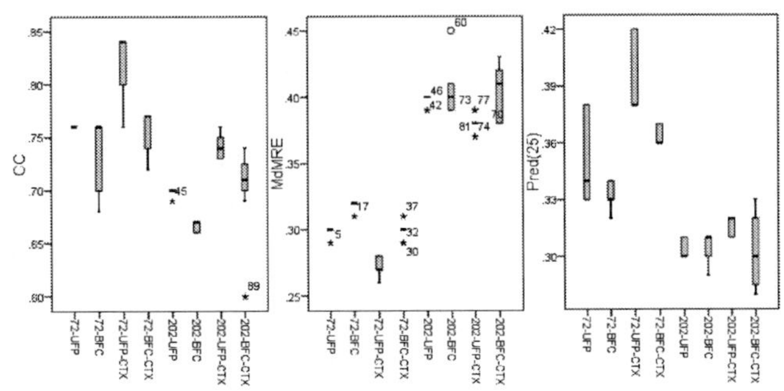

Fig. 2. Box-plots with Results of Performance Metrics

The proposed framework evaluated learning schemes (preprocessing + attribute selection + learning algorithms) in order to select the best prediction models based on performance metrics. The most recurrent learning schemes selected by each dataset are presented in Table 7. For the 72-UFP dataset, Log + ForwardSelection+ M5-Rules models were selected in 12% of total models evaluated. For the 72-BFC dataset, Log + BestFirst + M5-Rules was selected in 51% of total models evaluated. In 72-UFP-CTX dataset, Log + LinearForwardSelection + SMOreg was selected in 33% of total models evaluated. And for the 72-BFC-CTX dataset, ForwardSelection + SMOreg was selected in 31% of total models. For the 202-UFP dataset, ForwardSelection + SMOreg models were selected in 62% of total models evaluated. For the 202-BFC dataset, BackwardElimination + SMOreg was selected in 35% of total models evaluated and LinearForwardSelection + SMOreg in 26%. In 202-UFP-CTX dataset, LinearForwardSelection + SMOreg was selected in 51% of total models evaluated. And finally, for the 202-BFC-CTX dataset, Log + BestFirst + SMOreg was selected in 66% of total models.

Table 7. Prediction Models Learning Schemes

72-UFP				72-BFC				72-UFP-CTX				72-BFC-CTX			
DP	AS	LA	%	DP	AS	LA	%	DP	AS	LA	%	DP	AS	LA	%
Log	FS	M5P	12.0	Log	BF	M5P	50.7	Log	LFS	SMO	33.2	None	FS	SMO	30.7
None	LFS	DT	7.6	Log	LFS	M5P	17.7	None	FS	LR	18.3	None	LFS	M5R	18.6
Log	FS	SMO	6.5	Log	BE	M5P	5.8	None	LFS	SMO	8.8	None	BE	M5R	6.2
Log	FS	AR	5.4	None	BF	M5P	5.5	None	FS	SMO	5.6	Log	FS	SMO	4.1
Log	LFS	LMS	5.4	Log	FS	M5P	5.3	Log	FS	SMO	5.1	None	BF	SMO	4.1
202-UFP				202-BFC				202-UFP-CTX				202-BFC-CTX			
DP	AS	LA	%	DP	AS	LA	%	DP	AS	LA	%	DP	AS	LA	%
None	FS	SMO	62.1	None	BE	SMO	34.4	None	LFS	SMO	51.2	Log	BE	SMO	65.5
Log	FS	SMO	9.0	None	LFS	SMO	26.0	Log	LFS	SMO	18.3	None	BE	SMO	6.9
None	FS	LMS	4.5	Log	LFS	SMO	14.9	Log	BF	SMO	3.8	Log	BF	SMO	6.4
None	BF	SMO	3.1	None	FS	SMO	5.9	None	BF	SMO	3.1	Log	FS	SMO	3.8
None	BE	SMO	2.8	None	BF	SMO	4.0	None	FS	SMO	2.6	Log	BE	M5P	2.9

Prediction models based on basic functional components (BFC) were evaluated. For models based on BFC without context attributes, all BFC were selected as predictors in 60% of the models for the 72-BFC dataset, and in 72% of the models for the 202-BFC dataset. A model based on external inputs (EI) + external outputs (EO) + internal logical files (ILF) + external interface files (EIF) was selected in 22% of the models for the 72-BFC dataset, and a model based on EO + External inquiries (EQ) + ILF + EIF was selected in 10% of the models for the 202-BFC dataset. For models based on BFC and context attributes, models based on a subset of BFC were selected more frequently. A model based on EI + EO was selected in 32% of the models, a model based on EQ was selected in 17%, a model based on EI + EO + ILF + EIF was selected in 17%, and a model based on EI + ILF was selected in 14% of the models for the 72-BFC-CTX dataset. For the 202-BFC-CTX dataset, a model based on EI + EO + ILF + EIF was selected in 15% of the models, a model based on EI in 10% of the models, and a model based on EO + EQ + ILF in 8% of the models. In practice, results indicate that some effort models based on BFCs instead of UFP could be created. However, based on the variability of the selected components, further research evaluating simplified models based on a subset of basic functional components (BFC) should be conducted to identify which components perform better to predict effort.

5.1 Threads of validity

Internal validity: The limited size and characteristics of the sub-dataset used in some analyses may be a threat to internal validity. Data were filtered to make sure only desirable and high level quality information were used in the analysis and robust techniques were used to investigate correlations and prediction models. It is necessary to validate other learning scheme configurations. We will need to conduct experiments that include other genetic configurations (population and generations with different sizes), a larger search space and including additional datasets. **External validity**: The results of this study only considered the ISBSG R12 database. It is necessary to do more experimentation with other kinds of databases that present different structure and characteristics. The software project datasets used in our experiments were based on the business application domain. **Construction validity**: In the selection of the learning scheme combination, only the correlation coefficient was used by the elitism technique. Our main issue has been the runtime of the framework with the datasets, mainly the duration of execution of the fitness function. However we are working in a distributed solution.

6 Conclusions and Future Work

In this paper, a genetic approach selected the best learning scheme for predicting per dataset using the elitism technique. The learning scheme's performance was measured with different metrics: CC, MMER, MBRE, MdMRE and Pred25. The final performance per dataset is determined by the context configuration (random selection, missing values, imbalance dataset, outliers, other machine learning strategies, among others). This is the main reason why there is no single best learning scheme for all datasets. Each dataset had a different context configuration and hence a different learning scheme; this is the main goal of our framework: to try select the best learning scheme combination for a dataset.

The results of this benchmarking study partially confirm the results of previous studies in the field. Simple, understandable regression techniques with log transformation of attributes perform as well as nonlinear techniques. Moreover, according to our results, SMOreg that implements a support vector machine for regression presents an opportunity to improve some prediction models. We agreed with [8] regarding that although data mining and artificial intelligence techniques can make a contribution to the set of software effort estimation models, these still could not replace expert judgment. Both approaches should be seen as complementary. Prediction models can be adopted to check the expert estimations. The selection of a proper estimation technique can have a significant impact on the performance and it should be selected according the specific set of data used for the prediction.

For a future study, a replication of the experiment using different datasets and the complete rigorous statistical testing procedure described in [8] should be conducted to test the results of the benchmarking experiment and confirm the results presented above. The framework could also be enhanced to automate the statistical analysis for selected models. For example, a Friedman test

[26] could be used to evaluate if all techniques perform equivalently. If not, a posthoc Bonferroni-Dunn test [27] could be automated to compare the models and identify which of the models performance is better. To compare the performance of two models on a single dataset, other techniques such as nonparametric the Wilcoxon Matched Pairs test [28], parametric T-test [29], and standard T-test could be automated in the framework. Furthermore, we would like to work with more learning schemes adding more attribute-selector methods, learning algorithms and additional data preprocessing techniques such as MathExpression (mean, max, min, sd, count, sum) or AddExpression (log, abs, cos, exp, sqrt, floor, ceil, rint, tan, sin), PCA, BOX-COX among others. Additionally we plan to conduct more experimentation with different genetic configurations, for example, 30 and 50 populations and generations, or changing the $N - PASS$ parameter. Finally, with the objective of improving the runtime performance, we plan to implement our approach using parallel or distributed programming.

Acknowledgments This research was supported in part by the University of Costa Rica (No. 834-B5-A18), the National University of Costa Rica, and the Ministry of Science, Technology and Telecommunications (MICITT). Our thanks to The International Software Benchmarking Standards Group (ISBSG).

References

1. Moløkken, K., Jørgensen, M.: A review of software surveys on software effort estimation. In: Proceedings of IEEE International Symposium on Empirical Software Engineering ISESE. (2003) 223–230
2. Boehm, B.: Software engineering economics. Volume 197. Prentice-hall Englewood Cliffs (NJ) (1981)
3. Albrecht, A.J.: Measuring application development productivity. In: Proceedings of the Joint SHARE/GUIDE/IBM Application Development Symposium. Volume 10. (1979) 83–92
4. Jeng, B., Yeh, D., Wang, D., Chu, S.L., Chen, C.M., et al.: A specific effort estimation method using function point. Journal of Information Science and Engineering **27** (2011) 1363–1376
5. Albrecht, A.J., Gaffney Jr, J.E.: Software function, source lines of code, and development effort prediction: a software science validation. IEEE Transactions on Software Engineering (1983) 639–648
6. Jones, C.: Function points as a universal software metric. ACM SIGSOFT Software Engineering Notes **38** (2013) 1–27
7. Jorgensen, M., Shepperd, M.: A systematic review of software development cost estimation studies. IEEE Transactions on Software Engineering **33** (2007) 33–53
8. Dejaeger, K., Verbeke, W., Martens, D., Baesens, B.: Data mining techniques for software effort estimation: a comparative study. IEEE Transactions on Software Engineering **38** (2012) 375–397
9. Mittas, N., Angelis, L.: Comparing cost prediction models by resampling techniques. Journal of Systems and Software **81** (2008) 616–632
10. Kitchenham, B., Mendes, E.: Why comparative effort prediction studies may be invalid. In: Proceedings of the 5th International Conference on Predictor Models in Software Engineering. PROMISE '09, New York, NY, USA, ACM (2009) 4:1–4:5
11. Malhotra, R.: Comparative analysis of statistical and machine learning methods for predicting faulty modules. Applied Soft Computing **21** (2014) 286–297

12. Witten, I.H., Frank, E.: Data Mining: Practical machine learning tools and techniques. Morgan Kaufmann (2005)
13. Song, Q., Jia, Z., Shepperd, M., Ying, S., Liu, J.: A general software defect-proneness prediction framework. Software Engineering, IEEE Transactions on **37** (2011) 356–370
14. Murillo-Morera, J., Jenkins, M.: A software defect-proneness prediction framework: A new approach using genetic algorithms to generate learning schemes. In: The 27th International Conference on Software Engineering and Knowledge Engineering, SEKE 2015, Wyndham Pittsburgh University Center, Pittsburgh, PA, USA, July 6-8, 2015. (2015) 445–450
15. Quesada-López, C., Jenkins, M.: Function point structure and applicability validation using the isbsg dataset: a replicated study. In: Proceedings of the 8th ACM/IEEE International Symposium on Empirical Software Engineering and Measurement, ACM (2014) 66
16. Mendes, E., Lokan, C., Harrison, R., Triggs, C.: A replicated comparison of cross-company and within-company effort estimation models using the isbsg database. In: Software Metrics, 2005. 11th IEEE International Symposium, IEEE (2005) 10 pp.–36
17. Seo, Y.S., Bae, D.H., Jeffery, R.: Areion: Software effort estimation based on multiple regressions with adaptive recursive data partitioning. Information and Software Technology **55** (2013) 1710–1725
18. Quesada-López, C., Jenkins, M.: An empirical validation of function point structure and applicability: A replication study. In: CIBSE 2015 - XVIII Ibero-American Conference on Software Engineering. (2015) 418–431
19. Mendes, E., Lokan, C.: Replicating studies on cross-vs single-company effort models using the isbsg database. Empirical Software Engineering **13** (2008) 3–37
20. González-Ladrón-de Guevara, F., Fernández-Diego, M.: Isbsg variables most frequently used for software effort estimation: A mapping review. In: Proceedings of the 8th ACM/IEEE International Symposium on Empirical Software Engineering and Measurement, ACM (2014) 42
21. Quesada-López, C., Jenkins, M.: Function point structure and applicability: A replicated study. Journal of Object Technology **In press** (2016)
22. Hill, P.: Practical Software Project Estimation: A Toolkit for Estimating Software Development Effort & Duration. McGraw Hill Professional (2010)
23. Lavazza, L., Morasca, S., Robiolo, G.: Towards a simplified definition of function points. Information and Software Technology **55** (2013) 1796–1809
24. Lokan, C., Mendes, E.: Cross-company and single-company effort models using the isbsg database: a further replicated study. In: Proceedings of the 2006 ACM/IEEE international symposium on Empirical software engineering, ACM (2006) 75–84
25. Demšar, J.: Statistical comparisons of classifiers over multiple data sets. The Journal of Machine Learning Research **7** (2006) 1–30
26. Friedman, M.: A comparison of alternative tests of significance for the problem of m rankings. The Annals of Mathematical Statistics **11** (1940) 86–92
27. Dunn, O.J.: Multiple comparisons among means. Journal of the American Statistical Association **56** (1961) 52–64
28. Wilcoxon, F.: Individual comparisons by ranking methods. Biometrics bulletin (1945) 80–83
29. Hastie, T., Tibshirani, R., Friedman, J., Franklin, J.: The elements of statistical learning: data mining, inference and prediction. The Mathematical Intelligencer **27** (2005) 83–85

Análise Linguístico-Científica dos Termos "Esforço" e "Custo" e sua Relação com o Software: Um Estudo Qualitativo Apoiado pela Linguística de *Corpus*

Thiago Silva-de-Souza[1], Thiago Moreira da Silva[2] e Guilherme Horta Travassos[1,3]

[1] Programa de Engenharia de Sistemas e Computação (PESC),
Instituto Alberto Luiz Coimbra de Pós-Graduação e Pesquisa de Engenharia (COPPE),
Universidade Federal do Rio de Janeiro (UFRJ) – Rio de Janeiro-RJ, Brasil
[2] Faculdade de Letras,
Universidade Federal do Rio de Janeiro (UFRJ) – Rio de Janeiro-RJ, Brasil
[3] Pesquisador CNPq
thiagosouza@cos.ufrj.br, thiago.letras.ufrj@gmail.com, ght@cos.ufrj.br

Resumo. Modelos de estimativa de esforço e custo para projetos de software têm sido investigados há mais de 50 anos. Ao longo deste período, diferentes modelos foram propostos, utilizando as mais variadas técnicas de estimativa e considerando os mais diversos fatores, com o objetivo de alcançar melhores níveis de acurácia. Entretanto, percebe-se que grande parte dos trabalhos nessa área apresenta os termos "esforço" e "custo" como sinônimos, ao mesmo tempo em que relacionam fatores de custo ao esforço do projeto, potencializando inconsistências e ambiguidades, o que contribui para aumentar as ameaças à validade de constructo em estudos primários e, principalmente, secundários. Este trabalho, portanto, apresenta uma análise apoiada em pressupostos linguísticos dos termos "esforço" e "custo", através de recortes gramaticais de análise de como ambos os termos são utilizados, na materialidade linguística, em Engenharia de Software, com o objetivo de fornecer subsídios para uma melhor compreensão desses termos na referida área. Desta forma, foi realizada uma análise etimológica, visando resgatar o significado original das palavras "esforço" e "custo", e uma análise de *corpus*, baseada em amostras de *corpora* do Inglês, bem como, sobre os artigos indexados pela Scopus, com o objetivo de questionar o significado de ambos os termos no contexto da Engenharia de Software. Desta forma, os resultados apresentados servem para apoiar a identificação e classificação dos fatores que afetam o esforço e o custo de projetos de software, bem como, permitem aprimorar a realização de estudos qualitativos no campo de conhecimento em questão.

Palavras-chave: engenharia de software, estimativa de esforço, estimativa de custo, linguística de *corpus*.

1 Introdução

Nos últimos anos, diversos trabalhos têm apontado a necessidade de se consolidar a terminologia utilizada na área de Engenharia de Software (ES) [23, 30, 31]. Neste contexto, surge, por exemplo, o *Guide to the Software Engineering Body of*

Knowledge (SWEBOK) [6], conduzido pela IEEE *Computer Society*, com a intenção de categorizar e definir os conceitos relacionados à Engenharia de Software. No entanto, ainda não se pode observar na literatura técnica larga aceitação do SWEBOK, ou de instrumentos equivalentes. O motivo para esta constatação pode estar relacionado ao fato do SWEBOK representar "escolas de pensamento" específicas e por se basear em opiniões de especialistas, deixando de considerar as evidências experimentais [1].

A comunidade de Engenharia de Software Experimental, em especial, considera a definição de uma terminologia comum em Engenharia de Software como fundamental para uma melhor compreensão dos objetos de estudo [31] e melhor comunicação dos achados para a indústria e para as futuras gerações de pesquisadores [23]. O uso de termos imprecisos pode potencializar inconsistências, promover ambiguidades e levar a observações inapropriadas dos objetos de estudo, aumentando, assim, as ameaças à validade de constructo em estudos primários e, especialmente, em estudos secundários.

A motivação deste trabalho está relacionada à inconsistência conceitual observada em um estudo secundário conduzido pelo primeiro e terceiro autores a respeito de fatores que influenciam o esforço em teste de software [25], no qual foram definidas, entre outras, as seguintes questões de pesquisa:

- *Q1: O que se entende por esforço em teste de software e como ele pode ser medido?*
- *Q1.1: De acordo com o entendimento de Q1, que fatores influenciam o esforço em teste de software?*

Para respondê-las foi definida uma *string* de busca (Fig. 1) com base na abordagem PICO [21] e com palavras-chave identificadas a partir do conhecimento prévio dos pesquisadores e derivadas de sete artigos de controle selecionados através de uma busca *ad hoc*.

(("software testing" OR "software test" OR "testing of systems" OR "system test" OR "system testing" OR "software verification" OR "software validation" OR "verification & validation" OR "software evaluation" OR "software quality" OR "test activities" OR "testing activities" OR "test activity" OR "testing activity" OR "test planning" OR "test design" OR "test automation" OR "automated test" OR "test execution" OR "manual test" OR "test case" OR "test specification" OR "testing process" OR "testing project" OR "testing projects" OR "test project" OR "test projects") **AND** ("software test estimation" OR "effort estimation" OR "cost estimation" OR "estimate the cost" OR "effort prediction" OR "cost prediction" OR "effort measurement" OR "cost measurement" OR "execution effort" OR "time estimation") **AND** ("factor" OR "factors" OR "variable" OR "predictor" OR "indicator" OR "indicators" OR "driver" OR "drivers" OR "measure" OR "measures" OR "model" OR "models" OR "approach" OR "method" OR "process" OR "technique" OR "techniques" OR "metric" OR "metrics"))

Fig. 1. String de busca utilizada.

É possível observar no trecho "*... effort estimation" OR "cost estimation" OR "estimate the cost" OR "effort prediction" OR "cost prediction" OR "effort measurement" OR "cost measurement ...*" que os termos "*effort*" (esforço) e "*cost*" (custo) tiveram que ser tratados como sinônimos, combinados par a par com os termos "*estimation*", "*prediction*" e "*measurement*". Isso se deveu a observação dos autores de que os termos esforço e custo são utilizados na literatura técnica de Engenharia de Software de modo intercambiável [18, 19].

Após remover as duplicatas e aplicar os critérios de inclusão e exclusão, foram selecionados 33 trabalhos de um total de 550 artigos retornados. Logo após, iniciou-se a etapa de extração das informações de interesse do estudo. Ao tentar responder a questão Q1, observou-se que a literatura da área trata o conceito de esforço de forma tácita: apenas quatro dos 33 trabalhos selecionados apresentaram alguma definição sobre o que é esforço em teste de software. Mesmo assim, as definições apresentadas são incompletas e controversas, aumentando a incerteza sobre o objeto de estudo.

Em seguida, para selecionar e classificar os fatores que afetam o esforço em teste de software (questão Q1.1), era necessário ter uma definição sobre o que é "esforço". Tendo em vista que os artigos selecionados não forneceram resposta à questão Q1 e que a *string* de busca utiliza termos em Inglês, foi utilizada a primeira definição de esforço do dicionário de Cambridge: "atividade física ou mental necessária para alcançar algum objetivo" [7]. Com base nesta definição, procedeu-se a etapa de codificação utilizando o método *Grounded Theory* [27]. Nesta etapa, observou-se que, além da grande diversidade conceitual presente nos trabalhos selecionados, havia fatores que afetavam o "custo" do projeto, segundo a definição do mesmo dicionário [7], sendo atribuídos ao "esforço" necessário para realizá-lo. Percebeu-se ali um problema: "esforço" e "custo" não possuem necessariamente uma relação de sinonímia e, dependendo do contexto, podem assumir significados diversos, podendo levar a interpretações equivocadas. Este fenômeno de ausência de clareza conceitual pode, ainda, aumentar o nível de ruído inerente a *strings* de busca utilizadas em estudos secundários, bem como, dificultar a interpretação dos textos selecionados em função do nível de subjetividade e eventual ambiguidade dos termos.

Este trabalho, portanto, tem como objetivo principal investigar o significado dos termos "esforço" e "custo" em Engenharia de Software, enfatizando suas possíveis diferenças e eventuais relações. Uma compreensão mais precisa desses termos e dos conceitos associados pode contribuir para a redução de fatores de confusão na definição de modelos de estimativa de esforço e, consequentemente, torná-los mais representativos e fidedignos com eventual influência positiva em sua acurácia. Para alcançar uma maior clareza conceitual destes dois referidos termos e identificar possíveis inconsistências, a Linguística, em suas diversas subáreas, mostra-se como uma ciência que pode trazer importantes contribuições para solução do problema.

Em complemento, acreditamos que o protocolo de investigação utilizado neste trabalho, tendo em vista seu caráter interdisciplinar e contemporâneo para a Engenharia de Software, pode ser de utilidade para outros estudos qualitativos que, de forma semelhante, enfrentem dificuldades relacionadas à falta de uma terminologia comum no tópico de ES em investigação.

O restante deste artigo está organizado da seguinte maneira: a seção 2 apresenta o referencial teórico sobre estimativa de esforço e custo em projetos de software sob uma perspectiva histórica; a seção 3 descreve a metodologia de pesquisa utilizada e os principais resultados encontrados neste trabalho; a seção 4 discute o resultados encontrados, ressaltando o significado dos termos "esforço" e "custo" em ES; por fim, a seção 5 destaca as conclusões e direcionamentos de trabalhos futuros.

2 Referencial Teórico-Histórico

A literatura técnica sobre estimativa de esforço e custo em software é vasta, compreendendo um período de cerca de mais de 50 anos. Por esse motivo, e considerando a necessidade de se compreender em qual contexto a terminologia da área surgiu e evoluiu, esta seção apresenta o referencial teórico de um ponto de vista histórico. Tal abordagem serve, ainda, para identificar possíveis motivos para a atual confusão conceitual entre os termos "esforço" e "custo".

Segundo Jones [17], os pioneiros da área de estimativa de custo de software foram Barry Boehm e Larry Putnam, tendo iniciado seus trabalhos no final da década de 1960. Entretanto, os primeiros trabalhos nessa área datam do início da década de 1960, de autoria de membros da *System Development Corporation* (SDC), uma divisão da *RAND Corporation*, que desenvolvia projetos para órgãos vinculados ao Departamento de Defesa dos Estados Unidos [16, 12, 13]. Esses trabalhos faziam parte de um projeto patrocinado pela *Air Force Electronic Systems Division* cujo objetivo era identificar mecanismos para reduzir e estimar os **custos** de produção dos programas de computador daquela divisão militar [16].

O trabalho pioneiro de Heinze, Claussen e LaBolle [16] fez um levantamento dos fatores que afetam o **custo** de gerenciamento de projetos de desenvolvimento de software, com base em dados de sete projetos. Tais fatores foram divididos em três grupos: conteúdo técnico, ambiente e recursos. Este trabalho usou, pela primeira vez, o termo "*man-month*" (homem-mês) para o contexto de software, denotando a ideia de quantidade de trabalho humano realizado por unidade de tempo, de forma semelhante ao que era usado àquela época na manufatura. No ano seguinte, os trabalhos de Farr e Nanus [12] e Farr e Zagorski [13] apresentaram cerca de 50 fatores que teriam alguma influência sobre o **custo** do software. Tais fatores foram divididos em sete categorias, que incluíam fatores relacionados ao trabalho a ser feito ("requisitos e projeto operacionais" e "projeto e produção do programa"), aos recursos disponíveis ("equipamentos de processamento de dados" e "equipe de programação") e ao ambiente de trabalho ("processos de gerenciamento", "ambiente de desenvolvimento" e "instalações, serviços e suprimentos") [12, 13]. É possível, portanto, perceber nas categorias apresentadas a intenção dos trabalhos da SDC: desenvolver um modelo de **custo**, onde a mão-de-obra empregada é apenas um dos componentes. Essa percepção é corroborada, em especial, pelas seguintes categorias apresentadas:

- "Equipamentos de processamento de dados": considera o custo relacionado ao hardware necessário para desenvolver e testar o software;
- "Ambiente de desenvolvimento": considera, entre outros fatores, os custos decorrentes das viagens realizadas pela equipe de desenvolvedores;
- "Instalações, serviços e suprimentos": considera os custos do espaço físico, serviços de reprodução e material de escritório.

Vale frisar que os trabalhos da SDC associam o termo "*man-month*" ao termo **custo** e não a esforço. Esforço (*effort*) é utilizado nesses trabalhos com a acepção de "projeto". Os autores justificam a utilização de "*man-month*" como unidade de medida de **custo** em detrimento a uma unidade monetária (dólar) pelo fato desta última sofrer variações em função de salários diferenciados, câmbio e despesas gerais [13].

Nas décadas seguintes, os trabalhos de Boehm e Putnam ganharam destaque, tendo sido referenciados por inúmeros outros pesquisadores. O trabalho de Putnam e Myers [22] apresenta equações relacionando tamanho, esforço, tempo, produtividade e qualidade. Putnam utiliza a unidade de medida "*man-month*" com o mesmo sentido empregado nos trabalhos da SDC: tempo dedicado por determinada quantidade de mão-de-obra exclusivamente ao projeto, sem levar em conta o tempo com interrupções no trabalho. Entretanto, Putnam associa o termo "*man-month*" ao termo "*effort*" e não a "*cost*", como feito nos trabalhos da SDC. Já o modelo COCOMO, proposto por Boehm [3, 4] já indicava seu foco sobre o **custo** ao utilizar o termo "*cost*" no acrônimo que o nomeia - *Constructive Cost Model*. Além disso, o modelo é baseado em uma série de fatores, denominados "*cost drivers*" (fatores de **custo**), que são levados em conta em um conjunto de equações que incluem o esforço (medido em homens-mês), produtividade, cronograma e disponibilidade de pessoal. O **custo**, por sua vez, também é tratado em homens-mês tendo em vista as diferenças entre as organizações e considerando que homem-mês é uma unidade mais estável que o dólar. O **custo** em homens-mês deve ser, então, multiplicado por um valor monetário definido por cada organização para cada homem-mês empregado no projeto.

Os fatores de **custo** do COCOMO contemplam atributos relacionados ao produto a ser desenvolvido, hardware utilizado, recursos humanos e características do projeto. Diferentemente do que é percebido nos trabalhos da SDC, o modelo COCOMO, apesar de se designar um modelo de **custo**, não considera os custos indiretos do desenvolvimento de software, como aqueles relacionados às instalações e ao material de escritório. Os fatores de **custo** contemplados pelo modelo COCOMO estão concentrados nos gastos relacionados diretamente ao desenvolvimento do software, em especial aqueles gastos que irão afetar a quantidade de homens-mês do projeto. Pode-se levantar a hipótese de que esta característica do COCOMO tenha influenciado os modelos de estimativa subsequentes a focar apenas em fatores diretamente relacionados ao custo de desenvolvimento, especialmente o custo com mão-de-obra, em detrimento dos custos indiretos do projeto.

Essa percepção de que "esforço" e "custo" são tratados como termos equivalentes em ES pode ser observada nos trabalhos de Mendes [18, 19], quando a autora, ao definir o conceito de estimativa de esforço, cita "... estimativa de esforço, também conhecida como estimativa de custo (ou *costimation*)..." e quando a autora, ao descrever o conceito de "fatores de custo", diz que "... são os fatores que se acredita estar associados com o esforço...". Essa visão é ratificada pelo trabalho de Grimstad, Jørgensen e Moløkken-Østvold [15], que mostra que a terminologia a respeito de estimativa de esforço é raramente utilizada de forma consistente em um grande conjunto de livros-texto e artigos da área de Engenharia de Software.

3 Metodologia da Pesquisa

3.1 Relevância e questões de pesquisa

Considerando sua natureza interdisciplinar, este trabalho buscou apoiar-se na Linguística, a ciência que se ocupa dos estudos da linguagem. Fuzer e Cabral [14] definem a linguagem como "um recurso para fazer e trocar significados" ou "a instanciação de um potencial amplo de significados que pode (...) construir experiências". A ponte com a literatura de ES torna-se evidente uma vez que o fenômeno que se busca elucidar neste trabalho é o uso inconsistente dos vocábulos "custo" e "esforço". Estes dois termos são palavras e, como tais, parte constituinte da linguagem. É válido, então, dizer que, como expressões de linguagem, estes termos são usados para fornecer informações, de acordo com a definição de Fuzer e Cabral [14]. É importante a busca por perceber se tais termos evocam sempre as mesmas noções, ou seja, fornecem sempre as mesmas informações no contexto em que são usados (na literatura de Engenharia de Software), podendo, portanto serem usados de forma intercambiável ou se esta literatura ora usa-os em relação de sinonímia e ora como fornecedores de informações semelhantes, mas não idênticas a fim de promover maior nível de exatidão a modelos de estimativa.

Em suma, algumas questões são pertinentes, uma vez que a relação entre "esforço" e "custo" nem sempre é clara. São estes sempre sinônimos, podendo ser trocados sem prejuízo de significado, ou a relação construída entre eles é de hiponímia? Entende-se por hiponímia a relação entre "itens lexicais específicos e gerais, de forma que o primeiro esteja "incluído" no segundo [9]. Isto é, no plano conceitual, "esforço" estando incluído em "custo", aquele sendo parte deste mas não sendo exatamente a mesma noção. Uma vez que os autores na literatura em questão não fornecem sempre definições prévias do que entendem por "esforço" e o que entendem por "custo", busca-se identificar na construção textual indícios da relação entre estes lançando mão de pressupostos linguísticos. Neste cenário, pode-se estabelecer as seguintes questões de pesquisa para este trabalho:

- *QP1: Qual a relação linguística entre os termos "esforço" e "custo" em Engenharia de Software?*
- *QP2: Como a Linguística pode apoiar na resolução de confusões terminológicas em Engenharia de Software?*

A relevância de tal relação interdisciplinar entre a Engenharia de Software e a Linguística está em identificar inconsistências conceituais (ora os termos evocam noções semelhantes, ora não) que podem comprometer os modelos de estimativa de esforço que apresentam tais inconsistências. Para isto, recortes de análise de diferentes áreas da Linguística provam sua valia. Uma vez desenvolvida a argumentação no tocante ao auxílio de pressupostos linguísticos, a metodologia de análise é relatada. O primeiro recorte que é apresentado neste trabalho é de natureza etimológica.

3.2 Análise Etimológica

A etimologia é definida como o estudo da origem e história da forma e da significação das palavras [9]. Etimologicamente, as palavras "esforço" e "custo" provêm da mesma origem: o Latim Vulgar [10, 29]. O Latim Vulgar era a língua falada pelo povo em geral (a *plebe ignara*) no Império Romano, de maneira espontânea, coloquial e sem preocupação com normas gramaticais [5]. Idiomas românicos como o Português, o Espanhol e o Francês foram originados a partir do Latim Vulgar e, por tal proximidade linguística, a análise etimológica das palavras "esforço" e "custo" foi conduzida com base em um dicionário etimológico do Português [10], complementado por um dicionário etimológico do Inglês [29].

A palavra "esforço" é derivada de **exfortiare*[1] [10, 29]. O prefixo *ex*, presente em palavras como "êxodo" e "exorcismo", significa "para fora". O radical *forti*, é uma derivação da palavra *fortis*, que remete ao significado de "força". Já o sufixo *are* era usado para designar verbos que indicavam ação. Desta forma, o termo **exfortiare* foi provavelmente usado com o significado de "ação de dispender força" para realizar algum trabalho.

"Custo", por sua vez, vem da palavra **costare* [10, 29]. O prefixo *cos* é derivado da palavra latina *com*, que significa "em". O radical *stare*, derivado do vocábulo **sta*, significa "situar" ou "posicionar" e provém do tronco linguístico protoindo-europeu (PIE) [29], o ancestral comum entre os idiomas falados na Europa. Portanto, a acepção original de **costare* era "estar situado em". Entretanto, no século XIII, sua acepção foi estendida, passando a significar "preço" ou "valor" a ser pago [29].

Já o termo "homem-hora", e todas as suas derivações (homem-dia, homem-mês, homem-ano, pessoa-hora, pessoa-mês, etc.), não possui registros etimológicos precisos. O dicionário Merriam-Webster [20], por exemplo, indica que o primeiro registro desse termo data de 1912, enquanto que o Dictionary.com [11] informa que isto ocorreu entre 1915 e 1920. No entanto, é possível encontrar trechos de pronunciamentos proferidos no Parlamento Britânico no final do século XIX citando o termo homem-hora. Nesses registros é possível observar que o termo é empregado com a noção de quantidade de trabalho realizada por uma pessoa durante uma hora, como era comum no contexto da Revolução Industrial.

3.3 Análise de *Corpus*

Para compreender quais significados são atribuídos aos termos e, consequentemente, esboçar alguma teoria, torna-se necessário avaliar grandes volumes de informação, dada a quantidade de variáveis de contexto envolvidas. Para tal, é imprescindível utilizar ferramentas computacionais que possam facilitar o trabalho de organização e interpretação das evidências linguísticas. Neste cenário surge a Linguística de *Corpus*, uma área da Linguística que se apoia em ferramentas computacionais para coleta e análise de *corpus* [28]. Trata-se de um método quantitativo e probabilístico para apoiar estudos naturalmente qualitativos. Um *corpus*, por sua vez, é uma coletânea de registros textuais ou falados, necessariamente em formato eletrônico, compilados e organizados criteriosamente para serem objetos de pesquisa linguística [28].

Para realizar análises sobre *corpora* (o plural de *corpus*) é necessário utilizar ferramentas específicas para tal. Ferramentas para análise de *corpus* geralmente trazem uma série de recursos para apoiar análises linguísticas. A ferramenta utilizada neste trabalho, o *Sketch Engine* [26], possui uma série de recursos, sendo os seguintes os mais importantes no contexto deste trabalho:

- Concordanciador: capaz de exibir concordâncias do termo pesquisado, isto é, os fragmentos de texto nos quais o termo investigado está inserido [28].

---

[1] O asterisco usado antes da palavra serve para indicar que esta não se encontra documentada, sendo, portanto, hipotética [10].

Cada concordância é apresentada de acordo com o padrão *Key Word in Context* (KWIC), onde o termo pesquisado é apresentado de forma destacada dentro do fragmento ou contexto [26].

- *Thesaurus*: utilizado para identificar termos similares ao termo pesquisado, exibindo-os em um *ranking* de frequência [26]. Este recurso pode ser útil para identificar relações de sinonímia entre palavras.
- *Word Sketch*: permite comparar termos em função de relações lexicográficas que possuem com outros termos, o que pode ser útil para estudos voltados à sintaxe.

Tais recursos foram utilizados nas análises de *corpora* feitas neste trabalho. As seções 3.3.1 e 3.3.2 apresentam, respectivamente, uma análise dos termos "*effort*" e "*cost*" em um *corpus* de propósito geral e em um *corpus* preparado para retratar a linguagem utilizada na área de estimativa de esforço e custo de software.

3.3.1 Análise da frequência e relação entre termos no *British National Corpus*

Como já defendido na seção 3.1, as noções que as palavras evocam são construídas na sua relação com o todo, o contexto em que estão inseridas. É arriscado realizar análises numéricas que se encerram apenas em si mesmas. Isso não significa dizer que a frequência com que determinadas palavras são usadas de maneira relacionada não é relevante. Estes dados numéricos não devem ser conclusivos em si só, mas apontam caminhos de análise.

Ao lidar com a construção de uma relação entre palavras em termos estatísticos, os autores deste trabalho recorreram ao *British National Corpus* (*Corpus* Nacional Britânico), um banco de ocorrências de palavras na Língua Inglesa, composto por mais de 100 milhões de palavras, acessado via *Sketch Engine*. Ao se inserir o termo "*effort*" no *Thesaurus* deste *corpus,* as duas palavras que mais se aproximam em frequência e relação são "*attempt*" (tentativa) e "*initiative*" (iniciativa), enquanto que as palavras que apresentam maior proximidade com "*cost*" são "*price*" (preço) e "*value*" (valor). Esta estatística, como dito anteriormente, não basta. No entanto, estes dados apontam para a realidade de que nem sempre "esforço" e "custo" são necessariamente intercambiáveis sem prejuízo de significado, uma vez que o termo "*cost*" não aparece na lista de termos similares ao termo "*effort*" e vice-versa. Ainda, de maneira geral, os termos semelhantes a cada uma das duas palavras também não são os mesmos, como evidenciado nas figuras Fig. 4 e Fig. 5.

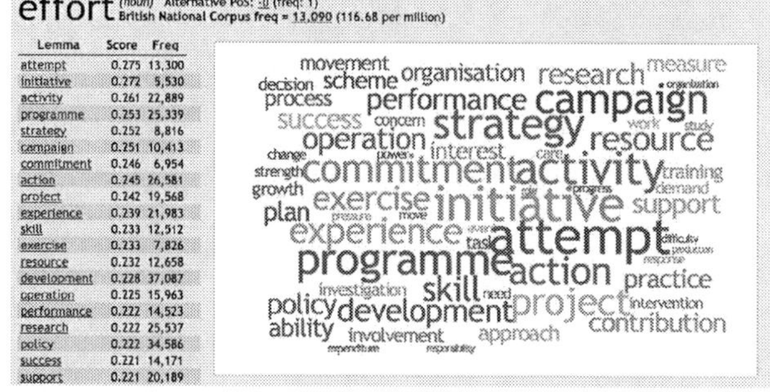

Fig. 2. Termos similares ao termo "*effort*" no *British National Corpus*.

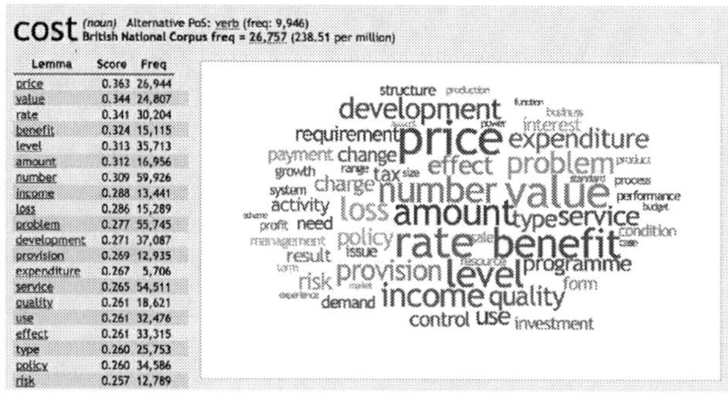

Fig. 3. Termos similares ao termo "*Cost*" no *British National Corpus*.

3.3.2 Análise sobre o *Corpus* de Estimativa de Esforço e Custo de Software

A análise da frequência e relação entre palavras feita na seção 3.3.1 foi de natureza numérica. Esta, apesar de instigante é inconclusiva em si mesma. Na tentativa de trazer o contexto para a análise de *corpus* e superar a limitação de uma análise desprovida de uma esfera contextual, um *corpus* específico foi criado com auxílio da ferramenta *Sketch Engine* [26]. Esse *corpus* foi nomeado como *Effort and Cost Estimation Corpus* (ECEC) e todas as ocorrências nele compiladas são oriundas de trabalhos da área de Engenharia de Software.

O ECEC foi carregado com os três relatórios da SDC citados na seção 2 [16, 12, 13], bem como, com artigos indexados pela máquina de busca Scopus. A escolha da Scopus foi motivada pela ampla cobertura oferecida em trabalhos relacionados à Computação. Desta forma, foi submetida a *string* de busca "*TITLE-ABS-KEY("software effort estimation" OR ("software cost estimation" OR ("software effort prediction" OR "("software cost estimation")"* na base da Scopus, retornando 769 ocorrências. O processo de inclusão dos artigos deu-se pela leitura do título e resumo das ocorrências, resultando em 731 ocorrências pré-selecionadas. Em seguida, considerando um nível de confiança de 95% e um intervalo de confiança de 8%, a amostra utilizada para carregar o ECEC contemplou 126 artigos escolhidos aleatoriamente dentre os 731 pré-selecionados.

Em relação a seu tamanho, o ECEC possui pouco mais de um milhão de palavras, distribuídas em 45.300 sentenças. Quanto à sua tipologia, o ECEC pode ser classificado de acordo com os seguintes critérios [24]:

- Modo: *escrito*, uma vez que o *corpus* é formado por livros e artigos técnicos.
- Tempo: *sincrônico*, porque representa um período específico de tempo.
- Seleção: *de amostragem* (*sample corpus*), já que o *corpus* é constituído por uma amostra finita da linguagem.
- Conteúdo: *especializado*, considerando que os textos são de uma área de conhecimento específica.
- Autoria: *de aprendiz*, tendo em vista que os autores deste *corpus* não são falantes nativos do idioma dos textos que o compõem.
- Finalidade: *de estudo*, já que pretende-se descrever o conteúdo deste *corpus*.

Neste *corpus* específico, nota-se que – conforme sugerido pelas Fig. 4 e Fig. 5 – "*cost*" é a palavra que mais se relaciona como similar a "*effort*" e vice-versa. O *corpus* nos sugere que existe forte aproximação no uso destas duas palavras no campo da Engenharia de Software.

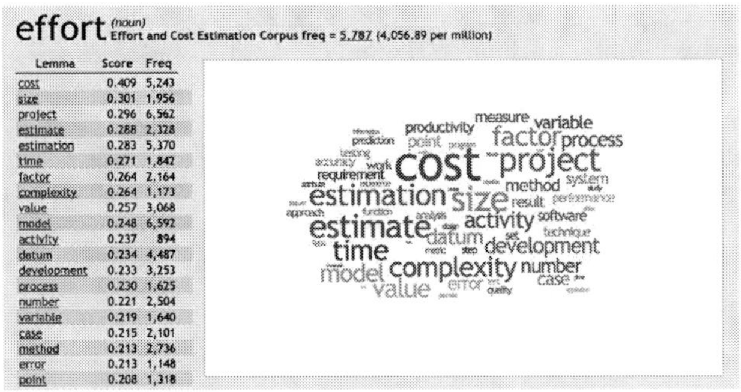

Fig. 4. Termos similares ao termo "Effort" no *Effort and Cost Estimation Corpus*.

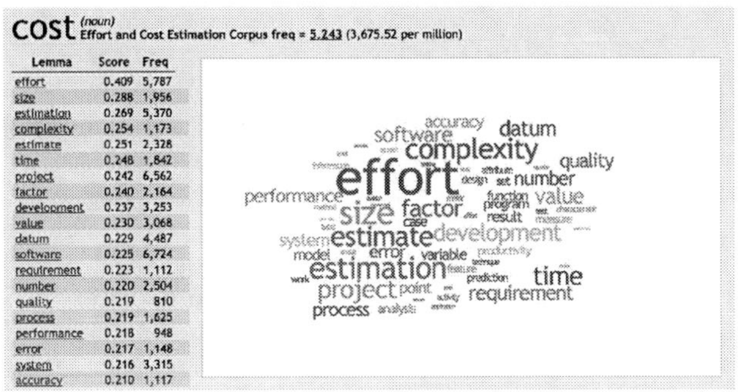

Fig. 5. Termos similares ao termo "Cost" no *Effort and Cost Estimation Corpus*.

Aqui cabe trazer a pergunta: esta forte relação entre estas duas palavras na definida área do conhecimento é construída apenas por aproximação, sem que as duas signifiquem o mesmo? Em suma, qual é a natureza da relação entre estes dois termos na engenharia de software: **sinonímia** (eles abarcam as mesmas noções) ou **hiponímia** (no plano conceitual, um está "contido" no outro, assim como "gato" está contido em "animal")? No intuito de coletar evidências que apontem para respostas a essas perguntas, foram utilizadas quatro concordâncias (fragmentos) do ECEC para análise.

- Concordância 1: "*... proposed a model for **effort and cost estimation** in agile software development by using regression analysis...*"

Na concordância 1, os termos que são foco desta análise não estão mais isolados. Antes, eles estão situados em um contexto de construção de significado e isto possibilita uma análise mais bem estruturada. Recorremos a um recorte sintático para a análise da expressão textual apresentada.

A sintaxe pode ser definida como o "termo tradicional para o estudo das regras que regem a maneira como as palavras se combinam para formar as sentenças de uma língua" [9]. Existe um conceito na Sintaxe, o conceito de coordenação, que pode sugerir a forma como os dois termos são tratados aqui. Por coordenação entende-se "o processo de combinação de dois constituintes de mesma natureza para a produção de um terceiro elemento, maior e do mesmo tipo" [8]. É justamente um processo de coordenação que une "*effort*" e "*cost*". Estes dois elementos estão exercendo a função de modificar, fornecer informação sobre o termo "*estimation*" (estimativa). Ou seja, o texto não fala de qualquer estimativa, mas somente de uma estimativa de custo e de esforço. Isto equivale a afirmar que "*effort*" e "*cost*" têm seu eixo de rotação e sua função de existência centrados no termo "*estimation*". Os termos "*effort*" e "*cost*" não são dependentes um do outro para existir. Ambos são subordinados ao termo "*estimation*" e independentes entre si. Os significados dos dois termos coordenados são distintos um do outro, ou seja, a forma como os elementos aqui referidos são justapostos sintaticamente sugere que estes têm significados diferentes. A conjunção que os coordena ("*AND*") reforça tal argumentação, uma vez que adiciona um conceito a outro. Pelo menos nesta concordância e em mais dez outras presentes no ECEC, **custo** e **esforço**, embora relacionados, são tratados como conceitos distintos.

- Concordância 2: "*Software **effort estimation** (SEE) is the prediction about the amount of **effort** required to make a software system and its duration [1]. SEE first appeared in 1950s (...) having the objective of developing useful models that constructively explain the development life-cycle and accurately predict the **cost** of developing a software product... Since then, there were developed a lot of models for the **effort and cost estimation**.*"

Na concordância 2, os dois termos são usados separadamente. Tal passagem é iniciada com uma definição de estimativa de esforço, sem que o conceito de esforço seja claramente explicitado. Posteriormente, tem-se a ocorrência de custo. A questão central aqui é: no fragmento citado, nenhum dos dois termos é definido. Não existe a expressão do que se entende por custo e esforço. Pode-se interpretar custo, por exemplo, como "soma de recursos financeiros que é necessária para se desenvolver um produto de software", ainda sem muita certeza. Já esforço pode ser interpretado como "desprendimento de energia". Esta energia, por sua vez, poderia ser definida como tempo, recursos tecnológicos ou ambos. Nada está claro. Finalmente, "custo" e "esforço" são novamente coordenados, como na concordância 1, sugerindo que estes evocam noções distintas, embora relacionadas.

- Concordância 3: "*The financial success of a project can depend on the ability of the software manager to estimate the* ***cost*** *of software development accurately, prior to the start of the project.* ***Software cost and effort estimation*** *will never be an exact science. Too many variables - human, technical, environmental, political - can affect the ultimate* ***cost*** *of software and the* ***effort*** *needed to develop it.*"

No fragmento 3, alguns fatores que afetam o custo e o esforço do desenvolvimento de um produto de software são elencados. Uma questão se torna pertinente, uma vez que estes termos aparecem coordenados, sugerindo que abarcam conceitos relacionados, porém, distintos: os fatores elencados afetam igualmente "custo" e "esforço"? Ou alguns fatores afetam apenas o custo e outros somente o esforço?

- Concordância 4: "*The main criterion for including a journal paper in our review is that the paper describes research on software development* ***effort or cost estimation****. Papers related to estimation of software size, assessment of software complexity, or identification of factors correlated with software development effort, are only included if the main purpose of the studies is to improve software development* ***effort or cost estimation****.*"

Na quarta concordância, ambos os termos aparecem coordenados modificando e fornecendo informações a respeito do termo "*estimation*". Todavia, o elemento que os coordena – ou seja, que os põe lado a lado sem um exercer função sobre o outro mas ambos exercendo função de especificar "*estimation*" – não é mais "*AND*" e sim "*OR*". O valor semântico deste último elemento deixa margem para a interpretação de custo e esforço como sendo sinônimos. Ou seja, a literatura poderia se valer de ambos em relação de sinonímia. Os dois termos aqui não são coordenados como evocando conceitos distintos, como em concordâncias anteriores, mas sim como evocadores dos mesmos conceitos. Este tipo de relação é observado em outras seis concordâncias.

Estes fragmentos são parte de uma amostra maior que evidencia a falta de consenso a respeito do tipo de relação entre estes dois vocábulos na Engenharia de Software. A linguagem coordena estes elementos dando forma linguística e observável àquilo que está no plano dos conceitos, no plano semântico. É, então, através da análise da forma que se evidencia a falta de clareza conceitual.

4 Resultados e Discussão

Como mencionado na seção 1, o estudo secundário que motivou este trabalho fez uso de definições de dicionário para definir o conceito de esforço em software e, consequentemente, identificar os fatores que o afetam [25]. No entanto, é importante ressaltar que a presença de diversas entradas no dicionário, por si só, evidencia que as palavras podem evocar múltiplos significados. É arriscado selecionar qualquer uma das definições sem contemplar o contexto em que estas palavras ocorrem, pois existe uma dependência de sentido evocado entre a palavra e o contexto em que é utilizada.

Quanto à questão de pesquisa QP1, do ponto de vista linguístico, pode-se observar que não há consistência no uso dos termos "esforço" e "custo" no contexto de software. Ora esses termos apresentam relação de sinonímia, ora de hiponímia e, por vezes, nenhuma dependência. Considerando uma perspectiva quantitativa, para que tais termos possam ser considerados equivalentes eles deveriam variar juntos, na mesma direção e na mesma intensidade, o que não é percebido na literatura da área.

Entende-se neste trabalho por "esforço" como a ação de dispender energia para realizar uma atividade física ou mental necessária para alcançar algum objetivo. Tal conceito, no entanto, é por vezes tratado como "custo" em Engenharia de Software. A área de Economia, por sua vez, apresenta o conceito de custo de forma consistente, como sendo o gasto financeiro relativo à aplicação de recursos (humanos, equipamentos, insumos) no processo de criação de um produto ou serviço [2]. Os custos ainda podem ser classificados em fixos ou variáveis, conforme a variação da quantidade de trabalho, o que é incomum observar nos trabalhos de ES.

Pode-se observar também que, respondendo à questão QP2, a linguística de *corpus* possibilita ao pesquisador apoiar-se em traços linguísticos reais e em grande quantidade para tentar realizar generalizações conceituais ou esboçar teorias em áreas carentes de uma terminologia consistente, como a Engenharia de Software.

As principais ameaças à validade deste estudo estão relacionadas ao uso de *corpora* de diferentes contextos para realizar análises semânticas e ao fato de analisar fragmentos específicos de um *corpus* para estabelecer percepções gerais. Quanto à primeira ameaça, trata-se do risco assumido quando se quer avaliar se a linguagem utilizada em uma área específica está de acordo com as acepções gerais. E quanto à segunda ameaça, é importante destacar que os fragmentos analisados apresentam fenômenos linguísticos recorrentes em diversas concordâncias do mesmo *corpus*.

5 Conclusão

Este trabalho aplicou princípios da Linguística em busca de uma definição consistente dos termos esforço e custo na área de Engenharia de Software. No entanto, os resultados indicam que os referidos termos são utilizados de forma inconsistente na literatura técnica da área, apresentando relações de dependência em alguns trabalhos e sendo totalmente distintos em outros, o que pode representar uma ameaça à validade dos modelos de estimativa de esforço e custo propostos em ES.

O conceito de esforço em ES deve levar em conta que desenvolver software é uma tarefa que envolve técnica, criatividade e raciocínio lógico e não pode ser confundida com tarefas previsíveis e repetitivas típicas da manufatura, usualmente medidas em homem-hora. Neste sentido, quando modelos são intitulados "de estimativa de custo" passam a impressão de que todos os custos do projeto estão sendo considerados. No entanto, ao representar custo como "homem-hora", tais modelos de estimativa se tornam incoerentes, pois passam a representar valor financeiro como eventual esforço humano, medido em função do tempo de alocação de pessoas em atividades criativas.

Neste cenário, entendemos que o conceito de custo tradicionalmente utilizado em Economia mostra-se adequado para ser utilizado na ES. Por sua vez, esforço deve ser observado através da energia despendida para a realização de atividades de criação nos projetos de software. A confusão conceitual entre fatores de esforço e custo representa uma ameaça à validade dos modelos de estimativa disponíveis em ES e pode contribuir para reduzir sua acurácia.

Referências Bibliográficas

1. Apshvalka, D., Wendorff, P. *Reflections on the Body of Knowledge in Software Engineering*. Vol. 1, em *Advances in Information Systems Development*, 995-1006. Springer, 2006.
2. Barbosa, C. *et al. Gerenciamento de custos em projetos*. 5. ed. Rio de Janeiro: FGV, 2014.
3. Boehm, B. *Software engineering economics*. Upper Saddle River: Prentice Hall, 1981.
4. Boehm, B. *et al. Software cost estimation with COCOMO II*. Upper Saddle River: Prentice Hall, 2000.
5. Botelho, J. M. "Causas e consequências da dialetação da língua latina. Um pouco de história externa da língua portuguesa." *Cadernos do XIV Congresso Nacional de Linguística e Filologia*. Rio de Janeiro: CiFEFiL, 2010. 231-243.
6. Bourque, P., Fairley, R. E. *SWEBOK: Guide to the Software Engineering Body of Knowledge*. Los Alamitos, CA: IEEE Computer Society, 2014.
7. Cambridge University Press. *Cambridge English Dictionary & Thesaurus*. 2015. http://dictionary.cambridge.org.
8. Celce-Murcia, M., Larsen-Freeman, D. *The grammar book: an ESL/EFL teacher's course*. Stamford: Heinle Cengage Learning, 1999.
9. Crystal, D. *Dicionário de linguística e fonética*. Rio de Janeiro: Jorge Zahar, 2008.
10. Cunha, A.G. *Dicionário etimológico da língua portuguesa*. 4. ed. Rio de Janeiro: Lexikon, 2013.
11. Dictionary.com. *Dictionary.com*. 2015. dictionary.reference.com.
12. Farr, L., Nanus, B. *Factors that Affect the Cost of Computer Programming - volume I*. Technical Report, Santa Monica: System Development Corporation, 1964.
13. Farr, L., Zagorski, H. J. *Factors that Affect the Cost of Computer Programming - volume II*. Technical Report, Santa Monica: System Development Corporation, 1964.
14. Fuzer, C., Cabral, S. R. S. *Introdução à grmática sistêmico-funcional em Língua Portuguesa*. Campinas: Mercado de Letras, 2014.
15. Grimstad, S., Jørgensen, M., Moløkken-Østvold, K. "Software effort estimation terminology: The tower of Babel." *Information and Software Technology*, 48, n. 4 (2006): 302-310.
16. Heinze, K., Claussen, N., LaBolle, V. *Management of Computer Programming for Command and Control Systems: a Survey*. Technical Report, Santa Monica: SDC, 1963.
17. Jones, C. *Estimating software costs: bringing realism to estimating*. 2nd edition. New York: McGraw-Hill, 2007.
18. Mendes, E. *Cost estimation techniques for web projects*. Hershey: IGI Publishing, 2008.
19. Mendes, E. *Practitioner's knowledge representation: a pathway to improve software effort estimation*. Heidelberg: Springer, 2014.
20. Merriam-Webster. *Merriam-Webster: Dictionary and Thesaurus*. 2015. www.merriam-webster.com.
21. Pai, M. *et al.* "Systematic Reviews and meta-analyses: An illustrated, step-by-step guide." *The National Medical Journal of India* 17, n. 2 (2004): 86-95.
22. Putnam, L. H., Myers, W. *Five core metrics: the intelligence behind successful software management*. New York: Dorset House Publishing, 2003.
23. Rainer, A. *et al.* "Teaching Empirical Methods to Undergraduate Students Working Group Results." *Empirical Software Engineering Issues*. Heidelberg: Springer, 2007. 158-162.
24. Sardinha, Tony Berber. *Linguística de Corpus*. Barueri: Manole, 2004.
25. Silva-de-Souza, T., Ribeiro, V. V., Travassos, G. H. "Estimativa de Esforço em Teste de Software: Modelos, Fatores e Incertezas." *Libro de Actas - XX Congreso Argentino de Ciencias de la Computación (CACIC)*. Buenos Aires, 2014.
26. Sketch Engine. *Sketch Engine*. 2015. https://www.sketchengine.co.uk (acesso em nov. de 2015).
27. Strauss, A., Corbin, J. *Basics of Qualitative Research: Techniques and Procedures for Developing Grounded Theory*. 2. ed. London: SAGE Publications, 1998.
28. Tagnin, S. E. O. *O jeito que a gente diz: combinações consagradas em Inglês e Português*. Barueri: Disal, 2013.
29. The Online Etymology Dictionary. *The Online Etymology Dictionary*. 2001. http://www.etymonline.com (acesso em nov. de 2015).
30. Wohlin, C. "Writing for Synthesis of Evidence in Empirical Software Engineering." *Proceedings of the 8th ACM/IEEE ESEM*. New York, NY: ACM, 2014.
31. Zelkowitz, M. V. "Data sharing enabling technologies working group results." *Empirical Software Engineering Issues*. Heidelberg: Springer, 2007. 108-110.

An Empirical Evaluation of Automated Function Points

Christian Quesada-López, Denisse Madrigal, Marcelo Jenkins

Center for ICT Research, University of Costa Rica, San Pedro, Costa Rica
{cristian.quesadalopez, denisse.madrigal, marcelo.jenkins}@ucr.ac.cr

Abstract. Background: Function point analysis (FPA) has become widely used to measure software functional size in the industry. FPA is usually performed manually, which is a time consuming and expensive process. Automated Function Point (AFP) specification states the guidelines for automating FPA counting from software source code, generally consistent with current FPA practices. **Objective:** This paper analyzes the relationships between FPA and AFP measures and measurement process. This includes total function points and basic functional components (BFC) size. The goals are to evaluate accuracy, reproducibility, perceived ease of use, usefulness, and intention to use and to understand the nature of the differences between measures. **Method:** A controlled experiment was conducted to evaluate the FPA and AFP measurement process with 14 participants (E1). We have subsequently conducted two replications of the original experiment with 12 participants each (E2 and E3). Statistical analyses were conducted to find differences between the methods regarding effectiveness and adoption properties. **Results**: Participants using FPA performed as well as participants using AFP to measure total functional size. Treatment and control groups did not differ significantly in terms of accuracy and reproducibility ($p<0.05$) throughout E1, E2 and E3. FPA presented similar accuracy to AFP for each replication. Participants between experiments performed different; data function (DF) results show an important difference between methods. **Conclusions**: The results confirm the potential for developing automation tools for function point counting that could produce more consistent measurement results; however, this process should be conducted carefully, depending on the implementation of a given requirements specification, AFP could produce different results. Although encouraging results were obtained, further research is needed to confirm performance results and to draw more conclusions on the perceived adoption properties.

Keywords. Functional size measurement, function points, function point analysis, FPA, automated function points, AFP, experimental procedure, replication.

1 Introduction

Research about functional size measurement (FSM) automation has become relevant in last years. Automating function points counting has been studied by several researchers, this involves benefits such as savings in time and costs, and better reliability and repeatability of measures [1]. Besides, an automated function point measurement could become a standard component of the software development and maintenance process and could generate reliable historical project data for benchmarking [2].

Functional size methods are used to measure the logical view of the software from the users' perspective by counting the amount of functionality to be delivered. These measures can be used for a variety of purposes, such as project estimation, quality assessment, benchmarking, and outsourcing contracts. Additionally, functional size measurements are used for budgeting, tracking progress, negotiating modifications, sizing deliveries, estimating portfolio size, managing productivity, and managing defect density. Software sizing has proved to be a task with impact in many stages of the software life cycle; since the early ones, in which estimations are done, to those in which final product is revised and people try to quantify real effort.

The Function Point Analysis (FPA) counting manual is one of the mostly used FSM methods in the software industry [3], but it is hardly automatable. Recently, the Object Management Group (OMG) released the Automated Function Point (AFP) specification [4]. AFP provides a standard for automating function point measurement according to the counting guidelines of the International Function Point User Group (IFPUG). According to OMG, this method ensures automation, consistency and verifiability. However, it is difficult to evaluate new proposals on a practical level due to the lack of rigorous empirical validation for new functional size measurement (FSM) methods and the absence of systematic evaluation could explain the low adoption rate of the new proposed FSM methods [5]. Conducting research in this direction could help understand the real benefits of applying an automated measurement process and determine how accurate, reliable, efficient and reproducible it is. Empirical evidence about the relationships between AFP and FPA measures are needed [1]. FSM automation is an attractive approach. Nevertheless, to independently demonstrate the accuracy of a FSM procedure, a standard verification protocol has to be used. Such protocol would ensure that the measurement process produces the right measurement results [6]. In general, formal, automated and validated FSM procedures are required, but measures should be audited to guarantee their quality.

This paper reports on an experiment that analyzes the relationships between FPA and AFP measures and measurement process in terms of performance properties (accuracy, reproducibility), and adoption properties (perceived ease of use, perceived usefulness and intention to use). This study was carried out at the University of Costa Rica with a group of 14 participants. Two subsequent replications were conducted with 12 participants each. The structure of this paper is organized as follows. Section 2 provides the foundations about function point methods. Section 3 presents related work on empirical studies assessing FSM methods. Section 4 describes the empirical study, and Section 5 analyses the results of the experiment. Finally, Section 6 discusses findings and outlines the conclusions.

2 Functional Size Measurement

Many functional size measurement (FSM) methods have been proposed to quantify the size of software based on functional user requirements (user's perspective). Functional size is defined as "a size of the software derived by quantifying the functional user requirements" [7].

Function point analysis (FPA) [8] was the first proposal for a FSM and it is one of the most used FSM methods in the industry. The International Function Point User Group Function Point Analysis (FPA) [9] is a refinement of the very first method for functionality measurement proposed by Allan Albrecht [8]. FSM methods analyze software requirements, transactions and data that are meaningful to the final user, which are identified and classified in a set of basic functional size components (BFC) and counted according to a defined complexity criteria. The BFC are mapped to numerical values and the sum of them constitutes the functional size. In FPA the user requirements are identified, classified and counted in a set of basic functional size components (BFC). These BFC are data functions and transactional functions. They represent data and operations that are relevant to final users. Data functions (DF) are classified into internal logic files (ILF) and external interface files (EIF). Transactional functions (TF) are classified into external inputs (EI), external outputs (EO), and external inquires (EQ). A function point analysis in FPA involves the identification of these five BFC types: EI, EO, EQ, ILF, and EIF. Each BFC contributes in the FPA counting that depends on its complexity. Details about this method can be found in FPA manual [9]. In this standard, some decisions are left to measurers. This yields variations of measures done by different measurers on the same application. This has also made particular researchers label FPA a method with partial subjective results [1]. Even though IFPUG now certifies counters, FPA is still considered a very time consuming and expensive method [2]. To take advantage of the benefits of software size measurement through function points counting, is necessary to provide a solution that generates measures faster and without human subjectivity.

The Automated Function Point (AFP) specification [4] provides a manual for automating function point measurement according to the counting guidelines of the International Function Point User Group (IFPUG). This specification may differ from IFPUG counting practice manual at points where subjective judgments have to be replaced by the rules needed for automation, and it is applicable to the functional sizing of transaction-oriented software applications. Particularly those with data persistency from source code. This method is the first manual that ensures the repeatability and consistency of the counting technique [4]. Besides, this process ensures automation and verifiability. An automated method for counting function points reduces the cost of counting and the inherent inconsistency of manual counts. AFP cannot be applied in any stage of the software life cycle other than those in which source code is already available. It would be useful when estimating maintenance effort or as a tool to generate reliable and consistent historical project data. In the long term this could impact budgeting, progress tracking, estimation of portfolio size, defect density management and other common tasks in software management [6]. Details about this specification can be found in AFP manual [4].

3 Related Work

The most important objective in evaluating a FSM method is to assess its effectiveness and efficiency in sizing the application. Jacked and Abran [10] proposed a process that includes a step to validate the functional size of a measured application and to verify that measurement rules were correctly applied. Abrahao and Pastor [11] proposed an evaluation method based on ISO FSM standard part 3. They include objective and subjective measures; performance-based and perception-based respectively. In this way, they also show how relevant it is to evaluate FSMs not only in terms of efficacy but from user's perception

Several studies have proposed measurement procedures for different FSM methods. Some of these use IFPUG FPA. The major motivation of these papers is to automate functional size measurement from a specific input artifact in different phases of the software life cycle. The effectiveness of automated counting has been rigorously tested by few studies; many of the results reported are synthetic cases. Both the total unadjusted function points (UFP) count and the UFP count of the BFCs are important. None of these studies reported the use of a specific verification protocol. Reporting the accuracy of the results in different levels of the counting process, and understanding the nature of the differences between these results, becomes significant when trying to improve and calibrate the counting procedures and the automated tools [6]. Soubra et al. [6] state that very little work has been conducted on verifying measurement results produced by FSM automation. They proposed a verification protocol designed to provide evidence of the accuracy of an automated FSM tool. The protocol states that all the details of the measurement steps must be kept for traceability purposes.

In a previous work [2], we presented a comparison between FPA and AFP methods by conducting an experiment. That experiment and the one we are presenting here, take into account performance and adoption properties. Including accuracy, reproducibility, and perceived ease of use, usefulness, and intention to use. Nevertheless this new experiment includes two subsequent replications of the original experiment, leading to the analysis of three experiments. We based this analysis on the verification protocol proposed in [12]. In this protocol a top down evaluation is required in order to identify differences in measurement results. These differences can also show counting differences in the measurement process that help evaluators identify what the causes of the measurement errors are, if there were any errors The protocol was adapted from [6], general phases proposed were used and adapted according to the counting guidelines of IFPUG FPA; recommendations from [4] were also included.

4 Description of the Empirical Study

In this section, details about the methodology for conducting the experiments are provided. A controlled experiment was conducted to evaluate the FPA and AFP measurement process with 14 participants (E1). We subsequently conducted two replications of the original experiment with 12 participants each (E2 and E3). The structure of this paper follows the reporting guidelines for experimental replications proposed by Carver

[13]. We included all details about the original study as well as the replications in this paper and we detailed results of individual studies as well as analysis across multiple studies. The authors of the original study conducted the replication process, thus current replication is internal [14]. Combined results from a family of replications are interesting because all studies are related and investigate related questions. The aggregation of replication results will be useful for software engineers to draw conclusions and consolidate findings about similar research questions [13]. The motivation for conducting two replications of the original experiment [2] is to examine whether the findings can be replicated in different settings (software application size and requirements), and different level of support (training and measurement guidelines), reporting lessons learned from the original experiment.

4.1 Objective

This paper analyzes the relationships between FPA and AFP measures and the measurement process. This includes the analysis of total function points (UFP) and basic functional components (BFC) size. The goals were to evaluate accuracy, reproducibility, perceived ease of use, usefulness, and intention to use. The analysis of the measurement results was conducted using a specific accuracy verification protocol [12] in order to identify differences reported by applying one or more FSM processes.

4.2 Hypothesis and Variable Selection

We tested the following hypotheses to address our research questions:

- H_{01}: There is no difference between the **accuracy** of FPA and AFP measures.
- H_{02}: There is no difference between the **reproducibility** of FPA and AFP measures.
- H_{03}: There is no difference between the **accuracy** of FPA and AFP BFC measures.
- H_{04}: There is no difference between the **reproducibility** of FPA and AFP BFC measures.
- H_{05}: There is no difference between the **adoption properties** of FPA and AFP process.

For each participant, metrics were collected to test the preceding hypotheses. By using the same comparable metrics, we supported comparison of findings across the original experiment and subsequent replications. The independent variable was the FSM method used by subjects to size the web applications: FPA or AFP. The dependent variables were total functional size, basic functional components size, and perceived ease of use, perceived usefulness, and the intention to use. Metrics used in this study were based on [2, 11, 15, 18, 19].

- Accuracy (quantitative, ratio): The closeness of the agreement between the result of a measurement and the true value. The functional size calculated by an expert represented the "true value". The following metrics were collected: magnitude of relative error (MRE), magnitude of error relative (MER), balanced relative error (BRE), and number of predictions within % of the actuals ($Pred_n$). AFP and FPA total function points and basic functional components size measures were collected for each subject.

- Reproducibility (quantitative, ratio): The closeness of the agreement between the results of successive measurement of the same product carried out under the same conditions. It refers to the use of the method on the same product and environment by different subjects. To evaluate the degree of variation in reproducibility, the difference in absolute value between the count produced by a subject and the average count produced by the other subjects in the sample, relative to his average count for the same FSM method was used. AFP and FPA total function points and basic functional components size measures were collected for each subject.
- Perceived ease of use (ordinal scale): the degree to which a person believes that using a particular method would be free of effort. This construct measures the perceptual judgment about the effort required to learn, use and apply the FSM method. The items were formulated as a five-point Likert scale using an opposing statements question format, as it was done in [2,11,15]. Perceived ease of use was measured using five evaluation items. Easiness to identify and count BFC were measured using two evaluation items for each component.
- Perceived usefulness (ordinal scale): the degree to which a person believes that a particular method will be effective in achieving its intended objectives. This construct measures the perceptual judgment about the effectiveness of the FSM method. The items were formulated as a five-point Likert scale using an opposing statements question format. Perceived usefulness was measured using five evaluation items.
- Intention to use (ordinal scale): the degree to which a person intends to use a particular method. This construct measures the perceptual judgment about the performance of the FSM method. The items were formulated as a five-point Likert scale using an opposing statements question format. Intention to use was measured using three evaluation items.

4.3 Selection of Subjects

The empirical studies were conducted in a graduate metrics course in three different periods (E1: II-2014, E2: I-2015, and E3: II-2015). Each group of participants applied the IFPUG FPA and OMG AFP methods to measure the same software application. Subjects reported all measurement details. The subjects were chosen based on convenience and were professionals working on Costa Rican software companies with similar backgrounds in software engineering. Researchers conducted the study as an online activity during the course. The completion of the assignment for this study was mandatory for all the students. The exercises performed as part of the study were graded and represented a significant percentage (25%) of the final grade. Participants were asked to report their experience in academic and work-related categories. The subjects were mainly from computer science (CS) background, 93% were from CS, 5% from other areas, 2% did not respond. Most of participants (80%) reported 0-2 years' experience in software project management processes. Between studies, participants have comparable experience across categories, minimizing potential biases.

4.4 Experimental Design

The experimental design is one factor with two treatments. The factor is the FSM method and the treatments are FPA and AFP methods. The treatments correspond to the two levels of the independent variable: the use of AFP versus FPA sizing an application. Among the experiments, similarities and differences in some environment settings are set up.

For each method, each experiment included two tasks, the measurement (FSM) process task and the post measurement survey. In the FSM process task, each subject used guidelines and rules of the method to measure a specific application. Data were collected on a results sheet provided. The data were later used to evaluate accuracy and reproducibility. In the post-measurement survey the subjects were asked to complete a questionnaire to evaluate perception properties. The instruments used to conduct this experiment include:

- Experimental object: includes the requirements specification document and source code for the software applications. The specification document describes the requirements for the system using the standard IEEE Recommended Practice for Software Requirements Specifications [16] based on [2, 15]. The requirements were described in terms of functionality. A detailed specification of requirements was provided. The applications source code was developed in C# .Net based on [15]. The design architecture is model-view-controller (MVC). For the FPA method the counting process was applied manually using the requirements document. For the AFP method, the measurement process was partially supported by the features provided by the solution explorer of the Visual Studio Professional 2013 IDE.
- Training materials: include a set of instructional slides that describe the FSM method and the measurement procedure, and a measurement example used in the training sessions. Besides, a measurement guideline for each FSM method was provided in order to conduct the counting, and analyze the measurement process and results. Finally, a technical manual and user manual of the application was provided as well.
- Survey instrument: includes 14 closed questions. Perceived adoption properties were computed with results of questions formulated as a five-point Likert scale.

The subjects were not aware of the aspects under study. They were informed that the researchers wanted to study the measurement process of the FPA and AFP methods but they did not have knowledge of the study´s research questions. From their perspective, they were solving a course exercise. All participants were guaranteed anonymity. All experimental instruments were prepared in advance and all experimental materials had been used in previous studies [2, 15].

The experiment was performed online over specific period of time, as part of a graduate-level metrics course, and the students were graded on the exercise. The experiment was run following these steps: (1) Participants attended four training sessions (2) Measurement task materials and the experimental objects were presented and experimental tasks were explained. (3) Participants measured the application based on the requirements document with the FPA method and/or based on the source code with the AFP specification. They reported all specific measurement results. (4) Survey about perceived properties was conducted. Participants measured the application after they had been taught several software measurement concepts.

The original experiment and replications differed in some aspects related to the setting of the study. In Table 1, differences in context factors for each experiment are reported. Specific sets of instructions, reference material, and requirement documents and source code were provided depending on the process experiment (E1, E2, E3). In Experiment (E1), a between-subject design was conducted for the reason that the time for the experiment was limited. The initial 14 subjects were randomly assigned to two groups with the same number of subjects. Each group worked with a different FSM method and no blinds were applied (group 1: FPA method [n=7], group 2: AFP method [n=7]). In Experiment 2 (E2) and Experiment 3 (E3), within-subjects designs were conducted. This design is an experiment in which the same group of subjects serves in more than one treatment. In E2, the 12 subjects first worked with the FPA method (FPA method [n=12]), and second with the AFP method (AFP method [n=12]). In E3, the 12 participants first worked with the AFP method (AFP method [n=9]), and second with the FPA method (FPA method [n=12]). In replication E3, three measurement results were removed because they were not completed.

Table 1 Experimental settings

	Original Study (E1)	**Replication-1 (E2)**	**Replication-2 (E3)**
Participants	14 graduate students	12 graduate students	12 graduate students
Design	Between-subject	Within-subjects	Within-subjects
Training session	Two training sessions per method (3 hours each one)	Two training sessions per method (1 hour each one)	One training session per method (1 hour each one)
Guidelines	IFPUG, TM, OMG	IFPUG, TM, SM, OMG	MPLR, OMG
Activity time	Take-home activity, 2 weeks per method	Take-home activity, 1 week per method	Take-home activity, 2 weeks per method
Application domain and Size	Transactional application. FPA: 101 UFP. AFP: 115 AFP.	Transactional application. FPA: 144 UFP. AFP: 115 AFP.	Transactional application. FPA: 152 UFP. AFP: 164 AFP.
Application documents	FPA: IEEE specification document, Database model, and class model.	FPA: IEEE specification document.	FPA: IEEE specification document. Labeled requirements.
Other changes	NA	Post task survey to evaluate measurement process.	Post task survey to evaluate measurement process.

IFPUG: IFPUG CPM [9].TM: Total Metrics FPA Basics IFPUG CPM 4.3. OMG: OMG AFP Specification 1.0 [4]. SM: Software Metrics FPA Training Course. MPLR: Measurement procedure for labeled requirements.

4.5 Threats to Validity

Internal validity: The effect of natural variation in human performance can influence the study outcomes. Differences among subjects were reduced selecting subjects with similar level of experience in FSM methods. The effect of experiment artifacts can influence the study outcomes. The same requirement specification and source code were used for all subjects, for each method in each experiment, and all of them for the same domain and functional characteristics. Although the small number of subjects for experiment is a threat, the fact that the subjects are industry practitioners is an advantage for the study. They were expected to deliver many data as part of their work with the course. Thus, there is a risk that the data is faked or simply not correct due to mistakes. Two of the researchers of this study applied FPA and AFP to count functional size used as a "true value". They are not CFPS certified. **External validity:** Although the applications were small, from 101 to 152 UFP, requirements and source code were a very similar example of the practices in a real case in the industry. The subjects were mainly analysts, developers and testers. They are not the population that normally uses FSM measurement methods; however, they are very familiar with software engineering practices. Although subjects' lack of experience in applying FSM methods could cause variances in counting, we expected similar performance among participants. All tasks were in the context of FPA and AFP methods in the information systems domain. Participants have been used in empirical studies to evaluate new methods with similar results to experienced professionals for the application of new methods [17]. **Construction validity:** Reliability of measures is an important consideration to draw valid conclusions about the outcomes. The dependent variables used in this study to evaluate the effectiveness of FSM methods are based on ISO 14143-3 [18], and the technology acceptance model (TAM) [19] adapted in [11].

5 Analysis and Interpretation

5.1 Descriptive Statistics

Table 2 shows descriptive statistics for the functional size in function points (FPA [UFP] and AFP), accuracy (MRE, MER, and BRE), and reproducibility. The results from each replication are presented. Participants using AFP performed as well as participants using FPA. AFP presented similar accuracy than FPA for each experiment (E1, E2 and E3). MMRE for AFP was 7.45% and for FPA was 6.36% in E1. In E2, AFP was 15.00% and FPA was 20.43%. Finally, in E3, AFP was 12.67% and FPA was 8.61%. The same similarities between methods were presented for MdMRE, and mean and median for MER and BRE. The analysis of these metrics is important because if the subject overestimates the size, then MRE is suitable to precisely evaluate the accuracy of size. While MRE ranges from 0 to infinity in case of overestimate, MER ranges from 0 to 1 despite the large difference between the actual and estimated. BRE is used to evaluate the accuracy of estimation in a balanced way. In E1 the number of predictions within 10% of the actuals $Pred_{10}$ was 57% for AFP and 72% for FPA. In E2 $Pred_{10}$ was 34% for AFP and 17% for FPA. In E3 $Pred_{10}$ was 45% for AFP and 75% for FPA. In terms of reproducibility, the same similarities were presented (FPA was 6.92% and AFP was 9.28% for E1, FPA was 23.38 % and AFP was 14.78% for E2, and FPA was 2.93% and AFP was 7.28% for E3).

Accuracy (MRE), and reproducibility were analyzed per each basic functional component (BFC), FPA and AFP methods were compared. Appendix A reports descriptive statistics for BFC of each method. Data functions (DF), transactional functions (TF), internal logic files (ILF), external interface files (EIF), external inputs (EI), external outputs (EO), and external inquires (EQ) are also reported. To analyze AFP and FPA components, we compared AFP EO against FPA EO+EQ [4]. Participants using AFP performed as well as participants using FPA to count transactional functions (TF). AFP TF presented similar accuracy that FPA TF for each experiment (E1, E2 and E3). Counting TF, MMRE for AFP was 11.4% and for FPA was 8.2% in E1. In E2, AFP was 13.3% and FPA was 13.6%. Finally, in E3, AFP was 12.5% and FPA was 5.9%. The same similarities between methods were presented for MdMRE. In terms of reproducibility, the same similarities were presented (FPA was 10.8% and AFP was 10.6% for E1, FPA was 13.01 % and AFP was 15.0% for E2, and FPA was 3.8% and AFP was 4.8% for E3). In E1 the number of predictions within 10% of the actuals $Pred_{10}$ was 42.9% for AFP and 71.4% for FPA. In E2 $Pred_{10}$ was 58.3% for AFP and 33.3% for FPA. In E3 $Pred_{10}$ was 12.5% for AFP and 75% for FPA.

Table 2 Functional size descriptive statistics

	Stu	Size		MRE (%)		MER (%)		BRE (%)		Rep (%)	
	dy	AFP	FPA	AFP	FPA	AFP	FPA	AFP	FPA	AFP	FPA
Mean	E1	108	95	7.45	6.36	8.64	7.22	8.66	7.24	9.28	6.92
	E2	107	137	15.00	20.43	17.15	24.64	17.89	25.96	14.78	23.38
	E3	143	165	12.67	8.61	15.59	7.80	15.59	8.61	7.28	2.93
Me-dian	E1	112	96	3.48	4.95	3.36	5.21	3.48	5.21	7.14	6.88
	E2	104	140	13.48	19.10	13.37	18.83	14.32	20.96	12.25	21.52
	E3	146	165	10.98	8.55	12.33	7.88	12.33	8.55	4.56	2.03
Std. Dev.	E1	10	7	7.39	6.41	9.34	7.71	9.32	7.70	4.71	4.90
	E2	19	34	9.67	11.39	12.83	18.87	13.17	18.56	12.88	11.77
	E3	14	6	8.51	4.17	12.62	3.55	12.62	4.17	7.63	2.86

AFP: OMG Automated Function Points. FPA: IFPUG Unadjusted Function Points. Rep: Reproducibility.

MRE: Magnitude of relative error. MER: Magnitude of error relative. BRE: Balanced relative error

Participants using AFP performed different as participants using FPA to count data functions (DF). AFP DF presented different accuracy that FPA DF for each experiment (E1, E2 and E3). Counting DF, MMRE for AFP was 27.2% and for FPA was 3.6% in E1. In E2, AFP was 33.6% and FPA was 64.9%. Finally, in E3, AFP was 4.2% and FPA was 22.3%. In terms of reproducibility, the same differences were presented. In E1 the number of predictions within 10% of the actuals $Pred_{10}$ was 57.1% for AFP and 85.7% for FPA. In E2 $Pred_{10}$ was 33.3% for AFP and 16.7% for FPA. In E3 $Pred_{10}$ was 75.0% for AFP and 33.3% for FPA. Between experiments, significant variation in the accuracy of external outputs and external queries were presented between E2 (AFP=16% and FPA=77%) and E3 (AFP=16% and FPA=16%). Besides, for internal logic files, there were differences between E1 (AFP=24% and FPA=3%) and E3 (AFP=4% and FPA=31%). In the same way, reproducibility also showed differences between experiments.

Figure 1 shows frequencies for the adoption properties of AFP and FPA (UFP). The adoption properties analyzed are perceived ease of use (PEOU), perceived usefulness

(PU), and intention to use (ITU). Additionally participants were asked about perceived ease to automate (AUT) the FSM method. Results from each method and across experiments shows similar results for PEOU (means between 2.51 and 2.91), ITU (means between 2.57 and 3.20), and AUT (means between 1.86 and 2.78). All measures indicate lower values than the neutral value (Neutral=3) indicating lower adoption properties for both methods. Perceived usefulness (PU) shows differences between methods in E1 and E2. In E1 participants perceived AFP (mean=3.63) more useful than FPA (mean=2.94), and in E2 participants perceived FPA (mean=3.47) more useful than AFP (mean=2.93). E3 did not show differences.

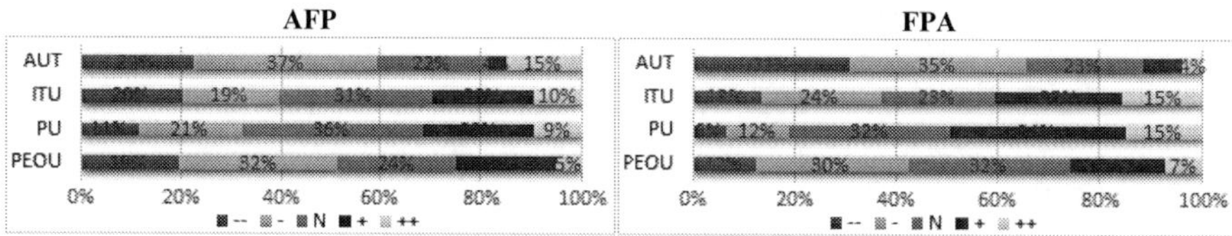

Figure 1 Adoption properties

5.2 Hypothesis Testing

Results from each experiment below are presented and discussed for the hypotheses given in Section 4.2. One way ANOVA was used to test accuracy (MRE) and reproducibility hypotheses. All assumptions were tested. The factor is the measurement method (AFP and FPA). Results with $p < 0.05$ are considered significant for our analysis.

Based on the results showed in Table 3, we found AFP and FPA measurement method accuracy and reproducibility for the combined data were not significantly different. There is not enough evidence to reject the H_{01} null hypothesis (p=0.857). There is no difference in the accuracy of FPA and AFP measurement results. Besides, there is not enough evidence to reject the H_{02} null hypothesis (p=0. 821). There is no difference in the reproducibility of FPA and AFP measurement results. In the same way, individual experiment (E1, E2, E3) results were not significantly different. Results support the claim that AFP produces the same accurate and reproducibility measurement results as FPA for total count.

Differences in the accuracy and reproducibility of FPA and AFP BFC measurement results were tested. Mann-Whitney Test was used to compare the means of each BFC. Based on the results showed in Appendix B, there is not enough evidence to reject the H_{03} null hypothesis. There is no difference in the accuracy of FPA and AFP measurement results for TF (p=0.369) and DF (p=0.206) for combined data. Besides, there is not enough evidence to reject the H_{04} null hypothesis. There is no difference in the reproducibility of FPA and AFP measurement results for TF (p=0.931) and DF (p=0.980) for combined data. Between experiments, participants using AFP performed different as participants using FPA to count data functions (DF). Significant differences were found in all experiments for data functions accuracy. Different levels of support to participants (training and measurement guidelines) impact the results. The use of a measurement procedure for labeled requirements could be one of the reasons why FPA performs better and was considered the easiest method to automate in E3. The use of more specific guidelines and documentation improves the measures. FSM procedures for AFP should be developed and tested to improve accuracy and repeatability between automated processes.

Table 3 Results of One-way ANOVA AFP versus FPA method

Metrics / Studies		Combined		E1		E2		E3	
		Means	p-value	Means	p-value	Means	p-value	Means	p-value
Accuracy	AFP	0.123	0.857	0.074	0.792	0.150	0.219	0.125	0.185
(MRE)	FPA	0.127		0.064		0.205		0.087	
Reproduc-	AFP	0.111	0.821	0.092	0.413	0.150	0.117	0.073	0.085
ibility	FPA	0.117		0.071		0.232		0.030	

Based on the results showed in Appendix C, we found that most of the AFP and FPA measurement method adoption properties were not significantly different. There is not enough evidence to reject the H_{05} null hypothesis for perceived ease of use (PEOU, p=0.155), intention to use (ITU, p=0.182), and easy to automate (AUT, p=0.331). Methods present lower adoption properties for this sample of subjects. We found the FSM method to be a significant factor in Perceived usefulness (PU) for E1 (p=0.002), and E2 (p=0.019), thus, we reject the H_{05} null hypotheses. However, between experiments one group was in favor of AFP and the other in favor of FPA, further analysis should be conducted to analyze this results. Participants were asked about the easiness to identify and count each basic functional component. Based on the tests, there was not difference between AFP and FPA methods (EI [p=0.653], EO and EQ [p=0.438], ILF [p=0.212], EIF [p=0.354]). Considering the perceived adoption properties, FPA and AFP present the same results in perceived ease of use and intention to use. However, only 25% of the participants think the models proposed in AFP could be constructed easily. None of the participants have ever used a case tool that makes these kinds of analysis.

6 Conclusions

This paper described a controlled experiment and subsequent replications to compare the FPA and AFP functional size measurement methods. The goal was to evaluate and compare the measurement process of both methods on several performance and adoption properties. Results support the claim that AFP produces equal accurate and reproducible measurement results as FPA when considering measures as a whole. This was proved by results given in combined data and analysis of results between experiments. In a more fine-grained analysis and looking at combined data results, we proved that FPA and AFP measurement of BFC components also present the same accurate and reproducible results. Nevertheless this does not happen when analyzing results between experiments. Data function (DF) particular results show an important difference between methods. The results confirmed the potential for developing automation tools for function point counting that could produce more consistent measurement results in conformance with the FPA counting guidelines. However, this process should be conducted carefully, if measurement results are compared to each other.

The main sources of inaccuracy of measurement results between FPA and AFP were: different classification of outputs (some external queries were classified as external outputs in FPA). In AFP, queries are always classified as outputs. AFP rules seem to be consistent to classify inputs, outputs and logic files. AFP classified any transaction that updates data tables as an input. AFP identified different logical files than FPA, in some cases, for example, AFP separate database tables that are joined in a FPA logical file. Differences in number of referenced files for ILF. AFP measurement results present differences depending on the implementation of a requirement specification. For example, inheritance implementation has an impact in the detection of logical files in AFP. In AFP different number of elements were identified because participants set up different naming conventions and include different set of input artifacts in the measurement analysis. AFP presents some differences with FPA and depending on the implementation of a given requirements specification AFP could produce different results. With the verification protocol, IFPUG FPA and OMG AFP measurement processes were evaluated and compared from different software artifacts. Participants were able to identify differences and the source of inaccuracy in a systematic way, and they traced the implementations of a given functional requirements.

Automation of functional size procedures provides opportunities for user requirements traceability and software visualization from the user's perspective. We agreed that keeping specifications aligned with the implementation is a good practice that should always be applied, independently from the need to get functional measures [1]. Furthermore, a suitable representation of the specifications can help reduce the cost of keeping them aligned with implementation and more easily to be counted. Although encouraging results were obtained, further research is needed to confirm performance results and to draw more conclusions on perceived adoption properties. Empirical evidence about the relationships of FPA and AFP and the accuracy of automated counting tools is still needed. More analysis about the relationships between the measures obtained by the two methods for the same software application is needed. Case studies using more complex applications or real software applications from the industry should be conducted.

Acknowledgments. This research was supported by V.I. at University of Costa Rica No. 834-B5-A18, and Ministry of Science, Technology and Telecommunications (MICITT).

References

1. Lavazza, L. (2015, May). Automated function points: critical evaluation and discussion. In *Proceedings of the Sixth International Workshop on Emerging Trends in Software Metrics*, 35-43. IEEE Press.

2. Quesada-López, C., Jenkins, M. (2015, April). An evaluation of functional size measurement methods. In *Proceedings of the XVIII Ibero-American Conference on Software Engineering*, 151-165.
3. Garmus, D., & Herron, D. (2001). Function point analysis: measurement practices for successful software projects. Addison-Wesley Longman Publishing Co., Inc.
4. Object Management Group, Automated Function Points (AFP) Version 1.0, January 2014, OMG Document Number: formal/2014-01-03, http://www.omg.org/spec/AFP.
5. Abrahao, S., Poels, G., & Pastor, O. (2004, August). Assessing the reproducibility and accuracy of functional size measurement methods through experimentation. In *Empirical Software Engineering, 2004. ISESE'04*, 189-198. IEEE.
6. Soubra, H., Abran, A., & Ramdane-Cherif, A. (2014, October). Verifying the Accuracy of Automation Tools for the Measurement of Software with COSMIC-ISO 19761 Including an AUTOSAR-Based Example and a Case Study. In *Software Measurement and the International Conference on Software Process and Product Measurement (IWSM-MENSURA), 2014 Joint Conference of the International Workshop on,* 23-31. IEEE.
7. ISO. (2007). ISO/IEC 14143-1- Information Technology - Software measurement - Functional Size Measurement. Part 1: Definition of Concepts.
8. Albrecht, A. J. (1979, October). Measuring application development productivity. In Proceedings of the Joint IBM Application Development Symposium, 10, 83-92.
9. ISO. (2009). ISO/IEC 20926, Software and systems engineering - Software measurement – IFPUG functional size measurement method.
10. Jacquet, J. P., & Abran, A. (1997, June). From software metrics to software measurement methods: a process model. In *Software Engineering Standards Symposium and Forum, 1997. Emerging International Standards. ISESS 97, Third IEEE International,* 128-135. IEEE.
11. Abrahao, S., Poels, G., & Pastor, O. (2004, September). Evaluating a functional size measurement method for Web applications: an empirical analysis. In *Software Metrics, 2004. Proceedings. 10th International Symposium,* 358-369. IEEE.
12. Quesada-López, C., & Jenkins, M. (2015). Applying a Verification Protocol to Evaluate the Accuracy of Functional Size Measurement Procedures: An Empirical Approach. In *Product-Focused Software Process Improvement*, 243-250. Springer International Publishing.
13. Carver, J. C. (2010, May). Towards reporting guidelines for experimental replications: A proposal. In *International Workshop on Replication in Empirical Software Engineering Research*, Cape Town, South Africa: IEEE.
14. Shull, F. J., Carver, J. C., Vegas, S., & Juristo, N. (2008). The role of replications in empirical software engineering. *Empirical Software Engineering*, 13(2), 211-218.
15. Abrahao, S. M., & Director-Lopez, O. P. (2004). On the functional size measurement of object-oriented conceptual schemas: design and evaluation issues (Doctoral dissertation). Universidad Politécnica de Valencia (Spain).
16. IEEE Computer Society. Software Engineering Standards Committee, & IEEE-SA Standards Board. (1998). IEEE Recommended Practice for Software Requirements Specifications. Institute of Electrical and Electronics Engineers.
17. Salman, I., Misirli, A. T., & Juristo, N. (2015, May). Are students representatives of professionals in software engineering experiments?. *InProceedings of the 37th International Conference on Software Engineering*. 1, 666-676. IEEE Press.
18. ISO. (2003). ISO/IEC TR 14143-3:2003 Information technology. Software measurement - Functional size measurement - Part 3: Verification of functional size measurement methods.
19. Davis, F. D. (1989). Perceived usefulness, perceived ease of use, and user acceptance of information technology. MIS quarterly, 319-340.

Appendix A. Basic functional components descriptive statistics

	Study	MRE (%)				Rep (%)				MRE (%)							Rep (%)						
		TF		DF		TF		DF		EI		EO, EQ			ILF		EI		EO, EQ			ILF	
		AFP	FPA	AFP	FPA	AFP	FPA	AFP	FPA	AFP	FPA	AFP	FPA	FPA	AFP	FPA	AFP	FPA	AFP	FPA	FPA	AFP	FPA
Mean	E1	11.4	8.20	27.2	3.60	10.6	10.8	35.1	7.30	12.9	5.40	28.6	N A	18.3	24.0	3.60	12.7	7.90	26.6	N A	23.5	30.4	7.30
	E2	13.3	13.6	33.6	64.9	15.0	13.1	41.5	58.6	21.6	19.6	24.8	84.6	69.6	34.9	47.2	20.7	11.9	29.9	9.70	87.9	43.7	59.3
	E3	12.5	5.90	4.20	22.3	4.80	3.80	7.40	14.8	7.30	10.2	26.7	20.8	11.5	4.20	31.3	9.00	6.30	21.8	24.0	12.6	7.40	31.7
Median	E1	11.9	4.10	9.70	0.00	7.20	11.4	20.0	4.30	9.50	2.10	33.3	N A	12.0	9.70	0.00	14.6	6.10	7.70	N A	21.0	17.2	4.30
	E2	7.70	17.2	24.2	75.0	10.5	11.9	16.9	59.9	9.50	18.3	14.3	100	75.0	32.3	75.0	15.2	10.5	22.9	87.2	87.7	15.8	67.4
	E3	12.7	5.20	0.00	21.4	2.70	4.00	5.00	18.7	4.00	8.90	21.7	5.00	6.30	0.00	25.0	4.50	6.10	14.6	5.50	8.30	5.00	19.6
Std. Dev.	E1	11.5	9.20	35.3	9.40	9.70	6.40	37.0	7.80	11.0	8.80	23.8	N A	26.0	27.3	9.40	9.70	8.10	25.4	N A	25.8	28.9	7.80
	E2	12.3	8.80	32.8	39.6	13.2	9.00	37.5	36.5	23.3	11.0	28.1	69.4	41.8	32.4	43.2	18.4	8.10	28.6	49.7	62.0	37.0	39.7
	E3	5.80	4.30	7.70	19.2	5.70	2.40	4.50	10.5	9.90	7.00	20.2	36.3	13.4	7.70	28.5	10.8	4.70	19.8	43.8	14.6	4.50	26.9
Min	E1	0.00	0.00	0.00	0.00	0.70	0.70	10.1	4.30	0.00	0.00	0.00	N A	0.00	0.00	0.00	1.50	1.40	3.90	N A	1.60	7.00	4.30
	E2	0.00	0.90	9.70	0.00	0.20	1.10	4.80	9.70	2.40	0.00	4.80	0.00	7.70	9.70	0.00	4.00	2.10	5.00	10.9	2.80	15.4	10.2
	E3	0.00	0.00	0.00	0.00	0.30	0.10	5.00	2.90	0.00	0.00	0.00	0.00	0.00	0.00	0.00	1.40	0.60	2.60	0.90	1.20	5.00	6.40
Max	E1	33.3	21.9	103	25.0	27.7	19.0	116	25.0	33.3	25.0	71.4	N A	76.0	80.6	25.0	28.2	25.5	63.6	N A	74.8	92.0	25.0
	E2	32.1	27.6	100	100	33.9	36.3	100	100	69.0	39.4	100	194	130	100	100	55.6	27.2	100	145	215	100	100
	E3	18.9	12.9	16.7	50.0	16.7	7.40	14.6	26.6	29.0	23.3	66.7	120	45.8	16.7	75.0	32.7	14.0	57.8	149	45.0	14.6	78.0
P_{25}	E1	0.00	1.40	9.70	0.00	0.70	6.10	17.6	4.30	7.10	0.00	2.40	N A	4.00	9.70	0.00	1.50	3.60	7.70	N A	3.90	17.2	4.30
	E2	1.50	4.50	9.70	27.7	2.80	7.80	13.7	15.5	3.60	12.0	8.30	21.1	39.4	9.70	6.30	6.60	6.10	7.60	14.0	33.9	15.5	11.3
	E3	11.1	1.60	0.00	3.60	0.40	1.80	5.00	3.50	0.00	3.60	15.4	0.00	4.20	0.00	0.00	1.40	1.70	7.90	0.90	4.20	5.00	6.40
P_{75}	E1	16.7	20.5	32.3	0.00	15.3	17.3	41.9	4.30	21.4	4.20	33.3	N A	16.0	32.3	0.00	18.6	8.70	50.0	N A	32.8	40.0	4.30
	E2	26.5	19.8	35.5	100	29.9	15.7	79.8	96.7	34.5	27.8	23.8	152	100	35.5	100	39.1	16.2	46.4	110	100	83.3	98.9
	E3	17.2	10.1	12.5	43.8	7.90	5.70	12.2	25.4	11.7	16.1	38.8	40.0	12.5	12.5	50.0	14.3	11.0	39.2	41.3	10.9	12.2	46.7

AFP: OMG Automated Function Points. FPA: IFPUG Unadjusted Function Points. Rep: Reproducibility.

MRE: Magnitude of relative error. MER: Magnitude of error relative. BRE: Balanced relative error

$$MRE_i = \frac{|ActualEffort_i - EstimatedEffort_i|}{ActualEffort_i}$$

$$MER_i = \frac{|ActualEffort_i - EstimatedEffort_i|}{EstimatedEffort_i}$$

$$BRE_i = \frac{|ActualEffort_i - EstimatedEffort_i|}{\min(ActualEffort_i, EstimatedEffort_i)}$$

$$Pred(n) = \frac{100}{N}\sum_{i=1}^{N}\begin{cases} 1 \ if\ MRE_i \le \frac{n}{100} \\ 0 \quad otherwise \end{cases}$$

$$Rep_i = \frac{|AverageOthers - Subject_i|}{AverageOthers}$$

Appendix B. Results of Mann-Whitney Test AFP versus FPA BFC

Accuracy (MRE)		TF		DF		EI		EO+EQ		ILF	
		Means	p-value	Means	p-value	Means	p-value	Means	p-value	Means	p-value
Combined	**AFP**	0.125	0.369	0.171	0.206	0.151	0.766	0.225	0.748	0.230	0.952
	FPA	0.094		0.346		0.126		0.430		0.294	
E1	**AFP**	0.114	0.748	0.272	**0.016**	0.130	0.081	0.282	0.368	0.241	**0.016**
	FPA	0.082		0.035		0.052		0.182		0.035	
E2	**AFP**	0.131	0.794	0.203	**0.017**	0.215	0.469	0.165	**0.002**	0.349	0.830
	FPA	0.136		0.649		0.195		0.770		0.472	
E3	**AFP**	0.125	**0.011**	0.402	**0.006**	0.072	0.213	0.267	**0.050**	0.042	**0.020**
	FPA	0.059		0.224		0.101		0.161		0.312	
Reproducibility		**TF**		**DF**		**EI**		**EO+EQ**		**ILF**	
		Means	p-value	Means	p-value	Means	p-value	Means	p-value	Means	p-value
Combined	**AFP**	0.108	0.931	0.242	0.980	0.151	0.189	0.230	0.949	0.319	0.846
	FPA	0.088		0.300		0.089		0.392		0.216	
E1	**AFP**	0.107	0.748	0.351	**0.009**	0.127	0.397	0.268	0.351	0.302	**0.009**
	FPA	0.105		0.070		0.080		0.207		0.070	
E2	**AFP**	0.150	0.773	0.301	0.062	0.207	0.340	0.745	**0.006**	0.436	0.886
	FPA	0.129		0.587		0.120		0.216		0.280	
E3	**AFP**	0.047	0.907	0.075	0.527	0.064	0.816	0.218	0.179	0.078	**0.002**
	FPA	0.037		0.148		0.088		0.182		0.317	

Appendix C. Results of One-way ANOVA for adoption properties between methods

Metrics / Studies		Combined		E1		E2		E3	
		Means	p-value	Means	p-value	Means	p-value	Means	p-value
PEOU	AFP	2.59	0.155	2.51	0.126	2.52	0.386	2.76	0.915
	FPA	2.79		2.91		2.71		2.78	
PU	AFP	2.97	**0.002**	3.63	**0.002**	2.93	**0.019**	3.04	0.675
	FPA	3.39		2.94		3.47		3.14	
ITU	AFP	2.80	0.182	2.57	0.402	2.72	0.359	3.07	0.673
	FPA	3.06		2.90		3.03		3.20	
AUT	AFP	2.19	0.331	1.86	1.000	2.73	0.18	2.78	0.793
	FPA	2.52		1.86		2.00		2.68	

PEOU: perceived ease of use. ITU: intention to use. PU: perceived usefulness. AUT: easy to automate.

A Systematic Mapping of Data Generation for Integration Software Testing

Maria A. S. Brito, Marcos P. Santos,
Simone R. S. Souza, and Paulo S. L. Souza

University of São Paulo,
400, Trabalhador São-Carlense Avenue, 13.560-970, São Carlos, Brazil
{masbrit,marcos,srocio,pssouza}@icmc.usp.br

Abstract. Different techniques have been proposed to test software artifacts and source code. Integration testing, however, has not been sufficiently applied to all types of systems that require high-quality evaluation. This paper summarizes approaches proposed to test data generation for integration testing identifying gaps and opportunities for further research. We conducted a systematic mapping study in order to discover how data generation for integration testing is supported by existing approaches. A subjective evaluation of the studies was also carried out to evaluate them in terms of quality. As a result of the systematic mapping we found 38 primary studies, published between 1996 and 2015. Most of them focus on specification-based coverage, and to a lesser extent, code coverage. The following trends were identified: increased use of UML models and concern regarding automated test data generation. Gaps were found in the use of gray-box approaches, mutation testing, data generation tools, and experimental validation studies. The study's findings enable researchers to attain an overview of existing approaches and identify points that require further attention. Future research work should look at cost and effectiveness of such approaches.

1 Introduction

Testing is used to insure quality by revealing defects in the software and models [1]. It concerns executing a program or model with data input and comparing actual and anticipated outputs based on software specification. After the unit test even if each unit has an expected output, when integrated into a system, the interactions between units can result to incorrect outputs [2]. Integration testing exercises the communication among units of the software to evaluate the communication among them.

The project of test cases is essential in the testing activity and significantly impact the quality of the test. Integration test cases are more complex, more expensive to develop, and harder to generate and maintain than unit test cases [3].

Systematic mappings and reviews have been conducted in unit testing to identify approaches to test data generation. Unit level test data generation do not consider the global variables declared outside of a function, communication among components and interfaces [4, 5]. In integration level the sequences of calls for a set of objects exercise them in different states, and can reveal errors that occur only when an object of a class is in specific state [6]. An effective approach to the generation of test data is essential to integration testing. Accordingly, the present study has conducted a systematic mapping, presented in this paper intending to close these gap.

The overall goal of the study is present a systematic mapping study conducted to obtain primary studies about test data generation for integration testing. We want to answer the questions: 1) What approaches have been defined for data generation for integration testing?; and 2) How can these approaches be classified?

The remainder of the paper is organized as follows: Section 2 summarizing concepts and definitions used in the paper. Section 3 describes the systematic mapping process undertaken, including planning, conduction and findings. Section 4 addresses the quality analysis; Section 5, threats to validity and Section 6 summarizes the study and provides recomendations for further research.

2 Background

An adequacy criterion establishes requirements to be satisfied by a test set for a specific program and are based on structural (or white-box), functional (or black-box), and defect-based testing techniques. They use different representations of the specification or program to generate test data. One of the critical tasks in any software test activity is the generation of test data.

The specification-based adequacy criterion uses the specification to generate test data. Among the techniques used to generate test data some are applied directly to the requirements, as informal techniques, that not use any rigorous of formal methods, or formal techniques such as random test generation and cause-effect graphing [7]. Several other notations using Unified Modeling Language (UML) [1] such as sequence, activity diagrams, and others can be used.

The more formal is the specification, the higher are the chances of automating the test-generation process. For example, specifications using Finite State Machines (FSMs), timed automata, and Petri nets can be input to a data test generator. However, a significant manual effort is required when generating test cases from use cases or textual specifications [7].

There also exist technniques to generate tests directly from the code. Code coverage adequacy criteria include control and data flow testing. Control flow testing uses a program control structure, represented by its control flow graph to generate test cases. Data-flow testing observes the definitions and uses of variables in control flows.

[1] http://www.uml.org/

3 Systematic Mapping

Systematic literature studies can address reviews and maps. Systematic reviews evaluate the literature to address research questions and thereby establish evidences. Compared to literature reviews, it has a more rigorous methodology than analysis studies within a given research field. Systematic mapping studies differ from systematic review primarily by obtaining evidence in a domain to be plotted at a high level of granularity. This secondary study reviews primary studies related to a research topic, identifies areas for more primary studies to be conducted [8]. The present study categorizes the mapping stages in three main phases, i.e., planning, conducting, and results.

3.1 Planning

The study follows the approach proposed by Kitchenham and Charters [8], and its research questions were based on PICOC criteria, with also govern the criteria for studies inclusion. Its Population are primary studies about integration testing; its Intervention are data generation approaches for integration testing; Comparison was not applied to this study; its Outcome is a classification of test data generation approaches for integration testing and; its Context focuses on test data generation defined to integration testing.

The study identifies and summarizes findings related to data generation for integration testing and proposing answers to the following questions:

1. RQ_1: What approaches have been defined for data generation for integration testing?
2. RQ_2: How can these approaches be classified?

The search string used in the automatic search was constructed based on two terms extracted from the research questions (RQ_1 and RQ_2) and comprises the keywords *test data generation* and *integration test*. Synonymous or terms of similar meaning combined by boolean operators *AND* and *OR* composed the final string:

(("test data generation" OR "test data generator" OR "data generation" OR "test case generation" OR "test case generator" OR "case generation" OR "generate test data" OR "generate test case") AND ("integration test" OR "integration testing" OR "component test" OR "component testing" OR "interface test" OR "interface testing"))

The string was further defined according to the particular syntax of each search engine. The databases that index the principal conferences and journals in software engineering were selected to obtain the primary studies [9]. Table 1 shows seven search engines and indexing systems selected. Automatic searches were performed on the title, abstract, and keywords fields.

Table 1. Automatic Sources.

ACM Digital Library - (<http://portal.acm.org>)
Compendex - (<http://engineeringvillage2.org>)
IEEEXplore Digiral Library - (<http://ieeexplore.ieee.org>)
ScienceDirect - (<http://sciencedirect.com>)
Scopus - (<http://scopus.com>)
Web of Science - (<http://isiknowledge.com>)
SpringerLink - (<http://link.springer.com/>)

After the search, the studies were selected based on preliminary and final selections. A manual search based on references from the selected studies was conducted after the final selection. The inclusion criterion (IC_1) was that the study describes at least one approach to test data generation for integration testing. Studies that met at least one of the following criteria were excluded: EC_1, unavailable in electronic format; EC_2, results analogous to other studies'; EC_3, not published in English; EC_4, not a published paper, e.g., posters, summaries, tutorials, theses, and dissertations; EC_5, fails to address integration testing; EC_6, an empirical evalutation of an data generation approach to integration testing.

After all selections had been made, a quality evaluation of the studies was conducted for the inclusion of other relevant data. Punctuation was not used as an exclusion criterion, but only to estimate the quality of included studies. The following questionnaire was used to evaluate study quality, with one point awarded for each affirmative response.

1. Does the study provide a structured abstract [10]?
2. Has the approach been clearly exposed?
3. Does the study provide references to download the artifacts used in the validation?

3.2 Conduction

The conduction phase began on September 12, 2015, with the search in electronic databases, obtained 201 studies. Two researches were used in the selection process for obtaining independent assessments. In the first phase, abstracts, titles, and keywords were analysed based on inclusion and exclusion criteria. Keywords were indentified to construct a classification schema (Table 2) to summarize points of interest. The classification schema was constructed based on studies selected to improve the summarization of results. After the first phase were selected 89 primary studies. In the second phase, following the analyses of the full text of each study, 27 were selected for mapping. The references of the selected studies were then analysed and eleven additional studies were included. These studies were available in the digital libraries used in this study, but for obtain them was required the inclusion of the terms: black-box, component interaction testing, testing object-oriented components, subsystem level, communication diagram, test sequence, test set generation, generate test case, and test generation in the search string. Some of these terms could improve the search and results, but others would leave it complex and longest. This result shows lack of standardization in the area when many terms are used to reference the same information.

They, ($S_2, S_3, S_4, S_5, S_7, S_8, S_9, S_{10}, S_{12}, S_{17}$, and S_{18}) were not returned in the first search because the terms of the search string were not present its title, abstract or keywords, however, it treats test data generation for integration testing and is related to the research questions.

Table 2. Classification Scheme Constructed and Used in our Study.

RQ	Attribute	Answer	Multiple selection
1	Title		
	Authors		
	Affiliation		
	Year		
	Publication	conference proceeding, journal, symposium, colloquium, workshop	
2	Type	solution proposal, validation research, evaluation research, experience papers, philosophical papers, opinion papers, other	x
	Integration	collaborative, bottom-up, top-down	
	Test technique	white-box, gray-box, black-box	
	Adequacy criterion	specification-, code-, or defect-based	
	Testing tool	yes, no	
	Specification Type	UML, formal, other, none	x
	Validation	yes, no	
	Type	controlled experiment, experiment, case study, example, none	
	Variable	defect detection, time, test data, other	x
	artifact	program, model	
	Number	0 - infinite	
	Language	C, C++, Java, other	
	Size	1 - infinite	

JabRef was used to support the selection processes of the studies and Microsoft Excel was adopted for the data extraction. The quality of the studies was assessed after the selection process.

3.3 Results

This section addresses the answers to the two research questions. It details evidences for RQ_1 and categorization for RQ_2 compiled in structured format.

***RQ*$_1$: What approaches have been defined for data generation for integration testing?** The Table 3 provides information about the 38 primary studies. According to Wieringa et al. [11], all studies are proposals of solution. Most studies had been published in journals (47.4%) and conferences (36.8%). Interactions among different research groups were observed in only 32.1% of the cases ($S_2, S_3, S_4, S_6, S_7, S_{12}, S_{16}, S_{18}, S_{19}, S_{24}, S_{25}, S_{29}, S_{34}, S_{37}$).

Table 3. Primary Studies Overview.

Id	T	Year	Author(s)	Id	T	Year	Author(s)
S_1[25]	C	1996	Watanabe, A. and Sakamura, K.	S_{20}[26]	C	2007	Li, Z. and Maibaum, T.
S_2[23]	C	1997	Bertolino, A. et al.	S_{21}[27]	W	2007	Benz, S.
S_3[21]	S	1999	Buy, U. et al.	S_{22}[28]	J	2007	Gupta, M. et al.
S_4[22]	S	2000	Hartmann, J. et al.	S_{23}[29]	J	2008	Rocha, C.R. and Martins, E.
S_5[30]	C	2000	Abdurazik, A. and Offutt, J.	S_{24}[15]	C	2008	Zhou, H. et al.
S_6[12]	C	2001	Tsai, W.T. et al.	S_{25}[18]	J	2008	Robinson-Mallett, C. et al.
S_7[20]	J	2001	Chen, H.Y. et al.	S_{26}[31]	C	2009	Saglietti, F. et al.
S_8[32]	C	2001	Linzhang, W. et al.	S_{27}[33]	S	2009	Fan, Xin et al.
S_9[34]	C	2001	Chevalley, P. and Thevenod-Fosse, P.	S_{28}[35]	J	2009	Brito, P.H. S. et al.
S_{10}[36]	C	2001	Liu, W. and Dasiewicz, P.	S_{29}[14]	J	2010	Swain, S.K. et al.
S_{11}[37]	C	2002	Di Lucca, G.A. et al.	S_{30}[38]	J	2010	Ogata, S. and Matsuura, S.
S_{12}[6]	C	2002	Martena, V. et al.	S_{31}[39]	W	2010	Saglietti, F. and Pinte, F.
S_{13}[40]	J	2004	Lugato, D. et al.	S_{32}[41]	C	2011	Kang, J.S. and Park, H-S.
S_{14}[42]	Co	2005	Chen, Y. et al.	S_{33}[43]	J	2011	Houhamdi, Z. and Athamena, B.
S_{15}[44]	J	2005	Briand, L.C. et al.	S_{34}[13]	J	2012	Mattiello-Francisco, F. et al.
S_{16}[16]	J	2006	Jun-yi, L. et al.	S_{35}[4]	J	2013	Hossain, M.I. and Lee, W.J.
S_{17}[45]	J	2006	Samuel, P. et al.	S_{36}[5]	C	2013	Khan, S.A. and Nadeem, A.
S_{18}[24]	J	2006	Robinson-Mallett, C. et al.	S_{37}[17]	J	2014	Swain, R.K. et al.
S_{19}[19]	J	2006	Bogdanov, K. et al.	S_{38}[46]	J	2015	Damasceno, A.C. et al.

Note: conference proceedings (C), journals (J), colloquiums (Co), workshops (W), and symposiums (S).

***RQ*$_2$: How can these approaches be classified?** A bubble plot of the systematic mapping is shown in Figure 1. Each bubble contains the number of studies shown in the pair of categories corresponding to its coordinates. The studies are organized by test technique and grouped by publication year and coverage type.

The studies were published after 1996 indicating a recent research area with possibility of gaps. Black-box approaches were the most frequently used. Different notations can be used to model the system behavior for data test generation [47]. According to the bubble plot, data generation approaches using specification-based coverage are most common, and state-based diagrams and formal specifications, are the most frequently used. In this graph some studies used several diagrams.

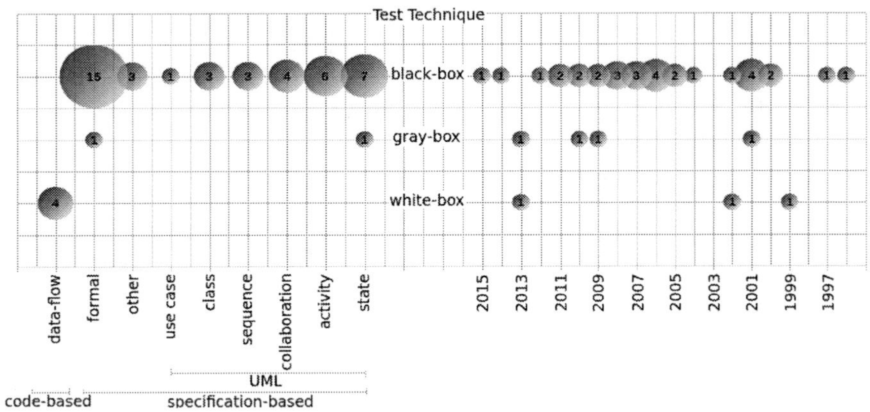

Fig. 1. Primary Study Bubble Plot.

Note: Other includes: fluxogram (S_{33}) and approaches that do not use models (S_3 and S_{32}).

UML is the most commonly model used to specification, comprises 47.4% ($S_4, S_5, S_8, S_9, S_{10}, S_{11}, S_{13}, S_{15}, S_{17}, S_{20}, S_{23}, S_{24}, S_{26}, S_{27}, S_{29}, S_{30}, S_{31}, S_{37}$). Studies using several included state (44.4%), activity (33.3%), collaboration (22.2%), class (16.7%), sequence (16.7%), and use case diagram (5.5%). Studies that used formal models were 42.1%, viz., $S_{13}, S_{18}, S_{19}, S_{22}, S_{25}, S_{34}, S_{38}$ (state transition-based notations), S_7 and S_{20} (contract), S_4, and S_{28} (CSP), S_{28} (B method), S_{21} (CTT formalism), S_2 (CHAM), S_{16} (Petri network), S_6 (Thin threads), and S_1 (Z notation). One study used UML model and state transition categories.

The types of code-based coverage are based on data-flow ($S_{12}, S_{14}, S_{35}, S_{36}$). Defect-based coverage was not the main objective of any primary studies and was used in S_{31} and S_9 to evaluate the test data generated from mutations in programs and state machines not criterion to generate the test data.

Test data can be generated manually or automatically. Tools to automatically generate test data were described in 50% of the primary studies ($S_2, S_4, S_6, S_7, S_8, S_9, S_{12}, S_{13}, S_{15}, S_{17}, S_{20}, S_{21}, S_{26}, S_{29}, S_{30}, S_{31}, S_{34}, S_{36}, S_{38}$). 21% of the studies

($S_3, S_5, S_{10}, S_{16}, S_{18}, S_{24}, S_{27}$ and S_{35}) automated only one part of the execution of the approach. However, any study have a tool that can be downloaded.

In the validation of the proposed approaches, the following variables were evaluated: communication, timing deviations, number of defects revealed, and other metrics. Experiments for the validation of the test data generation approaches were reported in 5.3% of the studies (S_1, S_{29}). These experiments, however, cannot be deemed "controlled experiments" since sufficient data regarding statistical analysis, variables, and comparisons was not provided. Furthermore, 47.4% of the studies ($S_2, S_3, S_4, S_5, S_8, S_{10}, S_{11}, S_{13}, S_{16}, S_{17}, S_{18}, S_{20}, S_{25}, S_{26}, S_{27}, S_{30}, S_{32}, S_{33}$) reported examples, 42.1% ($S_7, S_9, S_{12}, S_{14}, S_{15}, S_{19}, S_{21}, S_{22}, S_{23}, S_{24}, S_{28}, S_{31}, S_{34}, S_{35}, S_{37}, S_{38}$) case studies; 5.3% ($S_6, S_{36}$) no validation.

Regarding the number of artifacts used during the validation, 10.5% of the studies ($S_1, S_{26}, S_{29}, S_{35}$) used three; 10.7% ($S_{19}, S_{24}, S_{38}$), two; and the rest (67.8%) used 1. Artifacts in source code level were in Java ($S_9, S_{20}, S_{29}, S_{31}$), the C++ ($S_{12}$ and S_{14}) and the ASP (S_{11}) languages. S_{35} did not describe the language used. Only three studies described the size of the programs used in the lines of code (LOC). The largest program used in S_9 had 6500 LOC, S_{12} used a program with 496, and S_{35} had 82 LOC.

4 Analysis of Quality

Structured abstracts can facilitate the understandig of papers and they are composed of a standard set of headings to support the author in providing the key elements of the study [10]. A patterned abstract contributes to the conduction of secondary studies, as systematic mapping, because in the searchs and preliminar phase, the inclusion or exclusion of a study is based on its abstract. During the quality evaluation, the abstracts were analysed based on the work of Budgen et al. [10]. The set of headings of our quality evaluation was composed of five keywords (background, aim, method, results, conclusions). A summary with results is illustrated in Figure 2.

No study analysed provided structured abstract and all were scored with 0 point in this criterion. 47.4% of the studies adopted three keywords, background, aim and method ($S_2, S_4, S_6, S_7, S_8, S_9, S_{11}, S_{12}, S_{14}, S_{15}, S_{20}, S_{21}, S_{23}, S_{26}, S_{28}, S_{34}, S_{35}, S_{38}$), 21% included four keywords, background, aim, method and conclusions ($S_5, S_{10}, S_{22}, S_{24}, S_{27}, S_{33}, S_{36}, S_{37}$), 10.5% described other three keywords, aim, method and conclusions ($S_1, S_{16}, S_{18}, S_{29}$), 7.9% included two keywords, aim and method (S_{17}, S_{31}, S_{32}). 7.9% used other two keywords, background and aim (S_{13}, S_{19}, S_{30}), 2.6% or one study used four keywords, aim, method, results and conclusions (S_{25}), and 2.6% or one study, S_3, do not present abstract. This result shows the difficulty during the conduction of secondary studies, when the initial phase is based on electronic seach. When there is no standardization in writing some keywords can be omitted and this way the searches does not return these studies.

For the second quality criterion, all studies shown clear exposition of the test data generation approach. This criterion was analysed based on the expertise of the two reviewers. The studies were scored with 1 point in this criterion. The third criterion evaluated whether the studies provided references for the access to the artifacts used in the validation. This criterion was introduced because reproducibility is a relevant criterion facilitating the replication of studies and helping with other experimental evaluations, however only one study S_{38} provided references for the free access to the artifacts used in the experiments [46]. Studies that used real applications in case studies were 21.5% ($S_{34}, S_{23}, S_{31}, S_{11}, S_{12}, S_{38}, S_{25}, S_{19}$).

Based on the three quality criteria 37 studies obtained 1 point and one study obtained 2 points for a maximum of 3 points.

5 Threats to Validity

Construct validity defines how well the measures used in a study validate its results, i.e., do the operational definitions of the variables properly reflect the theoretical concepts? In the case of this study, it concerns adequacy of the keywords used in constructing the search string to select studies to address the research questions. To mitigate threats in this regard, the string was validated by a broad range of studies and executed in six leading databases. An additional search was conducted from the references in selected studies to enhance comprehensiveness.

As the selection of studies and extraction of data involve interpretation and judgment on the part of the reviewer, these procedures could be regarded as posing a threat of subjective bias. To minimize that risk, the selection and extraction processes were performed independently by two researchers. In some moments there was divergence of opinion between the researchers that were solved with meetings and discussions about the inclusion or exclusion of studies. A research protocol based on guidelines proposed by Kitchenham and Charters [8] was developed and followed.

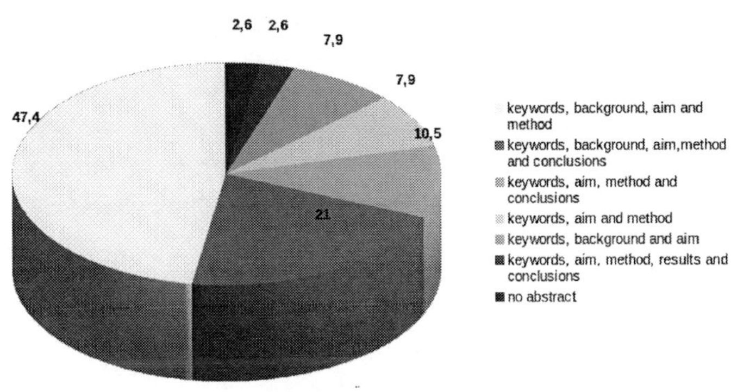

Fig. 2. Set of Headings of the Quality Evaluation.

Internal validity concerns factors that can affect inferences regarding causal relationships. It does not pertain to most descriptive studies such as this mapping study, which did not investigate cause and effect. Accordingly, any threat in this regard is minimal, if any. External validity lies at the heart of research design. Its principal criterion relates to generalization, i.e., to what populations, settings, and other variables can a study's results be generalized? We believe our review protocol enabled us to attain a representative study sample.

6 Discussion and Concluding Remarks

This study provides an initial systematic mapping of data generation for integration testing. The study finds test data generation is an increasingly active area of research as indicated by an expanding number of published studies. The most commonly used testing technique is black-box, resulting in specification-based coverage as the most used. This behavior was expected because at integration level, the objective is to verify the interfaces among components, the source code is often not available in reusable components or only very abstract specifications are available to derive test data facilitating the application of black-box testing. White- and gray-box techniques to generate integration test data could be more fully explored when possible.

Many types of models were used to describe specifications of the programs. UML models were the most commonly used, followed by formal models. Among UML models, there is a tendency to use state and activity diagrams. State diagrams explore the behavior of a use case or an object, whereas activity diagrams are variations of state diagrams that focus on the flow of actions and events[2]. State and activity diagrams together can provide control flow and event-oriented state change informations. Despite the fact that a small number of data generation tools was obtained, the authors indicate additional tools will be forthcoming. More experimental studies were anticipated, but, in general, the authors describe case studies for validation of their proposals.

Notwithstanding such research gaps, however, the reviewed studies show advancement in the development of techniques of automated test data generation. Nevertheless, challenging problems remain to be investigated and analysed, and we intend to evaluate the cost and effectiveness of such techniques.

Acknowledgments. This research received funding from the Brazilian government agencies FAPESP under processes 2013/03459-4 and 2013/01818-7 and CAPES under process DS-8435201/M.

[2] http://www.cs.toronto.edu/ jm/340S/PDF2/StateD.pdf

Bibliography

[1] G. J. Myers and C. Sandler. *The Art of Software Testing*. John Wiley & Sons, 2004. ISBN 0471469122.

[2] IEEE standard for software and system test documentation. *IEEE Std 829-2008*, pages 1–150, July 2008.

[3] M. Pezze, K. Rubinov, and J. Wuttke. Generating effective integration test cases from unit ones. In *Int. Conf. on Software Testing, Verification and Validation*, pages 11–20, March 2013.

[4] M.I. Hossain and W.J. Lee. A scalable integration testing approach considering independent usage pattern of global variables. *Int. Journal of Software Eng. and its Applications*, 7(3):195–204, 2013.

[5] S. A. Khan and A. Nadeem. Automated test data generation for coupling based integration testing of object oriented programs using evolutionary approaches. In *Int. Conference on Information Technology: New Generations*, pages 369–374, 2013.

[6] V. Martena, A. Orso, and M. Pezzé. Interclass testing of object oriented software. In *Int. Conf. on Engineering of Complex Computer Systems*, pages 135–, 2002.

[7] Aditya P. Mathur. *Foundations of Software Testing*. Addison-Wesley Professional, 1st edition, 2008.

[8] B. Kitchenham and S. Charters. Guidelines for performing systematic literature reviews in software engineering. Technical Report EBSE 2007-001, School of Comp. Science and Mathematics, 2007.

[9] T. Dyba, T. Dingsoyr, and G. K. Hanssen. Applying systematic reviews to diverse study types. In *Symp. on Emp. Soft. Eng. and Measurement*, pages 225–234, 2007.

[10] D. Budgen, A. J. Burn, and B. Kitchenham. Reporting computing projects through structured abstracts: A quasi-experiment. *Emp. Softw. Eng.*, 16 (2):244–277, April 2011.

[11] R. Wieringa, N. Maiden, N. Mead, and C. Rolland. Requirements engineering paper classification and evaluation criteria: a proposal and a discussion. *Requir. Eng.*, 11(1):102–107, December 2005.

[12] W. T. Tsai, X. Bai, R. Paul, W. Shao, and V. Agarwal. End-to-end integration testing design. In *Int. Comp. Software and Applications Conference*, pages 166–171, 2001.

[13] F. Mattiello-Francisco, E. Martins, A. R. Cavalli, and E. T. Yano. InRob: An approach for testing interoperability and robustness of real-time embedded software. *J. of Systems and Software*, 85(1):3–15, 2012.

[14] S. K. Swain, D. P. Mohapatra, and R. Mall. Test case generation based on state and activity models. *J. of Object Technology*, 9(5):1–27, 2010.

[15] H. Zhou, Z. Huang, and Y. Zhu. Polymorphism sequence diagrams test data automatic generation based on OCL. In *Int. Conference for Young Computer Scientists*, pages 1235–1240, 2008.

[16] J.-y. Li, H.-f. Gong, J.-p. Hu, B.-j. Zou, and J.-g. Sun. Class hierarchical test case generation algorithm based on expanded EMDPN model. *J. of Central South University of Technology*, 13(6):717–721, 2006.
[17] R. Swain, V. Panthi, D.P. Mohapatra, and P.K. Behera. Prioritizing test scenarios from UML communication and activity diagrams. *Innovations in Systems and Software Engineering*, 10(3):165–180, 2014.
[18] C. Robinson-Mallett, R.M. Hierons, J. Poore, and P. Liggesmeyer. Using communication coverage criteria and partial model generation to assist software integration testing. *Software Quality Control*, 16(2):185–211, 2008.
[19] K. Bogdanov, M. Holcombe, F. Ipate, L. Seed, and S. Vanak. Testing methods for X-machines: a review. *Formal Aspects of Computing*, 18(1): 3–30, 2006.
[20] H.Y. Chen, T.H. Tse, and T.Y. Chen. TACCLE: A methodology for object-oriented software testing at the class and cluster levels. *ACM Trans. Softw. Eng. Methodol.*, 10(1):56–109, January 2001.
[21] F. Jabeen and M. Jaffar-ur Rehman. A framework for object oriented component testing. In *Symposium on Emerging Technologies*, pages 451–460, Sept 2005.
[22] J. Hartmann, C. Imoberdorf, and M. Meisinger. UML-based integration testing. In *SIGSOFT Int. Symposium on Software Testing and Analysis*, pages 60–70, 2000.
[23] A. Bertolino, P. Inverardi, H. Muccini, and A. Rosetti. An approach to integration testing based on architectural descriptions. In *International Conference on Engineering of Complex Computer Systems*, pages 77–84, Sep 1997.
[24] C. Robinson-Mallett, R.M. Hierons, and P. Liggesmeyer. Achieving communication coverage in testing. *SIGSOFT Softw. Eng. Notes*, 31(6):1–10, November 2006.
[25] Thi-Quynh Bui and Oum-El-Kheir Aktouf. On-line testing of software components for diagnosis of embedded systems. In *World Academy of Science Engineering and Technology*, volume 22, pages 330–336, 2007.
[26] Z. Li and T. Maibaum. An approach to integration testing of object-oriented programs. In *Int. Conf. on Quality Software*, pages 268–273, 2007.
[27] S. Benz. Combining test case generation for component and integration testing. In *Int. Workshop Advances in Model Based Testing*, pages 23–33, 2007.
[28] M. Gupta, J. Fu, F.B. Bastani, L.R. Khan, and I.-L. Yen. Rapid goal-oriented automated software testing using MEA-graph planning. *Software Quality Journal*, 15(3):241–263, 2007.
[29] C. R. Rocha and E. Martins. A method for model based test harness generation for component testing. *J. of the Brazilian Computer Society*, 14(1):7–23, 2008.
[30] W. Damm, H. Hungar, B. Josko, T. Peikenkamp, and I. Stierand. Using contract-based component specifications for virtual integration testing and architecture design. In *Design, Automation Test in Europe Conference Exhibition*, pages 1023–1028, 2011.

[31] F. Saglietti, F. Pinte, and S. Sohnlein. Integration and reliability testing for component-based software systems. In *Euromicro Conf. on Software Eng. and Advanced Applications*, pages 368–374, 2009.

[32] A. Fin, F. Fummi, and D. Signoretto. The use of SystemC for design verification and integration test of IP-cores. In *International ASIC/SOC Conference*, pages 76–80, 2001.

[33] X. Fan, J. Shu, L. Liu, and Q. Liang. Test case generation from UML subactivity and activity diagram. In *Int. Symposium on Electronic Commerce and Security*, volume 2, pages 244–248, 2009.

[34] P. Chevalley and P. Thevenod-Fosse. Automated generation of statistical test cases from UML state diagrams. In *International Computer Software and Applications Conference*, pages 205–214, 2001.

[35] P.H.S. Brito, R. De Lemos, C.M.F. Rubira, and E. Martins. Architecting fault tolerance with exception handling: Verification and validation. *J. of Computer Science and Technology*, 24(2):212–237, 2009.

[36] W. Liu and P. Dasiewicz. Component interaction testing using model-checking. In *Electrical and Computer Engineering. Canadian Conference on*, volume 1, pages 41–46, 2001.

[37] G. A. Di Lucca, A. R. Fasolino, F. Faralli, and U. De Carlini. Testing web applications. In *Int. Conf. on Software Maintenance*, pages 310–319, 2002.

[38] S. Ogata and S. Matsuura. A method of automatic integration test case generation from UML-based scenario. *WSEAS Trans. on Information Science and Applications*, 7(4):598–607, 2010.

[39] F. Saglietti and F. Pinte. Automated unit and integration testing for component-based software systems. In *Int. Workshop on Security and Dependability for Resource Constrained Embedded Systems*, 2010.

[40] D. Lugato, C. Bigot, Y. Valot, J.-P. Gallois, S. Gerard, and F. Terrier. Validation and automatic test generation on UML models: the AGATHA approach. *Int. J. on Software Tools for Technology Transfer*, 5(2-3):124–139, 2004.

[41] J.S. Kang and H.S. Park. RPIST: Required and provided interface specification-based test case generation and execution methodology for robot software component. In *Int. Conference on Ubiquitous Robots and Ambient Intelligence*, pages 647–651, 2011.

[42] Y. Chen, S. Liu, and F. Nagoya. An approach to integration testing based on data flow specifications. In *Int. Conf. on Theoretical Aspects of Computing*, pages 235–249, 2005.

[43] Z. Houhamdi and B. Athamena. Structured integration test suite generation process for multi-agent system. *Journal of Computer Science*, 7(5):690–697, 2011.

[44] L.C. Briand, Y. Labiche, and J. Cui. Automated support for deriving test requirements from uml statecharts. *Software & Systems Modeling*, 4(4): 399–423, 2005.

[45] P. Samuel, R. Mall, and P. Kanth. Automatic test case generation from UML communication diagrams. *Information and Software Technology*, 49 (2):158–171, 2007.

[46] A.C. Damasceno, P.D.L. Machado, and W.L. Andrade. Testing real-time systems from compositional symbolic specifications. *Int. Journal on Software Tools for Technology Transfer*, pages 1–19, 2015.
[47] M. Utting, A. Pretschner, and B. Legeard. A taxonomy of model-based testing approaches. *Softw. Test. Verif. Reliab.*, 22(5):297–312, August 2012.

Evidências sobre Configurações de Algoritmos Genéticos para Geração Automática de Dados de Teste

Ricardo F. Vilela[1], Paulo S. L. Souza[1], Marcio E. Delamaro[1], Simone R. S. Souza[1]

Instituto de Ciências Matemáticas e de Computação (ICMC/USP)
São Carlos/SP, Brazil, 13560-970
ricardovilela@usp.br, pssouza@icmc.usp.br,
delamaro@icmc.usp.br, srocio@icmc.usp.br
http://www.icmc.usp.br

Resumo *Contexto*: A geração automática de dados de teste tem como intuito diminuir os esforços gastos na atividade de teste. Uma técnica amplamente utilizada para essa atividade é o Algoritmo Genético (AG), devido a sua característica de otimização e busca. Entretanto, a forma como os parâmetros de configuração são definidos pode influenciar nos resultados obtidos. *Objetivo*: Este trabalho apresenta um mapeamento sistemático definido para investigar, catalogar e classificar como os AGs são configurados nas pesquisas realizadas que usam AG para geração de dados de teste. *Método*: Uma busca sistematizada por artigos foi conduzida considerando trabalhos publicados até Maio/2014. *Resultados*: Os resultados indicam que existe uma variedade de configurações possíveis em relação aos parâmetros e operadores dos AGs e dependendo da configuração, diferentes resultados podem ser atingidos. Esses resultados fornecem subsídios para a construção de uma proposta de configuração adequada para a geração automática de dados de teste.

Palavras-chave: Teste de Software, Algoritmos Genéticos, Geração de dados de teste, Mapeamento Sistemático.

1 Introdução

O teste de software tem como objetivo verificar a presença de defeitos nos programas, sendo utilizado para aumentar a garantia de qualidade do software em desenvolvimento. Para isso, um conjunto de técnicas e critérios de teste são definidos para auxiliar a atividade de teste. A diferença entre as técnicas está na informação utilizada para gerar os casos de teste (entrada de um programa e sua saída esperada). Dentre as técnicas existentes, destacam-se: funcional, estrutural e baseada em erros. Neste trabalho é considerada apenas a técnica estrutural para o projeto de casos de teste.

A técnica estrutural utiliza aspectos estruturais do código-fonte para orientar a seleção de casos de teste exigindo a execução de partes ou de componentes elementares do programa. A ideia central no teste estrutural não é testar todas as possibilidades de entrada de um software, e sim as mais representativas. Sendo assim, é possível exercitar todos os comandos e todas as condições pelo menos uma vez para cada um de seus valores possíveis (verdadeiro ou falso) [1].

Ainda assim, na maioria dos casos, a determinação de quais entradas selecionar é feita manualmente, com base no conhecimento do software e experiência do testador. Embora a automatização dessa atividade (seleção de dados de teste) seja muito desejada, não existe um algoritmo de propósito geral e eficiente que seja capaz de gerar automaticamente e a baixo custo um conjunto de teste efetivo. Nem mesmo é possível determinar automaticamente se esse conjunto existe [2,3].

Apesar das limitações, técnicas têm sido propostas para geração automática de dados de teste, as quais, em geral, são guiadas por critérios de teste [2]. Umas das técnicas mais simples e baratas é a geração aleatória, a qual tem como objetivo selecionar pontos específicos do domínio de entrada de forma aleatória até que o critério de teste seja satisfeito (ou coberto). O problema principal dessa técnica é que ela não garante que trechos importantes do código serão executados.

Técnicas de computação evolutiva também são aplicadas para lidar com as limitações da atividade de teste [2]. Como exemplo, os testes evolucionários utilizam em sua maioria algoritmos genéticos (AGs) para geração de dados de teste, entretanto, para gerar bons indivíduos (dados de teste capazes de revelar defeitos ou atender determinados critérios de teste) um AG precisa ser configurado adequadamente, tarefa essa não trivial. Como exemplo, um tamanho inapropriado de população pode dificultar a seleção de bons indivíduos no espaço de busca, além disso, uma taxa inadequada de mutação pode permitir que o AG convirja muito cedo para mínimos locais (indivíduos subótimos) não alcançando ótimos globais (melhores indivíduos do espaço de busca). Além disso, uma taxa inapta de cruzamento pode não gerar bons indivíduos para novas gerações do AG.

Nesse sentido, diferentes configurações podem ser definidas e a questão em aberto é decidir qual delas escolher para obter melhores resultados. Este artigo contribui nesta direção apresentando um mapeamento sistemático sobre trabalhos de geração automática de dados de teste por meio de AGs. Neste mapeamento foram considerados artigos que utilizaram a técnica estrutural para derivação dos casos de teste, por ser uma técnica amplamente conhecida e utilizada na automatização do teste de software.

O intuito é investigar, catalogar e classificar a forma como os AGs são configurados de modo a fornecer subsídios sobre resultados de diferentes configurações. Além disso, outro objetivo é identificar as características das aplicações utilizadas nos experimentos dos estudos de casos. Este trabalho está organizado da seguinte forma: na Seção 2 são apresentados os principais conceitos sobre a geração automática de dados de teste por meio de AGs. A Seção 3 apresenta o protocolo utilizado para condução do mapeamento. Na Seção 4 são apresentadas as respostas encontradas para as questões de pesquisa, bem como a discussão sobre as mesmas. Por último na Seção 6 são apresentadas as conclusões do trabalho.

2 Geração Automática de Dados de Teste com Algoritmos Genéticos

A geração automática de dados de teste consiste em gerar automaticamente entradas para um determinado programa, no intuito de exercitar partes relevantes do código de um programa. Embora a geração de dados de teste seja desejável, essa tarefa é indecidível, pois existem restrições inerentes à atividade de teste que impossibilitam automatizar toda a etapa de geração de dados de teste.

Entre as restrições, destacam-se: **i) Correção coincidente**: Ocorre quando o programa em teste possui um defeito que é revelado por um dado de teste, um estado de erro é produzido, mas por coincidência um resultado correto é obtido, ou seja, essa característica implica em uma má avaliação do dado de teste pelo AG, uma vez que, a otimização do AG ocorre baseada na aptidão dos indivíduos (dado de teste), essa avaliação do dado de teste pode prejudicar novas gerações; **ii) Caminho ausente**: Corresponde a uma determinada funcionalidade requerida para o programa, mas que por algum motivo não foi implementada, ou seja, o caminho desejado não existe no programa. Dessa forma, o AG pode passar por diversas gerações na tentativa de obter um dado de teste que exercite uma função que não existe no programa; e **iii) Caminhos não executáveis**: Ocorre quando não existe um conjunto de dados de entrada para exercitar um caminho de determinado programa. Esses caminhos são gerados pelos critérios e quando o AG é aplicado ocorre o mesmo problema anterior, onde o AG insistentemente busca sem sucesso gerar dados para exercitar esse caminho [2].

A geração de dados de teste com algoritmos genéticos utiliza conceitos da computação evolutiva, que se baseia na evolução natural das espécies. Com essa técnica pode-se ter várias soluções que se encaixam em problemas com dificuldade na obtenção de resultados ótimos. Quando se implementa um AG é preciso representar o espaço de busca do problema e suas possíveis soluções de forma computacional e encontrar a função de aptidão que é usada para avaliar quão boa é uma dada solução. O algoritmo genético parte da premissa de que dada duas soluções com resultados aproximados para um determinado problema, essas duas soluções combinadas podem conduzir a outra melhor [4].

A geração de dados de teste com algoritmos genéticos geralmente se encontra classificada em duas categorias: função de avaliação baseada na cobertura, onde a avaliação é realizada com base na cobertura de cada dado de teste; e função de avaliação orientada a um objetivo, onde a função é especificada de acordo com um objetivo que é, geralmente, a cobertura de um elemento particular. Operadores genéticos como *crossover* e mutação são utilizados para a construção de novas soluções a partir de soluções antigas, de tal maneira que, para muitos problemas a população melhora constantemente. O operador *crossover* pode ser entendido da seguinte forma: dadas duas cadeias **a** e **b**, compostas por 6 variáveis (genes),

$$(a1, a2, a3, a4, a5, a6) \text{ e } (b1, b2, b3, b4, b5, b6),$$

as mesmas representam duas soluções para um determinado problema. Um ponto de *crossover* é escolhido aleatoriamente para gerar novas soluções. Neste exemplo considera-se que o ponto escolhido seja 2. A nova geração será composta pelos seguintes indivíduos:

$$(a1, a2, \mathbf{b3}, \mathbf{b4}, \mathbf{b5}, \mathbf{b6}) \text{ e } (b1, b2, \mathbf{a3}, \mathbf{a4}, \mathbf{a5}, \mathbf{a6}),$$

A maioria das aplicações utilizam cadeias compostas por apenas 0s e 1s, por facilitar a tarefa e por vantagens impostas por esta abordagem. Outro operador utilizado para geração de novos indivíduos é a mutação. O operador de mutação oferece a oportunidade de alcançar espaços de busca não alcançados pelo *crossover*. Cada gene da cadeia é examinado e possui uma pequena probabilidade de ocorrer uma alteração arbitrária em sua estrutura. Para ilustrar a situação, considere um individuo composto por 10 genes:

1001010100,

após aplicação desse operador, suponha que o terceiro e oitavo gene sofram uma mutação. A sequência obtida após a mutação resulta no novo individuo:

10**1**1010**0**00

Além da aplicação de operadores os indivíduos também são escolhidos com base em uma função de aptidão. A função de aptidão avalia cada indivíduo com base no problema a ser otimizado. Após a avaliação, diferentes abordagens são utilizadas para seleção desses indivíduos, dentre elas podemos destacar: **i) Roleta**: onde as habilidades de todos os indivíduos são calculadas e os valores obtidos corresponderão, proporcionalmente, aos setores de uma roleta. Assim, quando realizado o sorteio os maiores setores possuirão maiores chances de serem selecionados; **ii) Aleatória**: Consiste em escolher indivíduos da população de forma aleatória; **iii) Torneio**: Um número n de indivíduos são escolhidos aleatoriamente formando uma sub-população. Dessa forma, o indivíduo selecionado dependerá de uma probabilidade k definida previamente; e **iv) *Stochastic Universal Sampling*- SUS**: Semelhante a seleção por roleta, mas para selecionar n indivíduos, utiliza n agulhas igualmente espaçadas, girando-as em conjunto.

Como a geração automática de dados de teste é um problema de otimização, diversos estudos apresentam abordagens utilizando AGs para geração de dados de teste, e utilizam como função de aptidão determinados critérios de teste.

3 Mapeamento Sistemático

Para a realização deste estudo os autores seguiram as instruções propostas por Kitchenham et al. (2007) para produção de revisões sistemáticas. O objetivo deste trabalho é encontrar evidências sobre a configuração de AGs aplicados à geração automática de dados de teste em acordo com critérios estruturais [5]. Para isso foram estabelecidas as seguintes questões de pesquisa:

- **RQ1 Qual a configuração de AGs utilizada para geração de dados de teste?** O objetivo desta questão é levantar informações sobre o tamanho da população inicial, taxas de mutação e *crossover*, número de gerações utilizado, métodos de seleção utilizados e o número de repetições nos experimentos realizados.

– **RQ2 Quais os tipos de aplicações ou *benchmarks* utilizados como sistemas em teste (*System under testing*-SUT) para a avaliação dos AGs?** Pretende-se descobrir quais os principais programas utilizados pelos estudos e qual a complexidade desses programas.

3.1 Estratégia de Busca e Critérios de Seleção

A realização das buscas por estudos experimentais que possam responder questões de pesquisa contou com cinco repositórios de artigos:*SCOPUS Database*, *ACM Digital Library*, *IEEE Xplore Digital Library*, *Science Direct* e *Compendex*. Em cada base de dados, foi utilizada uma cadeia contendo palavras chave e seus respectivos termos relacionados. Além disso, foram utilizados operadores do tipo "*OR*" e "*AND*" para refinar a cadeia de busca. Os principais termos buscados foram: *Test Generation**, *Genetic Algorithm** e *Structural Testing**.

Em adição aos termos de busca, critérios de inclusão e exclusão foram definidos de modo a guiar o processo de seleção dos trabalhos, conforme apresentado na Tabela 1. As fases 1 e 2 correspondem a forma como são aplicados os critérios de inclusão e exclusão e a ordem de execução.

Tabela 1: Critérios de Seleção.

Critérios de Inclusão			Critérios de Exclusão		
CI	Fase	Critério	CE	Fase	Critério
CI-1	1	Apresentar no titulo, resumo ou palavras-chave os termos de busca;	CE-1	1	Artigos duplicados;
CI-2	2	Apresentar estudos experimentais sobre geração automática de dados de teste;	CE-2	1	Artigos não disponibilizados;
CI-3	2	Apresentar o método de execução realizado;	CE-3	2	Não apresentar a descrição do experimento;
CI-4	2	Apresentar a configuração do AG para geração automática de dados de teste;	CE-4	2	Teses, propostas, dissertações e relatórios técnicos.

3.2 Processo de Seleção

As buscas foram realizadas em maio de 2014, sendo identificados 172 trabalhos. Na Figura 1 é apresentada proporção de trabalhos encontrados em cada repositório de artigos.

Após reunir os trabalhos encontrados foi verificado a importância de cada estudo para o mapeamento. Sendo assim, os critérios de inclusão e exclusão

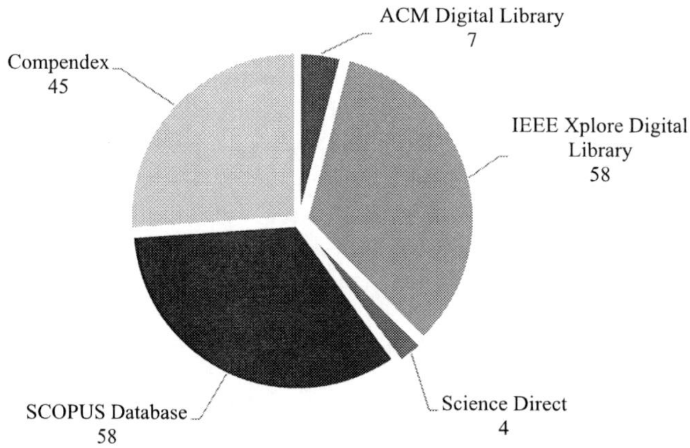

Figura 1: Trabalhos encontrados por cada repositório de artigos.

apresentados foram utilizados para refinar a busca. A Figura 2 apresenta o processo de busca realizado e os resultados obtidos em cada fase.

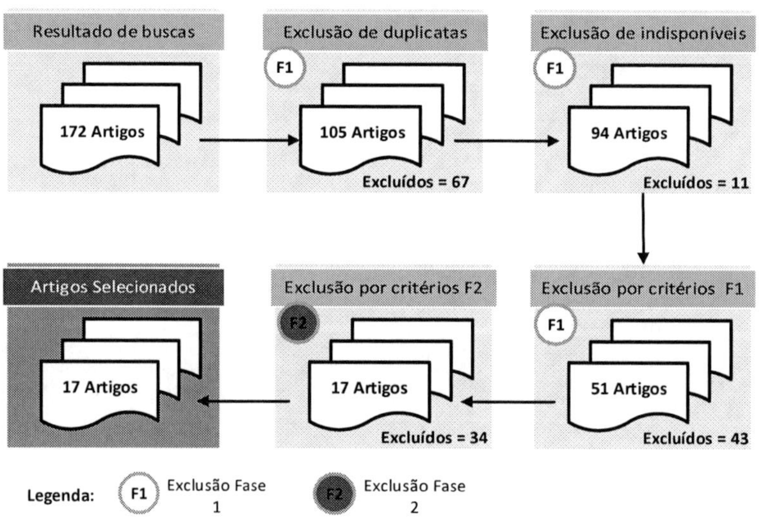

Figura 2: Processo de buscas.

Na primeira fase foi realizada a exclusão dos trabalhos duplicados, ou seja, aqueles trabalhos que foram retornados por mais de uma base de dados. Desse modo, após a exclusão desses trabalhos ainda havia 105 trabalhos remanescentes. Além da exclusão dos trabalhos duplicados, também foram excluídos aqueles trabalhos que não estavam disponíveis nas bases (11), os quais em sua maioria disponibilizavam apenas o resumo e informações sobre autores, restando 94 trabalhos para revisão de resumos e palavras-chave.

Nesta etapa, o critério de inclusão *CI-1* foi aplicado para refinar os estudos identificados, desta forma, apenas os trabalhos que tratavam a geração automática de dados de teste por meio de AG foram selecionados. Além disso, outro aspecto observado foi a técnica de teste utilizada, ou seja, apenas os trabalhos que utilizaram a técnica estrutural para guiar a geração foram selecionados. Desse modo, ao final desta etapa foram selecionados 51 trabalhos para a fase 2. Nesta fase foi realizada a leitura na íntegra e de acordo com os critérios de seleção definidos, 17 trabalhos foram selecionados, conforme Tabela 2.

Tabela 2: Estudos Selecionados.

ID	Ref	Título	Ano
#1	[6]	Automatic generation of basis test paths using variable length genetic algorithm	2014
#2	[7]	Dynamic white-box software testing using a recursive hybrid evolutionary strategy/genetic algorithm	2013
#3	[8]	Test Data Generation for Software Testing Based on Quantum-Inspired Genetic Algorithm	2013
#4	[9]	Applying Genetic Algorithm to Increase the Efficiency of a Data Flow-based Test Data Generation Approach	2012
#5	[10]	An Approach for Search Based Testing of Null Pointer Exceptions	2011
#6	[11]	A Multi-Objective Genetic Algorithm to Test Data Generation	2010
#7	[12]	A Strategy for Evaluating Feasible and Unfeasible Test Cases for the Evolutionary Testing of Object-oriented Software	2008
#8	[13]	GA-based Multiple Paths Test Data Generator	2008
#9	[14]	An Automatic Software Test-Data Generation Scheme Based on Data Flow Criteria and Genetic Algorithms	2007
#10	[15]	Applying Particle Swarm Optimization to Software Testing	2007
#11	[16]	Batch-Optimistic Test-Cases Generation Using Genetic Algorithms	2007
#12	[17]	Improving Evolutionary Real-Time Testing by Seeding Structural Test Data	2006
#13	[18]	A dynamic optimization strategy for evolutionary testing	2005
#14	[19]	A Unified Fitness Function Calculation Rule for Flag Conditions to Improve Evolutionary Testing	2005
#15	[20]	Automatic Test Data Generation for Data Flow Testing Using a Genetic Algorithm	2005
#16	[21]	Data Generation for Path Testing	2004
#17	[22]	Using a Genetic Algorithm and Formal Concept Analysis to Generate Branch Coverage Test Data Automatically	2004

4 Resultados

Nesta seção são apresentados os resultados obtidos por meio dos estudos classificados, para cada uma das questões de pesquisa de interesse apresenta-se a classificação dos dados em relação aos estudos.

- **RQ1 - Qual a configuração de AGs utilizada para geração de dados de teste?**

Os estudos mostraram diversas configurações dos AGs na geração automática de dados de teste. Além disso, um fato interessante foi os autores afirmarem utilizar tentativa e erro para configuração dos AGs [13] [10] , o que implica em altos esforços para configurar o AG, reforçando ainda mais a relevância deste estudo para novos trabalhos.

Na Tabela 3 são apresentados os resultados extraídos dos estudos selecionados. Na coluna **ID** encontram-se as identificações dos estudos com base na Tabela 2. Nas colunas **TamPOP** e **TaxaMutação** são apresentadas as populações utilizadas em cada estudo e as taxas de mutação empregadas, respectivamente. A taxas identificadas de *crossover* são apresentadas na coluna **TaxaCrossover** e os números de gerações utilizados por cada estudo são exibidos na coluna **NGerações**. Adicionalmente, o método de seleção e o número de execuções realizados nos estudos são apresentados nas colunas **MSeleção** e **NExecuções**, respectivamente. Os trabalhos que não apresentaram informações para algumas das subquestões de pesquisa são descritos como (N/A) na tabela.

Tabela 3: Configurações identificadas nos estudos.

ID	TamPOP	TaxaMutação	TaxaCrossover	NGerações	MSeleção	NExecuções
#1	10	0.15	0.8	50-100	Roleta	10
#2	50-1000	0.05	0.9	N/A	Roleta	N/A
#3	30	0.05	0.9	100	Roleta	100
#4	10	0.1	N/A	N/A	Roleta	N/A
#5	100	N/A	0.9	10000	Roleta	10
#6	50-100	0.2	0.8	50-100	Roleta	10
#7	5	0.1-0.34-0.8	0.1-0.33-0.8	200	Torneio	20
#8	30	0.1-0.3	0.5-0.9	100	Roleta	10
#9	50	0.4-0.5	0.4-0.5	2000	Roleta	15
#10	40	0.000001-0.1	1.0	200	SUS	30
#11	100	0.5	0.75	1000	N/A	N/A
#12	240	0.01-0.005	0.9	N/A	SUS	10
#13	100	0.1	0.5	250	Aleatório	N/A
#14	49	0.02	0.2	10000	N/A	N/A
#15	4-8-10	0.15	0.8	100	Roleta	N/A
#16	N/A	0.1	0.7	50	Aleatório	20
#17	250	0.4	0.8	50	N/A	N/A

Após a tabulação dos dados foi possível realizar análises estatísticas no intuito de fornecer informações para novos estudos. Dessa forma, foi utilizada estatística descritiva para esta análise, empregando os seguintes métodos: i) média - valor que aponta para onde mais se concentram os dados de uma distribuição; ii) moda - valor que detém o maior número de observações, o qual ocorre com maior frequência em um conjunto de dados; iii) mínimo - menor valor do conjunto de dados; e iv) máximo - maior valor do conjunto de dados. Na Tabela 4 são apresentados os resultados dos métodos empregados. Para a subquestão (Métodos de Seleção) foi calculada apenas a moda, uma vez que não foi possível calcular os demais métodos para o tipo de dado investigado.

Tabela 4: Estatística descritiva.

Questões/Métodos	Média	Moda	Min	Max
TamPOP	111.8	100	4	1000
TaxaMutação	0.15	0.1	0.000001	0.8
TaxaCrossover	0.674	0.9	0.1	1.0
NGerações	1626	100	50	10000
MSeleção	-	Roleta	-	-
NExecuções	23	10	10	100

Com base nos dados analisados pode-se observar que o tamanho da população mais utilizado pelos autores é de 100 indivíduos e a variação entre o tamanho da população diverge de um valor mínimo de 4 indivíduos para um tamanho máximo de 1000 indivíduos. A grande diferença entre os tamanhos identificados de população demonstra a ausência de uma padronização para o tamanho da população em AGs com o foco na geração automática de dados de teste. Obviamente os estudos acabam por utilizar configurações diferentes devido às características dos SUTs selecionados, entretanto, como serão apresentados nos resultados da RQ2, muitos trabalhos utilizam os mesmos SUTs para avaliação do AG, ainda assim, as configurações entre estes trabalhos são distantes. Como exemplo os trabalhos #2 e #4 empregam o SUT $TriangleClassification$ para avaliação de suas abordagens, para o qual são utilizados os tamanhos $(50 - 1000)$ e (10) nos respectivos trabalhos.

A taxa de mutação mais utilizada foi de 0.1, enquanto a média utilizada assume um valor de 0.15. A variação entre as taxas vai de uma taxa mínima de 0.000001 para uma máxima de 0.8. Assim como na população, os resultados identificados na taxa de mutação entre os trabalhos selecionados também são distantes para os SUTs em comum. Em adição, alguns dos trabalhos investigados foram encontradas altas taxas de mutação, nas quais o AG provavelmente comportou-se semelhantemente como um algoritmo aleatório, pois com uma taxa alta de mutação não é possível evoluir os indivíduos de forma eficaz durante as gerações. Além disso, no trabalho #7 foram utilizadas taxas de mutação iguais e superiores a taxa de *crossover*, ação esta não recomendada para configuração de AGs [4].

A taxa de *crossover* mais utilizada foi de 0.9, ao passo que, a média identificada foi de 0.674. A variação entre as taxas foi de um mínimo de 0.1 para um máximo de 1.0. Em complemento aos aspectos levantados sobre a configuração de AGs, para a taxa de *crossover* foram identificadas altas taxas, as quais podem ter prejudicado os resultados do AG. Como exemplo, o trabalho #10 apresentou a taxa de 1.0 para *crossover*, ou seja, 100% dos indivíduos em todas as gerações realizaram o cruzamento para gerar novas populações. Desse modo, essa configuração pode impossibilitar a ação de uma importante técnica do AG, o elitismo. O elitismo tem como objetivo manter os melhores indivíduos para gerações posteriores. Portanto, se o intervalo de geração (porcentagem da população que pode ser substituída na próxima geração) utilizado não garantir a permanência desses indivíduos, a otimização do AG será prejudicada.

O tamanho da população e as taxas de *crossover* e mutação são de grande importância para configuração de um AG, pois a forma como os indivíduos são criados a cada geração está ligada principalmente a esses três parâmetros. Diante disso, é importante investigar quais combinações diferentes existem para esses tipos de parâmetros. Na Figura 3 é apresentado um gráfico de bolhas, o qual exibe a quantidade de trabalhos que utilizaram determinadas combinações entre os fatores população-mutação e população-*crossover*.

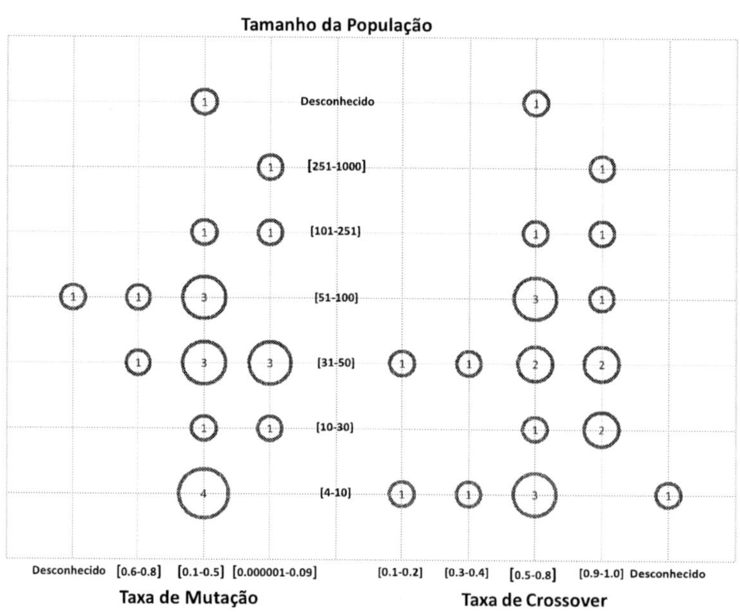

Figura 3: Gráfico de bolhas dos parâmetros população, mutação e *crossover*.

Outra questão importante sobre a configuração de AGs é o método utilizado para selecionar os indivíduos, nos quais serão aplicados os operadores genéticos. Como pode ser observado na Tabela 4, o método mais utilizado para seleção de indivíduos é a Roleta, sendo utilizado por 9 dos 14 estudos analisados. Esse método garante que os melhores indivíduos possuirão mais chances de serem selecionados para aplicação dos operadores, entretanto, em grandes cromossomos essa abordagem pode demandar um alto custo computacional para gerar os intervalos e posteriormente percorre-los.

Assim como as outras questões de pesquisa, o número de gerações utilizados para produzir uma população ótima de indivíduos também influencia no desempenho do AG. Assim, com base nos dados extraídos foi possível identificar que a maior parte dos estudos analisados utilizam 100 gerações para criação dos indivíduos. A variação entre os trabalhos em relação ao número de gerações é de um mínimo de 50 gerações para um máximo de 10000 gerações. O número de gerações de um AG é visto como um dos critérios de parada do algoritmo, ou seja, quando o número de gerações é alcançado o AG finaliza a execução. Diante disso, o valor estabelecido para o número de gerações pode influenciar no tempo despendido para o AG encontrar uma solução ótima. Como exemplo, o trabalho #5 define 10000 gerações para uma execução do AG, dessa forma, em um extenso espaço de busca (domínio de entrada) de um SUT, o custo para gerar os indivíduos pode ser demasiadamente alto se os demais critérios de parada não forem alcançados.

Para que os algoritmos sejam devidamente avaliados é necessário que existam repetições do experimento, pois com apenas uma execução, os resultados podem não refletir evidências corretas sobre a eficácia de um AG. Dessa forma, com as repetições é possível obter uma média dos resultados baseada em todas a execuções realizadas.

Neste mapeamento 41% dos trabalhos investigados não apresentaram o número de execuções realizadas, entretanto, com base nos demais trabalhos foi possível identificar que o número de repetições mais utilizado nos trabalhos é de 10 execuções, enquanto a média calculada assume um valor de 23 indivíduos. A variação entre o número de execuções diverge de um valor mínimo de 10 execuções para um tamanho máximo de 100 execuções. Definir a quantidade de repetições para avaliação dos resultados não é uma tarefa trivial, apesar disso, na literatura são exigidas pelo menos 10 execuções [23].

– **RQ2 - Quais os tipos de aplicativos ou *benchmarks* utilizados como SUT para a avaliação dos AGs?**

Assim como a configuração dos algoritmos genéticos, outra tarefa importante é a escolha de SUTs para avaliação do AG, ou seja, o fato de um AG gerar dados que exercitem boa parte de um determinado SUT não significa que o mesmo possa ser utilizado para geração de dados de outros programas de forma satisfatória. Um dos principais fatores que contribuem para uma efetiva avaliação de AGs com o foco na geração de dados de teste é a variação no tamanho de espaço de busca e a complexidade dos algoritmos. A Tabela 5 apresenta os SUTs utilizados nos estudos selecionados. Na coluna **Sistema em teste** são apresentadas as aplicações identificadas e na coluna **ID** os trabalhos que utilizaram cada SUT. Devido à limitação de espaço, apenas as aplicações utilizadas por dois ou mais estudos são apresentadas neste trabalho.

Tabela 5: Relação de SUTs identificados.

Sistema em teste	ID
Triangle Classification	#1, #2, #3, #4, #8, #10, #13, #16
ValidDate	#3,#4
Quadratic equation	#4,#10
Bubble-sort	#2,#8
Minimum-maximum	#2,#8

Como pode ser observado, dentre os SUTs mais utilizados pelos estudos o *Triangle Classification* e o *ValidDate* apresentam maiores índices de ocorrência. Dessa forma, os resultados obtidos podem auxiliar na escolha de SUTs para avaliar a geração de dados de testes por meio de AGs. Outro aspecto importante observado foi o tipo de sistema em teste utilizado, ou seja, é possível perceber que a maioria dos estudos utilizam sistemas simples para avaliação das abordagens propostas. Essa característica pode não destacar a eficácia de um AG, pois com SUTs de baixa complexidade com pequenos espaços de busca, a solução pode ser facilmente encontrada por algoritmos de menor complexidade e com menor tempo de execução, como exemplo a geração aleatória.

5 Ameaças à validade

Neste estudo foram considerados apenas estudos primários que utilizam a técnica estrutural para geração automática de dados de teste, ao passo que existem diferentes técnicas de teste de software. Apesar disso, considerando que os algoritmos genéticos necessitam de objetivos para guiar a otimização, acredita-se que, em sua maioria, os trabalhos utilizam aspectos relacionados a estrutura do código para guiar seleção de indivíduos (dados de teste).

Os trabalhos selecionados durante o estudo (sem duplicação) representam aproximadamente 16% dos estudos investigados inicialmente (17 de 105), ou seja, os resultados foram extraídos de uma pequena amostra da população, além disso, muitos dos trabalhos selecionados não oferecem todas as descrições requeridas para este mapeamento. No entanto, considerando que o objetivo deste estudo é descobrir as lacunas existentes na configuração dos AGs, e que 43 estudos foram excluídos por não apresentar a descrição do experimento, este resultado comprova a importância deste estudo e ressalta a necessidade de uma sistematização no processo de configuração de AGs.

6 Conclusão

A geração de dados de testes por meio de algoritmos genéticos vêm sendo amplamente empregada para diminuir os esforços gastos na atividade de teste, e não só apenas para critérios de teste estrutural. Dada a eficácia que os AGs possuem na geração de dados de teste, a configuração dos mesmos deve ser realizada de forma consistente, pois a eficácia dos dados de teste gerados está estritamente ligada a forma como os algoritmos genéticos são estruturados.

A otimização neste contexto considera diferentes objetivos, uma vez que, a característica de cada programa diverge de acordo com o seu paradigma e, além disso, as técnicas de teste utilizadas consideram diferentes informações. Os resultados obtidos neste trabalho inferem uma necessidade de métodos/abordagens que possam apoiar a efetiva configuração de AGs para geração automática de dados de teste, as quais, devem considerar as técnicas envolvidas juntamente com os critérios utilizados, os tipos e características dos sistemas em teste (como programas concorrentes e sequenciais) e as restrições presentes na geração de dados de teste.

Neste sentido, um modo efetivo para essa configuração poderá diminuir o custo para otimização, sendo este um dos principais desafios em técnicas de otimização, melhorar a qualidade do conjunto de teste gerado e contribuir para melhoria de qualidade dos softwares sob teste. Os resultados obtidos podem ser um ponto de partida para novos estudos empíricos realizados na área, oferecendo uma visão sobre a configuração AGs na geração de dados de teste.

Com esse objetivo, este trabalho oferece uma análise dos dados catalogados sobre a configuração dos AGs e apresenta os principais *benchmarks* utilizados na literatura para avaliação. Como trabalhos futuros, pretende-se investigar o impacto de diferentes funções de avaliação na geração de dados de teste e analisar diferentes espaços de busca nos *benchmarks* utilizados. Além disso, também pretende-se realizar estudos utilizando AGs para geração automática de dados de teste para outros domínios de aplicação, como por exemplo, programas concorrentes. A ideia é verificar se essas configurações também se aplicam a esse domínio de programas e quais resultados são obtidos.

Referências

1. Pressman, R.: Software Engineering: A Practitioner´s Approach. 7 edn. McGraw Hill, Inc., New York, NY, USA (2010)
2. Delamaro, M.E., Maldonado, J.C., Jino, M.: Introdução ao Teste de Software. Elsevier (2007)
3. McMinn, P.: Search-based software test data generation: A survey: Research articles. Software Testing Verification and Reliability **14** (2004) 105–156
4. Luke, S.: Essentials of Metaheuristics. second edn. Lulu (2013) Available for free at http://cs.gmu.edu/~sean/book/metaheuristics/.
5. Kitchenham, B., Charters, S.: Guidelines for performing systematic literature reviews in software engineering. Technical Report EBSE 2007-001, Keele University and Durham University Joint Report (2007)

6. Ghiduk, A.S.: Automatic generation of basis test paths using variable length genetic algorithm. Information Processing Letters **114** (2014) 304 – 316
7. Panchapakesan, A., Abielmona, R., Petriu, E.: Dynamic white-box software testing using a recursive hybrid evolutionary strategy/genetic algorithm. In: IEEE Congress on Evolutionary Computation. (2013)
8. MAO, C., YU, X.: Test data generation for software testing based on quantum-inspired genetic algorithm. International Journal of Computational Intelligence and Aplications **12** (2013)
9. Mahajan, M., Kumar, S., Porwal, R.: Applying genetic algorithm to increase the efficiency of a data flow-based test data generation approach. Software Engineering Notes - SIGSOFT (2012)
10. Romano, D., Di Penta, M., Antoniol, G.: An approach for search based testing of null pointer exceptions. In: Software Testing, Verification and Validation (ICST), 2011 IEEE Fourth International Conference on. (2011) 160–169
11. Pinto, G., Vergilio, S.: A multi-objective genetic algorithm to test data generation. In: Tools with Artificial Intelligence (ICTAI), 2010 22nd IEEE International Conference on. Volume 1. (2010)
12. Ribeiro, J.C.B., Rela, M.Z., de Vega, F.F.: A strategy for evaluating feasible and unfeasible test cases for the evolutionary testing of object-oriented software. In: Proceedings of the 3rd AST. (2008)
13. Ahmed, M.A., Hermadi, I.: Ga-based multiple paths test data generator. Computers & Operations Research **35** (2008) 3107–3124 Part Special Issue: Search-based Software Engineering.
14. Andreou, A., Economides, K., Sofokleous, A.: An automatic software test-data generation scheme based on data flow criteria and genetic algorithms. In: IEEE Conf. on Computer and Information Technology. (2007)
15. Windisch, A., Wappler, S., Wegener, J.: Applying particle swarm optimization to software testing. In: Proc. of the 9th Conference on Genetic and Evolutionary Computation. (2007) 1121–1128
16. Sofokleous, A., Andreou, A.: Batch-optimistic test-cases generation using genetic algorithms. In: 19th IEEE International Conference on Tools with Artificial Intelligence. Volume 1. (2007) 157–164
17. Tlili, M., Sthamer, H., Wappler, S., Wegener, J.: Improving evolutionary real-time testing by seeding structural test data. In: IEEE Congress on Evolutionary Computation. (2006) 885–891
18. Xie, X., Xu, B., Shi, L., Nie, C., He, Y.: A dynamic optimization strategy for evolutionary testing. In: 12th Asia-Pacific Software Engineering Conference - APSEC. (2005)
19. Liu, X., Liu, H., Wang, B., Chen, P., Cai, X.: A unified fitness function calculation rule for flag conditions to improve evolutionary testing. In: Proceedings of the 20th International Conference on Automated Software Engineering, NY, USA (2005)
20. Girgis, M.: Automatic test data generation for data flow testing using a genetic algorithm. Journal of Universal Computer Science **11** (2005) 898–915
21. Mansour, N., Salame, M.: Data generation for path testing. Software Quality Control (2004) 121–136
22. Khor, S., G.P.: Using a genetic algorithm and formal concept analysis to generate branch coverage test data automatically. In: Proceedings of IEEE international conference on Automated software engineering, Washington, USA (2004) 346–349
23. Ali, S., Briand, L.C., Hemmati, H., Panesar, R.K.: A systematic review of the application and empirical investigation of search-based test case generation. IEEE Trans. on Software Engineering (2010)

Software Development Initiatives to Identify and Mitigate Security Threats – A Systematic Mapping

Paulina Silva[1], René Noël[2], Mauricio Gallego[3], Santiago Matalonga[4], and Hernán Astudillo[1]

[1] Universidad Técnica Federico Santa Mara
pasilva@alumnos.inf.utfsm.cl
hernan@inf.utfsm.cl
[2] Universidad de Valparaíso, Chile
rene.noel@uv.cl
[3] Universidad de Quindío, Colombia
mauriciogallego81@gmail.com
[4] Universidad ORT Uruguay, Uruguay
smatalonga@uni.ort.edu.uy

Abstract. The effective building of secure software systems has been addressed by security experts and software development experts through several techniques for identifing and mitigating security threats. Many techniques had been theoretically developed, however, for most of these proposals there is few empirical evidence of its application in building secure software systems. A systematic mapping has been conducted to cover the existent technologies for identification and mitigation of security threats. A total of 10 different techniques covering threats identification and 8 covering the mitigation of threats were found. All the initiatives were integrated to at least one activity of the Software Development Lifecycle (SDLC), while 7 show signs of being adopted in the industry. The mapping found only 15 studies that covered 11 different iniatiatives. Only two techniques presented scientific evidence of its results through controlled experiments, while others selected studies presented informal case studies or examples.

Keywords: Security Patterns, Architectural Tactics, Security Threats, Secure Software Development, Systematic Mapping

1 Introduction

Security is a main interest topic in Information Technologies nowadays, and is considered a Quality Attribute of a System by software engineering (ISO 25010). From this point of view, several initiatives, like techniques, models and tools, have been proposed in order to add architectural and design decisions through the Software Development Life Cycle (SDLC) [31]. Some of these initiatives aim to help software engineers in the identification of security threats such as Attack Trees [26], the elicitation of security requirements with Misuse Cases [27], and the definition of security goals as in Secure Tropos [16], while others allow software engineers to mitigate these security threats or satisfy security requirements, by reusing security design decisions [1],[6], or supporting the decision making process [33]. However, the impact of these techniques, methods and models is hard to assess, considering the nature of software development process, the lack of standards to measure software security from the point of view of the software developer, and the difficulty of defining security requirements in an effective, clear and unambiguous way [10]. Also, the application of these proposals could be hard to replicate in real contexts, due to the dependence on the software process activities, artefacts and practices required as preconditions, that may vary between software development organizations or even between projects in the same organization. This paper presents a systematic mapping [22] to characterize techniques, methods, tools and processes proposed in Security and Software Engineering Journals, which at least show an example of the application of these proposals. A software engineering systematic map (SM) is a defined method to build a classification scheme and structure a software engineering field of interest. We focused in journals in order to cover studies reporting long term research in initiatives and accumulated scientific evidence. The goal of the study is to identify these proposals, characterize them by level of empirical evidence of its application, identify their use of software artefacts or notations, and identify the stage of the SDLC that these proposals support. The rest of the paper goes as follows: Section 2 presents the related work, reporting previous work of the authors in software security design studies, relevant systematic mapping publications that support our approach to answer our research questions, and some proposals of techniques, methods and tools that initially guided our search. Section 3 presents the design of the systematic mapping, while section 4 presents details of the execution and results. Threats to validity are reviewed in section 5. Finally, section 6 presents main conclusions and high level answers to our research questions.

2 Related Work

Authors have conducted several studies aiming to explore software design decisions for developing secure software systems. An experimental approach was initially taken to compare software security tactics and security design patterns [18], and several questions arose when trying to operationalize the identification and mitigation of security threats. These questions guided the authors to search for some security threat identification methods with demonstrated efficiency to be added to the experimental process, as a previous step to apply security tactics or patterns. In a first search based on a survey of techniques [31] and snowballing through it main references, no methods with scientific evidence of its impact were found, which motivated the present systematic mapping. Authors choose a well explained methodology for a first experimental approach to threats identification: Misuse Activities [3]. Results of applying this identification method can be found in [19], which show statistically significant differences when performing a guided identification process versus an ad-hoc approach. Also, authors have on going research initiatives to explore the importance of software artefacts over security decisions [14], and the structure of the Architectural Tactics for security decisions [7]. Whether a number of methodologies exist as mentioned in [31], the study [32] in which the security expert's opinion about the State-of-Practice of initiatives in the software development process was analized, revealed that a lot of them do not surpass the State-of-Art even if they are considered good practices. The study establishes requirements for a methodology for building secure systems, including that proposals must consider the compatibility of the technique with the commercial environment of developers and their current skills.

A software engineering systematic mapping (SM) is a defined method to build a classification scheme and structure a software engineering field of interest. When working with SM, it is difficult not to relate them to Systematic Reviews (SR or SLR). The main difference between them lies, according to [22], relays in the definition of goals, breadth, validity issues and implications of the studies; also, a SLR is more ambitious and rigorous than a SM. In [24] a series of rigorous guidelines to make a systematic mapping are presented, this directives constitute a well defined method for the revision of the mapping, with the potential to reach close to a high-quality systematic review. An example of the application of SM to answer research questions similar to the motivations of this study is presented in [5]: a SM is done with the goal of finding information about usability evaluation methods, which have been used by researchers to evaluate web applications and their relationship with the web development process. Main results are the identification of most reported methods, and research gaps aiming to the validations of these methods. The study in [9] presents a work in which a systematic revision is done with the goal of finding a trend in the definition of quality in the Model Driven Engineering. Main contribution of the study is the identification of a variety of multiple quality interpretations as consequence of the diversity in MDE compliance works.

Previous initiatives for documenting existing security techniques, methods, tools and methodologies can be found in [31]. Also, a field study to identify requirements for a methodology for building secure systems can be found in [32].

3 Methodology/Research Design

The aim of this investigation is to cover the existent initiatives and experience reports seen as methodologies, methods, techniques and tools, for identification and mitigation of security threats during Software Development in order to build Secure Systems. An "initiative" is a method, technique, proposal or methodology, among others. No comparison or evaluation is done between the studies, so we could classify this work as a **Systematic Mapping study** (SM). In a SM we do not consider specific outcomes or experimental designs in our study, since we look for a broad overview of the research area as a whole; this is also why this study is not a systematic review. In order to design and operate the study, we followed the guidelines proposed by Petersen [22], and the documented the protocol following Biolchini et al. definitions [2].

3.1 Research Questions

As commented in the related work section, no systematic mappings or reviews were found when searching for technologies for security threats identification and mitigation. Based on this main objective, we elaborated the following research questions:

1. What are the existing initiatives or methods of identifying security threats and attacks?
2. What threat identification methods are related to Security Tactics?
3. What other Mitigation Methodologies exist when developing Software, to conceive Secure Systems?

The first question is the main research question, while the second and third are secondary research question.

3.2 Identification of Population, Intervention and Amplitude

We followed P.I.C.O. [21] structure to define the search string, by defining a search string according the **Population**, **Intervention**, **Comparison** and **Output**, but since our work is a Systematic Mapping we follow the considerations presented in [22], which suggests only use Population and Intervention.

- Population: Software Development or Design related work
  Keywords: "software", "design", "engineering".

- Intervention Control: Security threat identification or mitigation methodologies/initiatives/guidelines
  Keywords: "security","threat", "attack", "identificate", "mitigate", "minimize", "elicitate", "elicitation".
  Keywords: "model", "guideline", "checklist", "method" and "methodology".

We excluded some words:

- "System": It is a word that encompasses a lot of research areas.
- Use of "Service" or "System" for population: returns results from other areas, which are of no use to this work.
- Plural words were not used in the search string.
- Complete words were not used, we use the prefixes of them.

3.3 Construction of a Search String

Table 1: Keywords used in the Search String

Term	**keywords obtained and synonyms**
P	("software" OR "design" OR "engineer" OR "develop")
I	("securit" OR "privacy" OR "integrity" OR "confidential" OR "availabil" OR "accountabil") AND ("threat" OR "risk" OR "attack" OR "requirement" OR "vulnerabil") AND ("identif" OR "mitig" OR "minimiz" OR "elicit" OR "enumer" OR "review" OR "assur") AND ("model" OR "metric" OR "guideline" OR "checklist" OR "template" OR "approach" OR "strateg" OR "method" OR "methodolog" OR "tool" OR "technique" OR "heuristic")
String	**(P AND I)**

The initial keywords were found out by asking our experts and using the control studies we defined in section 3.2; synonyms were added to the keywords already found. The keywords that represent the core of the research are: "Threat", "Attack", "Identify" and "Mitigate". As we mentioned in section 3.2, we used the prefixes of the word as a consequence of our search procedure's definition. This is further discussed in section in section 3.6.

3.4 Source Selection

Works should be available on the web, through open access or subscription based journals (those we could get access to). The language selected for the studies is English. The list of journals was proposed and reviewed by four researchers from different domains (software engineering, software security, distributed systems and software architecture), two of them not related to the research team. The Source Identification List is shown in Table 2.

3.5 Inclusion/Exclusion Criteria

The Study Type selected consist of articles related to Secure Software Development, and articles selected by the Inclusion Criteria (Table 3). Studies with at least one Exclusion criteria were not selected.

Two readers evaluated each study. We used the following acceptance criteria in case the evaluators do not agree which studies should be accepted.

Table 2: Source Selection

Journal Name	Link
Journal Computers & Security	www.journals.elsevier.com/computers-and-security/
Journal Information and Software Technology	http://www.journals.elsevier.com/information-and-software-technology/
Journal of Systems and Software	http://www.journals.elsevier.com/journal-of-systems-and-software/
Journal of Universal Computer Science	www.jucs.org/
Journal of System Architecture	http://www.journals.elsevier.com/journal-of-systems-architecture/
Requirements Engineering	http://link.springer.com/journal/766
IEEE Transaction on Software Engineering	http://www.computer.org/csdl/trans/ts/index.html
IEEE Transactions on Dependable and Secure Computing	http://www.computer.org/web/tdsc
International Journal of Secure Software Engineering	http://www.igi-global.com/journal/international-journal-secure-software-engineering/1159
Information Security Technical Report	http://www.sciencedirect.com/science/journal/13634127
Journal of Information Security and Applications	http://www.journals.elsevier.com/journal-of-information-security-and-applications/

Table 3: Inclusion/Exclusion Criteria

Inclusion Criteria	Exclusion Criteria
Studies from [2000 to 2015[	Being older than 2000 (]− to 2000[)
The paper mentions the Quality Attribute "Security" in some part of the work	Non-related Security article. Methodological proposals where security is not specified
Empirical or Experimental studies or Proposals (Methodological Definitions, Applied Case Studies or Experimental Application of Identification and Mitigation). – Is there a concern to formalize? No matter if it was successful or not. – Informal technical reports are useful (if it was wrote by someone of field)..	Non Empirical or Experimental studies. Complete proceedings or books without specifying the articles. Exclude Thesis if is not the publicated version.
Applicable techniques during Software Development/Conception	Techniques used when a System is already deployed. Techniques related to certificate or security modeling or risk assessment. Articles not related to development or assurance of systems, for example, curriculum proposals or Security Quality Assurance
Discusses about strategies	No mention of strategies
Discusses about methods	No mention of methods

- If the two readers accept: The study is included.
- If one reader accepts and one is in doubt: The study will be discussed in group.
- If the two readers excluded the study: The study is not included
- All conflicts were reviewed by a third researcher.

While the two readers are evaluating, they should document the rationale for excluding the article.

3.6 Search Strategy/Procedure

Our search strategy was to explore software development and software security journals, in order to cover studies reporting long term research in initiatives and accumulated scientific evidence.

1. We searched through studies from digital Journals. We selected the following information: Volume, Issue, URL (for the Journal-Volume), Title and Abstract.
2. All this information was saved in an Excel file, one file for each Journal revised.
3. From the Excel sheet where the studies are, we used a filter created by a Macro made in Visual Basic.
4. **First Filter:** This was done by searching with the **Search String** within the Abstract, and selecting those that had those terms in it. The Search String was created with the terms identifying the Population and Intervention. We manually evaluated the strength of the filter with one of the Journals used (IJSSE).
5. **Second Filter:** By reading again the title and abstract, we filter against the Inclusion and Exclusion Criteria (Table 3).
6. If any irrelevant or duplicate study appear, they should be removed.
7. **Third Filter:** From the second filter, we did a quick scan of the articles and tried to categorize them in the following cases: empirical evidence/experimentation, case study, proposal or systematic review. In this high level revision of the accepted papers we viewed Abstract, Introduction, Development of the work, Data obtained, Conclusions and other relevant sections of the paper; we considered that the abstract was not enough to judge a paper.
8. **Fourth Filter:** This is done by reading the complete text of the studies that were accepted by the third filtering. The fourth filtering is executed according to the Inclusion and Exclusion Criteria (Table 3). In this step, we tried to take some information that could help to speed up the Data Extraction.

4 Conducting the Systematic Mapping

Table 4: Selected papers from first filtering (27-07-15)

Journal	**Number of Articles Found**
Journal Computers & Security	29
Journal Information and Software Technology	19
Journal of Systems and Software	14
Journal of Universal Computer Science	6
Journal of System Architecture	6
Requirements Engineering	12
IEEE Transaction on Software Engineering	8
IEEE Transactions on Dependable and Secure Computing	10
International Journal of Secure Software Engineering	14
Information Security Technical Report	6
Journal of Information Security and Applications	3
Total	**127**

The trial was done on 27-07-15 according to all the previous sections, we found out the results presented in table 4. To obtain such results, we did the first phase filtering as its explained in section 3.6. No duplicate articles were found. Table 5 summarizes the quantity of articles selected in each phase. In the first phase filtering, the identification of the papers was performed in each Excel of the Journal selected, in total 127 papers were identified by filtering its abstract with the Search String. In the second phase, 41 papers were filtered by the inclusion/exclusion criteria, and 0 were duplicated. After discussing between the revisors, we decided to add 1 more article, so a total of 42 papers went to the third phase filtering. The third filter was done by scanning 15 studies, which remained in the list after fully reading them and extracting the necessary information.

Table 5: Resume of number of papers Selectedd in each phase

Stage	**Number of Articles**
First Filter: In Abstract by Search String	127
Second Filter: Articles selected by inclusion criteria	41
After discussion between revisors	42
Dupplicates	0
Third Filter: Lightly reading to other sections of the paper	15
Four Filter: Articles kept after full reading and Extraction	15

4.1 Data Extraction

The 15 papers selected by our approach are described briefly in Table 6 (final page).

From these we found that 11 different methodologies exist within these 15 papers selected, which are:

- KAOS: goal-oriented methodology with Faily et al. [4] (IJSSE).
- Secure Tropos: Agent-Driven Methodologies with Mouratidis et al. [17] (IJSEKE) and Kalloniatis et al. [12] (Requirements Engineering).
- Aspect-Oriented Risk-Driven Development (AORDD) methodology with Georg et al. [8] (IEEE Trans. of SE).
- SQUARE: security quality requirements engineering with Suleiman et al. [28] (Requirements Engineering).
- Information System Security Risk Management with Matulevicius et al. [15] (JUCS).
- Aspect-Oriented Petri Nets with Xu et al. [33] (IEEE Trans. of SE).
- Attack Trees with Karpati et al. [13] (Information and Software Technology) and Opdahl et al. [20] (Information and Software Technology).
- Misuse cases Karpati et al. [13] (Information and Software Technology), Opdahl et al. [20] (Information and Software Technology) and Sindre et al. [27] (Requirements Engineering).
- Practical method based on reusable requirement repository with Toval et al. [29] (Requirements Engineering).
- Model-Driven Architecture/Security with Snchez et al. [25] (JUCS) and Trujillo et al. [30] (Information and Software Technology).
- Ontology-engineering methodology with Razzaq et al. [23] (Computers & Security).

4.2 Analysis

After applying the first and second filter, then discussing between the revisors those papers where existed doubts about them, eliminated dupplicates and finally applied other two filters to get a list of papers that complied our inclusion and exclusion criterias, we analyzed them so our research question could be answered. Regarding the data obtained in the extraction (Table 6), we found out that the case study type was prevalent among other study types, followed by examples. Only 2 papers had experimental data and analysis, both of them had the same author [20], [23] (Figure 1).

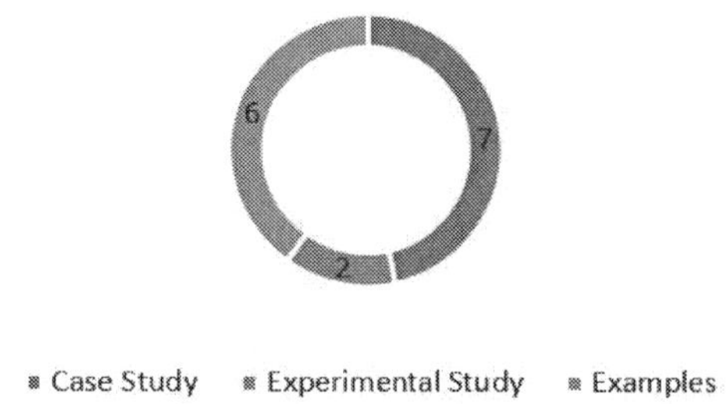

Fig. 1: Study types

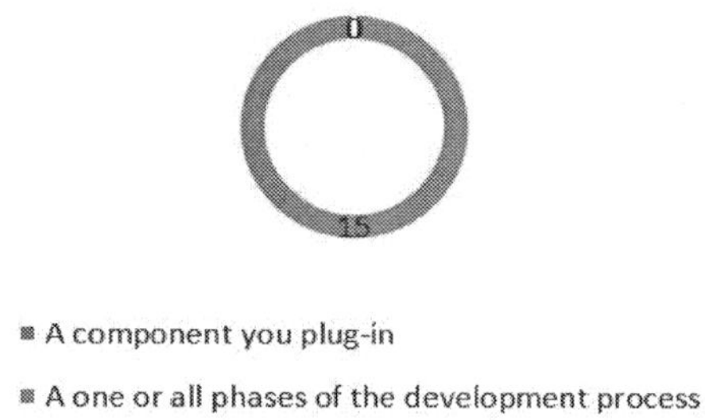

Fig. 2: Security considered as...

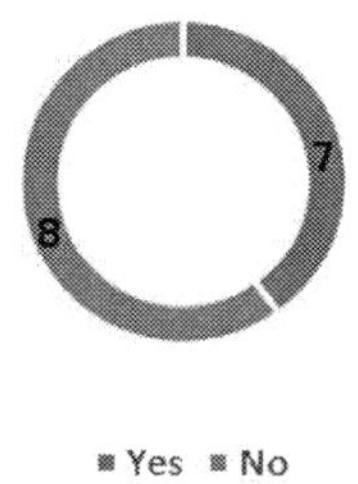

Fig. 3: Adoption of initiatives in the Industry

We were interested in knowing how they approached to security in the proposal, if it was thought as a part of the development process or maybe they just considered it as a software component. We can see in Figure 2 that none of the work we selected added security as if it was a software component. Another fact we discovered is that some initiatives found in the selected papers, 7 of 15 seem to be used within an industrial environment (Figure 3).

Most interesting findings can be summarized in the following lines:

- From 11 different papers [4], [8], [12], [13], [17], [20], [15], [27], [28], [30], [33], we found that different types of modelling languages were used. The most used were: UML, Attack Trees, Petri Nets and i*/Tropos based approaches.
- A petri based modelling approach of threats [33] shows the progressive and transversal intrinsic nature of security threats.
- SQUARE [28] delivers a set of artifacts, threats and vulnerabilities, from which is possible to get an impact analysis, the probability of occurring and risk level from it. With this is possible to categorize and prioritize security requirements, which allows to analyze the security requirements of the software from the beginning.
- [29] defines a repository of reusable generic requirements which minimize the time of developing in subsequent projects when using the practical methodology the propose. SIREN extends the MAGERIT methodology, conformes to the ISO 15408 or Common Criteria Framework, and also is based on IEEE standards.
- One approach work on how to prove that security was implemented in a project to the stakeholder [4]. They take into account the "usability" of the software as a part of the integration of stakeholders, to make explicit the security to them.

4.3 Answers to Research Questions

Part of the work is to answer our Research Question in Section 3.1, the answer to them are:

1. What are the existing initiatives or methods of identifying security threats and attacks?
   - From these methodologies, papers which identify Security Threats were [4], [8], [11–13], [17], [20, 25], [15], [27–29], [33], with a total of 10 different types of techniques.
   - Additionally, these techniques considered the Domain of the problem as a first step into getting security threats.
   - According to the results obtained with this work we can say there are a plethora of methods for identifying security threats.
   - In spite of the results, there is no clear distinction for defining threats and attacks, every article read has at least a different conception of the Threat and Attack concepts.
   - From the initiatives found, we can see that most part of them take into account security threats analysis within the requirement discipline.
   - Some of them have the business concern as the primary focus, and others are worried about satisfying the functional requirements in the most secure way. In the same way, there are not that many initiatives that are taken into account in the industrial environment.
   - Finally, we can relate to the work of Whyte and Harrison [32], which states the lack of implementation initiatives within the industry, which is clearly showed in the results above.
2. What threat identification methods are related to Security Tactics?
   With the search and extraction done, we could not find anything related to Security Tactics.
3. What other Mitigation Methodologies exist when developing Software, to conceive Secure Systems?
   - As some of the methodologies gave proposals to identify security threats/attacks, not everyone gave mitigation methodologies.
   - In [8] they use AOM (Aspect-Oriented Modeling) methodology and techniques to specify generic security mitigation mechanism models. With a set of these security mechanisms, they perform a trade-off analysis between them to improve the security in the design.
   - The view in the Risk analysis model in [4], compresses goal trees arising from risk responses, thereby making it easier to trace risks to mitigating responses, the requirements they treat, and the countermeasures they refine.
   - Mitigation on web based attacks [23] is based in the complete understanding of the domain and context of information contents to be processed, and the ability to filter them on the basis of their effects on the target web application, with the help of policies; which is done through the process of reasoning and intelligent decision making.
   - [33] uses threat mitigations (security features or assurance techniques) for mitigating specific security threats, PrT net-based aspects is the technique used to model threat mitigations.
   - [13], [20], [27] mentions that a Use Case can be a countermeasure for a Misuse Case, in which the first reduces the Misuse Cases chance of succeeding; they are called security use cases.
   - [15] uses Risk treatment-related concepts or decisions, requirements and controls defined and implemented to mitigate the risks. A risk treatment is the treatment decision for a risk.

5 Threats to Validity/Limitations of this Study

Throughout the execution of the protocol, we took care to reduce the threats that could invalidate the results obtained. We present those threats identified, and try to explain what we did to mitigate them (or chose to accept).

5.1 Threat of missing Literature

In the beginning we were using web search engines to get the conference and journal papers, like IEEEXplore, ACM, Spinger, and others. But we decided not to used them because every one of them had different forms to build a search string; which could lead to different kinds of search. Also we found that some web search platform changed the maximum quantity of keywords, so this gave us a big limitation. We changed our focus to ensure a more stable population, allowing the replication of the study. Also, we focused in journals in order to cover studies reporting long term research in initiatives and accumulated scientific evidence. We decided to do a "manual" search within the Journals we knew and had the access to get the material needed. To obtain all the articles within a Journal, we built a script[5] based on Python to download all the information needed to identify an article within a Journal (URL, Volume, Title, Abstract, etc.). To obtain the selected articles, we used Excel macros to filter according to the abstract, with the keyword obtained by the Population and Intervention. To mitigate the possible threat within the procedure to extract papers from the Journals and the filtering within the excel list made with abstract, we did:

- Executed the script at least everyday, for 2 weeks, to compare and see if the results obtained had not changed.
- Executed the macro, with our keywords every time we got a new list from the execution of the script.
- We observed that there were no changes.

We may have filtered out some studies when selecting papers in a time interval. We mitigate this by looking the earliest date in which software development processes (an in consequence all sort of initiatives too) started to become popular. UML and RUP were created on the nineties, but started to become popular in the early 2000.

5.2 Threat of Selection Bias

The selection of papers during the systematic mapping procedure was done by three researchers; two of them performed the selection process by following our guideline in section 3.6. Both researchers applied the inclusion and exclusion criteria, compared results and resolve conflict following the definitions stated in the research protocol. Both researchers applied the inclusion and exclusion criteria, compared results and resolved conflicts following the definitions stated in the research protocol. A third person was in charge of managing the selection and intervining whenever a resolutions was difficult to make by the other two.

5.3 Threat of Inaccuracy of data extraction

This threat was mitigated by the iterative nature of the execution of the protocol, the peer review applied with the 2 extractors and a third reviewer in case of conflicts.

[5] Python scripts, datasheets and macros on: `https://github.com/pasilvagh/SM-fondecyt2015`

6 Conclusions

A Systematic Mapping was planned and operated in order to identify technologies for security threats identification and mitigation. We covered 11 main software development and security journals, published between years 2000 and 2015 (July). From a total of 10.838 articles, 127 were analyzed following the research protocol. A total of 15 studies presented technologies of security threats identification and/or mitigation, and evidence of its applicability. A total of 10 different techniques covering threats identification and 8 covering the mitigation of threats were found. All the initiatives were integrated to at least one activity of the Software Development Lifecycle (SDLC), while 7 show signs of being adopted in the industry. The mapping found only 15 studies that covered 11 different initiatives. Only two techniques presented scientific evidence of its results through controlled experiments, while others selected studies presented informal case studies or examples. Some of the initiatives are focused on the Requirement Engineering discipline, using software and knowledge reuse or other techniques to create security requirement that could mitigate the threats related to them. A plethora of methodologies exists that try to take into account security within the development process, but they seem to be just proposals without an opportunity for their evaluation within an industrial setting.

This study allowed us to find a range of articles related to our Research Questions, mainly to elicitation of Security Threat and Mitigations. From this studies allowed us to identify only 2 studies with experimental research approach [20, 13], being both a replications of the same experiment. Both studies differed on the experimental subjects: the first time was done with students and the second, with practitioners, in an industrial setting. We did not found more papers with experimental approaches to validate or explore software security technologies.

Within the methodologies and tools found, they all define security in at least one phase and at least 8 techniques in two phases of software development lifecycle. Although there are many forms in which security could be introduced in the software development, the most repeated form was in the search of requirements or security requirements. Elicitation of threats does not always involve a whole methodology, for example Misuse Case and Attack Trees are techniques contextualized in the requirement analysis activities, but not involved in a whole development methodology. [13], [20] concludes with the experimentation that Attacks Trees have a better usability and identifies more security threats than Misuses Cases, although the threats identified by both were different and complementary. This finding guides us to think that there is a research gap on the comparation of threat identification techniques, in order to assess their impact and complementarity. Most of the studies supported the requirements stage of the SDLC, while eight of them seemed to support other development activities. However, proposals were not clear in how they integrate to the rest of the SDLC. Proposal [30], elicit security requirements based on business and organizational goals, in contrast with the majority who elicits from functional requirements. This guides us to think that the scenario based requirements analysis is more suitable for security analysis, but further research is required to validate this idea.

Studies have shown that there is no common agreement with some word definition or language in the Security Community [8], [12], [13], [17], [15], [23], [27]. Some studies presented security domain models to define the domain in which a threat could be related to others entities, others just used a definition already used by others, either way, we realized that the definition of the term "threat" depends on the methodology and it is not a global concept, as some with poor experience in security could have thought. For example, some would define the term "threat" as a way to misuse something in a way it is not supposed to, others may think that a threat is a temporal sequence of attack steps, or even some could not consider this construct and they only use the term "attack". This suggest the necessity of a common conceptual model focused on identification and mitigation of security threats, to conform a unified vocabulary for future research in technologies for building secure software systems. Finally, in the light of the results of this SM, and consistently with our original concerns - the lack of scientific evidence in initiatives presented in [31] and the fullfillment of the recommendations described in [32] - we have identified a research gap in the formalization of the application and validation of secure software development initiatives.

References

1. Bass, L.: Software architecture in practice. Pearson Education India (2007)
2. Biolchini, J., Mian, P.G., Candida, A., Natali, C.: Systematic Review in Software Engineering. Engineering 679(May), 165–176 (2005)
3. Braz, F., Fernandez, E., VanHilst, M.: Eliciting security requirements through misuse activities. In: Database and Expert Systems Application, 2008. DEXA '08. 19th International Workshop on. pp. 328–333 (Sept 2008)
4. Faily, S., Fléchais, I.: Towards Tool-Support for Usable Secure Requirements Engineering with CAIRIS. International Journal of Secure Software Engineering 1(3), 56–70 (2010)
5. Fernandez, A., Insfran, E., Abrahão, S.: Usability evaluation methods for the web: A systematic mapping study. Inf. Softw. Technol. 53(8), 789–817 (Aug 2011)
6. Fernandez, E.B.: Security patterns in practice: designing secure architectures using software patterns. John Wiley & Sons (2013)
7. Fernandez, E.B., Pedraza-garcía, G.: Revisiting architectural tactics for security pp. 1–9 (2014)
8. Georg, G., Anastasakis, K., Bordbar, B., Houmb, S.H., Ray, I., Toahchoodee, M.: Verification and Trade-Off Analysis of Security Properties in UML System Models. IEEE Transactions on Software Engineering 36(3), 338–356 (May 2010)
9. Giraldo, F., Espana, S., Pastor, O.: Analysing the concept of quality in model-driven engineering literature: A systematic review. In: Research Challenges in Information Science (RCIS), 2014 IEEE Eighth International Conference on. pp. 1–12 (May 2014)
10. Gollmann, D.: Facets of security. In: Priami, C. (ed.) Global Computing. Programming Environments, Languages, Security, and Analysis of Systems, Lecture Notes in Computer Science, vol. 2874, pp. 192–202. Springer Berlin Heidelberg (2003)
11. Irvine, C.E., Levin, T., Wilson, J.D., Shifflett, D., Pereira, B.: An Approach to Security Requirements Engineering for a High Assurance System *. Requirements Engineering 7(4), 192–206 (Dec 2002)
12. Kalloniatis, C., Mouratidis, H., Islam, S.: Evaluating cloud deployment scenarios based on security and privacy requirements. Requirements Engineering 18(4), 299–319 (Apr 2013)
13. Karpati, P., Redda, Y., Opdahl, A.L., Sindre, G.: Comparing attack trees and misuse cases in an industrial setting. Information and Software Technology 56(3), 294–308 (Mar 2014)
14. Márquez, G., Silva, P., Noel, R., Matalonga, S., Astudillo, H.: Identifying emerging security concepts using software artifacts through an experimental case. In: Workshop on Advanced Software Engineering (WASE), a track of the 22th JCC (2015)
15. Matulevicius, R., Mouratidis, H., Mayer, N., Dubois, E., Heymans, P.: Syntactic and semantic extensions to secure tropos to support security risk management. J. UCS 18(6), 816–844 (2012)
16. Mouratidis, H., Giorgini, P.: Secure tropos: a security-oriented extension of the tropos methodology. International Journal of Software Engineering and Knowledge Engineering 17(02), 285–309 (2007)

17. Mouratidis, H., Islam, S., Kalloniatis, C., Gritzalis, S.: A framework to support selection of cloud providers based on security and privacy requirements. Journal of Systems and Software 86(9), 2276–2293 (Sep 2013)
18. Noel, R., Pedraza-garcia, G., Astudillo, H., Fernandez, E.B.: An Exploratory Comparison of Security Patterns and Tactics to Harden Systems. 12 Workshop on Experimental Software Engineering (2014)
19. Noel, R., Pedraza-Garcia, G., Astudillo, H., Matalonga, S., Encina, O.: Comparando patrones de seguridad y tácticas de seguridad para construir sistemas seguros: Identificando amenazas de seguridad. In: XVIII Ibero-American Conference on Software Engineering (2015)
20. Opdahl, A.L., Sindre, G.: Experimental comparison of attack trees and misuse cases for security threat identification. Information and Software Technology 51(5), 916–932 (2009)
21. Pai, M., McCulloch, M., Gorman, J.D., Pai, N., Enanoria, W., Kennedy, G., Tharyan, P., Colford, J.M.: Systematic reviews and meta-analyses: an illustrated, step-by-step guide. The National medical journal of India 17(2), 86–95 (2004)
22. Petersen, K., Feldt, R., Mujtaba, S., Mattsson, M.: Systematic mapping studies in software engineering. In: Proceedings of the 12th International Conference on Evaluation and Assessment in Software Engineering. pp. 68–77. EASE'08, British Computer Society, Swinton, UK, UK (2008)
23. Razzaq, A., Anwar, Z., Ahmad, H.F., Latif, K., Munir, F.: Ontology for attack detection: An intelligent approach to web application security. Computers & Security 45, 124–146 (Sep 2014)
24. Sampaio, A.: Improving systematic mapping reviews. SIGSOFT Softw. Eng. Notes 40(6), 1–8 (Nov 2015)
25. Sánchez, Ó., Molina, F., García-Molina, J., Toval, A.: Modelsec: a generative architecture for model-driven security. J. Univ. Comput. Sci 15(15), 2957–2980 (2009)
26. Schneier, B.: Attack trees. Dr. Dobbs journal 24(12), 21–29 (1999)
27. Sindre, G., Opdahl, A.L.: Eliciting security requirements with misuse cases. Requirements Engineering 10(1), 34–44 (Jun 2004)
28. Suleiman, H., Svetinovic, D.: Evaluating the effectiveness of the security quality requirements engineering (SQUARE) method: A case study using smart grid advanced metering infrastructure. Requirements Engineering 18(3), 251–279 (2013)
29. Toval, A., Nicolás, J., Moros, B.n., García, F.: Requirements Reuse for Improving Information Systems Security: A Practitioners Approach. Requirements Engineering 6(4), 205–219 (Jan 2002)
30. Trujillo, J., Soler, E., Fernández-Medina, E., Piattini, M.: An engineering process for developing Secure Data Warehouses. Information and Software Technology 51(6), 1033–1051 (Jun 2009)
31. Uzunov, A.V., Fernandez, E.B., Falkner, K.: Engineering Security into Distributed Systems: A Survey of Methodologies. Journal of Universal Computer Science 18(20), 2920–3006 (2012)
32. Whyte, B., Harrison, J.: State of Practice in Secure Software: Experts Views on Best Ways Ahead. IGI Global
33. Xu, D., Nygard, K.: Threat-driven modeling and verification of secure software using aspect-oriented Petri nets. IEEE Transactions on Software Engineering 32(4), 265–278 (Apr 2006)

Table 6: Brief description of the papers

Reference	Initiative name	Initiative resume
[4]	CAIRIS	Create security models that are automatically generated from specified, declarative data rather than via direct manipulation.
[33]	Threat-Driven Modelling of Secure Software	Use aspect-oriented extension to Predicate/Transition (PrT) nets, as a rigorous formalism for threat-driven modeling and verification.
[8]	Aspect-Oriented Risk-Driven Development (AORDD)	The AORDD Methodology has two steps that must occur prior to any analysis. Create system functional models, using the UML 2.0 and perform a risk assessment of the system.
[29]	SIREN (SImple REuse of software requiremeNts)	In order to use the security profile properly, the Elicitation phase must start by studying the threats to the assets of the system.
[11]	Multilevel Secure LAN	A multidimensional threat model that accounts for developmental and operational phases of system evolution and considers both physical and non-physical threats is presented. Physical threats to the system are explicitly addressed in the requirements engineering process.
[27]	Misuse Case	Identify critical assets in the system. Define security goals for each asset. Identify threats. Identify and analyze risks. Define security requirements for the threats to match risks and protection costs, preferably aided by a taxonomy of security requirements.
[28]	SQUARE	SQUARE consists of nine steps: agree on Definitions, identify security goals, develop artifacts to support security requirements definitions, perform risk assessment, select requirements elicitation technique, elicit the security requirements, categorize the security requirements, prioritize the security requirements, and inspect the security requirements.
[12]	Secure Tropos and PriS	The process consists of three iterative activities: organizational analysis, Security and Private Requirements Analysis, and selection of deployment model.
[25]	ModelSec	ModelSec proposes a generative architecture based on a chain of model transformations involving several security models at different levels of abstraction.
[15]	Secure Tropos	Supports development of IS (information systems) through four phases: early and late requirements, architectural and detailed design. Language application includes three major stages.
[17]	SPEM, Secure Tropos and PriS	Three main activities of the framework: the Security and Privacy Cataloguing, the Security and Privacy Analysis, and the Selection of Cloud Service Provider. The proposed framework consists of a language and a process that is focused on the requirements engineering stage.
[20]	Attack Trees and Misuse Cases	A pair of controlled experiments was performed. In each experiment, the participants used the two techniques individually on two different threat identification tasks.
[30]	SEDAWA: Secure Engineering process for DAta Warehouses	The secure engineering process is proposed with the purpose of defining secure requirements and transforming them in order to develop secure Data Warehouses.
[13]	Attack tres and Misuse case	The participants were randomly assigned to one of four experiment groups.
[23]	Methontology	The life cycle activities of Methontology are composed of specification, conceptualization, formalization, implementation and maintenance activities.

Um *Survey* sobre Evolução de Esquemas e Uso de Sistemas Gerenciadores de Bancos de Dados

Tauany Lorene Santana Santos[1], Methanias Colaço Júnior[1,2], Camila Oliveira Carvalho[1], André Vinícius R. P. Nascimento[2], Marcos Barbosa Dósea[1]

1 Núcleo de Pesquisa e Prática em Inteligência Competitiva – NUPIC, DSI. Universidade Federal de Sergipe (UFS). Itabaiana, Sergipe, Brasil.

2 Programa de Pós Graduação em Ciências da Computação (PROCC). Universidade Federal de Sergipe (UFS). São Cristóvão, Sergipe, Brasil.

{tauany.lorene,camila.x17,andreviniciusnascimento,marcosdosea}@gmail.com, mjrse@hotmail.com

Resumo. Um tipo particular de mudança que afeta diretamente o código de um software é a evolução de esquemas de banco de dados. Modificar um esquema implica avaliação de impacto, ou seja, identificar todos os locais do sistema que podem ser afetados por cada mudança, para adaptá-los à nova realidade. Este artigo apresenta os resultados de um *survey*, com empresas brasileiras, acerca da utilização de bancos de dados e o tratamento dado à evolução de seus esquemas. Como resultados, o *Microsoft SQL Server* foi evidenciado como o Sistema Gerenciador de Banco de Dados (SGBD) mais utilizado entre as empresas pesquisadas. Em paralelo, o número de mudanças realizadas anualmente nos esquemas é alta, segundo 41,37% dos entrevistados. Apesar da grande maioria dos entrevistados (87,32%) realizar controle de mudanças, principalmente de forma manual (44,78%), eles não analisam os impactos causados (72,36%). Isto pode estimular mais investimentos da indústria e pesquisas sobre como elaborar melhores abordagens para automatização deste processo.

Palavras-Chave. Manutenção, Banco de Dados, Evolução de Esquemas, Análise de Impacto.

1 Introdução

Ao construir e manter um sistema de informação, seja ele de médio ou grande porte, um dos principais problemas é a necessidade de mudanças que surgem inevitavelmente ao longo do tempo. Um tipo particular de mudança, que pode ter consequências graves para o resto dos sistemas de aplicação, é a evolução de esquemas de banco de dados [11].

A projeção de um esquema de banco de dados é uma atividade evolutiva da Engenharia de Software que requer várias iterações e, mesmo depois de ser concluído, o esquema de banco de dados continua a mudar ao longo do tempo [15]. Um esquema de banco de dados precisa estar em evolução, a fim de se adaptar às mudanças de requisitos, corrigir erros e melhorar o seu desempenho. Embora a evolução do esquema torne mais fácil o entendimento e manutenção do banco de dados, por outro lado, é um risco que muitas empresas preferem evitar.

A evolução de um esquema traz modificações na estrutura do banco de dados, o que acarreta uma problemática para os desenvolvedores e empresas quanto aos efeitos de cada mudança sobre as aplicações ao redor do sistema. "Quando uma mudança de esquema ocorre, a consistência entre o esquema, o banco de dados e as aplicações deve permanecer." [6].

Os bancos de dados são ambientes que evoluem continuamente por meio da adição, atualização e remoção frequente de construções de projeto. Além disso, o problema torna-se mais grave com o crescimento de sistemas de informação *web* e dos bancos de dados de projetos de "*big science*", nos quais o rápido avanço do conhecimento e a participação ativa de muitos interessados têm acelerado o ritmo de evolução dos esquemas [5].

Essa aceleração gera complexidade, custo e tempo de inatividade, representando a fonte de problemas recorrentes no ciclo de vida dos *softwares*, bem como um dos principais obstáculos que entravam as atualizações de *software* [9].

Essas atualizações contínuas dos esquemas são necessárias para garantir que o mesmo reflita os requisitos com a maior precisão possível em todos os momentos [5]. Para tanto, é sabido que a tentativa de alcançar mudanças corretas é a atividade dominante na indústria de software de aplicação [11]. Porém, encontrar impactos das alterações de esquema sobre as aplicações e apresentá-las de forma adequada é particularmente desafiador [6].

Neste artigo, apresentamos um *survey*, com empresas brasileiras, acerca da utilização de bancos de dados e o tratamento dado à evolução de seus esquemas. Foi utilizado um questionário que consiste em 16 questões e divide-se em três blocos. O primeiro trata da utilização dos bancos de dados. O segundo bloco tem questões sobre a evolução e análise de esquemas. Por fim, o terceiro bloco de perguntas caracteriza o entrevistado.

O questionário foi disponibilizado por meio da internet (https://pt.surveymonkey.com/s/LHTY3DC), e pessoas da comunidade de Engenharia de Software foram convidadas a respondê-lo. Foi obtida uma amostra de 270 respostas.

Os resultados indicaram que o SGBD *Microsoft SQL Server* é o Sistema Gerenciador de Banco de Dados mais utilizado entre as empresas pesquisadas. Além disso, a grande maioriadas empresas realiza controle de mudanças (87,32%), principalmente de forma manual (44,78%), mas não realizam a análise de impacto causada pelas mudanças de esquemas (72,36%).

O restante do trabalho está estruturado como segue. A Seção2 apresenta os trabalhos relacionados. Na Seção3, é abordado desde o objetivo do *survey*, passando pela seleção de participantes, instrumentação e operação, até a análise e interpretação dos resultados colhidos. Por fim, a Seção4 apresenta as conclusões que puderam ser extraídas desse estudo, bem como sugestões de possíveis trabalhos futuros.

2 TRABALHOS RELACIONADOS

Não foram encontrados *surveys* científicos com o mesmo objeto de pesquisa deste artigo, inclusive tratando da utilização de SGBDs no Brasil. Este fato aumenta a importância dos dados aqui apresentados. Além disso, nosso trabalho difere de grande parte dos *surveys* apresentados na área de computação, pois possui uma amostra relativamente maior, considerando profissionais entrevistados, e por ter uma amostragem probabilística, a qual pode ser representativa da população de interesse. A seguir, alguns trabalhos moderadamente relacionados.

Li [7] apresentou um *survey* sobre evolução de esquemas de bancos de dados orientados a objetos. Houve uma avaliação e vistoria de alguns artigos sobre a evolução de esquemas de bancos de dados em geral, além de uma série de trabalhos de pesquisa e algumas teses de doutorado dedicadas a várias questões relacionadas com a evolução de esquemas. Nas conclusões, foi destacada que a evolução de esquemas para bancos de dados orientados a objetos surgiu como uma área de investigação séria. Além disso, as constantes mudanças do mundo real envolvem a evolução de bancos de dados em todos os aspectos, com ênfase para integridade semântica, capacidade de evolução do esquema e compatibilidade de aplicativos.

Curino [5] propõe um projeto que procura desenvolver métodos e ferramentas para automatizar o processo de evolução de esquemas de dados. Para atingir este objetivo, os autores criaram o sistema PRISM, o qual fornece uma linguagem de Operadores de Modificação de Esquema (*Schema Modification Operators* - SMO), para expressar de forma concisa as mudanças de esquema, bem como ferramentas para avaliar os efeitos de tais mudanças. O objetivo é que os administradores de banco de dados utilizem a nova linguagem para especificar as alterações do novo esquema e, em seguida, façam uso do PRISM para (i) prever e avaliar os efeitos de alterações de esquema, (ii) reescrever consultas antigas, realizar atualizações on-line e adaptar os aplicativos para trabalhar com a nova versão do esquema, (iii) migrar os dados e (iv) documentar todas as mudanças realizadas.

Karahasanovic [6] apresentou uma ferramenta de visualização para análise de impacto de evolução de esquema de dados em aplicações orientadas a objetos. A ferramenta *Schema Evolution Management Tool* (SEMT) recebe como entrada arquivos de código Java e de banco de dados, e, em seguida, identifica as relações entre os componentes (pacotes, classes, interfaces, métodos e campos), os quais são exibidos como um gráfico. Os autores realizaram um experimento controlado com estudantes para avaliar a ferramenta em relação à produtividade e satisfação do usuário. Os resultados indicaram que identificar os impactos na granularidade mais fina reduz o tempo e os erros cometidos para realizar as mudanças de esquema, e, além disso, os usuários aprovaram a ideia de visualização dos impactos.

Estes trabalhos instigam a investigação de como empresas brasileiras estão tratando este assunto e se as ferramentas existentes estão sendo utilizadas. Além disso, estimulam a criação de hipóteses sobre a necessidade de novas ferramentas para este fim. A seção seguinte apresenta, detalhadamente, os passos referentes à realização do *survey*.

3 SURVEY

Esta seção apresenta todas as etapas referentes à realização da pesquisa de campo (*survey*), desde seu objetivo, passando pela seleção de participantes, instrumentação, operação, até a análise e interpretação das respostas coletadas.

3.1 Objetivo

O objetivo geral deste *survey* é mapear a utilização de bancos de dados e o tratamento dado à evolução de seus esquemas, em empresas brasileiras. Este objetivo é formalizado usando parte do modelo GQM proposto por Basili e Weiss [3], como apresentado por Van Solingen e Berghout [14]: **Analisar** a utilização de Bancos de Dados Relacionais, **com o propósito de** caracterizar, **com respeito à** utilização de técnicas de análise de impacto de evolução de esquemas de dados, **do ponto de vista** de desenvolvedores de software, administradores de dados e bancos de dados, **no contexto de** empresas que utilizam SGBDs relacionais no Brasil. Baseado nesse objetivo, foram formuladas as seguintes questões de pesquisa:

RQ1. Qual o SGBD mais usado entre as empresas?

RQ2. Qual a frequência de mudança nos esquemas de banco de dados?

RQ3. Como é realizado o controle de mudanças nos esquemas de banco de dados?

RQ4. Como é feita a análise de impacto das mudanças nos esquemas de banco de dados?

Essas questões de pesquisa foram utilizadas para derivar as perguntas do questionário, analisadas nas próximas seções.

3.2 Planejamento

Formulação de Hipótese

Para avaliar as questões de pesquisa, serão utilizadas métricas baseadas em frequências, perfazendo o número de respostas por SGBD (RQ1), por quantidade de mudanças ao ano (RQ2), por tipo de controle (RQ3) e por forma de analisar o impacto de mudanças (RQ4).

Tendo o objetivo e métricas definidas, será ainda considerada a hipótese de que a há uma relação entre a falta de controle das mudanças de banco de dados ou o uso de uma ferramenta de controle não especialista com a falta de análise de impacto de mudanças. Desta forma, a hipótese que queremos testar é:

HIPÓTESE

H0: Empresas analisam impacto de mudanças independente do tipo de controle que fazem.

H1:A análise de impacto depende do tipo de controle exercido.

Seleção de Participantes e Cálculo do Tamanho da Amostra

A amostragem será aleatória simples, porém, considerando uma estratificação de profissionais de TI com envolvimento com esquemas de dados, presentes em listas de discussões nacionais e grupos vinculados a profissionais de tecnologia. Como exemplos, listas de discussão e profissionais identificados associados à Sociedade Brasileira de Computação e à DAMA *(Data Management Association)* Brasil. Também foram usados grupos profissionais nacionais de Engenharia de Software da rede social Linkedin, na qual é possível identificar e confirmar a existência da maioria dos profissionais.

Desta forma, buscou-se estabelecer uma amostra que se identificasse com o universo, preservando as mesmas características de interesse presentes na população.

Apesar da representatividade da nossa amostra só dizer respeito aos profissionais presentes nas listas de discussão selecionadas, calculamos o tamanho da amostra, levando em consideração o número estimado de profissionais de Tecnologia da Informação do Brasil: 1.300.000 profissionais [4]. Isso envolve inclusive profissionais que não interessam a essa pesquisa. Contudo, se considerarmos a presença de profissionais de todos os estados nas redes sociais, uma amostra com tamanho mínimo estimado, baseado na população de profissionais do Brasil, aumenta a confiabilidade na tendência dos dados. Além disso, este número será mais que suficiente para representar estatisticamente a população total presente nas listas selecionadas.

O cálculo foi realizado utilizando a Ferramenta SPSS – IBM [12] e considerando proporções, isto é, percentual da população em relação ao que está sendo avaliado. Como a variância não é conhecida, estima-se a maior variância possível numa proporção de 50% que são favoráveis ao que está sendo avaliado (1/2) e 50% (1/2) desfavoráveis. Logo, 0,5 x 0,5 = 0,25 (variância usada no cálculo) [8]. Também foi considerado um nível de significância de 0,05, perfazendo um índice de confiabilidade de 95% e uma margem de erro de 6%. A margem de erro de uma pesquisa aumenta à medida que a população diminui. Alargamos os limites, considerando e esperando amostras pequenas, encontradas em trabalhos relacionados, na área de Engenharia de Software. Finalmente, se forem feitas 100 pesquisas para o mesmo fim e com a mesma metodologia, em 95 delas os resultados estariam dentro da margem de erro utilizada. O valor calculado foi de 267 participantes, o qual foi estabelecido como meta para o nosso *survey*.

Metodologia

Foi projetada a execução de um piloto com profissionais, Engenheiros de Software, os quais tivessem uma relação direta com modelos de dados e bancos de dados, na realização das suas tarefas diárias.

A amostra para o piloto deve ser menor, com fins de identificar possíveis problemas e inconsistências nas perguntas. Esse pré-teste é necessário e visa melhorar o instrumento da pesquisa, sendo executado da mesma forma como será aplicado. A seleção de quem irá participar do pré-teste é flexível, entretanto, recomenda-se que as pessoas sejam razoavelmente adequadas para as perguntas [2].

Para que fosse garantida uma presença de respostas de diversos estados brasileiros, projetou-se distribuir o tamanho da amostra pelas regiões do Brasil. Para que o número pudesse ser dividido por 5 regiões, o tamanho da amostra foi arredondado para 270 (54 por região). Desta forma, apesar de, provavelmente, existirem regiões que atendam melhor ao apelo de responder ao survey, existiu a meta perseguida de conseguir respostas de empresas de todas as regiões. Além disto, respostas vindas da mesma empresa foram filtradas e selecionada a mais completa, perfazendo uma resposta para cada empresa que contribuiu.

Alguns cuidados adicionais foram tomados, devido à pesquisa ser feita pela internet [1]: o tempo gasto pelo respondente não deve ser superior a 10 minutos; o tempo de navegação entre uma página e outra não deve ultrapassar oito segundos; linguagem clara e abertura em qualquer *browser*.

Por fim, foi garantida a aleatoriedade, pois todos os profissionais presentes nas listas usadas tiveram a mesma chance de responder ao questionário. Isto foi garantido por meio dede sorteio para os convites, sem a conveniência de alguma disponibilidade especial de profissionais e sem escolha de profissionais específicos.

Instrumentação

O questionário (https://pt.surveymonkey.com/s/LHTY3DC) foi desenvolvido na ferramenta especialista *SurveyMonkey* [13] e distribuído por meio da internet. Contém uma apresentação inicial, em seguida as perguntas referentes à utilização de Banco de Dados e o tratamento dado à Evolução de seus Esquemas e, por fim, a última etapa, na qual é feita a caracterização do entrevistado e da empresa.

3.3 Operação

Aplicação

Nesta etapa, acontece a efetiva realização da pesquisa. Tudo que foi planejado nas etapas anteriores passa agora a concretizar-se.

Inicialmente, um piloto do questionário foi aplicado a 10 profissionais definidos na metodologia e selecionados por julgamento, os quais não participaram do *survey*, mas contribuíram para modificações, tornando o questionário mais claro e objetivo.

Em seguida, foram elencados os profissionais das listas e, utilizando uma tabela de números aleatórios, foram sorteados e convidados 270 profissionais, considerando o tamanho mínimo da amostra, calculado em 267, e considerando um percentual uniforme para cada região. Quando um convidado declinava da resposta, era sorteado e convidado outro. Após dois meses de convites e disponibilidade do *survey*, entre janeiro e fevereiro de 2015, foram contabilizadas 270 respostas, 244 sem nenhuma questão em branco.

Coleta e Validação de Dados

Mesmo tendo sido utilizado uma ferramenta especialista para a construção de *surveys*, foi verificado se os resultados eram realmente coerentes com os apontados pela mesma, assim como o total de respostas. Além disso, como formas de validação, foram averiguados os e-mails dos participantes, os estados a que eles pertenciam, bem como confirmada a existência da empresa apontada.

3.4 Análise e Interpretação dos Dados

Resultados Brutos

Foram elaboradas 8 questões para identificar o perfil dos entrevistados. Quanto à posição que os entrevistados ocupam nas empresas (vide Figura1), tivemos em primeiro lugar o cargo de Analista (32,79%), seguidos de Programadores (19,67%), DBAs (19,26%), Gerentes (14,75%), Administradores de Dados (2,87%), além daqueles que ocupam mais de um cargo ou mesmo outra posição (10,66%). O baixo número de Administradores de Dados encontrados pode indicar uma negligência brasileira com uma importante função, responsável pela qualidade dos modelos de dados corporativos.

A Figura 2 aponta o nível de formação que os entrevistados possuem.

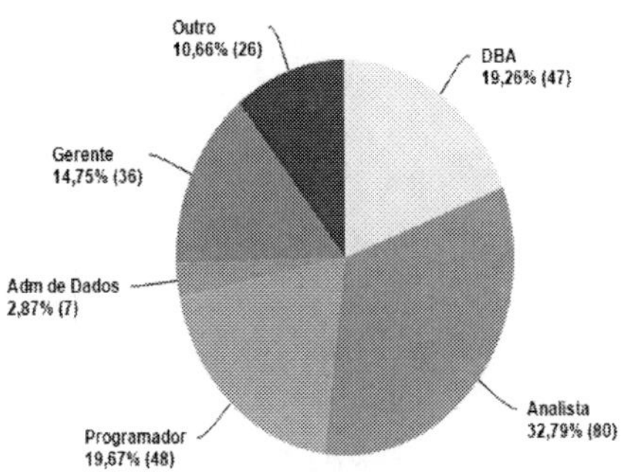

Fig. 1. Posição dos entrevistados

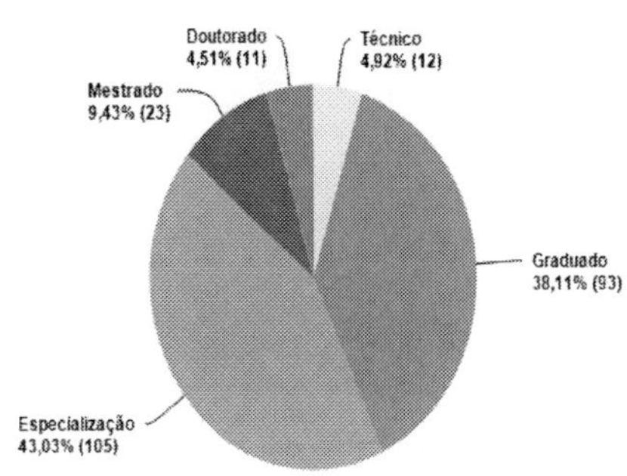

Fig. 2. Nível de formação

A maioria numérica entrevistada possui mais de 10 anos de experiência (30,34%), fato importante para confiabilidade e propriedade das respostas. Apenas 10,66% possuem até 3 anos.A Figura3mostra as demais distribuições.

Com relação à caracterização das empresas, 53,09% dos entrevistados trabalham em empresas de Tecnologia da Informação. 47,33% são empresas com mais de 250 funcionários, 20,58% possuem entre 10 e 49, 19,24% de 50 a 249, e apenas 12,79% de 1 a 9 fucionários. Leia-se, empresas grandes, pequenas, médias e micro, respectivamente.As empresas do setor Privado aparecem em 68,31% das respostas, assim como mostra a Figura 4.

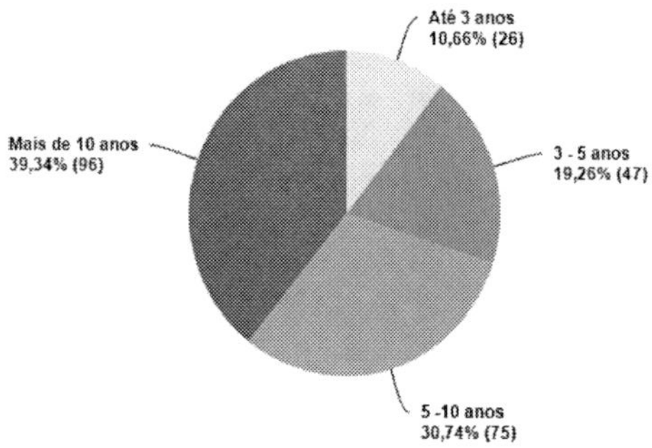

Fig. 3. Experiência dos entrevistados

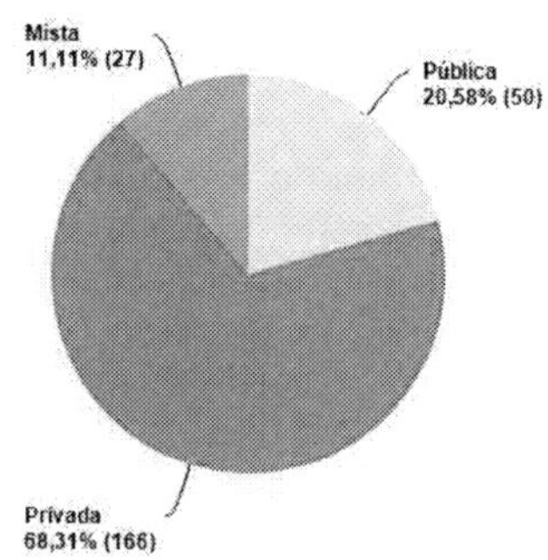

Fig. 4. Tipo das empresas.

Para responder à questão de pesquisa 1 (RQ1), foi elaborada uma questão que averiguou a a utilização de Sistemas Gerenciadores de Banco de Dados (SGBDs). Neste contexto, percebe-se a liderança do *Microsoft SQL Server* (62,08%), seguido pelo *Oracle* (43,12%), *MySQL* (34,20%), *PostgreSQL* (29,74%), além de outros. Alguns entrevistados apontaram a utilização de mais de uma opção. A Figura 5 aponta os demais dados. Se considerarmos a margem de erro de 6%, o MySQL pode ocupar o segundo lugar, bem como o PostgreSQL a terceira posição.O primeiro e segundo colocados ficaram alinhados com o *2015 Gartner Magic Quadrant for Operational Database Management Systems* [16], divulgado em outubro de 2015.

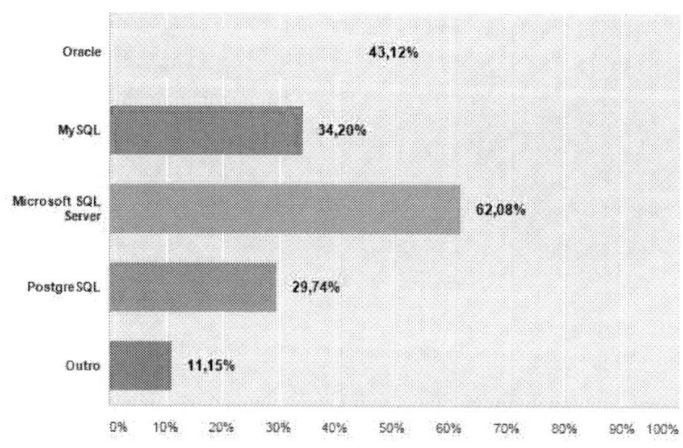

Fig. 5. Utilização dos SGBDs

Análises dos Resultados

Os dados que foram recolhidos e analisados serão apresentados a seguir, juntamente com comparações e observações, em exibições gráficas apropriadas para a melhor compreensão.

Ainda sobre a questão de pesquisa 1 (RQ1), como apresentado anteriormente, 62,08% da amostra utilizam Microsoft SQL Server, logo, foi possível perceber claramente que a maioria provém de empresas privadas e com mais de 250 funcionários, como é possível perceber nas Figuras 6 e 7, que descrevem a distribuição de usuários por tipo de empresa e por quantidade de funcionários, respectivamente.

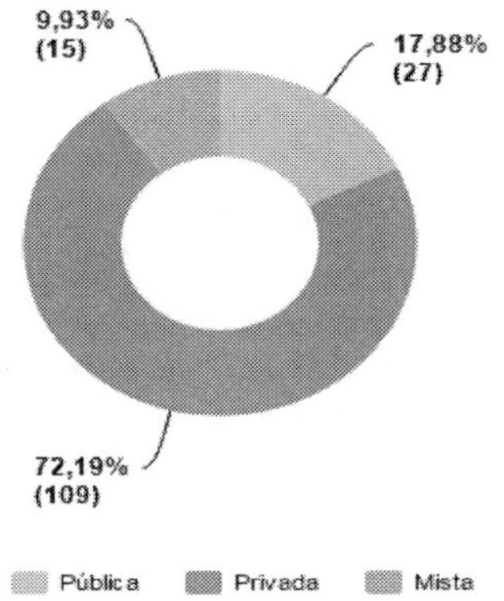

Fig. 6. Usuários do Microsoft SQL Server por Tipo de Empresa

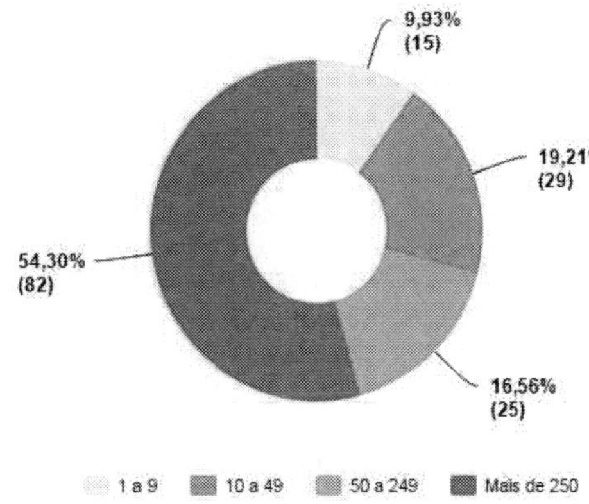

Fig. 7. Usuários do Microsoft SQL Server por Quantidade de Funcionários

Para uma melhor caracterização, foi feito um cruzamento da posição do entrevistado com a sua experiência. As Figuras 8 e 9 apresentam esta relação. Percebe-se, na primeira Figura, que aqueles com mais de 10 anos de experência ocupam o cargo de Gerente, já aqueles com até 3 anos são, em sua maioria, programadores. Este é um fato interessante, desde que isto não seja refletido no salário. No Brasil, é necessário se tornar um Gerente para obtenção de um salário maior[3]. Em muitos casos, perde-se um grande Analista ou Programador e ganha-se um péssimo Gerente.

A segunda Figura aponta que aqueles com maior número de sistemas mantidos são DBAs ou Gerentes.

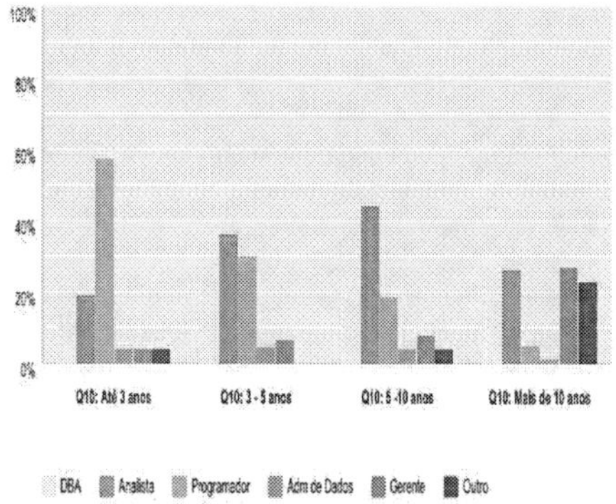

Fig. 8. Posição x Experiência

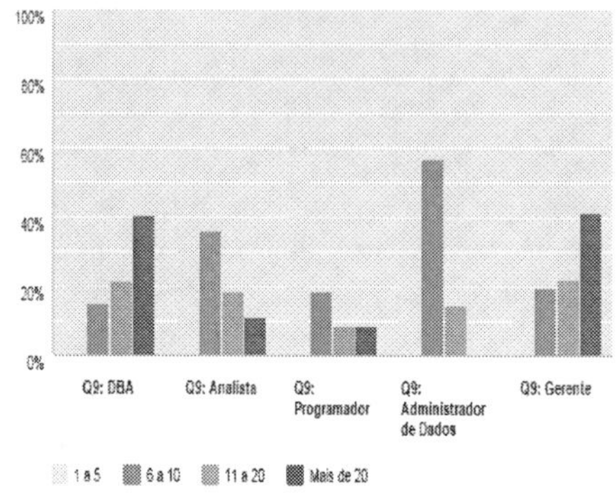

Fig. 9. Posição x Experiência (Número de Sistemas)

Para responder à questão de pesquisa 2 (RQ2), foram elaboradas 2 perguntas. 78,73% das respostas apontam que existem bases de dados sendo utilizadas por mais de um esquema. 68,27% dizem que existe controle de mudanças nos esquemas entre os ambientes de homologação, produção e desenvolvimento.

A frequência de mudanças que ocorrem nos esquemas de dados foi considerada Alta (Mais de 6 mudanças ao ano) por 41,37% dos entrevistados, Média (3 a 6 mudanças ao ano) por 24,90% e Baixa (0 a 2 mudanças ao ano) pelos demais 33,73%. A frequência de mudanças alta evidencia a necessidade de controle e análise de impacto.Isto é feito? Esta pergunta foi dividida nas questões de pesquisa 3 e 4, respondidas a seguir.

Para responder à questão de pesquisa 3 (RQ3), foram elaboradas 3perguntas. A Figura 10 apresenta os dados levantados sobre como é realizado o controle de mudanças nos esquemas de Banco de Dados. A maioria dos entrevistados divide-se entre as opções: Manualmente (44,78%) e Utilizando Ferramenta (40,30%). Concluindo, assim, que a grande maioria (87,32%) realiza o controle de mudanças.

A classe de ferramenta mais utilizada para o controle dessas mudanças é o Sistema de Controle de Versão (CVS, Subversion, etc.) (35,07%), seguida de Ferramentas Específicas para Evolução em Esquemas (18,28%). Como mostra a Figura 11.

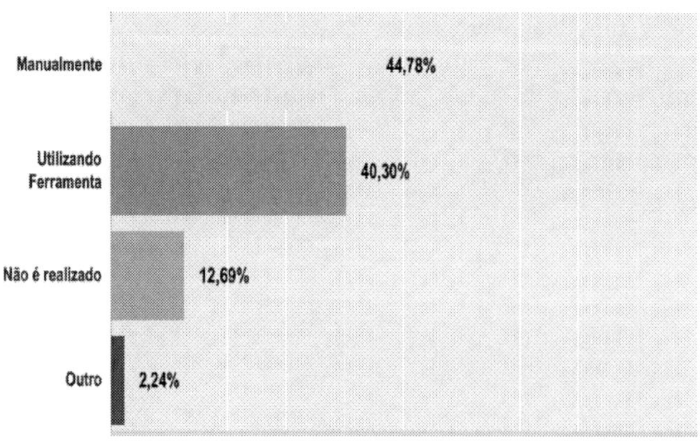

Fig. 10. Controle de mudanças

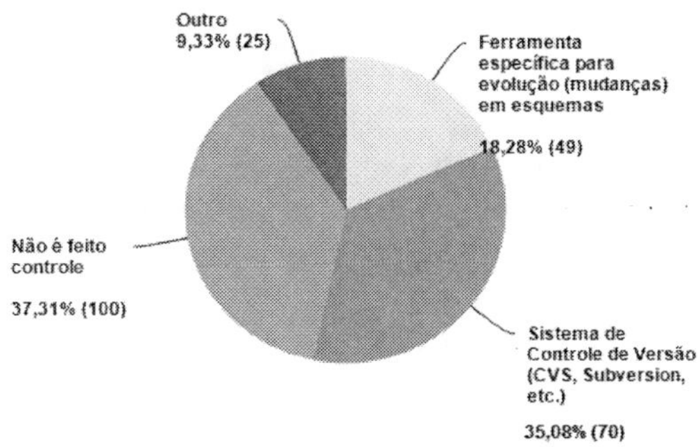

Fig. 11. Ferramenta utilizada para controle de mudança

Para responder à questão de pesquisa 4 (RQ4) e também ser possível o teste da hipótese apresentada no planejamento, foram elaboradas 2 perguntas. O percentual das empresas que afirmam fazer análise de impacto possui uma relação direta com o modo como é realizado o controle de mudanças. As empresas que não fazem controle de mudança (37,31%), juntamente com as empresas que fazem utilizando Sistemas de Controle de Versão (35,08 %), somam 72,38 % (vide Figura 11), percentual associado às empresas que afirmam não fazer análise de impacto (72,36 %) (vide Figura 13).

Para averiguar essa associação, também utilizando o SPSS [12], testamos a independência das variáveis, por meio de uma medida global chamada de χ^2 de Pearson (Qui-quadrado de Pearson) [10]. Este teste é apropriado para apoiar a análise de variáveis qualitativas, quando se deseja comparar as distribuições de frequências obtidas contra as frequências esperadas. Uma hipótese nula é levantada e testada: "as variáveis são independentes" (vide H0, no planejamento). Caso sejam encontradas diferenças significativas, então se deve rejeitar a hipótese nula em favor da hipótese alternativa: "as variáveis não são independentes" (vide H1, no planejamento), com um nível de significância tabelado.

Para este estudo, a rejeição da hipótese nula (H0), a um nível de significância de 0,05, representará que há evidências estatísticas de que as empresas que não controlam mudanças ou usam CVS não fazem análise de impacto. As frequências das respostas foram utilizadas como entrada para o teste. O resultado revelou o valor de 4,46 para χ^2, para 1 grau de liberdade e com um *p-value* entre 0,05 e 0,025, abaixo do nível de significância adotado, concluindo-se que devemos rejeitar a hipótese nula. Ou seja, há uma associação entre as variáveis.

É possível abstrair uma justificativa, para o fato de a maioria das empresas que utiliza Sistemas de Controle de Versão, no controle das mudanças, não faz análise de impacto. O simples histórico de mudanças, encontrado nos Sistemas de Controle de Versão, é insuficiente para rastrear impactos em sistemas ou em seus artefatos, causados pela evolução de esquemas.

Ainda neste contexto, 70,65% daqueles que realizam o controle de mudanças, com Sistema de Controle de Versões (CVS), e 84,44% dos que não realizam controle afirmam que não é realizado análise de impacto nas mudanças causadas pela evolução de esquemas. Na Figura 12, a primeira barra, parte azul, representa o percentual (70,65%) de empresas que **não** realizam análise de impacto, mas fazem controle de mudanças usando algum tipo de CVS. Na segunda barra, a parte azul representa o percentual (84,44%) de empresas que **não** realizam controle de mudanças e nem tão pouco fazem análise de impacto.

Aqueles que afirmaram realizar a análise de impacto de mudançasforam perguntados sobre qual ferramenta utilizam. Foram citados nomes como: Infosphere Data Architect e Jazz, para Controle de Versão; PL SQL Developer; Power Designer; Linkbase; Toad Data Analysts e o Data Modeler; Enterprise Data Archtect; Ferramenta CASE System Architect; SqlQUeryStress e Extended Events; SQLImpacte e SQLyog.

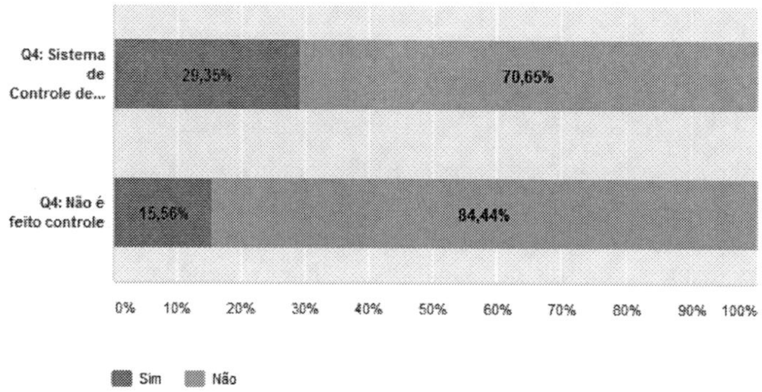

Fig. 12. Realização da Análise de Impacto (S ou N) por aqueles que realizam controle de mudanças, com Sistema de Controle de Versões, e pelos que não realizam o controle.

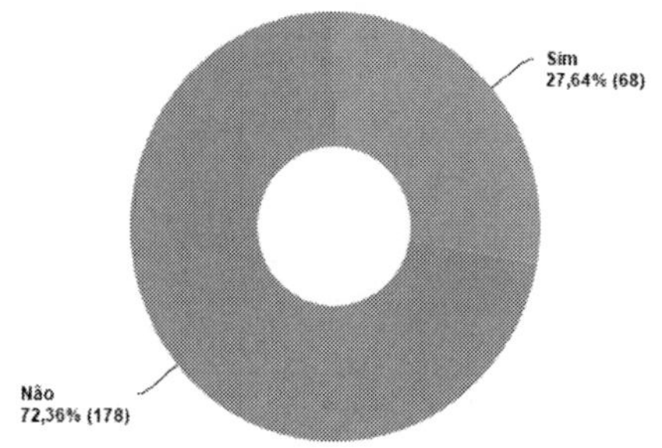

Fig. 13. Análise de Impacto na Evolução de Esquemas

Ainda com relação às empresas que afirmam fazer análise de impacto, existem fortes indícios que, desse percentual, uma parcela não faça efetivamente análise de impacto. Essa observação pode ser retirada da análise das ferramentas apontadas. Em sua maioria, as ferramentas apontadas não possuem características que permitam fazer a análise de impacto a partir de mudanças de esquemas, embora quase todas elas possam verificar mudanças entre *baselines*.

Finalmente, apesar da frequência de mudanças alta evidenciar necessidade de análises, destacamos mais uma vez que 72,36% não analisam o impacto dessas mudanças (vide Figura 13), dado relevante, levando em consideração a importância apresentada quanto à realização dessa análise.

Ameaças à Validade

Diferentes problemas podem ser ocasionados durante a participação dos indivíduos no questionário:

- Instrumentação adequadamente preparada **(validade interna)**: Os participantes responderam ao questionário sem nenhuma supervisão, assim, há a probabilidade dos mesmos não terem entendido uma questão específica. Para mitigar esse tipo de problema, um piloto foi realizado.
- População representativa **(validade externa)**: A variedade dos participantes que responderam ao questionário foi significativa, contudo, podem existir tipos de profissionais que não participam de grupos de discussão em redes sociais.
- Distribuição do conjunto de participantes **(validade de conclusão)**: A experiência dos profissionais ou as funções podem afetar os resultados, entretanto, tanto os mais experientes quanto os cargos de maior interesse ocupados pelos participantes do questionário estão distribuídos.

4 CONCLUSÃO E TRABALHOS FUTUROS

Este trabalho apresentou resultados de um levantamento quantitativo que pode ser usado por gestores de empresas para a tomada de decisão, bem como por pesquisadores da área para direcionar suas pesquisas de acordo com a demanda observada. Foi constatado que 62,08% utilizam o SGBD Microsoft SQL Server, seguido pela Oracle (43,12%), e que 87,32% realizam controle de mudanças, principalmente de forma manual (44,78%), mas 72,36 % não realizam a análise de impacto causada pelas mudanças de esquemas. Fatores que podem ser considerados decisivos para a consistência entre o esquema, o banco de dados e as aplicações. A ausência da avaliação de impacto gera resistência para realização de mudanças nos esquemas. Isso é provocado principalmente pela falta de estimativas sobre recursos, custos e cronogramas para execução dessas mudanças.

A principal barreira vencida neste trabalho foi a difícil tarefa da aplicação de uma pesquisa de campo (*survey*), levando em consideração a preocupação constante com a veracidade nas respostas dadas pelos participantes. Se compararmos o tamanho da amostra aqui apresentada, validações de origem e análises estatísticas, com outros trabalhos relacionados da área de Tecnologia da Informação, apresentamos uma confiabilidade acima da média, para a representatividade dos dados.

Como trabalhos futuros, sugere-se a validação de algumas informações acerca dos motivos para a falta de gerenciamento das mudanças em esquemas e análise de seus impactos no ambiente de Engenharia de Software, por meio do desenvolvimento ou adaptação de ferramentas, validando-as em estudos de casos reais e experimentos na indústria. Destaca-se, também, a necessidade de ampliar pesquisas de campo na área, com o objetivo de encontrar lacunas como as aqui identificadas.

Esta pesquisa científica não garante nenhum produto aqui listado, bem como não afirma que outros produtos não possam atender a necessidades semelhantes, considerando contextos específicos.

Por fim, está em fase de desenvolvimento uma ferramenta para detecção e análise de impacto na evolução de esquemas de dados em SGBDs relacionais. A ferramenta identificará, nos códigos das aplicações, possíveis impactos em função da evolução de esquemas. Esta adota uma abordagem baseada em cadastro de metadados. Todo e qualquer artefato, ao ser produzido, poderá ser vinculado a elementos de um esquema de dados, sejam eles um esquema, uma tabela, um atributo, um índice ou uma restrição. Uma vez vinculados, comparações entre *baselines* de esquemas podem identificar as mudanças que ocorreram e selecionar os artefatos diretamente ou indiretamente afetados pelas mudanças.

Referências

1. Aaker, D. A., Kumar, V. and Day, G. S. (2001). Pesquisa de Marketing. 1. ed. São Paulo: Atlas
2. Babbie, E. (1999). Métodos de Pesquisas de Survey Tradução Guilherme Cezarino. Belo Horizonte: Ed. UFMG, 519 p.
3. Basili, V. and Weiss, D. (1984). A Methodology for Collecting Valid Software Engineering Data. In: *IEEE Transactionson Software Engineering*. vol.10(3): 728-738. November.
4. BRASSCOM. (2014). O Mercado de Profissionais de TI no Brasil. http://www.brasscom.org.br/.
5. Curino, C., Moon, H. J. and Zaniolo, C. (2009). Automating Database Schema Evolution in Information System Upgrades. In: *HotSWUp*, pp. 1-5.
6. Karahasanovic, A. and Sjøberg, D.I.K. (2001). Visualizing Impacts of Database Schema Changes -- A Controlled Experiment. *Proceedings of the IEEE Symposium on Visual/Multimedia Approaches to Programming and SE.,* (pp. 358-365) Stresa, Italy.
7. Li, X. (2012). A Survey of Schema Evolution in Object-Oriented Databases. School of Information Systems, Technology and Management. Sydney, Australia.
8. Mcdaniel, C. and Gates, R. (2003). Pesquisa de Marketing. São Paulo, Pioneira Thomson Learning.
9. Papastefanatos, G., Vassiliadis, P., Anagnostou, F. and Vassiliou, Y. (2007). Hecataeus: A What-IfAnalysis Tool for Database Schema Evolution. *In 9th International* DaWaK, Regensburg, Germany, 3-7 September, 2007, LNCS 4654, pp. 23–33.
10. Plackett, R. L. (1983). Karl Pearson and the Chi-Squared Test. International Statistical Review (International Statistical Institute (ISI)).
11. Sjoberg, D (1993). Quantifying Schema Evolution. *Information and Software Technology*, vol. 35, no. 1, pp. 35-44.
12. SPSS. (2014). IBM software. http://goo.gl/eXfcT3.
13. SurveyMonkey (2014). https://pt.surveymonkey.com/.
14. Van, S. R and Berghout, E. (1999). The Goal/Question /Metric Method: A practical guide for quality improvement of software development. Mc Graw-Hill.
15. Zaniolo, C., Ceri, S., Faloutsos, C., Snodgrass, R. T., Subrahmanian, V., Zicari, R. (1997). Advanced Database Systems. Morgan Kaufmann Publishers Inc., San Francisco, California, Chapter 17, pp. 437-438.
16. Magic Quadrant for Operational Database Management Systems (2015). https://www.gartner.com/doc/3147919/magic-quadrant-operational-database-management/.

This page intentionally left blank.

Track3: Workshop on Requirements Engineering (WER 2016) Preface

Welcome to the 19th edition of the Workshop on Requirements Engineering (WER 2016), held in Quito, Ecuador from April 27th to 29th as a track of CIbSE 2016.

WER is the main Ibero-American research event on requirements engineering. The 2016 edition continues the tradition, started in 1998, of gathering the Ibero-American community on this area for discussing the most recent research advances and new research lines and for further trying jointly to tackle requirements engineering challenges and research problems.

The international program committee of WER 2016 consisted of 43 experts from academia and industry from 16 countries. We received 46 abstract submissions, which were finally materialized in 29 valid submissions from seven different countries. Each paper was reviewed by three members of the program committee and, after some online discussions, 15 papers were accepted for presentation at the Workshop, 12 as full papers and 3 as short papers. The accepted papers deal with reviews of the state of the art, requirements engineering in practice, knowledge-based approaches, goal modeling, and processes and requirements, among other topics. WER 2016 consists of four sessions for paper presentation.

We would like to thank the authors of the submitted papers, the members of the program committee, and the additional reviewers for their invaluable contribution towards realizing WER 2016, the rest of members of the CIbSE 2016 organization committees for their constant support, Universidad de las Fuerzas Armadas ESPE for hosting the Workshop, and the rest of sponsors for financially supporting the Work-shop.

Last but not least, we hope that you enjoy WER 2016.

Lidia López and Eduardo Kinder Almentero
WER 2016 PC co-chairs

Program Committee

Aiko Yamashita, Mesan y Simula Research Laboratory, Noruega
Alejandro Oliveros, Universidad de Tres de Febrero, Argentina
Alejandro Maté, Universidad de Alicante, España
Alicia Martínez, Centro Nacional de Investigación y Desarrollo Tecnológico, México
Amador Durán Toro, Universidad de Sevilla, España
André Leal, Universidade Federal Rural do Rio de Janeiro, Brasil
Antonio Oliveira, Universidade do Estado do Rio de Janeiro, Brasil
Carla Silva, Universidade Federal de Pernambuco, Brasil
Carlos Cares, Universitat de La Frontera, Chile
Carme Quer, Universitat Politècnica de Catalunya, España
Clara Ayora, Universidad Politécnica de Valencia, España
Cristina Palomares, Universitat Politècnica de Catalunya, España
Daniel Berry, University of Waterloo, Canadá
Daniel Méndez Fernández, Technische Universität München, Alemania
Dolors Costal, Universitat Politècnica de Catalunya, España
Fernanda Alencar, Universidade Federal de Pernambuco, Brasil
Giovanni Giachetti, Universidad Diego Costales, Chile
Gladys Maquera, Universidad Peruana Unión, Perú
Gladys Kaplan, Universidad Nacional de La Matanza, Argentina
Gonzalo Génova, Universidad Carlos III de Madrid, España
Graciela Hadad, Universidad Nacional del Oeste, Argentina
Isabel Brito, Instituto Politécnico de Beja, Portugal
Jaelson Castro, Universidade Federal de Pernambuco, Brasil
José Luis de La Vara, Carlos III University of Madrid, España
Juan Sánchez, Universitat Politècnica de València, España
Judith Barrios, Universidad de los Andes, Venezuela
Juan Pablo Carvallo, Universidad del Azuay, Ecuador
Julio Leite, Pontifícia Universidade Católica do Rio de Janeiro, Brasil
Leandro Antonelli, Facultad de Informática, UNLP, Argentina
Luiz E. G. Martins, Universidade Federal de São Paulo, Brasil
Luiz Marcio Cysneiros, York University, Canadá
Lyrene Silva, Universidade Federal do Rio Grande do Norte, Brasil
Marcela Ridao, Universidad Nacional del Centro de la Provincia de Buenos Aires, Argentina
Marcela Ruiz, Centro de Investigación de Métodos de Producción de Software, España
Márcia Lucena, Universidade Federal do Rio Grande do Norte, Brasil
Maria Lencastre, Universidade de Pernambuco, Brasil
Nathalie Aquino, Universidad Católica Nuestra Señora de la Asunción, Paraguay
Nelly Condori-Fernández, Vrije Universiteit Amsterdam, Paises Bajos
Oscar Pastor, Universitat Politècnica de València, España
Raúl Mazo, Université Paris 1 Panthéon - Sorbonne, Francia
Renata Guizzardi, Universidade Federal do Espírito Santo, Brasil
Sergio España, Utrecht University, Holanda
Uirá Kulesza, Universidade Federal do Rio Grande do Norte, Brasil
Vera Werneck, Universidade do Estado do Rio de Janeiro, Brasil

WER INDEX

Session 1: Goal Oriented Requirements Engineering

Session 2: Requirements Specification

Session 3: Requirements Analysis

Session 4: Literature review and survey

Scalability of iStar: a Systematic Mapping Study

Paulo Lima[1], Jéssyka Vilela[1], Enyo Gonçalves[12], João Pimentel[3], Ana Holanda[14], Jaelson Castro[1], Fernanda Alencar[1], Maria Lencastre[3]

[1]Universidade Federal de Pernambuco (UFPE)
[2]Universidade Federal do Ceará (UFC)
[3]Universidade de Pernambuco (UPE)
[4]Instituto Federal do Acre (IFAC)

{plc2, jffv, ejtg, jhcp, acah, jbc}@cin.ufpe.br
fernanda.ralencar@ufpe.br
mlpm@ecomp.poli.br

Abstract. Since its first proposal in the nineties, the i* framework has been used to requirements specification in many domains, such as healthcare, telecommunication, and air traffic control. After the modeling of different examples and case studies, it has been observed that i* models become dramatically more difficult to understand and analyze as they grow larger. This issue has led us to investigate scalability in the context of the i* framework, by means of a systematic mapping study. A total of 119 papers were analyzed, in order to understand how scalability is perceived by the i* research community, which proposals have considered this topic, and what open issues still need to be addressed. We found that scalability issues are indeed perceived as relevant and that further work is still required, even though many potential solutions have already been proposed. This study can be a starting point for researchers aiming to further advance the treatment of scalability in social goal models.

Keywords: Systematic Mapping study, Scalability, iStar, i*, Goal Models.

1 Introduction

The i* framework is a modeling language used in Requirements Engineering (RE) to develop models that represent requirements actors and systems [1]. Requirements are represented by dependencies of interest, through goals, softgoals, resources and tasks. The i* language has been used in several situations [1], such as telecommunications, air traffic control, agriculture, e-government, healthcare and business process.

Unfortunately, i* is not suitable for modelling complex cases or involving many parts [3]. The limitation in scaling i* is identified as one of their biggest barriers for industrial adoption [1] [3]. If i* could make possible a good modelling of large and complex cases, there would be greater adoption of i*. Therefore, the i* framework requires solutions and means to address its scalability [2] [3].

This paper aims to map the studies that addressed i* scalability issue. In order to meet our goal, we conducted a systematic mapping study to identify the primary studies on the scalability of i*, following a predefined review protocol. We identified 119 papers about i* scalability and analyzed the distribution of these studies, definitions, mentions for artifacts to address it; how the researchers community perceive the i* ability to scale and, if there are open issues related in this theme.

This goal is important to support researchers in the i* community since i* models can become complex and could be difficult to decompose into smaller pieces [3]. The number of papers that mentioned i* scalability (or near attribute) may serves to future systematic reviews. Moreover, the comparisons between approaches to address i* scalability are necessary.

This paper is structure as follows: Section 2 discusses related works, the study design is presented in Section 3, the results related to each research question are reported in Section 4. Section 5 presents the discussion of the results. Section 6 shows the conclusions and future work of this paper.

2 Related Work

The scalability of i* is an issue addressed by many researchers. However, we identified only two secondary studies that synthesize i* and its scalability: [2] outlined published research on i* in general, commenting also the question of scalability, and [3] present many great challenges and i* problems, including scalability notation.

The first work [2] cites some approaches proposed to improve the scalability. This work reviews the approaches adopted by the i* framework and reports their application in various fields. The authors of this paper explained that models need to reflect software in their social characteristics of complex systems. They argue that i* has a scalability limitation. The second work [2] [3] exposed the scalability as one of the great challenges of i*. It argues that scalability and complexity are two characteristics that i* does not support well and proposed a set of concepts to help improve it.

In order to understand the progress that has been made in integrating goal models with downstream system development, [26] conducted a systematic survey to investigate what approaches exist which map/integrate/transform goal-oriented languages to other software artefacts or languages. They produced a roadmap summarizing 174 publications. They also comment the lack of widespread industrial adoption of goal-oriented models that could be attributed to several factors including the scalability and usability challenges in complex models which are not easily decomposable.

Horkoff and Yu [4] use three available tools implementing seven similar analysis procedures for goal satisfaction to analyze three sample goal models. They performed a comparison to understand the ways in which procedural design choices affect analysis results, and how differences in analysis results could lead to different recommendations over alternatives in the model.

After analyzing these studies, we can notice that scalability is a desirable quality. However, this question is addressed in a broad sense and it becomes difficult to categorize possible evidence since it not possible to replicate those results. Therefore, it is necessary to know all the works published more systematic way. Accordingly, our work presents the results of systematic mapping study conducted to investigate the scalability of i*. We analyzed the distribution of these studies, definitions, mentions for artifacts to address it; how the researchers community perceive the i* ability to scale and, if there are open issues related in this theme. In the next section, we describe our research protocol.

3 STUDY DESIGN

The purpose of this paper is to map the studies that addressed i* scalability. Being a systematic mapping, it provides a summary of evidence related to the topic, by applying explicit methods and systematic search, critical appraisal and synthesis of selected information [6].

We conducted this systematic mapping study following the guidelines of Kitchenham and Charters [5], while also observing the methodology of other systematic mappings that were recently published in well-known software engineering journals, such as the Journal of Systems and Software, the Empirical Software Engineering journal and the Requirements Engineering journal. From these mappings we obtained insight on creating search queries and on defining inclusion and exclusion criteria.

This research was performed with the following steps: (1) identification of the need for a systematic mapping; (2) formulation of focused research questions; (3) the comprehensive, exhaustive search for primary studies; (4) identification of the data needed to answer the research questions; (5) data extraction; (6) summary and synthesis of study results; (7) interpretation of the results to determine their applicability; and (8) report writing.

The study design described in this section was validated by experienced researchers and adjusted accordingly prior to its execution.

3.1 RESEARCH QUESTIONS

This paper aims to answer the following research questions:

- RQ1: What studies mention the issue of i* scalability?
- RQ2: Which are the scalability definitions in the context of i*?
- RQ3: Which are the types of contributions that have been published to support the i* scalability?
- RQ4: What is the perceived judgment on the scalability of i*?
- RQ5: Are there open issues?

The first research question (RQ1) focuses on identifying the works that address the scalability of the i*. The second research question (RQ2) relates to the conceptualization of scalability. The third research question (RQ3) quantifies which mechanisms have been proposed in order to handle scalability, such as metamodels, formalization, modelling processes, visual constructors, and algorithms. The fourth research question (RQ4) summarizes published findings on whether the scalability of i* is considered to be satisfactory or not. The fifth research question (RQ5) summarizes evidences about potential open issues mentioned in the selected studies. Therefore, this paper aims to synthesize information about the i* language regarding its scalability.

3.2 EXCLUSION AND INCLUSION CRITERIA

The selected studies were primary publications that present any discussion or study about the scalability of i*. The exclusion and inclusion criteria adopted are presented in Table 1 and Table 2 respectively.

Table 1. Exclusion criteria.

ID	Definition
EC01	Studies not captured by the keywords in search engines.
EC02	Studies published before 1990.
EC03	Unreadable files (files corrupted).
EC04	Studies not written in English.
EC05	Studies that do not mention i* or variants.
EC06	Studies that do not mention scalability (and similar terms) of i* or (variants)
EC07	Non-Scientific studies (notes, index, editorials, prefaces).

Table 2. Inclusion criteria.

ID	Definition
IC01	Studies that were not eliminated by the exclusion criteria.
IC02	Texts published between 01/01/1990 and 31/12/2014.
IC03	Studies that address some of the study questions
IC04	Theoretical or empirical work will be included.

3.3 SOURCES SELECTION AND SEARCH

The search strategy included only electronic databases and was validated by experts on the requirements engineering area. By using a search string, the following electronic repositories were surveyed: Science Direct, ACM Digital Library, IEEE Xplore, Engineering Village, Scielo and World Scientific. Figure 1 shows the number of papers identified at each search engine and the steps taken to select a subset of papers.

We developed the search string by specifying the main terms used about this topic, the derivation form constructors and synonyms arising from the research questions, previously readings from known studies, consulting from experienced researchers in the field and dictionaries or glossaries.

We performed pilot searches to refine the keywords in the search string using trial and error. After some iterations, we settled on the following search string:

("iStar" OR "i-star" OR "i star" OR "Yu, e" OR "Yu e" OR "GRL" OR "Tropos") AND ("goal-oriented" OR "goal-directed" OR "agent-oriented" OR "requirements engineering" OR "software requirements") AND (model OR diagram*) AND (scal* OR modul* OR complex* OR compreh* OR underst* OR evolu* OR large OR huge OR big OR siz* OR enormous OR immense); Publication Year: 1990 – 2014*

The first set of or-clauses refers to i*, some of its variants (GRL and Tropos), or the i* proponent (Eric Yu). The second or-clause refers to its use: goal-oriented approaches, agent-oriented approaches, or requirements approaches. Then, it is made explicit that we are interested in models or diagrams. The last or-clause defines our focal point: scalability and its related attributes, such as modularity, complexity, and size. The time period was limited to from around the i* creation until the beginning of this mapping. Considering that each search engine has their own syntax to perform automatic searches, the above search string had to be adapted to each one of them. All the search string variations used in this study, as well as other details of the mapping, are available at our website[1].

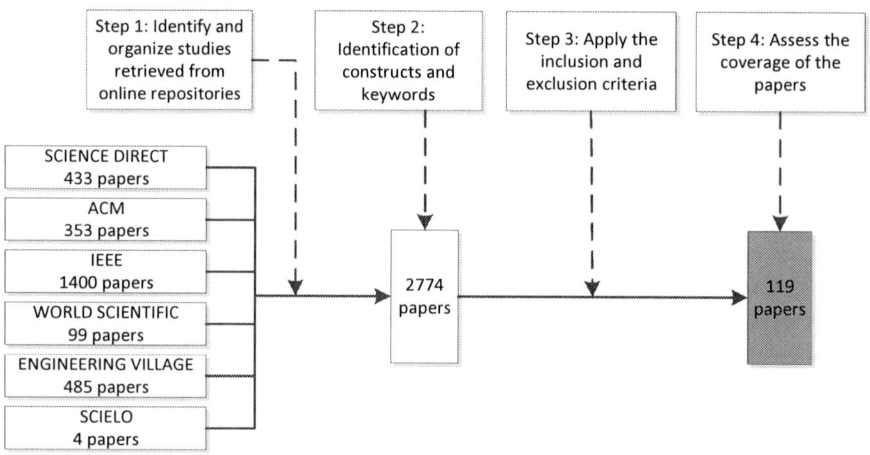

Figure 1. Paper selection.

After applying these steps, a total of 119 studies met the inclusion criteria and their data were extracted. The extraction was performed aiming to answer the research questions described in Section 3.1. The list of selected papers is presented in our website. In the next section, we present the results obtained.

3.4 THREATS TO VALIDITY

This section describes some threats that may be mitigated in future replications of this study and other aspects that must be taken into account when analyzing the re-

[1] www.cin.ufpe.br/~ler/supplement/wer2016

sults described in this paper [8]. We will base our discussion of threats to validity on the categories used by Wohlin et al. [7] but we will only go into details for the categories that we consider important for our study.

Internal validity was enhanced using triangulation in some parts of the method. We consulted experienced researchers to validate the research design and its understanding. Their feedback and the trials contributed to reduce threats.

Threats regarding construct validity required some extra care. This was necessary since the term scalability is an abstract word that has many definitions and the word i* is difficult to insert in the search engines. Hence, to minimize threats of this nature, we discussed synonyms and written alternatives for both terms (for example iStar for i*). We also related potential previous definitions for scalability under the supervision of experienced researchers.

External validity is concerned with establishing the generalizability of the systematic mapping results, which is related to the degree to which the primary studies are representative for the review topic [8]. The external validity (portability, transference) of this study was strengthened by the structure of the extracted data. It was also supported by detailing the research method in order to allow future comparative generalizations.

Regarding the empirical reliability, we tried to run a systematic mapping based on existing guidelines and on similar studies already published and accepted by the academic community.

4 RESULTS

The purpose of this research is to map, in the context of Requirements Engineering, the publications about the i* framework related to its scalability of. In the next sections, we present the answers for our research questions.

4.1 RQ1: What studies mention the issue of i* scalability?

We found 119 studies that mention i* scalability or at least one of its related concepts, such as modularity, complexity, and size. Considering the research types proposed by [9] and also used by [8], we identified that 45 studies can be considered empirical, i.e. they were classified in one the following types: evaluation research, validation research and solution proposals (see Figure 2).

We can notice that the number of studies on i* scalability has increased since 2005, peaking at 19 publications in 2011. Figure 3 shows the relationship between the search sources and the number of excluded and included studies.

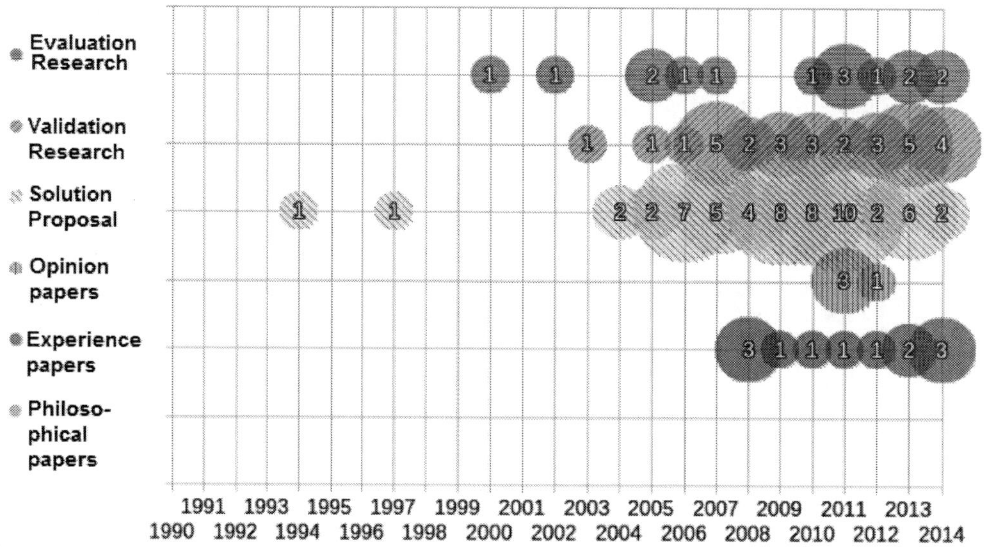

Figure 2. Selected studies distributed over quantity, year of publication and research categories.

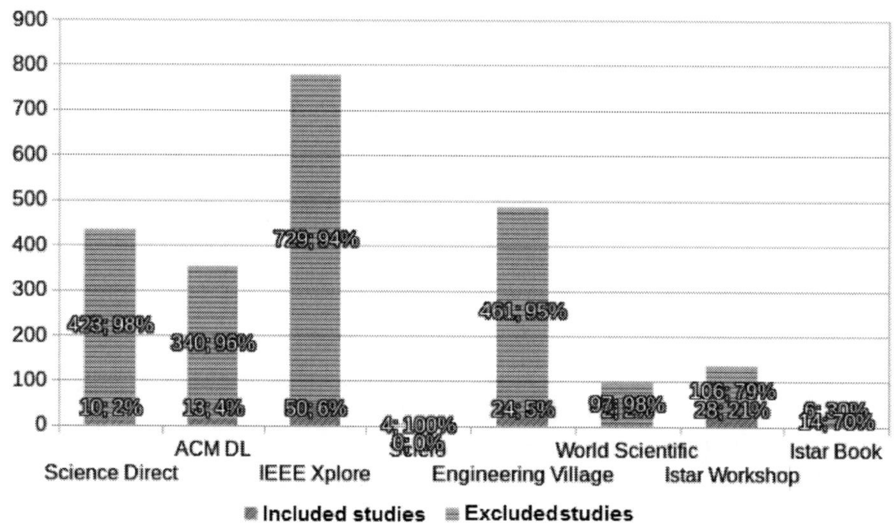

Figure 3. Number of included and excluded studies per search sources.

4.2 RQ2: Which are the scalability definitions in the context of i*?

From the selected studies, we identified 10 works that provide some definition of the term scalability. These definitions are shown in Table 3. In addition, 11 studies had, in their research objective, the study of scalability or related attributes, such as modularity.

Table 3. Scalability definitions extracted from the selected studies. The full reference of each study is available at www.cin.ufpe.br/~ler/supplement/wer2016

Study Id	Definition or Characterization
[S25]	"Scalability was defined by the number of goal levels and number of variants."
[S61]	"able to have models at different levels of abstraction so that both domain experts and developers alike can get an idea of the overall system behavior or focus on a particular part of the system in more detail if required."
[S66]	"is able to handle numerous Agents in an application."
[S78]	"the property of reducing or increasing the scope of methods, processes, and management according to the problem size (. . .) Inherent in this idea is that software engineering techniques should provide good mechanisms for partitioning, composition, and visibility control. It includes the ability to scale the notation to particular problem needs, contractual requirements, or even to budgetary and business goals and objectives."
[S84]	"the reduced complexity of goal graphs (. . .), the ability to group goal graphs with concerns, the encapsulation provided by concerns, the ability to use parameterized point cut expressions in AoGRL, and the simpler update tasks for AoGRL suggest that AoGRL models are more scalable than GRL models."
[S97]	"measures the methodology's support for designing systems that are scalable. It means that the system should allow the incorporation of additional resources and software components with minimal user disruption."
[S98]	"The degree to which the modeling framework can be used to handle applications of different sizes. Scalability also measures extensibility, the degree to which the inclusion of new modeling elements leaves the understandability of models unaffected. This feature is causally related to refinement and modularity."
[S102]	"features in the technique to scale with the size and complexity of the system under assessment. Examples: Abstraction, refinement, decomposition, different formats, types or versions of technique."
[S104]	"ability of both the approach as well as the specifications to serve for a variety of project sizes and constraints, need to be easily modifiable."
[S111]	"large organizational models (depending on the domain and their description) become complex and inconsistent due to bad labeling and irrelevant information."

4.3 RQ3: Which are the types of contributions that have been published to support the i* scalability?

From the set of selected studies, we identified 150 mentions to different types of contributions to improve the scalability of i* (Figure 4). This includes repetitions to the same technique as well as more than one type of contribution in the same study, i.e., a single paper may be classified in more than one category.

We separate contributions in four categories: metamodels or formalisms (24 mentions), modeling processes (52 mentions), visual constructors (41 mentions), and software or algorithms (33 mentions).

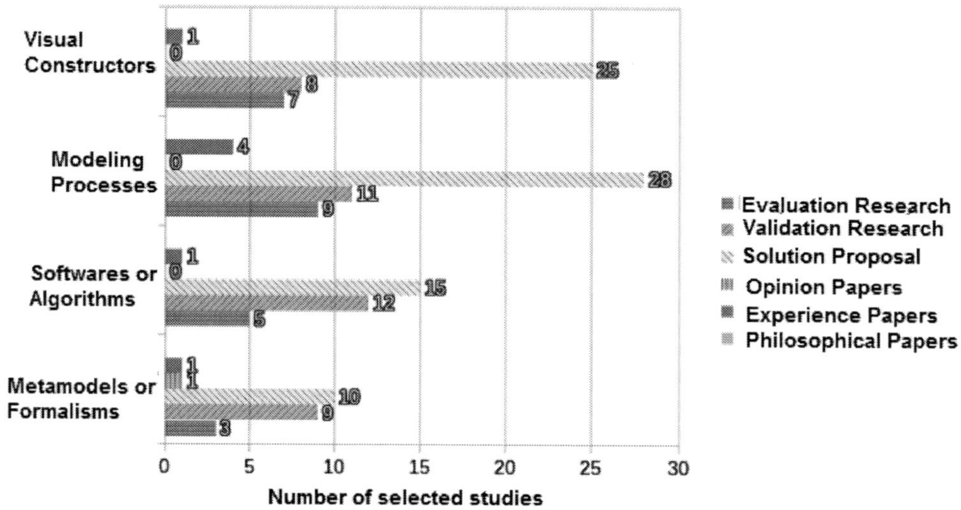

Figure 4. Types of contributions per type of research method.

4.4 RQ4: What is the perceived judgment on the scalability of i*?

According to the selected studies, we identified that i* does not have a good treatment regarding its scalability. In all research types categories (Figure 5), there were quantitatively more studies that reported bad impression on the i* models supporting scalability (62 studies). On the other hand, only eight studies judged the scalability of i*as being well treated. Finally, 49 studies did not mention any information about this question.

In relation to the research types categories (Figure 5), there are five Validation studies, one Evaluation study and two Solution Proposal studies category considering that scalability is well treated. On the other hand, eighteen Validation studies, eight Evaluation studies, twenty nine Solution Proposal studies, three Opinion Papers, and four Experience studies classified the scalability of i* as not being well handled.

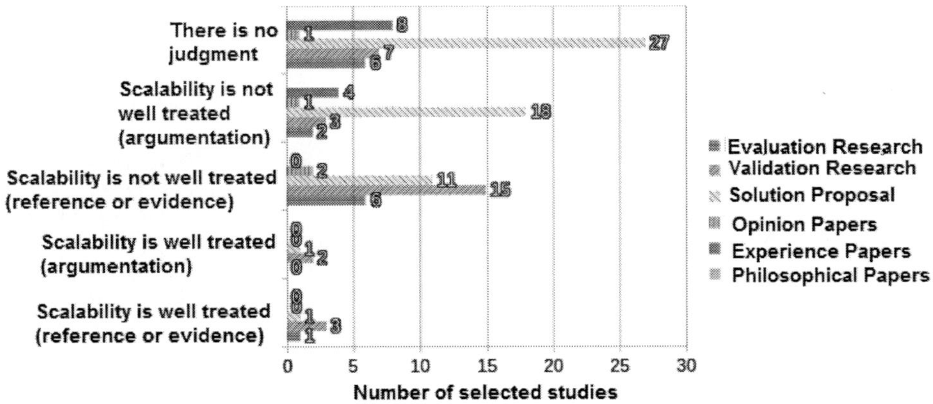

Figure 5. How the i* scalability is perceived.

4.5 RQ5: Are there open issues?

We identified 93 studies that present open issues and related future works about the scalability of i*. Regarding the research types categories (Figure 6), 47 Solution Proposal studies, 24 Validation studies, 11 Evaluation studies, 7 Experience studies, and 4 Opinion papers indicate open issues. On the other hand, 26 studies did not mention open issues. From these results, we concluded that there are indeed open issues on the topic.

4.6 Studies indicated by experienced researchers

After consulting experienced researchers, they pointed out 8 studies that were not captured by our systematic mapping study. The indicated studies were [10], [11], [12], [13], [14], [15], [16], and [17]. Most of these studies are PhD theses, which explains why they have not been captured by our search.

It is important to note that these studies are not inserted in the answers for our research questions since it is outside of our scope to use techniques such as manual inclusion and snowballing. Therefore, the results presented above correspond to the studies exclusively returned by our research protocol.

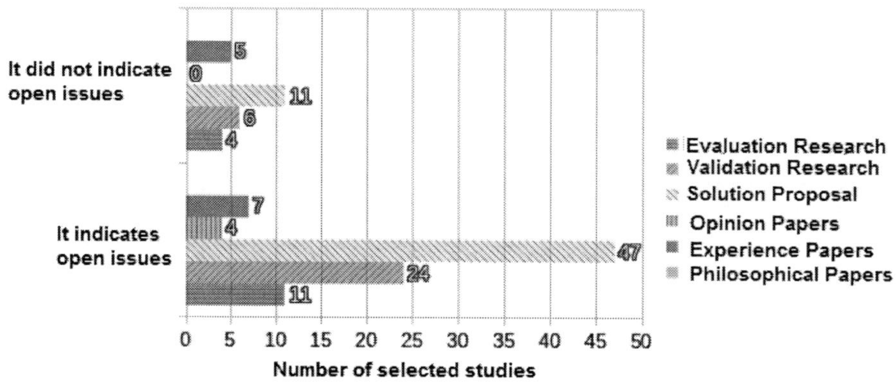

Figure 6. Number of papers that mentions open issues about the i* scalability per research category.

5 DISCUSSION

In this Section, we first discuss the scalability treatments of some of the reviewed papers, in order to provide an overview of approaches that have been proposed. Lastly, some general limitations and recommendations are presented.

Maté et al [25] defined modules for i* models. On an empirical evaluation comparing between regular models and models with modules, the authors observed increased scalability and improved understandability (considering the number of errors) on the latter, even though it took longer to understand them.

Pastor et al [24] presented an empirical evaluation of i* with respect to different concerns, including modularity, complexity management, and scalability. Both modularity and scalability were considered to be not supported, whereas complexity management was considered to be not well supported.

Alencar et al [18] extended i* with aspectual elements aiming to improve the modularity of its models. By distributing repeating elements on aspectual actors it is possible to increase the separation of concerns, with the disadvantage of being necessary to learn new elements in order to use this approach. With increased modularity and separation of concerns, the models are expected to be more scalable.

Previously, Mussbacher et al [22] have also investigated the adoption of aspectual concepts in the context of i*-based models. The proposal was evaluated by comparing three approaches for modeling an example system: regular GRL; monotonic GRL; and aspect-oriented GRL. The latter presented better results in terms of modularity, understandability, reusability, and maintainability, even though it presented an increased vocabulary size.

Oliveira et al [21] defined SDsituations, a modularity construct explicitly aimed at improving the scalability of i* models. SDsituations aggregate different elements of i* models, and each SDsituation is related to other SDsitutations through logical, temporal or sequential, and physical dependencies.

The approach from Dalpiaz et al [19] allows designing adaptive socio-technical systems. Here, instead of considering the scalability of the models themselves, it was analyzed the scalability of the adaptation algorithms that take i* models as input.

Similarly, Aydemir et al [20] assessed the scalability of its algorithms for model evolution. Moreover, it explicitly takes some precautions in order to improve its visual scalability, such as high visual distance between different kinds of elements and one-to-one correspondence between symbols and concepts.

Horkoff and Yu [23] address the problem of performing an interactive analysis of large goal models by highlighting specific elements depending on the current analysis step.

The following limitations on the overall research about i* scalability were identified: lack of evaluation research on the topic; scarcity of i* models from the industry; there are many papers on the topic, but no clear recommendations on which approach to adopt on different contexts; lastly, some relevant publications are not readily available, preventing wider adoption of the proposed approaches.

In order to improve future research on the topic, the following actions are suggested: make large and complex models publicly available; interact with the industry in order to create and publish models of real systems; make the resources of scalability experiments publicly available; define metrics and exemplars for comparing different approaches.

6 CONCLUSIONS AND FUTURE WORK

In this paper we present a systematic mapping on the scalability of the i* framework. A total of 119 papers were analyzed, resulting on the characterization of the research topic. Based on this study, it was possible to discover the different ways that scalability is considered in the i* community, as well as different mechanisms that have been proposed in order to tackle scalability issues.

We presented 10 concepts related to scalability presented in the selected papers. The contribution types were classified in metamodels or formalisms, processes, visual constructors, and software, and the respective amount of contributions on each type were presented. The existent judgments about the scalability of i* were classified by the following scale: there is no judgment, scalability is not well treated (argumentation); scalability is not well treated (reference or evidence); scalability is well treated (argumentation) and scalability is well treated (reference or evidence).

Regardless of the fact that there are several papers on the topic, it could be observed that the scalability of the i* framework still have many open issues. In future work, we expect to perform a more detailed analysis of the selected papers and to establish mechanisms for comparing different approaches.

Acknowledgments

The following Brazilian institutions have supported this work: FACEPE, CAPES and CNPQ.

References

1. E. Yu. Social modeling and i*. In: Conceptual Modeling: Foundations and Applications, Lecture Notes in Computer Science, vol. 5600, pp. 99–121, 2009.
2. X. Franch. Fostering the adoption of i* by practitioners: Some challenges and research directions. In: Intentional Perspectives on Information Systems Engineering, pp. 177–193, 2010.
3. X. Franch. The i* framework: the way ahead. In: sixth international conference on Research Challenges in Information Science (RCIS), 2012. pp. 1–3.
4. J. Horkoff; E. Yu. Comparison and evaluation of goal-oriented satisfaction analysis techniques. Requirements Engineering, v. 18, n. 3, 2013, pp. 199-222.
5. B. Kitchenham, S. Charters. Guidelines for performing systematic literature reviews in software engineering. In: EBSE Technical Report EBSE-2007-01, 2007
6. K. Petersen, R. Feldt, S. Mujtaba, M. Mattsson. Systematic Mapping Studies in Software Engineering. In: Proceedings of the International Conference on Evaluation and Assessment in Software Engineering (EASE), 2008. pp. 68–77.
7. C. Wohlin et al. Experimentation in software engineering: An introduction. Norwell, MA: Kluwer Academic, 2000.
8. D. Dermeval, J. Vilela, Ig Bittencourt, J. Castro, S. Isotani, P. Brito, A. Silva. Applications of ontologies in requirements engineering: a systematic review of the literature. Requirements Engineering, pp. 1-33, 2015.
9. R. Wieringa; N. Maiden; N. Mead; C. Rolland. Requirements engineering paper classification and evaluation criteria: a proposal and a discussion. In: Requirements Engineering, vol. 11, n. 1, 2006, pp. 102–107.
10. C. Cocca. Towards Improved Visual Support for i* Modelling. diploma thesis, Faculty of Information Studies – University of Toronto, Toronto, Canada (2007), http://www.collectionscanada.gc.ca/obj/thesescanada/vol2/002/ MR27330.PDF
11. H.E Esquivel. A Service-oriented Approach for the i* Framework. Ph.D. thesis, University of Trento, Italy; Universitat Politècnica de Valéncia, Spain (2008), http://hdl.handle.net/10251/3305
12. C. Gralha; M. Goulão; J. Araújo. Identifying modularity improvement opportunities in goal-oriented requirements models. In: Advanced Information Systems Engineering, Lecture Notes in Computer Science, vol. 8484, 2014, pp. 91–104.
13. C. Leica. Scalability Concepts for i* Modelling and Analysis. diploma thesis, Department of Computer Science – University of Toronto, Toronto, Canada (2005), http://www.collectionscanada.gc.ca/obj/thesescanada/vol2/002/mr02471.pdf
14. M. J. N. R Lucena. STREAM: a systematic process to derive architectural models from requirements models. Ph.D. thesis, Centro de Informática, Universidade Federal de Pernambuco (2010).
15. D. Moody; P. Heymans, R. Matulevicius. Visual syntax does matter: improving the cognitive effectiveness of the i* visual notation. In: Requirements Engineering, vol. 15, n. 2, 2010, pp. 141–175.

16. D. Moody. The physics of notations: Toward a scientific basis for constructing visual notations in software engineering. In:IEEE Transactions Software Engineering, vol. 35, n. 6, 2009, pp. 756–779.
17. J. Z. You. Using meta-model-driven views to address scalability in i* models. diploma thesis, Department of Computer Science – University of Toronto, Toronto, Canada (2004), http://www.collectionscanada.gc.ca/obj/s4/f2/dsk4/etd/MQ95286.PDF
18. F. Alencar, J. Castro, M. Lucena, E. Santos, C. Silva, J. Araújo, A. Moreira. Towards modular i* models. Proceedings of the 2010 ACM Symposium on Applied Computing. pp. 292–297, 2010.
19. F. Dalpiaz, P. Giorgini, J. Mylopoulos. Adaptive socio-technical systems: a requirements-based approach. In: Requirements Engineering, vol. 18, 2013, pp. 1–24.
20. F. Aydemir, P. Giorgini, J. Mylopoulos, F. Dalpiaz. Exploring alternative designs for sociotechnical systems. Eighth International Conference on Research Challenges in Information Science, pp. 1–12, 2014.
21. A. Oliveira, J. Leite, L. Cysneiros, C. Cappelli. Eliciting multi-agent systems intentionality: from language extended lexicon to i* models. XXVI International Conference of the Chilean Society of Computer Science, pp. 40–49, 2007.
22. G. Mussbacher, D. Amyot, J. Araujo, A. Moreira, M. Weiss. Visualizing aspect-oriented goal models with aogrl. Second International Workshop on Requirements Engineering Visualization, 2007.
23. J. Horkoff, E. Yu. Visualizations to support interactive goal model analysis. Fifth International Workshop on Requirements Engineering Visualization, pp. 1–10, 2010.
24. O. Pastor, H. Estrada, A. Martínez. Strengths and weaknesses of the i* framework: An empirical evaluation. Social Modeling for Requirements Engineering, chapter 18, pp. 607–643, 2011.
25. A. Maté, J. Trujillo, X. Franch. Adding semantic modules to improve goal-oriented analysis of data warehouses using i-star. Journal of Systems and Software 88, pp. 102 – 111, 2014.
26. J. Horkoff, T. Li, F. Li; M. Salnitri, E. Cardoso, P. Giorgini, J. Mylopoulos, J. Pimentel. Taking goal models downstream: A systematic roadmap. In: Eighth International Conference on Research Challenges in Information Science (RCIS), 2014, pp.1-12, 2014.

Transformação do Modelo i* em User Stories: uma abordagem para documentação ágil baseada nas razões, intenções e NFR

Celso Agra[1], Denise Assis[2], Aêda Sousa[3], Aline Jaqueira[4], Márcia Lucena[4], Teresa Maciel[5] e Fernanda Alencar[3]

[1] Centro de Estudos e Sistemas Avançados do Recife, Recife, Brasil
[2] Universidade de Pernambuco, Recife, Brasil
[3] Universidade Federal de Pernambuco, Recife, Brasil
[4] Universidade Federal do Rio Grande do Norte, Natal, Brasil
[5] Universidade Federal Rural de Pernambuco, Recife, Brasil

clasf@cesar.org.br, dabs@ecomp.poli.br, {aedasousa, alineopj, marcia.lucena, tmmaciel, fernandaalenc}@gmail.com

Abstract. Na documentação ágil, razões, intenções e requisitos não funcionais nem sempre são considerados a contento durante o ciclo de vida de desenvolvimento de um produto. A não consideração desses aspectos pode prejudicar a qualidade do sistema, levando a dificuldades na manutenção e no gerenciamento dos requisitos. Para mitigar o problema, este trabalho propõe a transformação do modelo i* (iStar), que naturalmente considera razões, intenções e requisitos não funcionais desde as fases iniciais, através das *user stories*. A transformação é realizada através de um conjunto de diretrizes que inclui o *design rationales* na documentação ágil. Para análise da proposta, considerou-se os exemplos propostos por Eric Yu na concepção do i*. Como resultado, é apresentada uma documentação que considera razões, intenções e requisitos não funcionais, evitando assim a construção de requisitos desnecessários e minimizando o impacto das mudanças de requisitos.

Keywords. métodos ágeis; modelo de transformação; i*; *user stories*; razões; intenções; requisitos não funcionais; *design rationales*; engenharia de requisitos orientada a objetivos.

1 Introdução

O desenvolvimento de *software* ágil está sendo aplicado cada vez mais na indústria e também se tornando um assunto popular no meio acadêmico [9]. Isso significa que a adoção de práticas ágeis é uma alternativa realmente viável aos modelos tradicionais existentes. Os métodos ágeis contribuem para o desenvolvimento de software, fornecendo uma visão clara do sistema mesmo em ambientes que apresentam constantes mudanças. A metodologia ágil permite desenvolver sistemas que terão seus requisitos alterados ou que ainda não estão bem definidos, além de limitar-se a documentar apenas o essencial para a manutenção e construção do software. Entretanto, existem alguns desafios, que serão abordados a seguir, e que requerem uma atenção na construção de requisitos para sistemas apoiados pelos métodos ágeis. A documentação ágil está sendo bastante questionada, pois ainda não há um consenso sobre a melhor forma de documentar e compartilhar informações através de um meio eficiente.

Para Hoda, Noble e Marshall [5], os métodos ágeis não possuem uma definição clara do que é uma documentação necessária para o produto de software e, portanto, a falta dessa compreensão causa problemas para definir o necessário para o produto final. Em [13], é afirmado que uma vez realizada a documentação, é preciso mantê-la e atualizá-la sempre que houver mudanças de requisitos, o que gera um custo extra durante o desenvolvimento de software. De acordo com [15], a comunicação verbal é suscetível a perda de informações durante o ciclo de vida do produto, pois em muitos casos, as razões e intenções do sistema não são lembradas, nem documentadas pela equipe. Por último, [9] afirma que os problemas apresentados em projetos, documentação e código, estão normalmente relacionados com a negligência da equipe, pois não possui conhecimento em produzir uma documentação apropriada para o projeto. Logo, a documentação ágil ainda apresenta lacunas a serem preenchidas, pois os documentos gerados nem sempre atendem as necessidades do projeto, e em alguns casos, não possuem uma visão clara e explícita das razões, intenções, arquitetura, requisitos funcionais e não-funcionais, para o sistema proposto.

É comum que projetos ágeis não utilizem uma documentação vasta e nem uma modelagem abrangente para representar requisitos e as necessidades do software. Isso pode dificultar a análise de informações complexas e na compreensão dos conflitos da solução, além de fornecer uma base limitada para avaliar o impacto das mudanças dos requisitos [10]. Assim, é preciso ter uma visão geral do sistema antes da fase de projeto e implementação, focando na fase de análise de requisitos, e identificando os objetivos do sistema proposto. A documentação ágil possui lacunas que precisam ser exploradas para garantir a completude das informações, sem ferir, no entanto, os valores do manifesto ágil [1]. De acordo com [13], uma documentação que abrange um alto nível abstração dos requisitos, fornece as razões e as justificativas para as decisões das funcionalidades e, portanto, permite que os *stakeholders* compreendam as intenções de cada ação do sistema. Os documentos que expressam as razões e justificativas para as decisões do sistema são conhecidos como *design rationales*.

Para [8], os documentos de *design rationale* precisam ser representados na forma de modelos e estão associados com a *Goal-Oriented Requirement Engineering* (GORE), que define os objetivos de forma clara e compreensível para os *stakeholders* [14]. A modelagem GORE apresenta metas organizacionais e os porquês das necessidades de um determinado sistema [2], ou seja, definem as razões e as intenções. Alguns modelos ainda possuem a representação de requisitos não funcionais [8].

Este trabalho apresenta uma proposta de transformação do modelo i* em *user stories* para suprir as necessidades encontradas na documentação ágil, como a construção de uma documentação baseada nas razões, intenções e requisitos não funcionais. O uso de uma abordagem GORE como um documento de *design rationale* contribui para evitar que requisitos desnecessários possam ser desenvolvidos, além de mitigar o impacto das mudanças desses requisitos. Escolhemos o i* por ser uma abordagem GORE, que possui uma modelagem bem consolidada com apoio de ferramentas adequadas [2]. Além disso, o i* é adequado para representar os objetivos organizacionais e as possíveis interações entre os atores, utilizando conceitos como metas e metas-flexíveis (*softgoals*) [12].

2 Framework i*

O *framework* captura os requisitos intencionais utilizando relacionamentos estratégicos entre os atores. Assim, o *framework* fornece um entendimento das razões ou dos "porquês" que se aplicam aos requisitos do sistema [11]. O *framework* está dividido em dois modelos: o *Strategic Dependency* (modelo SD ou modelo estratégico de dependências); e o *Strategic Rationale* (modelo SR ou o modelo estratégico de razões).

2.1 Elementos do i*

O *framework* i* possui elementos utilizados em ambos modelos (SD e SR). Assim, alguns conceitos relacionados aos elementos foram definidos da seguinte forma:

- Ator: é representado pelo elemento (i) da Figura 1. Para o modelo i*, o ator possui intenções (visão externa) e capacidades (visão interna). Além disso, pode se relacionar com outros atores através das relações de dependências.
- Tarefa: realiza tarefas e operações de um determinado ator ou relacionamento, que serão realizadas. Uma tarefa, representada pelo elemento (ii) da Figura 1.
- Recurso: pode ser caracterizado como um recurso físico que pode ser obtido por um ator. Um recurso está representado pelo elemento (iii) da Figura 1, e pode caracterizar um documento, por exemplo.
- Meta: representa os objetivos intencionais de um ator. Uma meta está representada pelo elemento (iv) da Figura 1.
- Meta-flexivel: representa as metas relacionadas a qualidade ou objetivos secundários. Uma meta está representada pelo elemento (v) da Figura 1 e pode caracterizar um requisito não funcional.

Figura 1: Representação dos elementos do i*

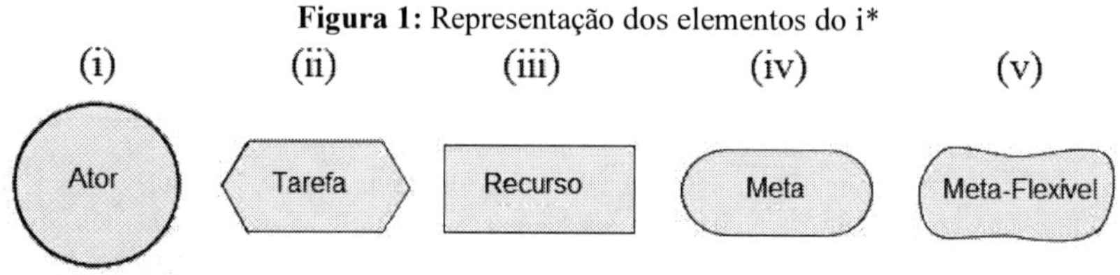

2.2 Modelo SD

Este modelo está focado nos relacionamentos intencionais entre os atores, pois cada ligação representa uma dependência entre eles, e é representado por nós e ligações (ou conectores). Os nós são representados pelos atores, que se dividem em dois grupos: o *depender*, um ator dependente de um determinado elemento (denominado *dependum*); e o *dependee*, que representa o ator que fornece o elemento para o *depender*. As ligações são as dependências entre os atores, e são representadas por elementos intencionais (*Intentional Elements*), como as metas (*goals*), as metas flexíveis (*softgoals*), os recursos (*resources*) e as tarefas (*tasks*).

A Figura 2 apresenta uma representação de um modelo SD. Nesse caso, teremos uma ligação entre os atores *depender* e *dependee* através do *dependum*. Nesse caso, o depender necessita do *dependee* para realizar ou executar o *dependum*.

Figura 2: Análise realizada em um modelo SD apresentando os atores *depender* e *dependee*, e o elemento intencional do *dependum*

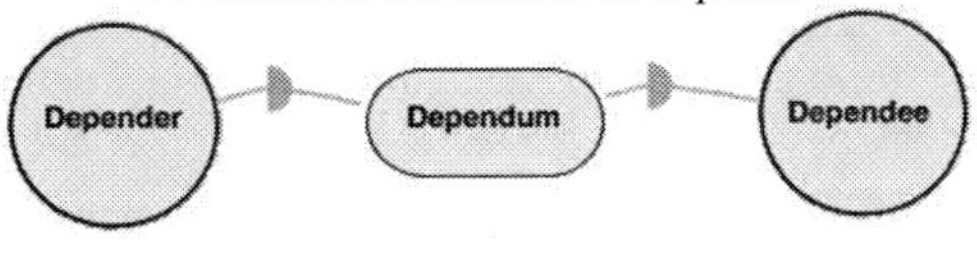

2.3 Modelo SR

O modelo SR expande a descrição de um determinado ator e mostra as suas razões associadas e suas dependências. Esse modelo apresenta todas as justificativas envolvidas em suas interações, e fornece um apoio para modelar as razões de cada ator em seus relacionamentos intencionais [2]. Nesse caso, o modelo SR representa os elementos internos do modelo i*. O *framework* possui diversas variações provenientes da evolução do modelo devido a necessidade de realizar uma melhoria desse *framework*. Para a proposta deste trabalho, resolvemos utilizar o modelo tradicional SR, baseado no trabalho de [16]. A Figura 3 mostra como essas ligações são utilizadas.

- Task-decomposition: representado pelo ítem (i) da Figura 3. Uma tarefa pode ser decomposta em partes, que podem representar qualquer um dos quatro tipos de elementos, como meta-flexível, tarefa, recurso e meta.
- Contribution: representado pelo item (ii) da Figura 3. Está relacionado com a contribuição de uma determinada meta-flexível (*softgoal*) ou requisito não funcional.
- Means-Ends: representado pelos itens (iii), (iv) e (v) da Figura 3. O relacionamento entre o meio (*means*), que pode ser uma tarefa ou uma meta a ser realizada, e o fim (*end*), que pode ser um objetivo, uma tarefa ou um recurso a ser alcançado, de acordo com o elemento fim.
    - **Figura 3:** Representação do modelo SR do i* tradicional baseado em [16]

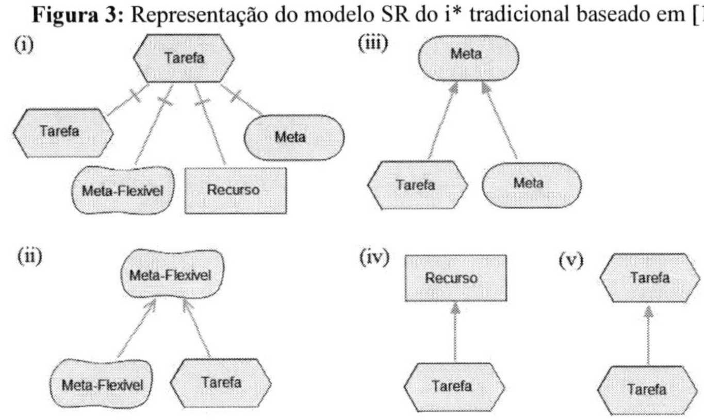

2.4 Caso de exemplo

A Figura 4 apresenta um modelo i* baseado em [16]. Trata-se de um caso de organizador de reuniões, onde um responsável deverá determinar a data e o local da reunião para os demais participantes. O modelo está dividido em três atores com suas respectivas necessidades e atividades. Como forma de identificação, foram acrescentados para esse modelo, numerações para os elementos intencionais, e siglas para os atores do sistema.

- **Criador da reunião:** Deve perguntar a todos os participantes sobre as suas respectivas disponibilidades para a reunião durante um intervalo de tempo, baseado nas agendas pessoais. Esse intervalo de tempo contém um conjunto de datas excluídas de acordo com as respostas dos participantes.
- **Organizador de reunião:** Propõe uma data que não esteja no conjunto de datas excluídas e deve estar de acordo com as datas de preferência dos participantes.
- **Participante da reunião:** Devem concordar com a data de reunião uma vez que a data aceitável seja encontrada.

Figura 4: Representação do modelo i* referente ao exemplo do organizador de reuniões.

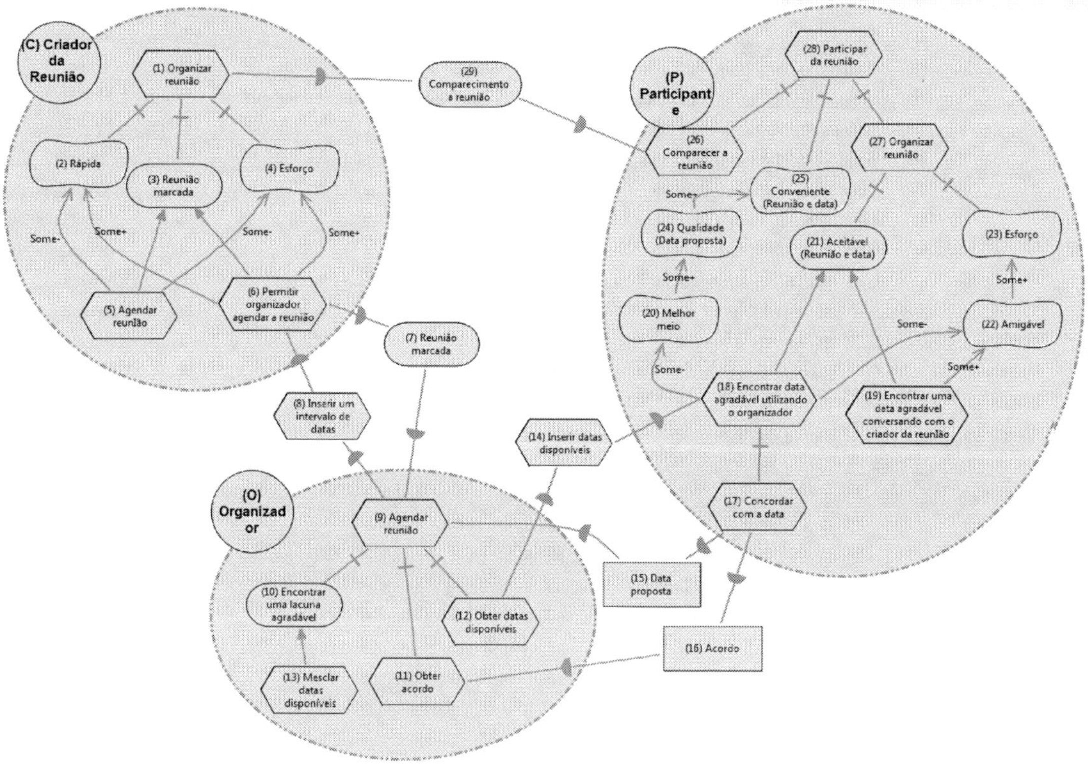

2.5 Análise Cross-impact

A análise *cross-impact* constitui na compreensão do valor semântico das ligações de dependência do modelo i*. Os modelos SR facilitam na identificação da análise *cross-impact* através do uso de ligações *means-ends* para *softgoals* [16]. Inicialmente, foi utilizado apenas para compreender as metas afetadas a partir de um meio.

A Figura 5 apresenta um exemplo da análise *cross-impact*, através de um sistema de contas a pagar. O ator cliente depende do sistema para "pagar pelo item". O ator fornecedor depende da ação do cliente junto ao sistema, para alcançar o objetivo "item pago". Além disso, o fornecedor também depende do sistema para que o pagamento seja realizado imediatamente. O ator tesoureiro depende do sistema para obter um bom fluxo de caixa. Por fim, o ator auditor depende do sistema para o controle contábil. Para esse caso, podemos ver que as ligações do *softgoals* são afetadas pelas ações do ator "Contas a pagar". As *tasks* "pagar quando receber item" e "pagar quando faturar", deverão afetar a *softgoal* "controle contábil" através da ligação de dependência, que pode ser representada semanticamente como uma ligação *contribution*.

Figura 5: Abordagem *cross-impact*.

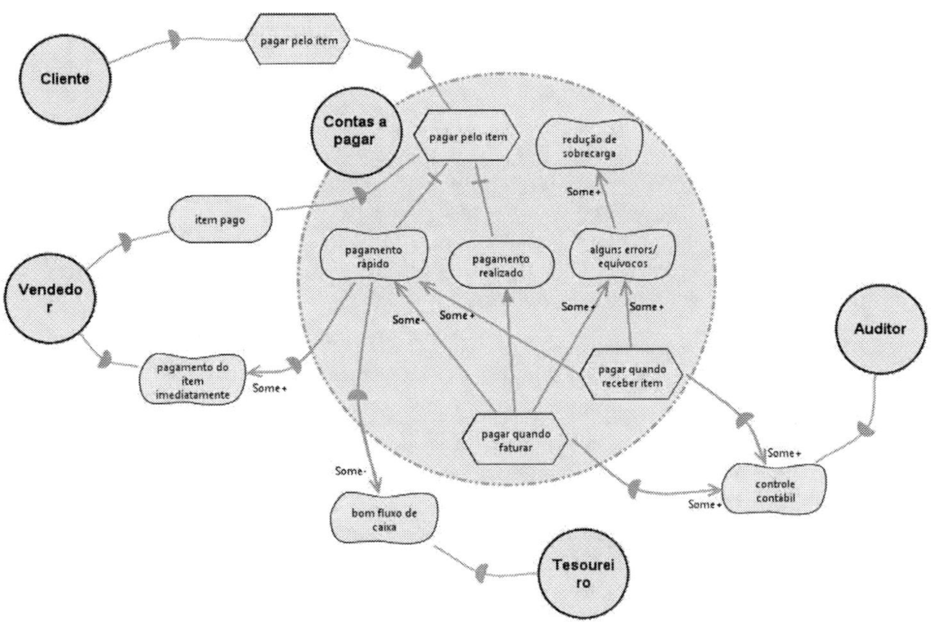

A análise *cross-impact* deve ser aplicada para cada ligação entre os elementos e atores, e é parte crucial para as transformações propostas neste trabalho.

De acordo com a Figura 5, é possível garantir uma relação de *cross-impact* com os elementos e ligações de dependências. Assim, realizamos uma análise das ligações para os demais elementos intencionais, como *goal*; *softgoal*; *resource*; e *task*.

Para cada ligação dos elementos do i* foi realizado uma análise semântica das ligações de acordo com as regras do modelo SR que estão baseadas na análise *cross-impact*. A Figura 6 apresenta apenas duas transformações baseadas na análise semântica. A análise possui um total de 64 combinações de ligação, considerando 4 elementos possíveis para o *depender*, 4 elementos para o *dependum* e os 4 elementos possíveis para o *dependee*.

Figura 6: Aplicação das regras de transformação dos conflitos semânticos

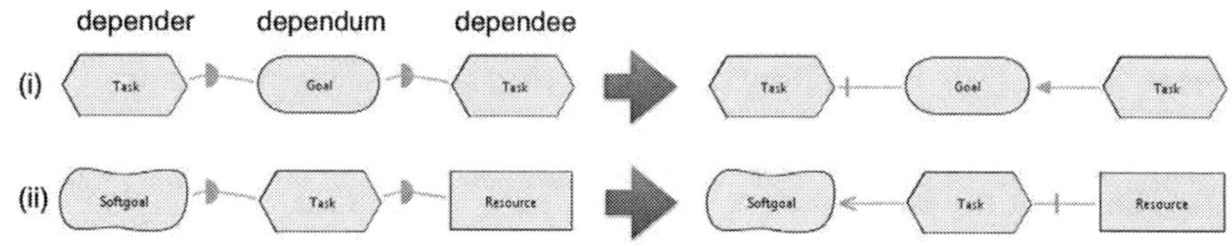

No primeiro caso (elemento i da Figura 6), temos os elementos intencionais relacionados com a ligação do modelo SD, onde a *task* representa o elemento interno do *depender*, o *goal* representa o elemento *dependum*, e por fim, a outra *task* representa o elemento interno do ator *dependee*. A transformação poderá substituir as ligações de dependência do modelo SD, por ligações do modelo SR, de acordo com as regras semânticas. Assim, a ligação entre a *task* e o *goal*, sendo estes elementos do *depender* e *dependum* (nessa ordem), poderão ser substituidos por uma ligação *task-decomposition*, enquanto a ligação entre a *goal* e *task*, como *dependum* e *dependee*, será uma ligação *means-ends*.

Para o segundo caso (elemento ii da Figura 6), o *softgoal* deverá representar o elemento interno do *depender*, a *task* representa o *dependum*, e por fim, o *resource* representa o outro elemento interno do *dependee*. A análise da Figura 6 é sempre realizada da esquerda para a direita. A ligação entre o *softgoal* e a *task*, poderá ser substituida por uma ligação *contribution*, enquanto a ligação entre a *task* e o *resource*, será substituida por uma ligação *task-decomposition*.

3 Proposta das diretrizes

Um conjunto de diretrizes são utilizadas para transformar o modelo i* em *user stories*. Assim, é possível estabelecer uma documentação para os métodos ágeis, baseada nas razões, intenções e requisitos não funcionais.

As diretrizes são divididas em duas etapas que foram propostas neste trabalho. A primeira etapa do processo baseia-se na transformação dos modelos SD em SR, para gerar um conjunto de modelos temporários, que deverão servir como entrada para a fase posterior. A segunda etapa utiliza o resultado da primeira etapa para transformar os modelos gerados em *user stories*.

A Figura 7 apresenta uma visão completa do fluxo do processo através da notação de modelagem de processos de negócio (BPMN). O processo apresenta um conjunto de diretrizes separadas em macro atividades: transformar modelos SD em modelos SR; e transformar modelos SR em *user stories*. Cada macro atividade é representada na Figura 7 como um agrupamento (região pontilhada) das atividades.

Figura 7: Fluxo do processo utilizando notação BPMN

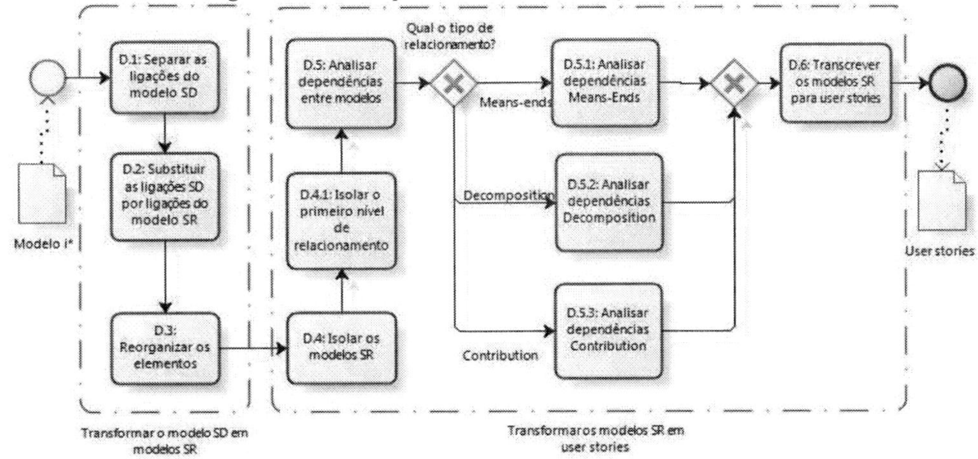

As seguintes diretrizes serão apresentadas para a primeira fase do processo "transformar modelos SD em modelos SR":

- **D.1:** Separar as ligações do modelo SD em *requirements path*
- **D.2:** Substituir as ligações SD por ligações SR
- **D.3:** Identificar o início de cada *requirement path*

A segunda fase "transformar modelos SR em *user stories* "deverá realizar as transformações de acordo com as seguintes diretrizes:

- **D.4:** Isolar os modelos SR, de cada *requirement path*
    - **D.4.1:** Cada modelo deve ser isolado considerando apenas o primeiro nível de relacionamento
- **D.5:** Analisar as dependências entre os modelos
    - **D.5.1:** Analisar dependências *Means-Ends*
    - **D.5.2:** Analisar dependências *Decomposition*
    - **D.5.3:** Analisar dependências *Contribution*
- **D.6:** Transcrever e transformar os modelos em *user stories*

3.1 D.1 - Separar as ligações do modelo SD em *requirements path*

Primeiramente, é preciso separar os relacionamentos em partes para que possam ser caracterizadas como uma especificação de requisitos. Nesse caso, cada dependência e seus respectivos relacionamentos internos devem ser analisadas para cada um dos atores. Essa estrutura é denominada *requirement path*.

O requirement path trata-se de uma representação de um requisito considerando um fluxo baseado em um *dependum* específico, sendo este o principal elemento para identificar essas representações. Assim, um *requirement path* é composto de um *dependum* e os elementos internos associados aos atores *depender* e *dependee*, incluindo relacionamentos internos como o *means-ends*, *contribution* e *decomposition*.

Devemos separar o modelo i* em grupos de acordo com os *dependums* do modelo. Assim, os elementos separados serão agrupados em *requirement paths*. Considerando o exemplo da Figura 4, os seguintes elementos estarão elegíveis para este agrupamento: 7 (reunião marcada); 8 (inserir um intervalo de datas); 14 (inserir datas disponíveis); 15 (data proposta); 16 (acordo); e 29 (comparecimento a reunião).

A Figura 8 apresenta a extração de um *requirement path* do modelo i* referente ao caso de exemplo da Figura 4. Assim, selecionamos apenas o grupo relacionado ao *dependum* 7 (reunião marcada) que será transformado em *user stories* posteriormente.

Figura 8: *Requirement path* referente ao *dependum* 7 (Reunião marcada)

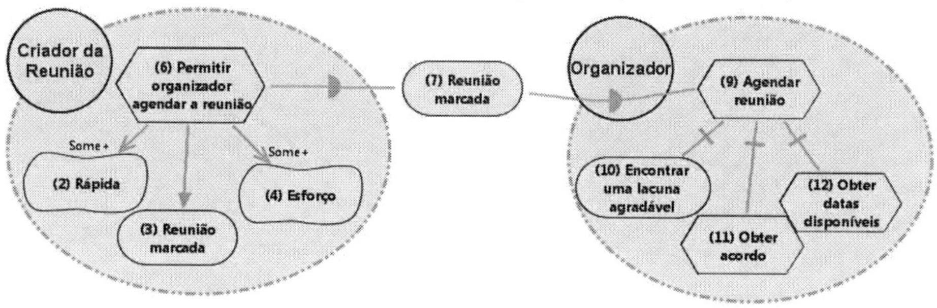

3.2 D.2 - Substituir as ligações SD por ligações SR

Após separar o elemento em um *requirement path*, é preciso substituir as ligações dos relacionamentos de dependência (do modelo SD) pelos conectores do modelo SR, através do conceito apresentado pela análise *cross-impact*. As ligações do modelo SD devem ser substituídas pelas ligações do modelo SR, para facilitar a compreensão dos requisitos gerados pelo i*. A Figura 9 apresenta o resultado dessas alterações para facilitar a compreensão e a construção das *user stories*.

Figura 9: Transformação do modelo i*, após a aplicação das diretrizes D.1 e D.2

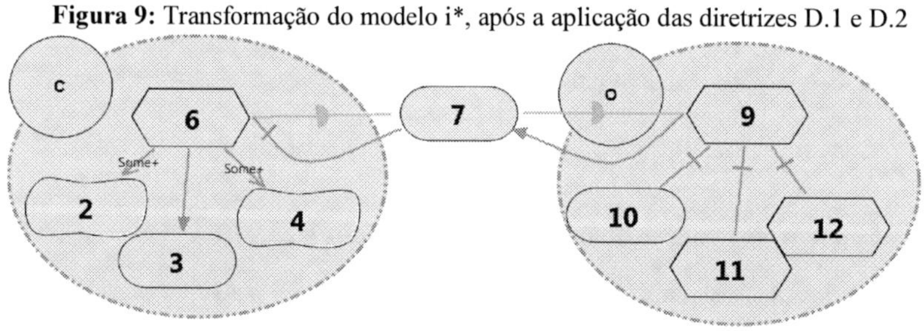

3.3 D.3 - Identificar o início de cada *requirement path*

Por último, os modelos são reorganizados verticalmente para melhorar na compreensão da abordagem e em seguida identificar o início de cada *requirement path*. Para o caso da Figura 9, é possível identificar onde um *requirement path* inicia e como ele deverá afetar os demais elementos. Assim, o caso deve iniciar a partir da ação de número 9 (Agendar reunião) pelo ator "O" (Organizador da reunião).

3.4 D.4 - Isolar os modelos SR, de cada *requirement path*

Com essa estrutura aplicada pelas diretrizes anteriormente citadas, é possível realizar a segunda parte da transformação. Para isso, é preciso isolar os modelos SRs e seus respectivos relacionamentos. Nesse caso, cada *requirement path* deverá ser dividido em pequenas partes. Cada parte extraída deverá gerar uma *user story*. Os demais elementos serão caracterizados como uma nova *user story* e uma relação de dependência com a *user story* existente.

A diretriz D.4.1 deve considerar apenas no primeiro nível de relacionamento. Assim, deverão apenas fazer parte do relacionamento de um nível: *means-end*, apenas quando se tratar do elemento "*means*"; *decomposition*, apenas quando o elemento analisado estiver sendo decomposto; *contribution*, apenas quando o elemento analisado for o agente contribuinte. A diretriz D.4.1 procurar limitar-se apenas ao primeiro nível para que possa ser gerado modelos mais simples possíveis. Isso deve resultar em user stories simples, com o foco apenas em uma ação, objetivo, recurso ou requisitos não funcionais. Isso torna o modelo i* legível e compreensível para a proposta.

A Figura 10 apresenta a transformação do *requirement path* após isolar os elementos em até um nível de relacionamento. A partir de então, teremos duas representações do modelo SR, do *framework* i*, que deverão transformar-se em *user stories*. O elemento 7 (reunião marcada) do modelo i* US01, não está contido no ator "C" (criador da reunião) pois o mesmo pertence ao ator "O" (organizador da reunião). Essa representação apenas demonstra que há uma dependência entre as duas *user stories*.

Figura 10: Transformação do modelo i*, após a aplicação das diretrizes D.4 e D.4.1

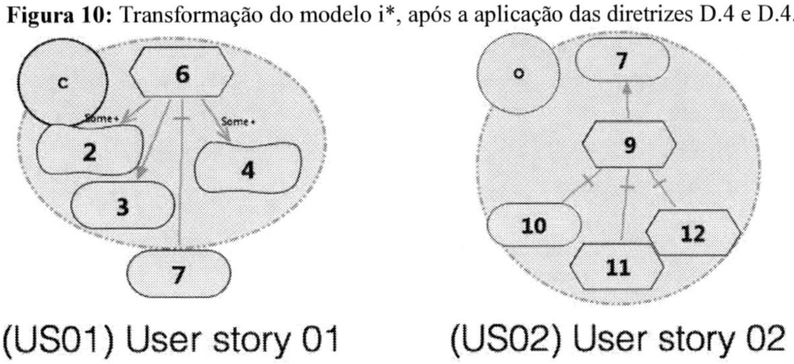

3.5 D.5 - Analisar as dependências entre os modelos

Analisar as dependências entre os modelos de acordo com os elementos que estão sendo utilizados, ou seja, se o elemento analisado estiver vinculado a um outro modelo SR isolado, então teremos uma dependência.

De acordo com a Figura 10, temos que o modelo i* US01 depende que o ator "O" (organizador da reunião) do modelo US02, alcance o objetivo 7 (reunião marcada), para que possa então, realizar a tarefa 6 (permitir organizador agendar reunião).

3.6 D.6 - Transcrever e transformar os modelos em *user stories*

Por fim, devemos transcrever os modelos i* em *user stories*, que deverão ser utilizadas no desenvolvimento de sistemas. Além disso, esses artefatos estarão transcritos em uma estrutura denominada story cards.

3.7 Construção de uma estrutura de Story Card

As *story cards* contém uma pequena descrição de uma funcionalidade de valor para um *stakeholder* [4]. Além disso, as *story cards* podem conter testes de aceitação, entre outras informações relevantes para a equipe de desenvolvimento. Para este trabalho, optamos pela estrutura tradicional, adicionando dois aspectos: as dependências entre as *user stories*; e a relação com os requisitos não funcionais. A estrutura de uma *story card* baseia-se nos conceitos de [4] e [7], e possuem as seguintes informações:

- **ID:** Identificador da *user story*, geralmente caracterizado por uma numeração ou código (ex.: US01.1)
- **Descrição:** Apresenta a descrição da *user story*, no formato padrão (ex.: "como <papel> eu quero <ação> para <meta>").
- **Critérios de Aceitação:** Realiza a validação da *user story*. Se todos os testes de aceitação estiverem de acordo com o que foi solicitado, então a *user story* também estará de acordo (Campo opcional)
- **Dependências:** Apresenta dependências entre as *user stories* (Campo opcional)
- **Requisitos não funcionais:** Apresenta informações sobre as metas-flexíveis (*softgoals*) ou requisitos não funcionais (Campo opcional)

Os quadros Quadro 1 e Quadro 2, apresentam as transformações dos modelos US01 e US02 respectivamente.

Quadro 1: Modelo US01 transcrito em forma de *user story*

ID: US01
Descrição: Como um "criador da reunião", eu quero "permitir organizador agendar a reunião", para obter uma "reunião marcada"
Critérios de Aceitação: • precisa ter uma "reunião marcada"
Dependências: Depende de US02, para alcançar o objetivo "precisa ter uma "reunião marcada"
Requisitos não funcionais: • Contribui com em ser "rápida" • Contribui com o "esforço"

Quadro 2: Modelo US02 transcrito em forma de *user story*

ID: US02
Descrição: Como um "organizador", eu quero "agendar reunião", para obter uma "reunião marcada".
Critérios de Aceitação: • Alcançar o objetivo "Encontrar uma lacuna agradável" • Realizar a atividade "obter acordo"

• Realizar a atividade "obter datas disponíveis"

4 Discussão

A partir do resultado deste trabalho, é possível compreender que conjunto das diretrizes de transformação do modelo i* para *user stories* é uma abordagem complementar e sem obrigatoriedade com a metodologia ágil. Assim, a abordagem auxilia na documentação ágil para mitigar os desafios encontrados, como o impacto e as constantes mudanças, além da construção de requisitos desnecessários.

Um projeto que utiliza Scrum, por exemplo, pode ser dividido em fases para que inicialmente seja elicitado requisitos a partir do modelo i*, e em seguida, gerar *user stories*. A abordagem apenas contribui e auxilia na construção de *user stories* com uma visão de alto nível, baseada em uma modelagem focada nos objetivos organizacionais, razões, intenções e requisitos não funcionais.

As limitações do modelo estão focadas nos elementos que não conseguem ser mapeado pelos *requirement paths*. Nesse caso, esses elementos não poderão estar presentes nas *user stories*, pois não caracterizam dependências e estão incorporados dentro das limitações dos atores, ou seja, são ações internas, e precisam ser estudadas com cautela pelos analistas de negócios, sobre a sua necessidade.

5 Trabalhos Relacionados

Nesta seção, apresentamos os trabalhos relacionados com a proposta. Esses trabalhos foram utilizados como meio para compreender a problemática e aplicar as regras de transformação do modelo i* em *user stories*.

[6] utilizou um conjunto de heurísticas para enriquecer as *user stories* transformando as mesmas em modelos i*. Os modelos i* contribuem como uma forma de documentação dos requisitos no ambiente ágil que podem ser visualizados de forma abrangente com seus relacionamentos de acordo com o ambiente de negócios. A principal preocupação está relacionada com a falta de documentação no ambiente de desenvolvimento ágil, pois isso é um dos principais desafios da metodologia.

[17] utilizou um conjunto de heurísticas para transformar modelos i* em *user stories*, incluindo informações que antes não eram capturadas pelos métodos ágeis, como os requisitos não funcionais, as razões, motivações e intenções dos papéis (ou atores) com suas respectivas metas e ações. A limitação do trabalho apresentou ausência dos casos de exemplo, e utilizou apenas um estudo de caso em ambiente controlado. Isso resultou em uma abordagem limitada, para a evolução da técnica proposta.

[18] propõe uma nova linguagem de modelagem, denominada Scrum i*, para projetos que utilizam métodos ágeis, em especial o Scrum. Esta nova linguagem visa simplificar a técnica i*, para ser integrada ao Scrum. Além disso, procura avaliar a viabilidade, benefícios e desafios para adoção da nova linguagem de modelagem em um ambiente industrial. Mesmo tratando-se da transformação do modelo i*, obtemos

apenas uma abordagem que foca na metodologia de um projeto, enquanto que a abordagem deste trabalho está focada na documentação e nos artefatos gerados.

6 Considerações Finais e Trabalhos Futuros

A documentação ágil ainda não definiu qual a melhor forma de documentar e compartilhar informações de forma eficiente. Em muitos casos, a falta de uma documentação necessária, que possua razões, intenções e requisitos não funcionais para o sistema proposto pode ocasionar em uma documentação incompleta, além de construir requisitos desnecessários e aumentar o impacto das mudanças desses requisitos.

A metodologia ágil possui alguns desafios na fase de documentação, o que pode causar problemas na comunicação e na qualidade do produto [6], assim como o aumento do escopo, do custo e do tempo. Outro desafio está relacionado com a eficácia da comunicação entre as partes interessadas, que depende de diversos fatores como a disponibilidade do cliente, o consenso entre os grupos de clientes e a confiança entre o cliente e os desenvolvedores, principalmente durante a fase inicial de um projeto [3]. Dessa forma, uma abordagem baseada em *design rationale*, pode fornecer requisitos mais compreensíveis para o desenvolvimento de software, através de uma modelagem que possa fornecer uma visão geral do sistema a ser desenvolvido.

Este trabalho apresenta uma proposta de transformação do modelo i* em *user stories* para produzir uma documentação baseada nas razões, intenções e requisitos não funcionais. A partir da identificação do problema, foi possível constatar a necessidade da aplicação das diretrizes de transformação da proposta. Assim, trata-se de uma proposta complementar para a Engenharia de Requisitos, integrando o conceito de *design rationale*, representado pelo framework i*, com a documentação ágil.

Os modelos GORE podem ser facilmente relacionados com projetos ágeis, sendo incluídos como uma abordagem complementar, para evitar constantes mudanças nos requisitos ou o desenvolvimento de funcionalidades desnecessárias para o projeto. Além disso, a modelagem GORE pode ser utilizada como uma documentação prévia dos projetos ágeis. Isso implica que os métodos ágeis podem estabelecer um padrão de documentação que contribua na compreensão dos requisitos do sistema. Essa documentação prévia é denominada *design rationale*.

Como trabalhos futuros, podemos destacar as seguintes atividades: (i) Construção de uma solução automatizada, através de uma linguagem específica de domínio (DSL, ou *Domain Specific Language*) para realizar uma transformação de acordo com os modelos i*. Essa solução poderá contribuir com os analistas de negócios e os *stakeholders* na construção de um produto com um grau de certeza das funcionalidades produzidas; (ii) Aplicar a proposta em casos reais, utilizando times de desenvolvimento de software especializados em métodos ágeis. Para isso, um conjunto de pesquisas deverão ser realizadas através de questionários e estudos de campo, utilizando a solução automatizada; (iii) A proposta de transformação ainda possui uma visão limitada diante das possíveis variações da especificação dos requisitos não funcionais. Assim, um estudo aprofundado da semântica e sintaxe do modelo i*, focado nos requisitos não funcionais deverá ser realizado para contribuir com as diretrizes de transformação do modelo i* para *user stories*.

References

1. Agile Manifesto (2001), http://www.manifestoagil.com.br/, [Online; accessado em 01/09/2015]
2. Alencar, F., Marin, B., Giachetti, G., Pastor, O., Castro, J., Pimentel, J.: From i* requirements models to conceptual models of a model driven development process. Lecture Notes in Business Information Processing pp. 99–114 (2009)
3. Cao, L., Ramesh, B.: Agile requirements engineering practices: An empirical study. Software, IEEE 25(1), 60–67 (2008)
4. Cohn, M.: User Stories Applied: For Agile Software Development. Addison-Wesley Professional (2004)
5. Hoda, R., Noble, J., Marshall, S.: How much is just enough?: Some documentation patterns on agile projects. In: Proceedings of the 15th European Conference on Pattern Languages of Programs. pp. 13:1–13:13. EuroPLoP '10 (2010)
6. Jaqueira, A., Lucena, M., Alencar, F.M.R., Castro, J., Aranha, E.: Using i * models to enrich user stories. In: iStar'13. pp. 55–60 (2013a)
7. Jeffries, R.: Essential xp: Card, conversation, confirmation. http://goo.gl/2e8VXG (2001), [Online; accessado em 01/09/2015]
8. López, C., Cysneiros, L.M., Astudillo, H.: Ndr ontology: Sharing and reusing nfr and design rationale knowledge. In: Managing Requirements Knowledge, 2008. MARK '08. First International Workshop on. pp. 1–10 (2008)
9. Prause, C.R., Durdik, Z.: Architectural design and documentation: Waste in agile development? In: Software and System Process (ICSSP), 2012 International Conference. (2012)
10. Read, A., Briggs, R.O.: The many lives of an agile story: Design processes, design products, and understandings in a large-scale agile development project. In: System Science (HICSS), 2012 45th Hawaii International Conference on. pp. 5319–5328 (2012)
11. Santander, V., Castro, J.: Deriving use cases from organizational modeling. In: Requirements Engineering, 2002. Proceedings. IEEE International Conference on. pp. 32–39 (2002)
12. Santander, V.F.A., Castro, J.: Developing use cases from organizational modeling. In: WER. pp. 246–265 (2001)
13 Sauer, T.: Using design rationales for agile documentation. In: Enabling Technologies: Infrastructure for Collaborative Enterprises, 2003. WET ICE 2003. Proceedings. Twelfth IEEE International Workshops on. pp. 326–331 (2003)
14. Sen, A., Hemachandran, K.: Elicitation of goals in requirements engineering using agile methods. In: Computer Software and Applications Conference Workshops (2010)
15. Stettina, C.J., Heijstek, W.: Necessary and neglected?: An empirical study of internal documentation in agile software development teams. SIGDOC '11. pp. 159–166. (2011)
16. Yu, E.S.K.: Modelling Strategic Relationships for Process Reengineering. Ph.D. thesis, University of Toronto (1995)
17. NETO, T. C. de L. Enriquecendo as Histórias de Usuários com a Abordagem i*. 2014
18. SCHEIDEGGER, M. E. dos Santos de. Integrando Scrum e a Modelagem de Re- quisitos Orientada a Objetivos por meio do SCRUM i*. Dissertação (Mestrado) — Universidade Federal de Pernambuco, Recife, PE, 2012.

An empirical study on the use of context annotations and flow expressions to specify the behavior of context-sensitive systems

Jéssyka Vilela[1], Jaelson Castro[1], João Pimentel[12], Enyo Gonçalves[13]

[1]Universidade Federal de Pernambuco (UFPE)
[2] Universidade de Pernambuco (UPE)
[3] Universidade Federal do Ceará (UFC)

{jffv, jbc, jhcp, ejtg }@cin.ufpe.br

Abstract. Context-Sensitive Systems (CSS) must detect variations in their operating context and adapt their behavior in response to such variations. Accordingly, the specification of the required context and the behavior of the tasks of such systems is a complex and labor-intensive task, which calls for systematic methods. In previous work, we have presented the GO2S (GOals to Statecharts) process to derive the behavior of context-sensitive systems from requirements models. In this paper, we report the findings of an empirical study conducted with twenty-two professionals. We examine how they perceive the complexity of the notations for context and for behavior specification, as well as the complexity of the GO2S process. The study findings showed that approximately 81% of the subjects specified the behavior correctly, whereas 97% identified the contextual variation points correctly. Moreover, according to the subjects' feedback, the notations for behavior and context specification and the GO2S process have a moderate complexity. Finally, we conclude this work by showing promising research opportunities underexplored in current research.

Keywords: Context-sensitive systems, Context Annotations, Flow expressions, GO2S Process, Behavior, Empirical study.

1 Introduction

Context-Sensitive Systems (CSS) monitor the environment and the level of satisfaction of its goals. They detect changes and react to context to provide services and relevant information to their users [1]. Accordingly, in order to satisfy its goals, the system should adapt its behavior, supporting different variants that enable itself to operate in varying contexts.

Many researchers have recognized the importance of context modeling for an effective adaptation such as [1][2][3]. However, the specification of what needs to be monitored as well as the adaptation mechanism in such applications is a challenging task due to their dependence on varying contextual elements, which need to be made explicit.

In order to design the behavior of context-sensitive systems, several steps must be taken. In previous work [4][5] we have presented the GO2S process, a systematic approach for deriving the behavior (expressed in statecharts) of context-sensitive systems, from requirements models (described as goal models). A complete description of GO2S can be found in our website[1].

The GO2S is an iterative process centered on the incremental refinement of a goal model, which is used to obtain different views of CSS, namely: design, contextual, and behavioral views. The GO2S process has a step to perform the context specification through context annotations in a goal model and refinements as well as another step to specify the system's behavior through flow expressions.

This paper contributes with an empirical study, which main purpose is to get initial feedback from industry professionals (subjects). We conducted it in order to understand the complexity of context annotations and flow expressions used to specify the behavior of context-sensitive systems. Moreover, we evaluated the complexity of GO2S process.

We consider the study results as particularly useful for the following audience: software engineers that develop CSS and want to improve their development method, since it reveals first insights on the benefits and limitations of the GO2S process; and researchers in requirements engineering and CSS who want to define research questions and set up hypotheses for future independent empirical investigations.

The remainder of this paper is structured as follows. The requirements model of the system analyzed in this study is presented in Section 2. In Section 3, we discuss related work. Section 4 gives an overview of the research method used. Section 5 presents the findings. Threats to validity are addressed in Section 6. We discuss the study results in Section 7. Last but not least, we draw conclusions and present future work in Section 8.

2 Background

The GO2S process uses context annotations in a contextual goal model [3] to perform context specification. The behavior specification is defined through flow expressions [7]. Flow expressions area particular flavor of regular expressions and can be used to describe the system behavior through its goals and tasks in a goal model.

In this study, we used a small version of the Smart Home system [6]. This system has been designed to make life easier for people with dementia problems and provide continuous care to them, ensuring their safety and comfort. In order to achieve that, the smart home has to act in response to the context.

The contextual goal model of the Smart Home system annotated with flow expressions is presented in Figure 1. The main goal of the system is to control the home for the patient: people with dementia suffer from serious problems with memory. As a result of these problems, a patient may forget to maintain a healthy family

[1] http://www.cin.ufpe.br/~ler/supplement/jffv/wer2016/

environment. The features of the system are the control of gas leaking, management of temperature, protection against theft and entertaining the patient.

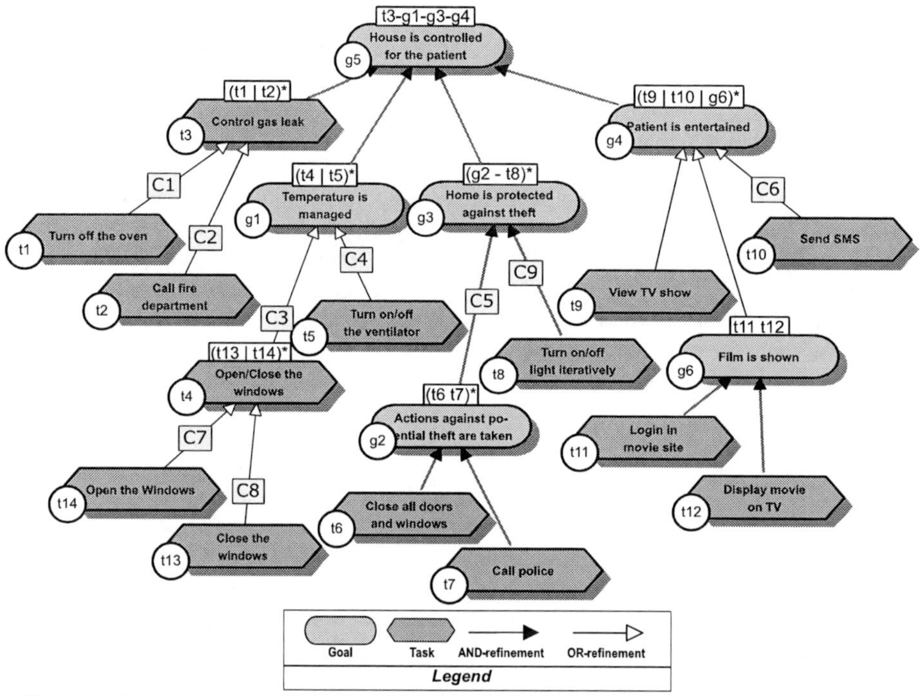

Figure 1. The contextual goal model of the Smart Home system annotated with flow expressions.

3 Related Work

The contextual goals models were analyzed in two systems (smart home and museum-guide) in the work of [6]. The study subjects were analysts that already were familiar with emerging computing paradigms scenarios and had a good expertise in goal modeling. The results of this work showed that the contextual goal model was easy to understand and the framework provided a useful systematic way to analyze contexts. Moreover, the relation between goals and context was strong in certain systems; the context specification could be a subject to viewpoints (in some other cases, it was debatable if a certain context was a statement or a fact) [6].

The use of flow expressions to specify the behavior of systems has been accepted and successfully used in many frameworks [7][8][9]. As evidence of the notation usefulness, [8] exhibited the application of flow expressions in many areas including the modeling of concurrent programs, the description of operating system architectures, the specification of synchronization problems and solutions, the flow and description of command languages, and systems analysis. We relied on this notation in the GO2S process to specify the behavior of context-sensitive systems and to derive contextualized statecharts.

The work of [7] explores the flow expressions in their multi-dimensional approach that exploits inherent variability of the design space. In this work, alternative refinements are considered for the same intermediate problem, resulting in multiple solutions (statecharts) from a single initial problem (requirements).

The flow expressions were also adopted in the work of [9] to propose a conceptual distinction between Design-time Goal Models (DGMs) - used to design a system - and Runtime Goal Models (RGMs) – deployed in the analysis of the system's runtime behavior with respect to its requirements. In their work, RGMs extend DGMs, In essence, they define some additional states and flow expressions as well as historical information about the fulfilment of goals.

4 RESEARCH METHOD

Our study has an investigative focus; hence, the purpose of this study was not to test hypotheses, but to explore what subjects' opinions and attitudes are with regard to a carefully selected set of research questions. We, therefore, designed our study to be explorative in nature, choosing a qualitative approach. As an exploratory study, it can help the identification of further research questions, as well as the definition of hypotheses that can be tested by means of analytical studies [17][10]. In this section, we discuss our research questions, the study design, its subjects, the data gathering methods and the data analysis approach.

4.1 RESEARCH QUESTIONS

This study strives to answer the following research questions:

RQ1: How do the subjects perceive the complexity of the contextual goal model and flow expressions?

RQ2: How do the subjects perceive the complexity of the GO2S process steps?

RQ3: What are the benefits stated by the subjects of the contextual goal model and flow expressions as well as the steps of the GO2S process?

RQ4: What challenges are related to the use of the GO2S process?

4.2 STUDY DESIGN

This study was conducted in April of 2015 and it consisted of four phases: profiling, training, study and post-study (see Figure 2). In the first phase, we identified the subjects' profile, current job and previous experiences through an online questionnaire. The findings from this phase are presented in Section 4.3.

The second phase consisted on training. In this phase, we provided a 3 hours training to the subjects about the GO2S process and its modeling notation.

For the study itself (third phase), we prepared a set of resources: a goal model of a simplified version of the Smart Home System, without context annotations nor flow expressions (adapted from [6]); a textual description of the system behavior; a reference guide with a summary of the activities and the notations used by the GO2S process; and the slides used for their training. All the resources were provided in Portuguese and are available at our website[2].

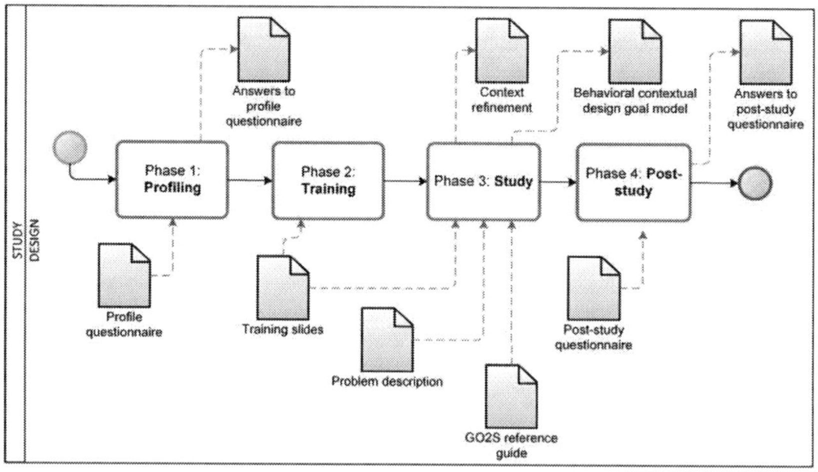

Figure 2. Study Design.

After the training, in the study itself (Phase 3) we asked the subjects to work in a project of a Smart Home system. It consisted in applying the GO2S process to perform the context and flow expressions specification. The subjects had to identify and refine the nine context annotations and eight flow expressions presented in Figure 1.

The last phase of our study consisted in applying a structured and self-administrated questionnaire with the twenty-two subjects in order to obtain their feedback about the GO2S process and its notation. After the study, we collected all the artifacts and answers from the subjects. All questionnaires were reviewed and analyzed – none was rejected due to incompleteness or errors.

4.3 STUDY SUBJECTS

The subjects were twenty-two professionals, i.e. they were working in the industry at the time when we conducted the experiment, with experience ranging from 1 to 15 years. The subjects, students of a professional master course, were invited by email. Their profile, current job and previous experiences were obtained with a pre-study questionnaire. The subjects have different background, i.e. they attended different undergraduate courses. The most studied course was *Information Systems*, followed by *Computer Science* and *Systems Development and Analysis*.

[2] http://www.cin.ufpe.br/~ler/supplement/jffv/wer2016/

The professional experience time of the subjects is presented in Figure 3. They have different degrees of experience. Notice that 50% of the subjects had more than one year of experience when the experiment was conducted.

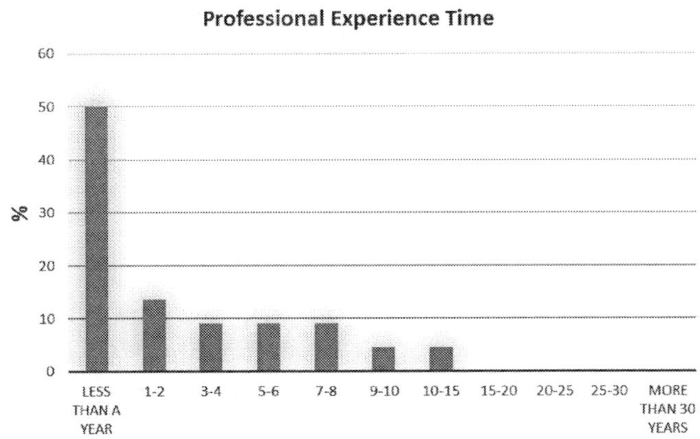

Figure 3. Professional Experience Time of the subjects.

We also wanted to understand the professional experience in software engineering of the subjects. Therefore, we asked them about their job history. This was a multiple selection question and the collected data are presented in Figure 4. Most subjects were Developer and System Analyst.

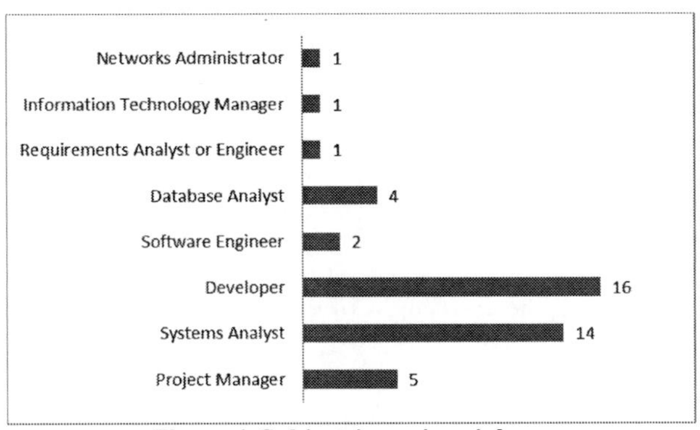

Figure 4. Subjects' previous jobs.

4.4 DATA GATHERING METHODS

In our study, we used a structured and self-administered questionnaire [9] for collecting the data from the subjects. Hence, all subjects were exposed to the same questions. The idea of using structured questionnaire was to control the input that triggered the subjects' answers so that their outputs can be reliably compared [9]. We emailed to the subjects the invitations for answering the pre-study questionnaire applied in order to obtain the subjects' profile and professional experience.

The subjects' answers about the complexity of the notations and the GO2S process were collected in a self-administrated questionnaire, which included a mix of close-ended and open-ended questions. This questionnaire was available online. The open-ended questions gave the subjects the possibility to provide a rationale for their decisions. The close-ended questions followed two well-known and widely used Likert scales [9]. The first one was Very Easy, Easy, Reasonable, Difficult and Very Difficult. The second one was Totally Agree, Agree, Indifferent, Disagree and Totally Disagree. The original questionnaires can also be found in our website.

4.5 DATA ANALYSIS

The analysis of data can be performed either quantitatively or qualitatively. According to [11], each one of these approaches can be classified in four dimensions: the qualitative analysis of qualitative data, the quantitative analysis of qualitative data, the qualitative analysis of quantitative data and the quantitative analysis of quantitative data.

For the analysis of our results, we relied on the quantitative analysis of qualitative data. The analysis of the subjects' profile included the construction of the profile matrix, or simply, the data matrix, which is a table of cases and their associated values [9].

Our analysis of the close-ended questions was performed through a quantitative analysis of quantitative data. This analysis was performed through mathematical analysis of the numeric data. The open-ended questions were analyzed by a quantitative analysis of the qualitative data. The subjects' statements were structured and displayed in an Microsoft Excel spreadsheet based on the selected key aspects using the coding technique. The traceability between the statements and the raw data were also established.

5 FINDINGS

In this section, we analyze the correctness of the models generated by the subjects as well as our research questions.

5.1 Correctness of the models

In relation to the correctness of context annotations specified in the contextual goal model, we observed that the number of context annotations specified correctly, i.e. annotations specified as described in the requirements document, was 97.53% with a standard deviation of 22.32%. We observed that some subjects specified more contexts than described in the specification. The average amount of contexts specified in excess by the subjects had a mean of 1.64% with a standard deviation of 3%. Moreover, the mean of flow expressions specified correctly was 80.95% with a standard deviation of 18.09%.

Figure 5 presents the boxplot of these two variables investigated: (a) context representation and (b) flow expressions. After analyzing this figure, we found 1 potentially outlying observation at the context representation since that subject did not specify correctly any context (bottom-center of Figure 5.a).

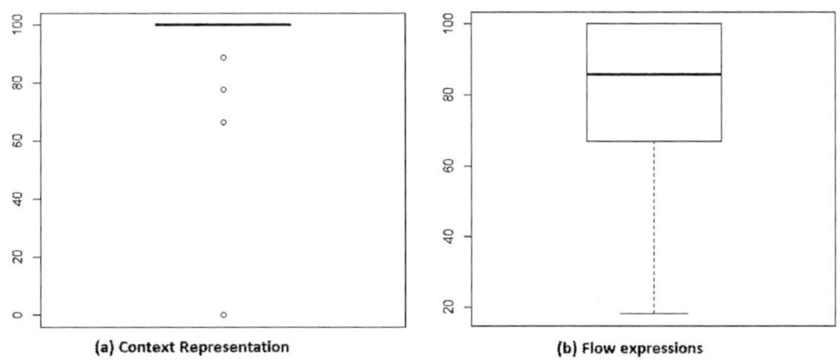

Figure 5. Correctness of context annotations and flow expressions.

However, after deeper investigation of the work, we did not find any justification for rejecting such observation. In relation to the specification of the flow expressions, we had none outliers.

5.2 RQ1: How do the subjects perceive the complexity of the contextual goal model and flow expressions?

The subjects classified the complexity of the notation for context specification using a Likert scale. The findings are shown in Table 1. The majority of subjects (63.6%) stated that it was of Reasonable complexity and 22.7% affirmed that it is Very Easy or Easy. In relation to the complexity of the flow expressions, 54.5% classified it as Reasonable and 31.8% as Very Easy or Easy.

Table 1. Complexity of the notations for context specification and flow expressions.

	Very Easy	Easy	Reasonable	Difficult	Very Difficult
Notation for context specification	1 (4.5%)	4 (18.2%)	14 (63.6%)	3 (13.6%)	0
Flow expressions	1 (4.5%)	6 (27.3%)	12 (54.5%)	3 (13.6%)	0

5.3 RQ2: How do the subjects perceive the complexity of the GO2S process steps?

We asked the subjects about different aspects of the GO2S process. The complexity of the process in general was classified by 72.7% of the subjects as Reasonable as depicted in Table 2. There were different opinions about the complexity of the Step 2, which corresponds to the specification of contextual variations points. 36.4% of the subjects stated that is Reasonable, although 31.8% classified it as Easy and 27.3% as Difficult. 45.5% subjects evaluated the complexity of the Step 3 (Specification of adaptation and monitoring) as Reasonable. On the other hand, 40.9% classified it as Difficult as presented in Table 2. The complexity of the Step 4 was evaluated by 59.1% as Reasonable and 27.2% as Very Easy or Easy.

Table 2. Complexity of the GO2S Process.

	Very Easy	**Easy**	**Reasonable**	**Difficult**	**Very Difficult**
GO2S Process	0	1 (4.5%)	16 (72.7%)	5 (22.7%)	0
Step 2 of GO2S	0	7 (31.8%)	8 (36.4%)	6 (27.3%)	1 (4.5%)
Step 3 of GO2S	0	3 (13.6%)	10 (45.5%)	9 (40.9%)	0
Step 4 of GO2S	1 (4.5%)	5 (22.7%)	13 (59.1%)	2 (9.1%)	1 (4.5%)

5.4 RQ3: What are the benefits stated by the subjects of the contextual goal model and flow expressions as well as the steps of the GO2S process?

In relation to the subjects' opinion about the following statement: "*The use of flow expressions makes the creation of statecharts more systematic*", 86.4% of the subjects agree (68.2% or Totally agree - 18.2%) with this statement. These findings are shown in Figure 6.

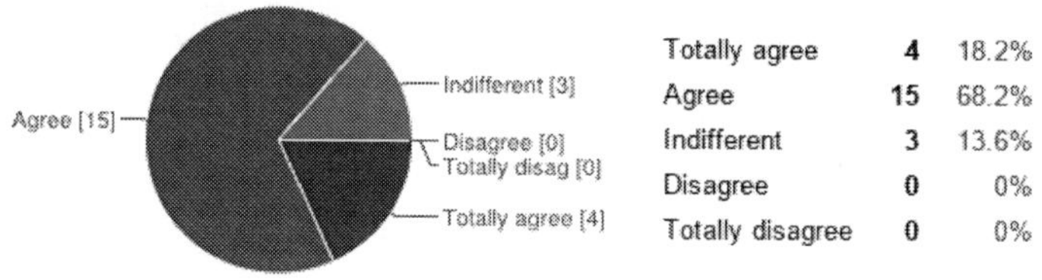

Figure 6. Flow expressions makes the creation of statecharts systematic.

The GO2S process is still an emerging methodology for derivation of the behavior of context-sensitive systems, and many benefits have not yet been fully realized or evaluated.

Hence, we analyzed which benefits of the GO2S process are perceived by the subjects, with the following open-ended question: "*In your opinion, which is the main benefit of this process?*" We extracted some codes from the subjects' answers (see Figure 7) using the coding technique. Coding is an essential part of the analysis when we are dealing with qualitative information.

We identified seven categories of benefits: accuracy of the statecharts specification, understanding the system's behavior, organization of the generated statecharts, requirements elicitation, the systematization of the derivation process, facilitates understanding of the problem domain and the system, mapping between tasks and states.

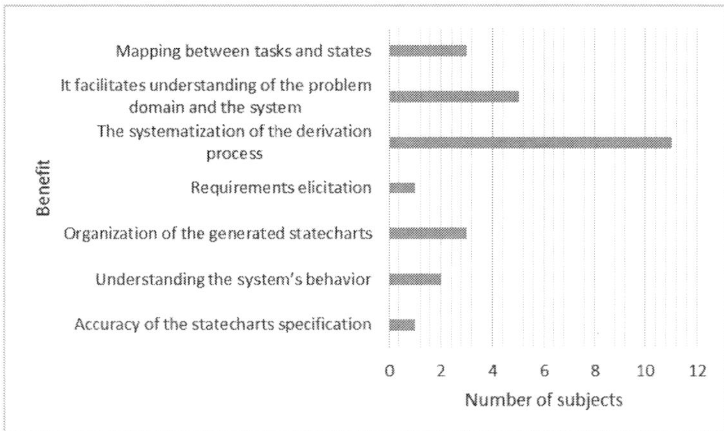

Figure 7. Benefits of the GO2S Process.

We already expected some of these benefits since they constitute the motivation for the process. However, the benefit for requirements elicitation was a surprise for us, since it is not the GO2S purpose. It was assumed that the software engineer had already performed this phase. Hence, a goal model was available as an input to the process. There are some studies such as [14] dedicated to investigate the problem of context elicitation.

5.5 RQ4: What challenges are related to the use of the GO2S process?

The subjects reported some difficulties and challenges about the use and specification of the GO2S process as well as training time. The majority (68.2%) said that they had more difficulty in step 2 (specification of contextual variation points) followed by step 3 (specification of adaptation and monitoring) with 54.5% while 50% had difficulty in step 5 (statechart derivation and refinement). These findings are depicted in Figure 8.

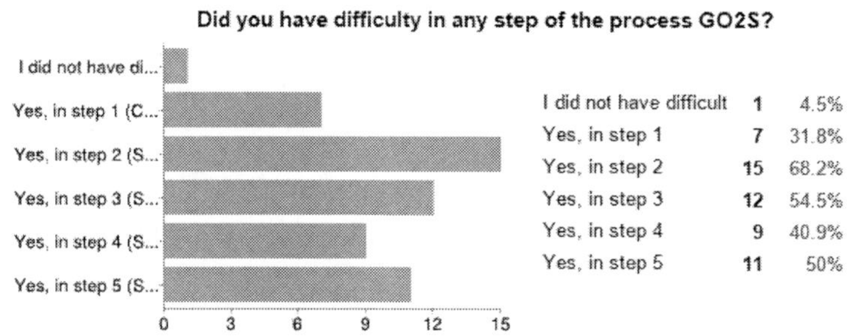

Figure 8. Difficulties in the use of the GO2 process.

The subjects also reported some difficulties regarding the study execution such as little experience in the use of the process, the identification of tasks to be performed at each step of the process, little time of training and the complexity of some steps of the GO2S process. The codes of the difficulties described in the subjects' opinions about the study execution are presented in Figure 9.

One subject complained about not making the material of the training available before the study. We made this call since we want all subject to have the same training time and level of knowledge, so we could draw reliable conclusions and avoid maturation effects. In the next section, we discuss threats to validity.

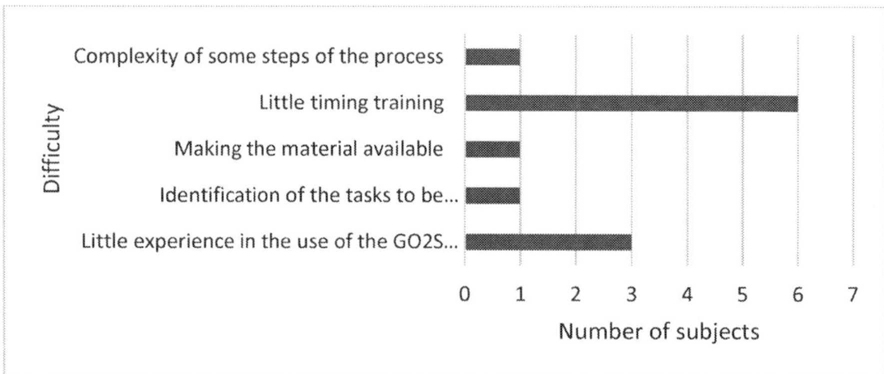

Figure 9. Difficulties reported in the study execution.

6 THREATS TO VALIDITY

We will base our discussion of threats to validity on the threat categories used by Wohlin et al. [12]. Due to space limitation we will only go into details for the threat categories that we consider most important for our study.

The conclusion validity is concerned with threats against being able to draw the correct conclusions about the relationship between treatment and observations. In relation to the statistical power, it should be noted that the purpose of the study was not to perform statistical testing of hypotheses, as this study is qualitative in nature.

The internal validity concerns the threats due to something else than the treatment influencing the observations. We minimized threats related to instrumentation due to bad forms, diagrams, score sheets etc. since the questionnaires had a straightforward layout, common to the questionnaires used in most cases where the Likert scale is used.

The construct validity addresses if the study be able to reflect the real world phenomena that we want to observe. We minimized threats related to instructions to the subjects since all of them got the same training with the same material and same instructor. Hence, differences in the study results can thus not stem from the instructions.

The external validity is related to the ability of generalization of the study results. We acknowledge that the limited number of subjects does not allow generalization outside the scope of the study. On the other hand, we expect that the results, including the subjects' feedback, can be used as guidelines to better improve the GO2S process. Besides, we believe that they are considerable contributions. This study can guide other studies in order to evaluate alternative approaches for context and behavior specification.

7 DISCUSSION

In this paper, we present the design and the findings of an empirical study conducted to understand the complexity of the notations for context and behavior specifications as well as the steps of the GO2S process. The study used a self-administrated questionnaire for collecting data from the subjects [17].

The questionnaire had a mix of close-ended and open-ended questions [17]. The close-ended questions have as advantages the efficiency and the unambiguity. The possible answers for the close-ended questions were exhaustive and mutually exclusive since we want the subjects to check just one answer. We used open-ended items for those aspects that we want to get more feedback from the subjects. Besides, we made short questions and tried to avoid loaded and double-barreled questions [17]. A double-barreled question is a single question asking about more than one issue, but that only allows for one answer. Moreover, we gave some training to the subjects so they to understand and answer the questions we want to investigate.

The research findings showed that 97% of the subjects identified appropriately the context annotations and 81% the flow expressions correctly. Moreover, according to the subjects' answers, the notations as well as the GO2S process have a reasonable perceived complexity.

Moreover, the subjects reported some benefits of the GO2S process such as the mapping between tasks and states. They also indicated that it facilitates the understanding of the problem domain and the system, the systematization of the derivation process. Moreover, it contributes to the requirements elicitation, organization of generated statecharts, as well as to understanding the system's behavior. Last but not least, it improves the accuracy of the statecharts specification.

The GO2S has a certain degree of complexity since it requires knowledge of several different notations such as goal models, context annotations and refinements, flow expressions and statecharts. Hence, the subjects classified the complexity of GO2S as reasonable.

Although the subjects were concerned with its reasonable complexity, such classification may be due to the little time available for training the subjects and execution of the study. Moreover, it is important to highlight that the subjects had no contact with these notations before this study.

A common issue with the reporting of empirical studies is the publication bias. This concept refers to the problem that positive results are more likely to be published than negative results [13]. However, the concept of positive or negative results sometimes depends on the viewpoint of the researcher. Accordingly, it is important to report difficulties such as little time for training and reasonable complexity in proposals, so that improvements can be investigated and improved in future works. Therefore, we believe that some results presented in this paper could not be interpreted as a drawback for adopting the process.

Finally, further replication by independent groups is necessary, and also new studies must be carried out with larger samples of subjects.

8 CONCLUSIONS AND FUTURE WORK

In this paper, we presented the findings of an empirical study conducted with twenty-two professionals to analyze the complexity of context annotations presented in goal models, along with flow expressions that specify the behavior of context-sensitive systems. Moreover, the steps of the GO2S process were also analyzed.

The findings presented in this study can be useful to the software engineering community, since it gathers evidences of the feasibility and of the benefits of using the context annotations of goal models to specify the context of context-sensitive systems. Besides, the subjects reported significant benefits in using flow expressions and the GO2S process to specify the behavior of context-sensitive systems, such as systematization of the process, better understanding of the problem domain and of the system itself; and good organization of the generated statecharts.

As future work, we expect to develop a case tool to support the process. It could be used to produce the goal model as well as to guide the application of the GO2S process, generating its different views (design, contextual and behavioral) of our process and implementing the statechart derivation. A prototype tool with some of these functionalities has already been developed [15].

Finally, the analysis of properties of the statecharts generated with the GO2S process is necessary. These properties can include completeness, correctness, deadlocks, and state reachability, as well as the satisfaction of quality attributes. We expect to be able to perform some of these analyses using ontological mechanisms, considering their suitability for requirements engineering as identified in previous work [16].

Acknowledgments

The following Brazilian institutions have supported this work: FACEPE, CAPES and CNPQ. The authors would like to express their gratitude to all those involved in this study.

References

1. V. Vieira; P. Tedesco; and A. C. Salgado. Designing context-sensitive systems: An integrated approach. In Expert Systems with Applications vol. 38, n. 2, pp. 1119-1138, 2011.
2. R. de Lemos et al. Software engineering for self-adaptive systems: A second research roadmap. In: Software Engineering for Self-Adaptive Systems II. Springer Berlin Heidelberg, pp. 1-32, 2013.
3. R. Ali; F. Dalpiaz; and P. Giorgini. A goal-based framework for contextual requirements modeling and analysis. Requirements Engineering, v. 15, n. 4, pp. 439-458, 2010.
4. J. Vilela; J. Castro; J. Pimentel. Deriving the behavior of context-sensitive systems from contextual goal models. In: Proceedings of the 30th SAC, 2015, pp. 1397-1400
5. J. Vilela; J. Castro; J. Pimentel, P. Lima. On the behavior of context-sensitive systems. In: Proceedings of the 18th WER, 2015, pp. 632-645.
6. R. Ali. Modeling and Reasoning about Contextual Requirements: goal-based framework. 2010. PhD Thesis, Universita degli Studi di Trento.
7. J. Pimentel et al. From requirements to statecharts via design refinement. In: Proceedings of the 29th Symposium of Applied Computing (SAC), pp. 995–1000, 2014.
8. A. C. Shaw. Software descriptions with flow expressions. IEEE Transactions on Software Engineering, n. 3, pp. 242-254, 1978.
9. F. Dalpiaz; A. Borgida; J. Horkoff; J. Mylopoulos. Runtime goal models: Keynote. In Seventh International Conference on Research Challenges in Information Science (RCIS), pp.1-11, 2013.
10. E. Sikora; B. Tenbergen; K. Pohl. Industry needs and research directions in requirements engineering for embedded systems. Requirements Engineering, v. 17, n. 1, p. 57-78, 2012.
11. H. R. Bernard. Social research methods: Qualitative and quantitative approaches. Sage, 2012.
12. C. Wohlin et al. Experimentation in software engineering: An introduction. Norwell, MA: Kluwer Academic, 2000.
13. B. Kitchenham; S. Charters. Guidelines for performing systematic literature reviews in software engineering. In: 2.3 EBSE Technical Report. EBSE. 2007.
14. C. A. T. Batista and C. T. L. L. S. Schuenemann. Um Processo Criativo de Elicitação de Contextos para Sistemas Sensíveis ao Contexto. In: Anais do XI Simpósio Brasileiro de Sistemas de Informação (SBSI). 2015.
15. J. Pimentel; J. Vilela; J. Castro. Web tool for Goal modelling and statechart derivation. In: 23rd International Requirements Engineering Conference (RE), 2015, pp.292-293.
16. D. Dermeval, J. Vilela, Ig Bittencourt, J. Castro, S. Isotani, P. Brito, A. Silva. Applications of ontologies in requirements engineering: a systematic review of the literature. Requirements Engineering, pp. 1-33, 2015.
17. H. R. Bernard. Social research methods: Qualitative and quantitative approaches. Sage, 2012.

Uma solução baseada em ontologia para o tratamento de erros em modelos construídos na linguagem i*

Heyde Francielle do Carmo França[1,2], Renato de Freitas Bulcão Neto[1]
1 Departamento de Informática – Universidade Federal de Goiás (UFG)
{heydecarmo, renato}@inf.ufg.br
2 Instituto Federal Goiano – Campus Rio Verde (IF Goiano)
heyde.franca@ifgoiano.edu.br

Abstract. The i* language faces problems regarding the quality of requirements models, which include typical mistakes of misuse of its constructs, the presence of ambiguities on the interpretation of those constructs and the complexity of the resulting i* models. This paper proposes the extension of an ontology-based representation for i* models aiming at preventing the most well-known errors while constructing such models. Results demonstrate an approximate coverage of 70% of those common errors in the context of a case study.

Keywords: Requirements Engineering, Goal, i* Language, OntoiStar, OWL.

1 Introdução

A técnica GORE (*Goal-Oriented Requirements Engineering*) captura e representa as reais intenções de *stakeholders* por meio de metas que devem ser satisfeitas, provendo uma maneira natural de estruturação de documentos de requisitos complexos [1]. Dentre as linguagens para modelagem de requisitos baseadas em GORE, destaca-se a linguagem i* dados os benefícios para a modelagem de requisitos como, por exemplo, acrescentar o entendimento das intenções e motivações dos membros da organização envolvida, promover uma rastreabilidade entre as funcionalidades do sistema e os requisitos, e permitir a análise de caminhos alternativos que podem ser seguidos para a satisfação de requisitos [3], [11], [13].

Apesar das vantagens que a linguagem i* apresenta, a literatura aponta problemas quanto à qualidade dos modelos produzidos nessa linguagem: a complexidade dos modelos resultantes, erros típicos de mau uso de construtores e a presença de ambiguidades na interpretação desses construtores [4], [8], [9]. Estes dois últimos problemas estão interrelacionados, pois o mau uso de seus construtores, em geral, acontece por erros de interpretação da sintaxe e da semântica da linguagem i* [11].

Em [5] foi proposta a ontologia *OntoiStar* de forma a não apenas estruturar, mas também fornecer semântica aos construtores da linguagem i*, porém sem tratar erros típicos em modelos i*, como erros envolvidos na definição de atores, dependências e relacionamentos entre atores. Esses erros comumente encontrados estão resumidos em um documento denominado catálogo de erros frequentes da linguagem i* [2], [4].

Este artigo relata a extensão da ontologia *OntoiStar* usando a semântica da linguagem OWL, com vistas a reduzir a ocorrência de erros descritos no catálogo de erros frequentes [2], [4] em modelos de requisitos construídos na linguagem i*. Ontologias podem ser utilizadas para resolver este tipo de problema, pois definem um vocabulário de representação que captura os conceitos e relações de um domínio, e um conjunto de axiomas que restringem a sua interpretação [7]. Para validação da proposta foi utilizado o cenário *Media Shop*, adaptado de [2] e [6], utilizado como ilustração de modelos i* em vários artigos da área.

Este artigo está estruturado como se segue: a seção 2 apresenta a extensão da ontologia *OntoiStar* para tratar erros em modelos i*, e a seção 3 descreve conclusões, limitações e trabalhos futuros.

2 Extensão da ontologia *OntoiStar*

Com base no catálogo de erros frequentes descritos em [2] e discutidos em [4] e [14], foram elaborados e incluídos axiomas e restrições na *OntoiStar* para prevenir a ocorrência desses erros. Para isso, utilizou-se a semântica de construtores OWL e o editor *Protégé* integrado ao raciocinador *Pellet*. Todos os exemplos apresentados seguem a modelagem do cenário *Media Shop* que inclui uma loja de vendas de diferentes tipos de itens (livros, jornais, revistas, cds, etc) que pode ser visto com mais detalhes em [2], [6]. Para fins de implementação das restrições apresentadas a seguir foi utilizada como referência a evolução do i* original[1], o que justifica a configuração empregada no tratamento dos erros 4 e 8 descritos nesta seção.

Erro 1: Atores dentro da fronteira de outro ator - a classe *ActorBoundary* da *OntoiStar* representa a fronteira de um ator. Para eliminar a possibilidade da existência de mais de um ator dentro dessa fronteira, a classe *ActorBoundary* foi redefinida para que apresente os relacionamentos *has_Actor_Bondaury* e/ou *has_Actor_boundary_elements* com exatamente 0 atores. Assim, o ator do *ActorBoundary* será o único dentro do relacionamento, permitindo apenas relacionamento com elementos da classe *InternalElement*. Após essa redefinição ser inserida na *OntoiStar*, o raciocinador *Pellet* integrado ao *Protégé* notifica que uma inconsistência é detectada ao se tentar reproduzir o erro da Figura 2, ligando-se os atores *Medi@* e *Bank_Cpy* por meio de *has_Actor_Boundary*.

Erro 2: Conexão de um *InternalElement* para um *ActorBoundary* - a classe *ActorBoundary* não deve possuir nenhum relacionamento direto do tipo *contribution* ou *dependency* com um *InternalElement*. As redefinições de classe apresentadas na Tabela 1 evitam a existência de relacionamentos do tipo *DependencyRelationship* ou *InternalElementRelationship* com a classe *ActorBoundary*. As regras foram criadas usando *DependableNode* em vez de *InternalElement*, pois assim garante que não poderão existir esses relacionamentos, nem com itens da classe *InternalElement*, nem com a classe *Actor*.

[1] Disponível em: http://istar.rwth-aachen.de/tiki-index.php?page=iStarQuickGuide

Erro 3: Dependência de ator - deve-se usar *DependencyRelationships* apenas para expressar dependências entre um membro da classe *Actor* e um *InternalElement*; não deve usar relacionamentos do tipo *InternalElementRelationShip* para representar dependências. Para evitar este erro, criaram-se as restrições descritas na Tabela 2. O símbolo * representa as possibilidades de um tipo de construtor, i.e. *source* e *target*.

Tabela 1. Condições para que não haja conexão entre *InternalElement* e *Actor Boundary*

has_Dependency_DependerLink_*-ref exactly 0 DependableNode
has_Dependency_DependeeLink_*-ref exactly 0 DependableNode
has_Dependency_DependumLink_*-ref exactly 0 DependableNode
has_InternalElement_MeansEndLink_*-ref exactly 0 DependableNode
has_InternalElement_AndDecompositionLink_*-ref exactly 0 DependableNode
has_InternalElement_ContibutionLink_*-ref exactly 0 DependableNode

Tabela 2. Condições para que não haja relacionamentos do tipo *InternalElementRelationship* para representar uma dependência entre um *Actor* e um *InternalElement*.

has_InternalElement_MeansEndLink_*-ref exactly 0 InternalElement
has_InternalElement_AndDecompositionLink_*-ref exactly 0 InternalElement
has_InternalElement_ContibutionLink_*-ref exactly 0 InternalElement
has_InternalElement_DecompositionLink_*-ref exactly 0 InternalElement
has_InternalElement_OrDecompositionLink_*-ref exactly 0 InternalElement

Erro 4: Refinando metas - uma meta não pode ser ligada diretamente a outra meta. Esta deve ser decomposta utilizando uma ligação do tipo *MeansEndLink*, e estas ligações só podem ligar tarefas a metas. Seguem na Tabela 3 as redefinições de classes para prevenir que este erro ocorra.

Erro 5: *Link* de dependência interna - não devem ser realizadas relações de dependência entre um *InternalElement* dentro da fronteira de um ator. Pode haver um *Dependum* que se origina externamente à fronteira do ator ligando-se a um *InternalElement* de dentro da fronteira, mas nunca uma relação de dependência entre dois *InternalElement* internos à fronteira. Para garantir que este erro não ocorra foi acrescentada uma redefinição na classe *ActorBoundary* como mostra a Tabela 4.

Erro 6: *Link* de dependência externa - não se deve usar um *link* de dependência entre dois atores sem um *Dependum*. Ou seja, um ator não pode estar diretamente ligado a outro ator. Para garantir que esse erro não ocorra foram inseridas as seguintes redefinições nas classes *DependeeLink* e *DependerLink*, conforme ilustra a Tabela 5.

Tabela 3. Condições para que uma tarefa só possa ser decomposta utilizando ligações do tipo *MeansEndLink* e que só possa ser decomposta em metas.

has_InternalElement_MeansEndLink_*-ref exactly 0 Resource
has_InternalElement_MeansEndLink_*-ref exactly 0 Softgoal
has_InternalElement_MeansEndLink_*-ref exactly 0 Plan
has_InternalElement_MeansEndLink_*-ref exactly 0 Service
has_InternalElement_MeansEndLink_*-ref exactly 0 Process

Tabela 4. Regra para certificar-se que um *Depender* não se origine na fronteira de um ator.

has_Dependency_DependerLink_source-ref exactly 0 InternalElement

Tabela 5. Regras para certificar-se que um *Dependee* e um *Depender* não se conectem diretamente a outro ator.

has_Dependency_DependeeLink_*-ref exactly 0 Actor
has_Dependency_DependerLink_*-ref exactly 0 Actor

Erro 7: *Link* de contribuição interna - um *ContributionLink* só deve ser usado para conectar um *IntentionalElement* a uma *Softgoal*. Para garantir que esse erro não ocorra foi inserido na classe *ContributionLink* as redefinições da Tabela 6.

Tabela 6. Regras inseridas para garantir que um *ContributionLink* só conecte um *InternalElement* somente a *Softgoal*.

has_InternalElement_ContibutionLink_*-ref exactly 0 Goal
has_InternalElement_ContibutionLink_*-ref exactly 0 Process
has_InternalElement_ContibutionLink_*-ref exactly 0 Service

Erro 8: *Link MeansEnd* interno - os *links* do tipo *MeansEnd* só podem ser utilizados para ligar *Tasks* a *Goals*. Para garantir que este relacionamento seja utilizado de forma correta foram inseridas as seguintes redefinições na classe *MeansEndLink* da ontologia *OntoiStar*, descritas na Tabela 7.

Tabela 7. Regras inseridas para garantir que um *MeansEndLink* só conecte *Tasks* a *Goals*.

has_InternalElement_MeansEndLink_*-ref exactly 0 Resource
has_InternalElement_MeansEndLink_*-ref exactly 0 Softgoal
has_InternalElement_MeansEndLink_*-ref exactly 0 Plan
has_InternalElement_MeansEndLink_*-ref exactly 0 Service
has_InternalElement_MeansEndLink_*-ref exactly 0 Process

Erro 9: Ator sem ligação ou com ligação incorreta - não deve existir no modelo um ator sem uma ligação de dependência ou *ActorRelationship*, e os relacionamentos entre atores devem obedecer às regras:

- *IsA* – relacionamentos apenas entre atores do mesmo tipo;
- *Plays* – relacionamentos apenas entre um agente e um papel;
- *Covers* – relacionamentos apenas entre uma posição e um papel;
- *Occupies* – relacionamentos apenas entre uma posição e um agente; e
- *INS* – relacionamentos apenas entre um agente e outro agente.

Vale ressaltar que as redefinições de classes descritas na Tabela 8 garantem apenas que os relacionamentos estão corretos, mas não garantem que não exista um ator sem ligação. Isto ocorre porque não é possível criar uma regra de obrigatoriedade de existência de um tipo de relacionamento utilizando a expressividade dos construtores da linguagem OWL. Sendo assim, o erro 9 é coberto apenas parcialmente.

Tabela 8. Regras para garantir ligações corretas entre atores.

has_Actor_ IsALink _*-ref exactly 1 Actor
has_Actor_ PlaysLink _*-ref exactly 1 Role
has_Actor_ PlaysLink _*-ref exactly 0 Agent
has_Actor_ PlaysLink _*-ref exactly 0 Position
has_Actor_ CoversLink _*-ref exactly 0 Role
has_Actor_ CoversLink _*-ref exactly 1 Agent
has_Actor_ CoversLink _*-ref exactly 0 Position
has_Actor_ OccupiesLink_*-ref exactly 0 Role
has_Actor_ OccupiesLink_*-ref exactly 1 Agent
has_Actor_ OccupiesLink_*-ref exactly 0 Position
has_Actor_ InstanceOfLink_*-ref exactly 1 Actor

A Tabela 9 resume as restrições acrescentadas à *OntoiStar* em uma representação em lógica de 1ª ordem: Ax (instância da classe *Actor*) e conceitos *Internal Elements* como T (*Task*), R (*Resource*), G (*Goal*), S (*Softgoal*), PL (*Plan*), SE (*Service*), PR (*Process*), IE (*InternalElement* ou (T ∨ R ∨ G ∨ S ∨ PL ∨ SE ∨ PR)).

Tabela 9. Representação axiomática referente a cada um dos erros tratados.

Erro 1	A1 ^ (*has_ActorBoundary* ∨ *has_Actor_boundary_elements*) ^ (T ∨ R ∨ G ∨ S ∨ PL ∨ SE ∨ PR ^ ¬ A_2)
Erro 2	A1 ^ (*has_ActorBoundary*) ^ (¬ (*DependencyRelationship* ∨ *InternalElementRelationship))*^ (T ∨ R ∨ G ∨ S ∨ PL ∨ SE ∨ PR ^ A_2)
Erro 3	A1 ^ (*DependencyRelationship* ^ (¬ *InternalElementRelationship))* ^ (T ∨ R ∨ G ∨ S ∨ PL ∨ SE ∨ PR ^ ¬ A_2)
Erro 4	T1 ^ (*has_InternalElement_MeansEndLink**) ^ (G ∨ ¬ (T ∨ R ∨ S ∨ PL ∨ SE ∨ PR ^ A_2))
Erro 5	ActorBoudary ^ ¬ (*has_Dependency_DependerLink_source-ref*) ^ (T ∨ R ∨ G ∨ S ∨ PL ∨ SE ∨ PR)
Erro 6	*(DependeeLink* ∨ *DependerLink*) ^ *has_Dependency_DependeeLink** ^ (¬ A_1)
Erro 7	*ContributionLink* ^ *has_InternalElement_ContributionLink** ^ (S ^ ¬ (T ∨ R ∨ G ∨ PL ∨ SE ∨ PR)
Erro 8	*MeansEndLink* ^ *has_InternalElement_MeansEndLink** ^ (G ^ ¬ (T ∨ R ∨ S ∨ PL ∨ SE ∨ PR)
Erro 9	A1 ^ *has_Actor_ IsALink** ^ (A2 ^ ¬ (Agent ∨ Role ∨ Position) A1 ^ *has_Actor_ PlaysLink* * ^ (Role ^ ¬ (Agent ∨ A2 ∨ Position) A1 ^ *has_Actor_ CoversLink* * ^ (Role ^ ¬ (Agent ∨ A2 ∨ Position) A1 ^ *has_Actor_ OccupiesLink* * ^ (Position ^ ¬ (Agent ∨ A2 ∨ Role) A1 ^ *has_Actor_ InstanceOfLink* * ^ (Agent ^ ¬ (Position ∨ A2 ∨ Role)

3 Conclusões e trabalhos futuros

Há trabalhos que exploram a sintaxe e a semântica da linguagem i*, como a iStarML [12], baseada em XML, e a *OntoiStar*, baseada em OWL. No entanto, essas soluções não resolvem erros típicos em modelos i*, como aqueles envolvidos na definição de atores, dependências, relacionamentos entre atores.

A extensão proposta à *OntoiStar* verifica a consistência de modelos i* à medida em que são criados, não permitindo a criação de modelos com aproximadamente 70% dos erros supracitados. Soma-se ainda a vantagem dessa solução também suportar a interoperabilidade entre variantes da linguagem i*.

Os erros do catálogo que não foram contemplados são mais subjetivos (ex.: uso de nome indequado para ator) e/ou mais difíceis de tratar apenas com a expressividade dos construtores da linguagem OWL. Em função dessa limitação, pretende-se realizar como trabalho futuro a utilização de regras SWRL (*Semantic Web Rule Language*) [10], que estendem a capacidade de expressão e de inferência da linguagem OWL.

AGRADECIMENTOS

Ao Programa Institucional de Capacitação Docente do Instituto Federal de Educação, Ciência e Tecnologia Goiano (PICSS IF Goiano), pelo financiamento da pesquisa.

Referências bibliográficas

1. Lamsweerde, A.V.: Goal-oriented Requirements Engineering: A Guided Tour. In: Fifth IEEE International Symposium on Requirements Engineering, 249-262, (2001)
2. Santos, E.B.: Uma Proposta de Métricas para Avaliar Modelos i*. Dissertação (Mestrado). UFPE, (2008)
3. Horkoff, J., Yu, E.: Detecting Judgment Inconsistencies to Encourage Model Iteration in Interactive i* Analysis. In: Fifth International i* Workshop, p. 20-25, (2011)
4. Souza, C., Souza, C., Alencar, F.M.R., Castro, J., Figueiredo, E., Cavalcanti, P.: Avaliação de Modelos i* com o Processo Airdoc-i. In: ERBR13, 1, (2013)
5. Najera K., Martinez, A., Perini, A., Estrada, H.: An Ontology-Based Methodology for Integrating i* Variants. In: 6h International i* Workshop, 1-6, (2013)
6. Castro, J., Kolp, M., Mylopoulos, J.: Towards Requirements-driven Information Systems Engineering: The Tropos Project. Information Systems, Elsevier Science Ltd., Oxford, UK, v. 27, n. 6, 365-389 (2002)
7. Nardi, J. C., Falbo, R. A.: Uma ontologia de Requisitos de Software. In: CIbSE, 111-124 (2006)
8. Nunes, C. M.: Uma Linguagem de Domínio Específico para a Framework i*. Dissertação (Mestrado). Universidade Nova de Lisboa (2009)
9. Malta, Á., Soares, M., Santos, E., Paes, J., Alencar, F.M.R., Castro, J.: iStarTool: Modeling Requirements Using the i* Framework. In: CEUR Workshop Proceedings, 163-165 (2011)
10. Horrocks, I., Patel-Schneider, P.F., Boley, H., Tabet, S., Grosof, B., Dean. M.: SWRL: A Semantic Web Rule Language, Available online at http://www.w3.org/Submission/SWRL/
11. Guizzardi, R.S.S., Franch, X., Guizzardi, G.: Applying a foundational ontology to analyze means-end links in the i* framework. In: Meeting of the RCIS, IEEE, 1-11 (2012)
12. Cares C., Franch, X.: iStarML: Principles and Implications. In: 5th International i* Workshop, 8-13, (2011)
13. Yu, E.: Modelling Strategic Relationships for Process Reengineering. Tese (Doutorado). Canadá: University of Toronto, Department of Computer Science (1995)
14. Souza, C., Alencar, F. M. R., Guedes, G., Soares, M., Souza, C., Ramos, R. A., Castro, J.: AIRDoc-i*: um processo para avaliação de modelos i*. In: 15th Workshop em Engenharia de Requisitos (WER), 1-4, (2012)

Especificação de Requisitos no Domínio de Sistemas de Informação com o Uso de Padrões

Leonardo Barcelos[1,2], Rosângela Penteado[1]

[1] Departamento de Computação – Universidade Federal de São Carlos, UFSCar – Programa de Pós-Graduação em Ciência da Computação – Campus São Carlos/SP – Brasil
[2] Departamento de Ciências Exatas e da Terra – Universidade do Estado de Minas Gerais, UEMG – Bacharelado em Sistemas de Informação – Unidade Frutal/MG – Brasil
{leonardo.barcelos, rosangela}@dc.ufscar.br

Abstract. The requirement elicitation is the first step to obtain quality software, requiring constant interaction among stakeholders. The requirements in the information systems domain have similar characteristics, such as the CRUD operations. Reusing knowledge obtained in previous projects, requirement patterns can be elaborated to facilitate the complete and consistent specification of system requirements in that domain. This paper shows a set of functional requirement patterns and business rules elaborated to help the software engineer in the writing of the requirements document. The non-functional requirements were not considered in this project. A computational support was developed, based on that set of patterns, to facilitate the organized and complete writing of the requirements document. Case studies are presented with the use of the computational support.

Keywords: requirements document; requirement patterns; system information domain; computational support based on requirement patterns

1 Introdução

Contextualização: Problemas relacionados com a Engenharia de Requisitos (ER) são amplamente reconhecidos por afetar a qualidade do software e impactar a eficácia do processo de desenvolvimento de software [1]. Estima-se que descobrir e corrigir um problema após a entrega do software pode ser 100 vezes mais caro do que se essa correção ocorrer durante as fases iniciais do desenvolvimento [2]. Nesse sentido, há relatos que a completa compreensão e especificação de requisitos estão entre as tarefas mais difíceis enfrentadas por um engenheiro de software [3].

Chernak [4] relata que na indústria de TI, existem três formas principais de documentação de requisitos, sendo a ER tradicional (48%), a dirigida por casos de uso (28%), a de métodos ágeis (11%) e as demais abordagens que representam 13%. Observa-se que a ER tradicional corresponde a principal forma para a documentação de requisitos. Contudo, normalmente os requisitos são especificados usando linguagem natural, o que pode resultar em problemas como ambiguidade e incompletude [5].

Dentre os problemas comuns na elicitação de requisitos pode-se citar a dificuldade dos *stakeholders* em expressar suas necessidades e a dos engenheiros de software, sem experiência do domínio do cliente, em entendê-las completamente [6]. Geralmente, o produto de software desenvolvido não atende às reais necessidades dos *stakeholders*, gerando retrabalho, aumento do custo, a insatisfação ou até o cancelamento do projeto.

Motivação: A reutilização de software pode contribuir para o aumento da produtividade, uma vez que conduz à: a) melhoria do tempo de colocação do produto no mercado; b) melhoria da qualidade do produto; e c) redução do custo de desenvolvimento [4]. A aplicação de abordagens de reúso desde a fase inicial do projeto pode ajudar aos engenheiros de software na elicitação, validação e documentação dos requisitos do software, tendo como consequência uma especificação completa, consistente e sem ambiguidade [7] [8].

Padrões de software têm sido usados nas mais variadas áreas, para captar e reutilizar o conhecimento previamente adquirido. Seus usos mais conhecidos são na arquitetura, no projeto de componentes e na implementação. Neste trabalho o enfoque é o uso de padrões na engenharia de requisitos.

Um Padrão de Requisito de Software (PRS) corresponde a um artefato que fornece orientações sobre como especificar requisitos, funcionais, não funcionais e regras de negócio, de forma que possam ser reusados em contextos e problemas bem definidos [9].

No desenvolvimento de software existem requisitos que são de natureza similar ou que aparecem com frequência na maioria dos softwares, o que indica um possível padrão [9]. Outras fontes para identificação de padrões incluem conhecimentos adquiridos a partir de pesquisas de campo, conhecimento individual de engenheiros de software, normas e melhores práticas ou quaisquer outros artefatos de software [10].

Um padrão possui uma estrutura de apresentação que corresponde à formalização e documentação para captar e reutilizar o conhecimento. Há várias formas de se apresentar um padrão. Em geral, quatro elementos são essenciais: nome do padrão (descrição geral da aplicabilidade), problema (o que pretende resolver), solução (descrição de como obter o resultado desejado) e consequências (implicações com o uso do padrão) [11].

O uso de padrões auxilia engenheiros de software na reutilização de soluções de sucesso para desenvolver novos projetos [11], eliminando a redundância de definição de um conjunto de requisitos para cada projeto de software, o que reduz a carga de trabalho e a habilidade necessária para a comunicação entre os *stakeholders*.

Problema: Em função da evidente importância e os problemas enfrentados no processo de ER, observa-se a existência de algumas lacunas de pesquisa em relação à especificação do documento de requisitos (DR), para que o mesmo seja completo, consistente e sem ambiguidade. A reutilização de requisitos com o uso de padrões pode ser uma alternativa viável para aumentar a qualidade da especificação dos requisitos no desenvolvimento de software.

Quando o engenheiro de software conta com um apoio computacional para a elicitação de requisitos e a escrita do DR com o uso de padrões, pode-se garantir também a uniformidade das informações, além do aumento da produtividade uma vez que há um guia a ser seguido.

Este trabalho tem por objetivo apresentar um conjunto de padrões elaborados para a especificação de requisitos funcionais e regras de negócio no domínio de Sistemas de Informação (SI), bem como um apoio computacional elaborado com base nesses padrões para a confecção de um DR. Padrões para requisitos não funcionais não estão no escopo deste projeto, sendo que alguns podem ser encontrados em [12].

Contribuições: As principais contribuições são: a) um catálogo de padrões para a elicitação e a escrita de requisitos funcionais e de regras de negócio no domínio de SI; b) um apoio computacional com base no conjunto de padrões que favorece a escrita completa e consistente dos requisitos obtidos dos *stakeholders*, gerando um DR padronizado, com instâncias específicas do sistema em elaboração; c) um repositório de requisitos elaborado a partir dos padrões descritos em a); d) a possibilidade de escrita de novos padrões a partir de uma estrutura elaborada.

Atualmente, o processamento de informação corresponde a maior área de aplicação de software, o que justifica a seleção do domínio de SI para a elaboração de padrões propostos neste trabalho. A relevância na elaboração desses padrões justifica-se em razão da similaridade encontrada quando da descrição de diferentes sistemas de SI.

Organização do trabalho: Este trabalho está dividido em seis seções, além desta de introdução. Na Seção 2 são apresentados os trabalhos relacionados com o uso de padrões na especificação de requisitos. Na Seção 3 são feitas considerações sobre conceitos em SI. Na Seção 4 são apresentados e comentados os padrões elaborados para o domínio de SI. Na Seção 5 é apresentado o apoio computacional desenvolvido para a elaboração de documentos de requisitos com base nos padrões exibidos na Seção 4. Na Seção 6 são apresentados os resultados da avaliação do uso do apoio computacional e dos padrões elaborados. Na Seção 7 são comentadas as considerações finais e sugestões de trabalhos futuros.

2 Trabalhos Relacionados

Withall [9] apresenta um catálogo com trinta e sete padrões de requisitos organizados em oito domínios (fundamental, informação, entidade de dados, função do usuário, desempenho, flexibilidade, controle de acesso e comercial). Cada padrão atende a uma funcionalidade específica desses domínios, porém, alguns padrões compartilham e integram informações. A maioria dos padrões atende à especificação de requisitos não funcionais e técnicos, sendo alguns também para requisitos funcionais.

Roher e Richardson [10] sugerem a incorporação de padrões de requisitos de sustentabilidade no processo de engenharia de requisitos, a fim de facilitar a escrita do DR para determinados tipos de requisitos de sustentabilidade. Esses padrões, nem sempre são tratados nos SI.

Wei et al. [13] fornecem um *template* para a escrita de padrões de requisitos de segurança de software, elaborado com base nos padrões de projeto de Gamma et al. [11] e os padrões de requisitos de Withall [9]. O padrão "*hazard control command*", por exemplo, é aplicável na especificação de requisitos de segurança crítica nos níveis de A-C, sendo que esses níveis correspondem ao grau de severidade do risco, sendo o nível A – catastrófico, B – crítico e C – significativo.

O estudo de Li et al. [14] consiste na apresentação de dois padrões de requisitos de projetos típicos para sismologia computacional: o padrão de simulação e o padrão de acesso a dados. Os autores relatam que esses padrões podem beneficiar a especificação de projeto futuros e na redução de custos de desenvolvimento.

Franch et al. [15] apresentam o *framework* PABRE (*PAttern-Based Requirements Elicitation*), que foi projetado para apoiar a reutilização de requisitos por meio de padrões. Esse *framework* consiste de um metamodelo que descreve os principais conceitos usando a noção de padrão, um método para conduzir os processos de elicitação e documentação de requisitos, um catálogo de padrões e uma ferramenta de apoio à gestão e utilização do catálogo. Esses padrões atendem principalmente a requisitos não funcionais e de gestão de documentos, que estão fora do escopo deste projeto.

O estudo de Palomares et al. [16] apresenta dois padrões de requisitos não técnicos, elaborados por meio do *framework* PABRE. Além disso, os autores afirmam que esses padrões integram um catálogo maior, que atualmente contém 37 padrões de requisitos não técnicos, 29 padrões de requisitos não funcionais e 47 padrões de requisitos funcionais que se aplicam ao domínio de gestão de documentos e que foram construídos a partir de documentos de requisitos de projetos anteriores. Esses padrões de requisitos funcionais não são aplicáveis ao domínio de SI comerciais.

Os padrões encontrados nesses trabalhos relacionados, em sua maioria, são para a especificação de requisitos não funcionais, que propicia reúso do padrão na integra em diferentes domínios, sem qualquer alteração. Para os requisitos funcionais isso não ocorre, uma vez que há necessidade de especificar detalhes para o sistema em desenvolvimento [17]. Contudo, observa-se que no domínio de SI, existe similaridade na especificação dos requisitos funcionais independentemente do tipo de sistema. Essa similaridade pode ser encontrada, por exemplo, na manutenção de dados (CRUD), nos relatórios gerenciais, nas transações comerciais, entre outras funções.

3 Conceitos em Sistemas de Informação

Em documentos de requisitos de SI é comum encontrar requisitos funcionais que especificam operações para processamento, manutenção e consulta de dados, tais como criar, ler, atualizar e excluir informação.

Em razão da existência de diferentes interesses, especialidades e níveis em uma organização, os sistemas são classificados em tipos, sendo os mais comuns: sistemas de processamento de transações (SPT), sistemas de informação gerencial (SIG) e sistemas de apoio a decisões (SAD) [18]. Os SPTs são usados para registrar transações básicas da organização, tais como registro de pedidos de venda, de reservas de hotel, de vendas, de manutenção do registro do cliente etc. Os SIGs usam os dados armazenados pelos SPTs para fornecer informações aos gerentes e tomadores de decisões, como exemplo pode-se citar um relatório de pedidos semanal e a lista de reservas do hotel em um determinado período. Os SADs são usados para dar apoio à tomada de decisões em problemas específicos, contribuindo para responder questões como: Qual o impacto na programação de produção caso ocorra duplicação nas vendas em dezembro? Os SADs usam informações internas dos SPTs, SIGs e frequentemente recorrem a informações de fontes externas [19].

Os requisitos funcionais desses tipos de sistemas, na maioria dos casos, requerem a definição de regras de negócio específicas. Na perspectiva de SI, uma regra de negócio é uma declaração que define ou restringe alguma circunstância do negócio [20].

Wiegers e Beatty [20] identificam cinco tipos principais de esquemas de classificação de regras de negócio, que apresentam uma forma típica de escrita, como apresentado a seguir:

- **Fatos**: são declarações significativas sobre a forma de execução do negócio em questão. Um fato descreve associações ou relacionamentos entre importantes termos do negócio. Exemplo: Todo pedido tem uma taxa de entrega.
- **Restrições**: são declarações que restringem as ações que o sistema ou seus usuários podem realizar. Exemplo: Um estudante só pode tomar emprestado, concomitantemente, de um a três livros.
- **Ativadores de Ações**: são regras que disparam alguma ação se condições específicas forem verdadeiras. Exemplo: Se a retirada do livro não ocorrer dentro do prazo determinado, então a reserva é cancelada.
- **Inferências**: são regras que derivam novos fatos a partir de outros fatos. Geralmente são escritas no padrão "se / então", no entanto, a cláusula "então" simplesmente fornece um fato ou conhecimento e não uma ação a ser tomada. Exemplo: Se o usuário não devolve um livro emprestado dentro do prazo estabelecido, então ele torna-se um usuário pendente.
- **Computações**: são regras de negócio que definem cálculos que transformam dados existentes em novos dados usando algoritmos ou fórmulas matemáticas específicas. Podem ser expressas como fórmulas matemáticas, descrição textual, tabelas, etc. Exemplo: Aplica-se um desconto progressivo se mais do que 10 unidades forem adquiridas. De 6 a 10 unidades, o desconto é de 10%. A compra de 11 ou mais unidades tem um desconto de 20%.

Esses conceitos foram utilizados neste trabalho, entretanto na definição dos padrões de regra de negócio a classificação acima não foi utilizada. Contudo, o engenheiro de software deve conhecê-los de forma a elaborar um DR completo e sem ambiguidade, observando a especificação dos requisitos funcionais, não funcionais e das regras de negócio de um sistema de software.

Na seção seguinte é apresentada a metodologia usada para a elaboração dos padrões de requisitos.

4 Elaboração de Padrões de Requisitos de Software para o Domínio de Sistemas de Informação

A metodologia usada para a elaboração dos padrões constou das seguintes etapas:

1. **Obtenção de diferentes documentos de requisitos**: foram obtidos documentos de requisitos fictícios utilizados na academia, como material didático de disciplinas, em instituições de ensino (UFSCar, USP e UEMG) e outros que estão disponibilizados na literatura especializada, bem como, na web.

2. **Organização dos Requisitos**: os requisitos de diferentes documentos do domínio de SI foram organizados por tipo de operação. Exemplos: manutenção de dados (inclusão, remoção, alteração, consulta), processamento de transação (compra, venda, devolução, etc.), impressão ou listagem de relatórios gerenciais, etc. Os requisitos que realizam a mesma operação foram os selecionados a se tornarem um padrão.
3. **Análise dos Requisitos**: para cada tipo de operação, os requisitos foram analisados para identificar se estavam completos e não possuíam ambiguidade, bem como identificar as partes do texto que deveriam ser fixas e as partes variáveis.
4. **Especificação do Padrão**: foi definida a aplicabilidade e a solução do padrão para atender a especificação de um conjunto de requisitos similares (Quadro 1). Além disso, para apoiar o engenheiro de software na utilização do padrão, para cada parâmetro (parte variável do requisito) do *template* foram estabelecidas sugestões de valores e a multiplicidade para orientar a quantidade de valores de preenchimento (ex. a multiplicidade 1..*, indica que o parâmetro pode possuir um ou muitos valores).
5. **Estabelecimento de Relação entre os Padrões**: definição da relação do padrão em questão com outros padrões. Essa relação pode orientar e/ou alertar o engenheiro de software na utilização de outros padrões que complementem a especificação, quando da aplicação de um determinado padrão, proporcionando completude no DR.

Para atender ao domínio de SI, neste projeto, foi estabelecida uma estrutura de apresentação de padrões com base na estrutura do Gamma et al. [11], apresentada no Quadro 1.

Quadro 1. Estrutura Adotada para Apresentação dos Padrões

Elemento	Descrição
Nome	Especifica o nome do padrão, que deve ser único e refletir a aplicabilidade do padrão.
Domínio	Corresponde ao domínio de aplicação do padrão.
Propósito	Descreve o objetivo da aplicação do padrão.
Problema	Descreve a situação em que o padrão pode ser aplicado.
Consequência	Descreve as consequências de se utilizar o padrão.
Tipo	Especifica o tipo de requisito: funcional, não funcional ou regra de negócio.
Solução	Apresenta um *template* para a especificação da parte fixa e variável do requisito que o padrão deve representar. A parte fixa apresenta um texto padrão para a especificação do requisito. A notação <...> é usada para descrever a parte variável que é denominada de parâmetro e deve ser substituída pelos dados pertinentes ao requisito a ser elaborado.
Padrões Relacionados	Especifica os padrões relacionados que são complementares ao padrão em questão. Esse elemento contribui para o engenheiro de software na indicação de outros possíveis padrões que podem ser usados quando ocorrer o uso do padrão em questão.

A seguir são apresentados dois dos padrões elaborados a partir dos requisitos obtidos: Processar Transação (processamento de transação) no Quadro 2 e Condição de Execução (regra de negócio) no Quadro 3.

Quadro 2. Padrão de Requisito Funcional: Processar Transação

Nome	Processar Transação
Domínio	Sistemas de Informação
Propósito	Processar e armazenar informação de uma transação.
Problema	Estabelecer quais dados da transação devem ser armazenados.
Consequência	A especificação de um requisito que descreve a necessidade de um usuário de processar uma transação e armazenar sua informação.
Tipo	Funcional
Solução	**Template**: Permitir o processamento de <transação> de <entidade>, com o armazenamento dos seguintes atributos: <atributos>. **Parâmetro**: <transação> nome da transação que contém informações do domínio (1). <entidade> nome da entidade que descreve o tipo de transação (1). <atributos> nome dos atributos da entidade que devem ser armazenados (1..*). **Sugestões de Parâmetros:** <transação> venda <entidade> produto <atributos> número, data, cliente, produto, preço unitário e preço total. **Exemplo da Descrição do Requisito:** - Permitir o processamento de venda de produto, com o armazenamento dos seguintes atributos: número, data, cliente, produto, preço unitário e preço total.
Padrões Relacionados	Informação Requerida, Condição de Execução, Limite de Execução, Calculo de Valor e Recuperar Informação.

Quadro 3. Padrão de Regra de Negócio: Condição de Execução

Nome	Condição de Execução
Domínio	Sistemas de Informação
Propósito	Estabelecer as condições permitidas para uma determinada operação.
Problema	Especificar as condições específicas da operação.
Consequência	A especificação de um requisito que descreve uma regra de negócio que estabelece as condições de execução de uma determinada operação.
Tipo	Regra de Negócio
Solução	**Template**: A <operação> somente deve ser permitida se <condição> **Parâmetro**: <operação> nome da operação que deseja estabelecer uma condição (1). <condição > descrição da condição para a execução da operação (1..*). **Sugestões de Parâmetros:** <operação> reserva <condição> se houver estoque suficiente, houver vagas suficientes para atende-la. **Exemplos da Descrição do Requisito:** - A reserva somente deve ser permitida se houver vagas suficientes para atende-la.
Padrões Relacionados	-

No Quadro 4 é apresentado o catálogo de padrões elaborado para o domínio de SI que atende às operações básicas de manutenção e consulta de dados, o processamento de transações, a consulta/impressão de relatórios gerenciais e o estabelecimento de regras de negócios. Na primeira coluna consta o tipo do padrão, na segunda tem-se o nome do padrão, e a consequência é exibida na terceira coluna.

Não foram gerados padrões para atender aos requisitos para SADs em razão da especificidade que eles possuem.

Quadro 4. Catálogo de Padrões de os para o Domínio de Sistemas de informação

Tipo	Nome	Consequência
Operações Básicas	Incluir Informação	A especificação de um requisito que descreve a necessidade de um usuário de armazenar informação de uma entidade de dados.
	Alterar Informação	A especificação de um requisito que descreve a necessidade de um usuário de alterar determinados dados de uma entidade de dados.
	Excluir Informação	A especificação de um requisito que descreve a necessidade de um usuário de excluir informação de uma entidade de dados.
	Recuperar Informação	A especificação de um requisito que descreve a necessidade de um usuário de recuperar informação de uma entidade de dados por meio da descrição de parâmetros.
Processamento de Transações	Processar Transação	A especificação de um requisito que descreve a necessidade de um usuário de processar uma transação e armazenar sua informação.
Informações Gerenciais	Especificar Consulta Gerencial	A especificação de um requisito que descreve a necessidade de um usuário de emitir consultas de informações gerenciais em tela ou impresso.
Regras de Negócio	Informação Requerida	A especificação de um requisito que descreve uma regra de negócio que estabelece as informações requeridas por uma determinada operação.
	Condição de Execução	A especificação de um requisito que descreve uma regra de negócio que estabelece as condições de execução de uma determinada operação.
	Limite de Execução	A especificação de um requisito que descreve uma regra de negócio que estabelece limites específicos de execução de uma determinada operação.
	Calculo de Valor	A especificação de um requisito que descreve a necessidade de um usuário de descrever um determinado cálculo matemático, requerido em uma operação.

5 Apoio Computacional Para a Elaboração de Documentos de Requisitos Com o Uso De Padrões

Palomares et al. [21] afirmam que há dificuldade de utilizar padrões sem um apoio computacional para direcionar o engenheiro de software. Em especial também relatam a opinião dos participantes sobre o reúso com base em padrões de requisitos de software. Um dos quesitos avaliados foi quanto aos fatores críticos para a introdução de um catálogo de padrões de requisitos. Dois pontos principais foram citados: a necessidade de um método de uso bem definido e uma ferramenta de apoio.

Neste projeto após criar os padrões de requisitos funcionais e de regras de negócio, considerando as observações de Palomares et al. [21], foi também desenvolvido o processo de uso e um apoio computacional a fim de auxiliar engenheiros de software na atividade de elicitação de requisitos com a utilização dos padrões elaborados. Ressalta-se novamente que os requisitos não funcionais não fazem parte do escopo deste trabalho.

O processo de uso consiste na utilização do apoio computacional para a instanciação dos padrões a fim de elaborar documentos de requisitos de SI com os objetivos anteriormente citados. Os passos que devem ser seguidos são:

1. **Seleção do Padrão**: de acordo com a necessidade do cliente, o engenheiro de software seleciona, no apoio computacional, o padrão adequado para esse tipo de problema. Essa escolha sempre é confirmada com o cliente. Se o padrão atende aos requisitos solicitados, o engenheiro de software avança para o passo seguinte.
2. **Especificação das partes variáveis**: o engenheiro de software informa ao cliente as variabilidades que existem para a solução do padrão selecionado. O cliente pode escolher entre as opções que satisfaz ao seu sistema, fornecendo as informações pertinentes a partir do conjunto de sugestões cadastradas para o padrão no apoio computacional. No entanto, existe a possibilidade do cliente informar o que deseja e essas serem posteriormente incorporadas como variabilidades.
3. **Especificações complementares**: o engenheiro de software identifica junto ao cliente a existência de alguma regra de negócio da operação em questão e/ou algum requisito funcional complementar. Em ambos os casos um padrão pode ser utilizado para complementar a especificação. Dessa forma, volta-se aos passos 1 e 2 para a especificação dos requisitos complementares. O engenheiro de software também pode propor algum requisito complementar por meio das sugestões de padrões relacionados fornecidas pelo apoio computacional.

O apoio computacional para a elaboração do DR no domínio de SI possui três módulos: i) o de especificação e gestão dos padrões, que geralmente fica sob a responsabilidade de um engenheiro de software com mais experiência; ii) o de instanciação dos padrões durante a elicitação de requisitos; e iii) o de funcionalidade básica inerente à manutenção de usuário, cliente e projeto.

Com o módulo de especificação e gestão de padrões (Fig. 1) é possível realizar a manutenção dos padrões. Na definição do *template* da solução, para cada parâmetro que representa a parte variável do padrão, é fornecido: a) um tipo, que está associado a um conjunto de sugestões de preenchimento que pode ser usado na instanciação do padrão; b) uma descrição que orienta o correto preenchimento do parâmetro; c) a multiplicidade que orienta a quantidade de valores permitidos para o parâmetro.

Os padrões são apresentados em uma estrutura de árvore organizada pelo tipo de padrão, que, atualmente, podem representar requisitos funcionais e regras de negócio.

Para realizar a especificação do padrão as abas Informações Básicas e Padrões Relacionados são utilizadas. Os padrões relacionados com o padrão em questão são descritos por meio da aba com o respectivo nome.

O módulo de instanciação de padrões (Fig. 2) possui quatro abas. As mesmas são apresentadas em detalhes nos próximos tópicos:

- **Informações Básicas**: apresenta as informações de aplicabilidade e solução do padrão.

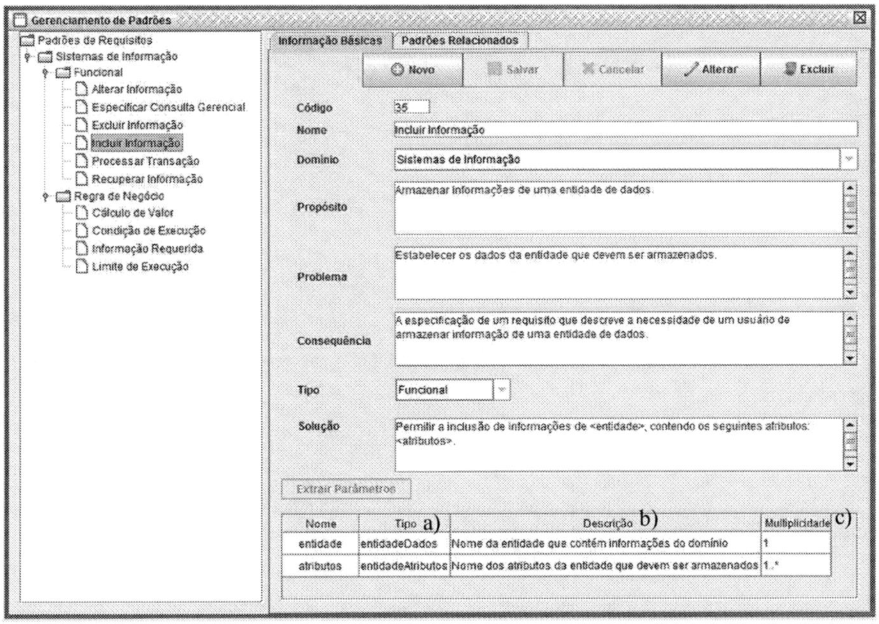

Fig. 1. Módulo de Especificação e Gestão de Padrões

- **Elaboração**: usada para a especificação de um requisito por meio do padrão escolhido. As letras colocadas na Fig. 2 tem o objetivo de guiar o leitor, assim são as mesmas utilizadas a seguir. Nessa aba é apresentado: a) um campo para descrição do requisito; b) o *template* da solução; c) uma lista com os parâmetros; d) uma lista de sugestões organizada em categorias de sugestões; e) ao selecionar a categoria de sugestão, uma lista de possíveis valores é apresentada. O Padrão Incluir Informação está sendo instanciado para a inclusão de clientes, como pode ser visto na Fig 2. Nesse exemplo, o parâmetro *<atributos>* é preenchido com valores que correspondem aos atributos de cliente. Com a seleção desse parâmetro são fornecidas algumas categorias de sugestões, como venda, produto, pessoa, etc. Ao selecionar uma dessas sugestões, outras são apresentadas para o preenchimento do parâmetro. Após essas seleções, o botão [+] deve ser pressionado para que os valores selecionados sejam atribuídos ao parâmetro. Caso seja necessário um valor de preenchimento diferente dos sugeridos, a especificação desses novos valores é feita por meio do botão [Novo]. A finalização da especificação de um requisito, ou seja, com o preenchimento de todos os parâmetros, é realizada ao pressionar o botão [Salvar].
- **Requisitos**: apresenta todos os requisitos do projeto; permite a seleção do requisito para a edição ou exclusão; permite a geração do DR, no formato *pdf*; permite o estabelecimento de relacionamento (rastreabilidade) entre os requisitos; e fornece sugestões de padrões relacionados com o requisito instanciado.
- **Reúso**: apresenta os requisitos já instanciados em outros projetos, que foram elaborados pelo padrão selecionado. Esses requisitos podem ser reusados no projeto atual ao invés de serem especificados com o uso de um padrão.

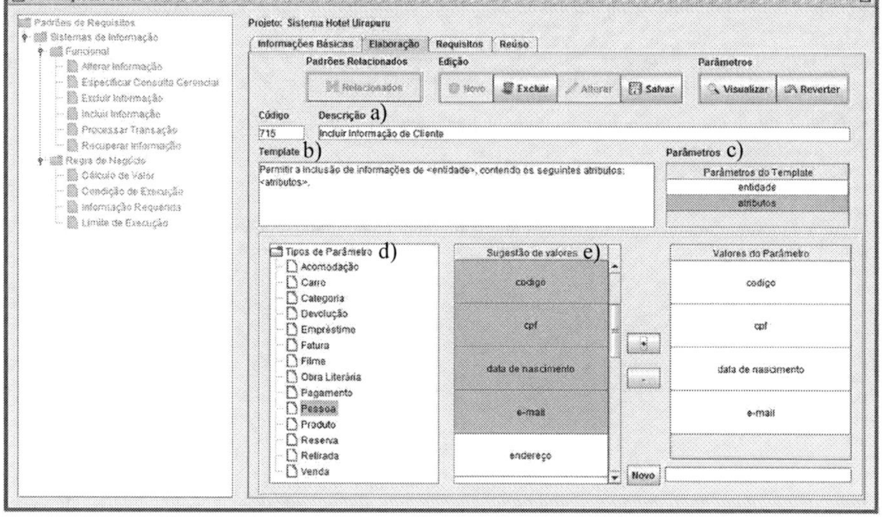

Fig. 2. Módulo de Instanciação de Padrões

Uma versão simplificada do DR resultante da instanciação dos padrões apresentados anteriormente é apresentada na Fig. 3. Os requisitos funcionais são identificados pela sigla "RF" e as regras de negócio pela sigla "RN". A coluna da tabela "Depende de" apresenta a dependência entre os requisitos. No exemplo em questão, o requisito RF2 depende do requisito RF10.

Identificador:	Descrição	Depende de:
RF1	Permitir a inclusão de informações de Cliente, contendo os seguintes atributos: codigo, nome, endereço e cidade.	
RF2	Permitir o processamento de Venda de Produto, com o armazenamento dos seguintes atributos: código, data da venda, cliente, produto, quantidade, valor unitário e valor total. RN2.1. A venda de produto somente deve ser permitida se houver estoque suficiente	RF10

Fig. 3. Documento de Requisitos de Exemplo

O apoio computacional foi desenvolvido na linguagem Java [22] utilizando o banco de dados MySQL [23].

Este trabalho difere dos demais apresentados na Seção 2, pois: a) permite a escrita padronizada de um DR com requisitos funcionais e regras de negócio para sistemas específicos no domínio de SI. Por exemplo, o padrão que especifica o cadastro de um novo registro de uma entidade, pode ser usado para a elaboração de um sistema de hotel, um sistema de farmácia ou qualquer outro e terá no DR a especificação completa desse requisito; b) com o uso do apoio computacional o DR é elaborado completamente em formato *pdf*; c) o engenheiro de software pode reusar especificações de requisitos construídas em sistemas anteriores modificando alguns atributos ou não. Por exemplo, uma especificação para a reserva em um hotel, pode ser recuperada do repositório e reusada em um outro sistema de hotel. Há a possibilidade de reusar essa função para qualquer sistema que a realize de forma similar, por exemplo, um sistema de reserva de livros, carros, produtos, etc.; d) novos padrões de requisitos podem ser elaborados usando a estrutura de apresentação.

6 Avaliação da Aplicação dos Padrões com o Apoio Computacional

Para avaliar a abordagem proposta quanto à completude dos padrões e usabilidade do apoio computacional, foram realizados estudos de casos com estudantes de graduação dos cursos de Bacharelado em Ciência da Computação e de Engenharia Elétrica da UFSCar, campus de São Carlos/SP e do curso de Sistemas de Informação da UEMG, unidade de Frutal/MG.

Estudo de caso 1: participaram quarenta e dois estudantes divididos em oito grupos e cada um com um projeto relacionado a serviços oferecidos pela UFSCar como: biblioteca, restaurante universitário, locação de quadra, inscrição em disciplina, etc. Previamente, os estudantes haviam elaborado um DR de modo *ad hoc*, com sistemas simples e com poucos requisitos.

Os padrões de requisitos de software e o apoio computacional foram apresentados, bem como um treinamento com um sistema exemplo com requisitos diferentes dos que constavam dos documentos de requisitos elaborados pelos estudantes.

Em seguida foi solicitada a elaboração do DR do sistema em desenvolvimento pelo grupo, agora utilizando o ferramental apresentado. Após essa atividade, os estudantes responderam a um questionário, a fim de identificar a porcentagem de requisitos especificados com o uso do apoio computacional, se o DR ficou mais completo e se o apoio computacional é de fácil utilização. O resultado obtido foi: na média, 93% dos requisitos foram especificados. Em razão da falta de conhecimento mais aprofundado dos padrões existentes, alguns requisitos não foram especificados por meio deles; 87% dos participantes afirmaram que o DR ficou mais completo, com novos requisitos e regras de negócio; e 75% avaliaram que o apoio computacional foi de fácil utilização.

Estudo caso 2: foi realizado em duas disciplinas da UFSCar, sendo uma: i) composta por estudantes da ciência da computação com conhecimentos mais avançados sobre requisitos e desenvolvimento de sistemas para dispositivos móveis e ii) com estudantes do curso de engenharia elétrica, com conhecimentos iniciais sobre requisitos, que desenvolveram sistemas simples. Os estudantes estavam distribuídos em grupos e cada um desenvolvendo sistemas do domínio de SI. Nesse estudo os DR foram elaborados após o conhecimento e treinamento com os padrões de requisitos e apoio computacional, entretanto sem terem escrito o DR de modo *ad hoc*. Os resultados obtidos foram os seguintes:

i) Sistemas desenvolvidos para dispositivos móveis; 15 grupos com quatro estudantes em cada grupo; 46% dos grupos notaram que é possível reutilizar totalmente os requisitos na elaboração do DR e 26% citaram que o reúso é parcial. O reúso dos padrões proporcionou na média, em 20% dos grupos a especificação de mais de 90% dos requisitos; 27% especificaram de 50% a 90%. Além disso, 80% concordam que há facilidade no uso do apoio computacional.

ii) Sistemas de informação simples; 7 grupos com total de 24 estudantes; 70% dos grupos notaram que é possível reutilizar totalmente os requisitos na elaboração do DR e 10% citaram que o reúso é parcial. O reúso dos padrões proporcionou na média, em 20%

dos grupos a especificação de mais de 90% dos requisitos; 30% especificaram de 50% a 90%. Além disso, 60% concordam que há facilidade no uso do apoio computacional.

Estudo de caso 3: participaram trinta e quatro estudantes do curso de Sistemas de Informação da UEMG, divididos em treze grupos. Os projetos eram relacionados a sistemas reais desenvolvidos em empresas que os estudantes atuam. Como ocorreu no estudo de caso 1, os DR foram primeiramente elaborados de modo *ad hoc* e após a apresentação dos padrões e do apoio computacional foram refeitos.

Os resultados obtidos foram: 54% dos grupos notaram que é possível reutilizar totalmente os requisitos na elaboração do DR e 38% citaram que o reúso é parcial. O reúso dos padrões proporcionou na média, em 38% dos grupos a especificação de mais de 90% dos requisitos; 46% especificaram de 50% a 90%. Além disso, 61% concordam que há facilidade no uso do apoio computacional.

Há indícios, pelos resultados obtidos após a realização dos estudos de caso e com as respostas obtidas nos questionários, que os padrões elaborados auxiliaram a confecção de um DR mais completo. Outros estudos devem ser realizados, principalmente com sistemas reais em empresas para que resultados mais conclusivos sejam obtidos. Em razão da limitação de espaço o questionário aplicado não é apresentado neste artigo.

7 Considerações Finais

Este artigo apresentou uma abordagem para escrita de documentos de requisitos no domínio de SI com base em padrões de requisitos. Essa abordagem foi desenvolvida com base no reúso de conhecimento de projetos do domínio de SI. Os padrões elaborados auxiliam principalmente aos engenheiros de software menos experientes, fornecendo uma base para a escrita de DR mais completos e consistentes.

Para facilitar o uso dos padrões foi criado um apoio computacional em uma plataforma Java com o banco de dados MySQL que direciona o engenheiro de software no uso de padrões e na confecção de um DR com completa checagem da dependência existente entre os requisitos funcionais bem como a completa especificação de regras de negócio. Os requisitos não funcionais ainda não estão disponíveis no apoio apresentado. O apoio computacional, bem como os padrões elaborados e os questionários utilizados nos estudos de caso estão disponíveis no endereço http://advanse.dc.ufscar.br/tools.html.

Como citado na Seção 6, os resultados obtidos com a realização de estudos de caso com estudantes de cursos de graduação em duas instituições públicas, evidenciou a facilidade de uso do apoio computacional. Também pode ser notado que os padrões elaborados colaboraram para que os requisitos funcionais fossem especificados com maior segurança, considerando que há a possibilidade de verificação de dependência entre esses requisitos. Dessa forma, um engenheiro de software menos experiente conta com a verificação de dependência entre requisitos e a completa especificação das regras de negócio, ou mesmo do reúso de especificações realizadas em projetos anteriores. Assim, o DR produzido é mais completo e abrangente.

Como trabalhos futuros, novos padrões podem ser elaborados e inseridos no apoio computacional a fim de aumentar a taxa de reúso. Com o uso do apoio computacional mais intenso, podem ser realizadas melhorias quanto a sua funcionalidade e usabilidade. Uma melhoria prevista é a extensão do módulo de instanciação de padrão, permitindo o estudo da incorporação de novos valores para o conjunto de valores sugeridos para os parâmetros, com base nos novos valores fornecidos pelos *stakeholders*. Outra extensão é a elaboração de padrões que atendam aos requisitos não funcionais. Considera-se também que estudos mais aprofundados sejam realizados a fim de que possam ser reusados requisitos funcionais já especificados por outros autores. A inclusão desses requisitos não funcionais deve ocorrer no apoio computacional bem como a realização de experimentos controlados a fim de verificar a eficácia da proposta.

Referências

[1] M. Niazi e S. Shastry, "Role of requirements engineering in software development process: an empirical study," *Multi Topic Conference, 2003. INMIC 2003. 7th International,* 2003.

[2] B. Boehm e V. R. Basili, "Software Defect Reduction Top 10 List," *Computer (IEEE),* 2001.

[3] R. S. Pressman, Engenharia de Software - Uma Abordagem Profissional, 7ª ed., Porto Alegre/RS: McGraw-Hill, 2011.

[4] Y. Chernak, "Requirements Reuse: The State Of The Practice," *IEEE International Conference on Software Science, Technology and Engineering,* 2012.

[5] A. Fatwanto, "Software Requirements Specification Analysis Using Natural Language Processing Technique," *International Conference on Quality in Research,* pp. 105-110, 2013.

[6] I. Sommerville, Engenharia de Software, São Paulo: Pearson Addison-Wesley, 2007.

[7] S. Ketabchi, N. K. Sani e K. Liu, "A Norm-Based Approach towards Requirements Patterns," *IEEE Annual Computer Software and Applications Conference,* 2011.

[8] C. Palomares, C. Quer e X. Franch, "PABRE-Man: Management of a requirement patterns catalogue," *IEEE Software Engineering Conference,* 2011.

[9] S. Withall, Software Requirement Patterns, Microsoft Press, 2007.

[10] K. Roher e D. Richardson, "Sustainability requirement patterns," *IEEE International Workshop on Requirements Patterns,* 2013.

[11] E. Gamma, R. Helm, R. Johnson e J. Vlissides, Padrões de Projeto, Porto Alegre/RS: Artmed, 1995.

[12] X. Franch, C. Palomares, C. Quer, S. Renault e F. Lazzer, "A Metamodel for Software Requirement Patterns," em *Requirements Engineering: Foundation for Software Quality,* Springer, 2010.

[13] C. Wei, B. Xiaohong e L. Xuefei, "A Study on Airborne Software Safety Requirements Patterns," *IEEE International Conference on Software Security and Reliability Companion,* 2013.

[14] Y. Li, C. Pelties, M. Käser e N. Nararan, "Requirements patterns for seismology software applications," *IEEE International Workshop on Requirements Patterns,* 2012.

[15] X. Franch, C. Quer, S. Renault, C. Guerlain e C. Palomares, "Constructing and Using Software Requirement Patterns," em *Managing Requirements Knowledge,* , Springer, 2013, pp. 95-116.

[16] C. Palomares, C. Quer, X. Franch, C. Guerlain e S. Renault, "A catalogue of non-technical Requirement Patterns," *IEEE International Workshop on Requirements Patterns,* 2012.

[17] C. Palomares, C. Quer, X. Franch, S. Renault e C. Guerlain, "A Catalogue of Functional Software Requirement Patterns for the Domain of Content Management Systems," *ACM Symposium on Applied Computing,* 2013a.

[18] R. M. Stair e G. W. Reynolds, Princípios de Sistemas de Informação, São Paulo: Pioneira Thomson Learning, 2006.

[19] K. C. Laudon e J. P. Laudon, Sistemas de Informação Gerenciais, São Paulo: Pearson Prentice Hall, 2007.

[20] k. Wiegers e J. Beatty, Software Requirements, Redmond, Washington: Microsoft Press, 2013.

[21] C. Palomares, X. Franch e C. Quer, "Requirements Reuse and Patterns: A Survey," em *Requirements Engineering: Foundation for Software Quality,* Springer, 2014.

[22] Java. [Online]. Available: http://www.java.com/pt_BR/. [Acesso em 2 Janeiro 2015].

[23] MySQL, "MySQL Documentation: MySQL Reference Manuals," [Online]. Available: http://dev.mysql.com/doc/. [Acesso em 02 Janeiro 2015].

A utilização da linguagem natural na especificação de requisitos: um estudo por meio das equações estruturais

Roberto Avila Paldês[1], Angelica Toffano Seidel Calazans[1], Ari Melo Mariano[1], Eduardo José Ribeiro de Castro[1], Bruno de Souza da Silva[1],

[1] Centro Universitário de Brasília, Distrito Federal, Brazil
{roberto.paldes, angelica.calazans, ari.mariano, eduardo.castro}@uniceub.br, bruno7317@gmail.com

Resumo. O objetivo deste estudo é analisar fatores de influência para a escolha da linguagem natural (LN) na especificação de requisitos. A metodologia adotada é de estudo descritivo, de abordagem quantitativa por meio de equações estruturais. O modelo teórico proposto baseia-se na Teoria Unificada de Aceitação e Uso da Tecnologia (UTAUT). Foi elaborado um questionário (α=0,817) com 17 perguntas para 50 analistas de requisitos. O instrumento de pesquisa foi validado e pode continuar a ser usado. Identificou-se que o motivo que leva os analistas a usar a LN na especificação é a expectativa de um rendimento elevado. A expectativa de esforço não pode ser confirmada com um fator de influência. Há um forte reconhecimento que o uso da LN leva a uma maior adesão às necessidades do cliente. Não se identificaram condições facilitadoras nas organizações que influenciem o comportamento de uso, o que pode indicar uma direção de aprimoramento efetiva.

Palavras chave. Requisitos de software. Especificação de requisitos. Linguagem natural. Equações estruturais.

1 Introdução

A Engenharia de Requisitos é parte fundamental do processo de desenvolvimento de *software*. Ela organiza a base para a construção de qualquer sistema pois oferece suporte às fases iniciais do seu ciclo de vida. A Engenharia de Requisitos compreende os processos de obtenção, refinamento e verificação das necessidades do usuário, por meio do uso de técnicas sistemáticas e repetíveis a serem usadas para assegurar que os requisitos do software sejam completos, consistentes, relevantes e que atendam às necessidades do cliente [1].

O processo de obtenção das necessidades é um dos fatores chave de sucesso para um projeto de um sistema. Sua função principal é identificar todas as características e funções que o *software* a ser desenvolvido deve possuir, atuando como um contrato entre o cliente e o desenvolvedor. Esse processo gera a especificação de requisitos que é um dos primeiros artefatos tangíveis a serem produzidos. Este artefato serve de base para todas as etapas subsequentes do desenvolvimento, sendo utilizado pelos diversos participantes do processo, como patrocinadores, usuários, projetistas, programadores e testadores de software.

A especificação de requisitos é a etapa que engloba os conceitos definidos pelos especialistas de domínio e os relacionamentos entre eles [2]. Estes conceitos e seus relacionamentos devem ser escritos em uma linguagem entendida por todos participantes do processo de desenvolvimento de um software. A abordagem mais comum para redigir requisitos de um software é por meio de Linguagem Natural (LN). A LN pode assumir o papel de vetor pelo qual são transmitidos os requisitos. Usando frases bem estruturadas para descrevê-los – em oposição ao uso exclusivo de modelos amplamente usado atualmente – ela tem sido a forma mais utilizada para descrever requisitos [3] sendo complementada, às vezes, por outros tipos de notações, tais como diagramas, equações e modelos formais.

A utilização da LN facilita o entendimento dos requisitos, por ser simples e de fácil compreensão [4]. Uma vantagem da LN é sua capacidade de ser uma abordagem intuitiva na comunicação entre os *stakeholders* e adequada ao contexto de diversos clientes. Nesse contexto, a LN se reveste de importância ao se oferecer como uma linguagem de compreensão comum tanto pelo especialista do domínio da aplicação quanto pelo especialista em requisitos.

A LN também apresenta alguns aspectos negativos [5] [6]. Sua utilização pode resultar em especificações confusas requisitos funcionais e não-funcionais podem ser misturados em uma mesma especificação [2]. Algumas vezes há a necessidade de se descrever um requisito muito especificadamente e o documento acaba se tornando muito detalhado e, com isso, difícil de ler. Problemas como a imprecisão, dificuldade de compreensão e incoerência são comuns quando a LN é utilizada. Ela também possibilita múltiplas interpretações gerando ambiguidade e os modelos produzidos a partir dessa linguagem podem não contemplar as todas as características que o software deve possuir [7].

Os desafios não são novos. Já em 1995 a Conferência Internacional de Aplicações de Linguagem Natural para Sistemas de Informações consolidou as pesquisas da época sobre esse assunto. O assunto continua mantido um interesse persistente e crescente e muitas pesquisas têm sido realizadas englobando a LN e o processo de desenvolvimento de software. A tarefa de extrair informações uteis de dados não estruturados ainda apresenta desafios nos dias atuais [8].

Assim, para avaliar o impacto da escrita em LN nos dias atuais é necessário obter a percepção das pessoas que fazem uso desse recurso, os engenheiros ou analistas de requisitos e analistas de sistemas com essa atribuição. Modelos de percepção que envolvem tecnologia tem sido estudados para diferentes áreas [10][11][12] através da escala de medida UTAUT (*Unified Theory of Acceptance and Use of Technology*/Teoria Unificada de Aceitação e Uso da Tecnologia). Porém os estudos sobre UTAUT estão aplicados a Tecnologia de uma maneira geral, sendo necessário adaptar este estudo ao da LN. Entender os motivos da sua adoção ou não na engenharia de requisitos é necessário para contribuir na melhoria da técnica, assim como da relação das soluções trazidas pelos engenheiros e os usuários envolvidos nas diferentes etapas do processo.

Considerando o exposto, a presente pesquisa objetiva responder a seguinte questão de pesquisa: qual são as percepções dos profissionais de requisitos acerca da LN na especificação das necessidades de um cliente de um produto de software?

Para responder a essa questão, esse trabalho foi elaborado com o objetivo geral de analisar a influência das expectativas de desempenho e esforço, bem como as condições facilitadoras, com relação a utilização da LN na especificação de requisitos. Para isso, na seção 2 descreve-se sucintamente os processos da engenharia de requisitos para que suporte a sua contextualização dos conceitos da LN no ambiente de requisitos de software. Na seção 3 explica-se a metodologia utilizada na pesquisa, enquanto que na seção 4 disponibiliza-se os dados coletados e sua análise. Na seção 5 sintetizam-se as conclusões da pesquisa.

2 A Linguagem Natural na Engenharia de Requisitos

2.1 A especificação dos requisitos

Os requisitos podem ser definidos como as descrições do que o software deve fazer, os serviços que ele deve oferecer e as restrições ao seu funcionamento [2]. Segundo *The Guide to the Software Engineering Body of Knowledge* [13], o processo de Engenharia de Requisitos é composto de várias etapas, entre elas descobrir, analisar, documentar os requisitos e verificar as funções e restrições definidas. Para Sommerville [2] existem quatro atividades principais do processo de produção de requisitos: o estudo de viabilidade, a elicitação e análise, a especificação e a validação dos requisitos.

Na visão de Losada e Jaramillo [14], a elicitação de requisitos engloba a identificação, captura e integração requisitos decorrentes da comunicação entre um grupo de analistas e as partes interessadas, gerando descrições textuais e/ou gráficas que refletem os conceitos mais relevantes do domínio para o desenvolvimento de uma aplicação.

A fase de análise contribui para o sucesso do processo de desenvolvimento dos requisitos valendo-se de um processo de descoberta, refinamento, modelagem e especificação, onde se validam as informações obtidas e se identificam eventuais inconsistências [15]. É uma fase muito dependente de opiniões pessoais e de natureza subjetiva, considerando o nível de abstração do processo. Algumas partes interessadas podem apresentar dúvidas com relação a compreensão dos requisitos. Os *stakeholders* devem ser capazes de compreender os requisitos apresentados e entender o impacto desses requisitos de maneira eficiente e uniforme [16]. Para facilitar esse entendimento, os requisitos são geralmente escritos e mantidos em LN, que é uma forma de comunicação compartilhada por todos os atores do processo, ainda que a flexibilidade da LN traga também riscos de ambiguidade e desentendimento.

É indispensável a documentação organizada dos processos de requisitos para que uma organização possa defini-los e gerenciá-los, podendo utilizar a descrição de processos em linguagem com base em um léxico ampliado da linguagem [17].

Um resultado importante do fluxo dos requisitos é, portanto, a especificação de requisitos do software, um documento que descreve detalhadamente o conjunto de requisitos especificados para um produto de software [18]. Este documento pode recorrer à escrita, a modelos gráficos ou matemáticos, a cenários ou a protótipos. Admite, também a combinação de descrições em LN e modelos gráficos, buscando demonstrar de forma clara e flexível os requisitos do sistema [19].

2.2 A utilização da Linguagem Natural

No contexto da presente pesquisa, considera-se a Linguagem Natural o uso de frases bem estruturadas para descrever os requisitos de um sistema. Uma LN é elaborada naturalmente pelo ser humano, sem rigores de preparação [20]. É o idioma normalmente utilizado na comunicação em uma comunidade. O conceito se contrapõe ao emprego exclusivo de modelos na Engenharia de Requisitos, devido à necessidade de uma comunicação mais simples com os usuários.

A LN é caracterizada por sua enorme riqueza e capacidade de comunicação, sua flexibilidade e capacidade de utilizar com palavras e expressões, produzindo metáforas e ambiguidades [14]. A ambiguidade é um fenômeno intrínseco da LN [7], consistindo na capacidade de entender algo de mais de uma maneira ou sentido diferente. Assim, sugerem que a identificação de frases e palavras ambíguas é um aspecto crucial na comunicação humana.

As ferramentas linguísticas no apoio ao desenvolvimento de sistemas de software em geral e análise de requisitos, em particular, podem ajudar o analista a [21]: concentrar no problema e não na modelagem; interagir com outros atores; levar em conta os vários tipos de requisitos (organizacionais, funcionais, etc.); garantir a rastreabilidade desde os primeiros documentos produzidos; gerenciar com mais eficiência o problema das necessidades dos utilizadores em mudança.

Da mesma forma, o padrão IEEE 830 [1] aponta diversas propriedades para que a especificação de requisitos de software obtenha um bom nível de qualidade entre elas a isenção de ambiguidade e o uso da LN para a descrição de requisitos. Existem vários motivos para que os requisitos sejam escritos em LN [22] e permaneçam nessa linguagem: é uma forma de comunicação primária compartilhada por todos os atores do processo de desenvolvimento de software; os requisitos são especificados considerando diferentes níveis de abstração; a relação custo benefício, a necessidade de reação às mudanças de mercado, a rapidez necessária ao desenvolvimento do produto de software, são favoráveis à LN; oferece melhor apoio para a gestão de requisitos errados, incompletos ou parcialmente definidos; pode capturar propriedades externas dos requisitos, como as reais intenções dos usuários.

Requisitos em linguagens formais são úteis para verificar a coerência e verificar propriedades, mas são difíceis de especificar [23]. Como resultado, as partes interessadas (por exemplo, clientes, designers, engenheiros) muitas vezes preferem escrever requisitos em LN considerando a flexibilidade dessa linguagem. Os requisitos em LN podem ser escritos facilmente sem ônus de rigor formal.

Os requisitos são geralmente escritos e mantidos em LN, mas esses requisitos devem ser revistos e validados para melhorar a qualidade e minimizar a ambiguidade, imprecisão, imperfeição, conflito, inconsistência etc [22] e [24].

Por outro lado, os requisitos escritos em LN podem ser imprecisos, incompletos e ambíguos. A informalidade pode ajudar na discussão entre as partes interessadas no início do projeto, mas pode levar a confusão, inconsistência, a falta de automação, ambiguidade e a erros [23] [25],

Para evitar a ambiguidade, uma das soluções foi o desenvolvimento de um Léxico Estendido da Linguagem [26] tornando mais preciso o vocabulário utilizado na especificação de requisitos. Essa linguagem continua sendo utilizada por várias pesquisas para apoiar a modelagem de requisitos na linguagem corrente do contexto [27].

Segundo Bustos [5], alguns pesquisadores citam que a LN não é suficiente madura para ser aplicada na engenharia de requisitos. No entanto, várias propostas têm mostrado resultados promissores. Por exemplo, a mescla de especificações escritas em LN com as especificações escritas em linguagens formais, a utilização de Técnicas de processamento em LN para melhorar a qualidade das especificações de um modo semiautomático, indicando ao engenheiro de requisitos possíveis ambiguidades nas especificações, a Linguagem Natural para Serviços de Informações-intensivos da Web, a Linguagem Natural em Modelagem Conceitual focada em técnicas de modelagem baseadas em PNL para apoiar a aquisição de conhecimento do domínio de aplicação através de documentos e textos de análise [8] [5].

Outro desafio na especificação dos requisitos de software, utilizando da LN, é o grande volume de documentos gerados, notadamente em grandes projetos. A medida que cresce a documentação da especificação, aumentam as dificuldades com a interpretação, a consistência e a manutenção[6].

3 METODOLOGIA

O método adotado neste estudo foi descritivo, de abordagem quantitativa por meio de equações estruturais [28]. A modelagem por equações estruturais é uma técnica estatística multivariada que valora as relações e predição entre variáveis identificadas na literatura como participantes de um constructo experimental. A medida que este constructo vai sendo validado, vai ganhando estabilidade na literatura [29].

O modelo teórico proposto baseia-se na Teoria Unificada de Aceitação e Uso da Tecnologia – Unified Theory of Acceptance and Use of Technology, UTAUT, apresentado na fig. 1. Esse modelo foi elaborado para explicar a aceitação de uma tecnologia por um indivíduo ou grupo [30].

Por meio da base teórica [28][29] e segundo o modelo [30], existem quatro fatores que poderão influenciar a aceitação de uma tecnologia que nesta etapa estão direcionados a aceitação da técnica:

- Expectativa de Desempenho: definida como o grau de ganho do usuário no desempenho de seu trabalho e ou atividade;
- Expectativa de Esforço: explicado pelo grau de energia aplicado para o uso do sistema;

- Influência Social: a influência dos diversos grupos aos quais pertence o usuário sobre o uso de determinada tecnologia; e
- Condições Facilitadoras: relacionada a infraestrutura operacional e técnica para suportar o uso desde sistema.

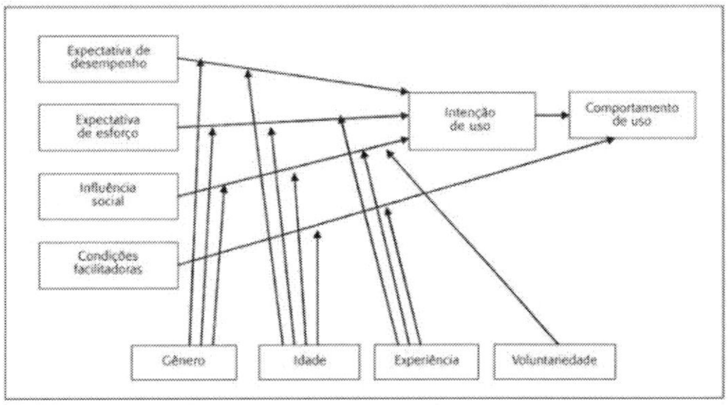

Fig. 1. O modelo UTAUT (Fonte: [30])

Estas variáveis aparecem como variáveis independentes que predizem a intenção de uso e o comportamento de uso formando relações traduzidas na teoria como hipóteses. Aparecem no modelo variáveis moderadoras como: gênero, idade, experiência e voluntariedade. Para este estudo, se realizou uma adaptação, conforme os objetivos do trabalho, como se observa na fig. 2. Por se tratar de um estudo inicial resolveu-se eliminar as variáveis moderadoras.

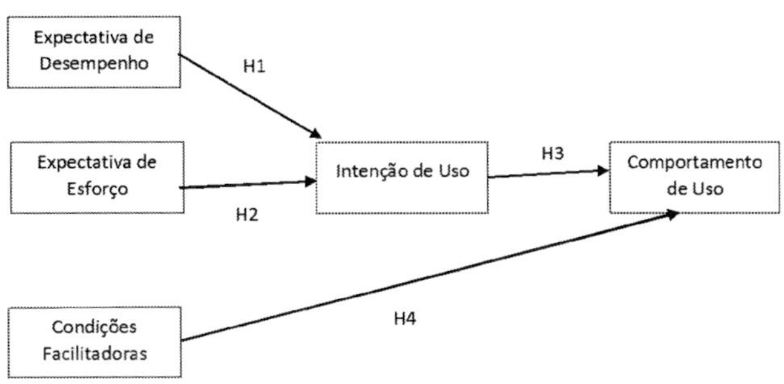

Fig. 2. - Modelo Adaptado do original UTAUT (Fonte: própria)

Assim, o modelo geral deste estudo apresenta algumas hipóteses adaptadas (e posteriormente validadas) para o escopo do presente estudo:

- H1: A expectativa de um rendimento elevado leva os analistas a usar a LN na Especificação de Requisitos.
- H2: A expectativa de um baixo esforço leva os analistas a usar a LN na Especificação de Requisitos.

- H3: O uso de LN na Especificação de Requisitos leva a uma maior adesão às necessidades do cliente.
- H4: A organização onde o analista trabalha estimula o uso da LN na Especificação de Requisitos.

Como instrumento de coleta de dados foi utilizado o questionário (Apêndice A) adaptado da escala de UTAUT, validado com (α=0,817). O instrumento possui 17 questões abrangendo as questões relacionadas a expectativa de desempenho, expectativa de esforço, condições facilitadoras objetivando identificar a intenção de uso dos utilizadores da tecnologia.

O questionário foi disponibilizado via Google Docs e enviado a analistas de requisitos de diferentes empresas do ramo de tecnologia em Brasília, entre os meses de maio e outubro de 2015. Foram consideradas as respostas de analistas de empresas de tecnologia localizadas em Brasília, Distrito Federal. A amostra foi de conveniência e foram respondidos 50 questionários. Identificou-se que 66% dos analistas respondentes eram homens e 34% mulheres, todos com idade média de 37 anos e 3 meses. A amostra apresentava uma média de experiência com requisitos de 7 anos e 3 meses.

Os participantes acessaram uma URL indicada e responderam a questões relacionadas indicando o grau de concordância com as afirmações expostas: 1 para discordo inteiramente, 2 para discordo em grande parte, 3 para discordo parcialmente, 4 para neutro, 5 para concordo parcialmente, 6 para concordo em grande parte e 7 para concordo inteiramente.

4 RESULTADOS E DISCUSSÃO

Trabalhar com a mensuração de modelos requer uma série de cálculos específicos que são aplicados em diferentes níveis. O software SmartPLS (*Smart Partial Least Square*) 3.2.3 auxilia na mensuração de modelos através de equações estruturais. O software [31] é uma ferramenta para modelagem de equações estruturais [28] e para a análise de experimentos que exijam múltiplas variáveis ou mesmo relacionar influência direta e indireta de diversos fatores.

Os resultados são agrupados em dois grupos: Confiabilidade e Validade do modelo que demonstram em que grau o modelo é valido e confiável, ou seja, se o modelo for aplicado em mais ocasiões tende a medir com precisão novamente (confiabilidade) e se ele mede o que se propõe medir (validade) e Valoração do modelo de medida que explica o poder de predição das variáveis independentes sobre a dependente (R2) e o grau de influência de cada variável nesta predição (Beta).

4.1 Confiabilidade e Validade do Modelo

A confiabilidade de Item está relacionada a maneira que os indicadores de correlacionam individualmente com suas variáveis. Espera-se que os itens sejam superiores a 0,707 [28].

Esta depuração é realizada uma a uma. Inicialmente, os indicadores EE1, EE2, FC3 e FC4 estavam abaixo de 0,707, porém ao realizar a depuração item a item o indicador FC3 aumentou seu índice para 0,705. Ao se tratar de uma pesquisa inicial resolveu-se manter o item. Uma vez depurado o modelo através da confiabilidade de item o resultado final do modelo (tabela 1).

Tabela 1. – Confiabilidade de Item Depurado

Indicador	Condições Facilitadoras (FC)	Expectativa de Esforço (EE)	Expectativa de Desempenho (PE)	Uso de Linguagem Natural (BI)	Utilidade na Especificação de Requisitos (IC)
BI1	0,000	0,000	0,000	0,870	0,000
BI2	0,000	0,000	0,000	0,944	0,000
BI3	0,000	0,000	0,000	0,927	0,000
EE2	0,000	0,705	0,000	0,000	0,000
EE3	0,000	0,932	0,000	0,000	0,000
EE4	0,000	0,909	0,000	0,000	0,000
FC1	0,910	0,000	0,000	0,000	0,000
FC2	0,928	0,000	0,000	0,000	0,000
IC1	0,000	0,000	0,000	0,000	0,903
IC2	0,000	0,000	0,000	0,000	0,916
PE1	0,000	0,000	0,737	0,000	0,000
PE2	0,000	0,000	0,731	0,000	0,000
PE3	0,000	0,000	0,809	0,000	0,000
PE4	0,000	0,000	0,709	0,000	0,000

Fonte: Própria

Quanto à confiabilidade de item (Tabela 2), a confiabilidade do modelo depende de outras três variáveis que são: Inflação da Variância (VIF) que explica a gravidade da multicolinearidade, pois em análises que envolvem regressão existe um risco de aproximação alta, gerando uma alta correlação entre variáveis o que poderia alterar resultados no modelo, aceitam-se índices menores que 10 [29]. Os outros dois índices de Confiabilidade dizem respeito a confiança composta e são expressas por dois índices que são Alpha de Cronbach e Confiabilidade Composta. Apesar de ambos os índice medirem o mesmo aspecto, normalmente a confiabilidade composta é menos rígido e muito utilizado em pesquisas iniciais. Neste caso se utilizará ambos os índices que devem ser maiores que 0,7. Para assegurar a Validade do modelo deve-se apresentar sua consistência interna. Deve-se esperar ao menos uma diferença de 50% da Variância Média Extraída (AVE), assegurando independência dos indicadores em relação as demais variáveis [29].

Tabela 2. - Resultados de Confiabilidade e Validade

Variável	VIF	CR	CA	AVE
Condições facilitadoras	1,088	0,916	0,816	0,916
Expectativa de desempenho	1,367	0,835	0,742	0,835
Expectativa de esforço	1,367	0,889	0,834	0.923
Uso da Linguagem Natural	1,088	0,938	0,901	0.938
Utilidade na especificação de requisitos	0,000	0,906	0,792	0,906

VIF(Inflação da Variância Interna), CR(Confiabilidade Composta), CA(Alpha de Cronbach), AVE (Variância Média Extraída). Fonte: Própria

Finalmente o último teste de validade é a Validade Discriminante (Tabela 3). Um modelo possui Validade Discriminante quando a raiz quadrada de AVE de cada variável latente é maior que as correlações das outras Variáveis Latentes.

Tabela 3. - Variância Discriminante

Variáveis	Condições Facilitadoras (FC)	Expectativa de Desempenho (EE)	Expectativa de Esforço (PE)	Uso de Linguagem Natural (BI)	Utilidade na Especificação de Requisitos (IC)
FC	**0,919**				
EE	-0,091	**0,747**			
PE	0,155	0,518	**0,855**		
BI	0,285	0,370	0,280	**0,914**	
IC	0,283	0,155	0,154	0,794	**0,910**

Fonte: Própria

Pode-se observar que o modelo cumpre com todos os índices de confiabilidade e validade, assegurando que o modelo é válido e confiável.

4.2 Valoração do Modelo Estrutural

Uma vez atestada a confiabilidade e validade do modelo, segue-se para a mensuração e resultados na análise. A valoração do modelo é realizada através da Análise do R^2 e do Beta. O R^2 explica em que grau a variável dependente é predita pela dependente (fig. 3).

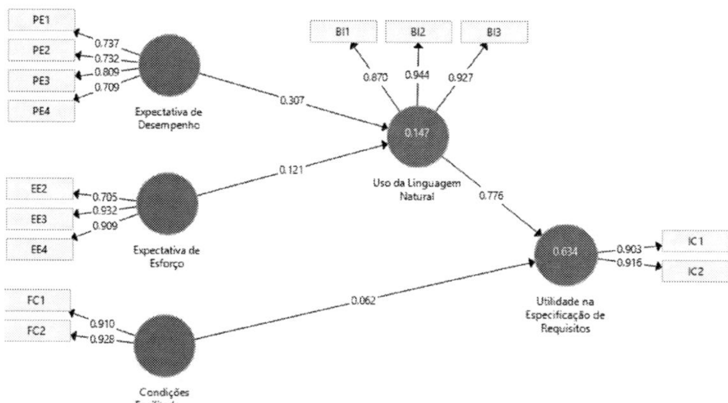

Fig. 3. - Modelo Mensurado (Fonte: própria)

Pode-se observar na fig. 3 que a LN é explicada pela Expectativa de Esforço e pela Expectativa de Desempenho em 14,7%, enquanto a Utilidade na Especificação de Requisitos que é o problema central deste estudo foi de predita em 63,4% pelas Variáveis

Uso da Linguagem Natural e Condições Facilitadoras. Para que seja aceitável a predição deve ser de ao menos 10%, sendo reveladora acima de 30% [29]. Neste caso pode-se se dizer que o estudo tem uma predição reveladora. Os percentuais são derivados dos números que aparecem no nomograma da fig. 3.

Uma vez apresentada o nível das predições é necessário apresentar o grau de influência de cada variável independente em sua dependente. Esta análise é desvelada através dos valores de Beta. A literatura [29] explica que para que as relações que se apresentam como hipóteses devem ter valor igual ou superior a 0,2 para serem significativas. Nesta ocasião apenas o Uso da Linguagem foi significativa para a Utilidade na Especificação de Requisitos, sendo que no Uso da Linguagem apenas a Expectativa de Desempenho é significante, podendo-se afirmar que apenas as relações significantes asseguram hipóteses verdadeiras.

Pode-se também mensurar o percentual de influência destas variáveis multiplicando a o Beta da Variável Latente por suas Correlações. Nesta ocasião (tabela 4). Expectativa do Desempenho colaborou 11,4% na predição do Uso da LN e o Uso da LN e a Utilidade na Especificação dos Requisitos foi de 61,6%.

Tabela 4. – Percentual de Influência das variáveis

Variáveis	Uso de Linguagem Natural	Utilidade na Especificação de Requisitos	Correlação das Variáveis Latentes	% de Explicação
Condições Facilitadoras	0,000	0,062	0,283	**1,8%**
Expectativa de Esforço	0,121	0,000	0,280	**3,4%**
Expectativa de Desempenho	0,307	0,000	0,370	**11,4%**
Uso da Linguagem Natural	0,000	0,776	0,794	**61,6%**

Fonte: Própria

Porém, mesmo revelando as hipóteses significantes da pesquisa, em estatística são necessários testes a fim de minimizar a possibilidade de erros nos resultados finais. Em correlações e regressões lineares devem ser avaliadas a possibilidade de Hipóteses nulas. Este teste é realizado através do p-valor. Para rejeitar a nulidade de uma hipótese o p-value deve ser menor ou igual a 0,5, sendo considerados resultados altamente significantes menores ou iguais à 0,01 [29].

Outro teste que também ratifica a significância das hipóteses é o valor T de Student (tabela 5). Para que os valores sejam significativos, exigem-se valores superiores ou iguais a 1,96 [32]. Pode-se perceber que as hipóteses aceitas também foram suportadas nos testes de nulidade (tabela 5).

Uma vez que o modelo foi apresentado como confiável e válido, demonstrando resultados relevantes, pode-se dizer que o estudo agrega valor à literatura sobre o tema. Com a finalidade de medir a bondade do ajuste ou a qualidade do modelo de medida um teste complementar pode ser realizado, uma ratificação dos relevantes resultados aqui obtidos.

A bondade de ajuste é realizada através do GOF (*Goodness of Fit*) e aceita-se valores de GOF maiores ou iguais a 0,5 [33]. Este índice é calculado através da Raiz quadrada da média de AVE multiplicado pela Raiz quadrada da média de R2. O resultado para esta análise foi 0,54 comprovando a qualidade do modelo aqui apresentado.

Tabela 5. – Teste de hipóteses

Hipóteses	P-value	T_value		Resultado
H1-Expectiva de Desempenho--> Uso de Linguagem Natural	0,356	0,598	*	Suportada
H2-Expectativa de Esforço--> Uso de Linguagem Natural	0,018	2,383	**	Não suportada
H3-Uso da Linguagem Natural--> Utilidade na Especificação de Requisitos	0,000	0,923	***	Suportada
H4-Condições Facilitadoras--> Utilidade na Especificação de Requisitos	0,550	9,078	*	Não suportada

*$p \leq .05$, **$p \leq .01$, ***$p \leq .001$

Fonte: Própria

Pode-se observar que as raízes quadradas de AVE foram superiores às cargas fatoriais dos itens, assim pode-se dizer que o modelo é válido e confiável, podendo ser usado em pesquisas futuras que adotem o mesmo instrumento e permitindo avaliar as hipóteses propostas.

Há, portanto, indicativos da visão dos analistas de requisitos com relação ao uso da LN na Especificação de Requisitos. Um dos fatores mais impactantes é a maior adesão às necessidades dos clientes (hipótese 3). Usando LN é provável que a comunicação entre as partes se torne mais transparente, aumentando a qualidade dos requisitos. Isso ratifica os achados citados em outras pesquisas [22].

Outro fator impactante é a expectativa de alto rendimento (hipótese 1). Com a melhor troca de informações entre as partes e, assim, evitando ruídos na comunicação é possível levantar os mesmos requisitos em menos tempo [23] e [25].

Por outro lado, foi encontrada uma baixa correlação entre a expectativa de um baixo esforço no uso da LN para a especificação de requisitos (hipótese 3). O resultado não surpreende, pois é preciso dedicar atenção, métodos e ferramentas para utilizar a LN de forma precisa e sem ambiguidades, sob o risco de produzir uma especificação de difícil leitura [2].

Apesar desses indicadores positivos quando às expectativas de contribuição, os analistas não encontram estímulos nas suas organizações para o uso da LN na especificação de requisitos (hipótese 1). A especificação formal de modelos para os requisitos pode estar sendo preferida pelas organizações para retratar os mesmos conceitos em um nível mais alto de abstração, facilitando a visualização do problema e da sua solução, a rastreabilidade entre os diversos modelos e a aproximação com a fase de desenvolvimento do software [34].

5 CONCLUSÕES

O objetivo geral deste estudo foi analisar a influência dos aspectos de desempenho, esforço, social e condições facilitadoras, com relação a utilização da LN na especificação de requisitos. Foram apresentados breves conceitos sobre Engenharia de Requisitos, requisitos e LN. Após o embasamento teórico foram mensurados os indicadores para saber quais as variáveis incidem mais sobre a opção de utilizar a LN para especificar requisitos. Após a formulação dos indicadores desenvolveu-se questionário com 17 perguntas, com a aplicação deste para engenheiros ou analistas de requisitos.

A pesquisa permitiu validar o instrumento de pesquisa utilizado, recomendando seu uso em pesquisas futuras que tenham o mesmo intuito. Ao mesmo tempo, foi identificada não só a percepção dos analistas de requisitos, mas também o grau que ela se manifesta. Um dos fatores mais impactantes foi a consciência da validade da LN para se obter uma maior adesão às necessidades dos clientes. Isso ratifica os achados citados em outras pesquisas [22]. Outro fator relevante é a expectativa de alto rendimento, pois com a melhor troca de informações entre as partes evitam-se ruídos na comunicação [23] e [25].

Os resultados indicam que os analistas de requisitos reconhecem, portanto, a importância do uso da LN. Por outro lado, os mesmos profissionais não identificam condições facilitadoras para sua utilização mais efetiva. A pesquisa permite mensurar, na realidade considerada, um percentual para essa percepção. Essa constatação permite, portanto, verificar que, a despeito do embasamento técnico e conceitual fornecido pelas pesquisas nos últimos anos, é preciso a realização de investigações científicas voltadas o apoio organizacional sobre a utilização a LN na especificação dos requisitos. Estudos futuros poderiam apontar quais são as razões para esse descompasso entre a visão técnica e a visão gerencial. Uma amostra maior, englobando outras regiões do país, podem complementar o estudo, pois ele é valido para a realidade identifica na capital federal do Brasil.

6 Referências

1. IEEE Std. 830: Guide to Software. Institute of Electrical and Eletronics Engineers, IEEE (1998)
2. Sommerville, I. Engenharia de Software. 9. ed. São Paulo: Prentice Hall (2011)
3. Mich, L., Franch, Franch, M, Pierluigi, N. Market research for requirements analysis using linguistic tools. Requirements Engineering Journal, 40-56 (2004)
4. Kroth, E. , Dessbesell, G. Emprego de técnicas de representação do conhecimento como forma de apoio à engenharia de requisitos. XVIII Congreso Argentino de Ciencias de la Computación (2012)
5. Bustos, R.G. Procesamiento de Lenguaje Natural en Ingeniería de Requisitos: Contribuciones Potenciales y Desafios de Investigación. CIbSE 2015 : Conferencia Iberoamericana de Software Engineering. Lima, 1-3 (2015)
6. Lopes, P.S. Uma taxonomia da pesquisa na área de Engenharia de Requisitos. Dissertação de Mestrado. Universidade de São Paulo (2002)

7. Kiyavitskaya, N., Zeni, N., Micha, L., Berry, D.M. Requirements for tools for ambiguity identification and measurement in natural language requirements specifications. Requirements Engineering, v. 13, n. 3, 207-239 (2008)
8. Martinez-Barco, P., Metais, E. , Liopis, F., Moreda, P. An overview of the Applications of Natural Language to Information Systems. Data & Knowledge Engineering, 109-112 (2013)
9. Web of Science. http://login.webofknowledge.com/
10. Ramírez-Correa, P. Uso de internet móvil en Chile: explorando los antecedentes de su aceptación a nivel individual. Ingeniare. Revista chilena de ingeniería, v. 22, n. 4, 560-566 (2014)
11. Farias, J., Lins, P., Albuquerque, P. A propensão de usuários à adoção de tecnologias: um estudo com usuários e não usuários do Progama Nota Legal no Distrito Federal. XI Simpósio Brasileiro de Sistemas de Informação, Goiânia (2015)
12. Visentini, M., Chagas, F., Bobsin, D. Análise Bibliométrica das Pesquisas sobre redes sociais virtuais publicadas em âmbito nacional. Anais do SEPE-Seminário de Ensino, Pesquisa e Extensão da UFFS 5.1 (2015)
13. SWEBOK. The Guide to the Software Engineering Body of Knowledge. Los Alamitos, California: IEEE Computer Society (2014)
14. Losada, B., Jaramillo, C. Transformación de lenguaje natural a controlado en la educción de requisitos: una síntesis conceptual basada en esquemas preconceptuales.Rev. Fac. Ing. Univ. Antioquia , mar, 132-145 (2014)
15. Castro, E.R, Calazans, A.T., Paldês, R.A., Guimarães, F.A. Engenharia de Requisitos: um enfoque prático na construção de software orientado ao negócio. Florianópolis: Bookess, (2014)
16. Sagara, V.B., Abiramib, S.. Conceptual modeling of natural language functional requirements. The Journal of Systems and Software, 25-41 (2014)
17. Fiorini, S.T., Leite, J.C., De Lucena, C.J. Organizando Processos de Requisitos. In: Workshop em Engenharia de Requisitos, 1-8 (1998)
18. Paula Filho, W. Engenharia de Software: fundamentos, métodos e padrões. Rio de Janeiro, LTC (2003)
19. Pressman, R. S.; Software Engineering: A Practitioner's Approach, 7 ed., McGraw Hill (2010)
20. Lima, Vania Mara Alves. Terminologia, comunicação e representação documentária. Dissertação de Mestrado. Universidade de São Paulo (1998)
21. Mich, L., Franch, M., Pierluigi, N.I. Market research for requirements analysis using linguistic tools. Requirements Engineering Journal, 40-56 (2004)
22. Sayão, M. Verificação e validação de requisitos: Processamento da Linguagem natural e agentes. Tese. Pontificia Universidade Catolica do Rio de Janeiro (2007)
23. Ghosh, S., Elenius, D., Li, W., Lincoln, P,. Shankar, N., Steiner, W. ARSENAL:Automatic Requirements Specification Extraction from Natural Language. Cornell University Library, Jul., 1-32 (2014)
24. Dorigan, J.A. Um modelo de processo de engenharia de requisitos para padronização e aumento da qualidade. Dissertação. Londrina: Universidade Estadual de Londrina (2013)
25. Yang, H., Roeck, A., Gervasi, V., Willis, A., Nuseibeh, B. Analysing Anaphoric Ambiguity in Natural Language Requirements. Requirements Eng, maio, 163-189 (2011)
26. Leite, J.C.S.P.; Franco, A.P.M. A Strategy for Conceptual Model Acquisition. In: International Symposium on Requirements Engineering, San Diego, Ca. Proceedings... IEEE Computer Society Press, p. 243-246 (1993)

27. Engiel, P., Pivatelli, J., Moura, P., Portugal, R., Leite, J.C. Um processo colaborativo para a construção de léxicos: o caso da divulgação de transparência. Anais do 18 WER, Lima, Peru (2015)
28. Chin, W. W. The partial least squares approach for structural equation modelling, en Methodology for Business and Management. Modern Methods for Business Research, 295-336, Hillsdale: Lawrence Erlbaum Associates (1998)
29. Ramírez, P.E.; Mariano, A.M., Salazar, E.A. Propuesta Metodológica para aplicar modelos de ecuaciones estructurales con PLS: El caso del uso de las bases de datos científicas en estudiantes universitarios. Revista ADMpg Gestão Estratégica, 7(2), artículo 15 (2014)
30. Venkatesh, V.; Morris, M. G.; Davis, G. B.; Davis, F.D. User acceptance of information technology: Toward a unified view, MIS Quarterly, 27(3), 425-478 (2003)
31. Smart PLS. http://www.smartpls.de/
32. Hair Jr, J.F. et al. A primer on partial least squares structural equation modeling (PLS-SEM). Sage Publications (2013)
33. Tenenahus, M. PLS path modeling. Computational statistics & data analysis, v. 48, n. 1, p. 159-205 (2005)
34. Da Silva, L.F., Leite, J.C. Uma Linguagem de Modelagem de Requisitos Orientada a Aspectos. Anais do VIII WER. Porto, Portugal, Junho 13-14, pp 13-25 (2005)

Apêndice A.

Construtos e indicadores do modelo

Expectativa de Desempenho PE1- A linguagem natural é útil na especificação de requisitos. PE2 - Utilizar a linguagem natural capacita-me a executar a especificação de requisitos mais rapidamente. PE3 - Utilizar a linguagem natural aumenta minha produtividade na especificação de requisitos. PE4 - Se eu uso a linguagem natural eu aumento minhas chances de ganhar uma promoção.	**Condições Facilitadoras** FC1 - Eu tenho os recursos necessários para usar a linguagem natural na especificação de requisitos. FC2 - Eu tenho o conhecimento necessário para usar a linguagem natural na especificação de requisitos. FC3 - A linguagem natural não é compatível com outros métodos que eu uso para especificar requisitos. FC4 - Uma pessoa específica (ou grupo) está disponível para prover-me assistência nas dificuldades com a linguagem natural.
Expectativa de Esforço EE1 - Minha interação com a linguagem natural é clara e compreensiva. EE2 - É fácil tornar-se experiente em usar linguagem natural para especificar requisitos. EE3 - É fácil usar a linguagem natural para especificar requisitos. EE4V- É fácil aprender a usar a linguagem natural.	**Uso de Linguagem Natural** BI1 - Eu pretendo continuar usando a linguagem natural para especificar requisitos no futuro. BI2 - Eu sempre tento usar a linguagem natural na especificação de requisitos. BI3 - Eu planejo continuar usando a linguagem natural frequentemente na especificação de requisitos.
Utilidade na Especificação de Requisitos IC1 - Eu já fiz uso da linguagem natural na especificação de requisitos. IC2 - Eu uso a linguagem natural na especificação de requisitos com muita frequência.	

Adaptado do modelo UTAUT

Calidad en la inspección de requerimientos de software: una propuesta de medición

Alex F. Armijos, Carlos Monsalve, Rubén H. Ullón, Ricardo D. Maya, and José A. Romero

Facultad de Ingeniería en Electricidad y Computación (FIEC)
Escuela Superior Politécnica del Litoral (ESPOL)
Campus Gustavo Galindo, Km 30.5 vía Perimetral, Guayaquil-Ecuador
{afarmijos,monsalve}@fiec.espol.edu.ec
{rullon,rmaya,joanrome}@espol.edu.ec

Resumen La inspección de software, dentro del análisis de requerimientos, consiste en un conjunto de pasos ordenados y coordinados que intenta detectar tempranamente defectos para prevenir la construcción de un software que no responda a las necesidades del usuario final. Sin embargo, aunque se sigan estos pasos, su calidad podría verse afectada por el perfil de los inspectores. La calidad en la inspección de software no ha sido estudiada a profundidad; es decir, no se ha definido claramente que mediciones de calidad realizar y cómo realizar comparaciones entre inspectores. El presente estudio propone, con bases estadísticamente probadas, una forma concreta para medir la calidad en trabajos de inspección realizados por inspectores con diferentes perfiles. El experimento fue diseñado basado en la norma IEEE 1028-2008 y consistió en inspeccionar casos de uso para un software de un organismo del gobierno ecuatoriano donde los inspectores tenían dos perfiles: estudiantes universitarios y profesionales de computación. Los resultados obtenidos presentan mejores índices de calidad en los profesionales. La medición de calidad de inspección propuesta podría mejorarse con experimentos adicionales y trabajos a futuro.

1. Introducción

Construir software libre de defectos es una aspiración que todo ingeniero o equipo de ingenieros de software desea. Con este fin, en el proceso de desarrollo de software se utilizan distintas técnicas que apoyen este objetivo. Una técnica ampliamente usada y estudiada es la inspección de software que tuvo su origen en 1976 cuando Fagan [1] realizó su primera propuesta enfocada en la inspección de código. Desde ese entonces la técnica de inspección de software ha tenido variantes con experimentos diversos que han mostrado su aplicabilidad en la industria. La importancia de la mencionada técnica radica en que mientras más defectos significativos se encuentren en una etapa temprana de la construcción del software, más posibilidades existen que el producto final responda a las necesidades funcionales. Por lo tanto, encontrar defectos en los Documentos de Especificación de Requerimientos de Software (DERS) durante el análisis de requerimientos reducirá el riesgo de producir software que no satisfaga las necesidades de usuarios y clientes finales.

Actualmente la norma IEEE 1028-2008 [2] establece una serie de pasos y recomendaciones que se deben cumplir para que una inspección (revisión sistemática de un artefacto) cumpla su cometido de encontrar defectos en los DERS. Sin embargo, estas recomendaciones sólo se enfocan en la detección de defectos mas no en medir la calidad del proceso de inspección; es decir, no plantea ningún indicador que refleje la cantidad de defectos detectados por el inspector que son realmente defectos (eficacia) y el esfuerzo demandado por la inspección(eficiencia). El mencionado esfuerzo corresponde a toda la inspección (revisión del artefacto) aunque este no tuviese defectos. La medición de la calidad de inspección es de utilidad pues permite realizar comparaciones de productividad y cambios en el proceso de inspección si fuesen necesarios (en los pasos o en los inspectores); y así, encontrar cada vez mayor cantidad de defectos en menor tiempo en los artefactos inspeccionados. Siendo la medición de la calidad de inspección de utilidad, entonces también resulta de interés el identificar los factores que podrían incidir en la calidad mencionada. Por un lado algunas métricas de inspección de software han sido resumidas por Nair, Suma y Tiwari [3] mientras que por otro, Monsalve, Ullón y Maya [4] plantean que se debe analizar si la experiencia de los inspectores es un factor que influye en el acierto de los defectos y en el esfuerzo requerido para la inspección.

El presente estudio tiene un doble objetivo: 1) analizar si los perfiles de los inspectores influyen en la calidad de la inspección; y 2) proponer un nuevo método de cálculo de la calidad de inspección que incluye tanto la eficacia de acierto al detectar defectos como la afectación del esfuerzo que toma detectar dichos defectos. El método propuesto es un modelo estadístico, y su aplicación en un caso de estudio y un experimento de inspección de DERS contribuye a responder si la experiencia de los inspectores influye en la calidad de detección de defectos. Tanto el caso de estudio como el experimento incluyen dos tipos de perfiles de los inspectores participantes: estudiantes y profesionales del área de computación. La hipótesis que formulamos es: *La calidad de inspecciones realizadas por profesionales es significativamente más alta que las realizadas por estudiantes.*

A continuación exponemos la estructura de esta investigación. En la sección 2 se expone lo relacionado al proceso de inspección, y los trabajos actuales para medir su calidad. La sección 3 explica el método de cálculo propuesto. La sección 4 explica la metodología con que se diseñó el experimento. La sección 5 analiza los resultados, las secciones 6 y 7 discuten y concluyen el trabajo.

2. Inspección y Calidad de Inspección

2.1. La Inspección

El proceso de inspección fue inicialmente propuesto por Fagan [1] para detectar defectos en el código construido; sin embargo, el uso de este proceso ha sido extendido a otros artefactos que intervienen en el proceso de construcción de software. La norma IEEE-1028-2008 detalla los documentos que pueden ser inspeccionados por este proceso. En esta norma también se detallan los roles involucrados: 1) Moderador, 2) Registrador, 3) Lector, 4) Autor y 5) Inspector; así como sus etapas: 1) Preparar el proceso, 2) Planificar el trabajo, 3)Revisar anticipadamente los procedimientos, 4) Revisar anticipadamente el producto a inspeccionar, 5) Preparar la inspección (inspección individual), 6) Inspeccionar (inspección conjunta), 7) Remodelar y 8) Culminar. El *moderador* realiza una labor de guía y de coordinación de las reuniones de inspección, el *registrador* toma nota de los defectos detectados, el *lector* parafrasea el documento, el *autor* explica o modifica el documento (de ser necesario) y el *inspector* detecta los defectos. La *preparación del proceso* define el mejor proceso de inspección para el trabajo deseado. Durante la *planificación del trabajo* se agenda las reuniones y se define el equipo de inspección. La etapa de *revisar anticipadamente los procedimientos* proporciona una introducción sobre el proceso a los participantes (de la inspección). La *revisión anticipada del producto a inspeccionar* aproxima el documento a los participantes. Durante la *preparación de la inspección se hace una inspección individual* del documento. El *inspeccionar* detecta los defectos en inspecciones conjuntas(en reuniones). La etapa de *remodelar* verifica que los puntos encontrados en la reunión de inspección estén concluidos. Finalmente, la etapa de *culminar* es cuando se termina el proceso mediante un criterio de salida.

2.2. Métricas de calidad de inspección

El aporte que realiza presente trabajo sobre lo revisado en la literatura (sobre métricas de calidad de inspección) consiste en que las métricas actualmente propuestas no consideran el nivel de impacto de los defectos al momento de definir las métricas de calidad de inspección; y por tanto estas métricas de calidad no penalizan las mediciones de acuerdo al grado del acierto que tuvieron los inspectores al encontrar defectos. Otra diferencia es que ninguna de las métricas propuestas integran en una sola métrica los conceptos de eficacia y eficiencia, sino que miden por separado acierto y eficiencia. Los trabajos relacionados a las métricas de calidad de inspección son: [5–11]. Nair y Suma en [6] proponen métricas de profundidad de inspección (DI) y un indicador de procesos de inspección (IPM). El DI relaciona los defectos encontrados en la inspección versus los encontrados en la fase de pruebas y el IPM es un indicador del esfuerzo. Estas métricas han sido aplicadas en [5–10] y su motivación consiste en partir de un factor de calidad en función de aciertos (efectividad) y cuánto tiempo toma encontrar defectos (eficiencia). Estas métricas incluyen parámetros de inspección como tiempo de preparación, tiempo de inspección, nivel de experiencia, cantidad de inspectores y complejidad. Por otro lado Saito *et al.* [11] midieron trabajos de inspección con un puntaje de calidad orientado a medir el acierto pero sin incluir el esfuerzo dentro de este.

2.3. Inspecciones y experiencia de los inspectores

Existen estudios relacionados con el mejoramiento de la efectividad del proceso de inspección que proponen cambios al proceso: [12, 13, 13–18]. McCarthy *et al.* [12] realizaron un análisis costo beneficio (de las reuniones colaborativas de inspección), sugiriendo que se omitan dichas reuniones ya que no son necesarias para el éxito del proceso. Por otro lado, Eickelmann*et al.* [13] crearon un simulador con datos de inspección recolectados (sobre inspecciones) por Motorola para identificar los factores que intervienen en la efectividad de la inspección, y concluyeron que si las horas de inspección son incrementadas, su efectividad tiende a disminuir. Esto también lo confirma Raz y Yaung [17] con la variante que el tamaño del producto inspeccionado también influye en la efectividad.

Otros estudios explican cómo influye la experiencia del inspector en la inspección de requerimientos. Estos estudios realizan comparaciones entre inspectores profesionales y estudiantes universitarios: [12, 19–22]. En un estudio comparativo de métodos de inspección, Porter y Votta [19] indican que los resultados de las inspecciones realizadas por estudiantes son similares a la de los profesionales, sugiriendo que por tanto es preferible hacer experimentos con estudiantes porque hacerlos con profesionales resulta costoso. En otro estudio, Albayrak y Carver [20] concluyeron que la experiencia en los inspectores tiene una relación positiva sobre la efectividad de la inspección. Por otro lado, Carver *et al.* [21] propusieron que los inspectores novatos participen como observadores de otros procesos de inspección para mejorar su nivel de acierto y así realizar procesos de inspección más efectivos.

Existen otros trabajos [16, 23–28] que exponen propuestas para mejorar la calidad de la inspección; sin embargo, ninguno de ellos realizan mediciones de esa calidad.

2.4. Adaptación de la Norma IEEE 1028-2008

El proceso para las inspecciones realizadas en el presente trabajo fue diseñado tomando como referencia la norma IEEE 1028-2008. Algunas etapas fueron consolidadas en una por lo que exponemos las etapas adaptadas y su correspondencia con lo indicado en la norma: 1) Planificación (Preparar el proceso y Planificar el trabajo); 2) Arranque (Revisión anticipada de los procedimientos y Revisión anticipadamente del producto a inspeccionar); 3) Preparación (Preparar la inspección); 4) Inspección; 5) Explicación (Remodelar); 6) Cierre (Culminar).

En la *preparación* fue realizada la inspección individual e intervino un miembro con el rol de *inspector*. En la *inspección* fue realizada la inspección conjunta e intervinieron: 1) un *inspector* que también hacía de *secretario* (conocido en la norma como *registrador*) y 2) un *inspector* que también participaba como *lector*. En la *explicación* los resultados de las inspecciones son revisados con el *autor*. El rol de *moderador* se mantuvo tanto para la *preparación* como para la *inspección*.

3. Método de Calidad propuesto

3.1. Calidad integral de inspección

La medición de calidad de inspección propuesta incluye en un mismo puntaje tanto un componente de esfuerzo como otro de eficacia de la detección de defectos; es decir, este trabajo propone una medición de la calidad integral. El primer componente está basado en el esfuerzo requerido para detectar los defectos (según el nivel de impacto de los defectos), mientras que el segundo está basado en el nivel de acierto en la detección de defectos (según el tipo de defecto y su nivel de impacto). Para ello, definimos un puntaje Q que será la calidad de inspección promedio para un grupo de inspecciones realizadas cada una sobre un artefacto. Este puntaje Q se define en el rango 0 a 100, siendo 100 el puntaje obtenido si todos los supuestos defectos encontrados por el inspector son aciertos y 0 para el caso en que el inspector no presenta acierto alguno. Un defecto encontrado por un inspector se considera acertado cuando este ha sido confirmado por el autor del artefacto inspeccionado, tanto en *Tipo de Defecto* (ortografía, redacción, ambigüedad, inconsistencia e incompleto) como en *Nivel de Impacto* (crítico o menor).

j	Tipo de Defecto	Nivel de Impacto	Valor Priorización	Penalidad
0	Acertado	Acertado	38.19	1.00
1	No Acertado	Acertado	33.40	0.87
2	Acertado	No Acertado	27.72	0.73
3	No Acertado	No Acertado	0.69	0.02

Cuadro 1: Penalidad a aplicar de acuerdo al desacierto del defecto.

Por cada desacierto ocurrido en la inspección se aplica una penalidad al puntaje cuyo valor podemos observar en el Cuadro 1. Estas penalidades se obtuvieron a partir del juicio de expertos en priorizar los tipos de aciertos y desaciertos en los resultados de inspección, tal como se explica en el siguiente párrafo. Por ejemplo, si el inspector acierta el tipo de defecto pero desacierta el nivel de impacto, entonces se le aplica la penalidad número 2 que es de 0.73. Los valores j indentifican la penalidad a aplicar.

Los valores de penalidades fueron calculados mediante una relación lineal aplicada sobre los valores de prioriación, asignando 1 al valor de priorización 38.19 (acierto en ambos criterios). Los valores de priorización fueron determinados a partir de una matriz de priorización generada a partir de una encuesta realizada a 11 expertos a los que se consultó cuál de los criterios (tipo de defecto y nivel de impacto) tenía más peso si se acertaba (o desacertaba) en cada defecto detectado. Para ello se realizaron los siguientes pasos: 1) Crear una matriz de priorización de importancia sobre los tipos de desaciertos; 2) Realizar un pilotaje del llenado de esta matriz por tres expertos; 3) Llenado de la matriz de priorización por 11 expertos mediante una encuesta electrónica; y 4) Definir los valores de penalización de acuerdo a las priorizaciones ingresadas por los expertos. Llamaremos P_j al elemento j del arreglo P que contiene las penalidades definidas en el Cuadro 1; donde j pertenece al rango *0..3*.

$$TCC_i * X_i + TMC_i * Y_i = 100 \tag{1}$$

La ecuación (1) es la base para determinar el aporte de cada defecto acertado (si no hubiese penalidad, por eso suma 100) al puntaje de calidad Q; siendo el subíndice i la inspección realizada en un artefacto, donde i se define en el rango *0..n-1*, siendo n artefactos inspeccionados. Es decir, cada uno de los n artefactos es inspeccionado una vez. X_i es el puntaje por acertar cada defecto de impacto crítico en la iésima inspección realizada; y TCC_i es la cantidad **t**otal de verdaderos defectos de impacto **c**rítico que tiene el artefacto **c**onfirmados por el autor en la iésima inspección realizada. Por otro lado, Y_i es el puntaje por acertar cada defecto de impacto menor en la iésima inspección realizada y TMC_i es la cantidad **t**otal de defectos de impacto **m**enor **c**onfirmados por el autor en la iésima inspección realizada . X, Y, TCC y TMC son arreglos de tamaño n.

$$K = \frac{X_i}{Y_i} \tag{2}$$

Para introducir la afectación del esfuerzo dentro del puntaje Q fueron separados por un lado los puntajes de los defectos de impacto crítico de los defectos de impacto menor. El motivo de esta división se debe al supuesto que encontrar un defecto de impacto crítico no toma el mismo esfuerzo que encontrar uno de impacto menor por lo tanto, no puede otorgarse el mismo puntaje. En la sección 5.1 explicamos la correlación que existe entre el esfuerzo y el nivel de impacto de los defectos detectados al realizar las inspecciones. Para utilizar esta correlación, definimos la constante K como la relación que existe entre el esfuerzo por encontrar un defecto de impacto crítico y el esfuerzo por encontrar uno de impacto menor. La sección 3.2 explica cómo calcular esta constante. Una vez obtenido este valor de K, podemos definir la relación entre el puntaje por acertar un defecto de impacto crítico (X_i) y uno de impacto menor (Y_i), para cada una de las inspecciones realizadas. Esta relación de puntajes se encuentra definida en la ecuación (2). Cada inspección tiene un par X_i,Y_i porque estos valores otorgan puntos a cada defecto y la cantidad de defectos detectados varía por cada inspección; por lo tanto, estos valores deben ser calculados para cada inspección. El método de cálculo sólo considera los falsos positivos, es decir defectos encontrados que el autor no confirmó. No se consideran los falsos negativos (defectos no detectados que el autor hubiese confirmado).

3.2. Cálculo de la constante K

Cada constante K puede definirse dependiendo de los grupos de inspecciones que deseemos comparar. Es decir, que para este trabajo vamos a definir dos constantes K: 1) desde el esfuerzo en las inspecciones realizadas por los estudiantes; y 2) desde el esfuerzo en las inspecciones realizadas por los profesionales.

La hipótesis planteada en este trabajo deberá ser contrastada para ambas K; es decir, encontrar sus valores y realizar una prueba de hipótesis para cada una.

Cada valor de K puede obtenerse con los coeficientes de una regresión lineal múltiple que explique el esfuerzo (variable dependiente) versus la cantidad de defectos críticos y menores (variables independientes). Es decir, cada K se calculará dividiendo el coeficiente correspondiente a los defectos de impacto crítico sobre el correspondiente a los defectos de impacto menor, coeficientes resultantes de la mencionada regresión.

3.3. Cálculo de los puntajes X y Y

Los puntajes para defectos de impacto crítico están dados por el arreglo X, mientras que los correspondientes a los de impacto menor están dados por Y. Cada X_i y Y_i (siendo i el subíndice correspondiente una inspección realizada sobre un artefacto en el rango de *0..n-1*) es hallado resolviendo el sistema de ecuaciones (1) y (2) para cada inspección realizada (una sobre cada artefacto).

3.4. Cálculo del puntaje de calidad integral Q

$$Q = \frac{\sum_{i=0}^{n-1} Q_i}{n} \tag{3}$$

El puntaje de calidad integral Q como se indica en la ecuación (3), está dado por el promedio de los puntajes de calidad calculados para cada una de las n inspecciones y cuyos valores están dados por QI_i.

$$QI_i = QC_i + QM_i \tag{4}$$

Para calcular QI_i(puntaje de calidad para cada inspección), como se indica en la ecuación (4), debemos obtener por un lado los puntajes de calidad de los defectos de impacto crítico (dado por QC_i) y por otro los de impacto menor (dado por QM_i) de cada *i-ésima* inspección. El valor de estos puntajes de calidad separados por el nivel de impacto se obtienen de las ecuaciones (5) y (6) respectivamente.

$$QC_i = \sum_{j=0}^{3} X_i * P_j * DC_{ij} \tag{5}$$

$$QM_i = \sum_{j=0}^{3} Y_i * P_j * DM_{ij} \tag{6}$$

Llamaremos DC_{ij} al elemento de la *i-ésima* fila y de la *j-ésima* columna de la matriz DC que contiene la cantidad de defectos detectados por el inspector y que los identificó como de impacto crítico de la *i-ésima* inspección y de la *j-ésima* penalidad de desacierto (penalidad enumerada en el Cuadro 1). La matriz

DC es utilizada para determinar cuántos defectos deben ser castigados con una determinada penalización. De la misma manera DM será la matriz que contendrá la cantidad de defectos de impacto menor, siendo del mismo tamaño de DC con los mismos subíndices i y j. En las ecuaciones (5) y (6) son aplicadas las penalidades cuyos valores se encuentran en el arreglo P, castigando los puntajes X_i y Y_i de la *i-ésima* inspección. Ejemplos de estos cálculos se presentan en el Cuadro 2 en la sección 5.

4. Metodología

Para probar la hipótesis en estudio exponemos el siguiente diseño metodológico.

4.1. Lineamientos de las inspecciones

Siguiendo la línea de la hipótesis planteada, es necesario realizar inspecciones utilizando inspectores profesionales por un lado e inspectores estudiantes por otro. Para ambos grupos de inspecciones se respetaron los siguientes lineamientos: 1) Asignación equitativa de cantidad de páginas de los artefactos (DERS) para cada inspector; 2) Cada sesión de inspección no duró más de 2 horas; 3) Los inspectores recibieron talleres sobre el proceso de inspección, uso del formulario de inspección y explicación de los documentos a inspeccionar (artefactos); 4) Los artefactos inspeccionados siempre provienen de un mismo grupo de DERS; 5) Se utilizó el mismo formulario (validado y probado en inspecciones previas); y 6) Cada defecto encontrado fue señalado en el artefacto y registrado en el formulario con un comentario. El autor sólo confirmó los defectos encontrados por los inspectores, es decir, él no detectó ningún defecto durante la *explicación*.

4.2. Artefactos inspeccionados

Las inspecciones realizadas por los profesionales fueron llevadas a cabo en un caso de estudio donde fueron inspeccionados 209 documentos de especificaciones de casos de uso pertenecientes a una institución del gobierno ecuatoriano para un proyecto de un sistema financiero nacional. En estas inspecciones fueron ejecutadas todas las etapas indicadas en la sección 2.4 y participaron dos grupos de profesionales en ciencias de la computación (grupo profesional 1 y 2). Los 209 casos de uso fueron asignados equitativamente (misma cantidad de páginas) para los 8 inspectores profesionales en ciencias de la computación. Como lo indican las etapas, el proceso de inspección fue preparado, las capacitaciones y aproximación a los casos de uso fueron realizadas y se procedió a realizar la inspección individual (etapa de *preparación*). Luego, en cuatro grupos de inspección los documentos de casos de uso fueron revisados en la inspección conjunta (etapa de *inspección*) donde los autores de los artefactos confirmaron por cada defecto detectado si el tipo de defecto y su nivel de impacto eran aciertos. En esta etapa intervinieron los siguientes roles: *secretario*, *lector* y *moderador*. A continuación, en la etapa de *explicación*, el autor realizó la confirmación de los defectos detectados por los inspectores. Esta confirmación fue el punto de referencia para penalizar el desacierto al aplicar el nuevo método de cálculo.

Las inspecciones realizadas por los estudiantes fueron llevadas a cabo en un experimento en una escuela politécnica ecuatoriana durante una sesión de clases de la asignatura de Ingeniería de Software con máximo 2 horas de duración (el mismo tiempo máximo que tuvieron las sesiones de inspección realizadas en el caso de estudio). Estas inspecciones solo consideraron las etapas de *planificación*, *arranque* y *preparación*(inspección individual). Debido a que el experimento sólo se podía realizar en una sesión de clases de 2 horas (por restricciones de la asignatura) era imposible inspeccionar los 209 documentos de casos de uso ya que habían sólo 23 estudiantes. Por lo tanto, para garantizar la igualdad de condiciones y poder comparar las inspecciones en el experimento fue necesario: 1) inspeccionar una muestra de 54 documentos casos de uso (tamaño de muestra calculado con el programa STATS) y asignar similar carga de inspección a cada inspector (19 páginas de casos de uso); y 2) considerar en las inspecciones realizadas por profesionales sólo los defectos detectados hasta la etapa de *preparación* (sólo se compararon hasta las inspecciones individuales).

Los 54 casos de uso fueron escogidos al azar respetando la distribución del tamaño de los 209 casos de uso: 79.90 % pequeños (menos de 10 páginas), 19.14 % medianos (entre 11 y 15 páginas) y 0.96 grandes (más de 16 páginas).

4.3. Instrumentos utilizados

Los instrumentos utilizados para medir las inspecciones fueron: 1) Formulario de inspección; 2) Documentos de especificación de casos de uso a inspeccionar; y 3) Método de cálculo de la calidad de inspección (Q).

5. Resultados

Acorde al diseño metodológico anteriormente expuesto, la calidad fue calculada para cada documento tanto para el caso de estudio como para el experimento. En esta sección se presentan los resultados para su posterior análisis y discusión. Un ejemplo de estos cálculos realizados son mostrados en el Cuadro 2.

i	Caso Uso	X	Y	TCC	TMC	DC_j				DM_j				QC	QM
						0	1	2	3	0	1	2	3		
0	No. 1	8.84	1.36	9.00	15.00	3.00	0.00	0.00	0.00	9.00	0.00	0.00	0.00	26.51	12.27
1	No. 2	35.06	5.41	1.00	12	1.00	0.00	0.00	0.00	8.00	1.00	1.00	0.00	35.06	51.95
2	No. 3	34.18	5.27	2.00	6.00	1.00	0.00	0.00	0.00	0.00	0.00	0.00	0.00	34.18	0.00

Cuadro 2: Ejemplo de cálculos realizados para obtener el puntaje Q en inspecciones profesionales del grupo 1 para K 6.48

5.1. Esfuerzo y nivel de impacto

Para aplicar este método de cálculo propuesto es necesario confirmar que existe una correlación entre el esfuerzo(variable dependiente) y las cantidades de defectos de impacto crítico y menor (variables independientes). Para ello, se ejecutó una prueba de Pearson entre las variables mencionadas resultando: $p < 0{,}05$ y $r = 0{,}493$ (para inspecciones estudiantes) y $p < 0{,}05$ y $r = 0{,}364$ (para inspecciones profesionales). Estos valores confirman la existencia de la correlación.

5.2. Constantes K

	Profesionales			Estudiantiles		
Variables	Coeficiente	t	valor p	Coeficiente	t	valor p
Intercepto	0.287299	7.952	1.05e-13	0.478567	6.629	2.28e-08
Crítico	0.009637	5.100	7.47e-07	0.082238	3.469	0.00109
Menor	0.008319	2.775	0.006	0.012697	2.319	0.02453

Cuadro 3: Regresión lineal múltiple en inspecciones estudiantiles y profesionales

Una vez realizada la confirmación de correlación en la sección 5.1, aplicamos regresiones lineales múltiples cuyos coeficientes resultantes se muestran en el Cuadro 3. Los valores de la prueba F de estas regresiones fueron: 1) inspecciones realizadas por los estudiantes $F(2,50) = 11{,}61$, $p < 0{,}001$ y $R^2 = 0{,}3171$; 2) inspecciones realizadas por los profesionales $F(2,214) = 16{,}43$, $p < 0{,}001$ y $R^2 = 0{,}1331$. Los modelos solo explican los datos al 32 % y 13 % respectivamente. El K correspondiente a los estudiantes fue $K = 0{,}082238/0{,}012697 = 6{,}48$. Como indicamos en la sección 3.2 dividimos entre el coeficiente de la regresión lineal múltiple del defecto de impacto crítico y el de impacto menor. Lo mismo fue realizado para el K de los profesionales: $K = (0{,}009637/0{,}008319) = 1{,}15$.

5.3. Puntajes de Calidad Obtenidos

	Media (Q)		Mediana		Max.		Desv.Est.		Q_1		Q_3	
Inspectores / K	6.48	1.15	6.48	1.15	6.48	1.15	6.48	1.15	6.48	1.15	6.48	1.15
Estudiantes	7.41	11.00	2.36	5.62	45.17	55.94	10.90	14.49	0.00	0.00	17.94	11.50
Profesionales1	40.51	38.86	38.24	42.08	100.00	100.00	35.89	33.63	0.14	0.06	68.29	73.90
Profesionales2	44.40	49.96	49.35	58.39	100.00	100.00	36.30	35.89	3.50	1.79	77.46	75.24

Cuadro 4: Resultados de Puntos de Calidad (la media corresponde a la Q final)

El Cuadro 4 describe los puntajes calculados para ambas K. Existen inspecciones realizadas por profesionales que no fueron penalizadas (100 % acierto) y obtuvieron 100 puntos. Las inspecciones de los estudiantes no llegaron a 56 puntos. Las Q (que corresponde a la media) de los profesionales son superiores a la de los estudiantes y lo mismo se repite con las medianas.

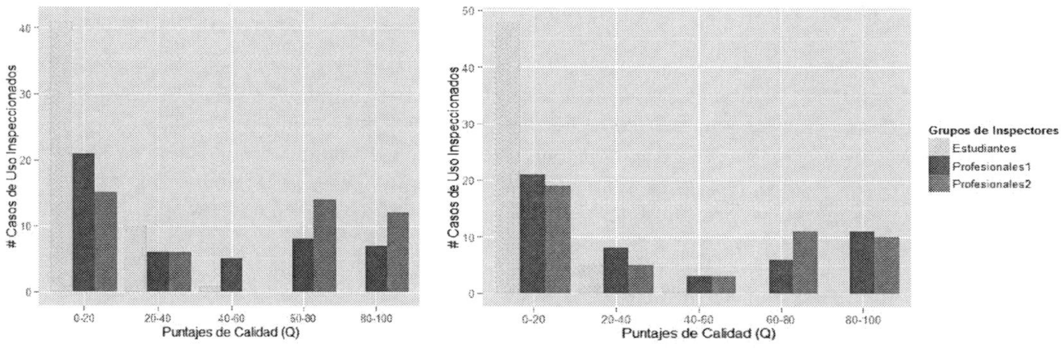

(a) K1.15 (b) K6.48

Figura 2: Puntajes de calidad Q calculados

En las Figuras 2a y 2b mostramos los números de casos de uso (inspecciones) según el puntaje obtenido. Para ambas K, la mayor cantidad de inspecciones obtuvieron puntajes inferiores a 20, sobretodo con las realizadas por estudiantes. En el resto de rangos de puntajes, los profesionales concentraron sus puntajes entre 60 y 100, donde no aparecen inspecciones estudiantes.

5.4. Hipótesis en estudio

La hipótesis en estudio es: *La calidad de inspecciones realizadas por profesionales es significativamente más alta que las realizadas por estudiantes.* Para poder probar esta hipótesis primero realizaremos la prueba de normalidad y homocedasticidad.

La prueba de Shapiro Wilk (prueba de normalidad) mostró un valor $p = 1{,}564e - 12$ para K = 6.48 y $p = 3{,}356e - 11$ para K = 1.15, ambos inferiores al nivel de significación 0.05; por lo tanto, concluimos que los puntajes calculados no siguen una distribución normal. La prueba de Levene (prueba de homocedasticidad) mostró un valor $p = 2{,}2e - 16$ para K = 6.48 y $p = 2{,}517e - 12$ para K = 1.15, ambos inferiores al nivel de significación 0.05; por lo tanto, concluimos que los puntajes calculados no tienen varianzas homogéneas.

Dado que los puntajes calculados no cumplen la normalidad, tampoco con la homocedasticidad, vamos a comparar 3 grupos (estudiantes vs profesionales grupo 1 y estudiantes vs profesionales grupo2), es pareada y de una cola, entonces para la prueba de hipótesis escogimos el Wilcoxon signed rank test. Si definimos a MD_{p1} como la mediana del puntaje de las inspecciones de los profesionales grupo 1, MD_{p2} como la mediana del puntaje de las inspecciones de los profesionales grupo 2 y MD_e como la mediana del puntaje de las inspecciones de los estudiantes; entonces las hipótesis nulas serán: $Ho1 : MD_{p1} \leq MD_e$ y $Ho2 : MD_{p2} \leq MD_e$. Los valores p del test fueron: 1) $p = 1{,}646e - 07$ para Ho1 y K=6.48; 2) $p = 2{,}754e - 08$ para Ho2 y K=6.48; 3) $p = 5{,}013e - 06$ para Ho1 y K=1.15; y 4) $p = 1{,}143e-07$ para Ho2 y K=1.15. Todos los valores p son inferiores al nivel de significación 0.05 por lo que rechazamos las *Ho* y concluimos que los puntajes Q de las inspecciones realizadas por profesionales si son superiores.

6. Discusión

Hemos comprobado que la calidad de inspección Q de los profesionales es mayor que la de los estudiantes. Esto podría parecer obvio; sin embargo, no teníamos una medida integral de calidad de inspección que corrobore qué tan distantes se encuentran estos dos perfiles de inspectores. A simple vista, podríamos pensar que la experiencia del inspector es un factor que influye en la calidad con que los documentos de especificación de casos de uso fueron inspeccionados. Sin embargo, se puede observar en las Figuras 1a y 1b que una gran cantidad de documentos inspeccionados por profesionales obtuvieron una medición de calidad de inspección inferior a 20 puntos, lo que indica que, seguramente, existen otros factores a más de la experiencia del inspector que influyen en las inspecciones.

Analizar los factores adicionales es una tarea a realizar a futuro que plantea sus propios retos. Podríamos partir analizando cuáles son los tipos de defectos que los inspectores profesionales no acertaron. La formación profesional no está asociada, necesariamente a la experiencia profesional y por lo tanto podría ser otro factor influyente. Alineado con lo investigado por Albayrak y Carver [20], podría ser que los inspectores de otras áreas ajenas a la computación sean más efectivos en la detección de defectos sobre documentos de especificación de casos de uso. Por lo tanto, a futuro también se podría realizar un estudio que compare los tipos de defectos involucrados en las inspecciones realizadas por profesionales de distintas áreas.

7. Conclusión

En este trabajo se desarrolló un caso de estudio donde participaron profesionales en ciencias de la computación realizando inspecciones de documentos de especificaciones de casos de uso de un sistema financieron nacional perteneciente a un ministerio del gobierno ecuatoriano. Luego, tomando estos mismos documentos se desarrolló un experimento en el que estudiantes universitarios (de una universidad politécnica ecuatoriana) hicieron trabajos de inspección sobre una muestra de estos documentos. La calidad de inspección de ambos grupos de inspecciones fueron comparadas. Para realizar las inspecciones, se siguió un proceso de inspección basado en la norma IEEE 1028-2008. Debido a las limitantes de tiempo, para el caso de las inspecciones realizadas por estudiantes sólo se consiguió llegar hasta la etapa de preparación (inspección individual), realizada en una sesión de clase de 2 horas. Para los profesionales, se consiguieron ejecutar todas las etapas pero solo se compararon con las inspecciones de estudiantes con los defectos encontrados hasta la etapa de preparación (inspección individual). Los defectos detectados por cada grupo de inspectores fueron clasificados según el acierto con el objetivo de penalizar por cada desacierto la calidad de inspección de cada documento. Cada inspección de un artefacto obtuvo una métrica de calidad que fue usada para realizar comparaciones entre los dos grupos de inspecciones. La significancia de las diferencias entre las métricas de calidad fue comprobada mediante una prueba Kruskal Wallis. Es importante estudiar si factores adicionales a la experiencia del inspector influyeron en que los estudiantes tengan menores métricas de calidad que los profesionales, o por qué ciertos profesionales obtuvieron bajas calidad en la inspección de algunos de artefactos. Trabajos futuros podrían responder si el dominio de formación profesional (no solo la experiencia del inspector) podría influir en la detección de defectos. Finalmente, otros trabajos pueden replicar el uso del método de cálculo de calidad propuesto y realizar adaptaciones (como ampliar los niveles de impacto) que permitan su generalización.

Agredecimientos. Los autores agradecen a la Ing. Cristina Barreto, estudiante de maestría de la Escuela Superior Politécnica del Litoral (ESPOL), por su valiosa contribución en el orden de priorización de los criterios al acertar los defectos en las inpecciones.

Referencias

1. Fagan: Design and code inspections to reduce errors in program development. In: The IBM Systems Journal. Volume 15. (1976) 182—211
2. IEEE: Ieee standard for software reviews and audits. In: IEEE Standard for Software Reviews and Audits. IEEE STD (2008) 1–52
3. Tiwari, T.G.N.V.S.P.K.: Significance of depth of inspection and inspection performance metrics for consistent defect management in software industry. The Institution of Engenieering and Technology (2012) 524–535
4. Carlos Monsalve, Rubén Ullón, R.M.y.J.R.: Dataseries: an efficient, flexible data format for structured serial data. Revista Latinoamericana de Ingeniería de Software **3** (2015) 111–116
5. Tiwari, T.G.N.V.S.P.K.: Significance of depth of inspection and inspection performance metrics for consistent defect management in software industry. IET Software **6** (2012) 524–535
6. Gopalakrishnan Nair, T.R., S.V.: Defect management using pair metrics, di and ipm. CrossTalk, J. Def. Softw. Eng **24** (2011) 22–27
7. Gopalakrishnan Nair, T.R., S.V.: A paradigm for metric based inspection process for enhancing defect management. ACM SIGSOFT SEN **35** (2010) 1
8. Li, Q., S.F.B.B.W.Q.: Improving the roi of software quality assurance activities: an empirical study. LNCS (2010) 357–368
9. Suma V., T.R.G.N.: Four-step approach model of inspection (fami) for effective defect management in software development. InterJRI Science and Technology **3** (2011)
10. T.R.Gopalakrishnan Nair, S.V.: Estimation of characteristics of a software team for implementing effective inspection process through inspection performance metric. American Society for Quality (ASQ) Journal, Software Quality Professional **13** (2011)
11. Saito, S. Takeuchi, M..H.M..K.T..A.M.: Requirements clinic: Third party inspection methodology and practice for improving the quality of software requirements

specifications. Requirements Engineering Conference (RE), 2013 21st IEEE International (2013)
12. McCarthy, Porter, S.V.: An experiment to assess cost-benefits of inspection meetings and their alternatives: a pilot study. Software Metrics Symposium 3rd International (1996)
13. Eickelmann, N.S. ; Schaumburg, I..R.F..J.B..A.A.: An empirical study of modifying the fagan inspection process and the resulting main effects and interaction effects among defects found, effort required, rate of preparation and inspection, number of team members and product 1st pass quality. Software Engineering Workshop, 2002. Proceedings. 27th Annual NASA (2002)
14. Amira A. Alshazly, Ahmed M. Elfatatry, M.S.A.: Detecting defects in software requirements specification. Alexandria Engineering Journal **53** (2014) 513–527
15. Albayrak, O.: An experiment to observe the impact of uml diagrams on the effectiveness of software requirements inspections. Empirical Software Engineering and Measurement in 3rd International Symposium on (2009)
16. Schilling, W.: Teaching software inspection effectiveness: An active learning exercise. Frontiers in Education Conference (FIE) (2012)
17. Tzvi Raz, A.T.Y.: Factors affecting design inspection effectiveness in software development. Information and Software Technology **39** (1997) 297–305
18. Kollanus, S.: Experiences from using icmm in inspection process assessment. Software Quality Journal **17** (2009) 177–187
19. Adam Porter, L.V.: Comparing detection methods for software requirements inspections: A replication using professional subjects. Empirical Software Engineering **3** (1998) 355–379
20. Özlem Albayrak, J.C.C.: Investigation of individual factors impacting the effectiveness of requirements inspections: a replicated experiment. Empirical Software Engineering **19** (2014) 241–266
21. Jeffrey Carver, Forrest Shull, V.B.: Can observational techniques help novices overcome the software inspection learning curve? an empirical investigation. Empirical Software Engineering **11** (2006) 523–539
22. McMeekin, D.A.;von Konsky, B..R.M..C.D.: The significance of participant experience when evaluating software inspection techniques. Software Engineering Conference, 2009. ASWEC '09. Australian (2009) 200–209
23. MacDonald, F.;Miller, J..B.A..R.M..W.M.: A review of tool support for software inspection. Computer-Aided Software Engineering Proceedings., Seventh International Workshop on (1995)
24. Harjumaa, L.;Tervonen, I..V.P.: Improving software inspection process with patterns. Quality Software, 2004. QSIC 2004. Proceedings. Fourth International Conference on (2004)
25. Stefan Wagner, T.S.: Software quality economics for defect-detection techniques using failure prediction. Newsletter ACM SIGSOFT Software Engineering **30** (2005) 1–6
26. Miroslaw Staron, Ludwik Kuzniarz, C.T.: An empirical assessment of using stereotypes to improve reading techniques in software inspections. Newsletter ACM SIGSOFT Software Engineering **30** (2005) 1–7
27. Stefan Biffl, Paul Grünbacher, M.H.: Factors affecting design inspection effectiveness in software development. Automated Software Engineering **13** (2006) 373–394
28. Gursimran S. Walia, J.C.C.: Using error abstraction and classification to improve requirement quality: conclusions from a family of four empirical studies. Empirical Software Engineering **18** (2012) 625–658

Um modelo para tratamento de ambiguidades em requisitos de evolução de sistemas jurídicos baseado em mapeamento conceitual

Luiz Gustavo Ferreira Aguiar, Rebeca Teodoro da Silva, Elias Canhadas Genvigir, José Augusto Fabri, Alexandre L´Erario

Universidade Tecnológica Federal do Paraná – Campus Cornélio Procópio

lgfaguiar@hotmail.com, rebeca.teodoro@gmail.com, elias@utfpr.edu.br, fabri@utfpr.edu.br, alerario@utfpr.edu.br

Abstract. O Domínio Judicial Brasileiro possui sistemas em processo de evolução, principalmente os sistemas de processo judicial eletrônico. A participação de diferentes usuários, concomitante às complexidades do direito, geram requisitos de evolução de software contendo ambiguidades. Este trabalho apresenta um modelo para captação e tratamento desses requisitos, através de *feedback* dos usuários, utilizando mapeamento conceitual. O modelo proporciona a delimitação do escopo do requisito e sua conceituação, sendo importantes contribuições para a compreensão do requisito, reduzindo a incidência de ambiguidades. Devido à complexidade do direito, a linguagem natural ainda é predominante para os requisitos, contudo, o mapeamento conceitual demonstra-se eficiente para a representação dos conceitos da área, bem como de fácil aprendizado.

Keywords: Software *Evolution*, Engenharia de Requisitos, Mapas Conceituais

1 Introdução

Um software bem sucedido é um produto de mudanças provindas de requisitos de desenvolvimento, tecnologias e conhecimento dos *stakeholders*, sendo estas responsáveis pela evolução do software [1]. Originalmente, a evolução de software surgiu como um fenômeno inesperado [2], mas que, com o decorrer dos anos, ganhou a atenção dos engenheiros de software, tornando-se o maior estágio do desenvolvimento de software, incluindo novas perspectivas como o desenvolvimento ágil, *open-source* e outros. Pesquisas tem sido realizadas, principalmente com foco na tarefa fundamental da evolução de software que é a mudança do software [1].

Ao tratar da mudança do software o *feedback* do usuário é fundamental para a melhoria da qualidade pois constitui-se de uma rica fonte de informações para a melhora de futuras versões do software, sendo a força motriz para a sua evolução [3]. No entanto, a principal fonte de defeitos em um software provém de uma análise deficiente dos requisitos [4–6].

O domínio judicial, amplia a perspectiva da questão da análise deficiente de requisitos dentro da evolução do software. Isso se deve à complexidade do direito e a ocorrência de ambiguidades, visto a existência e concorrência de múltiplas leis, estatutos e normativas [7], necessitando de métodos e ferramentas que auxiliem na análise dos requisitos de usuários e qualidade da evolução de seus softwares.

Propõe-se neste artigo um modelo de coleta e tratamento de requisitos para a evolução de software do domínio judicial, por meio de *feedback* dos usuários em mapas conceituais para contextos de sistemas judiciais, que permita a redução de ambiguidades e a melhoria na compreensão dos requisitos pelos engenheiros de software.

Atualmente, dentro do domínio judicial, devido a ocorrência de ambiguidades, esses requisitos são efetuados em linguagem natural [8], dentro de um processo *ad hoc* e propenso a erros [9]. Um modelo conceitual das leis e textos legais pode atuar como um orientador para a representação dos requisitos [10]. O mapeamento conceitual é uma técnica conhecida pela sua facilidade de uso e rápida implementação. Os Mapas Conceituais [11–13] estabelecem uma estrutura hierárquica baseada em conceitos, que permite ganho cognitivo e facilita a compreensão.

O presente artigo está organizado da seguinte forma: na sessão 2, apresenta-se a importância do *feedback* do usuário para a evolução de um sistema de software; na sessão 3, analisa-se a estrutura do Domínio Judicial Brasileiro, o processo judicial eletrônico e sua iminente necessidade de evolução; na sessão 4, a complexidade dos requisitos evolutivos do domínio judicial, no que tange a características de ambiguidade, é trabalhada; na sessão 5, apresenta-se e discute um modelo para captação dos requisitos evolutivos do domínio judicial utilizando mapeamento conceitual; por fim, na sessão 6, são realizadas considerações sobre o trabalho apresentado.

2 O papel do usuário na evolução do software

Para a Engenharia de Software, a evolução do software é a fase central do ciclo de vida do software, de forma que para um software ser bem sucedido, uma grande parcela de tempo e recursos são gastos na evolução, merecendo assim uma atenção especial dos pesquisadores [1].

A mudança é o princípio básico da evolução de um software, de modo que a evolução do software é o estágio do ciclo de vida onde são realizadas alterações substanciais. Tais mudanças podem ser abordadas de duas maneiras: de forma preventiva, onde é possível antecipar-se e preparar-se para o obvio, baseado em experiências passadas; ou de forma reativa, onde enfrenta-se mudanças inesperadas. Esta última, é essencial para a prática da evolução do software, necessitando de ferramentas e metodologias [14].

O envolvimento do usuário no processo de software mudou significativamente nas últimas décadas, passando de programadores e pessoal treinado para praticamente qualquer pessoa, implicando em mudança de atitude dos desenvolvedores em relação aos usuários [15]. Há uma distância maior entre os usuários e desenvolvedores, no entanto, é necessário manter o foco nos usuários para atender suas crescentes demandas, tornando o *feedback* do usuário cada vez mais importante para os desenvolvedores [16, 17].

O *feedback* do usuário contém informações importantes para os desenvolvedores, ajudando a melhorar a qualidade do software, bem como identificar recursos ausentes [15].

3 O sistema judiciário brasileiro e perspectivas de evolução dos sistemas de processo eletrônico

O sistema judiciário brasileiro é organizado em unidades autônomas, respeitando cada unidade federativa do Brasil [18]. Observando uma combinação de natureza judicial, localização física e grau de jurisdição, a estrutura do sistema judiciário brasileiro possui um número superior à 100 unidades [19].

Essa estrutura não possui uma coordenação central, tendo em vista que suas instancias são autônomas, inclusive quanto ao uso de recurso de tecnologia da informação [18]. O CNJ (Conselho Nacional de Justiça), visando auxiliar principalmente os tribunais que não possuem estrutura e recursos para desenvolver ou adquirir uma solução tecnológica de porte, desenvolveu sistemas de forma gratuita aos tribunais. Num primeiro momento disponibilizou o sistema Projudi[1], e atualmente, o PJe[2]. O sistema de processo eletrônico deve ser abrangente suficientemente para atender as várias instâncias do judiciário brasileiro, com seus milhares de usuários, com perspectivas e anseios de diferentes culturas e necessidades.

O PJe é um sistema em fase de evolução, e como já não bastasse os esforços pertinentes a tal fase, o sistema foi desenvolvido observando os ditames da Lei 5.869, porém, será substituída pela Lei 13.105, a partir de 16 de março de 2016, implementando mudanças substanciais quanto ao processo judicial.

Os sistemas de processo judicial eletrônico são sistemas complexos em plena evolução, inseridos em um contexto peculiar. Há perspectivas que apontam tais como ecossistemas de software (ECOS). Um ECOS é composto por sistemas e subsistemas de negócio que se interagem em um nicho específico de mercado. Com relação aos sistemas de processo judicial eletrônico, em especial o sistema PROJUDI, possuem uma complexa rede de interligações entre sistemas, atores, elementos técnicos, transacionais e sociais [20].

ECOS tem se tornado um tema de pesquisa relevante para a engenharia de software, principalmente no aspecto de estudo da evolução desses softwares. Assim, há grandes desafios também para a Engenharia de Requisitos, buscando alcançar concordância e compreensão acerca dos requisitos para sua evolução. Pesquisas tem sido realizadas no sentido de encontrar uma abordagem mais holística no tratamento dos requisitos dos usuários [21].

---

[1] Projudi – um sistema de informática que reproduz todo o procedimento judicial em meio eletrônico, substituindo o registro dos atos processuais realizados no papel por armazenamento e manipulação dos autos em meio digital [40].

[2] PJe - um sistema de processo judicial eletrônico capaz de permitir a prática de atos processuais, assim como o acompanhamento desse processo judicial, independentemente de o processo tramitar na Justiça Federal, na Justiça dos Estados, na Justiça Militar dos Estados e na Justiça do Trabalho [41].

4 Ambiguidades em requisitos evolutivos do Domínio Judicial

A forma como o direito é escrito pode criar uma barreira impenetrável para sua compreensão, até mesmo para profissionais do direito. Para cidadãos comuns, os textos legais até parecem escritos em língua estrangeira [22]. Pesquisas tem sido realizadas no sentido de nivelar o nível de linguagem entre as diversas camadas de pessoas envolvidas na dinâmica do direito [23].

A Hermenêutica Jurídica é responsável pelo estudo, definição e sistematização de métodos para determinar o sentido das expressões contidas nas normas jurídicas. A interpretação jurídica é a aplicação prática da hermenêutica, sendo gerida pelas suas descobertas e princípios. A interpretação de leis se torna mais completa quando coloca em crise o modelo representacional da linguagem, passando a considerar outros elementos além dos linguísticos em seus textos [24].

A principal mudança recente no direito é a perspectiva do chamado "destinatário-interprete", onde o receptor da mensagem passa a ter participação ativa no processo comunicativo [25]. Essa "viragem ontológica" tem sido a responsável pela construção de um novo paradigma filosófico no direito, sendo consequência da inevitável participação de elementos alheios a ciência pura do direito na interpretação de textos legais [26]. Esse novo paradigma coloca em confronto a até então consolidada, Teoria Pura do Direito[3], proposta por Hans Kelsen, responsável por grande parte do que hoje se entende por Direito Contemporâneo.

Neste novo paradigma, não é possível desvincular o direito de outros elementos em seu entorno. Concomitante a isso, a sociolinguística interacional, estabelece que quando o contexto não é observado, pode ser criada uma indeterminação. Apesar da existência de significados sociais pré-estabelecidos, a situação também cria conhecimento. As ambivalências e paradoxos são inerentes a língua como instrumento simbólico, de forma que o contexto é utilizado para solucionar as indeterminações [27].

As ambiguidades são um fenômeno cotidiano no direito. Entende-se como ambíguo um texto que comporta muitos sentidos, produzindo dúvida a respeito de uma norma ou texto legal. A ambiguidade é inerente a linguagem, porém, é possível identificar textos legais com graves ambiguidades, promovendo uma acentuada instabilidade e imprevisibilidade [25]. Em consequência disso, as ambiguidades são refletidas em todos os processos de comunicação do direito.

Diante de toda a complexidade inerente a linguagem do direito, de uma maneira especial pela ocorrências de ambiguidades, o processo de requisitos tem sido realizado de forma *ad hoc* [9], sendo os requisitos tratados e realizados em linguagem natural [8]. Há abordagens de métodos e ferramentas, que foram introduzidas nos últimos anos, contudo, tais se concentram em aspectos específicos, resolvendo apenas parcialmente os problemas, não se demonstrando adequados para a elicitação de requisitos legais [28].

---

[3] Para a Teoria Pura do Direito [42] os conceitos devem estar baseados exclusivamente no conteúdo das normas jurídicas positivas, devendo estar isentas de motivações, intensões, desejos e interesses das autoridades legisladoras.

Um sistema de software de sucesso deve ser capaz de evoluir com os requisitos dos *stakeholders* e ambientes onde o sistema opera [29]. O sistema de software deve se adaptar ao ambiente social onde os usuários formam suas opiniões e experiências [30]. Desta forma, uma sistemática eficaz para captar requisitos evolutivos é fundamental para o software se adaptar e melhorar [31].

Segundo a Norma ISO/IEC/IEEE 29148:2011, uma especificação de requisitos deve ser completa e inequívoca [32], auxiliando no diálogo e acordo entre os *stakeholders* acerca do que o software deve fazer. Entre várias recomendações, a norma defini que a especificação dos requisitos deve ser "não ambígua", permitindo apenas uma única interpretação. Assim, não se deve utilizar uma linguagem e/ou recursos que sejam técnicos demais que prejudiquem a compreensão dos *stakeholders*, nem muito simples e não estruturados que prejudiquem uma correta modelagem do sistema a ser desenvolvido.

A maioria dos defeitos de software são originados num processo de requisitos deficiente, e mais difíceis de reparar [4–6]. Estima-se que o processo de requisitos utiliza de 5 a 16% dos esforços do processo de desenvolvimento de software, porém o retrabalho para correção de erros utiliza cerca de 40 a 50%, o que indica se concentrados maiores esforços durante o processo de requisitos, levará a um menor retrabalho [33].

Os sistemas de processo judicial eletrônico encontram-se em processo de evolução, recebendo requisitos de diferentes usuários, com diferentes expectativas e objetivos, podendo ocorrer requisitos com conflitos de interpretação (ambiguidades). Se tais não forem tratados adequadamente, poderão comprometer a qualidade da evolução do sistema.

5 Tratando ambiguidades do Domínio Judicial usando Mapeamento Conceitual

Um modelo conceitual das leis e textos legais pode atuar como um orientador para a representação dos requisitos [10]. Assim, considera-se o uso de mapeamento conceitual para delimitar o contexto no qual o requisito está inserido, permitindo identificar os conceitos relacionados com o mesmo, representando adequadamente as necessidades dos usuários. Os mapas conceituais propostos por Novak e Gowin [11, 13] estabelecem uma estruturação hierárquica dos conceitos que são apresentados numa diferenciação progressiva e reconciliação integrativa, estruturados conforme a Teoria da Aprendizagem Significativa proposta por David Ausubel [34, 35], contribuindo de maneira eficiente para a construção do conhecimento [36].

Tal proposta é uma importante ferramenta disponibilizada pela Engenharia e Gestão do Conhecimento [37], sendo aplicada em áreas diversas, como melhoria de processos de software [38], e também em para o tratamento de requisitos de sistema do domínio jurídico [39].

Tendo em vista que os Mapas Conceituais facilitam a aprendizagem criando quadros de conhecimento, que permitem não somente que o conhecimento seja utilizado em novos contextos, mas também permite sua retenção [12]. Tal característica levou a considerar a hipótese de seu uso como ferramenta de apoio a um modelo de comunicação de requisitos para sistemas do domínio jurídico existentes.

Assim, propõe-se um modelo de captação de requisitos, tendo como meta o auxílio na interpretação das solicitações/requisitos para sistemas existentes do domínio jurídico. Adota-se o mapeamento conceitual como auxílio no nível de comunicação, produzindo um modelo de comunicação onde os requisitos produzidos por usuários e especialistas do domínio jurídico dentro de um contexto conceitual. Ao incluir o mapeamento conceitual, espera-se reduzir o número de ambiguidades e falhas na interpretação e compreensão dos requisitos, quando se comparado aos requisitos produzidos de maneira textual.

O modelo proposto oferece ao usuário uma opção para que o mesmo informe uma nova solicitação durante o uso do sistema. Essa nova solicitação será realizada dentro de um mapeamento conceitual apresentado pelo sistema, relacionado a funcionalidade do sistema que está sendo utilizada no momento. Essa requisição deve ser realizada de modo textual, sem a necessidade de o requisitante "construir" o mapeamento conceitual. Ao terminar de descrever sua solicitação, a mesma será encaminhada para a equipe de desenvolvimento para análise. Esse processo é realizado conforme disposto pelo diagrama apresentado na figura 1.

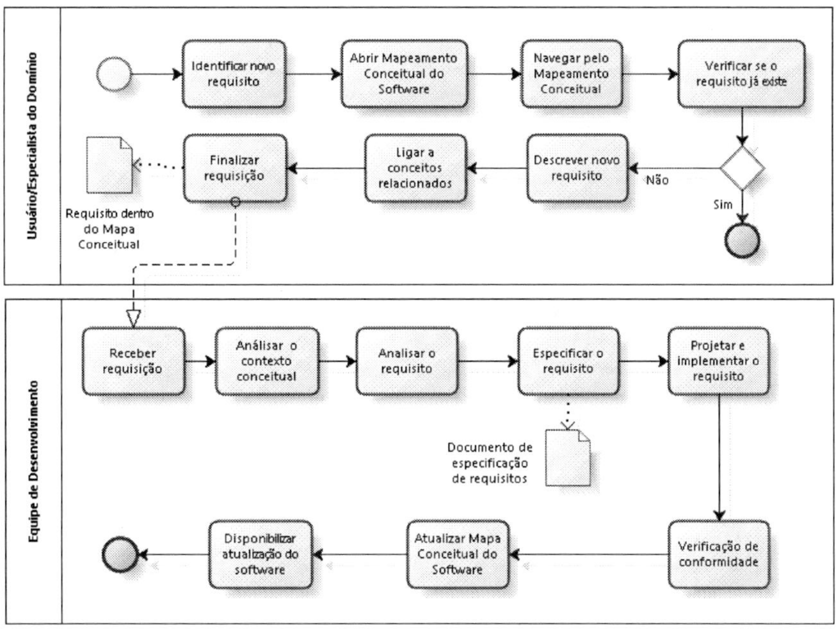

Fig. 1. Processo de criação de requisitos com mapeamento conceitual (Fonte: autoria própria)

Com esse procedimento, a equipe de desenvolvimento receberá o requisito dentro de um contexto conceitual. O artefato produzido é ilustrado pela figura 2. O mapeamento conceitual permitirá uma correta contextualização na qual o requisito foi inserido, permitindo uma melhor compreensão do mesmo.

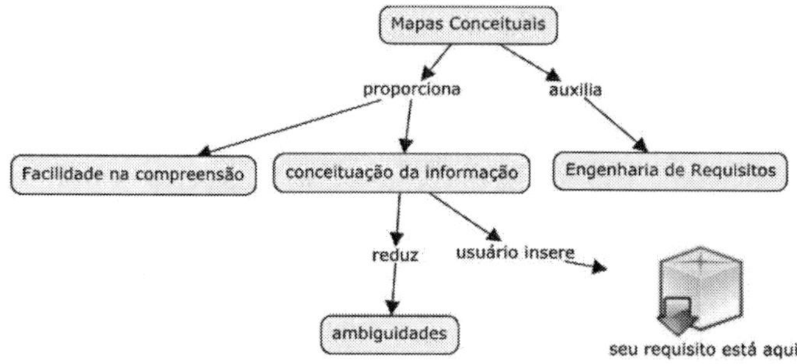

Fig. 2. Ilustração de requisito inserido dentro de mapeamento conceitual (fonte: autoria própria)

5.1 Proposta de Arquitetura de Sistema

Propõe-se um modelo de arquitetura a ser utilizada nos sistemas a seguirem a metodologia, que seja de fácil integração, tanto para desenvolvimento de novos sistemas, como para seu uso em sistemas existentes. Esse modelo de arquitetura baseia-se em um conceito modular, de forma que haverá um módulo responsável pela geração e gerenciamento dos mapas conceituais do sistema. Essa estrutura pode ser melhor visualizada pela figura 3.

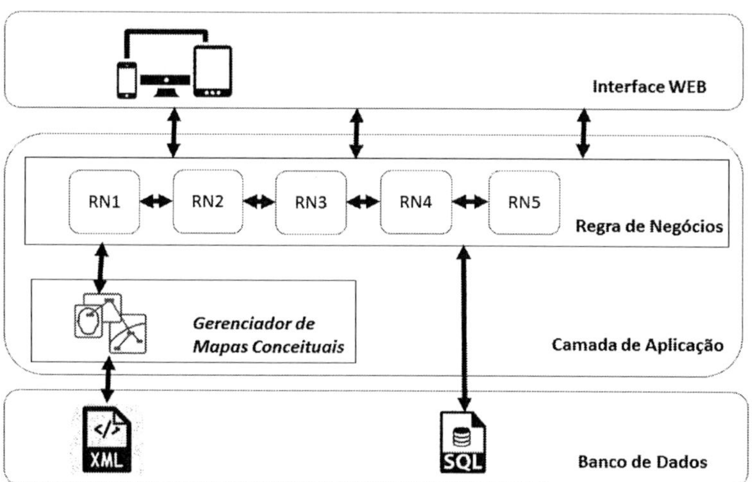

Fig. 3. Arquitetura de sistema em 3 camadas com gerenciador de mapas conceituais

A arquitetura apresentada pela figura acima apresenta a disposição de um sistema organizado em 3 camadas modulares. A primeira camada "Interface WEB" consiste na interface gráfica do usuário, disponível em HTML ou XHTML, portável para dispositivos *desktop*, bem como para dispositivos móveis como *tablets* e *smartphones*. Essa camada possui uma comunicação bilateral com uma segunda camada, a qual representa o sistema propriamente dito. Essa "Camada de Aplicação" possui um conjunto de módulos que implementam as regras de negócio do sistema, que por sua vez possui uma comunicação bilateral com uma terceira camada, contendo um banco de dados SQL. Ainda dentro de "Camada de Aplicação", possuímos um *framework* identificado como "Gerenciador de Mapas Conceituais", que possui uma comunicação bilateral com o conjunto de módulos de regras de negócio, bem como uma comunicação bilateral com uma base de dados XML.

O *framework* "Gerenciador de Mapas Conceituais" será acionado pelos módulos de regras de negócio no momento em que o usuário decidir fazer uma solicitação de sistema. Ao ser acionado, o *framework* irá identificar quais são os conceitos pertinentes as funcionalidades do sistema que estão sendo utilizadas no momento da solicitação, e irá realizar uma consulta a base de dados em XML acerca de tais conceitos, produzindo dinamicamente na sequência, um mapa conceitual para ser apresentado ao usuário, o qual irá realizar sua solicitação na forma descrita pela subseção anterior. Tais passos são apresentados no diagrama de atividades a seguir.

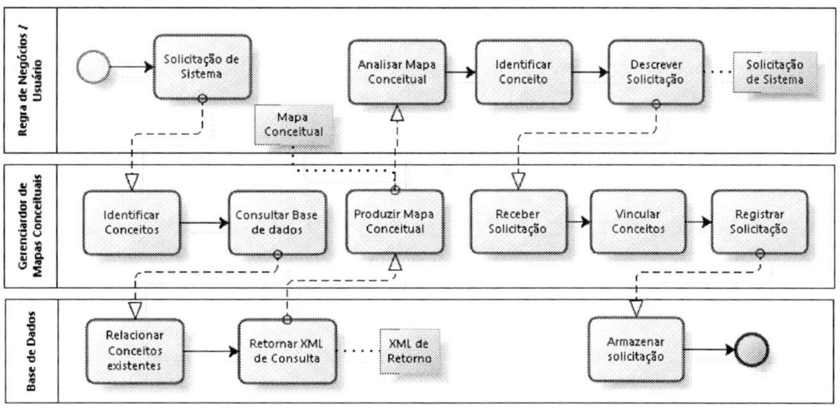

Fig. 4. Processamento de uma solicitação de sistema usando o "Gerenciador de Mapas Conceituais"

A base de dados em XML, com os conceitos do sistema, será alimentada sempre por uma analista de negócios e/ou analista de requisitos em momentos oportunos. Quando da criação de um novo sistema ou módulo, poderá ser alimentada a base de mapas conceituais durante o desenvolvimento do mesmo ou conforme o cronograma de implantação. Quando da integração em um sistema existente, essa alimentação poderá ser realizada gradualmente, sem prejuízos ao sistema, pois não é determinante que todos os conceitos estejam alimentados para que uma solicitação seja realizada.

Sempre que atendida uma solicitação, a base de dados em XML deverá ser examinada e atualizada, se for o caso, garantindo a consistência das funcionalidades do sistema com os conceitos inseridos na base de dados.

5.2 Exemplo prático do modelo proposto

Para uma melhor ilustração, considera-se o artigo 185[4] do CPC (Código de Processo Civil). Um advogado, utilizando o sistema de processo judicial eletrônico, possui uma relação de processos nos quais há intimações para serem verificadas, tal como apresentado pela figura 4. Cada intimação possui um prazo específico para cumprimento. As intimações após lidas, ficaram em uma lista de pendências para cumprimento. Porém, o advogado nota que uma determinada intimação recebida não possui prazo (ou realizada com prazo "zero"), e que assim, após abrir a intimação, a mesma não fica na lista de pendências do sistema, podendo assim cair em esquecimento. Considerando o disposto no artigo 185 do CPC, o advogado chega à conclusão que uma intimação deve necessariamente ter um prazo. Esse advogado decide realizar uma solicitação, na opção oferecida pelo sistema, conforme demonstrado pelo protótipo funcional apresentado na figura 5.

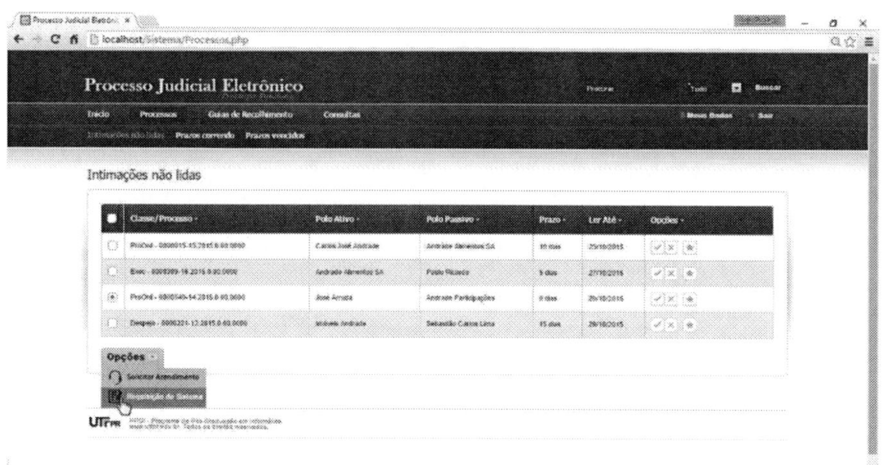

Fig. 5. Protótipo Funcional de um sistema de Processo Judicial Eletrônico – Realizar solicitação dentro da tela de Intimações não lidas

Ao advogado, quando requisitar uma solicitação de sistema, uma nova tela lhe é apresentada, contendo um mapa conceitual com os conceitos legais e normativos relacionados com a funcionalidade do sistema; conceitos de intimação no presente caso que foram observados quando do desenvolvimento do sistema até o presente momento. Assim, o advogado poderá examinar todos os conceitos, visualizando pelo mapa conceitual. Um exemplo de mapa conceitual para a funcionalidades de intimação é apresentado pela figura 6.

---

[4] Artigo 185 do CPC – "*Não havendo preceito legal nem assinação pelo juiz, será de 5 (cinco) dias o prazo para a prática de ato processual a cargo da parte*".

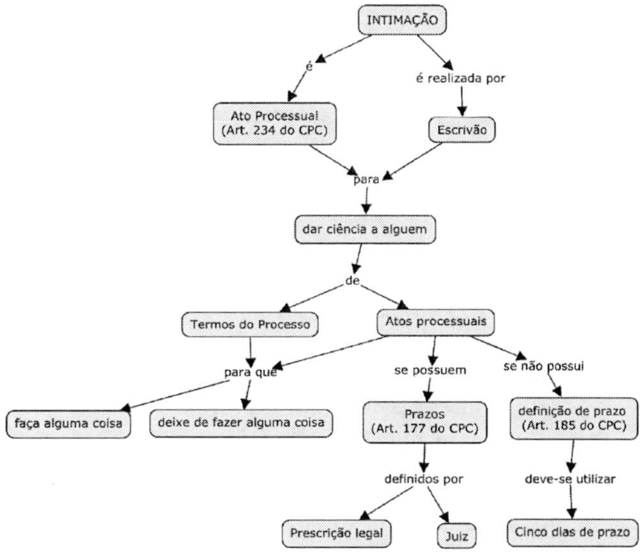

Fig. 6. Mapa Conceitual com definições e prescrições legais a respeito de "intimações"

Ao terminar de examinar o mapa conceitual, e identificado o conceito mais próximo da sua necessidade, o advogado seleciona o conceito. Neste momento o sistema abre uma caixa de texto para que o advogado apresente as informações que julgar necessárias. Ao final desse procedimento, um artefato é gerado pelo sistema e enviado aos analistas de requisitos do sistema. Tal artefato é ilustrado pela figura 7.

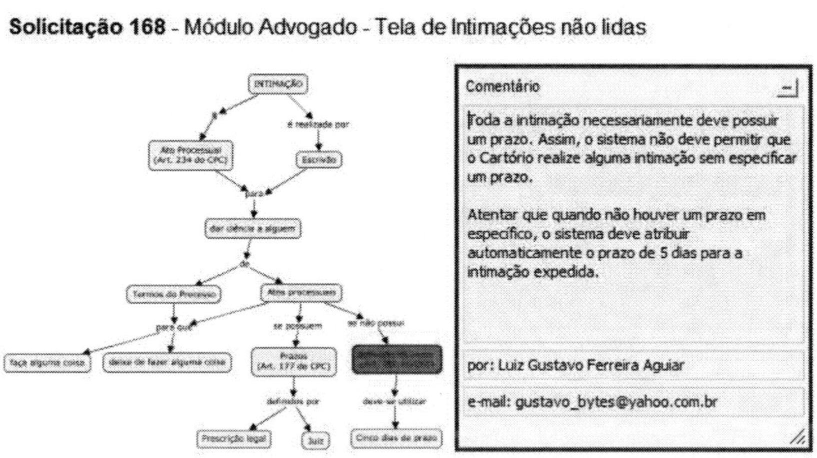

Fig. 7. Artefato de solicitação de sistema utilizando mapeamento conceitual

O artefato constante da figura 7 proporciona uma melhor compreensão conceitual da solicitação do usuário do sistema, permitindo ao analista de requisitos iniciar a leitura da solicitação contextualizado acerca do assunto referente a solicitação, reduzindo a margem de interpretações equivocadas, pois, mesmo que o usuário em sua descrição informações um tanto quanto desconexas, ou imprecisas, tendo em vista o mapeamento conceitual, as arestas são reduzidas pelo mapa, que reduz e especifica melhor o escopo da solicitação.

6 Considerações e trabalhos futuros

Os sistemas da área judicial encontram-se em um momento de evolução, em especial os sistemas de processo judicial eletrônico. A estrutura organizacional do Poder Judiciário Brasileiro apresenta diversas instituições autônomas com culturas e necessidades especificas. Para que os softwares possam atender bem tal estrutura, é fundamental a participação dos usuários, colaborando para a evolução dos softwares com seus conhecimentos e experiências. Processos de requisitos de forma *ad hoc* tem sido realizados, privilegiando o uso da linguagem natural para a especificação dos requisitos. Tal perspectiva, concomitante com as especificidades da linguagem do direito, que permitem uma variedade de interpretações, prejudica a especificação de requisitos, gerando ambiguidades.

Este artigo apresentou um modelo para a captação e tratamento de ambiguidades para requisito de evolução de sistemas jurídicos, tendo como fonte o *feedback* dos usuários. Considerou-se, como solução, o uso de Mapeamento Conceitual tendo em vista sua característica cognitiva que permite transmitir, de modo simples, o escopo no qual uma solicitação é realizada. Uma vez que, delimitado o escopo de uma solicitação, e apresentado conceitos relacionados a tal solicitação, são reduzidas as possibilidades de variadas interpretações, reduzindo assim as ambiguidades.

Os Mapas Conceituais conseguem expressar adequadamente os conceitos da área jurídica para a equipe de desenvolvimento [39], viabilizando assim o desenvolvimento do modelo apresentado.

Como trabalhos futuros pretende-se desenvolver um estudo experimental utilizando um protótipo funcional de um processo judicial eletrônico que implemente o modelo apresentado neste artigo. O objetivo do estudo será observar o ciclo de solicitações utilizando o mapeamento conceitual comparando os resultados das solicitações realizadas em linguagem natural *versus* o modelo apresentado neste trabalho.

Por fim, um *framework,* baseado na metodologia do modelo, poderá ser desenvolvido e disponibilizado para a comunidade para a implementação do método em sistemas já existentes e em sistemas ainda a serem desenvolvidos.

Referências

1. Rajlich, Václav. 2014. Software evolution and maintenance. In *Proceedings of the on Future of Software Engineering - FOSE 2014*, 133–144. New York, New York, USA, New York, USA: ACM Press. doi:10.1145/2593882.2593893.

2. Belady, L. a., and M. M. Lehman. 1976. A model of large program development. *IBM Systems Journal* 15: 225–252. doi:10.1147/sj.153.0225.

3. Carreno, Laura V Galvis, and Kristina Winbladh. 2013. Analysis of user comments: An approach for software requirements evolution. *Proceedings - International Conference on Software Engineering*: 582–591. doi:10.1109/ICSE.2013.6606604.

4. Bourque, Pierre, and Richard E. (Dick) Fairley. 2014. *Guide to the Software Engineering Body of Knowledge Version 3.0 (SWEBOK Guide V3.0)*. Edited by IEEE Computer Society. IEEE Computer Society.

5. Braude, E J, and M E Bernstein. 2010. *Software Engineering: Modern Approaches*. Wiley.

6. Brooks, Frederick P. 1995. No Silver Bullet — Essence and Accident in Software Engineering: 1–16.

7. Ghanavati, Sepideh, and Travis D Breaux. 2015. Comparing and Analyzing Definitions in Multi- jurisdictions. In *Requirements Engineering and Law (RELAW), 2015 IEEE Eighth International Workshop on*, 47–56. Ottawa. doi:10.1109/RELAW.2015.7330211.

8. Hassan, Wa ël, and Luigi Logrippo. 2008. Requirements and compliance in legal systems: a logic approach. *2008 Requirements Engineering and Law*: 40–44. doi:10.1109/RELAW.2008.8.

9. Breaux, Travis D., Matthew W. Vail, and Annie I. Antón. 2006. Towards regulatory compliance: Extracting rights and obligations to align requirements with regulations. *Proceedings of the IEEE International Conference on Requirements Engineering*: 46–55. doi:10.1109/RE.2006.68.

10. Siena, Alberto, John Mylopoulos, Anna Perini, and Angelo Susi. 2008. From laws to requirements. *Requirements Engineering and Law, RELAW'08*: 6–10. doi:10.1109/RELAW.2008.6.

11. Novak, Joseph D, and Alberto J Cañas. 2006. The Origins of the Concept Mapping Tool and the Continuing Evolution of the Tool. *Information Visualization Journal* 5: 175–184.

12. Novak, Joseph D, and Alberto J Cañas. 2008. *The Theory Underlying Concept Maps and How to Construct and Use Them*. Flórida.

13. Novak, J D, and D B Gowin. 1999. *Aprender a aprender (2 ed.)*. Coleção Plátano Universitária. Plátano Edições Técnicas.

14. Rajlich, V.T. 2001. Software evolution: a road map. In *Proceedings IEEE International Conference on Software Maintenance. ICSM 2001*, 6. Florence: IEEE Comput. Soc. doi:10.1109/ICSM.2001.972705.

15. Pagano, Dennis, and Bernd Bruegge. 2013. User involvement in software evolution practice: A case study. In *2013 35th International Conference on Software Engineering*

(ICSE), 953–962. San Francisco, CA: IEEE. doi:10.1109/ICSE.2013.6606645.

16. Ko, Andrew J., Michael J. Lee, Valentina Ferrari, Steven Ip, and Charlie Tran. 2011. A case study of post-deployment user feedback triage. In *Proceeding of the 4th international workshop on Cooperative and human aspects of software engineering - CHASE '11*, 1. New York, New York, USA: ACM Press. doi:10.1145/1984642.1984644.

17. Maalej, Walid, and Dennis Pagano. 2011. On the Socialness of Software. In *2011 IEEE Ninth International Conference on Dependable, Autonomic and Secure Computing*, 864–871. IEEE. doi:10.1109/DASC.2011.146.

18. Andrade, André, and Luiz Antonio Joia. 2012. Organizational structure and ICT strategies in the Brazilian Judiciary System. *Government Information Quarterly* 29, Supple: S32 – S42. doi:http://dx.doi.org/10.1016/j.giq.2011.08.003.

19. Andrade, Andre. 2008. Porque a Justiça não se comunica ? Um problema de estrutura organizacional. *Revista de Derecho nformático/Computer Law Magazine*.

20. Silva, Rebeca Teodoro da, Luiz Gustavo Ferreira Aguiar, and Elias Canhadas Genvigir. 2015. Ecossistema de Software no Contexto do Poder Judiciário - Apontamentos Sobre o ECOS Projudi no Estado do Paraná. In *9th WORKSHOP ON DISTRIBUTED SOFTWARE DEVELOPMENT, SOFTWARE ECOSYSTEMS AND SYSTEMS-OF-SYSTEMS*, 49 – 56. Belo Horizonte – MG, Brazil.

21. Valenca, George. 2013. Requirements negotiation model: A social oriented approach for software ecosystems evolution. In *2013 21st IEEE International Requirements Engineering Conference (RE)*, 393–396. IEEE. doi:10.1109/RE.2013.6636763.

22. Maley, Yon. 1987. The language of legislation. *Language in Society* 16: 25. doi:10.1017/S0047404500012112.

23. BAGNO, Marcos. 2006. *A norma oculta : língua e poder na sociedade brasileira*. 2ª Edição. São Paulo: Parábola.

24. Streck, Lenio Luiz. 1999. Hermeneutica Juridica e(m) crise.

25. SGARBI, ADRIAN. 2007. *TEORIA DO DIREITO PRIMEIRAS LIÇÕES*. Edited by LUMEN JURIS2. 1 Ed. Rio de Janeiro: LUMEN JURIS2.

26. SOUSA, Aline Delias. 2004. Direito e linguagem: a contribuição do neopositivismo lógico e da filosofia da linguagem ordinária para um direito transformador. *Revista Escrita Direito*.

27. MARTINS, Carla. 2002. A INDETERMINAÇÃO DO SIGNIFICADO NOS ESTUDOS SÓCIO-PRAGMÁTICOS: DIVERGÊNCIAS TEÓRICO-METODOLÓGICAS. *Delta*. doi:http://dx.doi.org/10.1590/S0102-44502002000100004.

28. Kiyavitskaya, Nadzeya, Alžběta Krausová, and Nicola Zannone. 2008. Why eliciting and managing legal requirements is hard. *Requirements Engineering and Law*: 26–30. doi:10.1109/RELAW.2008.10.

29. Nuseibeh, Bashar, and Steve Easterbrook. 2000. Requirements Engineering: A Roadmap. In *Proceedings of the conference on The future of Software engineering - ICSE '00*, 1:35–46. New York, New York, USA: ACM Press. doi:10.1145/336512.336523.

30. Godfrey, Michael W, and Daniel M German. 2008. The past, present, and future of software evolution. In *2008 Frontiers of Software Maintenance*, 129–138. IEEE. doi:10.1109/FOSM.2008.4659256.

31. Jiang, Wei, Haibin Ruan, Li Zhang, Philip Lew, and Jing Jiang. 2014. For User-Driven Software Evolution: Requirements Elicitation Derived from Mining Online Reviews. In , ed. Vincent S. Tseng, Tu Bao Ho, Zhi-Hua Zhou, Arbee L. P. Chen, and Hung-Yu Kao, 8444:584–595. Lecture Notes in Computer Science. Cham: Springer International Publishing. doi:10.1007/978-3-319-06605-9_48.

32. Standard, International. 2011. Systems and software engineering -- Life cycle processes --Requirements engineering. *ISO/IEC/IEEE 29148:2011(E)* 2011: 1–94. doi:10.1109/IEEESTD.2011.6146379.

33. Génova, Gonzalo, José M. Fuentes, Juan Llorens, Omar Hurtado, and Valentín Moreno. 2011. A framework to measure and improve the quality of textual requirements. *Requirements Engineering* 18: 25–41. doi:10.1007/s00766-011-0134-z.

34. Ausubel, David Paul, Joseph D Novak, and Helen Hanesian. 1980. *Psicologia educacional*. Interamericana.

35. Ausubel, David P. 2003. Aquisição e retenção de conhecimentos: uma perspectiva cognitiva. *Lisboa: Plátano* 1.

36. Tavares, Romero. 2007. Construindo mapas conceituais. *Ciências & Cognição*.

37. Fabri, José Augusto, Alessandro Silveira Duarte, Alexandre L'Erario, Rodrigo H. Cunha Palácios, Elias Canhadas Genvigir, and André Luís dos Santos Domingues. 2012. Aplicación de los mapas conceptuales en la definición y la institucionalización de los procesos para la producción de software. *Fifth Int. Conference on Concept Mapping*: 25 – 32.

38. Fabri, José Augusto, Alexandre L Erario, André Luis, and Marcelo S De Paula Pessôa. 2011. Knowledge Management and Concept Maps applied to Software Process Improvement. *6th Iberian Conference on Information Systems and Technologies (CISTI)*: 1 – 4.

39. Aguiar, Luiz Gustavo Ferreira, Elias Canhadas Genvigir, José Augusto Fabri, and Alexandre L´Erario. 2014. APLICAÇÃO DE MAPAS CONCEITUAIS PARA REGISTRO DE REQUISITOS DE SOFTWARE NO AMBIENTE JURÍDICO. In *Sixth International Conference on Concept Mapping*. Santos: Institute for Human & Machine Cognition.

40. Justiça, Conselho Nacional de. 2015. Sistema CNJ - Projudi.

41. Justiça, Conselho Nacinal de. 2015. Processo Judicial Eletrônico (PJe).

42. Kelsen, Hans. 2009. *Teoria Pura do Direito*. Edited by Wmf Martins Fontes. 8ª Edição. São Paulo: Wmf Martins Fontes.

Uso de un Léxico y Escenarios para Mitigar Amenazas a Requisitos en el Desarrollo Global de Software

Juan P. Mighetti[1], Graciela D. S. Hadad[2]

[1]DIIT, Universidad Nacional de La Matanza, Argentina
[2]Escuela de Informática, Universidad Nacional del Oeste, Argentina

jmighetti@unlam.edu.ar, ghadad@uno.edu.ar

Abstract. El desarrollo global de software se está difundiendo cada vez más en las organizaciones. Si bien brinda ventajas competitivas al aumentar la velocidad en las entregas del software y reducir costos por aprovechar recursos calificados más baratos, es una forma de trabajo compleja, donde amenazas provenientes principalmente de distancias geográficas y culturales pueden impactar negativamente en actividades y artefactos del proceso. La calidad de los requisitos suele deteriorarse debido a estas amenazas latentes no tratadas, propagando defectos en subsiguientes fases del desarrollo. Estas dificultades fueron estudiadas en un proyecto real de gran envergadura, desarrollado bajo esta modalidad de trabajo. Debido a ellas, se elaboró una propuesta utilizando un modelo Léxico y Escenarios para mitigar amenazas que afectan a los requisitos en esta modalidad distribuida. La propuesta fue aplicada en un nuevo proyecto real de similares características y, al compararlos en calidad y tiempos en requisitos, se obtuvieron resultados suficientemente promisorios.

Keywords: Desarrollo Global de Software, Amenazas, Comunicación, Proceso de Requisitos, Léxico Extendido del Lenguaje, Escenarios.

1 Introducción

Las especificaciones de requisitos son la entrada para las etapas siguientes del proceso de desarrollo de software, por lo que la calidad de las mismas es vital para obtener el producto de software apropiado y cumplir además con los plazos y costos establecidos. La producción de requisitos no es una actividad trivial ni monolítica [1], debiéndose encarar siguiendo un proceso definido que contemple las circunstancias propias del proyecto y del contexto de aplicación [2]. Un caso particular son los proyectos de desarrollo global de software (DGS), los cuales suelen estar afectados por diversas amenazas, tales como distancia geográfica y temporal, diferentes culturas e idiomas, y dificultades de comunicación, entre otros factores [3][4][5]. Estas amenazas latentes suelen impactar negativamente sobre los requisitos [4]. Para entender la dimensión de los requisitos dentro del proceso de software, se puede citar que los problemas asociados al proceso de ingeniería de requisitos son la principal causa de fracaso de proyectos de software [6].

Es importante conocer el nivel de exposición a amenazas con el que se trabaja bajo el DGS; dicho nivel dependerá de aspectos tales como el conocimiento del equipo de trabajo sobre el dominio del problema, la confianza existente entre todos los involucrados, y los intereses comunes o individuales que prevalecen. Conocer tardíamente estas amenazas y/o subestimarlas podría traer consecuencias nefastas para los requisitos, en primer lugar, y para todo el proyecto en general, tanto en calidad como en tiempos y costos. Anticiparlas y tomar las medidas adecuadas para su mitigación puede ayudar a conseguir los resultados esperados [5].

En tal sentido, se propone un proceso de requisitos basado en modelos escritos en lenguaje natural (LN), acompañado de un repositorio de gestión de conocimiento, con el fin de atacar principalmente problemas de comunicación, distancias, diferencia idiomática y conocimiento fragmentado. Esta propuesta se elaboró a partir de las dificultades detectadas y cuantificadas en un proyecto de DGS donde no se habían tomado medidas respecto a las amenazas propias de esta modalidad de trabajo. El proceso fue aplicado en un proyecto real en el mismo dominio y comparando los resultados alcanzados sobre la calidad de los requisitos y tiempos de las actividades involucradas se pudo determinar la mitigación de amenazas a requisitos lograda.

En la siguiente sección se describe un proceso de requisitos basado en modelos en LN y sus beneficios, y se presentan brevemente las amenazas potenciales que pueden afectar a un DGS. En la sección 3 se describen las amenazas identificadas en un proyecto real de DGS tras un análisis post-mortem del mismo. En la sección 4 se presenta la propuesta de mitigación de amenazas a requisitos y su aplicación en otro proyecto de similares características, analizando comparativamente la mitigación de amenazas a requisitos lograda. Al final, se exponen conclusiones y trabajos futuros.

2 Marco Teórico

Es bien conocido que los requisitos son un componente esencial para la generación de un producto software, y su correcta elaboración es vital dentro del proceso de software [7]. Si ocurre un defecto en esta fase, impactará en cascada en las demás fases del proceso de software deteriorando el producto en su totalidad [7]. Si a ello se suma que el DGS posee características distintivas que complejizan el proceso de software, esto compromete aún más las actividades de definición de requisitos [8].

2.1 Proceso de Requisitos basado en Modelos en Lenguaje Natural

La ingeniería de requisitos tiene un ingrediente social de carácter colectivo, dada la participación de una variedad de involucrados en un proyecto, los que suelen poseer diversas habilidades, conocimientos y vocabularios, que hacen que el entendimiento sea una tarea ardua. Para tener un proceso de ingeniería de requisitos exitoso es vital disponer de una buena comunicación entre las partes y comprender cabalmente el contexto del sistema a construir [9][10]. Es por ello que seguir un proceso de requisitos basado en modelos escritos en LN facilita esta comunicación. Los modelos Léxico Extendido del Lenguaje (LEL) y Escenarios poseen esta particularidad, que proporciona ventajas no solo al proceso de requisitos, sino a lo largo de todo el ciclo de vida del software, siendo un medio de comunicación de fácil entendimiento entre las partes [9]. El LEL es un glosario que define los términos utilizados en el contexto de aplicación [10]; cada término se define mediante su noción (denotación) y su impacto (connotación en ese contexto). Los escenarios son descripciones de comportamiento en un contexto dado y en un momento particular [9]; ese comportamiento se define mediante un conjunto de episodios, realizados por actores para cumplir un objetivo específico, y las excepciones que impiden ese cumplimiento. Se distinguen dos conjuntos de escenarios: i) los Escenarios Actuales (EA), que describen las situaciones observadas en el contexto de aplicación, y ii) los Escenarios Futuros (EF), que describen situaciones que se proyecta ocurrirán en el contexto con la introducción del software a construir. La Fig. 1 presenta 2 términos del LEL de un proyecto de DGS donde se propuso mitigar amenazas a requisitos. La Fig. 2 muestra un EF creado para dicho proyecto. Ambos ejemplos están escritos en inglés, por ser el idioma común adoptado, debido a las diferencias idiomáticas de los involucrados.

Symbol	***Policy / Contract***
Notion	• A written document containing the terms of the agreement between the insurer and the insured. • Instrument evidencing the agreement between the insured and the insurer.
Behavioral Response	• It defines the rules in general, particular or special ways that regulate the contractual relationship between the insurer and the insured. • It has a unique policy number. • It has an insured and policyholder and can be these two different entities. • The insured receives a printout after contracting the insurance. • It may be modified, terminated or extended. • Premium could not be collected by Insurance Company directly. All premiums are collected through agents. • The payment of the policy premium could be done by check, deposit, bank transfer.
Symbol	***Insured***
Notion	• Person, owner of the interest on which insurance risk is taken. • The person or organization that is covered by the insurance policy. • He may or may not be the beneficiary of the policy.
Behavioral Response	• He hires the policy with the insurer. • He can negotiate, terminate or extend the policy.

Fig. 1. Ejemplo de dos Términos del LEL

En general, existen jergas propias del contexto del problema, con palabras o frases que tienen un significado particular. No entender este lenguaje puede conllevar a defectos en las especificaciones de requisitos, que derivarían en re-trabajo por correcciones, reiterando verificaciones y validaciones. Entonces, el LEL mejora la comunicación entre los involucrados, al establecer como terminología común a utilizar la propia de los usuarios, lo que ayuda a entablar una buena relación con ellos, facilita la validación de modelos escritos en LN y minimiza las ambigüedades en los modelos que se generan, entre otros aportes [10].

Los escenarios permiten conocer el contexto de aplicación, unificar criterios sobre cómo se interactuará con el sistema, incrementar el compromiso de clientes y usuarios con el propio proceso de desarrollo, y entrenar a nuevos integrantes del equipo [9].

Title	*Pre processing Incoming payments*	
Goal	The Interface should process the payments associated to policies collected by other entities in name of the Insurance Company and registering the accounting entries into Intermediate Data Base.	
Context	**Temporal Location**	• Every day. • Brazil Time should be used for Interface schedule execution time
	Geographical Location	• Brazil
	Preconditions	• Existence of the Intermediate Data Base. • Access (user & Password) to the location where the file is stored in order to allow interface to log and read the file. • Access (user & Password) to the Intermediate Insurance Company Data Base to allow interface to record the registers. • Interface execution scheduled in Execution tool.
Actors	Bank entity (File), Insurance Company (Intermediate data base, processing interface)	
Resources	File with the collection, Intermediate Data Base, processing interface	
Episodes	1. The bank lets the file available for interface reading.	
	2. The interface invokes with the product parameter.	
	3. The interface invokes bank entity logging service.	
	4. The interface reads full file from bank entity.	
	5. The interface filters the rows by motor or other products specified.	
	6. The interface inserts data into the Intermediate Insurance Company Data Base taking into consideration the unique policy number.	
	7. The interface confirms the processing of the data and deliver status log.	
	8. The interface logoffs from the service.	
Exceptions	1. Error trying to access File (log error and INFORM EXECUTION PROBLEM).	
	2. Security error trying to access Intermediate Insurance Company Data Base (log error and INFORM SECURITY PROBLEM).	
	3. Error invoking centralized logging service (log error and INFORM EXECUTION PROBLEM).	
	4. Error invoking centralized error handling service (log error and INFORM EXECUTION PROBLEM).	

Fig. 2. Ejemplo de un Escenario Futuro

El proceso de requisitos basado en modelos en LN se desarrolla en 4 etapas [11]:

i. Comprender el vocabulario del contexto: crear, verificar y validar el LEL;
ii. Comprender el contexto actual: crear, verificar y validar Escenarios Actuales;
iii. Definir el contexto del software: crear, verificar y validar Escenarios Futuros;
iv. Explicitar los requisitos del software a partir de los Escenarios Futuros: crear, verificar y validar las especificaciones de requisitos (ver Fig. 3).

1. Introduction
2. Business Process and Business Rules
3. Solution Requirements
3.1 Business Function Requirements
3.1.1 Function 1: <description>.
3.1.2 Function 2: <description>.
……………………
4 Other Business Process Requirements
4.1 Organizational Requirements
4.2 Location Requirements
4.3 Data Requirements
4.4 Application Requirements
4.5 Technology Requirements

Fig. 3. Índice de una Especificación de Requisitos

Cabe aclarar que cuando se hace referencia a la creación de un modelo, ello involucra actividades de elicitación, modelado y gestión de los mismos. Por otro lado, debe notarse que todos los modelos utilizan la terminología definida en el LEL con hipervínculos a él, de manera tal de reducir la ambigüedad inherente a las descripciones en LN.

2.2 Amenazas del Desarrollo Global de Software

Si se considera que distribuir los equipos de trabajo es una decisión estratégica que persigue ventajas como reducción de costos y mayor competitividad, ella conlleva una alta inversión y fuertes desafíos [12], por lo que el impacto frente a un fracaso no será menor. Las organizaciones que abordan esta modalidad de trabajo deben contar con procesos estipulados, herramientas adecuadas, medios y formas de comunicación apropiadas, políticas claras, entre otros aspectos, para hacer frente a las diversas amenazas que rodean al DGS [13].

Las principales amenazas a las que está sometido el DGS [3][4][5][12][13] son: i) comunicación inadecuada, ii) diferencias culturales e idiomáticas, iii) distancia geográfica y temporal, y iv) problemas de gestión del conocimiento. Asimismo, se derivan otras amenazas que surgen de la combinación de las anteriores [14], siendo algunas no específicas del DGS pero que deben ser atendidas: v) falta de confianza e involucramiento; vi) carencia de conocimiento del dominio; vii) problemas técnicos o de herramientas; viii) ambigüedad, contradicciones y falta de claridad en las especificaciones; ix) objetivos individuales; y x) rotación del equipo de trabajo. Desconocer o subestimar estas amenazas puede impactar fuertemente en la calidad de los requisitos [14] y cuando se identifican en etapas distantes incrementarán significativamente los costos de resolución [15].

3 Análisis Post-Mortem de un Proyecto de DGS sin Mitigación de Amenazas

La propuesta que se presenta surge como consecuencia de haber identificado, en etapas tardías de un proyecto de software de gran envergadura, un impacto altamente negativo sobre la calidad del software, los plazos estimados y el presupuesto. Este proyecto en el dominio de seguros dispuso de un presupuesto de 9 millones de dólares, un plazo estimado de 10,5 meses y la participación de alrededor de 100 personas. Fue el primero de un programa, cuyos equipos de trabajo estaban dispersos en varios países: analistas en Buenos Aires (Argentina), desarrolladores en Pune (India), testers en Chennai (India), proveedores de configuración en Polonia y proveedores de equipos en Dinamarca. Los destinatarios del software de este primer proyecto estaban localizados en Caracas (Venezuela). El segundo proyecto, cuyos destinatarios estaban en San Pablo (Brasil), tuvo la misma distribución geográfica de equipos aunque con otra composición y otros integrantes. Sobre este segundo proyecto se aplicó la propuesta para mitigar amenazas a requisitos, en base a las dificultades detectadas en el proyecto cuyos usuarios estaban en Venezuela.

La estrategia de desarrollo de software para ambos proyectos consistió en que los analistas de Buenos Aires se movilizaban al país donde residían los usuarios para la elicitación y el modelado preliminar. En Buenos Aires se planificaba, especificaban los requisitos y se diseñaba. Posteriormente, se realizaba la transición a la fábrica de software en Pune para su desarrollo, en la cual las especificaciones de requisitos se asignaban a los desarrolladores y estos evacuaban sus dudas con los analistas.

Finalizado el desarrollo, se realizaban las pruebas de integración en Chennai; el equipo de testing despachaba los entregables al país destinatario del software, donde se realizaban las pruebas de certificación del software.

Ambos proyectos utilizaron un conjunto de métricas pre-definidas por la compañía de seguros, las que se calculaban en función de la información recopilada en cada actividad. La Tabla 1 solo presenta el sub-conjunto de métricas relacionadas con requisitos. La estimación de tiempos de las actividades se realizó en base a información histórica propia de la compañía. Las relacionadas con requisitos se estimaron por complejidad de especificación: Baja, Media y Alta, discriminando por analistas o desarrolladores con y sin conocimiento en el dominio de seguros. La complejidad de las especificaciones se estableció con la ayuda de un estimador basado en puntos de función.

Tabla 1. Métricas relacionados con requisitos, aplicadas en los proyectos Venezuela y Brasil

Código	Indicador	Definición	Fase	Unidad de Medida
DFE01	Creación de especificación	Tiempo promedio de creación de una especificación de requisitos	Análisis y Diseño	Día
DFA01	Aprobación de especificación	Tiempo promedio de aprobación de una especificación	Análisis y Diseño	Día
DFR01	Rechazo de especificación	Cantidad promedio de rechazos por especificación durante la aprobación de los usuarios	Análisis y Diseño	Numérica
TRATPT 01	Tiempo de transición a fábrica de software	Tiempo promedio de transición a fábrica por especificación	Transición a Fábrica	Hora
TRACP DF01	Preguntas por especificación	Cantidad promedio de preguntas por especificación de requisitos	Transición a Fábrica	Numérica
CERTN CFF01	% de defectos atribuibles a especificaciones	Porcentaje de no conformidades en especificaciones respecto al total de no conformidades	Pruebas: Certificación de usuarios	Porcentaje
CERTIN CPER01	Tasa de defectos por especificación	Índice de no conformidades por especificación, debido a defectos en requisitos	Pruebas: Certificación de usuarios	Numérica

Durante la certificación del software en el proyecto Venezuela, se identificaron numerosos rechazos por parte de los usuarios, que encendieron alarmas para avanzar con el siguiente proyecto, que se encontraba a punto de comenzar y cuyo destinatario era Brasil. Estos rechazos fueron debidamente documentados, los que provenían mayoritariamente de los requisitos. En base al análisis de las métricas procesadas, se elaboró una propuesta para reducir dichos rechazos en el proyecto Brasil.

En el proyecto Venezuela, se dispuso de 20 usuarios en Caracas, 13 analistas en Buenos Aires, 38 desarrolladores en Pune y 8 testers en Chennai. El 69% de los analistas no tenían conocimiento en el dominio de seguros, y el 66% de los desarrolladores tampoco. Se crearon 104 especificaciones: 43% de complejidad Baja, 35% Media y 23% Alta. Las especificaciones de baja complejidad tenían en promedio 18 páginas, las de media complejidad 48 páginas y las de alta complejidad 82 páginas. En cuanto al proceso de requisitos utilizado involucraba las siguientes actividades:

- Elicitación y análisis de los requerimientos del negocio.

- Creación del registro de requerimientos del negocio.
- Creación de la matriz de trazabilidad.
- Validación usando sesiones y aprobación formal de requerimientos del negocio.
- Priorización de requerimientos del negocio.
- Creación de las especificaciones de requisitos y su validación mediante sesiones.
- Aprobación formal de las especificaciones de requisitos.

3.1 Métricas calculadas en el proyecto Venezuela relacionadas con requisitos

A continuación se presentan las métricas obtenidas en el proyecto Venezuela. El valor de la métrica DFE01 presenta diferencias sustanciales entre los tiempos estimados y reales de creación de especificaciones. La Tabla 2 muestra, además, que el tiempo de creación de una especificación por un analista con experiencia en el dominio es claramente inferior al tiempo de creación por un analista sin experiencia.

Tabla 2. Variación de tiempo real respecto al estimado para crear especificaciones (días)

Complejidad	Tiempo Estimado		Tiempo Real		Variación	
	Expertos	Inexpertos	Expertos	Inexpertos	Expertos	Inexpertos
Baja	6	8	7	14	17 %	75 %
Media	10	18	13	29	30 %	61 %
Alta	15	20	22	32	47 %	60 %

El tiempo promedio real para la aprobación formal de cada especificación de requisitos por parte de los usuarios (métrica DFA01) fue excesivamente alto respecto al estimado, en promedio más del 60% de lo estimado (ver Tabla 3).

Tabla 3. Variación de tiempo real respecto al estimado para aprobar especificaciones (días)

Complejidad	Tiempo Estimado		Tiempo Real		Variación	
	Expertos	Inexpertos	Expertos	Inexpertos	Expertos	Inexpertos
Baja	2	5	3	9	50 %	80 %
Media	4	9	6	13	50 %	44 %
Alta	6	10	10	19	67 %	90 %

La cantidad promedio de rechazos durante la aprobación de las especificaciones de requisitos (métrica DFR01) fue considerablemente mayor para aquellas especificaciones creadas por analistas inexpertos frente a los expertos (ver Tabla 4), en promedio un 132% superior.

Tabla 4. Variación promedio de rechazos por especificación creada por categoría de analista

Complejidad	Promedio de rechazos por especificación		Variación de rechazos
	Analistas Expertos	Analistas Inexpertos	
Baja	2	5	150 %
Media	4	9	125 %
Alta	5	11	120 %

En la fase de transición a la fábrica del software, el solapamiento del horario laboral entre Buenos Aires y Pune era de solo 2 horas diarias y el idioma utilizado fue el inglés, el cual no era la lengua madre en ninguna de las dos locaciones. Cada desarrollador realizaba una lectura previa para familiarizarse con la especificación de requisitos asignada, para luego esclarecer dudas con el analista en una sesión limitada a esas 2 horas. Las herramientas de comunicación utilizadas fueron conferencia telefónica, video conferencia y una herramienta de gestión de preguntas y respuestas.

La Tabla 5 presenta los tiempos estimados y reales para la transición a fábrica por especificación y por categoría de analista (métrica TRATPT01). Las transiciones de analistas con manejo del dominio se mantuvieron cerca de los valores estimados, mientras que para los analistas sin conocimiento se incrementó en promedio casi 19% respecto al estimado. Los desarrolladores hicieron en promedio 13,2 preguntas por especificación para esclarecer dudas (métrica TRACPDF01). Los desarrolladores inexpertos elaboraron un 37% más de preguntas que los expertos. Esta falta de conocimiento del dominio y de la jerga hizo que gran parte del tiempo sincrónico se consumiera en esclarecer conceptos básicos.

Tabla 5. Variación de tiempo real respecto al estimado en la transición a fábrica (horas)

Complejidad	Tiempo Estimado		Tiempo Real		Variación	
	Expertos	Inexpertos	Expertos	Inexpertos	Expertos	Inexpertos
Baja	**8**	**11**	**8**	**13**	**0 %**	**18 %**
Media	**18**	**24**	**19**	**28**	**6 %**	**17 %**
Alta	**22**	**29**	**24**	**35**	**9 %**	**21 %**

En las pruebas de certificación del software, se reportaron 238 defectos clasificados según 9 orígenes, 98 de los cuales provenían de los requisitos (41% del total, métrica CERTNCFF01). Estos 98 defectos se originaban en 75 especificaciones de requisitos de las 104 creadas (72% del total de especificaciones), lo cual implicaba que algunas de ellas tenían más de un defecto asociado. De estas 75 especificaciones, el 73% habían sido creadas por analistas sin experiencia. La tasa de defectos en requisitos (métrica CERTINCPER01) fue 0,94 defectos por especificación.

En la Tabla 6 se han resumido las amenazas a las que estuvo afectado el proyecto Venezuela, identificándose las métricas relacionadas con requisitos asociadas a dichas amenazas. Se considera que gran parte de estas amenazas impactaron en los requisitos, dado que la mayoría de los defectos detectados en la certificación del software procedían de las especificaciones. Por otro lado, el proyecto sufrió fuertes desviaciones en el costo (incremento del 53% respecto al presupuesto) y el plazo del proyecto (incremento del 48% respecto de lo planificado). El mayor costo se vio reflejado como consecuencia del retraso en los tiempos, dado el tipo de contrato con el proveedor era necesario extender la contratación de todo el equipo, repercutiendo en el costo total. La extensión de tiempo surgió de manera indirecta por rechazos en la aprobación de especificaciones, cantidad de preguntas y tiempos de transición. Si bien la cantidad de defectos por especificación puede parecer baja, el gran insumo de tiempo y, por ende costo, ocurrió en las actividades de definición de requisitos.

La comunicación basada en diferentes léxicos tiene una mayor probabilidad de fracasar [9], lo que en este proyecto provino, por un lado, de la carencia de conocimiento del dominio por una gran parte del equipo de trabajo y, por otro, de las diferencias idiomáticas (castellano, hindú, inglés) y culturales, usando jergas locales particulares. Las consecuencias de la carencia del dominio se observaron, por ejemplo, en la interacción entre usuarios y analistas inexpertos, provocando un incremento sustancial en los tiempos de creación y aprobación de especificaciones y, por ende, en la cantidad de rechazos a las mismas. Asimismo, la comunicación sincrónica restringida afecta el vínculo entre involucrados en el DGS [4], evidenciado en el aumento de los plazos previstos de transición de analistas a desarrolladores.

Tabla 6. Amenazas identificadas en el proyecto Venezuela

Amenaza	Impactó en:
Comunicación inadecuada	• Creación de especificación de requisitos (DFE01) • Aprobación de especificación de requisitos (DFA01) • Rechazo de especificación de requisitos (DFR01) • Preguntas por especificación de requisitos (TRACPDF01) • Tiempo de transición a fábrica de software (TRATPT01)
Distancia geográfica y temporal	• Tiempo de transición a fábrica de software (TRATPT01) • Preguntas por especificación de requisitos (TRACPDF01)
Diferencias culturales e idiomáticas	• Tiempo promedio de transición a fábrica (TRATPT01) • Preguntas por especificación de requisitos (TRACPDF01)
Gestión del conocimiento	• Tiempo promedio de transición a fábrica (TRATPT01) • Preguntas por especificación de requisitos (TRACPDF01)
Falta de confianza e involucramiento	• Creación de especificación de requisitos (DFE01) • Aprobación de especificación de requisitos (DFA01) • Rechazo de especificación de requisitos (DFR01)
Carencia del dominio del problema	• Creación de especificación de requisitos (DFE01) • Rechazo de especificación de requisitos (DFR01) • Preguntas por especificación de requisitos (TRACPDF01) • Tiempo de transición a fábrica de software (TRATPT01)
Ambigüedad, contradicciones y/o falta de claridad en las especificaciones	• Rechazo de especificación de requisitos (DFR01) • Tiempo de transición a fábrica de software (TRATPT01) • Preguntas por especificación de requisitos (TRACPDF01) • % de defectos atribuibles a especificaciones (CERTNCFF01) • Tasa de defectos por especificación (CERTINCPER01)

4 Propuesta para Mitigar Amenazas a Requisitos en el DGS

El proceso de desarrollo de software seguido en el proyecto Brasil fue similar al de Venezuela, salvo que se incorporaron otras actividades de requisitos para ayudar en la mitigación de amenazas a requisitos identificadas en el proyecto Venezuela. La propuesta de utilizar modelos en LN: LEL, EA y EF, está fundamentada en la sub-sección 2.1, donde se resaltan los aportes de estos modelos a la comunicación entre involucrados, reducción de ambigüedades e imprecisiones, comprensión del problema y comprensión de qué debe hacer el futuro software en dicho contexto. El proceso de requisitos utilizado constó de (en *cursiva* se identifican las nuevas actividades):

- *Creación del Léxico Extendido del Lenguaje.*
- *Creación de los Escenarios Actuales.*
- *Almacenamiento del LEL y los EA en el repositorio de gestión del conocimiento.*
- *Validación usando sesiones y aprobación formal del LEL y EA.*
- Elicitación y análisis de los requerimientos del negocio.

- Creación del registro de requerimientos del negocio.
- Creación de la matriz de trazabilidad.
- Validación usando sesiones y aprobación formal de requerimientos del negocio.
- *Creación de los Escenarios Futuros.*
- *Almacenamiento de los EF en el repositorio de gestión del conocimiento.*
- *Validación usando sesiones y aprobación formal de los EF.*
- Priorización de requerimientos del negocio.
- Creación de las especificaciones de requisitos y validación usando sesiones.
- Aprobación formal de las especificaciones de requisitos.

Adicionalmente, se incorporaron actividades referidas a la evolución de estos modelos escritos en LN, y se utilizó un repositorio compartido por todos los involucrados, conteniendo dichos modelos.

El equipo de trabajo estuvo conformado por: 60 usuarios en San Pablo, 16 analistas en Buenos Aires, 47 desarrolladores en Pune y 8 testers en Chennai. Al igual que en el proyecto Venezuela hubo una proporción similar de analistas y desarrolladores sin conocimiento en el dominio de seguros. Esto se debió, en ambos proyectos, a la falta de recursos disponibles en los mercados laborales de Buenos Aires y Pune. Se crearon un LEL con 46 términos, 26 Escenarios Actuales, 97 Escenarios Futuros y 154 especificaciones de requisitos. La cantidad de páginas por especificación estuvo en proporciones afines al proyecto Venezuela, con una composición similar en cuanto a la complejidad de las mismas. Todos los modelos fueron redactados en inglés, dado la diversidad de idiomas de los equipos y con una terminología unificada al disponer de definiciones precisas a través del modelo LEL.

4.1 Métricas calculadas en el Proyecto Brasil

A continuación las Tablas 7 a 10 presentan los valores calculados para el proyecto Brasil, siendo Tablas equivalentes a las descriptas en la sub-sección 3.1. Para ambos proyectos se usaron los mismos tiempos estimados. Comparando las Tablas 2 y 7, se observan mejoras en los tiempos de creación de especificaciones respecto a tiempos estimados.

Tabla 7. Variación de tiempo real respecto al estimado para crear especificaciones (días)

Complejidad	Tiempo Estimado		Tiempo Real		Variación	
	Expertos	Inexpertos	Expertos	Inexpertos	Expertos	Inexpertos
Baja	6	8	6	10	0 %	25 %
Media	10	18	13	21	18 %	17 %
Alta	15	20	21	25	40 %	25 %

En la Tabla 8 respecto a la Tabla 3, se observa una baja importante en los tiempos de aprobación de especificaciones respecto a los estimados para analistas inexpertos. Del análisis de la duplicación de tiempo resultante en la aprobación de especificaciones simples creadas por analistas expertos, solo se ha podido concluir que el valor estimado de 2 días era realmente optimista. Por otro lado, se observa una disminución sustancial en el promedio de rechazos para especificaciones de media y alta complejidad creadas por analistas inexpertos frente a expertos (ver Tablas 4 y 9).

Tabla 8. Variación de tiempo real respecto al estimado para aprobar especificaciones (días)

Complejidad	Tiempo Estimado		Tiempo Real		Variación	
	Expertos	Inexpertos	Expertos	Inexpertos	Expertos	Inexpertos
Baja	2	5	4	6	100 %	20 %
Media	4	9	6	11	50 %	22 %
Alta	6	10	9	13	50 %	30 %

Tabla 9. Variación promedio de rechazos por especificación creada por categoría de analista

Complejidad	Promedio de rechazos por especificación		Variación de rechazos
	Analistas Expertos	Analistas Inexpertos	
Baja	2	5	150 %
Media	5	8	60 %
Alta	6	9	50 %

En la transición a fábrica en el proyecto Brasil, los tiempos reales frente a los estimados se redujeron aunque con poca significancia respecto al proyecto Venezuela (ver Tablas 5 y 10). Se redujo notoriamente la cantidad de preguntas de los desarrolladores respecto a Venezuela, siendo 8,5 preguntas en promedio por especificación. Se logró igualar la cantidad de preguntas de desarrolladores inexpertos frente a expertos, salvo para las especificaciones de alta complejidad.

Tabla 10. Variación de tiempo real respecto al estimado en la transición a fábrica (horas)

Complejidad	Tiempo Estimado		Tiempo Real		Variación	
	Expertos	Inexpertos	Expertos	Inexpertos	Expertos	Inexpertos
Baja	8	11	7	12	-13 %	9 %
Media	18	24	17	29	-6 %	21 %
Alta	22	29	24	34	9 %	17 %

En la certificación del software se detectaron 254 defectos, correspondiendo el 32% a defectos en requisitos. Estos defectos se originaron en 69 especificaciones de un total de 154, es decir, el 45% del total de especificaciones contenían defectos, valor muy inferior al de Venezuela. Al igual que en dicho proyecto, la mayor cantidad de especificaciones con defectos fueron creadas por analistas inexpertos. La tasa de defectos en requisitos por especificación fue de 0,53, casi la mitad de Venezuela.

4.2 Análisis Comparativo de Métricas de ambos Proyectos

Tanto los analistas con y sin experiencia en el dominio redujeron sus tiempos de creación de especificaciones de requisitos en el proyecto Brasil, independiente de la complejidad de la especificación (ver Tabla 11). En el caso de los analistas inexpertos la reducción de tiempos de creación respecto a Venezuela fue del 26%, mientras que para los expertos fue del 6%. En la aprobación formal de las especificaciones también se redujeron los tiempos, excepto para especificaciones de baja complejidad creadas por analistas expertos, que en valores absolutos se incrementó en 1 día, pudiendo considerarse poco significativo; algo similar se observa en la cantidad de rechazos de especificaciones de expertos. Hubo solo una mínima reducción en la cantidad de rechazos de especificaciones creadas por analistas inexpertos, aunque debe notarse que los rechazos en el proyecto Brasil se originaron en cambios o errores menores.

Tabla 11. Variación de mediciones de Brasil respecto a Venezuela en la creación y aprobación de especificaciones de requisitos

Complejidad	Tiempo de Creación		Tiempo de Aprobación		Rechazos en Aprobación	
	Analistas Expertos	Analistas Inexpertos	Analistas Expertos	Analistas Inexpertos	Analistas Expertos	Analistas Inexpertos
Baja	-14 %	-29 %	33 %	-33 %	0 %	0 %
Media	0 %	-28 %	0 %	-15 %	25 %	-11 %
Alta	-5 %	-22 %	-10 %	-32 %	20 %	-18 %

Se disminuyeron levemente los tiempos de transición a fábrica de software, mientras que hubo una reducción significativa en la cantidad de preguntas (ver Tabla 12). Lo primero se debe básicamente a la limitación de horas de solapamiento entre Buenos Aires y Chennai para la comunicación sincrónica. Los desarrolladores hicieron en promedio 13,2 preguntas por especificación en el proyecto Venezuela mientras que en el proyecto Brasil el promedio fue de 8,5 preguntas.

Tabla 12. Variación de mediciones de Brasil respecto a Venezuela en la Transición a Fábrica

Complejidad	Tiempo de Transición		Cantidad de Preguntas	
	Analistas Expertos	Analistas Inexpertos	Desarrolladores Expertos	Desarrolladores Inexpertos
Baja	-13 %	-8 %	-29 %	-44 %
Media	-11 %	4 %	-18 %	-40 %
Alta	0 %	-3 %	-40 %	-36 %

La Tabla 13 resume las métricas obtenidas para ambos proyectos, observándose mejoras significativas en varias de dichas métricas. Es notaria la disminución en el desvío del costo y plazo del proyecto Brasil, como la reducción casi a la mitad de la tasa de defectos por especificación en la certificación del software. En promedio hubo mejoras menos significativas en cantidad de rechazos en la aprobación y en tiempos de transición, siendo más sustanciales para los recursos sin experiencia en el dominio.

En base al análisis comparativo de resultados entre Venezuela y Brasil se observan indicios de mejoras importantes sobre ciertos aspectos y en otros casos mitigaciones parciales de amenazas a requisitos identificadas. Mediante el uso del LEL, que ancla el vocabulario del contexto manejado durante todo el proceso de software, se mejoró la calidad de la comunicación, se disminuyó la ambigüedad, contradicciones y/o falta de claridad en las especificaciones, y se mitigó parcialmente las diferencias culturales e idiomáticas. Mediante los EA y EF, se mejoró claramente las amenazas referidas a carencia del dominio, y a ambigüedad, contradicciones y/o falta de claridad en las especificaciones, presentando estas una tasa menor de defectos, debido principalmente a que los EF habían sido previamente validados y dichas validaciones se facilitaron por estar los EF escritos en el lenguaje propio de los usuarios. Al utilizarse modelos escritos en LN con un vocabulario unificado, se motivó la confianza e involucramiento de los equipos de trabajo. Estos modelos LEL, EA y EF permitieron mitigar parcialmente la amenaza referida a distancia geográfica y temporal, ya que fueron una fuente validada para crear las especificaciones de requisitos y, además, durante la transición a fábrica permitieron evacuar dudas o tomar decisiones rápidamente en forma individual, minimizando la cantidad de preguntas. Asimismo, un repositorio compartido con estos modelos facilitó la gestión del conocimiento.

Tabla 13. Comparación de mediciones entre los proyectos Venezuela y Brasil

Métrica	Venezuela	Brasil
Días promedio de creación de cada especificación	20	16
Días promedio de aprobación de cada especificación	10	8,2
Cantidad de rechazos en aprobación de especificaciones	6	5,8
Horas promedio de transición a la fábrica de software	21,2	20,5
Cantidad de preguntas por especificación de requisitos	13,2	8,5
Tasa de defectos por especificación (certificación)	0,94	0,53
Proporción de defectos en requisitos respecto al total de defectos (certificación)	41 %	32 %
Proporción de especificaciones con defectos respecto al total de especificaciones (certificación)	72 %	45 %
Desviación en el costo total estimado del proyecto	53 %	26 %
Desviación en el tiempo total estimado del proyecto	48 %	18 %

5 Conclusiones

El DGS se ha extendido ampliamente en la industria del software, y es por ello que debe prestársele la debida atención dado que, aún cuando presenta grandes beneficios, estos pueden reducirse por desconocer o desestimar sus características particulares, las que deben ser consideradas apropiadamente en el proceso de desarrollo. Esas particularidades pueden convertirse en amenazas que atentan contra la calidad del proceso y del producto [3][4][5][8][12][13]. Muchas de ellas afectan en mayor o menor medida a los requisitos, por lo que, su identificación es el primer paso hacia una estrategia proactiva de mitigación de las mismas. La propuesta que se ha presentado utilizando los modelos LEL, EA y EF [10][11] intenta aportar beneficios en la mitigación de amenazas sobre los requisitos en proyectos de DGS.

Ambos proyectos presentados, Venezuela y Brasil, poseían características similares desde la perspectiva técnica, pues se utilizaron los mismos procesos, métricas, modelo de estimación y herramientas. En base a las métricas calculadas para el proyecto Brasil, pudo evidenciarse que la incorporación de dichos modelos junto con un repositorio común conteniéndolos, permitió reducir las amenazas identificadas previamente en el proyecto Venezuela. Esta propuesta está alineada con lo planteado en [8], que expone la necesidad de un proceso de ingeniería de requisitos diferente para proyectos inmersos en el DGS. Las características de los proyectos Venezuela y Brasil son afines a muchos otros proyectos de DGS, según se evidencia en la literatura, lo que haría suponer que las mejoras alcanzadas en la calidad de las especificaciones de requisitos utilizando el LEL, los Escenarios y el repositorio compartido, también podrían obtenerse en proyectos similares. La propuesta de [3] se enfoca en el uso de ontologías y herramientas groupware para mejorar la comunicación, la comprensión del problema y la gestión de conocimiento. Recurrir al uso de ontologías es relativamente similar a las ventajas que proporciona el LEL, aunque éste se centra en el vocabulario específico del contexto, complementado con EA para una comprensión acabada del comportamiento en ese contexto.

Una posible mejora en la propuesta presentada es la creación de un LEL adicional que refleje el vocabulario utilizado en los EF y en las especificaciones de requisitos, debido a que en ellos pueden aparecer términos no definidos en el LEL inicial o modificar términos existentes, por cambios en los procesos del negocio o cambios tecnológicos al incorporar el software. Un punto propuesto a futuro es cómo el LEL y los EF podrían colaborar en entender la jerga y los flujos del sistema para el equipo de pruebas, tarea que muchas veces es encargada a otro proveedor.

Referencias

1. Nuseibeh, B., Easterbrook, S.: Requirements Engineering: A Roadmap. In: Future of SE Track 2000, pp. 35-46. Limerick, Ireland (2000)
2. Bucher, T., Klesse, M., Kurpjuweit, S., Winter, R.: Situational Method Engineering. In: Situational method engineering: fundamentals and experiences, pp.33-48. Springer (2007)
3. Aranda, G.N., Vizcaíno, A., Cechich, A., Piattini, M.: A Methodology for Reducing Geographical Dispersion Problems during Global Requirements Elicitation. In: 11th Workshop on Requirements Engineering, pp.117-127 (2008)
4. Damian, D.E., Zowghi, D.: RE challenges in multi-site software development organisations. Requirements Engineering Journal, 8(3),149-160 (2003)
5. Richardson, I., Casey, V., McCaffery, F., Burton, J., Beecham, S.: A Process Framework for Global Software Engineering Teams. Information and Software Technology, 54(11),1175-1191 (2012)
6. Niazi, M., Shastry, S.: Role of requirements engineering in software development process: an empirical study. In: 7th International Multi Topic Conference, pp. 402-407 (2003)
7. Nahar, N., Student, P.G.: Managing Requirement Elicitation Issues Using Step-Wise Refinement Model. International Journal of Advanced Studies in Computers, Science and Engineering, 2(5),27-33 (2013)
8. Zowghi, D.: Does Global Software Development Need a Different Requirements Engineering Process? In: International Workshop on Global Software Development - ICSE 2002, Orlando, Florida, pp.53-55 (2002)
9. Hadad, G.D.S, Kaplan, G.N., Oliveros, A., Leite, J.C.S.P.: Integración de escenarios con el léxico extendido del lenguaje en la elicitación de requerimientos: aplicación a un caso real. Revista de Informática Teórica y Aplicada (RITA), 6(1),77-103, Brasil (1999)
10. Leite, J.C., Doorn, J.H., Kaplan, G.N., Hadad, G.D., Ridao, M.: Defining System Context using Scenarios. Perspectives on Software Requirements, pp.169-199. Springer (2004)
11. Hadad, G.D.S.: Uso de Escenarios en la Derivación de Software. Tesis Doctoral, Facultad de Ciencias Exactas, Universidad Nacional de La Plata (2008)
12. Fryer, K., Gothe, M.: Global Software Development and Delivery. Trends and Challenges. IBM Developer Works, The Rational Edge (2008)
13. ul Haq, S., Raza, M., Zia, A., Khan, M.N.A.: Issues in global software development: A critical review. Journal of Software Engineering and Applications, 4(10),590--595 (2011)
14. Bhat, J.M., Gupta, M., Murthy, S.N.: Overcoming requirements engineering challenges: Lessons from offshore outsourcing. IEEE Software, 23(5), 38-44 (2006)
15. Westland, J.C.: The cost of errors in software development: evidence from industry, Journal of Systems and Software, Vol.62, pp.1-9 (2002)

Melhoria de Documentos de Requisitos: um mapeamento sistemático da literatura.

Roberto Azevedo[1], Aêda Sousa[1], Ricardo Ramos[2], e Fernanda Alencar[1]

[1]Universidade de Pernambuco, UPE, Recife, Brasil
{rcostape,fernandaalenc, aedasousa}@gmail.com

[2]Universidade Federal do Vale do São Francisco, UNIVASF, Juazeiro, Brasil
ricargentonramos@gmail.com

Resumo. Diversas técnicas são utilizadas, tanto pela indústria quanto pela academia, para a especificação de requisitos de um sistema de software. Dentre essas, destacam-se casos de uso e descrição textual que, como outras, apresentam problemas com relação a requisitos que foram abandonados; estruturas demasiadamente longas ou muito pequenas, pouco significativas e até desnecessárias; requisitos duplicados, fragmentados e espalhados. Tudo isso diminui a facilidade de entendimento, a modularidade e a reusabilidade do documento de requisitos, acarretando a inserção de erros nas fases posteriores do processo de desenvolvimento. Para esses casos, o quanto antes os problemas forem encontrados, menor será o custo para removê-los. Nesta pesquisa, utilizou-se o mapeamento sistemático da literatura como procedimento metodológico, com o objetivo de verificar, com bases em evidências, o estado atual de estudos sobre a melhoria de documentos de requisitos. A ideia foi verificar como essas melhorias foram validados e se utilizam alguma ferramenta de apoio. Diversos estudos propõem diferentes técnicas para avaliação e melhoria de documentos de requisitos por meio de refatorações e padrões, a fim de minimizar ou remover deficiências. Após análise dos estudos identificados, melhorias serão propostas à abordagem AIRDoc (Approach to Improve Requirements Documents), bem como o desenvolvimento de uma ferramenta para apoiar a execução do processo de forma efetiva.

Palavras-Chave. mapeamento sistemático, documentos de requisitos, melhoria, qualidade.

1 Introdução

A maioria dos problemas de software surge de deficiências na maneira em que os requisitos de software são elicitados, gerenciados e expressos [33]. Elaborar um documento de requisitos de software com qualidade é essencial para o sucesso de qualquer projeto de desenvolvimento de software, tendo em vista a importância da sua utilização em diversas etapas do projeto [37]. No entanto, a avaliação da qualidade de um documento de requisitos não é um processo simples, principalmente devido aos diversos tipos de propostas, abordagens, técnicas e ferramentas, muitas vezes contraditórias quando se trata dos atributos de qualidade a serem avaliados e as metodologias utilizadas [33].

A descrição textual, por meio da linguagem natural, é a principal representação utilizada nos documentos de requisitos elaborados na indústria, o que implica que os documentos de requisitos estejam suscetíveis à ambiguidade, ou seja, a mesma frase pode ser interpretada de várias formas diferentes [6]. Outra técnica bastante utilizada é o modelo de Caso de Uso, o qual permite modelar as necessidades dos usuários em um documento de requisitos, por meio da Descrição do Caso de Uso e de uma possível representação em um Diagrama de Casos de Uso. A modelagem de Casos de Uso é uma ferramenta poderosa para a captura de requisitos funcionais de sistemas de software, pois possibilitam especificar a interação entre o sistema de software e seus usuários [34]. Entretanto, por serem geralmente descritos por textos, significa que eles também são afetados por questões como a ambiguidade, redundância, inconsistência e incompletude.

Diversas pesquisas foram realizadas, a fim de lidar com esses problemas de qualidade do documento de requisitos. A literatura fornece modelos [37][38], diretrizes para a criação de requisitos de software [18], e listas de verificação para inspecionar Casos de Uso [36]. Outros buscam alguma forma de automatizar, com apoio de ferramentas, a detecção desses erros em documentos de requisitos descritos em Linguagem Natural [39].

A AIRDoc [13] propõe a utilização de métricas para a detecção de problemas recorrentes em documentos de requisitos especificados com Casos de Uso. Com a aplicação das métricas, um engenheiro (ou equipe de qualidade) identificará trechos no documento de requisitos que poderão ser melhorados com a utilização de um catálogo de refatorações de requisitos. Atualmente, a AIRDoc não é apoiada por ferramenta de automatização, o que dificulta sua utilização devido à quantidade de atividades necessárias para a sua correta aplicação.

Baseado nesse contexto, este trabalho reúne a síntese das informações de um mapeamento sistemático da literatura (MSL) cujo objetivo é verificar, por evidências, estudos focados na melhoria de documentos de requisitos; como as propostas foram validadas; e, se utilizam alguma ferramenta para automatização. O mapeamento inclui estudos a partir de 1986, ano em que os primeiros Casos de Uso foram divulgados à comunidade acadêmica por Ivar Jacobson [32], e segue um protocolo de pesquisa adaptado de Kitchenham [28]. A pesquisa iniciou com 3616 estudos, sendo 3297 resultantes de buscas automáticas a bases de dados acadêmicos e 319 do repositório do WER. Após a etapa de seleção, 27 trabalhos relevantes à pesquisa foram analisados, a fim de obter informações necessárias para responder as questões de pesquisa definidas.

O artigo está estruturado nas seguintes seções: a seção 2 apresenta o processo de mapeamento sistemático da literatura. Na seção 3 são descritos e analisados os resultados alcançados com a pesquisa. Na seção 4 são descritas possíveis ameaças à validade dos resultados. A seção 5 apresenta alguns trabalhos relacionados. E por fim, a seção 6 traz as conclusões dos estudos realizados e trabalhos futuros.

2 Método de Pesquisa

O Mapeamento Sistemático apresentado foi conduzido baseado na metodologia utilizada para a realização de uma revisão sistemática da literatura recomendada pela Kitchenham [28]. Algumas partes da metodologia utilizada no estudo foram apresentadas por outras revisões sistemáticas [29][30][35]. A Figura 1 apresenta o processo utilizado para a realização do MSL.

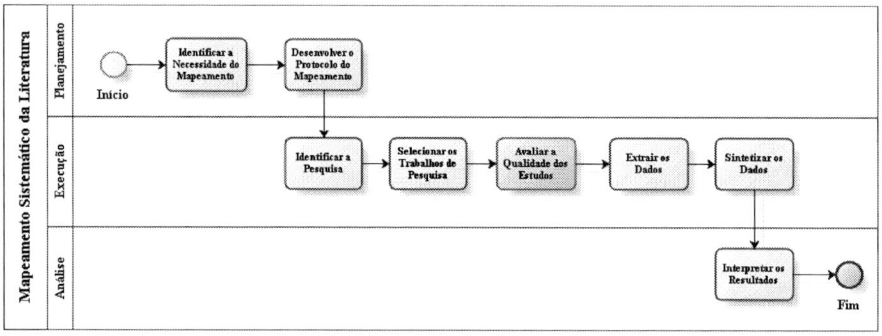

Fig. 1. Processo de Condução do Mapeamento Sistemático. Adaptado de [28].

2.1 Questões de Pesquisa e Contexto

Para verificar o estado atual de estudos com foco na melhoria de documentos de requisitos, três Questões de Pesquisa (QPs) foram formuladas com a sua respectiva descrição, conforme Tabela 1.

Tabela 1 - Questões de Pesquisa e Descrição.

Questão de Pesquisa	Descrição
QP1 – Como os requisitos são especificados nas abordagens?	Pretende-se identificar a forma como os requisitos são documentados (e.g., Modelos de Casos de Uso, Ponto de Vista, Descrição Textual) nas abordagens (técnicas, processos, frameworks, métodos) focadas na melhoria de documentos de requisitos. É importante, pois provê um conjunto de contribuições voltadas para problemas de pesquisa já conhecidos, os quais podem ser úteis para pesquisadores que estão interessados no uso de alguma dessas abordagens para melhoria de Documentos de Requisitos.
QP2 – Quais abordagens são apoiadas por ferramentas de automatização?	A resposta para esta questão permite identificar quais das abordagens têm alguma ferramenta que as apoiam. Importante investigar como essas ferramentas são utilizadas e o grau de automatização das mesmas.
Q3 – Existem transformações	Objetiva-se identificar as diferentes formas de melhoria

aplicadas a Documentos de Requisitos visando à melhoria destes?	nos documentos de requisitos, e.g., *Patterns*, Diretrizes (*Guidelines*), Refatorações, *Checklists*. Ajudar a identificar qual transformação de melhoria necessita de mais esforço e experiência do responsável pela melhoria de documentos de requisitos.

2.2 *Strings* de Busca

Baseado nas questões de pesquisas, termos e palavras-chaves são identificados, a fim de definir a *String* de busca. Algumas modificações e ajustes foram necessários para permitir a execução da *String* nos diversos mecanismos de busca utilizados. A Tabela 2 apresenta a *String* de busca utilizada nesse mapeamento.

Tabela 2 - *String* de Busca.

String
(quality AND (improvement OR evolution OR refactoring) AND ("software requirement" OR "functional requirement") AND ("requirement specification" OR "requirement document"))

2.3 Critério de Exclusão e Inclusão

O MSL conduzido nesse artigo tem como objetivo verificar estudos primários focados na melhoria de documentos de requisitos publicados entre os anos de 1985 e 2015. Estudos que não foram escritos em Inglês, bem como Revisões Sistemáticas, *Surveys* dentre outros estudos secundários foram descartados.

É importante fazer a distinção entre os conceitos de melhoria de documentos de requisitos, utilizado neste artigo, e validação. O objetivo da fase de validação é detectar, junto aos clientes, se os requisitos estão bem escritos, livres de ambiguidade e completos. Já a melhoria de documentos de requisitos realiza a verificação destes e outros problemas, porém ela é realizada pela equipe de desenvolvimento, sem a participação do cliente.

A Tabela 3 apresenta todos os Critérios de Inclusão e Exclusão utilizados no mapeamento.

Tabela 3 - Critérios de Inclusão e Exclusão.

#	Critérios de Inclusão
1	Estudos Primários
2	Estudos publicados entre Janeiro de 1985 até Novembro de 2015
3	Estudos que tenham como objetivo principal propor, explicitamente, alguma abordagem para melhoria de documentos de requisitos
#	**Critérios de Exclusão**
6	Estudos Secundários

7	Artigos curtos (<= 5)
8	Estudos Duplicados (apenas um será considerado)
9	Estudos que não tratam de abordagens de melhoria em documentos de requisitos
10	Estudo redundante de algum autor (a versão mais completa será considerada)
11	Artigos não inscritos em Inglês
12	Estudos não relacionados às questões de pesquisa
13	Estudo Inacessível
14	Estudos que não tratam de requisitos funcionais
15	Estudos que propõem melhorias em documentos de requisitos apenas na validação

2.4 Bases de Pesquisa

Foram utilizadas cinco bases de dados neste trabalho, sendo elas: IEEE Xplore, ScienceDirect, Scopus, SpringerLink e ACM Digital Library. Também foi realizada uma busca manual no Repositório do WER dos trabalhos publicados entre os anos de 1998 e 2015, os quais foram adicionados aos demais artigos.

2.5 Seleção dos Estudos

As buscas foram realizadas e os resultados passaram por 4 fases de seleção, conforme estabelecido no protocolo da pesquisa e apresentado na Figura 2.

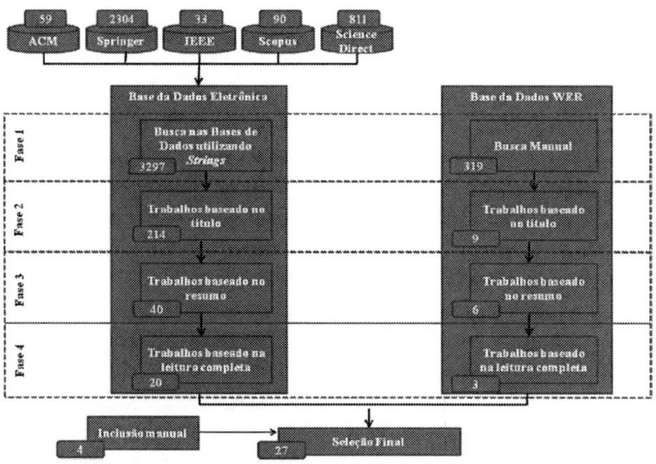

Fig 2. Fases para Seleção dos Trabalhos, adaptado de [30].

A partir dos resultados das buscas eletrônicas nas bases de dados, referente à Fase 1 do protocolo, foi utilizada a ferramenta StArt Tool[1], a qual facilitou a execução das demais fases do protocolo. Posteriormente, a Fase 2 do protocolo foi executada, na

[1] http://lapes.dc.ufscar.br/software/start-tool
[2] http://wer.inf.puc-rio.br/WERpapers/

qual os trabalhos tiveram seus títulos lidos, tendo como resultado 214 artigos dos 3297 iniciais. Em seguida, a Fase 3 consistiu em avaliar os resultados por meio da leitura dos resumos e disponibilidade por completo do artigo, sendo selecionados 40 dos 214. Na Fase 4, todos os trabalhos selecionados foram lidos por completo, restando para a seleção final 20 artigos. Para a busca manual no Repositório do WER[2], na Fase 2, foram lidos todos os 319 títulos dos artigos. A partir da leitura do título, apenas 9 artigos foram selecionados. Na Fase 3, foram selecionados 5 artigos, sendo um dos motivos de exclusão um estudo redundante. Por fim, na Fase 4, um artigo foi rejeitado por estar duplicado com um artigo selecionado na busca eletrônica e outro por não tratar do objetivo da pesquisa, restando apenas 4 artigos. Em complemento, 4 trabalhos foram incluídos manualmente. A Tabela 4 apresenta a lista dos estudos selecionados (busca eletrônica e busca manual). O identificador foi definido como Trabalho mais Sequência Numérica no formato (T#) sem levar em consideração ordem alfabética ou cronológica.

Tabela 4 - Estudos Selecionados.

ID	Ano	Título	Referência
T1	2015	A benchmarking process to assess software requirements documentation for space applications	[18]
T2	2005	Achieving high quality of use-case-based requirements	[3]
T3	2010	Ambiguity detection: Towards a tool explaining ambiguity sources	[6]
T4	2015	A methodology for the classification of quality of requirements using machine learning techniques	[11]
T5	2010	A method to evaluate the suitability of requirements specifications for offshore projects	[10]
T6	2008	Automated formal specification generation and refinement from requirement documents	[15]
T7	1989	Evaluation method for user requirements documents	[2]
T8	2010	Functional requirement improvements through size measurement: A case study with inexperienced measurers	[17]
T9	2014	Identifying duplicate functionality in textual use cases by aligning semantic actions	[4]
T10	2012	Improving the quality of software requirements specifications with Semantic Web technologies	[1]
T11	2010	Improving the quality of use case models using antipatterns	[9]
T12	2012	NLARE, a Natural Language Processing Tool for Automatic Requirements Evaluation	[7]
T13	2003	On the interplay between consistency, completeness, and correctness in requirements evolution	[20]
T14	2008	Practically relevant quality criteria for requirements documents	[16]
T15	2009	Quality improvement for use case model	[13]
T16	2008	Reducing Ambiguities in Requirements Specifications Via	[12]

		Automatically Created Object-Oriented Models	
T17	2006	Requirements quality control: a unifying framework	[14]
T18	2012	Supporting Learning Organisations in Writing Better Requirements Documents Based on Heuristic Critiques	[8]
T19	2014	Using model transformation to refactor use case models based on antipatterns	[5]
T20	2014	Using syntactic and semantic analyses to improve the quality of requirements documentation	[19]
T21	2005	A Content Analysis Technique for Inconsistency Detection in Software Requirements Documents	[22]
T22	2008	Can Rules of Inferences Resolve Coordination Ambiguity in Natural Language Requirements Specification	[23]
T23	2007	Requirements for Tools for Ambiguity Identification and Measurement in Natural Language Requirements Specifications	[21]
T24	2009	Ontologies in checking for inconsistency of requirements specification	[24]
T25	2001	An Automatic Quality Evaluation for Natural Language Requirements	[25]
T26	2001	An XML – based Approach for the Automatic Verification of Software Requirements Specifications	[26]
T27	2014	Rapid Requirements Checks with Requirements Smells: Two Case Studies	[27]

2.6 Avaliação da Qualidade

A avaliação da qualidade (QA) dos estudos selecionados foi obtida por meio de uma técnica de pontuação para avaliar a credibilidade, integridade e relevância dos estudos selecionados. O instrumento de avaliação utilizado é apresentado a seguir. As questões Q1, Q2, Q3, Q4 e Q5 foram adotadas e adaptadas a partir da literatura [29][30][35]. Este instrumento usa uma escala de pontuação com três graus (Sim = 1 ponto, Não = 0 ponto, e parcialmente = 0.5 pontos).

Tabela 5 - Critérios da Avaliação da Qualidade

# Critérios de Inclusão	Possíveis Respostas
1 O estudo descreve claramente o objetivo da abordagem, técnica, método ou processo?	S = 1, N = 0, P = 0.5
2 O estudo apresenta alguma ferramenta de automatização para tratar a melhoria de documentos de requisitos?	S = 1, N = 0, P = 0.5
3 O estudo explicita como a abordagem, técnica, método, processo ou ferramenta foi validado?	S = 1, N = 0, P = 0.5
4 As limitações do estudo são apresentadas?	S = 1, N = 0, P = 0.5
5 O estudo define quais os tipos de problemas que a abordagem trata?	S = 1, N = 0, P = 0.5

2.7 Extração dos Dados e Síntese

A fim de responder as Questões de Pesquisa deste trabalho, alguns dados específicos foram extraídos dos artigos selecionados, tais como: Identificador do Estudo, Autores, Título, Ano de Publicação e País, Contexto da Aplicação, Método de Pesquisa, Objetivos, Tipo de Contribuição, Forma de Especificação, Ferramenta Proposta, Validação e Tipos de Melhoria. Esses dados foram utilizados para realizar o fichamento dos estudos e responder as Questões de Pesquisa.

3 Análise dos Resultados

Nessa seção, são apresentados os resultados alcançados através da extração dos dados e as respostas das questões de pesquisa definidas. Foram identificados 27 estudos, conforme apresentado na Tabela 3.

3.1 Ano de Publicação

Tendo em vista que as primeiras aparições de Casos de Uso são datadas do ano de 1986 [32], foram considerados estudos publicados a partir do ano de 1985. A Figura 3 apresenta a quantidade dos trabalhos selecionados por ano de publicação. Pode-se verificar que a preocupação com a qualidade dos Documentos de Requisitos é constante, sendo realizadas pesquisas em praticamente todos os anos a partir de 2001. Isso se deve ao fato da importância que os Documentos de Requisitos têm em todo o processo de desenvolvimento de software.

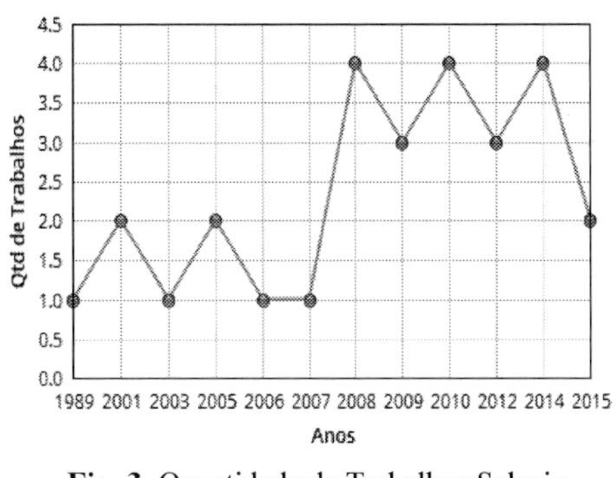

Fig. 3. Quantidade de Trabalhos Selecionados por ano de Publicação.

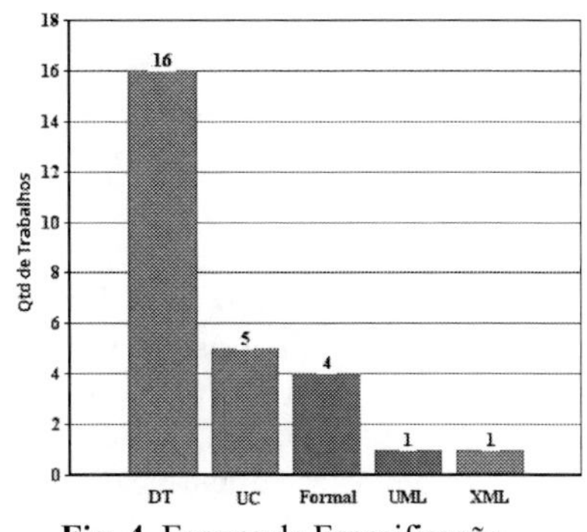

Fig. 4. Formas de Especificação.

3.2 QP1 – Como os requisitos são especificados nas abordagens?

O objetivo desta questão é identificar a forma como os requisitos são especificados, tais como Modelos de Casos de Uso, Ponto de Vista, Descrição Textual, nas abordagens focadas na melhoria de documentos de requisitos. A distribuição dos estudos dentro destas categorias é apresentada na Figura 4.

Pode-se verificar que 59,25% dos trabalhos analisados foram especificados utilizando Descrição Textual, tendo em vista esta ser a forma mais utilizada para especificação de requisitos funcionais [31]. Em seguida, tem-se a utilização de Modelos de Casos de Uso com 18,51%, valor relativamente baixo, dado a grande utilização desta técnica nos dias de hoje. Uma possível causa deste valor está relacionada com a *String* de busca utilizada. A inclusão do termo "Caso de Uso" possibilitaria encontrar mais resultados relevantes sobre esta técnica.

Em seguida, as especificações formais totalizaram 14,81%. Este valor, próximo da especificação por Casos de Uso, deve-se ao fato da formalização facilitar a checagem de problemas em Documentos de Requisitos de forma automática, uma vez que utilizam notações matemáticas para especificá-los.

3.3 QP2 - Quais abordagens são apoiadas por ferramentas de automatização?

A resposta para esta questão permite identificar quais das abordagens tem alguma ferramenta que as apoiam. É importante investigar como essas ferramentas são utilizadas e o grau de automatização das mesmas. A Tabela 6 apresenta como os trabalhos foram classificados de acordo com o grau de automatização que a ferramenta possibilita.

Tabela 6 - Ferramentas para automatização.

Tipo	Estudos	Quantidade	%
Automática	T03 T04, T06, T07, T09, T10, T11, T12, T18, T19, T20, T21, T25, T26	14	52%
Semi-automática	T13, T16, T23, T24, T27	5	19%
Manual	T01, T02, T05, T08, T14, T15, T17, T22	8	29%

Por automatização semi-automática, entende-se que algum grau de intervenção humana é utilizado no processo de melhoria, ou seja, alguma avaliação humana deve ser feita para que se obtenha algum resultado. Grande parte da automatização proposta pelos trabalhos é focada na detecção de problemas na especificação de requisitos, principalmente por meio da análise léxica e sintática das descrições textuais. Estes valores podem diferenciar bastante caso a busca fosse realizada em trabalhos de outras línguas diferentes do inglês, tendo em vista as características linguísticas de cada idioma.

É importante frisar que alguns trabalhos sugerem a utilização de mais de uma técnica para a detecção e correção de problemas em Documentos de Requisitos, como é o caso de T2, o qual combina, de forma sistemática, diretrizes para criação de Casos de Uso (prevenção), inspeções de Casos de Uso (detecção) e Simulação (problemas de consistência entre Casos de Uso). O estudo sugere ainda que a abordagem seja aplicada apenas para os Casos de Usos mais críticos, tendo em vista o esforço adicional necessário para aplicar as três técnicas.

3.4 QP3 – Existem transformações aplicadas a Documentos de Requisitos visando à melhoria destes?

O objetivo dessa questão é identificar as diferentes formas de melhoria nos documentos de requisitos, tais como: *Patterns*, Diretrizes (*Guidelines*), Refatorações, *Checklists*. Ela ajudará a identificar qual transformação de melhoria necessita de mais esforço e experiência do responsável pela melhoria de documentos de requisitos. A Tabela 7 apresenta essas informações.

Tabela 7 - Melhorias propostas.

Melhoria	Estudos	Quantidade	%
Checklist	T01	1	4,34%
Diretrizes	T02, T05, T08, T17	4	14,81%
Patterns / AntiPatterns	T11, T19	2	8,69%
Refatorações	T15	1	4,34%
Regras	T22	1	4,34%
Não Aplicável	T03, T04, T06, T07, T09, T10, T12, T13, T14, T16, T18, T20, T21, T23, T24, T25, T26, T27	14	51,85%

Pode-se verificar baseado no resultado encontrado, que a maioria das propostas, 51,85% dos estudos, não propõe um mecanismo de melhoria. Isso se deve ao fato desses trabalhos terem como proposta uma ferramenta para detecção automática de problemas na especificação dos requisitos.

Apesar de T11 e T19 terem um autor em comum, o que acarretaria na exclusão de algum deles de acordo com o critério de exclusão, eles foram mantidos na condução do mapeamento, tendo em vista que as propostas dos trabalhos são diferentes. Enquanto T11 propõe a definição de *Antipatterns*, a partir de um conjunto de regras pré-definidas que são aplicáveis para qualquer modelo de Caso de Uso, T19 propõe uma abordagem para transformação de modelos a partir da detecção de *Antipattern* e Refatoração. T19 lista um conjunto de 14 *Antipatterns* e 21 Refatorações. Essas Refatorações são as possíveis soluções para os *Antipatterns* detectados.

3.5 Resultado da Avaliação da Qualidade

A avaliação da qualidade dos estudos selecionados é útil para aumentar a precisão dos resultados dos dados extraídos. A Tabela 8 apresenta os valores obtidos baseado nas questões da avaliação da qualidade definidas na Tabela 5.

Tabela 8 - Resultado da avaliação da qualidade dos estudos selecionados, adaptado de [30].

ID	Q1	Q2	Q3	Q4	Q5	Total	ID	Q1	Q2	Q3	Q4	Q5	Total
T01	1	0	1	1	1	4	**T15**	1	0	1	1	1	4
T02	1	0	1	1	1	4	**T16**	1	1	1	1	1	5
T03	1	1	1	1	1	5	**T17**	1	0	0.5	0.5	1	3

T04	1	1	1	1	1	5	**T18**	1	1	0	1	1	4
T05	1	0	1	1	1	4	**T19**	1	1	1	1	1	5
T06	1	1	0.5	1	1	4.5	**T20**	1	1	1	0.5	0.5	4
T07	1	1	0.5	1	1	4.5	**T21**	1	1	1	0.5	1	4.5
T08	1	0	1	1	1	4	**T22**	1	0	1	1	1	4
T09	1	1	1	1	1	5	**T23**	1	0.5	1	1	1	4.5
T10	1	1	1	1	1	5	**T24**	1	1	0.5	1	1	4.5
T11	1	1	1	1	1	5	**T25**	1	1	1	1	1	5
T12	1	1	1	1	1	5	**T26**	1	1	0	1	1	4
T13	1	1	0.5	0.5	1	4	**T27**	1	1	1	1	1	5
T14	1	0	1	0	1	3							

	Q1	Q2	Q3	Q4	Q5	Total
Pontuação Média	1	0.69	0.82	0.89	0.98	4.38

Nenhuma pontuação ficou abaixo de 3, porém os trabalhos T14 e T17 necessitaram de uma nova análise baseado nos critérios de inclusão e exclusão, a fim de se garantir que a seleção dos estudos foi realizada de forma correta. A média geral da pontuação ficou em 4.38, o que é um valor aceitável para este mapeamento sistemático.

4 Validade da Pesquisa

Apesar da grande quantidade de artigos retornados pela pesquisa automática nas bases de dados, diversos trabalhos foram excluídos da fase de Extração de Dados devido à impossibilidade de acessá-los. Esses trabalhos poderiam contribuir para este mapeamento, permitindo uma conclusão mais precisa do mesmo.

Outro fator a ser considerado é a diferenciação entre avaliação e melhoria de documentos de requisitos. Enquanto o primeiro está focado em detectar possíveis problemas na especificação, o segundo se preocupa nas possíveis técnicas para corrigir esses erros. Com isso, alguns trabalhos não faziam muito bem essa diferenciação, o que pode ter ocasionado o descarte de muitos artigos durante a fase de Seleção.

Vários estudos secundários: revisões sistemáticas, *Surveys* dentre outros; já foram conduzidos [29;30;33], os quais podem trazer maiores detalhes para os resultados alcançados nesta pesquisa. Porém, os mesmos foram descartados de acordo com os critérios de exclusão do protocolo utilizado, tendo em vista a necessidade de se obter informações específicas de cada estudo primário.

5 Trabalhos Relacionados

Outros estudos secundários [29;30;33] também foram realizados, a fim de verificar ambiguidade, inconsistência, incompletude, omissões, dentre outros erros em documentos de requisitos em determinadas formas de especificação de requisitos.

Tiwari e Gupta [29] examinam estudos que tratam da evolução dos casos de uso, suas aplicações, avaliações de qualidade, questões abertas, e as direções futuras.

Foram analisados 119 artigos, verificando-se que cerca de vinte modelos de casos de uso foram propostos e aplicados a vários problemas de especificação de software tanto para descrições informais até as notações formais.

Ding et. al [30] buscam entender como as abordagens baseadas no conhecimento podem ser empregadas para melhorar a qualidade do Documento de Software. Foram selecionados e analisados 60 artigos, dos quais doze atributos de qualidade de documentos de software e nove categorias de benefícios do uso de abordagens baseadas no conhecimento em documentação de software foram identificados.

Saavedra et. al [33] apresentam um conjunto de atributos de qualidade normalmente encontrados em documentos de requisitos e quais trabalhos propõem diretrizes e modelos para detectar problemas nesses atributos.

A pesquisa aqui apresentada não focou em um formato específico de documento de requisito, nem em um conjunto limitado de atributos de qualidade. Buscou-se verificar, de forma abrangente, o estado atual de estudos focados na melhoria de documentos de requisitos e na existência de ferramenta de apoio para as abordagens existentes.

6 Conclusões e Trabalhos Futuros

O estudo permitiu observar que existem diversas pesquisas focadas na avaliação e melhoria dos Documentos de Requisitos. Ressalta-se que a maioria dos estudos selecionados está focada da detecção dos problemas existentes nos requisitos especificados, sendo essas avaliações realizadas automática, semi-automática e manualmente. Estas últimas por meio de técnicas bastante conhecidas, tais como Inspeções, Revisões e Técnicas de Leituras.

O mapeamento permitiu verificar, também, que todas as ferramentas propostas nos estudos selecionados estão focadas diretamente na detecção dos erros existentes no Documento de Requisitos, ou seja, não foi verificada qualquer ferramenta que apoiasse um processo de forma automatizada.

Como trabalho futuro, pretende-se realizar uma análise mais crítica dos resultados encontrados, buscando fazer comparações entre as abordagens, a fim de identificar aspectos positivos e negativos em cada uma delas. Pretende-se, ainda, desenvolver uma ferramenta para apoiar a execução da AIRDoc [13], possibilitando definir e otimizar o processo de forma efetiva. Esta ferramenta auxiliará engenheiros de software a avaliar a qualidade dos documentos de requisitos e propiciará a construção de softwares com menos erros e consequentemente, softwares construídos em menor tempo e mais baratos de serem mantidos. Por fim, será realizado um estudo qualitativo dos resultados encontrados, a fim de adicionar novas refatorações ao catálogo proposto pela AIRDoc.

Referências

[1] V. Castañeda, L. Ballejos, and M. L. Caliusco, "Improving the Quality of Software Requirements Specifications with Semantic Web Technologies," 2008.

[2] D. Cordes and D. Carver, "Evaluation method for user requirements documents," *Inf. Softw. Technol.*, vol. 31, no. 4, pp. 181–188, 1989.

[3] C. Denger, B. Paech, and B. Freimut, "Achieving high quality of use-case-based requirements," *Inform. - Forsch. und Entwicklung*, vol. 20, no. 1–2, pp. 11–23, 2005.

[4] A. R. M. A. Diaz-Pace, "Identifying duplicate functionality in textual use cases by aligning semantic actions," *Softw. Syst. Model.*, vol. NA, 2014.

[5] Y. A. K. El-Attar, "Using model transformation to refactor use case models based on antipatterns," *Inf. Syst. Front.*, vol. NA, 2014.

[6] B. Gleich, O. Creighton, and L. Kof, "Ambiguity detection: Towards a tool explaining ambiguity sources," *Lect. Notes Comput. Sci. (including Subser. Lect. Notes Artif. Intell. Lect. Notes Bioinformatics)*, vol. 6182 LNCS, pp. 218–232, 2010.

[7] C. Huertas and R. Juárez-Ramírez, "NLARE, a natural language processing tool for automatic requirements evaluation," *Proc. CUBE Int. Inf. Technol. Conf. - CUBE '12*, p. 371, 2012.

[8] E. Knauss, K. Schneider, "Supporting Learning Organisations in Writing Better Requirements Documents Based on Heuristic Critiques," *REFSQ 2012*: 165-171., 2012.

[9] M. E.-A. Miller, "Improving the quality of use case models using antipatterns," *Softw. Syst. Model.*, vol. 9, no. 2, 2010.

[10] S. Overhage, O. Skroch, and K. Turowski, "A Method to Evaluate the Suitability of Requirements Specifications for Offshore Projects," *Bus. Inf. Syst. Eng.*, vol. 2, pp. 155–164, 2010.

[11] E. Parra, C. Dimou, J. Llorens, V. Moreno, and A. Fraga, "A methodology for the classification of quality of requirements using machine learning techniques," *Inf. Softw. Technol.*, vol. 67, pp. 180–195, 2015.

[12] D. Popescu, S. Rugaber, N. Medvidovic, and D. M. Berry, "Reducing Ambiguities in Requirements Specifications Via Automatically Created Object-Oriented Models," *Innov. Requir. Anal. From Stakeholders' Needs to Form. Des.*, vol. 1, pp. 103–124, 2008.

[13] R. Ramos, J. Castro, F. Alencar, J. Araújo, A. Moreira, and R. Penteado, "Quality improvement for use case model," *SBES 2009 - 23rd Brazilian Symp. Softw. Eng.*, pp. 187–195, 2009.

[14] A. K. Sakkinen, "Requirements quality control: a unifying framework," *Requir. Eng.*, vol. 11, no. 1, 2006.

[15] G. C. Sampaio, "Automated formal specification generation and refinement from requirement documents," *J. Brazilian Comput. Soc.*, vol. 14, no. 1, 2008.

[16] T. Simon, J. Streit, and M. Pizka, "Practically Relevant Quality Criteria for Requirements Documents," *Itestra.De*, vol. 2, pp. 115–121, 2008.

[17] S. Trudel and A. Abran, "Functional Requirement Improvements through Size Measurement: A Case Study with Inexperienced Measurers," *2010 Eighth ACIS Int. Conf. Softw. Eng. Res. Manag. Appl.*, pp. 181–189, 2010.

[18] P. C. Véras, E. Villani, A. M. Ambrosio, M. Vieira, and H. Madeira, "A benchmarking process to assess software requirements documentation for space applications," *J. Syst. Softw.*, vol. 100, pp. 103–116, 2015.

[19] K. Verma, A. Kass, and R. Vasquez, "Using syntactic and semantic analyses to improve the quality of requirements documentation," *Semant. Web*, vol. 5, pp. 405–419, 2014.

[20] D. Zowghi and V. Gervasi, "On the interplay between consistency, completeness, and correctness in requirements evolution," Inf. Softw. Technol., vol. 45, no. 14, pp. 993–1009, 2003.

[21] N. Kiyavitskaya, N. Zeni, L. Mich, and D. M. Berry, "Requirements for tools for ambiguity identification and measurement in natural language requirements specifications," Requir. Eng., vol. 13, pp. 207–239, 2008.

[22] A. Fantechi and E. Spinicci, "A content analysis technique for inconsistency detection in software requirements documents," Proc. VIII Work. Requir. Eng., pp. 245–256, 2005.

[23] S. Tjong and D. Berry, "Can Rules of Inferences Resolve Coordination Ambiguity in Natural Language Requirements Specification?," Wer, pp. 205–210, 2008.

[24] P. Kroha, R. Janetzko, and J. E. Labra, "Ontologies in checking for inconsistency of requirements specification," 3rd Int. Conf. Adv. Semant. Process. - SEMAPRO 2009, pp. 32–37, 2009.

[25] F. Fabbrini, M. Fusani, S. Gnesi, and G. Lami, "An Automatic Quality Evaluation for Natural Language Requirements," REFSQ 2001 Proc. Seventh Int. Work. RE Found. Softw. Qual., vol. 1, pp. 150–164, 2001.

[26] A. Durán, B. Bernárdez, A. Ruiz, and M. Toro, "An XML – based Approach for the Automatic Verification of Software Requirements Specifications," Wer01, 2001.

[27] H. Femmer, D. M. Fernández, E. Juergens, M. Klose, I. Zimmer, and J. Zimmer, "Rapid Requirements Checks with Requirements Smells: Two Case Studies," Proc. 1st Int. Work. Rapid Contin. *Softw. Eng.*, pp. 10–19, 2014.

[28] B. Kitchenham, Procedures for Performing Systematic Reviews, Keele, Reino Unido, Keele University 33, 2004.

[29] S. Tiwari and A. Gupta, "A systematic literature review of use case specifications research," *Inf. Softw. Technol.*, vol. 67, pp. 128–158, 2015.

[30] W. Ding, P. Liang, A. Tang, and H. Van Vliet, "Knowledge-based approaches in software documentation: A systematic literature review," *Inf. Softw. Technol.*, vol. 56, no. 6, pp. 545–567, 2014.

[31] Denger,C.,Berry,D.M.,Kamsties,E.,2003.Higher quality requirements specifications through natural language patterns. In: Proceedings of the IEEE International Conference on Software—Science, Technology & Engineering(SwSTE'03), pp.1–11.

[32] I. Jacobson, Object-oriented development in an industrial environment, in: Proceeings of the Conference on Object-Oriented Programming, Systems, Languages & Applications, ACM, 1987, pp. 183–191.

[33] R. Saavedra, L. Ballejos, and M. Ale, "Quality Properties Evaluation for Software Requirements Specifications: An Exploratory Analysis," Wer.Inf.Puc-Rio.Br, pp. 1–14.

[34] A. Cockburn, Writing Effective Use Cases, vol. 1, Addison-Wesley, Boston, 2001.

[35] T. Dingsøyr and T. Dyba, "Empirical studies of agile software development: A systematic review," Inf. Softw. Technol., vol. 50, pp. 833–859, 2008.

[36] B. Anda, D. Sjøberg, M. Jørgensen, Quality and understandability of use case models, in: J. Knudsen (Ed.), ECOOP 2001 Object-Oriented Programming, Lecture Notes in Computer Science, vol. 2072, Springer, Berlin Heidelberg, 2001, pp. 402–428.

[37] Boehm BW (1984) Verifying and validating software requirements and design specifications. IEEE Software 1(1):75–88.

[38] WIEGERS, K. E.: "Software Requirements", Microsoft Press, Second Edition. (2003).

[39] U. S. Shah and D. C. Jinwala, "Resolving Ambiguities in Natural Language Software Requirements," ACM SIGSOFT Softw. Eng. Notes, vol. 40, no. 5, pp. 1–7, 2015.

Avaliação do Processo de Engenharia de Requisitos em Empresas de Desenvolvimento de Software

Flávia Belintani Blum Haddad, Elias Canhadas Genvigir,
José Augusto Fabri, Alexandre L' Erário

Universidade Tecnológica Federal do Paraná – Campus Cornélio Procópio

flaviablum@gmail.com, elias@utfpr.edu.br, fabri@utfpr.edu.br, lerario@utfpr.edu.br

Resumo. A demanda, em ascensão, pela produção de softwares sob medida e softwares destinados a um mercado geral gera uma preocupação com a forma como os softwares são desenvolvidos. Neste contexto, os processos de software contribuem com a definição de atividades a serem executadas pelas equipes, em cada uma das fases de desenvolvimento conduzindo a produção de softwares a fim de atender às necessidades dos clientes, dentro do prazo e custos pré-estabelecidos. Pesquisas apontam que entre 40 a 60 por cento dos defeitos e falhas nos softwares são atribuídos a incorreta definição dos requisitos e que corrigir erros no sistema pronto pode ser até 100 vezes mais caro do que se a correção ou a prevenção ocorrer durante a fase que envolve a engenharia de requisitos e a implementação do sistema. Portanto, esta pesquisa se destinou ao estudo de processos de engenharia de requisitos em empresas de desenvolvimento de software, por meio de um estudo de caso único com múltiplas unidades de análise. Os processos de engenharia de requisitos atuais das empresas pesquisadas foram modelados e avaliados com o auxílio de um quadro de avaliação de maturidade de processo, Uni-REPM (*Unified Requirements Engineering Process Maturity Model*). Na sequência, foram apresentadas, às empresas, normas e modelos de referências, tais como CMMI-DEV (*Capability Maturity Model Integration for Development*), ISO/IEC 12207, ISO/IEC 15288 e o Guia de boas práticas em engenharia de requisitos (REGPG), para que pudessem conhecer e propor a inclusão de práticas ao processo atual. A análise dos dados após o enquadramento no Uni-REPM possibilitou verificar quantas ações são necessárias para que cada empresa alcance um nível de maturidade conforme dispõe o quadro de avaliação de maturidade de processos de requisitos utilizado. A relevância da pesquisa se caracteriza pela aplicação do quadro Uni-REPM, disponível na literatura científica atual, em processos reais de engenharia de requisitos, ou seja, esta pesquisa contribui para a aproximação da ciência e da indústria por se tratar de uma pesquisa aplicada, além da busca constante pela melhoria de processos de software.

Palavras Chave: Melhoria de processo de requisitos, Avaliação, Maturidade.

1 Introdução

Pesquisadores da área de Engenharia de Requisitos (ER) têm buscado evidências de que a melhoria dos processos de ER resulta em um efeito positivo no desenvolvimento do software [1][2][3][4]. Ellis e Berry [1] concluíram que um processo de ER eficaz melhora todo o ciclo de vida de desenvolvimento, podendo conquistar, inclusive, um produto final com qualidade, que atenda às necessidades do cliente e que tenha sido construído dentro dos prazos e custos previstos.

As fases de processo de desenvolvimento de software propostas na ER são conhecidas como fundamentais para obtenção do resultado esperado de um projeto [5][2][6]. No entanto, na prática, as atividades de ER muitas vezes não são utilizadas ou não são aplicadas de forma adequada [7]

O desenvolvimento de software, seja um software sob medida ou softwares voltados para o mercado, enfrenta desafios, especialmente desafios relacionados às atividades de engenharia de requisitos. Os problemas ocorrem na maioria das vezes pela falta de processos bem definidos, pelo mau uso de ferramentas e métodos para gerir as atividades que envolvem os requisitos e pelo pouco envolvimento do usuário [8][9], portanto, há uma necessidade da busca por melhoria nestes processos[10].

Existem várias estruturas na literatura que visam suprir as lacunas entre as atividades de engenharia de requisitos praticadas pelas empresas e as melhores práticas que podem ser introduzidas ao processo atual da empresa. Pode-se citar como exemplo o Guia de boas práticas (REGPG) [11] e o Modelo de maturidade de processo (REPM) [12]. Já os modelos de avaliação como o CMMI [13], as normas ISO/IEC 12207 [14], ISO/IEC 15288 [15], o MPS-BR (Modelo de processo de software brasileiro) [16] e o SPICE [17] abrangem a engenharia de requisitos, porém de uma forma mais superficial, pois estão voltados para todos os processos contidos no desenvolvimento de software.

Como as organizações de software necessitam implementar de forma contínua tecnologias inovadoras e melhores práticas visando aumentar suas capacidades no desenvolvimento de software [18], o primeiro passo para a melhoria do processo de software é avaliar o estado atual do processo utilizado na indústria de software [19].

A seção 2 deste artigo apresenta a base teórica para o desenvolvimento da pesquisa, na seção 3 é detalhada a metodologia da pesquisa, na seção 4 é descrito estudo de caso, coleta e manuseio dos dados, a seção 5 apresenta a análise e discussão dos dados e conclui-se este trabalho na seção 5.

1.1 Questões da pesquisa

Este artigo aborda a utilização de um modelo de avaliação de processo de ER aplicado em empresas de desenvolvimento de software da região norte do Paraná, para verificação da maturidade do processo de ER e apontamento de pontos de melhorias. Acredita-se que com a execução e conclusão deste trabalho, as empresas selecionadas terão seu conhecimento ampliado quanto à existência de atividades específicas da engenharia de requisitos e poderão programar, gradativamente, a inclusão destas atividades em seus processos. Cientificamente, o registro desta pesquisa quanto a forma de aplicação do quadro de avaliação de maturidade de processo de ER: a disseminação do conhecimento sobre as atividades que envolvem a ER e os resultados obtidos poderão auxiliar empresas do mundo todo a conhecer melhor e aperfeiçoar seus processos de requisitos.

As contribuições mais evidentes realizadas neste estudo de caso, respondem a duas perguntas principais:

1. Os processos de engenharia de requisitos adotados pelas empresas de desenvolvimento de software (em regiões como a do Norte do Paraná) alcançam algum nível de maturidade?
2. Com a aplicação do quadro de avaliação de maturidade de processo de ER, é possível perceber diferenças entre empresas certificadas e empresas não certificadas?

2 Referencial teórico

2.1 Processo de software

O processo de software pode ser definido como a forma com que uma organização desenvolve seus produtos e serviços de apoio, definindo quais passos devem ser seguidos em cada fase da produção, apoiando a elaboração de estimativas, plano de desenvolvimento e medindo a qualidade e ainda que o processo deve começar com os resultados esperados, desenhando estes passos para o alcance dos resultados[20][21].

Para definição dos processos de software, Barreto [22] aponta alguns elementos que devem ser considerados: as características da organização, as necessidades do projeto, as técnicas e métodos a serem utilizados no desenvolvimento do software, a adesão às normas e modelos de referências e as restrições de tempo e recursos.

2.2 Engenharia de requisitos

A engenharia de requisitos é uma disciplina fundamental para o desenvolvimento de software [23]. O foco principal da Engenharia de Requisitos é documentar os requisitos, devidamente elicitados, para assegurar o entendimento de todos os envolvidos no projeto [24].

Em uma pesquisa realizada com gerentes de projeto, a engenharia de requisitos foi classificada como uma área de maior risco a ser gerenciado em um projeto [25]. A ER foi citada por Schimdt et al. [26] como sendo a fase mais problemática entre todas as atividades de engenharia de software. Por esses e outros motivos, empresas procuram melhorar seus processos através de projetos de melhoria, isso requer um esforço organizacional complexo, envolvendo toda a organização e muitas pessoas [27].

Svensson et al. [28] citam que satisfazer apenas os requisitos funcionais não garante o sucesso do produto final, para ajudar neste processo é fundamental encontrar e implementar os requisitos de qualidade. Priorizar requisitos de qualidade significa aumentar a chance de sucesso do produto, mas para isto é necessário encontrar, selecionar e planejar o uso dos requisitos mais adequados. Se os requisitos forem selecionados equivocadamente, os usuários podem não ter interesse no produto final [28].

2.3 Melhoria de processo de software

A melhoria de processo de software pode ser definida como a ação de compreender o processo de software que é utilizado dentro das organizações, e assim, conduzir a implementação de mudanças para que o processo atinja seus objetivos específicos, dentre estes, o aumento da qualidade do produto e a redução do custo de produção [21].

O principal objetivo da melhoria nos processos de software é aumentar a qualidade do software, dentro do orçamento e prazos previstos, refletindo positivamente na produtividade da organização[29].

A melhoria do processo pode ocorrer quando se aplica de forma consistente as práticas que produzem bons resultados e altera-se ou excluem-se as práticas que causam problemas [30].

Há diversos modelos, baseados em normas, que auxiliam na melhoria de processo de software. Neste trabalho são citados alguns deles.

2.3.1 Melhoria de processo de requisitos

Especificamente sobre a melhoria do processo de engenharia de requisitos, deve-se avaliar o processo de ER utilizado na empresa de desenvolvimento de software, a fim de encontrar pontos de melhoria [23]. Os modelos, padrões e normas de referências que possuem atividades relacionadas a ER podem contribuir na melhoria dos processos com a realização de práticas e sub práticas no desenvolvimento do projeto.

Podem-se citar as normas e modelos de referência como o CMMI-DEV [13], ISO/IEC 12207 [14], ISO/IEC 15288 [15] e MPS-BR [16] que sugerem atividades para o processo de desenvolvimento de software, tendo em vista a melhoria no processo, e por consequência a melhoria do produto.

Além destas normas e modelos de referência, a Engenharia de Requisitos pode contar com práticas apresentadas por pesquisadores como Sommerville e Ransom [3] que citam alguns exemplos de boas práticas a serem aplicadas na engenharia de requisitos.

Com exceção das boas práticas em ER mencionadas por Sommerville e Ransom [3], as normas e modelos de referência citados dispõem de atividades e tarefas a serem executadas em todos os processos de software, inclusive o processo de ER. A seguir será apresentado um quadro de avaliação de maturidade de processo voltado exclusivamente à engenharia de requisitos.

O modelo de maturidade de processo de engenharia de requisitos, REPM, foi elaborado para ser aplicado na indústria de desenvolvimento de software, porém com aplicabilidade em projetos de software feitos por encomenda, mas para que o modelo de maturidade pudesse abranger todos os tipos de projeto, incluindo os softwares produzidos para atender ao mercado, foi construído o Uni-REPM (*Unified Requirements Engineering Process Maturity Model*) [31].

Este quadro é um instrumento capaz de avaliar a maturidade do processo de engenharia de requisitos além de oferecer uma visão contemporânea do estado da arte na área, de forma que pesquisadores e profissionais podem utilizar as práticas propostas e empiricamente validadas [32].

2.4 Avaliação de processo de ER

O quadro de avaliação de maturidade de processo de engenharia de requisitos, Uni-REPM, foi desenvolvido a partir de uma revisão sistemática da literatura, onde foram selecionados alguns modelos e práticas existentes, tais como o CMMI (*Capability Maturity Model Integration)*, o REGPG (*Requirements Engineering Good Practice-Guide*), o REPM (*Requirements Engineering Process Model*) e o MDREPM (*Market-Driven Requirements Engineering Process Model*) [32].

O REPM foi elaborado para ser aplicado em indústrias de desenvolvimento de software, com aplicabilidade em projetos de softwares feitos por encomenda e o MDREPM foi construído visando os processos de requisitos para desenvolvimento de softwares voltados para o mercado. Mas pensando em um modelo de processo de engenharia de requisitos que pudesse abranger todos os tipos de projetos, foi desenvolvido um modelo universal, o Uni-REPM[31].

O Uni-REPM fornece uma solução simples e de baixo custo para identificação do estado do processo de ER, servindo como um instrumento de avaliação. Diferente do REPM, que atende apenas processos de ER para desenvolvimento de softwares feitos sob encomenda e do MDREPM, que atende softwares produzidos para o mercado, o Uni-REPM é híbrido, ou seja, pode ser aplicado em ambos cenários. Além de avaliar a maturidade dos processos de ER, contribui ainda para instrução dos profissionais da área sobre os benefícios resultantes de cada ação (prática de ER) executada e apresenta um caminho para melhoria dos processos de ER [32].

2.4.1Estrutura do Uni-REPM

O Uni-REPM, apresenta duas visões, uma visão do processo dividida em áreas de processo e uma visão por nível de maturidade. As ações foram dispostas de acordo com a área do processo, descrevendo um conjunto de práticas da engenharia de requisitos, consistentes e coerentes, onde as práticas em um nível dão subsídios para as práticas do nível seguinte [32].

As práticas descritas neste modelo de avaliação estão dispostas em 7 áreas de processos principais, denominadas MPAs (*Main Process Area*). Cada MPA por sua vez é subdividida em subáreas de processos, SPA (*Sub-process Area*) as quais contém ações estreitamente relacionadas. As ações são a menores unidades do modelo que mostram uma boa prática específica. Esta divisão permite que as organizações encontrem mais facilmente as práticas que dizem respeito a um determinado fenômeno, tornando o modelo fácil de navegar [32].

As áreas de processos do Uni-REPM correspondem às principais áreas de processos da ER: Apoio Organizacional, Gerenciamento de Processos de Requisitos, Elicitação de requisitos, Análise de Requisito, Planejamento de Lançamento, Especificação e Documentação de Requisitos e Validação de Requisitos [32].

Para avaliar a maturidade dos processos de ER, o Uni-REPM possui 3 níveis de maturidade: básico, intermediário e avançado. A avaliação pode ser realizada em todo o processo de ER ou pode-se obter a maturidade de uma MPA isoladamente [32]. Cada ação recebe um nível de maturidade específico, e se todas as ações de um determinado nível são realizadas, significa que a organização possui um processo de ER consistente e coerente no nível em que foi classificada [10].

O objetivo de utilizar 3 níveis no Uni-REPM, ao invés de 5, como no REPM, é obter uma melhora significativa a cada mudança de nível do processo de ER. O nível básico busca um processo de requisitos que seja definido e repetível, preocupando-se com a relevante participação dos interessados na elicitação dos requisitos, na análise e na utilização de documentos padrões pré-definidos. Este nível não contempla a comunicação entre as partes envolvidas [32].

O nível intermediário engloba ações voltadas para as estratégias e metas do produto, definição de papéis e responsabilidades para execução de tarefas específicas, gestão de mudanças e priorização de requisitos. O nível avançado, que indicada maior grau de maturidade do processo, visa uma elicitação de requisitos mais avançada, garantia da qualidade, comunicação e entendimento comum entre as partes interessadas. No nível avançado busca-se também a reutilização de requisitos e evolução dos documentos [10].

O quadro de avaliação Uni-REPM pode ser encontrado em http://www.bth.se/tek/mdrepm.nsf/attachments/uniREPM_v09CR_pdf/$file/uniREPM_v09CR.pdf.

2.4.2 Avaliação

Para avaliação da maturidade de um processo de ER, devem-se mapear as ações presentes no modelo relacionando-as com as atividades do processo de ER real da organização. Para cada ação do Uni-REPM verifica-se se a organização realiza a atividade de forma completa (C), se realiza parcialmente ou não a realiza, o que a torna uma atividade incompleta (IC) e se atividade não for necessária ou possível de ser realizada em um determinado processo, considera-se como inaplicável (IA) [10].

O critério de avaliação IA foi definido, pois as características e ambientes das organizações e seus processos podem variar e algumas ações podem ser consideradas desnecessárias para aplicação em situações particulares. Se uma ação se encaixar em umas destas situações, e for classificada como incompleta, o processo pode não atingir determinado nível e pode ainda, ter alcançado o nível intermediário ou avançado, sem ter o nível básico realizado por completo. Portanto, a utilização do critério IA evita um resultado distorcido [10].

Após a elaboração do Uni-REPM, o modelo foi validado. Esta validação foi executada de forma estática, com a participação de especialistas da área e dinâmica, realizada em vários projetos de indústrias de softwares. Um dos itens validados está relacionado a sua aplicabilidade, principalmente na questão da utilização do critério "inaplicável" [10].

Foram estudadas quais ações são mais comumente consideradas inaplicáveis. A partir deste estudo foi definido o modelo de latência, ou seja, o número de ações consideradas inaplicáveis. Ficou caracterizado que em projetos de desenvolvimento de softwares sob encomenda, as ações da MPA de planejamento e liberação de requisitos, por padrão, são consideradas inaplicáveis [10].

Portanto, a natureza dos projetos é um fator que pode ser considerado para a utilização do critério "inaplicável" [10].

E ainda, ao considerar uma ação inaplicável a análise deve ser cuidadosa a fim de evitar que uma ação importante acidentalmente seja classificada como inaplicável.

Falta de tempo, de recursos ou desconhecimento não podem ser julgados como inaplicável [12].

Quanto ao resultado da avaliação, este pode ser interpretado em uma determinada MPA ou no processo todo de ER. Para definir qual nível a MPA ou o processo se encontra, todas as ações de um determinado nível devem ser satisfeitas, ou seja, devem estar assinaladas como "completa" ou "inaplicável". É importante analisar as ações marcadas como "incompletas" no nível acima da maturidade atual, pois indicará os esforços necessários para a melhoria do processo [10].

O Uni-REPM é sugerido como uma maneira fácil e barata de avaliar os processo de engenharia de requisitos em empresas de desenvolvimento de software, e portanto, foi selecionado para ser aplicado nesta pesquisa.

3 Procedimentos metodológicos

Para a realização desta pesquisa foi utilizado o conceito de estudo de caso. O estudo de caso utiliza-se de análise do ambiente de estudo ao invés da generalização estatística, isto é, o estudo de caso pode ajudar os pesquisadores a desenvolver uma teoria para entender outros casos, fenômenos ou situações semelhantes [34].

Segundo Yin [34], os estudos de caso podem ser aplicados em uma investigação exploratória para examinar acontecimentos contemporâneos. As fontes de evidência podem advir de observação direta, de uma série sistemática de entrevistas, análise de documentos e aplicação de questionários.

Dos quatro tipos básicos de estudo de caso apresentados por Yin [34], esta pesquisa terá um caso único incorporado, o processo de engenharia de requisitos, e múltiplas unidades de análise, as empresas selecionadas.

A escolha deste método se justifica, pois, o estudo de caso permite uma flexibilidade em relação ao objeto estudado [35]. Esta flexibilização ocorre quando, após a coleta dos dados quantitativos, o pesquisador modela o processo atual da empresa e avalia qualitativamente as atividades para enquadrar no Uni-REPM, a fim de verificar a maturidade dos processos de requisitos das empresas.

O quadro 1 apresenta o protocolo do estudo de caso da avaliação de processos de ER, nas unidades de análise selecionadas.O protocolo elaborado para auxiliar no desenvolvimento do estudo de caso descreve os procedimentos e as regras que devem ser seguidas para obtenção dos objetivos pretendidos [34].

Protocolo para desenvolvimento do estudo de caso	
Questão da pesquisa	Qual o nível de maturidade dos processos de engenharia de requisitos de software?
Estrutura teórica para desenvolvimento do estudo de caso	Referencial bibliográfico sobre processo de engenharia de requisitos e avaliação de processo de ER.
a) Locais a serem visitados b) Pessoa de contato c) Documentos analisados	a) Empresas de desenvolvimento de software da região norte do Paraná b) Gerentes de projeto ou Analistas de sistemas c) Processos de requisitos de software
Roteiro para desenvolvimento do estudo de caso	1. Caracterização da empresa pesquisada 2. Visão das atividades dos processos de engenharia de requisitos realizados nas empresas

	(modelagem do processo atual) 3. Avaliação e classificação dos processos de ER, por meio do Uni-REPM 4. Análise quantitativa dos dados, para responder às questões da pesquisa 5. Modelagem dos processos de ER das empresas com proposta de melhorias
Análise e validação do estudo de caso	As evidências foram coletadas por meio de entrevistas e análise dos documentos dos processos de ER utilizados pelas empresas pesquisadas. Os entrevistados validaram os processos de ER modelados após a coleta dos dados e os processos modelados após a sugestão de melhoria.

Quadro 1 - Protocolo para desenvolvimento do estudo de caso

4 Estudo de caso

O estudo de caso foi realizado entre os anos de 2013 e 2015, em 20 empresas de desenvolvimento de software da região norte do Paraná, com a participação dos alunos do programa de mestrado em informática da Universidade Tecnológica Federal do Paraná.Grande parte dos alunos do programa trabalha em empresas de desenvolvimento de software, fator que contribuiu de forma significativa para seleção das empresas, levantamento dos dados e para a aproximação entre indústria e academia.

As empresas foram selecionadas e classificadas em 3 grupos, sendo 2 grupos de acordo com a idade e o 3° grupo contendo apenas empresas que possuem certificação de processo de software.Para não divulgar as empresas, os nomes foram substituídos por números, de 1 a 20. O quadro 2 resume o perfil das empresas.

Classificação	Empresas	%
Grupo A (+ de 10 anos)	1, 2, 3, 4, 7, 8, 9, 10, 11, 12, 14, 15, 16, 17, 19, 20	80%
Grupo B (de 5 a 10 anos)	5, 6, 13, 18	20%
Grupo C (certificadas)	1, 2, 5, 7, 8, 9, 13, 14, 19	45%

Quadro 2. Classificação das empresas

Durante a entrevista, os participantes foram perguntados sobre o processo de requisitos utilizado na respectiva empresa, descrevendo-os. Todas as informações foram anotadas em tempo real de modo a garantir que o processo fosse modelado de acordo com o que de fato ocorre na empresa. Algumas empresas, além de descreverem o processo, apresentaram documentação auxiliar do processo atual da empresa. Um questionário, com questões abertas e fechadas foi aplicado a fim de obter dados quanto a idade da empresa, n° de colaboradores, certificação e conhecimento sobre processo de requisitos.

Após a coleta dos dados os processos atuais foram modelados utilizando a notação BPMN (*Business Process Modeling Notation*) [36] ou SPEM (*Software Process Engineering Metamodel*) [38]. A escolha do BPMN se justifica por ser uma linguagem de modelagem expressiva, formal e de fácil compreensão aos usuários finais e não apenas aos especialistas do domínio [37].Por sua vez a notação SPEM é caracterizada como uma linguagem utilizada em processos de desenvolvimento de software, baseada na UML. Tanto o BPMN quanto o SPEM são padronizadas pela OMG [39].

A figura 1 apresenta a modelagem do processo atual de ER de duas empresas participantes, sendo a figura 1a modelada com SPEM e a figura 1b modelada com BPMN. Ressalta-se que todas as empresas tiveram seus processos de requisitos modelados.

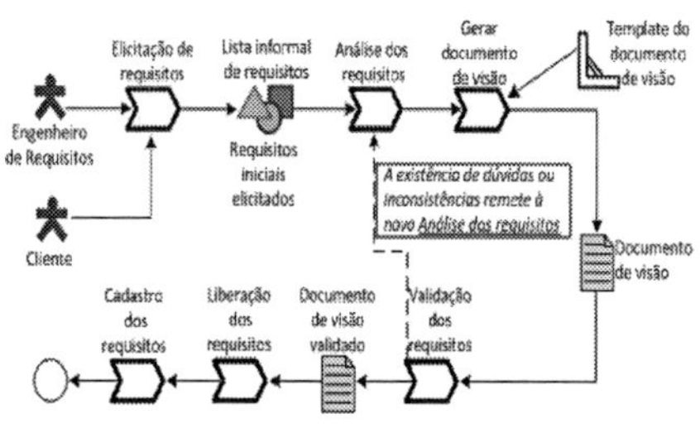

Figura 1a. Processo de ER com SPEM

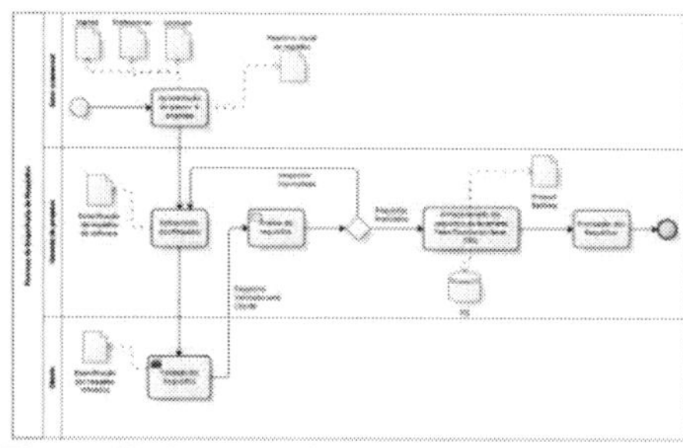

Figura 1b. Processo de ER com BPMN

Após a modelagem dos processos de ER das empresas, foi selecionado um quadro de avaliação de maturidade de processo de requisitos, o Uni-REPM. A seleção deste quadro se justifica, pois é um quadro de avaliação de processo de requisitos flexível, construído com base nas normas, modelos de referência e boas práticas citados neste artigo, localizado na literatura recente, sendo que este quadro já está validado em trabalho publicado no ano de2012 [10].

O enquadramento das atividades contidas no processo atual das empresas foi realizado de acordo com a função e artefatos gerados por cada atividade executada pela empresa em ação similar contida no Uni-REPM. No enquadramento do processo atual da empresa não foi considerado o critério IA (inaplicável). Este critério será utilizado para avaliação dos processos após a sugestão de atividades pelas empresas para obtenção do modelo de latência. O pesquisador teve um papel fundamental nesta etapa da pesquisa, pois a partir da modelagem do processo foram extraídas as informações necessárias para o enquadramento.

5 Análise e Discussão

Um dos resultados obtidos após o enquadramento do processo atual das empresas pode ser visualizado por meio da figura 2a e figura 2b, as quais representam, respectivamente, a análise do processo atual de duas empresas, ambas dos Grupos A e C (empresas nominadas 1 e 2), mas que não alcançam nenhum nível de maturidade proposto pelo Uni-REPM.

O gráfico da figura 2a aponta que de 29 ações do nível básico, a empresa realiza em seu processo atual9 ações, do nível intermediário, das 30 ações propostas pelo Uni-REPM, a empresa realiza 5 e do nível avançado, das 15 ações, a empresa realiza 4. Da mesma forma, a figura 2b retrata que a empresa 2 também não alcança o nível de maturidade básico do Uni-REPM, com 13 ações de 29 do nível básico, 4 ações de

30 do nível intermediário e 2 de 15 do nível avançado. Esta forma de apresentação possibilita uma visão global do processo atual em relação ao Uni-REPM. Em outra análise é possível dizer que a empresa 2, figura 2b, possui uma latência equivalente a 16 ações para alcançar o nível básico.

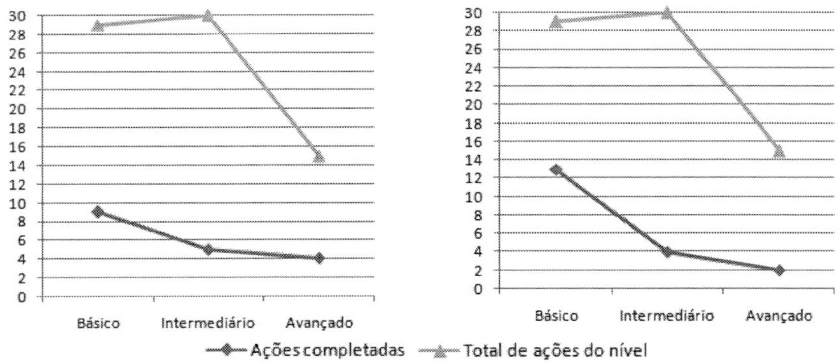

Figura 2a. Gráfico de latência - empresa 1

Figura 2b. Gráfico de latência - empresa 2

Outra forma de leitura dos dados pode se dar por meio da geração de gráfico em barra, onde são detalhadas quantas ações são realizadas em cada MPA, contidas em todos os níveis de maturidade. Um exemplo é apresentado nas figuras 3a e 3b, as quais correspondem, respectivamente às empresas 3 e 4, ambas do Grupo A, porém sem certificação.

São 7 áreas de processos principais que se repetem em cada nível de maturidade, porém diferenciam-se quanto às ações a serem realizadas em cada nível. Para facilitar a visualização do gráfico, foi uma utilizada uma abreviatura para cada uma das 7MPAs: AO - Ajuda Organizacional; GP - Gestão de Processo de Requisitos; ER - Elicitação de Requisitos; AR - Análise de Requisitos; PL - Plano de Lançamento; DR - Documentação de Requisitos; VR - Validação de Requisitos.

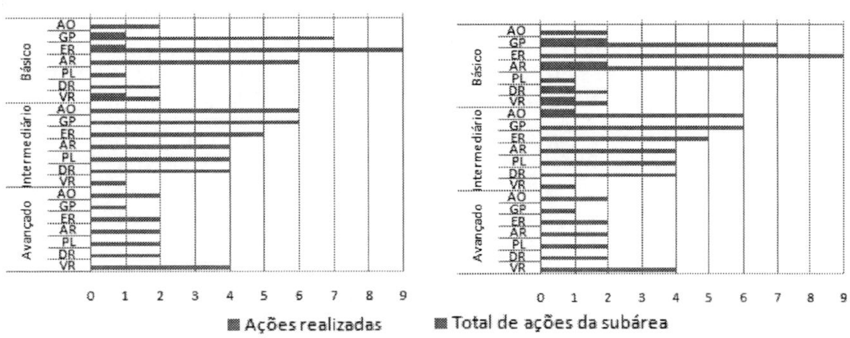

Figura 3a. Gráfico por MPA - empresa 3

Figura 3b. Gráfico por MPA - empresa 4

Ao aplicar o quadro de avaliação de maturidade de processo, pode-se ainda gerar gráficos individuais por área de processo principal (MPA), conforme demonstrado nas figuras 4a e 4b, referentes às áreas de Elicitação de Requisitos e Análise de Requisitos, respectivamente, do processo de ER da empresa 11, Grupo A, não certificada.

A empresa 11 precisa executar mais 5 ações da MPA de Elicitação de Requisitos para alcançar o nível básico desta MPA, 2 ações para atingir o nível intermediário e 2 para chegar ao nível avançado, conforme desenhado na figura 4a. Da mesma forma, ao observar a figura 4b, verifica-se que a empresa 11não executa nenhuma ação de Análise de Requisitos do nível básico e do nível avançado e para cumprir todas as ações do nível intermediário, precisa acrescentar apenas 1 ação deste nível, segundo o quadro Uni-REPM.

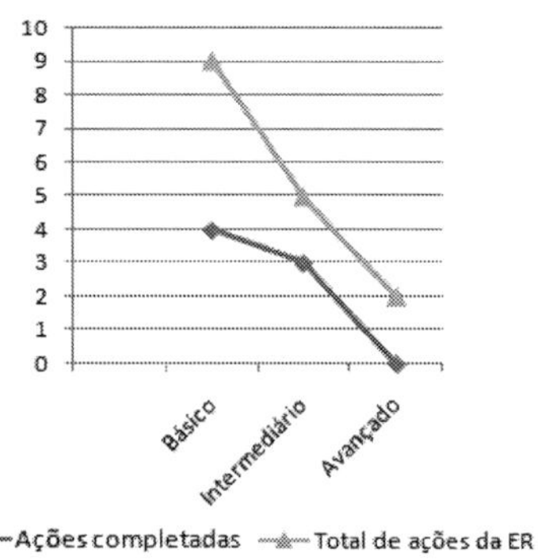

Figura 4a. Gráfico por SPA - ER

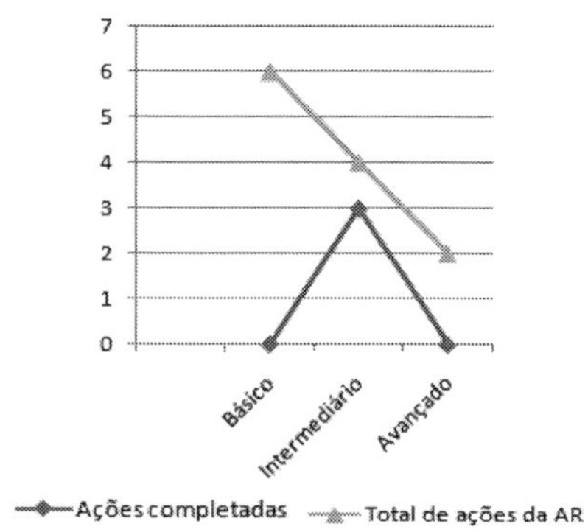

Figura 4b. Gráfico por SPA - AR

Na análise dos dados foi possível responder as duas questões desta pesquisa. Ao levantar, modelar e avaliar os processos de ER das empresas constatou-se que, de acordo com o Uni-REPM, nenhum processo de ER atingiu níveis de maturidade. As empresas com maior número de atividades no nível básico atingiram 45% do total de ações deste nível. As ações dos níveis intermediário e avançado tiveram um índice baixo de execução pelas empresas. A empresa de menor desempenho executa apenas 6,9% das ações propostas pelo Uni-REPM. Isto leva a análise de quem são estas empresas, qual a diferença entre as certificadas das demais?

A tabela 1 apresenta o resultado da análise comparativa entre empresas certificadas e empresas não certificadas, não levando em consideração o tempo de existência das empresas. A classificação das empresas de acordo com a idade e certificação pode ser visualizada no quadro 2. Observa-se que no nível básico as empresas certificadas executam o dobro de ações em relação as não certificadas, e executam 3 e 4 vezes mais ações, respectivamente nos níveis intermediário e avançado. Porém, o índice de ações realizadas nestes níveis chega no máximo a 16,6% no intermediário e 13,3% do avançado.

Tabela 1. Média e diferença (%) de ações realizadas

	Básico	Intermediário	Avançado
Com certificado	34	8	4
Sem certificado	17,6	2,6	0,6
Diferença	16,4	5,4	3,4

A média de atividades realizadas por todas as empresas é 9. Todas as empresas, com número de atividades maior que a média, possuem em seu quadro mais de 40 colaboradores, porém, o estudo também demonstrou que outras empresas com número de colaboradores superior a 40 não ultrapassam a média de ações realizadas por todas as empresas, o que leva a crer que o número de colaboradores não influencia diretamente na execução das atividades. Fortalece esta afirmação o fato de que duas empresas com menos de 40 colaboradores em seu quadro, executam atividades acima da média, sendo estas certificadas, o que indica que mesmo com menos colaboradores, seus processos se equiparem aos das empresas com mais de 40 colaboradores.

Foram analisadas ainda quais áreas possuem maior e menor número de atividades realizadas no processo atual das empresas. A análise demonstrou que as áreas de Elicitação de Requisitos (ER), seguida da área de Gestão de Processo de ER (GP) e Análise de Requisitos (AR) são as áreas que as empresas dão maior importância na execução de seus processos. Na área Plano de Lançamento de Requisitos (PL) apenas as empresas 1 e 2 empresas, ambas certificadas, executam uma e duas atividades respectivamente. Similar à área PL, a área de Ajuda Organizacional (AO) tem um baixo índice de atividades realizadas, sendo que apenas 3 empresas, sendo apenas 1 certificada, executa alguma ação nesta área.

Vale citar que na área de Documentação de Requisitos (D) das 9 empresas com certificação, apenas 6 realizam atividades nesta área e apenas 1 das empresas não certificadas executa alguma atividade proposta pelo Uni-REPM em seu processo.

6 Conclusão

Após a realização deste estudo de caso o trabalho está sendo continuado. Nesta segunda fase está sendo apresentada, às empresas, um conjunto de práticas dispostas nas normas e modelos de referência (CMMI, ISO, MPS-BR, SPICE, boas práticas) que compreendem as ações previstas no Uni-REPM. O objetivo desta atividade visa promover às empresas um ganho de conhecimento na área de requisitos. Tal prática está sendo organizada de forma que as empresas possam escolher atividades para aperfeiçoar os seus processos.

Os dados da segunda fase tem refletido uma melhoria do processo, após a agregação do conhecimento de novas práticas, sem a exigência do atendimento a um padrão ou norma.

Em relação ao estudo atual observa-se, no grupo estudado, que a realidade das práticas nas empresas, em relação ao número de atividades, está aquém das atividades estabelecidas por padrões, normas ou guias de boas práticas, elementos já bem conhecidos na área de pesquisa. Pode-se observar a possibilidade da realização de estudos que visem analisar a qualidade dos requisitos e outros artefatos gerados em processos como os apresentados, ou seja, com poucas atividades realizadas mesmo em contextos como elicitação ou gerenciamento de requisitos.

Conclui-se, com a realização deste estudo de caso, que as empresas certificadas, possuem processos com mais atividades que as não certificadas, mas em relação a maturidade dos processos, considerando o Uni-REPM como parâmetro avaliativo, todas precisam inserir novas atividades para melhoria dos processos.

A aplicação do quadro de avaliação de maturidade de processos de requisitos, Uni-REPM, em processos de empresas de desenvolvimento pode contribuir para que as empresas conheçam melhor os seus processos, identifiquem lacunas e busquem a inserção de novas atividades para melhoria do processo de ER, o que irá refletir no resultado final do produto de software.

Referências

1. Ellis, K, Berry,D.M.(2012).Quantifying the impact of requirements definition and management process maturity on project outcome in large business application development. *Requirements Engineering, 18*(3), 223–249.doi:10.1007/s00766-012-0146-3.
2. Génova, G., Fuentes, J. M., Llorens, J., Hurtado, O., Moreno, V. (2011). A framework to measure and improve the quality of textual requirements. *Requirements Engineering, 18*(1), 25–41. doi:10.1007/s00766-011-0134-z.
3. Sommerville, I. A. N.,Ransom, J. (2005). *An Empirical Study of Industrial Requirements Engineering Process Assessment and Improvement*, ACM, New York, USA *14*(1), 85–117. doi: 10.1145/1044834.1044837.
4. Sommerville, I. (2006) "Software Engineering". 8ª ed., São Paulo: Addison-Wesley.
5. Hofmann, H.F., Lehner, F. (2001) Requirements engineering as a success factor in software projects. IEEE Software 18(4):58–66.
6. Paech, B., Koenig, T., Borner, L., Aurum, A. (2005) An analysis of empirical requirements engineering survey data. In: Engineering and managing software requirements, Part 3. Springer, Berlin. pp 427–452.
7. Gürses, S., Seguran, M., Zannone, N. (2011). Requirements engineering within a large-scale security-oriented research project: lessons learned. *Requirements Engineering, 18*(1), 43–66. doi:10.1007/s00766-011-0139-7.
8. Juristo, N., Moreno, A., Silva, A. (2002) Is the European industry moving toward solving requirements engineering problems? IEEE Software 19(6): 70–77
9. Neill, C., Laplante, P. (2003) Requirements engineering: The state of the practice. IEEE Software 20 (6):40–45.
10. Svahnberg, M., Gorschek, T., Nguyen, T. T. L., Nguyen, M. (2012). Uni-REPM: validated and improved. *Requirements Engineering*. doi:10.1007/s00766-012-0148-1
11. Sommerville, I, Sawyer, P. *Requirements Engineering a good practice guide*. Johh Wiley & Sons Ltda. Boffins Lane, Chichster, England, 1998.
12. Gorschek, T., Gomes, A., Pettersson, A., Torkar, R. (2012) Introduction of a process maturity model for market-driven product management and requirements engineering. Journal of Software:Evolution and Process 23(1): 83–113.
13. Software Engineering Institute. CMMI for development: CMMI–DEV, v. 1.2, Carnegie Mellon University. 2006.
14. International Standard Organization.12207: systems and software engineering - software life cycle processes, [S.l.], 2008a.
15. International Standard Organization.15288: systems and software engineering - system life cycle processes, [S.l.], 2008b.
16. Softex. MPS.BR: melhoria de processo do software brasileiro. Guia geral, v. 1, 2006.
17. SPICE: Software process improvement and capability determination. http://www.sqi.gu.edu.au/spice/ (2011).
18. Cerderial, C.T (2008). Uma abordagem para gerência e avaliação de projetos de melhoria de processos de software do ponto de vista da Instituição de consultoria, M. Sc. COPPE. UFRJ, Rio de Janeiro.

19. Khurum, M., Aslam, K., Gorschek, T. (2008) A method for early requirements triage and selection utilizing product strategies, Piscataway, NJ, USA: IEEE, 2008, pp. 97---104.
20. Lepmetz, M., Mcbride, T., RAS, E. *Goal alignment in process improvement.* The Journal of Systems and Software 85 (2012) 1440– 1452.
21. Coleman, G., O'connor, R. *Using grounded theory to understand software process improvement: A study of Irish software product companies*. Information and Software Technology, Volume 49, Issue6, June 2007, Pages 654-667, ISSN 0950-5849.
22. Barreto, A. S. (2011). Software Process Definition : a Reuse-based Approach.J. UCS; 17(13):1765-1799.
23. Napier, N. P., Mathiassen, L., Johnson, R. D. (sep 2009). Combining Perceptions and Prescriptions in Requirements Engineering Process Assessment: An Industrial Case Study. IEEE Transactions on Software Engineering, v. 35, n. 5, p. 593–606.
24. Attarha, M. Focusing on the Importance and the Role of Requirement Engineering. Interaction Sciences (ICIS), 2011 4th International Conference, IEEE.
25. Beecham, S., Hall, T., Britton, C., Cottee, M., Rainer, A. "Using an Expert Panel to Validate a Requirement Process Improvement Model," J. Systems and Software, vol. 76, no. 3, pp. 251-275, 2005.
26. Schmidt, R., Lyytinen, K., Keil, M., Cule, P. Identifying Software Project Risks: An International Delphi Study. J. Management Information Systems, vol. 17, no. 4, pp. 5-36, 2001.
27. Mathiassen, L.,Ngwenyama, O. K., Aaen, I. "Managing Change in Software Process Improvement," IEEE Software, vol. 22, no. 6, pp. 84-91, Nov./Dec. 2005.
28. Svensson, R. B., Gorschek, T., Regnell, B., Torkar, R., Shahrokni, A., Feldt, R. (2011). *Prioritization of Quality Requirements : State of Practice in Eleven Companies*, 69–78.
29. Sharma, L., Sharm, N. (2012). *Software Process Improvement in Small Scale Organizations : An Empirical Study. International Conference on Recent Advances and Future Trends in Information Technology* 18–21.
30. Aggarwal, A. (2012). Design of Software Process Improvement Model, *49*(13), 30–34.
31. Svahnberg, M., Gorschek, T., Nguyen, T. T. L., Nguyen, M., Peterson, A., Gomes, A., Tejle, K. (2011). Requirements Engineering Process Maturity Model Uni-REPM. docengeneering: Blekinge Institute of Technology, Karlskrona,Sweden, 2011.
32. Svahnberg, M., Gorschek, T., Nguyen, T. T. L., Nguyen, M. (2013). Uni-REPM: a framework for requirements engineering process assessment. *Requirements Engineering*. doi:10.1007/s00766-013-0188-1
33. Robson, C. (2002) *Real World Research* (second edition).Oxford: Blackwell.
34. Yin, R. "Estudo de Caso". São Paulo. 3a. Edição. Bookman, 2005.
35. Wohlin, C.,Runeson, P.,Höst, M.,Ohlsson, M.C.,Regnell, B.,Wesslén, A. *Experimentation in Software Engineering*. New York. Springer, 2012. ISBN 978-3-642-29044-2 (eBook).
36. Object Management GroupBusiness Process Model and Notation (BPMN)" (2011). Disponível em: http://www.omg.org/spec/BPMN/2.0/PDF.Acesso: 20/02/2014.
37. Chinosi, M., Trombetta, A. (2012). Computer Standards & Interfaces BPMN : An introduction to the standard. *Computer Standards & Interfaces*, *34*(1), 124–134. doi:10.1016/j.csi.2011.06.002
38. Object Management Group. Software & systems process engineering meta-model specification,2008.Disponível em: <http://www.omg.org/spec/SPEM/2.0/PDF>.Acesso: 24/02/2014.
39. Portela, C., Vasconcelos, A., Silva, A., Sinimbú, A., Silva, E., Ronny, M., Oliveira, S. (2012) A Comparative Analysis between BPMN and SPEM Modeling Standards in the Software Processes Context, 330–339. doi:10.4236/jsea.2012.55039.

Trends and Needs in Requirements Engineering Research in Ibero-America: Insights from a Panel

Jose Luis de la Vara[1], Isabel Sofia Brito[2], Nelly Condori-Fernández[3], and João Araújo [4]

[1]Carlos III University of Madrid, Spain
[2]Instituto Politécnico de Beja, Portugal
[3]VU University Amsterdam, Netherlands
[4]Universidade Nova de Lisboa, Portugal
jvara@inf.uc3m.es, isabel.sofia@ipbeja.pt, n.condori-fernandez@vu.nl, joao.araujo@fct.unl.pt

Abstract. Some aspects characterise Requirements Engineering (RE) research from different regions, whereas others constrain RE and RE approaches should not disregard them. Within this context, this paper aims to provide new insights into the trends and needs in RE research in Ibero-America. We have analysed the results from a panel at WER 2015 on the characteristics in Ibero-America that RE research should consider, the topics successfully researched in the region, the topics not sufficiently researched, and the topics on which future research should focus. Among the conclusions, Ibero-America seems to have specific social and cultural characteristics that impact RE, research on goal-oriented RE and RE for web-based systems can be regarded as successful, how to improve requirements quality should have been further studied, and RE education and knowledge transfer must be addressed in the future.

Keywords: Requirements Engineering, trends, needs, future research, panel.

1 Introduction

Although Requirements Engineering (RE) is a global research area and people from all around the world have contributed to its development, some characteristics distinguish RE research from different regions. For example, North American universities are arguably the main contributors to requirements traceability [5]. These characteristics are indicators of the trends in RE research in different regions. Certain aspects also constrain software development and RE in specific regions nowadays, such as outsourced software development to India [3], and others are expected to impact RE research in the near future, such as new software security regulations in Europe [2]. If these aspects are disregarded, then RE research results will very likely not fulfil the needs in these regions.

This paper aims to provide insights into the trends and needs in RE research in Ibero-America. To this end, we have analysed the results from a panel at WER 2015 targeted at discussing these aspects. The panel addressed the following questions: (1) What characteristics in Ibero-America should RE research carefully take into account? (2) What RE topics have been successfully researched in Ibero-America? (3) What RE topics have not been sufficiently researched in Ibero-America? (4) What RE topics should be the main focus of Ibero-American RE research in the future?

Although panels have been arranged in many editions of RE-targeted conferences such as RE, REFSQ, and WER, and some of these panels have dealt with trends and needs in RE, we are not aware of any that has focused on these aspects for a specific region. Prior research has also argued for the relevance of considering regional characteristics for RE approach success [3], has shown that RE research topics have varied among regions [5], and has regularly proposed RE research agendas (e.g. [1]). However, most of this research has not focused on Ibero-America. Those publications that have studied Ibero-American aspects have only done it for a limited scope, such as papers at WER [7] or in Brazil [6], and not for all the panel questions. We aim to fill this gap by presenting the insights gained from the answers that people from several Ibero-America countries provided to the four questions formulated.

Three experts presented their opinion on these topics, over 20 people attended the panel, and several attendees actively participated in the discussions. According to the discussions at the panel, Ibero-America does seem to have specific characteristics that can affect RE, such as different, better communication skills when compared to other regions. Ibero-American RE research can be regarded as successful in some topics, but maybe just in a few cases. How to improve requirements quality and user experience have not been investigated enough in the past in Ibero-America, and future research must pay greater attention to how to finally materialise RE technology transfer, not only to industry but also to education institutions.

The rest of the paper is organised as follows. Section 2 describes the panel, Section 3 presents its results, and Section 4 summarises our conclusions.

2 Panel

We organised a panel at WER 2015 to answer the four questions presented in the introduction. Three experts accepted to participate as panellists. Jaelson Castro was the representative from academia in Latin America. He is very well known for his contributions to goal modelling. João Araújo was the representative from academia in Europe. He is very well known for his contributions to aspect-oriented RE and to model-driven RE. Juan José Miranda was the representative of the software industry. He is the President of the Peruvian Association of Software and Technologies. The moderator of the panel was Nelly Condori-Fernández.

Over 20 people attended the panel, from both industry and academia, and including well-known members of the RE community in Ibero-America such as Alejandro Oliveros, Julio Leite, Luis Olsina, and Óscar Pastor. The duration of the panel was around 70 minutes, and it was divided into six slots: one for panel introduction (five minutes), four for discussing the panel questions (around 15 minutes per question), and another to summarise and close the panel (five minutes). The first and the second authors took notes during the panel. A summary of the topics, the most discussed topics (topics discussed in more depth, argued by several participants and not only referred to by one), and initial conclusions were presented at the end of the panel.

3 Results

Table 1 summarises the panel results. For each panel question, the table lists the specific aspects discussed, including the controversial points. The aspects in bold correspond to the most discussed ones. The aspects are ordered first according to the depth with which they were discussed and second in alphabetical order. As can be observed, the attendees discussed challenges and the reasons for certain happenings.

The first question (**What characteristics in Ibero-America should RE research carefully take into account?**) is the most balanced in relation to the number of controversial and of non-controversial specific aspects, thus there might not be a clear agreement upon the existence of the characteristics. Two very different positions were presented at the beginning of the question slot: some participants indicated that there are relevant different characteristics and others strongly argued that such characteristics do not exist. As the discussion developed, the number of potentially relevant characteristics increased, which suggests that they indeed exist.

Among the differentiating characteristics, the existence of cultural differences that can affect RE and the fact that people from Ibero-America probably have better communication skills than people from other regions were the most discussed specific aspects. They might especially influence requirements elicitation and negotiation. Nonetheless, we wonder about the extent to which some characteristics are really Ibero-American. The financial situation is e.g. likely a result of the global economic crisis. It can also be analysed the extent to which the characteristics are different in Ibero-America and their actual impact on a RE approach.

Regarding the controversial aspects, some characteristics seem to be negative for RE. Lack of organization or discipline in the work probably hinder the RE process because this process must aim to be systematic. There is also a conflict between one panel participant that indicated that people in Ibero-America were innovative and another that indicated that they mostly follow trends from other regions. It remains an open question to us the extent to which the fact that several countries in South America are emerging economies, or will likely grow in the near future, affects RE.

It is very surprising to us that only three RE topics were mentioned as successfully researched in Ibero-America when discussing the second question (**What RE topics have been successfully researched in Ibero-America?**). Nonetheless, there seemed to be a general agreement upon their success at the end of the question slot. Even more interestingly, this is the question with the highest number of controversial specific aspects, with a stark difference with the number of non-controversial specific aspects. In our opinion, this is an indication of little agreement upon the extent to which RE research in Ibero-America has been successful. This question also has the highest number of specific aspects discussed in more depth.

Two very different positions were presented regarding the question: some participants indicated that success had occurred only in a few cases, and others disagreed and mentioned some examples. Prior studies suggest that goal oriented RE, model-based RE, and scenario-based RE are the most addressed approaches in WER [6, 7]. This is not surprising considering that, for instance, goal-oriented RE is one of the most researched topics in Brazil. We also believe that modelling and scenario topics have been successful research areas in Ibero-America because, in general, requirements modelling appears together with other topics such as elicitation [7].

The participants claimed that the RE community in Ibero-America is small and needs the presence of more students. A cross-cutting controversial point is the lack of knowledge and technology transfer. This is a serious problem not only in Ibero-America. An aspect that could be studied is how success should be characterised, e.g. number of publications or of citations, technology transfer, or benefits provided.

Table 1. Specific aspects discussed at the panel

1) What characteristics in Ibero-America should RE res. carefully take into account?	**2) What RE topics have been successfully researched in Ibero-America?**
1. **Better communication skills**, which facilitate the understanding of users, stakeholder needs, and goals 2. **Culture different to other regions** 3. Financial situation and economic characteristics of the region 4. History, related to e.g. having been part of Portugal and Spain 5. People are more innovative than in other regions 6. Sustainability needs *Controversial points* 7. **There are no relevant differences with other regions**; all the regions are the same for RE 8. Lack of organization and of systematic processes 9. People in the region have a bad reputation as a result of their behaviour 10. Ibero-America mostly follows trends from other regions	1. **Goal-oriented RE** 2. **RE for web-based systems** 3. Aspect-Oriented RE *Controversial points* 4. **RE community in Ibero-America is small and needs the presence of more students** 5. **Success only in a few cases** 6. **There is a lack of industry pull to assess success** 7. **Research results are not transferred to education, thus it is not successful** 8. Insufficient funding hinders success 9. No past RE research in Ibero-America can really be regarded as successful 10. RE research in Ibero-A. lacks recognition 11. Success is very limited when compared to the relative relevance and interest in other social areas (e.g., sports) 12. Success is biased because RE community in Ibero-A. does not evolve (same people)
3) What RE topics have not been sufficiently researched in Ibero-America?	**4) What RE topics should be the main focus of Ibero-A. RE res. in the future?**
1. **Communication means for the RE process** 2. **Requirements quality** 3. **Requirements representation languages** 4. **User experience** 5. Communication 6. Contextual aspects 7. Further automation of the RE process 8. Health 9. Multicultural aspects for RE 10. Multi-skill needs 11. RE and software architecture 12. Requirements assessment 13. Requirements validation 14. Sustainability 15. System scope elicitation *Controversial point* 16. There has been enough research; no important topic insufficiently researched	1. **Governance** 2. **Knowledge transfer**, both to industry and to education institutions 3. **Model quality** 4. **RE education** 5. Adaptive-systems requirements 6. Apps requirements 7. Business-IT alignment 8. Cloud requirements 9. Confidence in reqs.-based estimation 10. Domain specific languages 11. Evidence-based RE 12. Rapid requirements validation 13. RE for agile 14. RE in practice 15. Requirements and architecture 16. Resilience requirements 17. System scalability 18. User profile unification

Given the amount of RE publications that researchers in Ibero-America have produced [6, 7], someone might have expected a shorter list of topics for the third panel question (**What RE topics have not been sufficiently researched in Ibero-America?**). More surprisingly, we think that some topics have indeed been researched, e.g. automation. We wonder whether the reason for regarding these topics as insufficiently researched is that some specific problems need further investigation. Another possible explanation is that the corresponding results are not mature enough.

The communication means for the RE process is regarded as not been sufficiently researched in Ibero-America even though, as presented above, people from the region probably have better communication skills and requirements elicitation is a successful research topic. These communication means impact requirements elicitation and relate to characteristics that RE research should take into account. A possible explanation is the lack of research on requirements validation and negotiation [6, 7], which involves communication and addressing aspects related to user experience.

Requirements quality has been identified as an insufficiently investigated point, as well as requirements representation languages. The latter is surprising because of the extensive prior work on e.g. the use of models for goal-oriented, aspects-oriented, and business process-based RE [7]. It remains an open question why some topics have not been further researched. One might think of lack of background on the topics, but insufficient relevance for Ibero-America could also be a justification.

The fourth question (**What RE topics should be the main focus of Ibero-American RE research in the future?**) has the highest number of specific aspects discussed. We interpret it as evidence of the interest in deciding upon and proposing topics for future research. It is also noteworthy that no controversial point was discussed for this aspect. This suggests that future research is a clearly necessary aspect for RE in Ibero-America, in which little disagreement exists beyond on reaching a common opinion on the areas to research on.

References to most of the topics, implicitly or explicitly, can be easily found in research agendas, e.g. to quality [1]. Knowledge transfer to education institutions is an important issue to promote RE research results. University lecturers have the responsibility to integrate new RE research insights into our teaching, and to thereby extend the knowledge of the future generation of requirements engineers. Knowledge and technology transfer to industry would benefit from better advice on how to apply RE technologies more systematically [1].

The answers to this panel question refer to new software-intensive system types, e.g. apps, and to new requirements types, e.g. resilience. We regard these patterns as reasonable because such references are common. When comparing the topics mentioned in the fourth panel question with WER 2016 call for paper and CIbSE scope, we have found both similarities and difference with the panel participants' opinions on what future RE research in Ibero-America should focus on.

4 Conclusions

This paper presents trends and needs in RE research in Ibero-America based on the discussions during a panel. Ibero-America seems to have specific characteristics that RE researchers should consider. We argue that future RE research should pay further attention to the distinguishing social and cultural features of the region, identifying those that can affect the RE process and characterising the impact. Extensive research on RE has been conducted in Ibero-America and it can be regarded as successful on goal-oriented RE, RE for web-based systems, and aspect-oriented RE. On the other hand, how to improve requirements quality should have been further studied. Industry needs RE approaches that incorporate quality-targeted mechanisms in their requirements tools, e.g. metrics. Future RE research could also aim at tackling broad societal challenges such as sustainability [4], and the enhancement of RE education and knowledge transfer must be addressed. The teaching community should devise new means for RE education at both universities and companies.

This work may lead to the establishment of new partnerships in order to tackle the issues discussed, and help RE researchers focus their work on more relevant needs in Ibero-American. For industry, the results and conclusions reported are expected to help practitioners both identify aspects that must be considered in their RE processes and gain awareness of the relevant RE research results produced in Ibero-America.

Regarding the limitations of the results and conclusions presented, a reader must be aware that the insights presented strongly depend on the panel participants. They had a specific background and the representation from industry was limited. Anyway, we consider that the limitations are reasonable given the exploratory nature of a panel.

As future work, it could be valuable to replicate the panel in the future (e.g., at WER 2020) and compare the results. Systematic literature reviews could also provide a wider overview of the Ibero-American characteristics that can affect RE and of the RE research that has been conducted in the region.

Acknowledgments. We are grateful to the panellists and the rest of panel attendees. The research leading to this paper has received funding from Carlos III University of Madrid (2015/00261/001 project reference) and NOVA LINCS research center.

References

1. Cheng, B.H.C., Atlee, J.M.: Research Directions in Requirements Engineering. In: FOSE 2007, pp. 285-303
2. IT Governance: Majority of EU businesses unprepared for new cyber security legislation (online) http://www.itgovernance.eu/blog/majority-of-eu-business-unprepared-for-new-cyber-security-legislation/ (2015) (Accessed on Dec 3, 2015)
3. Khan, S.U., et al.: Barriers in the selection of offshore software development outsourcing vendors: An exploratory study using a systematic literature review. Information & Software Technology 53(7): 693-706 (2011)
4. Lago P.: Challenges and Opportunities for Sustainable Software. In: PLEASE 2015
5. Nair, S., et al.: A review of traceability research at the Requirements Engineering conference. In: RE 2013, pp 222-229
6. Oliveira, K., et al.: 25 years of Requirements Engineering in Brazil: a systematic mapping. In: WER 2013
7. Valaski, J., et al.: WER Overview: Retrospective, Trends and Relevance. CLEI Electron. J. 17(3) (2014)

Industrial Track (IT 2016) Preface

Shakespeare dialogs on Software Engineering: preface to Industrial Track at CIbSE2016

Carlos Cares[1] and Sabrina Marczak[2]

[1] Universidad de La Frontera, Departamento de Ciencias de Computación e Informática, Centro de Estudios en Ingeniería de Software (CEIS), Av. Francisco Salazar 01145, Temuco, Chile
[2] Pontifícia Universidade Católica do Rio Grande do Sul – PUCRS
Faculdade de Informática – Programa de Pós-Graduação em Ciência da Computação, Caixa Postal 1429 – 90.619-900 – Porto Alegre – RS – Brasil

carlos.cares@ceisufro.cl, smarczak@inf.pucrs.br

Most of outstanding writers have been pointed out as visionaries. Arthur C. Clarke in "2001: A Space Odyssey" described the Earth as a planet having too much orbiting artificial satellites in 1968. Julio Verne in "From the Earth to the Moon" anticipated over a 100 years in advance the men landing on the moon, in addition to remote controlled artefacts and submarines in other of his novels. Morgan Robertson enters to the list by "predicting" the Titanic tragedy in the novel "Futility, or the wreck of the Titan" fourteen years earlier. Shakespeare, certainly, is not on the list. In spite of that, he wrote of a wreck in his theatre play "The Tempest". The aim of this presentation is to offer a Software Engineering context to "The Tempest" and to suggest in it the role of software industry. However, in order to reduced space (irony), we have omitted a matching analysis and we will present just some Software Engineering history facts and some dialogs from this classic play.

The software crisis was early identified and some of symptoms were: projects running over-budget, projects running over-time, never-delivered software, and unmanageable projects.

> On a ship at sea: a tempestuous noise

...

- **Master**. Boatswain!
- **Boatswain**. Here, master: what cheer?
- **Master**. Good, speak to the mariners: fall to't, yarely, or we run ourselves aground: bestir, bestir.

More than 25 years later, the Chaos report from the Standish Group reported at 2000 that only 26% of projects were successful, 58% were challenged projects (over budget, over time, and/or requirements not met) and, the remaining 28% of cases projects were never delivered (failed projects).

> The ship is capsizing, Gonzalo is an honest old counselor of the rightful duke of Milan, both are in the ship.

- **Boatswain**. When the sea is. Hence! What cares these roarers for the name of king? To cabin: silence! trouble us not.
- **Gonzalo**. Good, yet remember whom thou hast aboard.
- **Boatswain**. None that I more love than myself. You are a counsellor; if you can command these elements to silence, and work the peace of the present, we will not hand a rope more; use your authority: if you cannot, give thanks you have lived so long, and make yourself ready in your cabin for the mischance of the hour

Few years later, Glass, Vessey, and Ramesh show in 2003 that preferred methods from software engineering research were conceptual analysis (43.5%), conceptual analysis using maths (10.6%), and proof of concepts (17.1%). Case study (2.2%), action research (0%), and ethnography (0%) were also considered in this study.

> The ship already wrecked, Adrian and Sebastian, members of nobility, have survived

- **Adrian**. Though this island seem to be desert, uninhabitable and almost inaccessible,
- **Sebastian**. Yet,
- **Adrian**. Yet,

Between 2004 and 2010, several approaches using the concept of "empirical software engineering" are proposed and are nowadays highly cited. Most of them formalize strict methods in order to generate evidence-based knowledge. Table 1 shows some of these work.

Table 1. Empirical Software Engineering References

- Sjøberg, Dag IK. *Guide to advanced empirical software engineering*. Eds. Forrest Shull, and Janice Singer. Vol. 93. Germany: Springer, 2008.
- Kitchenham, Barbara, et al. "Evaluating guidelines for reporting empirical software engineering studies." *Empirical Software Engineering* 13.1 (2008): 97-121.
- Runeson, Per, and Martin Höst. "Guidelines for conducting and reporting case study research in software engineering." *Empirical software engineering* 14.2 (2009): 131-164.
- Jedlitschka, Andreas, Marcus Ciolkowski, and Dietmar Pfahl. "Reporting experiments in software engineering." *Guide to advanced empirical software engineering*. Springer London, 2008. 201-228.
- Easterbrook, Steve, et al. "Selecting empirical methods for software engineering research." *Guide to advanced empirical software engineering*. Springer London, 2008. 285-311.Hove, Siw Elisabeth, and Bente Anda. "Experiences from conducting semi-structured interviews in empirical software engineering research." *Software metrics, 2005. 11th ieee international symposium*. IEEE, 2005.

> In the isle, all characters are nobility members

- **Sebastian**. A most high miracle!
- **Ferdinand**. Though the seas threaten, they are merciful; I have cursed them without cause.

[Kneels]

- **Alonso**. Now all the blessings of a glad father compass thee about! Arise, and say how thou camest here.
- **Miranda**. O, wonder! How many goodly creatures are there here! How beauteous mankind is! O brave new world, that has such people in't!

However, in spite of new or imported epistemological movements in Software Engineering, the same pessimistic cifres indicate that, once a time and today, there are successful software projects carry out by industry.

> In another part of the isle, Trinculo, a jester, and Stephano, a drunken butler, also survivors, have connected with Caliban, a native of grotesque body.

Caliban. I'll show thee the best springs; I'll pluck thee berries; I'll fish for thee and get thee wood enough. A plague upon the tyrant that I serve! I'll bear him no more sticks, but follow thee, thou wondrous man

Trinculo. A most ridiculous monster, to make a wonder of a poor drunkard! (Stephano)

Caliban. I prithee, let me bring thee where crabs grow; and I with my long nails will dig thee pignuts; show thee a jay's nest and instruct thee how to snare the nimble marmoset; I'll bring thee to clustering filberts and sometimes I'll get thee young scamels from the rock. Wilt thou go with me?

Of course, to apply basic software engineering adjectives, such as systematic, disciplined, and measurable would be a good idea as a research approach. However, in order to understand and live in the software engineering world, seems to be a better idea, at least from time to time, to leave our academic chairs and let guide us by "such people in it". Therefore, naturally emerge epistemological questions about software industry, is it object of study?, or is it a subjective knower? may it be both? and may it be both at the same time?

For sure after this analysis, Shakespeare will continue not being part of a predictive or futurist group of writers; however, if we follow "The Tempest" metaphor, at least we have to recognize values, approaches, and prejudices in our epistemological approaches. Moreover, a good philosophical exercise may be to look for the corresponding characters into software engineering discipline to some of non-presented characters, such as spirits and speaking dead people that also are part of this theatre play.

In the meanwhile, it is a really pleasure to us to present you the industrial track at CIbSE, software engineering approaches from "natives" and "survivors". All part of this "new brave new world" of software engineering research and development.

This second Industrial Track, part of the XIX Ibero-American Conference on Software Engineering (CIbSE 2016), have received 18 paper submissions from authors of 8 different countries. Between them we had papers written in each of the 3 official languages: English, Portuguese and Spanish. All the submitted papers were revised by at least 2 reviewers from the Industrial Track Program Committee. At the end of the reviewing process, 5 high quality papers were accepted to be published and presented at the Industrial Track, representing an acceptance rate of 28%. In the following table we summarize the participating countries.

Country	Submitted papers with authors from	Accepted papers with authors from
Cuba	7	0
Brasil	3	1
Chile	2	2
Colombia	2	0
Costa Rica	2	2
France	2	0
Perú	1	0
EEUU	1	1

We would like to acknowledge and thank all authors who submitted papers. You made this second Industrial Track possible by sharing your expertise with us. We also would like to thank all the members of the Program Committee, composed by experts with strong academic and industrial background from 8 different countries, for following an excellent and meticulous reviewing process. Your dedication has resulted in the selection of high-quality papers for the Industrial Track.

Welcome !

Industrial Track Program Committee

Ahilton Barreto, Brazilian National Development Bank, Brazil

Aiko Yamashita, Oslo and Akershus University College of Applied Sciences, Norway

César Pardo Calvache, Universidad EAFIT, Colombia

Marcos Kalinowski, UFF, Brazil

Ricardo Gacitúa, UFRO, Chile

Igor Steinmacher, Universidade Tecnológica Federal do Paraná, Brazil

Marcela Genero, University of Castilla-La Mancha, Spain

Jorge Díaz, CEIS Universidad de La Frontera, Chile

Pedro Rossel, Universidad Católica de la Santísima Concepción, Chile

Raúl Mazo, Paris1-Sorbonne University, France

Angélica Caro, Universidad del Bío-Bío, Chile

Daniel Endara, Lazos S.A., Chile

Roberto Arisaca, UNSA, Perú

Juan Carlos Araneda, Everis, Chile

Jorge Ibsen, ALMA, Chile

Gustavo Rossi, LIFIA-F. Informática – UNLP, Argentina

INDUSTRIAL TRACK INDEX

Aplicación del nivel 1 estándar ASVS de OWASP: un caso de estudio

Enrique Brenes[1] and Alexandra Martínez[2]

[1] Posgrado en Computación e Informática, Universidad de Costa Rica
enrique.brenes@ecci.ucr.ac.cr
[2] Escuela de Ciencias de la Computación e Informática, Universidad de Costa Rica
alexandra.martinez@ecci.ucr.ac.cr

Resumen Este caso de estudio explora la aplicabilidad del nivel 1 del estándar para verificación de la seguridad de aplicaciones de OWASP en el contexto de una aplicación web de la industria financiera. Dos analistas de calidad no expertos en seguridad se encargaron de ejecutar el nivel 1 del estándar, reportando en una bitácora varias métricas relativas a las pruebas realizadas, el esfuerzo requerido y las vulnerabilidades encontradas. Luego, el equipo de desarrollo corrigió las vulnerabilidades reportadas, registrando el esfuerzo de corregir cada vulnerabilidad. Finalmente, un grupo de expertos en seguridad realizó una evaluación de la aplicación, detallando sus hallazgos en un informe. Los resultados aportan evidencia de que el nivel 1 del estándar ASVS puede ser aplicado por analistas de calidad que no sean expertos en seguridad, mediante análisis manual de código y técnicas de pruebas de penetración con apoyo de herramientas. En el software bajo estudio, las vulnerabilidades de Control de acceso y Autenticación fueron las más frecuentes, de mayor severidad y con mayor esfuerzo de reparación. La evaluación realizada por expertos en seguridad ayudó a comprobar que la cobertura del nivel 1 del estándar fue alta a pesar de haber sido realizada por personal inexperto en pruebas de seguridad.

Keywords: Pruebas de seguridad; OWASP; ASVS; vulnerabilidades.

1. INTRODUCCIÓN

Las aplicaciones web están sujetas a características del ambiente en que se ejecutan como el acceso abierto y conexiones sin estado, por lo que su seguridad es un tema de preocupación creciente tanto en la academia como en la industria [8]. Cuando estas aplicaciones administran información sensible de personas y negocios, el tema de la seguridad se vuelve aún más crítico [2].

Una vulnerabilidad es un defecto de seguridad en el software que puede ser usado maliciosamente por un atacante para ganar acceso al sistema o a la red [1]. En el año 2013 el Proyecto Abierto de Seguridad de Aplicaciones Web (OWASP, por sus siglas en inglés), publicó las diez vulnerabilidades de seguridad más comunes en aplicaciones industriales, con base en un conjunto de datos de ocho firmas que se especializan en seguridad de aplicaciones. Estas vulnerabilidades son: inyección de código maligno, administración de la sesión, vulneración de la autenticación, *cross-site scripting*, referencias directas a objetos de forma insegura, exposición de datos sensibles, control de acceso, *cross-site request forgery*, utilización de componentes con problemas conocidos, y redireccionamiento y reenvíos no validados [3]. En el año 2014 el OWASP publicó la última versión del estándar para verificación de la seguridad de aplicaciones (ASVS, por sus siglas en inglés), el cual tiene tres niveles de verificación: oportunista (nivel 1), estándar (nivel 2) y avanzado (nivel 3) [4]. El nivel 1 contiene 45 verificaciones de seguridad divididas en 9 requerimientos.

Las pruebas de seguridad pueden ser utilizadas para identificar vulnerabilidades en una aplicación web. Las técnicas más utilizadas son las pruebas de penetración y el análisis de código [1]. Las pruebas de penetración consisten en ejecutar una aplicación web de forma remota para encontrar vulnerabilidades, con los mismos permisos que tendría un usuario final y sin saber cómo funciona la aplicación por dentro. El análisis de código consiste en revisar el código en busca de vulnerabilidades, sin ejecutarlo. Esta técnica es muy efectiva cuando es realizada por expertos en seguridad, aunque también existen herramientas automatizadas que apoyan el proceso.

Los objetivos de este estudio fueron: (1) investigar la aplicabilidad del nivel 1 del estándar ASVS a una aplicación web de la industria financiera, por parte de analistas de calidad del software no expertos en seguridad, (2) caracterizar las vulnerabilidades de seguridad encontradas y (3) analizar la efectividad en la cobertura del estándar. Para lograr estos objetivos, nos planteamos las siguientes preguntas de investigación:

RQ 1 ¿En qué grado se puede aplicar el nivel 1 del estándar ASVS? Esta pregunta se subdividió en tres preguntas:

- RQ 1.1 ¿Qué grado de experticia en seguridad necesita un analista de calidad para aplicar el nivel 1 del estándar ASVS?
- RQ 1.2 ¿Cuánto esfuerzo toma la aplicación del nivel 1 del estándar ASVS?
- RQ 1.3 ¿Cuáles herramientas pueden apoyar la aplicación del nivel 1 del estándar ASVS y en qué medida?

RQ 2 ¿Cómo se caracterizan las vulnerabilidades encontradas al aplicar el nivel 1 del estándar ASVS? Esta pregunta se subdividió también en tres preguntas:

- RQ 2.1 ¿De qué tipo y severidad son las vulnerabilidades encontradas?
- RQ 2.2 ¿Cuánto esfuerzo requiere corregir las vulnerabilidades encontradas?

RQ 3 ¿Qué tan efectiva fue la cobertura del nivel 1 del estándar ASVS? Esta pregunta se subdividió en 2 preguntas:

- RQ 3.1 ¿Cómo se caracterizan las vulnerabilidades descubiertas por los expertos, en términos de su tipo, severidad, nivel del estándar y esfuerzo de reparación?
- RQ 3.2 ¿En qué medida validan los hallazgos de los expertos la cobertura del nivel 1 del estándar ASVS lograda por los analistas de calidad?

2. Metodología

2.1. Contexto

El estudio se realizó entre agosto de 2014 y marzo de 2015, en la empresa que para efectos de este reporte llamaremos ServiciosFinancieros[3], la cual desarrolla sistemas de información financieros (el primer autor laboraba en esta empresa al momento de realizar el estudio). En particular, se escogió una aplicación desarrollada en un 85 %, que usaba C# .NET, Html5, Javascript y Google Angular, una arquitectura RESTFul y una base de datos Oracle. En el contexto de esta aplicación, la evaluación por parte de expertos en seguridad era un requisito para liberar a producción. Debido a que el desarrollo de la aplicación no había considerado aspectos de seguridad desde un inicio, se identificó el riesgo de que la evaluación final de seguridad descubriera vulnerabilidades difíciles de solucionar, comprometiendo la fecha de salida a producción, que ya había sido pactada. Para mitigar este riesgo, se optó porque los analistas de calidad de la empresa realizaran pruebas de seguridad apoyadas en el estándar ASVS, con la consigna de lograr una alta cobertura del nivel 1 de dicho estándar.

2.2. Procedimiento y roles

La aplicación del nivel 1 del estándar estuvo a cargo de dos analistas de calidad sin experiencia previa en pruebas de seguridad (uno de los cuales es el primer autor), quienes utilizaron análisis manual de código y técnicas de pruebas de penetración con apoyo de herramientas en la ejecución del estándar. Una vez terminada la ejecución del nivel 1 del estándar, el equipo de desarrollo procedió a corregir las vulnerabilidades encontradas. Una vez probadas las soluciones a todas las vulnerabilidades, un equipo de expertos en seguridad realizó una evaluación de la aplicación, documentando sus hallazgos en un informe. Dicho informe fue revisado y discutido por el equipo de desarrollo en conjunto con uno de los expertos en seguridad. Los hallazgos se solucionaron en las semanas siguientes. Finalmente, el equipo de expertos colaboró con un ciclo de pruebas adicional para confirmar que las vulnerabilidades reportadas ya no eran reproducibles.

2.3. Recolección de datos

Para almacenar los datos relevantes al estudio, se usaron tres bitácoras (hojas de cálculo). La *bitácora de progreso* especificaba, para cada verificación del estándar, su estado (si pasó o falló), la razón del estado y la técnica o herramienta usada. La *bitácora de vulnerabilidades* registraba, para cada vulnerabilidad encontrada por un analista de calidad o por un experto en seguridad, su categoría, estado, severidad, prioridad, descripción, correspondencia con el estándar

[3] La empresa del caso que se presenta no ha autorizado a difundir su nombre, pero los autores han mostrado suficiente evidencia al comité de programa para afirmar que el reporte se formula a partir de datos recogidos en terreno.

(nivel) y esfuerzo requerido para arreglarla. La *bitácora de esfuerzo* registraba el esfuerzo requerido (en horas) para ejecutar cada requerimiento del nivel 1 del estándar, así como el estado de su ejecución. La información acerca del tiempo requerido para ejecutar el estándar y de las vulnerabilidades reportadas, se extrajo del Microsoft Team Foundation Server, herramienta utilizada para el reporte de defectos y gestión del proyecto.

2.4. Análisis y procesamiento de datos

Para responder RQ 1 se tomaron como insumos la bitácora de progreso y la bitácora de esfuerzo. Se calculó el porcentaje de cobertura del nivel 1 del estándar contando las verificaciones que se pudieron realizar y las que no. Para RQ 1.1, se extrajo un detalle del perfil de los analistas encargados de ejecutar el estándar, el entrenamiento requerido y las limitaciones encontradas. Para RQ 1.2, se graficó el esfuerzo invertido en cada requerimiento del estándar, para visualizar cuáles requerimientos tomaron más tiempo. Para RQ 1.3, se contó la cantidad de verificaciones que fueron apoyadas por herramientas y se calculó la contribución de cada herramienta a la aplicación del estándar (cuántas verificaciones apoyó). Las herramientas fueron seleccionadas con base en las sugerencias de la guía de pruebas de OWASP[6]. Adicionalmente se incluyó AppScan [7], debido al amplio uso que tiene en la empresa donde se realizó el estudio.

Para responder RQ 2 se utilizó la bitácora de vulnerabilidades. Para RQ 2.1, se elaboraron gráficos con las vulnerabilidades encontradas por los analistas, agrupadas por requerimiento (tipo) y severidad. Para RQ 2.2, se graficó el esfuerzo requerido para resolver las vulnerabilidades, agrupado por requerimiento.

Para responder RQ 3 también se utilizó la bitácora de vulnerabilidades. Para RQ 3.1, el análisis fue muy similar al de RQ 2, con la adición de un gráfico de distribución de las vulnerabilidades según el nivel del estándar al que corresponden. Esta distribución permitió abordar RQ 3.2, mediante el conteo de las vulnerabilidades encontradas por los expertos en seguridad que debieron haber sido detectadas por los analistas de calidad.

3. Resultados

3.1. Resultados de RQ 1: aplicación del nivel 1 del estándar ASVS

Para el software estudiado, fue posible ejecutar el nivel 1 del estándar en un 98 %, según el reporte de los analistas. La única verificación que no se pudo ejecutar fue la de seguridad de las comunicaciones, por restricciones de infraestructura impuestas por el departamento de TI. El Cuadro 1 muestra el resultado de ejecutar las 45 verificaciones del nivel 1. Una verificación 'aprobada' significa que sí existía el respectivo control en la aplicación; una 'fallida' significa que se descubrió al menos una vulnerabilidad; y 'no aplica' significa que el control no existía en la aplicación por razones justificadas (no era una vulnerabilidad).

Cuadro 1. Resultados de la ejecución de las verificaciones del nivel 1 del estándar.

Estado de la verificación	Cantidad
Aprobada	24
Fallida	17
No aplica	3
No ejecutada	1
Total	45

RQ 1.1 - Grado de experticia en seguridad. Los analistas que ejecutaron el estándar tenían entre 2 y 3 años de experiencia en pruebas de software, pero no tenían experticia en pruebas de seguridad. Por lo tanto, se les dio un entrenamiento (de dos horas) sobre las diez vulnerabilidades más comunes reportadas por OWASP. Por otro lado, los analistas utilizaron características puntuales de las herramientas ZAP[5], AppScan, RequestMaker[9] y herramientas de desarrollo del navegador web para apoyar la aplicación del estándar. Cada analista tuvo dos días para adiestrarse en el uso de estas herramientas. En síntesis, el grado de experticia en seguridad que necesitaron los analistas de calidad para aplicar el nivel 1 del estándar fue muy poco (capacitación de 2 horas sobre las vulnerabilidades más comunes y 2 días para aprender a usar las herramientas).

RQ 1.2 - Esfuerzo de aplicación del nivel 1 del estándar. La aplicación del nivel 1 del estándar requirió un total de 95 horas. La Fig. 1 muestra la distribución del esfuerzo (en horas) por requerimiento del estándar. Los requerimientos "Administración de la sesión" y "Manejo de entradas maliciosas" representaron conjuntamente un 55 % del esfuerzo total.

Figura 1. Distribución del esfuerzo requerido para aplicar cada requerimiento del nivel 1 del estándar.

RQ 1.3 - Herramientas de apoyo a la aplicación del nivel 1 del estándar. Las herramientas contempladas en esta investigación apoyaron un 48 % de las verificaciones realizadas. Las herramientas fueron utilizadas con diversos propósitos, entre ellos, dar exhaustividad a las pruebas de inyección de código, atrapar tráfico HTTP, generar peticiones personalizadas al servidor y listar las *urls* del sitio para realizar pruebas de accesos no autorizados. La Fig. 2 muestra la contribución de cada herramienta a la aplicación del estándar, en términos de la cantidad de verificaciones que apoyó. AppScan resultó ser la que apoyó la mayor cantidad de verificaciones. En algunos casos, varias herramientas apoyaron una misma verificación.

3.2. Resultados de RQ 2: vulnerabilidades de nivel 1 del estándar

Se encontraron vulnerabilidades en 6 de los 9 requerimientos evaluados por los analistas de calidad, siendo "Autenticación" y "Control de acceso" los requerimientos con más vulnerabilidades. Es interesante que no se encontraran vulnerabilidades en el requerimiento "Manejo de entradas maliciosas", a pesar de ser el que encabeza la lista de vulnerabilidades más comunes de OWASP. Esto puede atribuirse a que durante el desarrollo de la aplicación, las pruebas funcionales validaron consistentemente que no se permitieran entradas maliciosas tanto a nivel de interfaz de usuario como a nivel de parámetros en las peticiones al servidor.

RQ 2.1 - Tipo y severidad de las vulnerabilidades. La severidad de las vulnerabilidades fue asignada por el Departamento de Seguridad de la empresa. El tipo de la vulnerabilidad está dado por el requerimiento al cual se asocia. La Fig. 3 muestra la cantidad y severidad de las vulnerabilidades encontradas por requerimiento (tipo). Los requerimientos "Autenticación" y "Control de acceso" exhibieron la mayor cantidad de vulnerabilidades y la mayor concentración de severidades críticas. "Control de acceso" concentró las vulnerabilidades de seve-

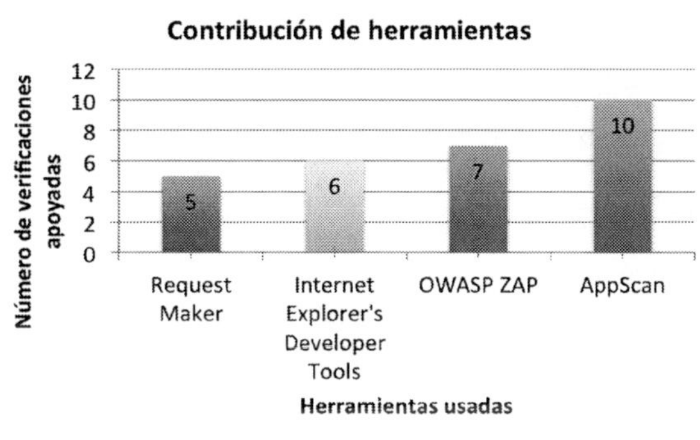

Figura 2. Contribución de cada herramienta a la aplicación del nivel 1 del estándar.

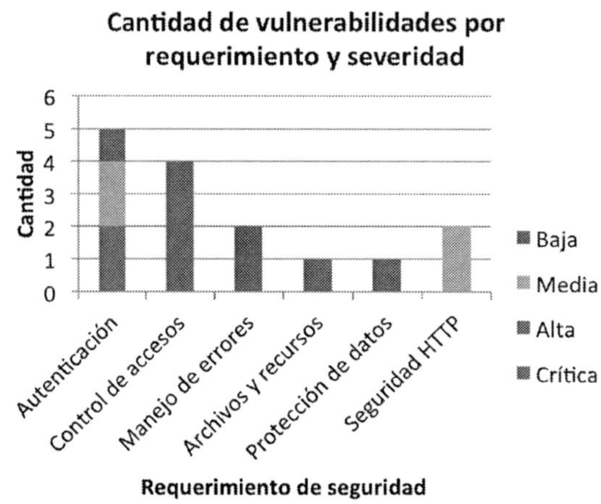

Figura 3. Severidad y cantidad de vulnerabilidades por requerimiento.

ridad más alta: 3 críticas y 1 alta. En total hubo 5 vulnerabilidades de severidad crítica, 3 de severidad alta, 4 de severidad media y 3 de severidad baja.

RQ 2.2 - Esfuerzo de corrección de las vulnerabilidades. La corrección de las 15 vulnerabilidades encontradas por los analistas requirió un esfuerzo equivalente a 55 días de trabajo (con 8 horas diarias). La Fig. 4 muestra la distribución del esfuerzo de corrección de vulnerabilidades por requerimiento. Un resultado notable es que el esfuerzo requerido para solucionar las vulnerabilidades en los requerimientos "Autenticación" y "Control de acceso" suma alrededor de 48 días, es decir, un 90 % del esfuerzo total.

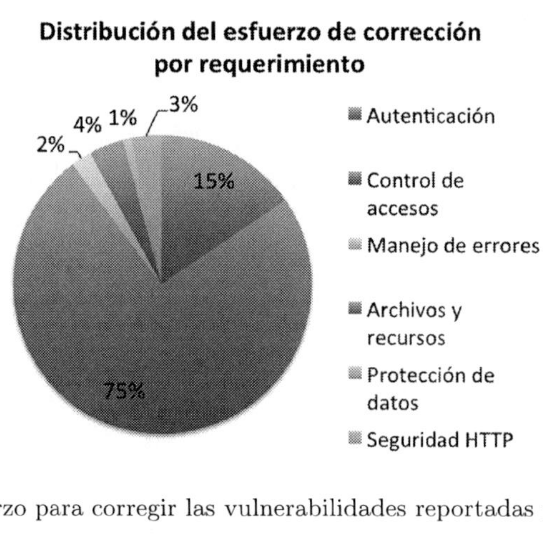

Figura 4. Esfuerzo para corregir las vulnerabilidades reportadas por los analistas.

3.3. Resultados de RQ 3: cobertura del nivel 1 del estándar ASVS

La evaluación realizada por los expertos en seguridad arrojó un total de 11 vulnerabilidades, de las cuales solo 3 correspondían al nivel 1 del estándar (y eran de baja severidad).

RQ 3.1 - Caracterización de las vulnerabilidades descubiertas por los expertos en seguridad. Los expertos en seguridad detectaron vulnerabilidades en los requerimientos de "Autenticación", "Control de accesos", "Lógica del negocio", "Seguridad de las comunicaciones", "Protección de datos", "Seguridad HTTP" y "Administración de la sesión". Una buena parte de las vulnerabilidades descubiertas tuvieron que ver con certificados de seguridad, cifrado de las comunicaciones, protocolos de seguridad en la capa de transporte y configuraciones del servidor de aplicaciones. El Cuadro 2 muestra la distribución de las vulnerabilidades detectadas por nivel del estándar y por severidad. Se observa que la mayoría (55 %) de las vulnerabilidades detectadas fue de nivel 2, y en mucho menor grado se detectaron vulnerabilidades de nivel 1 (27 %) y nivel 3 (18 %). También se observa que las vulnerabilidades de severidad media y baja representaron conjuntamente un 55 % del total, mientras que las de severidad alta representaron un 45 %. Un hallazgo muy interesante fue que el esfuerzo de corrección de estas vulnerabilidades (descubiertas por expertos) fue mucho menor (6,2 días) que el de las vulnerabilidades encontradas por los analistas de calidad (55 días). Esto se debe a que una gran parte de los hallazgos de los expertos se solucionaron a través de modificaciones en la configuración del servidor de aplicaciones y de su entorno de ejecución. Por ejemplo, vulnerabilidades relacionadas con los protocolos SSL, TLS y HTTPS fueron reportadas por los expertos y corregidas con facilidad. Por su parte, algunas vulnerabilidades reportadas por los analistas de calidad requirieron correcciones en todos los controladores de la aplicación, las cuales fueron muy costosas. El requerimiento que más esfuerzo de corrección necesitó fue "Protección de datos", con 2 días. El esfuerzo requerido para corregir las 3 vulnerabilidades de nivel 1 del estándar fue de tan solo 1,75 días, lo cual se considera bastante bueno pues no afectó significativamente el cronograma del proyecto. Estas 3 vulnerabilidades de nivel 1 fueron de severidad baja.

RQ 3.2 - Análisis de cobertura. La revisión por parte de los expertos en seguridad permitió identificar vulnerabilidades en el nivel 1 del estándar que los

Cuadro 2. Cantidad de vulnerabilidades reportadas por los expertos en seguridad, agrupadas por nivel y severidad.

Nivel del estándar	Sev. alta	Sev. media	Sev. baja	Total
Nivel 1 (Oportunista)	-	-	3	3
Nivel 2 (Estándar)	3	2	1	6
Nivel 3 (Avanzado)	2	-	-	2
Total	5	2	4	11

analistas de calidad pasaron por alto. Dicha evaluación también recalcó que las validaciones de los niveles 2 y 3 del estándar son necesarias para aprobar una evaluación de seguridad rigurosa. A continuación se listan los resultados más relevantes de la evaluación realizada por los expertos.

- Los expertos no lograron descubrir vulnerabilidades de severidad alta ni media en el nivel 1 del estándar (solo detectaron tres vulnerabilidades de baja severidad). Esto respalda que las pruebas realizadas por los analistas de calidad fueron altamente efectivas en cubrir el nivel 1 del estándar.
- El esfuerzo requerido para reparar las vulnerabilidades del nivel 1 del estándar detectadas por los expertos fue solo un 3 % del esfuerzo requerido para reparar las vulnerabilidades encontradas por los analistas de calidad. El esfuerzo total de reparación de todas las vulnerabilidades descubiertas por los expertos representó el 11 % del esfuerzo de reparación de las vulnerabilidades encontradas por los analistas. Este resultado fue el más importante desde el punto de vista del proyecto, ya que permitió liberar la aplicación a producción en la fecha prevista y con los arreglos exigidos por los expertos en seguridad.
- Los expertos lograron descubrir cinco vulnerabilidades de alta severidad en los niveles 2 y 3 del estándar, lo que realza la necesidad de someter la aplicación a una evaluación rigurosa por parte de expertos en seguridad, en lugar de conformarse con la cobertura del nivel 1 del estándar alcanzada por los analistas de calidad.

4. Conclusiones

Este trabajo exploró la aplicación del nivel 1 del estándar ASVS de OWASP a una aplicación web financiera. En una primera etapa, dos analistas de calidad sin experiencia previa en seguridad ejecutaron las verificaciones del nivel 1 del estándar, apoyados en herramientas existentes. En una segunda etapa, los desarrolladores corrigieron todas las vulnerabilidades encontradas por los analistas. En una tercera etapa, un grupo independiente de expertos en seguridad evaluaron la aplicación.

Los resultados de este estudio aportan evidencia de que para ejecutar el nivel 1 del estándar ASVS no es necesario tener experticia previa en el área de seguridad, pues los analistas de calidad que nunca habían hecho pruebas de seguridad fueron capaces de completar un 98 % del nivel 1 del estándar en 95 horas de esfuerzo.

En el contexto de la aplicación bajo estudio, la mayoría de las vulnerabilidades de nivel 1 encontradas por los analistas fueron de autenticación y control de acceso (ambas suman 9 de un total de 15 vulnerabilidades). Los requerimientos "Control de acceso" y "Autenticación" del estándar concentraron las vulnerabilidades de mayor severidad y mayor esfuerzo de corrección. Los demás requerimientos del nivel 1 del estándar presentaron vulnerabilidades con costos de corrección más bajos (por debajo de los dos días). Esto da pie para recomendar que las pruebas de control de acceso y autenticación se realicen en fases tempranas del desarrollo, evitando que sean detectadas tardíamente, cuando el costo de reparación es muy alto.

Asimismo, este caso de estudio revela que el nivel 1 del estándar ASVS deja por fuera una serie de verificaciones importantes (protocolos de seguridad, certificados de seguridad y cifrado), asociadas al requerimiento de "Seguridad de las comunicaciones", que son vitales para la puesta en producción de aplicaciones web con requerimientos altos de seguridad.

La evaluación realizada por el equipo de expertos detectó vulnerabilidades en el nivel 1 del estándar que los analistas de calidad no lograron encontrar. Sin embargo, dichas vulnerabilidades fueron reportadas con una severidad baja y tuvieron un esfuerzo de reparación menor a 2 días.

Referencias

1. Awang, N., and Manaf, A. Detecting vulnerabilities in web applications using automated black box and manual penetration testing. In *Advances in Security of Information and Communication Networks*, Springer Berlin Heidelberg (2013), 230–239.
2. Dukes, L., Yuan, X., and Akowuah, F. A case study on web application security testing with tools and manual testing. In *Southeastcon, 2013 Proceedings of IEEE* (April 2013), 1–6.
3. Foundation, T. O. Owasp top 10 - 2013. los diez riesgos mas criticos en aplicaciones web. `https://www.owasp.org/images/5/5f/OWASP_Top_10_-_2013_Final_-_Espa\%C3\%B1ol.pdf`, 2013. [Online; accessed Dec-2014].
4. Foundation, T. O. Application security verification standard (2014). `https://www.owasp.org/images/5/58/OWASP_ASVS_Version_2.pdf`, 2014. [Online; accessed Dec-2014].
5. Foundation, T. O. Owasp zed attack proxy project. `https://www.owasp.org/index.php/OWASP_Zed_Attack_Proxy_Project`, 2014. [Online; accessed Dec-2014].
6. Foundation, T. O. Testing guide introduction. `https://www.owasp.org/index.php/Testing_Guide_Introduction#Testing_Techniques_Explained`, 2014. [Online; accessed Dec-2014].
7. IBM. Ibm security appscan. `www.ibm.com/software/products/en/appscan`, 2014. [Online; accessed Dec-2014].
8. Mao, C. Experiences in security testing for web-based applications. In *Proceedings of the 2Nd International Conference on Interaction Sciences: Information Technology, Culture and Human*, ICIS '09, ACM (New York, NY, USA, 2009), 326–330.
9. Nurminen, J. Request maker download site. `https://chrome.google.com/webstore/detail/request-maker/kajfghlhfkcocafkcjlajldicbikpgnp`, 2014. [Online; accessed Dec-2014].

Herramienta para la generación automática de software en PHP

Leonardo Bravo, Beatriz Marín

Escuela de informática y telecomunicaciones,
Universidad Diego Portales, Chile
{leonardo.bravo,beatriz.marin}@mail.udp.cl

Resumen. El desarrollo tradicional de software requiere de programadores que realicen la codificación, por lo que el tiempo de trabajo podrían ser horas, semanas o meses, dependiendo las habilidades y buenas prácticas del equipo. Este trabajo presenta una herramienta que permite generar de forma automática una plataforma web a partir de un modelo conceptual, poniendo de manifiesto el desarrollo de software dirigido por modelos (MDD). La plataforma web generada por esta herramienta corresponde a una plataforma PHP, y no requiere de la intervención de un programador para poder ser puesta en producción, sólo bastará poseer un servicio web y una base de datos SQLite, disminuyendo así el tiempo de codificación.

1 Introducción

Hoy en día, nadie defiende la idea de programar en ensamblador, pues se consideran las ventajas de los lenguajes de programación de alto nivel [8]. De igual forma, MDD propone estar un paso más arriba en el nivel de abstracción con lo que respecta al desarrollo de software. La propuesta de MDD es generar un modelo definido por constructores conceptuales que permitan representar un software de forma completa, y en base a este modelo, generar de forma automática el código de un software en su totalidad, disminuyendo los tiempos de programación y aumentando la calidad del software generado [9].

Considerando que una herramienta MDD permite reducir tiempo y otros costos monetarios en el desarrollo de software, sería conveniente que se licenciara bajo software libre para facilitar su adquisición, estudio y perfeccionamiento.

El objetivo de la herramienta presentada en este documento es la generación automática de sitios web, para esto se ha seleccionado PHP [6] como lenguaje de programación para construirlos. La razón para usar PHP se debe a que desde el 2010 a la fecha es uno de los lenguajes más utilizados para el desarrollo de éstos [7], ya que más del 80% de los sitios web están programados con PHP.

El resto del artículo esta organizado como sigue: la sección 2 presenta un resumen de los trabajos relacionados, la sección 3 presenta el diseño del herramienta MDD que permite generar código en lenguaje PHP, la sección 4 presenta un caso de estudio que demuestra la aplicabilidad de herramienta, y finalmente, la sección 5 presenta las principales conclusiones y trabajos futuros.

2 Trabajos relacionados

Para identificar los trabajos relacionados, se realizó una revisión sistemática según el proceso definido por Kitchenham [2], para identificar de forma objetiva ¿qué editores gráficos que generen código existen?.

La búsqueda se realizó en las bibliotecas digitales de IEEE, Springer y ACM y se encontraron en total 123 documentos. Un resumen de las herramientas encontradas se presentan en [18] y un extracto de estos trabajos se pueden ver en la Tabla 1.

Tabla 1: Extracto de las herramientas encontradas

Nombre	**Descripción**
Application herramienta [10]	Codifica en Java de forma completa el software modelado, su lenguaje de modelado posee un modelo de presentación, para especificar elementos de interacción entre el software y el usuario, es opensource, por lo que se puede descargar y estudiar su código.
Rational Rose [11]	Codifica en Java de forma completa el software modelado, utiliza UML como lenguaje de modelado, posee una licencia restrictiva.
MoDisco Eclipse [12]	Esta basado en Eclipse, genera código en Java ejecutable completo, utiliza UML como lenguaje de modelado, es Opensource.
ArcStyler [10]	Codifica en Java y .Net de forma completa el software modelado, utiliza UML como lenguaje de modelado, es Opensource.
Kermeta [15]	Codifica bajo su propio lenguaje de programación (lenguaje interpretado), posee problemas de portabilidad, utiliza un lenguaje de modelado propio, no posee modelo de presentación, es Opensource.
WebRatio [1]	Genera código Java y HTML, utiliza el lenguaje de modelado WebML, es Opensource, orientado en la generación de sitio web.
ArgoUML [15]	Genera código PHP, esta basado en Elcipse, utiliza UML como lenguaje de modelado, es Opensource, orientado en la generación de páginas web.
PervGT [16]	Codifica en Java de forma completa el software modelado, esta construido sobre Eclipse Modeling Framework (EMF) [3] y Graphical Modeling Framework (GMF) [4], posee su propio lenguaje de modelado llamado PervML, orientado para el desarrollo de servicios web para demótica.
UML2PHP [19]	Genera automáticamente aplicaciones PHP completas a partir de diagramas de clase UML. La aplicación generada ofrece todas las funcionalidades CRUD (Create/Read/Update/Delete) básicas para mostrar y manipular los datos de la aplicación.

Estas herramientas MDD generan principalmente código en Java, utilizan lenguajes de modelado como UML ó OO-Method para el modelado del software y una minoría codifica de forma completa el software, requiriendo la intervención de un programador para crear un software que pueda ser puesto en producción.

Dentro de las herramientas observados no se encontró uno que fuera igual a la presentada en este documento, es decir una herramienta que genere sitios web dinámicos en PHP, que no requiera la intervención de un programador para completar el código, listo para ser puesto en producción, en base un lenguaje de modelado que posea un modelo de presentación.

3 Diseño de la herramienta

La herramienta propuesta consiste en un editor de modelos y un compilador a PHP, esta herramienta es llamada MetaWebDesign. El editor de modelos, utiliza un lenguaje de modelado basado en OO-Method [14] que posee constructores conceptuales para el modelado de un sitio web. El compilador a PHP, transformará el XML generado por el editor de modelos en un sitio web codificado sobre PHP y una base de datos SQL. En resumen, el editor de modelos permite modelar las clases, las interfaces gráficas como las páginas web, el formato con el que se presentará el contenido (tabla, combobox, imagen), junto con menús de navegación.

3.1 Editor de modelos

El editor de modelos fue construido como una aplicación de Eclipse utilizando los frameworks EMF [3] y GMF [4]. Para el lenguaje de modelado se construyó un metamodelo, presentado en la Figura 1.

El metamodelo presentado en la Figura 1, posee Clases que contendrán los objetos que administrará el sitio web; Servicios de creación, destrucción, modificación, visualización de un objeto, visualización de la población de objetos; atributos que pueden ser derivados o no derivados. Los atributos derivados serán los que nacen en función de los valores de otros atributos, por lo tanto se debe especificar una fórmula para generarlos. En el caso de la herramienta, esta fórmula tendrá la sintaxis SQL, en donde el nombre de las columnas serán los atributos y el nombre de las tablas son los nombres de las clases. Los atributos no derivados, son los que poseen un valor propio. Relaciones que permiten vincular clases entre sí se transformarán por el compilador en llaves foráneas dentro de la base de datos. Cada clase podrá poseer restricciones, que pueden condicionar la ejecución de un servicio de creación, actualización, según un valor establecido.

También, el metamodelo posee elementos que ayudarán a definir páginas o menús de navegación que permiten modelar elementos de interacción con el usuario. Dentro de una página se podrán desplegar atributos y definir cómo se presentarán (tabla, imagen, texto). Además, dentro de una página se podrán

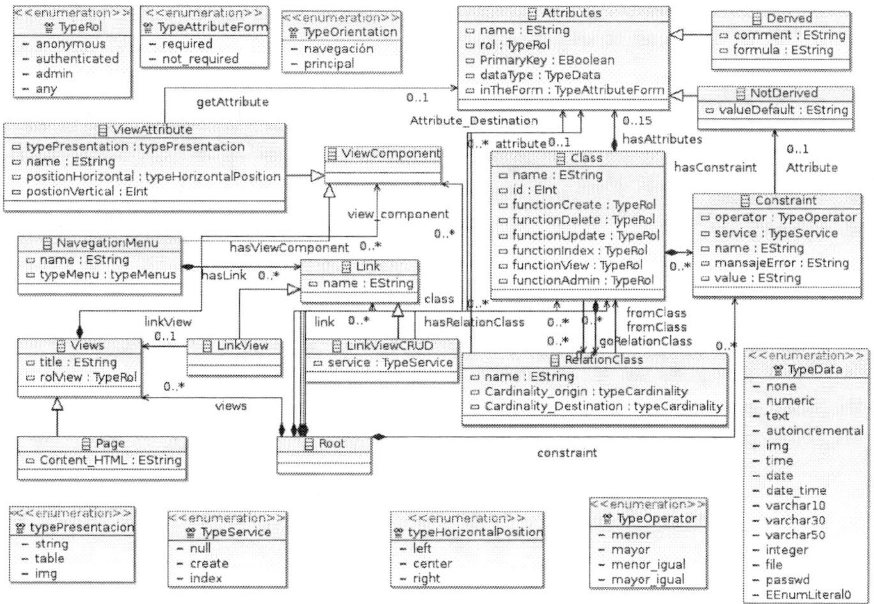

Fig. 1. Meta-modelo editor de modelos.

definir menús de navegación con links hacia vistas de servicios u otras páginas modeladas. Con los constructores conceptuales del metamodelo mencionados y utilizando GMF se ha creado el editor de modelos de la Figura 2.

El editor de modelos presentado en la Figura 2, posee un área de modelado indicada con un número uno; una paleta con los elementos de modelado indicada con el número dos; un área de configuración de los elementos modelados (asignación de nombre, tipos de variables, valores por defecto, entre otras) indicada con el número tres; una opción para compilar a PHP el modelo generado, indicada con el número cuatro.

Compilador El compilador se encuentra programado en Java y genera un sitio web programado en PHP usando como base el framework Yii para integrar el compilador con el editor de modelos. El compilador se ha diseñado como un plugin de eclipse, que carga como un botón sobre la barra de herramientas del editor de modelos, tal como se puede observar en la Figura 2.

El compilador utiliza código del framework Yii para la generación de los modelos, controladores y vistas de los servicios de creación, modificación, destrucción, visualización de un objeto, visualización de la población de objetos y la búsqueda de uno o más objetos. Sobre esta base generada, se procede a modificar la visualización de los servicios, cargando widgets para el despliegue

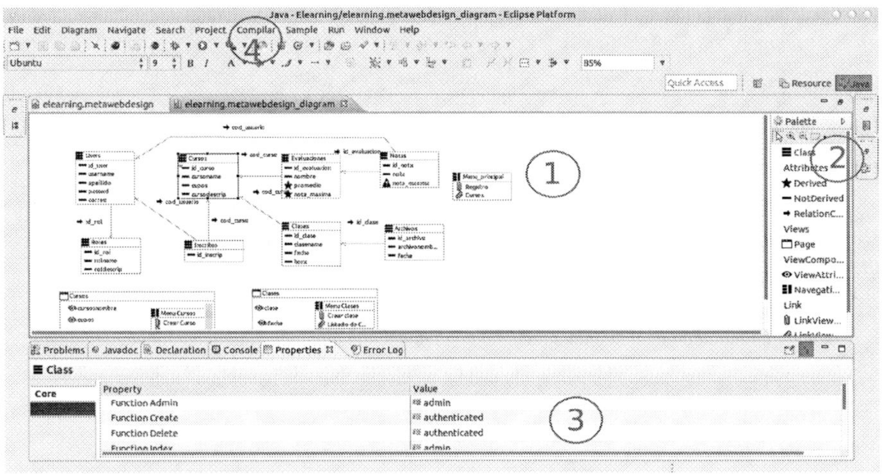

Fig. 2. Editor de modelos

de calendarios, hora y áreas de texto; modificar los modelos para la aplicación de restricciones; modificar los controladores para configurar el control de acceso a estos por parte de los usuarios; generar páginas modeladas y generar menús de navegación.

El compilador esta compuesto principalmente por los siguientes cinco módulos:

- **Compilar.java:** Este programa contiene todas las operaciones realizadas por el compilador, invoca al resto de los módulos programados. Es quien orquesta todo el proceso de compilación. Es capaz de detectar sitios web generados anteriormente, respaldándolos ante una nueva generación de código y también detecta uno o más proyectos generados por el editor de modelos ofreciendo la opción de seleccionar uno para ser compilado.
- **ReadModel.java:** Este programa se encarga de la validación y lectura del XML que contiene el modelo generado. Revisa la estructura del modelo, alertando e indicando dónde se está produciendo el defecto en el caso de que exista uno.
- **SQLite.java** Este programa se encarga de generar la base de datos del sitio web, con sus respectivas tablas, atributos, índices, llaves foráneas y vistas.
- **PHP.java:** Este programa se encarga de generar el código PHP, utiliza el framework Yii como base para la generación de los Modelos, Controladores y vistas de los servicios CRUD. Además, se encarga de modificar alguna de estas vistas añadiendo widgets para el despliegue de calendarios, imágenes, áreas de texto editables, DropDown, entre otras.
- **ExecuteShellComand.java:** Este programa se encarga de ejecutar procedimientos en Bash generados para la generación de la base de datos en SQLite,

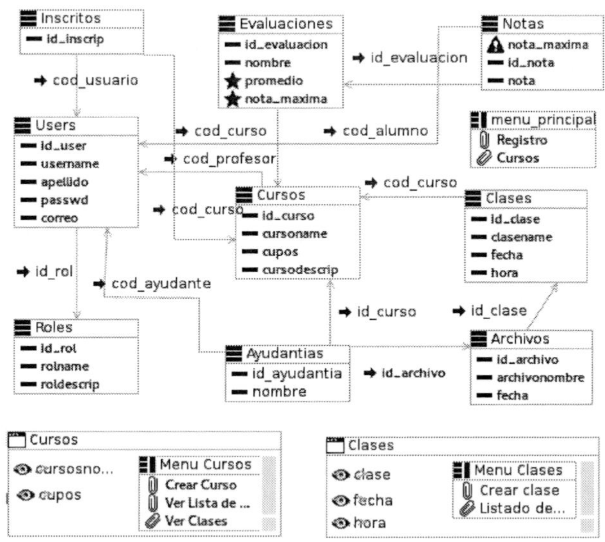

Fig. 3. Modelo Elearning

la inserción de datos, junto con algunas instrucciones para la configuración del sitio web.

La herramienta MetaWebDesign se encuentra disponible para la instalación y descarga en github, `https://github.com/MetaWebDesign`, bajo licencia GPL V3.

4 Caso de estudio

Para probar la herramienta MetaWebDesign, se ha diseñado un caso de estudio que consiste en una plataforma elearning, en la que profesores y ayudantes pueden administrar sus clases, subir material de estudio y llevar un registro de las evaluaciones realizadas. Cada curso posee una cantidad de clases, ayudantías, evaluaciones y documentos.

El sitio web elearning generado con la herramienta, modelado en la Figura 3, fue puesto a pruebas de validación y verificación de requisitos funcionales y no funcionales. Los resultados entregaron que éste cumple con un 100% de los requisitos funcionales, es decir cumple con 52 de 52 y un 85.71% de los requisitos no funcionales, es decir cumple con 6 de 7. El código generado se puede apreciar en la Figura 4, que corresponde a las vistas de creación, visualización de un objeto (una Clase), visualización de una población de objetos (Clases).

Los requisitos funcionales, consistieron en servicios de creación, modificación, destrucción, visualización de un objeto, visualización de la población de objetos,

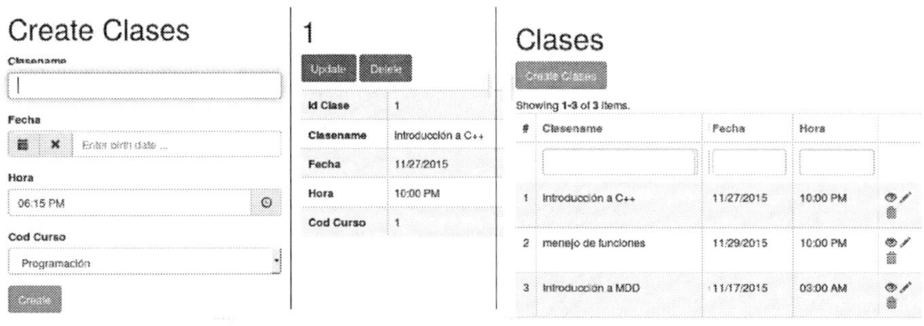

Fig. 4. Sitio web Elearning

búsqueda de un objeto, además de aspectos de navegación como links para crear clases, ayudantías y adjuntar archivos. Dentro de los requisitos no funcionales se encuentran aspectos como Seguridad (visualización horizontal, inyección SLQ, Cross site scripting, Cross site request), Mantenibilidad (Sitio web MVC), Portabilidad (sitio web responsivo), Usabilidad (navegación).

Si bien ha sido posible evaluar la aplicabilidad de la herramienta para el desarrollo de sitios web, la versión actual de esta posee algunas limitaciones en áreas que no fueron abordadas dentro de los alcances iniciales del proyecto. Dentro de las limitaciones, se encuentran:

- Sólo esta disponible para GNU Linux, debido a que el sistema operativo facilita por medio de procedimientos Bash la automatización de la instalación y configuración del entono de desarrollo web.
- No soporta una llave primaria compuesta, debido a que Yii por defecto trabaja sólo con un único identificador por clase.
- Sólo trabaja con base de datos SQLite, a futuro se podrían agregar opciones para PostgreSQL, MariaDB, entre otras.

5 Análisis General

A continuación se presenta un análisis general de MetaWebDesign respecto de las herramientas presentadas en la Tabla 1.

- **Application Framework**:
  - **Similitudes:**Genera código ejecutable completo, posee elementos de un modelo de presentación, es Opensource.
  - **Diferencias:**Genera código Java, utiliza un modelo estático, no esta orientado a aplicaciones web y no se encuentra vigente.
- **Rational Rose**
  - **Similitudes:** Genera código ejecutable completo.

    - **Diferencias:** No es Opensource, genera código en Java, utiliza lenguaje de modelado UML, el costo de adquisición puede ir desde los 7494 Euros, además no posee modelo de presentación.
- **MoDisco Eclipse**
    - **Similitudes:** Esta basado en Eclipse, es Opensource, genera código ejecutable completo.
    - **Diferencias:** Genera código en Java, utiliza lenguaje de modelado UML, orientado en la modernización de sistemas legacy y no posee modelo de presentación.
- **ArcStyler**
    - **Similitudes:** Genera código ejecutable completo.
    - **Diferencias:** No es Opensource, genera código a Java y .Net, utiliza lenguaje de modelado UML. No posee modelo de presentación y no se encuentra vigente.
- **Kermeta**
    - **Similitudes:** Genera código ejecutable completo, Opensource.
    - **Diferencias:** No posee modelo de presentación , genera código ejecutable bajo su propio lenguaje interpretado, lo que puede generar problemas de portabilidad o soporte de terceros, no posee modelo de presentación y no se encuentra vigente.
- **WebRatio**
    - **Similitudes:** Genera código ejecutable de forma completa, Opensource, posee modelo de presentación, genera código SQL
    - **Diferencias:** Utiliza el lenguaje de modelado WebML, genera código Java, HTML. Genera paginas web estáticas.
- **ArgoUML**
    - **Similitudes:** Genera código PHP, está basado en Eclipse.
    - **Diferencias:** Utiliza lenguaje de modelado UML. No posee modelo de presentación, no genera código completo.
- **PervGT**
    - **Similitudes:** Genera código ejecutable completo, es Opensource, posee un modelo de presentación, esta construido sobre EMF (Eclipse Modeling Framework) y GMF (Graphical Modeling Framework)
    - **Diferencias:** Genera código Java, utiliza un lenguaje de modelado propio llamado PervML, no esta orientado para aplicaciones web, esta orientado a la demótica. El proyecto no posee nuevas contribuciones desde el 2007.
- **UML2PHP**
    - **Similitudes:** genera automáticamente aplicaciones PHP completas a partir de diagramas de clase UML. El sitio web generado en PHP utiliza un framework para la generación de CRUD.
    - **Diferencias:** Los formularios y vistas posee una serie de widgets programados junto con temas responsivos y estilos usando Bootstrap, UML2PHP no.

6 Conclusiones

La herramienta MetaWebDesign es una opción para el desarrollo de sitios web, que por medio de las pruebas realizadas, demostró empíricamente ventajas en en el tiempo utilizado para la generación de código y la base de datos, tardando segundos, en comparación a un desarrollo tradicional, que hubiera tardado horas, días o meses, creando un software listo para poner en producción.

Utilizar un framework como Yii en el compilador ha facilitado la integración de widgets en formularios que hacen más operable el sitio web generado, y asegura que los datos ingresados posean un formato válido. El tener a disposición widgets ya programados ahorra horas de programación, concentrando los esfuerzos en la integración de éstos con las vistas, junto con generación y edición de componentes, según los aspectos modelados. También ha ayudado a poseer una arquitectura MVC entregando un orden en el código del proyecto, facilitando la ubicación de los componentes y funciones de éste, con el fin de realizar mantenciones para agregar nuevas características o corregir errores.

Como trabajo futuro, queda mejorar las validaciones realizadas por el editor de modelos, por ejemplo caracteres no válidos en los nombres, mejorar la forma de generar fórmulas en los atributos derivados, de manera que ésta se genere de forma automática, y mejorar el control de acceso según roles. Si bien MetaWebDesign cuenta con un sistema de administración de accesos a servicio y vistas según rol, también no posee medidas de control para la visualización horizontal. Además, se espera aplicar MetaWebDesign en casos reales.

7 Agradecimientos

Este trabajo ha sido financiado por Universidad Diego Portales y FONDECYT (Chile) bajo el proyecto TESTMODE Ref. 11121395.

Referencias

1. Brambilla, M., Comai ,S., Fraternali, P., Matera, M., "Designing web applications with webml and webratio", in Springer Human-Computer Interaction Series pp 221-261, 2008.
2. Kitchenham, B., Pretorius, R., Budgen, D., Orereton, B., Turner, M., Niazi, M., and Linkman, S.. Systematic literature reviews in software engineering - A tertiary study. Inf. Softw. Technol. 52, 8, pp 792-805, 2010.
3. Eclipse modeling framework, `http://www.eclipse.org/modeling/emf`
4. Eclipse graphical modeling framework, `http://eclipse.org/modeling/gmp/`
5. OWASP Foundation - Top 10 2013, `https://www.owasp.org/index.php/Top_10_2013-Top_10`
6. PHP , `www.php.net`
7. W3Techs, Historical trends in the usage of server-side programming languages for websites `http://w3techs.com/technologies/history_overview/programming_language`

8. Kahanwal, B. - "Abstraction level taxonomy of programming language frameworks", International Journal of Programming Languages and Applications, Volume 3, No. 4, pp. 1-12, 2013.
9. Selic, B., "The pragmatics of model-driven development," in IEEE Software, pp.19-25, Sept.-Oct. 2003.
10. Choi, J., Yang, S., Jeong, J. "Application framework for multi platform mobile application software development, 11th International Conference on "Advanced Communication Technology, 2009. ICACT 2009, Phoenix Park, 2009, pp. 208-213.
11. Afonso, M., Vogel, R. and Teixeira, J., "From code centric to model centric software engineering: practical case study of MDD infusion in a systems integration company," Fourth and Third International Workshop on Model-Based Development of Computer-Based Systems and Model-Based Methodologies for Pervasive and Embedded Software, 2006. MBD/MOMPES 2006, Potsdam, 2006, pp. 10 pp.-134.
12. Améndola, F., Favre, L., "Adapting CRM Systems for Mobile Platforms: An MDA Perspective, 2013 14th ACIS International Conference on "Software Engineering, Artificial Intelligence, Networking and Parallel/Distributed Computing (SNPD), Honolulu, HI, 2013, pp. 323-328.
13. Duarte, J., Tonanez, M., Cernuzzi, L., Lopez, O., "Evaluation of software development through an MDA tool: a case study," in IEEE Latin America Transactions, vol. 6, no. 3, pp. 252-259, July 2008
14. Pastor, O., Insfrán, E., Pelechano, V., Raúl, J. , Merseguer, J., "00-METHOD: An 00 Software Production Environment Combining Conventional and Formal Methods". Seminal Contributions to Information Systems Engineering 2013, pp 139-152
15. Liu, J., Mei, X., "A visual program modeling technology based on procedure blueprint, Proceedings 2013 International Conference, "Mechatronic Sciences, Electric Engineering and Computer (MEC), Shengyang, 2013, pp. 1697-1700
16. Riba, N., Cervantes, H., Eighth Mexican International Conference on "A MDA tool for the development of service-oriented component-based applications," Current Trends in Computer Science, 2007. ENC 2007., Michoacan, 2007, pp. 149-156
17. Tri, D., Tho, Q., 2012 Fourth International Conference on "Systematic Diagram Refinement for Code Generation in SEAM," Knowledge and Systems Engineering (KSE), Danang, 2012, pp. 203-210.
18. Bravo, L., Marín, B., Framework para el desarrollo de software en PHP en base a MDD, Universidad Diego Portales, 2015.
19. UML2PHP, `http://uml2php.com`

Evaluando la Creación de Pruebas Unitarias para un Sistema Legado mediante Microsoft Fakes y Dobles de Prueba

Mario Barrantes[1*] y Alexandra Martínez[2]

[1] Intel, Estados Unidos
mario.alberto.barrantes.quesada@intel.com
[2] Escuela de Ciencias de la Computación e Informática,
Centro de Investigaciones en Tecnologías de la Información y Comunicación,
Universidad de Costa Rica, Costa Rica
alexandra.martinez@ecci.ucr.ac.cr

Resumen Este artículo evalúa la creación de pruebas unitarias para un sistema de código legado usando dos técnicas alternativas: el *framework* de aislamiento Microsoft Fakes y el método de dobles de prueba. La organización en la cual se efectuó este estudio no realiza pruebas unitarias, lo cual deriva en un alto costo de mantenimiento para sus sistemas pues debe ejecutar pruebas de regresión manuales cuando se realiza un cambio. Se usó entonces uno de sus sistemas legados como caso de estudio para evaluar cuál técnica de inclusión de pruebas unitarias resultaba más ventajosa para la organización. En primer lugar, se analizó la mantenibilidad del sistema legado. En segundo lugar, se seleccionaron los métodos a probar con pruebas unitarias y finalmente, se desarrollaron las pruebas usando el *framework* Microsoft Fakes y el método de dobles de prueba. Durante el desarrollo y la ejecución de las pruebas, se recolectaron las métricas necesarias para la comparación de ambos métodos. Los resultados de este caso de estudio muestran que Microsoft Fakes posibilita el desarrollo de pruebas unitarias en código legado sin necesidad de cambiar el código productivo y en un menor tiempo de desarrollo que dobles de prueba, pero a un mayor tiempo de ejecución.

Keywords: Código legado, pruebas unitarias, Microsoft Fakes, dobles de prueba

1. Introducción

Las pruebas unitarias son una parte importante del proceso de desarrollo de software pues constituyen la retroalimentación más temprana que tiene el desarrollador sobre su código. Recordemos que un defecto detectado en desarrollo es de 3 a 10 veces más barato de arreglar que si es detectado en producción [4]. Adicionalmente, durante la etapa de mantenimiento del software, las pruebas

[*] La afiliación actual del autor es Intel, pero esta investigación se desarrolló como parte de su investigación de posgrado en la Universidad de Costa Rica

unitarias son un buen mecanismo para identificar rápidamente regresiones en el software. De ahí el interés en incorporar pruebas unitarias no sólo al nuevo software que se desarrolle sino también al software existente que está en mantenimiento. La creación de pruebas unitarias automatizadas es una práctica estándar en desarrollos modernos de software, no obstante, su incorporación a software existente sigue siendo un reto debido a que los componentes de software deben aislarse en unidades que puedan ser probadas de forma independiente y no es usual que el software existente soporte tal nivel de aislamiento si no fue diseñado para ello.

En este trabajo utilizaremos el término "código legado"para referirnos a código (software) sin pruebas unitarias, siguiendo la definición dada por Feathers [7]. El código legado generalmente tiene que ser adaptado para que se puedan ejecutar pruebas unitarias sobre él. Esta adaptación se conoce como refactorización, que es un proceso de reestructuración interna del código tendiente a mejorar su diseño, legibilidad o mantenibilidad, sin alterar su comportamiento externo [7].

Las técnicas tradicionales para resolver el problema de aislamiento de unidades de software en código legado se conocen con el término genérico de "dobles de prueba"(*test doubles* en inglés) [3] y consisten en simular componentes de software que interactúan con el software a probar en forma de dependencia. Existen distintos tipos de dobles de prueba, entre los cuales están: maniquí (*dummy*), auxiliar (*stub*), espía (*spy*), falsificación (*fake*) y simulacro (*mock*) [6]. Los maniquíes son el tipo más sencillo de dobles de prueba pues no contienen implementación y se usan como valores de parámetros (bien pueden ser nulos). Los auxiliares son implementaciones mínimas de interfaces o clases base y normalmente devuelven valores preestablecidos, que obligan al software bajo prueba a ejecutar caminos específicos. Los espías son auxiliares con capacidad de grabación y generalmente guardan información sobre las llamadas a métodos hechas por el software bajo prueba, para ser verificado luego por las pruebas. Las falsificaciones son implementaciones más complejas que ofrecen la misma funcionalidad que el componente real pero de una forma más sencilla y se usan principalmente cuando el componente real no está disponible aún, es muy lento o no puede usarse en el ambiente de pruebas debido a sus efectos secundarios. Los simulacros son creados dinámicamente mediante una biblioteca, en lugar de ser codificados por un desarrollador de pruebas (como los otros dobles de prueba).

Microsoft Fakes es el nuevo *framework* de aislamiento que introdujo Microsoft en el 2012, mediante el cual se pueden reemplazar partes de código con *stubs* o *shims* para fines de pruebas [2]. Un *stub* remplaza una clase con un sustituto pequeño que implementa la misma interfaz y típicamente se usa para llamadas dentro de una solución que se pueden desacoplar usando interfaces. Un *shim* modifica en tiempo de ejecución el código compilado para inyectar un sustituto y se usa para llamadas a ensamblados de referencia para los que el código no está bajo nuestro control. La mayor diferencia entre ambos elementos es que los *shims* modifican el ensamblado de la dependencia que necesitamos sustituir, mientras los *stubs* únicamente inyectan una dependencia distinta (ajustada a lo que se necesita) de una interfaz o abstracción existente.

2. Trabajo Relacionado

El problema de incluir pruebas unitarias en código legado ha existido desde hace tiempo. Algunas investigaciones se han enfocado en desarrollar y evaluar herramientas para crear automáticamente pruebas unitarias. Un ejemplo de esto es el estudio realizado por Ramler y otros [8], el cual desarrolló un experimento que comparaba pruebas manuales contra pruebas generadas automáticamente. Las pruebas unitarias manuales las realizaron 48 estudiantes de maestría por un lapso de 60 minutos, mientras que las pruebas automatizadas las generaron mediante la herramienta de pruebas unitarias Randoop. El estudio arrojó que los 48 estudiantes en una hora cubrieron el 32 % del código y encontraron 24 errores, mientras Randoop cubrió el 29 % del código y encontró 9 errores.

Otros trabajos de investigación se han centrado en desarrollar técnicas de objetos de simulación. Estos objetos frecuentemente se necesitan para realizar pruebas unitarias, así que se han desarrollado *frameworks* que facilitan su inclusión en pruebas unitarias a partir de clases ya existentes. Un ejemplo de esta línea de investigación es el modelo tabular propuesto por Kim y otros [5], que permite tener trazabilidad entre las diferentes llamadas a métodos o funciones del objeto de simulación mediante una pila de llamados manejados por una máquina de estados de interacción. Sin embargo, a pesar de que este modelo ayuda a crear más pruebas unitarias, el esfuerzo que requiere la preparación consume mucho tiempo. Otra técnica de objetos de simulación propuesta por Samimi y otros [9] es la simulación declarativa, un esquema en el que los desarrolladores escriben especificaciones de métodos en un lenguaje de alto nivel para el API simulado y un solucionador de restricciones ejecuta dichas especificaciones cuando los métodos son invocados. Si bien este enfoque puede acelerar la creación de pruebas unitarias, solamente existe una extensión para Java.

Todas estas técnicas intentan agilizar el proceso de creación de pruebas unitarias, sin embargo, están orientadas -en su mayoría- al desarrollo de software guiado por pruebas. Lastimosamente, en código legado no se puede aplicar el desarrollo guiado por pruebas. Es por ello que ha surgido interés en investigar sobre cómo incorporar pruebas unitarias a código legado. Un ejemplo de esta línea de investigación es el trabajo de Shihab y otros [11], que propone un nuevo concepto llamado "Mantenimiento guiado por pruebas", el cual provee una serie de heurísticas para trabajar en un proceso similar al desarrollo guiado por pruebas, pero con código legado.

3. Contexto

La Universidad de Costa Rica cuenta con un conjunto de sistemas informáticos creados por varias unidades de desarrollo de software institucional. El presente estudio fue desarrollado en una de estas unidades, que posee una extensa base de código legado en producción. La mayoría de este código no fue diseñado para ser probado mediante pruebas unitarias, sin embargo, está en constante mantenimiento, lo cual implica un alto costo pues se deben ejecutar pruebas de regresión manuales cada vez que se realiza un cambio sobre el código.

La unidad de desarrollo en cuestión, de ahora en adelante llamada "la organización", se beneficiaría en gran medida de la incorporación de pruebas unitarias a sus sistemas legados, ya que servirían como pruebas de regresión automatizadas, reduciendo el tiempo y el costo de mantenimiento de sus sistemas. Uno de los retos de incorporar pruebas unitarias a este código legado es el fuerte acoplamiento entre sus componentes de software. Para solventarlo, se debe recurrir a la refactorización, o bien, a un *framework* de aislamiento como Microsoft Fakes.

Esta investigación propone entonces utilizar uno de los sistemas legados de la organización como caso de estudio para evaluar dos técnicas de creación de pruebas unitarias: el *framework* Microsoft Fakes y el método de dobles de prueba con refactorización. Se espera que las conclusiones derivadas de este caso de estudio ayuden a la organización a elegir la técnica que les resulte más ventajosa.

4. Metodología

4.1. El sistema legado

El sistema legado escogido para este estudio es una aplicación web desarrollada en ASP.Net utilizando el lenguaje de programación Visual Basic. El sistema cuenta con 87 casos de pruebas manuales y funcionales documentados, pero ninguna prueba unitaria. El sistema utiliza un modelo típico de tres capas: la capa de presentación, la capa de lógica de negocios y la capa de acceso a datos. La capa de lógica de negocios accede a varios servicios web de otros sistemas de la organización. La mayor parte de la lógica del sistema se encuentra en la capa de lógica de negocios (como es usual), por lo que para efectos de los análisis realizados, métricas recolectadas y pruebas realizadas en el estudio, se usó solamente el proyecto de lógica de negocios del sistema legado.

4.2. Pasos de la metodología

El primer paso de la metodología de investigación fue realizar un análisis de mantenibilidad del sistema legado. El segundo paso fue seleccionar los métodos a probar del sistema legado. El tercer paso fue determinar las métricas que se recolectarían y utilizarían en la comparación de las técnicas de pruebas unitarias. El cuarto paso fue la creación y ejecución de las pruebas unitarias bajo ambas técnicas: Microsoft Fakes y dobles de prueba. A continuación se detalla cada paso de la metodología.

Análisis de mantenibilidad del sistema legado. La organización nos facilitó el código fuente del sistema legado así como documentos de diseño, de arquitectura y de pruebas del sistema. Con estos insumos, se procedió a estudiar la arquitectura del sistema y el código mismo. Se extrajeron las siguientes métricas de mantenibilidad: el índice de mantenibilidad, la complejidad ciclomática y el acoplamiento de clases. El 'índice de mantenibilidad'combina funciones de la complejidad ciclomática, el volumen Halstead y la cantidad de líneas de código por módulo [12]. La 'complejidad ciclomática' mide la cantidad de caminos linealmente independientes en el código [1]. El 'acoplamiento de clases' mide la cantidad de entidades que dependen de un determinado miembro de una clase [4]. Todas estas métricas permiten evaluar la facilidad o dificultad de realizar pruebas unitarias sobre un código.

Selección de los métodos a probar. Para poner en contexto el sistema bajo estudio, se sabe que este sistema fue desarrollado y ha sido parte de una organización dentro de la UCR por varios años y a través del tiempo se le han implementado cambios y arreglos. Para seleccionar los métodos a los cuales se les aplicarían pruebas unitarias, se definieron los siguientes criterios a satisfacer:

- El método debía estar en el proyecto de Lógica de Negocios del sistema, ya que en esta capa es donde se realiza la mayor parte de lógica del sistema.
- El método debía tener lógica y no ser un simple método de paso de datos. Durante la investigación se detectó que mucho código era generado automáticamente mediante plantillas básicas de conexión y acceso a la base de datos, por lo que esos métodos básicos fueron ignorados.
- El método debía tener más de un caso de prueba posible. En otras palabras, debía ser lo suficientemente complejo (en cantidad de ramificaciones) para aplicar al menos dos casos de prueba.
- El método debía poseer dependencias. Todos los métodos de la Lógica de Negocios tenían al menos una dependencia.

Después de aplicar estos criterios a los métodos de la capa de lógica de negocio del sistema legado, quedaron seleccionados los siguientes métodos:

1. **DeshacerRegistroTramitado**: este método tiene la lógica de deshacer una transacción realizada. Fue seleccionado debido a que pueden existir diferentes casos de prueba, por ejemplo, si se intenta deshacer un registro que no existe o que está vació, o cuando el registro tiene un monto.
2. **InsertarNotificar**: este método inserta un registro y notifica por correo electrónico. Fue seleccionado por que existen muchos casos de prueba que se pueden automatizar y además porque agrega varias dependencias, entre ellas: la base de datos y el servidor de correos electrónicos.
3. **ModificarNotificar**: este método modifica un registro y notifica por correo electrónico. Fue seleccionado por las mismas razones que el anterior.
4. **TotalRubrosPorEntidad**: este método calcula el total de rubros por entidad. Tiene muchas dependencias con tablas y estructuras de datos de la aplicación y también tiene muchas ramificaciones y posibles casos de prueba.

Elección de las métricas a recolectar. Se eligió recolectar las siguientes métricas sobre la creación y ejecución de las pruebas unitarias:

a. **Tiempo invertido en el desarrollo de las pruebas (TD)**: mide el tiempo de desarrollo de las pruebas unitarias, incluyendo el arreglo de los datos, la refactorización (de ser necesaria), las aserciones y la depuración. La medición de este tiempo se hizo de forma manual.

b. **Tiempo de ejecución de las pruebas (TE)**: mide el tiempo que toma ejecutar las pruebas unitarias. Como el tiempo de ejecución puede variar por factores no controlables (el estado del sistema operativo en el momento de correr las pruebas unitarias, el uso de la red, el uso del procesador, etc.), se tomó la decisión de ejecutar las pruebas diez veces y tomar el promedio de estas corridas.
c. **Cobertura de código (CC)**: mide el porcentaje de líneas de código del sistema legado cubiertas (o ejercitadas) por las pruebas unitarias. Este porcentaje se obtuvo mediante la herramienta de análisis de cobertura que ofrece la herramienta Visual Studio.
d. **Cantidad de líneas de código productivo modificadas (CCM)**: cuenta la cantidad de líneas de código productivo que tuvieron que ser modificadas, eliminadas o agregadas para incorporar pruebas unitarias.
e. **Total de líneas de código productivo (TC)**: cuenta el total de líneas de código productivo bajo prueba (en nuestro caso, se contabilizó sólo el código pertinente de la capa de Lógica de Negocios).
f. **Porcentaje de código modificado (PCM)**: es la razón de CCM a TC.

Creación y ejecución de pruebas unitarias. Para la creación de pruebas unitarias, primeramente se estudió la documentación tanto de Microsoft Fakes como del método de dobles de pruebas con refactorización. Una vez estudiadas y entendidas ambas técnicas, se procedió a aplicarlas sobre el código legado en cuestión. Las pruebas unitarias se diseñaron intentando alcanzar la mayor cobertura de código posible. Todas las pruebas fueron desarrolladas por un solo desarrollador (primer autor del artículo). Cada prueba se ejecutó diez veces, para efectos de medición del tiempo de ejecución.

5. Resultados y Discusión

Mantenibilidad del sistema legado. El cuadro 1 muestra el resumen (promedio, valor máximo y valor mínimo) de las métricas de mantenibilidad obtenidas sobre la capa de lógica de negocios del sistema legado, que contenía 172 miembros. Las métricas se obtuvieron mediante análisis estático de código usando la herramienta Visual Studio. Del cuadro 1 se observa que el promedio del índice de mantenibilidad es normal (el rango de valores de esta métrica es de 0 a 100), pero existen 22 miembros de clases con un índice de mantenibilidad por debajo de 35 (valores bajos representan código poco mantenible). La complejidad ciclomática promedio es baja, pero hay 28 miembros de clases que presentan una complejidad ciclomática mayor a 10 (un valor de complejidad ciclomática de 10 o menor es un buen indicador de código mantenible [13]). Por otro lado, el promedio de acoplamiento de clases es alto, lo cual refleja la existencia de 40 miembros de clases con acoplamiento mayor a 20 (un valor de acoplamiento de clases de 9 o menor indica código mantenible [10]).

Cuadro 1. Resumen de las métricas de mantenibilidad del sistema legado.

	Promedio	Max	Min
Indice de mantenibilidad	56.1	98	23
Complejidad Ciclomática	5.0	30	1
Acoplamiento de clases	10.3	42	0

Un estudio más detallado del código del sistema legado determinó que el alto acoplamiento de clases se debe a las dependencias que tiene la capa de lógica de negocios con la capa de acceso a datos, servicios externos que consume y otros utilitarios. Todas estas dependencias son consumidas utilizando implementaciones concretas y no existe inyección de dependencias.

Los resultados arrojados por este análisis de mantenibilidad muestran que el sistema legado tiene un alto acoplamiento de clases, lo cual advierte que el proceso de refactorización no será fácil. El nivel de acoplamiento de clases indirectamente permite estimar qué tanta refactorización de código será necesaria al crear pruebas unitarias con las técnicas tradicionales (como dobles de pruebas).

Creación y ejecución de las pruebas unitarias. Se diseñaron 14 pruebas unitarias sobre los 4 métodos seleccionados del sistema legado, para un total de 28 pruebas unitarias implementadas (14 con cada técnica). El cuadro 2 muestra las métricas recolectadas durante el desarrollo y la ejecución de las pruebas unitarias, tanto usando el *framework* Microsoft Fakes como el método de dobles de prueba con refactorización. Aquí, TD es el tiempo de desarrollo de la prueba unitaria en minutos y TE es el tiempo de ejecución de la prueba unitaria en milisegundos. Del cuadro 2 se concluye que el tiempo de desarrollo de las pruebas unitarias fue 3.3 veces mayor usando dobles de prueba, mientras que el tiempo de ejecución de las pruebas fue 2.8 veces mayor usando Microsoft Fakes.

Por otro lado, el porcentaje de cobertura de código (métrica CC) fue de 100 % en ambos casos. El total de líneas de código productivo (métrica TC) en la capa de lógica de negocio fue 35,347. La cantidad de líneas de código productivo modificadas (métrica CCM) fue 0 cuando se utilizó Microsoft Fakes y 3,445 cuando se usó dobles de prueba. El porcentaje de código modificado (métrica PCM) resultó en 0 % para Microsoft Fakes y 9.7 % para dobles de prueba.

Las diferencias en tiempo de desarrollo y tiempo de ejecución entre ambas técnicas se deben a la forma como trabaja cada una de ellas. En el caso de los dobles de prueba, el desarrollador debe crear manualmente los objetos de simulación y refactorizar el código, lo cual incrementa el tiempo de desarrollo, pero mejora el tiempo de ejecución. El tiempo de ejecución mejora porque el código con los objetos de simulación es compilado y por ende el ejecutor de pruebas no tiene sobrecarga adicional en tiempo de ejecución. En contraposición, cuando se usa Microsoft Fakes, el ejecutor de pruebas debe ensamblar los proyectos *fakes* creados por el *framework* junto con el código de la prueba unitaria antes de ejecutar la prueba. Entre más grande sea el ensamblado que se está falsificando con Microsoft Fakes, mayor será el tiempo de ejecución.

Cuadro 2. Métricas recolectadas sobre las pruebas unitarias. TD es el tiempo de desarrollo en minutos y TE es el tiempo de ejecución en milisegundos.

	Microsoft Fakes		Dobles de prueba	
Prueba unitaria	TD	TE	TD	TE
1	25	21	90	6
2	20	1	15	1
3	15	3	90	1
4	15	1	12	1
5	20	2	70	2
6	10	8	10	6
7	20	1	125	1
8	8	324	12	33
9	45	1	180	1
10	5	6	10	5
11	6	15	10	56
12	5	1	15	1
13	4	125	15	67
14	5	5	15	3
Total	203	514	669	184
Promedio	14.5	36.71	47.79	13.14

Vale la pena mencionar que el alto acoplamiento de clases detectado durante el análisis de mantenibilidad incidió en el tiempo de desarrollo de las pruebas que se hicieron con dobles de pruebas, pues estas requirieron una refactorización del 9.7 % del código legado productivo. Como el *framework* de aislamiento Microsoft Fakes no requirió modificar el código productivo (evitó refactorizar), el tiempo de desarrollo de las pruebas con esta técnica fue menor.

Valoración de las técnicas de pruebas. Las ventajas encontradas al utilizar el *framework* Microsoft Fakes fueron:

- Se pudieron crear pruebas unitarias sobre código legado sin necesidad de modificar el código productivo original, lo cual elimina el riesgo de regresiones.
- El tiempo de desarrollo de las pruebas fue bajo en comparación con dobles de prueba.

Las desventajas encontradas al utilizar el *framework* Microsoft Fakes fueron:

- El tiempo de ejecución de las pruebas fue alto en comparación con dobles de prueba.
- Al omitir el proceso de refactorización (el cual es saludable), permitió probar código que incumplía con principios de buen diseño de software.

Las ventajas encontradas al utilizar la técnica de dobles de prueba fueron:

- El tiempo de ejecución de las pruebas fue bajo en comparación con el de Microsoft Fakes.
- Requirió del proceso de refactorización, el cual es conveniente desde la perspectiva de buen diseño de software.

Por otro lado, las desventajas que se encontraron con dobles de prueba fueron:

- El tiempo de desarrollo de las pruebas fue alto en comparación con el de Microsoft Fakes.
- El riesgo a introducir nuevos defectos es mayor que con Microsoft Fakes, pues la refactorización es obligatoria para crear las pruebas.

6. Conclusiones

Esta investigación comparó el uso del *framework* de aislamiento Microsoft Fakes contra la técnica tradicional de dobles de prueba con refactorización, para agregar pruebas unitarias a un sistema de código legado. El sistema legado es una aplicación web para uso interno de la Universidad de Costa Rica, desarrollado por una unidad de desarrollo de software institucional.

En este trabajo se analizó la mantenibilidad del sistema legado, utilizando las métricas de índice de mantenibilidad, complejidad ciclomática y acoplamiento de clases. Dicho análisis señaló que el mayor problema de mantenibilidad del sistema legado en estudio era su alto acoplamiento de clases, el cual es producido por la falta de inyección de dependencias. Luego de este análisis, se seleccionaron cuatro métodos de la capa de lógica de negocio para ser probados mediante pruebas unitarias. Sobre estos métodos se implementaron 14 pruebas unitarias con Microsoft Fakes y con dobles de prueba. Durante su implementación, se recolectaron métricas sobre el tiempo de desarrollo y ejecución de las pruebas unitarias, así como sobre la cantidad de líneas de código que tuvieron que ser modificadas para crear las pruebas.

Los resultados indican que el *framework* Microsoft Fakes logró aislar las dependencias que tenía el código con servicios externos a los que la capa de lógica de negocio se conectaba, posibilitando así la creación de pruebas unitarias automatizadas sin necesidad de cambiar una sola línea de código productivo. (Se optó por aislar y no simular estos servicios ya que la simulación hubiese sido más costosa.) Los resultados también indican que la técnica de dobles de prueba logró crear pruebas unitarias automatizadas sobre el código legado, pero requirió la creación manual de los objetos de simulación y la respectiva refactorización del código productivo. En este caso de estudio, para usar la técnica de dobles de prueba se tuvo que modificar un 9.7 % del código productivo. Otro resultado interesante para este caso de estudio es que el tiempo de desarrollo de las pruebas unitarias con Microsoft Fakes fue 3.3 veces menor que con dobles de prueba, mientras que el tiempo de ejecución de las pruebas con Microsoft Fakes fue 2.8 veces mayor que con dobles de pruebas.

Finalmente, nuestra recomendación es utilizar el *framework* Microsoft Fakes en código legado que posea un alto nivel de acoplamiento de clases (mayor a 9) y que esté sujeto a mantenimientos pequeños. Por el contrario, en código legado con buenos indicadores de mantenibilidad (en especial, bajo acoplamiento de clases), se recomienda usar dobles de prueba ya que el esfuerzo de refactorización no sería muy grande. Similarmente, si el código legado va a sufrir cambios grandes, se recomienda utilizar dobles de pruebas para obtener un mejor diseño del software a través de la refactorización. Finalmente, para desarrollo de código nuevo se recomienda usar métodos tradicionales de dobles de prueba y refactorización, que ayuden a producir software con bajo acoplamiento de clases.

Agradecimientos

Agradecemos al Centro de Investigaciones en Tecnologías de la Información y Comunicación de la Universidad de Costa Rica por servir de enlace con la organización donde se efectuó el estudio, proveer la infraestructura tecnológica y brindar apoyo técnico durante la investigación. Agradecemos también a la organización que desarrolló el sistema legado aquí estudiado.

Referencias

1. J.L. Anderson. Using software tools and metrics to produce better quality test software. In *AUTOTESTCON*, pages 293–297, 2004.
2. Microsoft Corporation. *Exploring The Continuum Of Test Doubles*. Microsoft Corporation, 2007.
3. Microsoft Corporation. *Better Unit Testing with Microsoft Fakes*. Microsoft Corporation, 2013.
4. Michael Feathers. *Working Effectively with Legacy Code*. Prentice Hall, 2004.
5. Taeksu Kim, Chanjin Park, and Chisu Wu. Mock object models for test driven development. In *4th International Conference on Software Engineering Research, Management and Applications*, pages 221–228, 2006.
6. Steve McConnell. *Code Complete: A Practical Handbook of Software Construction, Second Edition*. Microsoft Press, 2004.
7. Gerard Meszaros. *xUnit Test Patterns: Refactoring Test Code*. Addison-Wesley, 2007.
8. R. Ramler, D. Winkler, and M. Schmidt. Random test case generation and manual unit testing: Substitute or complement in retrofitting tests for legacy code? In *38th Conference on Software Engineering and Advanced Applications*, pages 286–293, 2012.
9. Hesam Samimi, Rebecca Hicks, Ari Fogel, and Todd Millstein. Declarative mocking. In *Proceedings of the 2013 International Symposium on Software Testing and Analysis*, ISSTA 2013, pages 246–256, New York, NY, USA, 2013. ACM.
10. R. Shatnawi. A quantitative investigation of the acceptable risk levels of object-oriented metrics in open-source systems. *IEEE Transactions on Software Engineering*, 36(2):216–225, March 2010.
11. E. Shihab, Z. M. Jiang, B. Adams, A.E. Hassan, and R. Bowerman. Prioritizing unit test creation for test-driven maintenance of legacy systems. In *10th International Conference on Quality Software*, pages 132–141, 2010.
12. Diomidis Spinellis. *Code Quality: The Open Source Perspective*. Addison-Wesley Professional, 2006.
13. Arthur H. Watson, Thomas J. Mccabe, and Dolores R. Wallace. Special publication 500-235, structured testing: A software testing methodology using the cyclomatic complexity metric. In *U.S. Department of Commerce/National Institute of Standards and Technology*, 1996.

Tutorials Sessions CIbSE 2016 Preface

The Ibero-American Conference on Software Engineering CIbSE is a premier research forum on Software Engineering in Ibero-America. The main objective of this venue is to promote high-quality scientific research in the region, encouraging the researchers in this community to publish and discuss their work with scholars, professionals and students.

One of the components of CIbSE is the tutorials track. In this edition six proposal were received from countries like Spain, Sweden, Finland and the Netherlands. These tutorials have been arranged in the following sessions:

-"Agent-oriented modeling using i *" by Xavier Franch, Universidad Politécnica de Cataluña, Spain.

-"Combination of empirical methods in software engineering projects" by Marcela Fabiana Genero, Universidad de Castilla-La Mancha, Spain.

-"Creating domain specific languages (DSL)" by Jesús J. García Molina, Universidad de Murcia, Spain.

-"An introduction to software effort estimation, with focus on Web effort estimation" by Emilia Mendes, Blekinge Institute of Technology (BTH), Sweden; and University of Oulu, Finland

-"Design science research in information systems and software systems engineering" by Roel Wieringa, University of Twente, Netherlands.

-"Quantitative Methods for Experimental Software Engineering Synthesis" by Óscar Dieste, Universidad Politécnica de Madrid, Spain

We would like to thanks all the authors who submitted a tutorial proposal, they made possible this tutorial track by sharing their know-how with all of us. We would also like to thank to all the members of the organizing committee for their support, particularly to local and general chairs for made possible this edition of CIbSE.

Omar S. Gómez, 2016

TUTORIALS INDEX

Tutorial 1

Agent-oriented modeling using i *

Xavier Franch

Universidad Politécnica de Cataluña, Barcelona, España

Franch@essi.upc.edu

Abstract: i * is a goal-oriented approach consisting of a modeling language around which has helped to developed various methodologies and techniques. This tutorial will present the concepts of the language, including the recent iStar standard 2.0, covering purely notational, methodological, ontological and technological aspects. The tutorial will be interactive.

Tutorial 2

Combination of empirical methods in software engineering projects

Marcela Fabiana Genero

University of Castilla-La Mancha (Spain)

marcela.genero@uclm.es

Abstract: The main objective of this tutorial is to learn to select the most appropriate empirical method to validate the different technologies (processes, methods, devices, etc.) proposed in projects carried out in the context of software engineering. To this end, there will be an overview of the main empirical methods: experiments, surveys and case studies, analyzing the pros and cons of each. In addition, there is going to be a special emphasis in the fact that not always the application of a single method is sufficient, that sometimes it is necessary to combine many methods in order to achieve objectives.

Tutorial 3

Creating domain specific languages (DSL)

Jesús J. García Molina

University of Murcia (Spain)

jesus.gmolina@gmail.com

Abstract: The aim is to present the main techniques for building domain specific languages (DSL). First, construction techniques for textual DSL (External, Embedded and Fluent APIs) will be illustrated through several examples of DSL created in our group. Also, there will be shown some metamodel based tools that automate the creation of DSL (Language definition workbench), in particular we will contrast xtext, MPS and EMFText for textual DSL, and Sirius will be presented for graphical DSL. During the tutorial we will create a simple textual and graphical DSL. Also, issues related to the evaluation of DSLs and some recommendations for its creation will be discussed.

Tutorial 4

An introduction to software effort estimation, with focus on Web effort estimation

Emilia Mendes

Blekinge Institute of Technology and University of Oulu

emilia.mendes@bth.se

Abstract: Good effort estimates are essential to help project managers allocate resources and control costs & schedule, which in turn enables projects to be finished on time and within budget. The objective of this tutorial is to introduce the concepts related to effort estimation and also to detail the most common techniques that have been used by researchers who have investigated this area using models. All the examples given are based on effort estimation relating to Web projects.

Tutorial 5

Design science research in information systems and software systems engineering

Roel Wieringa

University of Twente,, Netherland

roelw@cs.utwente.nl

Abstract: The last ten years has seen a surge of interest in design science research in information systems, and of empirical research in software engineering. In this talk I present a framework for design science in information and software systems engineering that shows how in design science research, we iterate over designing new artifacts and empirically investigating these artifacts. To be relevant, the artifacts should potentially contribute to organizational goals, and to be empirically sound, research to validate new artifacts should provide insight into the effects of using these artifacts in an organizational context. The logic of both of these activities, design and empirical research, is that of rational decision making. I show how this logic can be used to structure our technical and empirical research goals and questions, as well as how to structure reports about our technical or empirical research. This gives us checklists for the design cycle used in technical research and for the empirical cycle used in empirical research. Finally, I will discuss in more detail what the role of theories in design science research is, and how we use theory to state research questions and to generalize the research results.

Tutorial 6

Quantitative Methods for Experimental Software Engineering Synthesis

Oscar Dieste

Universidad Politécnica de Madrid, Madrid, Spain

odieste@fi.upm.es

Abstract. Meta-analysis, or quantitative synthesis, is the branch of statistics aimed at combining the results of individual experiments into a single estimate of treatment effect. Meta-analysis is typically performed in the framework of Systematic Literature Reviews, but in SE it is also used to pool together the results of close replications (i.e.: families of experiments) conducted by the same researchers.

There are two broad types of meta-analysis techniques: individual- and aggregated-data. Individual-data meta-analysis uses the data collected for *each* experimental unit to calculate the global effect size. Usual statistical techniques (e.g.: ANOVA, regression, etc.) are used in this case. Aggregated-data meta-analysis takes a *single* value per experiment (e.g.: treatments' averages) instead. We will focus on this second group of techniques.

Aggregated-data meta-analysis techniques can be further divided into continuous and discrete data. Continuous data are the most frequent case in SE and include: Weighted mean difference (e.g.: Glass, Cohen and Hedges' effect sizes), response ratio (parametric and non-parametric), correlations, vote counting (statistically corrected) and omnibus tests for p-values. We will review one discrete data technique as well: The Mantel-Haenszel method for combining odds ratios.

The tutorial will have a practical orientation. We will introduce the minimal theoretical concepts needed to apply the techniques to some case studies. We will also learn how to use the R environment to make calculations and display the results using *forest plots*.

Keywords. Weighted mean difference, response, correlation, vote counting, omnibus tests, odds ratio, R

This page intentionally left blank.

Doctoral Symposium (DS 2016) Preface

The CIbSE 2016 Doctoral Symposium is an international forum for PhD students whose research area includes topics of Software Engineering, Requirements Engineering or Experimental Software Engineering to discuss their research goals, methodology, and early results, in a critical but supportive and constructive environment.

It will be performed in a one-day session. Selected students will present their work and receive constructive feedback both from a panel of experts and from other Doctoral Symposium students. The students will also have the opportunity to seek advice on various aspects of completing a Ph.D. and performing research in Software Engineering.

Gleison Santos, Juan Pablo Carvallo

PC co-chairs of the CIBSE Doctoral Symposium 2016

Program Committee

Gleison Santos, UNIRIO, Brazil

Jose Viterbo Filho, UFF, Brazil

Claudia Cappelli, UNIRIO, Brazil

Adriano Albuquerque, UNIFOR, Brazil

Juan Hernández, Universidad de Extremadura, España

Arilo Claudio Dias-Neto, UFAM, Brazil

DOCTORAL SYMPOSIUM INDEX

Impacto de las características personales de los programadores en la efectividad de Test-Driven-Development (TDD): Propuesta de una serie de replicaciones

Geovanny Raura.[1], Oscar Dieste.[2], Efraín R. Fonseca C.[1]
[1] Universidad de las Fuerzas Armadas ESPE, Sangolquí, Ecuador
[2] Universidad Politécnica de Madrid, Madrid, España
[1]{jgraura,erfonseca}@espe.edu.ec, [2]odieste@fi.upm.es

Resumen. Se han realizado diversos experimentos en empresas y academia acerca de Test Driven Development (TDD) una de las técnicas de desarrollo ágil ampliamente utilizado en la industria. En general, los experimentos no muestran un efecto positivo de TDD en la calidad del código o la productividad de los programadores. Se propone realizar una serie de replicaciones del experimento UPM 2014 efectuado por N. Juristo y su equipo [1], para reproducir sus resultados y secundariamente estudiar las características personales del desarrollador como la experiencia, la formación académica, el conocimiento del dominio y su influencia en la efectividad de TDD; mismas que no han sido consideradas en otros experimentos.

Palabras Clave: Test-Driven Development, TDD, Experimentación, Ingeniería de Software.

1 Introducción a la problemática de investigación

Las metodologías ágiles han venido ganando adeptos desde su introducción en la década de los 90, tal es así que actualmente se presentan como una de las aproximaciones más utilizadas para desarrollar software [2]. Las metodologías ágiles se basan en una serie de prácticas, tales como la programación por pares o el desarrollo dirigido por pruebas (TDD, por sus siglas en inglés) [3]. Estas metodologías pretenden aumentar la calidad del producto software y la productividad de los programadores. Varios estudios empíricos se han llevado a cabo con el propósito de comprobar las bondades de TDD, cuyos resultados al contrario de lo esperado, han puesto de manifiesto que estas prácticas pueden ser en ocasiones incluso perjudiciales (por ejemplo: la programación por pares puede reducir la productividad) [4].

El presente estudio se centra en la calidad externa del código y la productividad de los desarrolladores al utilizar la técnica TDD, dado que existen contradicciones en los resultados de múltiples estudios empíricos efectuados a nivel académico e industrial. Una reciente revisión sistemática de literatura [5] sugiere que TDD no posee efecto alguno, ni positivo ni negativo, sobre la productividad. Esto contrasta categóricamente las afirmaciones de sus proponentes, que son por ejemplo la mejora en la comprensión del código, eficiencia para encontrar defectos, entre otros [3].

Adicionalmente, y a diferencia de la práctica de la programación por pares, pocos estudios empíricos de TDD han considerado posibles variables moderadoras como la experiencia de los programadores, el conocimiento del dominio y su formación académica. Estas variables y su posible efecto, serán determinadas en el transcurso de la investigación.

2 Antecedentes y trabajos relacionados

Test-Driven-Development (TDD) es una técnica que cobra fuerza alrededor del manifiesto ágil publicado por un grupo de practicantes de software [3], como parte de la metodología de desarrollo Xtreme Programming (XP) [6] y propone que en lugar de realizar algún diseño o modelo de software, se debe enfrentar el desarrollo en base a la generación de pruebas unitarias antes de la generación efectiva del código.

Los estudios sobre la efectividad de TDD han sido sintetizados en diferentes revisiones sistemáticas de literatura [5], [6], [7], [8], [9], [10], [11], [12], [13], [1]. Estas revisiones reportan que los estudios primarios se han efectuado en su mayoría en el ámbito académico y en menor porcentaje en la industria; utilizando para ello, diferentes métodos de investigación tales como: experimentos, casos de estudio, estudios piloto, encuestas, entre otros. Aunque los factores analizados son varios, es de nuestro interés el análisis de la calidad externa y de la productividad.

La calidad externa de un sistema es medida usualmente como el número de casos de prueba pasados y el número de defectos por unidad de tamaño del código (por ejemplo, líneas de código, u otra medida adecuada). En el experimento original efectuado por N. Juristo y su equipo [1], esta medida representa el grado de corrección del código desarrollado por los sujetos y es analizada en función del número de historias de usuario implementadas correctamente. Se espera que TDD permita la fácil detección de errores en virtud de que el sistema es sometido a pruebas continuas a un nivel de grano-fino [8]

La productividad es expresada generalmente como una relación entre las entradas y salidas. En varios estudios sobre la efectividad de TDD, la productividad mide la velocidad de desarrollo del equipo, y es calculada como el número de unidades producidas en un determinado período de tiempo (días o meses) [7]. En el experimento original, la productividad representa la cantidad de trabajo correctamente realizado por los sujetos, como se define en la sección 5.

En cuanto a la calidad interna y externa, la figura 2 muestra los efectos positivos, negativos o neutros de TDD, reportados en la revisión sistemática de Mäkinen & Münch [11] sobre 19 publicaciones (Hay que precisar que en este estudio, la calidad externa hace referencia a estudios cualitativos que recogen opiniones subjetivas y del entorno).

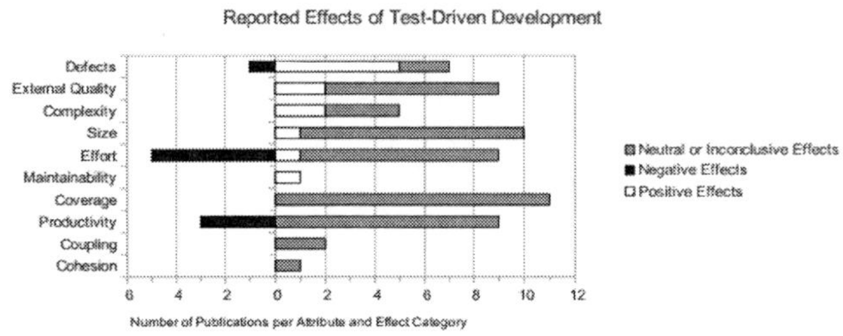

***Fig. 2** Efectos de TDD en los atributos de calidad (Figura tomada de [13])*

Como se observa en la figura 2, existen atributos de calidad que han sido en mayor o menor medida estudiados, como por ejemplo: la mantenibilidad ha sido un aspecto poco estudiado, en tanto que el esfuerzo es uno de los aspectos más estudiados. Se reporta además que la mayoría de estudios presentan resultados inconclusos o no concluyentes en diferentes aspectos investigados.

Estos resultados en general son similares a los hallazgos encontrados en [5], [8] y [9]; donde también se puede notar que existe una tendencia a pensar que TDD mejora la calidad externa. Sin embargo, la calidad interna y la productividad presentan diferentes conclusiones.

La tabla 1 resume por orden cronológico los resultados de las revisiones sistemáticas citadas y que muestran los efectos de TDD en la calidad externa y la productividad. Se debe mencionar que los estudios que informaron sobre la calidad interna han sido omitidos, dado que no son del interés de esta investigación. También se observa que Shull et al. [7] (*) resume los resultados de Turhan et al. [8]; por tal motivo, se muestra como un único estudio ya que sus conclusiones son similares.

TABLA 1. EFECTOS DE TDD EN LA CALIDAD EXTERNA Y PRODUCTIVIDAD DE ACUERDO A DIFERENTES ESTUDIOS.

Revisión	Año	Calidad Externa	Productividad
Kollanus [14]	2010	Experimento controlado: Sin diferencia Estudios de caso: Mejora Otros: Mejora **PROMEDIO: Mejora**	Experimento controlado: No concluyente Estudios de caso: reducción Otros: Mejora **PROMEDIO: Reducción**
Turhan et al. [9] Shull et al [8] (*)	2010	Experimento controlado: no concluyente Estudios piloto: Mejora Industria: Mejora **PROMEDIO: Mejora**	Experimento controlado: mejora Estudios piloto: no concluyente Industria: Disminución **PROMEDIO: No Concluyente**
Rafique & Misic [3]	2013	Experimento académico: sin diferencia Industria: Mejora Test Last: Mejora Iterative Test-Last: no concluyente (potencial disminución) **PROMEDIO: Mejora**	Experimento académico: mejora Industria: disminución Test Last: disminución Iterative Test-Last: no concluyente (potencial mejora) **PROMEDIO: No concluyente**
Munir et al. [10]	2014	Estudios de Alto Rigor y Alta Relevancia (A): Mejora Estudios de Bajo Rigor y alta Relevancia (B1): Mejora	Estudios de Alto Rigor y Alta Relevancia (A): disminuye Estudios de Bajo Rigor y alta Relevancia (B1): disminuye

		Estudios de Alto Rigor y baja Relevancia (B2): sin diferencia Estudios de Bajo Rigor y Baja Relevancia (C) : no concluyente **PROMEDIO: Mejora**	Estudios de Alto Rigor y baja Relevancia (B2): sin diferencia Estudios de Bajo Rigor y Baja Relevancia (C) : no concluyente **PROMEDIO: No concluyente**

En síntesis podemos indicar que los estudios citados reportan diferentes resultados sobre los efectos de TDD en la calidad y la productividad, dependiendo de los grupos investigados, del rigor y relevancia de los métodos de investigación utilizados y otros factores que en general no han permitido llegar a conclusiones sólidas.

3 Objetivos y aporte de la investigación

El objetivo general de la propuesta de investigación es estudiar la efectividad de TDD en base a las características personales particulares de cada programador; para lo cual se plantean los objetivos específicos indicados a continuación:

- Realizar una serie de replicaciones experimentales en la academia e industria, sobre la efectividad de TDD con grupos de programadores que posean diferentes características personales.
- Sintetizar las replicaciones mediante diversas técnicas tales como: Thematic Synthesis, meta-análisis, entre otras, con la finalidad de establecer los efectos de dichas características en la efectividad de TDD.
- Empaquetar y difundir los resultados experimentales a la industria de software.

4 Motivación para la realización de la investigación

Creemos que lo que subyace en los resultados aparentemente contradictorios sobre la efectividad de TDD, se debe a que no han sido consideradas las características personales de los sujetos como pueden ser: la experiencia y el conocimiento previo en TDD, su habilidad para realizar casos de pruebas, el conocimiento del dominio, la motivación, entre otros; lo cual se evidencia en la carencia de estudios referentes a estos aspectos.

Tomando como base la revisión sistemática de Turhan et al. [8], y luego de realizar un re-análisis, hemos podido comprobar en que al menos la experiencia (o el tipo de sujeto) si parece tener influencia en algunas variables, como la calidad externa y la productividad.

Para este re-análisis, hemos clasificado al estudio de Turhan et al [8] en función de la calidad de los experimentos, relacionando la experiencia del programador y la rigurosidad del proceso en la aplicación de TDD en 4 niveles (L0-L3); siendo L0 los experimentos de menor calidad y L3 los de mayor calidad. En este re-análisis, además hemos categorizado los valores MEJOR, PEOR, etc. utilizando una variable indicadora (dummy) de acuerdo al siguiente esquema:

MEJOR = 1,

MEZCLA = 0.5

SIN DIFERENCIA/INCONCLUSO = 0

PEOR = -1

La variable indicadora permite representar en un gráfico tipo box-plot los estudios de distribución que apoyan o están en contra de TDD. Si bien este procedimiento es equivalente al análisis llevado a cabo por Turhan et al., la diferencia es la naturaleza visual del procedimiento y la auto-evidencia de las conclusiones que pueden extraerse.

Es así que en las figuras 3 y 4 se puede observar que TDD al parecer mejora la calidad externa sólo para los sujetos sin experiencia. Para los sujetos con experiencia, TDD parece que empeora la calidad externa y además se observa que disminuye la productividad.

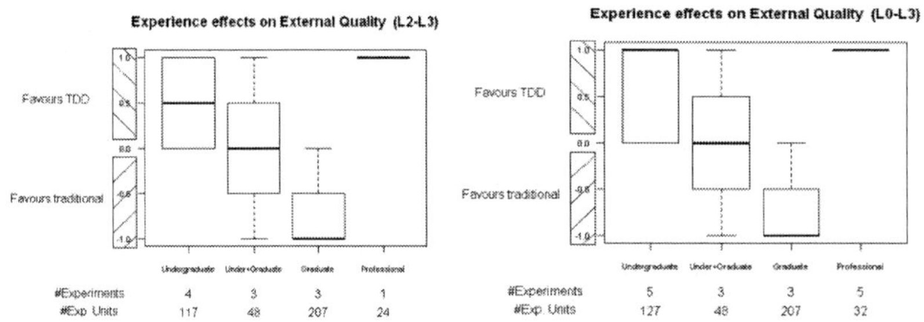

Fig3 Efectos de la experiencia sobre la calidad externa para estudios de alta calidad (izquierda) y para todos los estudios (derecha)

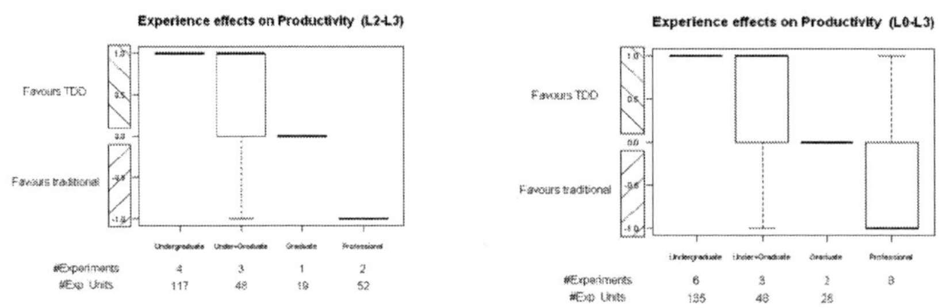

Fig4. Efectos de la experiencia sobre la productividad para estudios de alta calidad (izquierda) y para todos los estudios (derecha).

Aunque los estudios empíricos existentes en la industria muestran que TDD aumenta la calidad externa (Nótese el promedio de [5], [8], [9], [13] de la tabla1), sin embargo al considerar la experiencia o al menos los tipos de sujetos por separado, el estudio de Turhan et al. [9] muestra una tendencia a la baja. Como se aprecia en la figura 3, la calidad externa disminuye para los sujetos graduados y aumenta para los no graduados. Esto sugiere que los resultados positivos de TDD en la calidad externa pueden ser solo un efecto engañoso producto de la gran cantidad de estudios empíricos realizados en la academia, comparados con el menor número de estudios realizados en la industria. De hecho, y como se puede apreciar en la figura 3, el análisis de Turhan et al [8] sobre la efectividad de TDD en relación la calidad externa, es realizado con un único estudio en la industria para L2 y L3.

En cuanto a la productividad, como sugieren los estudios referidos en la tabla 1, la mayoría presentan resultados no concluyentes (Nótese el promedio de [5], [8], [9]). Sin embargo, en este re-análisis podemos notar en la figura 4 un claro patrón de tendencia hacia la disminución de la productividad cuando se considera la experiencia del sujeto.

Por lo tanto, parece que el tipo de sujeto es un mediador potencialmente interesante que se debe investigar con mayor detalle y rigurosidad desde luego desde el punto de vista de la experiencia, aunque tampoco se podría excluir a priori otras características, como el conocimiento del dominio o la formación académica, por citar dos características personales bien establecidas y estudiadas en la literatura.

5 Metodología de Investigación.

Se realizará una secuencia de replicaciones experimentales basadas en un experimento realizado por N. Juristo [1] y su equipo de la Universidad Politécnica de Madrid, sobre la los efectos de la aplicación de TDD en la calidad y la productividad de los desarrolladores. Inicialmente se utilizarán las mismas hipótesis y variables consideradas en este experimento para reducir las amenazas a la validez en la implementación de las replicaciones y para facilitar la comparación con el experimento original. Sin embargo, el diseño original será modificado a lo largo de las distintas replicaciones, en caso de ser necesario, para adecuarlo a los objetivos de la investigación.

La efectividad del desarrollo basado en TDD puede ser estudiada desde varias perspectivas. En el experimento original se han estudiado dos variables: la calidad externa (QLTY) y la productividad (PROD), junto con otras variables no relevantes para este trabajo. QLTY representa el grado de corrección del código desarrollado por los sujetos, y se define como:

$$QLTY = \frac{\sum_{i=1}^{\#tus} QLTY_i}{\#TUS} \tag{1}$$

donde QLTYi es la calidad de la historia de usuario i-ésima implementada por el sujeto. QLTYi se define como:

$$QLTY_i = \frac{\#Assert_i(Pass)}{\#Assert_i(All)} \tag{2}$$

mientras que #TUS (Tackled User Stories), es la cantidad de trabajo realizado en una tarea de desarrollo y se define como:

$$\#TUS = \sum_{i=1}^{\#us} \#Assert_i(Pass) \geq 0 \mapsto True \tag{3}$$

En ambos casos, #Asserti(Pass) representa el número de aserciones de jUnit (ya que el experimento se realizó utilizando el lenguaje de programación Java) correctamente ejecutados en la historia de usuario i-ésima.

PROD representa la cantidad de trabajo realizada por los sujetos, y se define como:

$$PROD = \frac{\#Assert(Pass)}{\#Assert(All)} \tag{4}$$

Las hipótesis de investigación serán:
H1: Cómo TDD afecta en la cantidad de trabajo realizado en comparación con la estrategia Test-Last?
H2: Cómo TDD afecta en la calidad externa en comparación con la estrategia Test-Last?
H3: Cómo TDD afecta en la productividad en comparación con la estrategia Test-Last?
H4: Qué características personales son moderadoras o mediadoras en H1, H2, H3?

Como variables independientes se consideran a las prácticas de desarrollo Test Driven Development (TDD) y Test Last Development (TLD) y como variables dependientes a la Productividad (PROD), la Calidad Externa (QLTY) y el número de Tackled User Stories (TUS).

Las características personales (CP) (como por ejemplo la experiencia de los sujetos, el conocimiento del dominio, su formación académica) serán identificadas durante el transcurso de la investigación como posibles moderadores o mediadores de las hipótesis H1, H2 y H3. Luego de la fase experimental, se realizará la síntesis de resultados.

6 Resumen del estado actual de la investigación y planificación de las etapas siguientes

6.1 Estado actual de la investigación.

En una primera etapa, se ha definido la problemática a través de una revisión inicial de literatura sobre estudios experimentales acerca de la efectividad de la técnica TDD. De esta revisión, se efectuó un re-análisis de los hallazgos presentados por las revisiones sistemáticas de literatura de Rafique & Misic [3] y Turhan et al. [9]; encontrando, que la experiencia del sujeto experimental es un aspecto interesante que se debe investigar con mayor detalle y rigurosidad.

En una segunda etapa, se ha planteado una serie de replicaciones experimentales, basadas en el experimento propuesto por Juristo et al. [15]. Dichas replicaciones se efectuarán en el marco de un proyecto de investigación, seguido de una síntesis de datos. Creemos que guiar la investigación desde esta perspectiva mejorará la generación de evidencias que puedan ser generalizadas en el ámbito de la Ingeniería de Software.

Hasta el momento se han llevado a cabo cuatro replicaciones del experimento original en el ámbito académico: una a nivel de postgrado en la Universidad de las Fuerzas Armadas ESPE de Ecuador extensión Latacunga la que contó con la participación de uno de los experimentadores originales, y tres replicaciones a nivel de grado: una en la Universidad de las Fuerzas Armadas ESPE extensión Sangolquí, otra en la Universidad Autónoma de Yucatán de México y una tercera en la Universidad Nacional de La Plata de Argentina. Los resultados obtenidos hasta ahora son prometedores, ya que a partir de ellos fue aceptada una publicación [14] en las XI Jornadas Iberoamericanas de Ingeniería de Software e Ingeniería del Conocimiento JIISIC – CEIS 2015.

6.2 Planificación de las siguientes etapas

Se encuentra planificado continuar con otra serie de replicaciones experimentales para el año 2016. En este caso, se prevé realizar más instancias a nivel de postgrado y en especial a nivel industrial, donde las condiciones del diseño experimental podrían variar significativamente respecto al experimento original. Como etapa final, se sintetizarán los resultados del conjunto de replicaciones obtenidas en los años 2014, 2015 y 2016; con la intención de difundir los resultados a la industria de software.

7 Bibliografía.

[1] N. Juristo, A. Tosun, O. Dieste, D. Fucci, S. Vegas, B. Turhan, H. Erdogmus, A. Santos, M. Oivo, K. Toro y J. Jarvinen, «An Industry Experiment on the Effects of Test-Driven Development on External Quality and Productivity,» *Submitted to Empirical Software Engineering,* 2015.

[2] B. Cartaxo, A. Araujo, A. S. Barreto y S. Soere, «The impact of scrum on customer satisfaction: An empirical study,» *Software Engineering (SBES) 2013 27th Brazilian Symposium on,* pp. 129-136, 2013.

[3] K. Beck, «Test Driven Development: By Example,» *Addison-Wesley Professional,* 2002.

[4] J. E. Hannay, T. Dyba, E. Arisholm y D. I. S, «he effectiveness of pair

programming: A meta-analysis Information and Software Technology,» *Software Engineering for Secure Systems Software Engineering for Secure Systems,* vol. 51, nº 7, p. 1110 – 1122, 2009.

[5] Y. Rafique y V. Misic, «The Effects of Test-Driven Development on External Quality and Productivity: A Meta-Analysis,» *Software Engineering, IEEE Transactions,* vol. 39, nº 6, p. 835–856, 2013.

[6] M. Hussan, M. Misagh y P. Kai, «Considering rigor and relevance when evaluating test driven development: A systematic review,» *Information and Software Technology,* vol. 56, pp. 375-394, 2014.

[7] F. Shull, G. Melnik, B. Turhan, L. Layman, M. Diep y H. Erdogmus, «What do we know about test-driven development?,» *IEEE Software,* vol. 27, nº 6, pp. 16-19, 2010.

[8] B. Turhan, L. Layman, M. Diep, H. Erdogmus y F. Shull, «How Effective is Test-Driven Development?,» de *Making Software What Really Works, and Why We Believe It*, O'Reilly Media, 2010, pp. 399-412.

[9] H. Munir y M. Moayyed, «Systematic Literature Review and Controlled Pilot Experimental Evaluation of Test Driven Development (TDD) vs.Test-Last Development (TLD),» 2012.

[10] A. Causevic, D. Sundmark y S. Punnekkat, «Factors Limiting Industrial Adoption of Test Driven Development: A Systematic Review,» *Software Testing, Verification and Validation (ICST),* pp. 337-346, 2011.

[11] M. Simo y M. Jürgen, «Effects of Test-Driven Development: A Comparative Analysis of Empirical Studies,» *Software Quality. Model-Based Approaches for Advanced Software and Systems Engineering,* vol. 166, pp. 155-169, 2014.

[12] S. Mäkinen y J. Münch, «Effects of Test-Driven Development: A Comparative Analysis of Empirical Studies,» *Software Quality. Model-Based Approaches for Advanced Software and Systems Engineering Lecture Notes in Business Information ,* vol. 166, pp. 155-169, 2014.

[13] S. Kollanus, «Test-Driven Development—Still a Promising Approach?,» *Quality of Information and Communication and Technology,* pp. 403-408, 2010.

[14] O. Dieste, E. Fonseca, G. Raura y P. Rodríguez, «Efectividad del Test-Driven Development: Un Experimento Replicado,» de *XI Jornadas Iberoamericanas de Ingeniería de Software e Ingeniería del Conocimiento JIISIC – CEIS 2015*, Riobamba Ecuador, 2015.

[15] K. e. a. Beck, «agilemanifesto.org,» 2001. [En línea]. Available: http://agilemanifesto.org.

[16] K. Beck y A. Cynthia, «Extreme Programming Explained: Embrace Change,» *Addison-Wesley Professional,* 2004.